A WORLD BANK COUNTRY STUDY

Tanzania at the Turn of the Century

Background Papers and Statistics

Government of the United Republic of Tanzania

The World Bank
Washington, D.C.

World Bank Country Studies are among the many reports originally prepared for internal use as part of the continuing analysis by the Bank of the economic and related conditions of its developing member countries and of its dialogues with the governments. Some of the reports are published in this series with the least possible delay for the use of governments and the academic, business and financial, and development communities. The typescript of this paper therefore has not been prepared in accordance with the procedures appropriate to formal printed texts, and the World Bank accepts no responsibility for errors. Some sources cited in this paper may be informal documents that are not readily available.

The findings, interpretations, and conclusions expressed in this paper are entirely those of the author(s) and should not be attributed in any manner to the World Bank, to its affiliated organizations, or to members of its Board of Executive Directors or the countries they represent. The World Bank does not guarantee the accuracy of the data included in this publication and accepts no responsibility for any consequence of their use. The boundaries, colors, denominations, and other information shown on any map in this volume do not imply on the part of the World Bank Group any judgment on the legal status of any territory or the endorsement or acceptance of such boundaries.

The material in this publication is copyrighted. The World Bank encourages dissemination of its work and will normally grant permission promptly.

Permission to photocopy items for internal or personal use, for the internal or personal use of specific clients, or for educational classroom use, is granted by the World Bank provided that the appropriate fee is paid directly to Copyright Clearance Center, Inc., 222 Rosewood Drive, Danvers, MA 01923, U.S.A., telephone 978-750-8400, fax 978-750-4470. Please contact Copyright Clearance Center prior to photocopying items.

For permission to reprint individual articles or chapters, please fax your request with complete information to the Republication Department, Copyright Clearance Center, fax 978-750-4470.

All other queries on rights and licenses should be addressed to the World Bank at the address above, or fax no. 202-522-2422.

ISBN: 0-8213-5061-7
ISSN: 0253-2123

Library of Congress Cataloging-in-Publication Data has been applied for.

CONTENTS

List of Tables

List of Figures

List of Boxes

Statistical Appendix Tables

ACKNOWLEDGMENTS

The preparation of this Country Study was undertaken jointly between the Government of Tanzania and the World Bank. The task managers, Mr. Benno Ndulu (Lead Specialist, World Bank) and Mr. Charles K. Mutalemwa (Permanent Secretary, Planning Commission, Government of Tanzania), would like to register their appreciation for the support received from a number of individuals and institutions who contributed to the preparation of this memorandum.

Overall guidance for the Country Study was provided by the Technical Team and the Steering Committee formed by the Government of Tanzania. The report was prepared under the general supervision of Messrs. Frederick Kilby, Peter Miovic, James W. Adams, and Ronald Brigish (World Bank), who also provided extensive comments on the various drafts.

The principal author for the *Synthesis of Key Messages* (World Bank, April 2001) is Mr. B. Ndulu (World Bank).[1] The current compilation has two parts, background papers and a statistical appendix. Principal authors of the individual sections are as follows:
- "Recent Macroeconomic Performance"—Mr. P. I. Mpango (University of Dar es Salaam).
- "What Matters Most for Growth?"—Mr. R. J. Utz (World Bank).
- "Combating Poverty, Ignorance, and Disease"—Messrs. L. Rutasitara and H. Mwinyimvua (University of Dar es Salaam).
- "Unleashing the Private Sector's Potential for Tanzania's Development"—Ms. P. Ahuja (World Bank).
- "Pacemakers for Sustainable Growth"—Messrs. R. J. Utz and B. Ndulu (World Bank).
- "Zanzibar's Economic Performance"—Mr. R. Mabele (University of Dar es Salaam).

Background papers and significant contributions to individual chapters were prepared by Ms. S. Dhar and Mr. B. Tarimo (World Bank); Messrs. L. Msongole, A. Mwakapugi, and U. Tenende (Planning Commission); Mr. N. S. Magonya (Vice President's Office); Mr. J. Massawe (Bank of Tanzania); Ms. N. Mbilinyi (consultant); and Mr. H. Semboja (Economic and Social Research Foundation).

Ms. S. Dhar and Mr. B. Tarimo (World Bank) acted as overall coordinators of the drafting team. Able research assistance was provided by Messrs. E. Mungunasi, G. Kabelwa, and J. Mduma (University of Dar es Salaam). Ms. R. Covington, Ms. L. James, and Ms H. Mannoro (World Bank) provided dedicated logistical support in Washington and Dar es Salaam. The final draft of the report was edited by Ms. S. Dhar (World Bank) and Ms. A. Faintich (consultant).

Given the pivotal role of agriculture in the Tanzanian economy, the decision was made early in the preparatory work to publish the background research on this sector as a separate report, *Agriculture in Tanzania since 1986: Follower or Leader of Growth* (June 2000). The main findings are summarized in "Transforming Agriculture into an Engine of Growth and Poverty Reduction". Messrs. C. Delgado and N.

---

[1] *Tanzania at the Turn of the Century: From Reforms to Sustained Growth and Poverty Reduction*, Country Study, Washington, D.C.; ISBN: 0-8213-4941-4; ISSN: 0253-2123.

Minot (International Food Policy Research Institute) were the principal authors of the June 2000 report. Background papers and significant contributions to individual chapters were made by Ms. J. Bitegeko, Messrs. A. Ngondo, and R. Mlay (Ministry of Agriculture and Cooperatives); Messrs. H. Amani, R. Mabele and W. Maro (University of Dar es Salaam); Mr. E. Wiketye (Institute for Development Management); Mr. R. Mfungahema (formerly of the Planning Commission); and Mr. J. Komba (formerly of the National Bureau of Statistics). Messrs. C. Courbois, O. Mashindano and K. Kazungu provided research assistance.

A draft of this Country Study was discussed at a review meeting held in Dar es Salaam in September 1999, with wide participation from the government, the World Bank, the donor community, the private sector, and academic and research institutions in Tanzania. Messrs. J. B. Raphael and Kibao (Zanzibar Planning Commission), and Ms. V. Leach (United Nations Development Programme/United Nations Development Assistance Framework) provided valuable comments. Peer reviewers for this CEM were Mr. David Bevan, (Oxford University); and Messrs. Enrique Rueda-Sabater, Peter Fallon, William Easterly, and Shantayanan Devarajan (World Bank). In addition, Mr. Alan Gelb, Chief Economist, Africa Region in the World Bank, made comprehensive comments on the entire Volume 1. In addition, the memorandum benefited from a review by the World Bank's Quality Assurance Group.

Finally, we acknowledge gratefully the generous financial support provided by the World Bank for the production of the overall report, and by the governments of Denmark and Sweden for the separate report focusing on agricultural development in Tanzania.

ACRONYMS AND ABBREVIATIONS

Government Fiscal Year
FY02 = July 1, 2001, to June 30, 2002

Currency Equivalents
Currency Unit: Tanzania Shilling (T Sh)

US$1 = T Sh 888.03 (June 2001)

CRDB	Cooperative and Rural Development Bank
EAC	East African Cooperation
EPZ	Export Processing Zone
ERP	Economic Recovery Program
ESAF	Enhanced Structural Adjustment Facility of the IMF
FAO	Food and Agriculture Organization of the United Nations
FDI	Foreign Direct Investment
f.o.b.	Free on Board
FY	Fiscal Year
GDP	Gross Domestic Product
GFCF	Gross Fixed Capital Formation
GNP	Gross National Product
HBS	Household Budget Survey
HDI	Human Development Index
HIPC	Heavily Indebted Poor Countries
HIV/AIDS	Human Immuno-Deficiency Virus/ Acquired Immune Deficiency Syndrome
HRDS	Human Resources Development Survey
ICT	Information and Communication Technology
IDA	International Development Association
IFC	International Finance Corporation
IMF	International Monetary Fund
MDF	Multilateral Debt Fund
MTEF	Medium-Term Expenditure Framework
NBC	National Bank of Commerce
NESP	National Economic Survival Program
NGO	Nongovernmental Organization
NIC	National Insurance Corporation
NMB	National Microfinance Bank
OCAG	Office of the Controller and Auditor General
ODA	Official Development Assistance
OECD	Organisation for Economic Co-operation and Development
PER	Public Expenditure Review
R&D	Research and Development
SADC	Southern Africa Development Community
SAP	Structural Adjustment Program
TANESCO	Tanzania Electric Supply Company
TAS	Tanzania Assistance Strategy

TAZARA	Tanzania-Zambia Railways Authority
TFP	Total Factor Productivity
TIC	Tanzania Investment Center
TRA	Tanzania Revenue Authority
T Sh	Tanzania Shilling
UNDP	United Nations Development Programme
VAT	Value Added Tax
ZIPA	Zanzibar Industrial Promotion Agency
ZSTC	Zanzibar State Trading Corporation

SUMMARY

Tanzania at the Turn of the Century: Background Papers and Statistics is the successor to the Country Economic Memorandum for Tanzania prepared in 1996 (World Bank 1996). The 1996 memorandum focused on the challenge of reforms and paid particular attention to the impact of reforms on growth, incomes and welfare in Tanzania. The current report draws out lessons from Tanzania's development experience of the past four decades, with emphasis on the period since the last report, and assesses the imperatives for higher sustained growth and better livelihood for its citizens in the future.

The 2000 memorandum is organized in three separate publications. The synthesis of the main results and key policy messages of in-depth analyses of Tanzania's development presented in the current compilation of background papers and statistics was published in April, 2001. A separate companion volume on agriculture was published in June 2000. The background papers presented in this Country Study reviews and assesses Tanzania's actual growth and poverty reduction performance against its large natural potential and against countries at a comparable stage of development, analyzes the main reasons behind the performance record, and then draws out the strategic and institutional imperatives for exploiting the country's vast potential for sustained growth and reduction of poverty in the long and medium term. The analysis focuses on development of the private sector and its increased role in scaling up overall growth and modernization of the Tanzanian economy. One chapter focuses on the Zanzibar economy and its development, even though Zanzibar is part of the union, because the policy and institutional framework for the island are distinct enough to merit separate attention. Also presented here are the statistical appendixes.

Current Status of Tanzania's Development

The study assesses Tanzania's current development status against the country's ambition, since independence, to rid the nation of three archenemies, poverty, ignorance, and disease. Forty years later, the war is far from being won, and Tanzania remains one of the 10 poorest countries in the world, even though it is endowed with a rich natural resource base, has easy geographical access to the international market, has had a peaceful and politically stable environment, and has managed to forge a cohesive national identity around a common language. Measured in domestic prices, real income per head is only about 30 percent higher than at independence. Poverty remains widespread and deep, with half of Tanzanians today living without access to the basic needs of livelihood. Poverty is concentrated in the rural areas, where approximately 70 percent of Tanzanians live, although urban poverty has also grown along with rapid urbanization and urban stagnation. Despite the fact that Tanzania's ranking based on the United Nations Development Programme Human Development Index is relatively better than that of its income level, the country has recently lost significant ground in international ranking.

Structural transformation in Tanzania has been extremely limited, and the achievements relative to expectations have been only marginal. Agriculture still dominates the economy. The share of agriculture in total production (45 percent), exports (75 percent), and employment (80 percent)—although lower than at independence—are higher than in most other developing countries. Tanzania's nondiversified economy hampers flexibility to withstand shocks when they occur.

Over the past four years, the Government of Tanzania intensified macroeconomic policy reforms with the aim of creating a more stable macroeconomic environment. These reforms were pursued with the understanding that such stability was necessary to achieve sustained growth, which is required to reduce the pervasive poverty in the country. As a result, Tanzania has progressed significantly in reestablishing macroeconomic stability. Inflation has fallen from levels in excess of 30 percent in 1995 to the current 6 percent; the exchange rate has remained reasonably stable despite the 15 percent depreciation in 1999; the amount of foreign exchange reserves has climbed from about 6 weeks of merchandise imports in 1995 to the current level of 18 weeks; and the overall fiscal balance, including grants, has had a surplus of between 0.8 percent and 1.2 percent of gross domestic product (GDP) in the past 3 years and is projected to remain in the low range of fiscal deficit, and thus accommodate propoor spending. In the medium term, however, this improvement will need to be grounded in a strong fiscal system to ensure sustained macroeconomic stability.

In parallel with the macroeconomic reforms, the Government of Tanzania also carried out structural reforms focusing on realigning the incentive structure toward increased exports, on using scarce foreign exchange more efficiently, on liberalizing markets for goods and services, and on reducing the involvement of the public sector in commercial activities. A large part of gross economic distortions has been dealt with effectively. Although still fragile and shallow, markets are relatively free, the parastatal sector and the civil service are considerably smaller, and a significant improvement in fiscal discipline has taken place, particularly in enforcing cash budgets. While such improvement must be sustained to instill confidence in investors and other economic agents, more effort is needed to bolster complementary structural policies and institutional structures for sustained growth and broad sharing of the benefits from growth. In a variety of institutional investor surveys, Tanzania scores lowest in the areas of structural policies and institutional quality. If the reforms proposed under the Programmatic Structural Adjustment Credit I are implemented as intended, the openness and liberal character of the economy will be on a solid base.

Main Factors Underlying the Slow Development in Tanzania

The report identifies the main factors behind the slow progress in Tanzania's development to be primarily inadequate capital accumulation and productivity growth, poor support for the transformation of agriculture, disrupted progress in building human capital, and delayed demographic transition. The contribution of physical capital accumulation to growth fluctuated significantly during the past four decades. Gross domestic investment in Tanzania increased from about 13 percent of GDP in 1964 to 30 percent in 1991, and then declined sharply to 18 percent in 1997. The decline was due mainly to a fall in public investment as a result of cutting down overall government spending and privatization. The response of private investment to reform measures has remained weaker than expected and has not compensated for the decline in public investment.

A striking feature of the Tanzanian growth experience is that when one juxtaposes the respective growth trends, investment and growth hardly seem to correlate. This was mirrored by the significant losses in investment productivity during the 1970s and early 1980s. It reduced the economywide rate of return from nearly 30 percent in the early 1970s to nearly 5 percent in the mid-1980s. The economy is only slowly recovering from that loss. Underutilization of capacity and poor investment choices were the main culprits. Actual capital accumulation was also much lower than implied by the investment rates because of the poor choices and incomplete projects affecting economywide returns to the investment. With better and more efficient use of its investment, Tanzania's per capita income in 1998 would have been 30 percent higher than what it actually was.

Poor support for the transformation of agriculture has limited the sector's dominant contribution to growth and poverty reduction. It has also limited progress in agricultural intensification and commercialization. Despite being the backbone of the economy and a source of livelihood for the majority of Tanzanians, agriculture was overtaxed during the control regime, and its revival is still constrained by inadequate public support for productivity growth in the sector and stagnant growth in agrobusiness. One of the reasons for slow intensification of agriculture is constrained access to inputs, credit, and timely advice based on sound research. The private sector has been slow in filling the gaps resulting from the withdrawal of public sector involvement in the delivery of these. The main constraints to commercialization relate to the poor availability of price information, poor infrastructure, undeveloped credit facilities, and weak competition in the markets. Underprovision and the poor condition of the rural road network and inadequate connectivity of this network to the main road arteries limit accessibility to markets and raise costs to producers, suppliers of inputs, and crop marketers. The lack of clearly defined and coordinated strategies among the various government institutions for the development of agriculture, and of rural development more broadly, has constrained the development of a coherent strategy for the transformation of agriculture.

Progress in building human capacity was not sustained in Tanzania. Despite the government's efforts to strengthen human capabilities through increased access to formal education, the contribution of human capital to growth declined from 0.3 percent during the 1960s to 0.1 percent during the 1980s. While Tanzania was successful in expanding access to primary education, high dropout and failure rates at the Primary School Leaving Examination resulted in a high share of the population lacking the necessary skills and knowledge to be able to engage gainfully in a modern economy. Tanzania's attainment rates in secondary and higher education are among the lowest in Sub-Saharan Africa. In fact, the data indicate that the share of Tanzania's population with at least some formal postprimary education had declined from 5 percent at independence to 3.2 percent by 1990. A major cause for low enrollment levels is the relatively high cost of secondary and tertiary education relative to income levels in Tanzania. While 80 percent of poor children and 100 percent of the rich complete grade 1, only 40 percent of the poor complete grade 7, compared with 75 percent of the rich.

The HIV/AIDS pandemic poses a major threat for eroding gains made in human development for the past four decades. The rate of HIV infection is estimated to have reached 8.1 percent in Tanzania. HIV/AIDS is not merely a health problem, but also an economic development problem. It has begun eroding the expected longevity of productive life from the peak of 52 years in 1988 to 48 years currently. It is depleting disproportionately the productive and skilled segment of the population, thereby raising the dependency ratio. The HIV/AIDS pandemic is also increasingly claiming a large share of public resources to care for the terminally ill. For example, it has been recently estimated that it takes resources that could educate nine primary school pupils to take care of one AIDS patient. In addition, families and communities bear much of the cost of taking care of children orphaned by AIDS.

Delayed demographic transition has resulted in an excessive burden on the labor force. At 50 percent, the dependency ratio in Tanzania is too high to support adequate saving levels. In combination with a population growth rate averaging 3 percent over the past four decades, it puts immense pressure on the existing labor force to provide for dependents and undermines progress in living standards. The pressure of rapid expansion of demands on the limited capacity of the economy to support the rapidly increasing livelihood needs is a major drawback to growth and poverty reduction. Tanzania, like the majority of African countries, has not embarked on a demographic transition to lower population growth and attaining a more mature age structure. Higher growth of the economy and education are therefore important elements in the effort to stem rapid growth of the population.

Imperatives for Higher Growth and Poverty Reduction

In looking forward, the memorandum takes as a point of departure Tanzania's intention to build on the strengths of peace, unity, and self-esteem and to break with the past weaknesses, as amply exposed in the *Tanzania Vision 2025* and the reform programs pursued for the last decade and a half. During the reform period, Tanzania has achieved macroeconomic stability, is making steady progress in reorienting its economy to a market-based operation, and creating space for exploiting the large potential of private sector initiative. Much as the payoff from these efforts has still to be fully realized, Tanzania Vision 2025 expresses both hope and determination in ridding the country of poverty, disease, and ignorance. It seeks to do so by achieving high and sustained growth, at an average of 8 percent, and halving abject poverty by 2010 and eliminating it by 2025. Furthermore, Tanzania aims to develop a modern, export-led economy and leap into the category of middle-income country.

Long-Term Strategy for Higher Sustained Growth and Poverty Reduction

Both cross-country experience and the high growth recorded in the 1960s indicate that Tanzania can sustain a 6–7 percent rate of growth by exploiting its natural resource potential, sustaining peace, and staying the course of reforms. It will require maintaining an investment rate of 25 percent (not a difficult task given historical rates achieved in Tanzania) and, even more important, raising investment productivity to levels achieved in the 1960s. To increase Tanzania's growth performance, it is necessary to raise the private investment response and enable efficient business operations. Sustained macroeconomic stability, reduced cost of doing business, fair competition, and privatization constitute the main criteria for achieving these results. Given the small size of the Tanzanian economy, growth will only be sustainable if it is firmly rooted in exploiting the domestic resource base, international competitiveness, and the aggressive pursuit of new export opportunities.

Increases in productivity will only be possible if close attention is paid to the acquisition, adoption, and use of various forms of knowledge, including technical know-how. Foreign direct investment, an appropriate communication and information infrastructure, and an improved level of educational attainment are key elements in facilitating productivity gains through knowledge. In light of Tanzania's low postprimary education attainment, it is imperative that measures be put in place to increase the incentives and returns for undertaking such investments. Given the government's limited capacity, it is wise for it to focus on increased public support in areas where externalities are large, such as primary education and preventive health care. Private sector and community participation in the delivery of postprimary education and health will enable higher levels of attainment and cost-effectiveness.

Structural transformation can be expected to occur alongside accelerated growth. Although the secondary and tertiary sectors (for example, tourism and mining) will likely continue to grow at significantly higher rates than agriculture, this does not imply that growth of these sectors should come at the absolute expense of agriculture or manufacturing. Agriculture will, for the foreseeable future, remain the backbone of the economy, and only a prospering agriculture sector can provide the basis for sustainable poverty reduction and accelerated growth in the other sectors. The memorandum estimates that, to achieve the 6–7 percent overall growth, agriculture should grow at 5 percent annually, a considerable increase from the current 3–4 percent growth rate. The prominence of this sector in overall growth and poverty reduction in Tanzania is underscored by the fact that it dominates income generation and has the highest forward linkages and consumption spin-off effects to the rest of the economy, compared with other sectors. T Sh 1 worth of income generated in agriculture generates a T Sh 1.80 increase in overall GDP, compared with T Sh 1.20 if the same income were generated in light industry. In contrast with the past initiatives, support for the transformation of agriculture should hinge on a cohesive, long-term strategy that targets intensification and commercialization. Apart from more effective research and extension, there will be a need for better rural roads to lower costs of access to markets and inputs, better education to facilitate adoption of improved husbandry, increased private credit to fill gaps left by the collapse of public credit institutions, lower and more transparent taxation, and greater contestability of markets.

The industrial sector similarly remains the backbone of modernization. Despite the massive closure of failed public enterprises, industry has managed to continue posting a growth rate, on average, of 5 percent or more in the past decade, implying that new and surviving firms are growing much faster to more than compensate for failing firms. What is needed is to enhance the skill profile for a modern labor force in order to support the buildup of export competence to break into new markets and withstand global competition in a world increasingly becoming dependent on information technology for productivity growth.

Tanzania's rich-resource endowment offers the opportunity to garner additional growth from more intensive exploitation of its resource base. Exports of nontraditional agricultural commodities, increased activity in the mining sector, and expansion of tourism are three areas that already have registered relatively high growth rates in recent years, but these areas still have substantial potential for additional growth in the near future. It is, however, imperative to take measures that increase the linkages with the rest of the economy.

Low density and poor quality of infrastructure is a critical constraint to market integration and efficiency, given the sparse distribution of economic activity in Tanzania. The resource requirements for developing the needed standards of roads, rail, shipping, telecommunication, and power are immense. Support for improving infrastructure is one area where external assistance can play the most effective role in promoting growth and alleviating poverty in Tanzania. However, unlike in the past, where such support is provided for public investment, it ought to be tied to clear commitments in the budgetary provision for recurrent maintenance costs and should complement a dominant private provision of these services. Most critical in this regard is strengthening the management capability of the government to prioritize road investment and develop an effective maintenance system that pays greater attention to cost-effectiveness.

Medium-Term Strategy for Scaling Up Growth and Reducing Poverty

Finally, the report identifies elements of a medium-term strategy for achieving long-term targets of Tanzania's National Development Vision 2025. These necessarily center on sustainable reduction of the poverty that afflicts half of the country's population. The memorandum identifies four pillars of the strategy for the immediate future: a poverty-reducing growth strategy; a cost-effective and improved system for delivery of better-quality public service; containment of the spread, and management of the impacts, of the HIV/AIDS pandemic; and a governance structure that promotes accountability and social inclusion and that upholds basic rights to a decent livelihood.

The imperatives identified for long-term growth are applicable for the medium-term strategy to raise growth. During the initial phase of scaling up, growth should focus on raising productivity, particularly in agriculture, while benefits from an improved policy environment take root and lead to a higher private investment response in the key sectors identified earlier as pacemakers for growth. To ensure that benefits from higher growth are shared widely, the focus of the strategy will be to expand opportunities for the poor to gainful employment. Higher growth of agriculture, a vibrant informal sector and micro-, small-, and medium-size enterprises are particularly pertinent for such broadly based growth. For the poor, improved access to basic education and primary health services is of highest priority to help bolster their income-earning capabilities.

Building competencies and strengthening accountability for improved public service delivery is an important element of the strategy. Enhanced cost-effectiveness in public service delivery entails three main areas of action: improving strategic prioritization of expenditure, adopting a results orientation as the main approach for monitoring the effectiveness of public spending; and strengthening competencies and institutional capacity for managing public service programs prudently, particularly at the local government level. In this regard, the Tanzania Assistance Strategy and the Medium-Term Expenditure Framework provide the vehicles for setting strategic priorities, budgeting, and monitoring effectiveness. The Public Service Reform Program is the main vehicle for encouraging a results orientation, better incentives, and capacity building in the public service.

Containing the spread and managing the impacts of the HIV/AIDS pandemic is of critical and immediate importance for Tanzania's development. The pandemic is most rampant in the productive, prime age cohort of 15–59. Recent estimates put the loss in potential growth due to the effects of the pandemic in Tanzania at 0.7 percent of GDP annually. The actions identified include adoption of a multisectoral national policy on HIV/AIDS; provision of financial resources for cross-sectoral actions against HIV/AIDS in the context of the Medium-Term Expenditure Framework; strengthening the capacity and increasing resource availability to the National Aids Control Committee and the National Aids Control Program to enable better research, extensive surveillance, and intensive public education campaigns; introduction of public health, HIV/AIDS, and peer education in schools; intensive involvement of the local communities, political leaders, nongovernmental organizations, donors, and religious groups in mass education and campaigns against the epidemic, as well in dealing with the increasing number of orphans; and availability of affordable treatment of the already infected population.

Building a more transparent, accountable, and tolerant governance system is also a key element of the strategy. As Tanzania continues its efforts in building democracy, social inclusion—which is a basis for meaningful participation in the development process by all concerned citizens—will increasingly become a right. The ongoing devolution of responsibilities for managing development to local governments and community organizations, and bringing accountability systems into the public domain augur well for promoting inclusiveness. Sustaining freedom of media and improving the flow of information through better and more effective means of communication constitute key forms of strategic actions to this end. In a corrupt environment, the poor are particularly vulnerable to injustice, as they cannot afford the means for paying off dishonest officials. Apart from dealing with grand corruption, which typically raises the cost of doing business and discourages investment, the country must pay attention to petty corruption in the courts, law enforcement, taxation, education, and health at the local level. The anticorruption strategy will need to scale up attention to this level of corruption.

It can be done, play your part. **What is needed is national resolve to proceed, with increased attention paid to effectiveness in application of resources, and in creating a conducive environment and a space for private initiative.**[2]

---

[2] Taken from an address by President Mwalimu Julius K. Nyerere on the Tanganyika Five-Year Plan and Review of the Plan in May 1964.

BACKGROUND PAPERS

1. Background Information

The United Republic of Tanzania consists of the area formerly known as Tanganyika, which is now mainland Tanzania; and Zanzibar, which is made up of the islands of Unguja and Pemba. Tanganyika became a sovereign state on December 9, 1961, and a republic the following year. Zanzibar became independent from the United Kingdom on December 19, 1963, and named the People's Republic of Zanzibar after the revolution of January 12, 1964. Tanganyika united with Zanzibar on April 26, 1964, to form the United Republic of Tanganyika and Zanzibar, renamed the United Republic of Tanzania on October 29, 1964.

Geography and Resources

Tanzania is endowed with a rich natural resource base and easy access for international trade. It has a total area of 945,000 square kilometers, of which 883,000 square kilometers are land; 881,000 square kilometers in the mainland and 2,000 square kilometers in Zanzibar. Inland waters occupy 62,000 square kilometers. With about 46 percent of the total land area being arable, the country has a rich potential for agriculture. Tanzania also has a large hydropower potential and a wide range of mineral deposits, including gold, diamonds, tin, iron ore, uranium, phosphates, coal, gemstones, nickel, and natural gas deposits. The terrain of the country varies, as does the climate and agro-ecological zones. The terrain consists of plains along the coast, a plateau in the central area, and highlands in the north and south. The vast majority of the population lives inland, far away from the coastline. The climate varies from tropical along the coast to temperate in the highlands. On average the country gets an annual rainfall of 1,000 millimeters. The wide diversity in the agroclimatic zones minimizes the countrywide risk of weather-related crop failures.

Good land and climate notwithstanding, the country has managed, according to 1993 estimates, to put only 6.7 percent of its land area under cultivation, of which only 1,500 square kilometers is under irrigation and 1 percent is under permanent crops. Of the remaining land area, 40 percent is under permanent pasture, 38 percent is under forests and woodland, and about 15 percent is under other uses. However, this low use rate masks the fact that population densities vary widely, creating pressure on land, especially in the fertile highlands of northern Tanzania and in the cities. Moreover, deforestation and overgrazing threaten desertification of a sizeable proportion of woodlands in the country.

Income and Human Development

Despite its potential and rich resource endowment, Tanzania is among the least industrialized countries in the world. Almost four decades after it became independent, the country has not sufficiently exploited its potential and resources for the benefit of raising the standard of living of its citizens. Real growth has been stagnant, and poverty has remained pervasive and deep. Tanzania's gross national product (GNP) of US$265 per capita is low and far less than Sub-Saharan Africa's and East Asia's averages of US$500 and US$970, respectively. About half of Tanzania's citizens are poor. Average life expectancy, at 48 years, is also low and below the Sub-Saharan Africa average of 52.5 years. Other vital statistics show that the infant mortality rate is 99 per 1,000 live births, and the total fertility rate is 5.5 children per woman.

Thirty-two percent of Tanzania's population aged 15 years and above is illiterate. Although the ratio of gross enrollment (those who enter at level 1 regardless of age) in primary school to the total eligible population is officially estimated at 76 percent, the ratio for net enrollment (those who are enrolled in school at the official school age as defined by the national education system) is 56.7 percent. In Tanzania it takes an average of 9.4 years instead of the expected 7 years to complete primary education, the extra 2.4 years being due to dropouts and repetition, especially at standard 4 level. The gross enrollment ratio in secondary schools is only 5 percent, far lower than the 27 percent average for Sub-Saharan Africa and 69 percent average for East Asia. This low enrollment ratio is based on six years of secondary education. If the widely used standard of four years of secondary education is adopted, the gross enrollment ratio rises to 9 percent, but is still significantly lower than the African average. Table 1.1 presents selected indicators for comparison of Tanzania with selected other countries and regions.

Table 1.1. *Selected International Comparative Indicators, Selected Locations and Years, 1960–97*

Indicator	Period	Tanzania	Kenya	Uganda	Sub-Saharan Africa	East Asia
Income and welfare						
GNP per capita	1997	210	330	320	500	970
Human development index (HDI) ranking	1997	36	46	33	38	88
Rank (per capita income)–rank HDI	1997	21	5	–19	—	—
Infant mortality per 1,000 live births	1960	147	124	133	166	84
	1994	85	70	121	97	17
Population with access to safe water	1990–95	38	53	38	51	93
Daily calorie intake	1992	2,021	2,075	2,161	2,096	3,107
Adult illiteracy 1995						
Male	1995	21	14	26	34	9
Female	1995	43	30	50	53	24
Gross enrollment ratios						
Primary	1980	93	115	50	78	111
	1996	76	85	74	77	118
Secondary	1980	3	20	5	15	43
	1996	5	24	12	27	69
Initial conditions						
Population (millions)	1997	31	28	20	—	—
Growth of population (percent)	1965–97	3.1	3.4	2.9	2.8	1.8
Density per square kilometer	1997	34	47	96	25	108
Land locked	n.a.	No	No	Yes	—	—
Infrastructure						
Paved roads (percent)	1997	4	14	—	16	10
Electric power consumption, 1996 per capita, kilowatt hours	1996	59	126	—	439	624
Telephones per 1,000	1997	3	8	2	16	10
Communications						
Ethno-linguistic index	1960	0.93	0.83	0.9	0.65	—
Newspapers per 1,000	1996	4	9	2	12	—
Radios per 1,000	1996	278	108	123	196	184
Fax machines per 100	1996	—	0.1	0.2	—	0.4

—Not available.
n.a. Not applicable.
Source: World Bank data.

4

Population

Although on average there is no population pressure on land, delayed demographic transition is holding back development. Tanzania has a total population of about 31 million people, of whom 30.1 million live on the mainland and about 900,000 live in Zanzibar. The crude birth and death rates are 41 and 14 per 1,000 people, respectively. The population of Tanzania has quadrupled over the last five decades, from 7.7 million in 1948 to 31 million in 1998. On the basis of the latest intercensus data, the current population growth rate is estimated at 2.8 percent, implying an annual increase of about 840,000 people per year. Tanzania's population has a higher proportion in the younger age groups than in the older age groups. The proportion of the total population that is under age 15 is about 47 percent, the proportion between 15 and 64 is 49 percent, and the proportion above age 65 is 4 percent. The median age is a low 16.4 years, and the dependency ratio rose from 98 in 1967 to 106 in 1996, indicating a rising and unsustainable burden for adults to fend for the dependent population.

The average population density for mainland Tanzania is 34 people per square kilometer, having increased from 8 people per square kilometer in 1948. This average hides much wider subnational differentials. According to the 1988 census analysis, population density in the different administrative regions ranged from 9.8 people per square kilometer to 976.9 people per square kilometer. Across districts the variation of population density was even wider, ranging from 1.4 people per square kilometer for Babati district in Arusha region to 1,579.4 people per square kilometer for Ilala district in the Dar es Salaam administrative region.

The population of Tanzania is predominantly rural, accounting for 76 percent of the total. The share of the urban population in total, however, has been rising rapidly as a result of a combination of high population growth and migration from rural to urban areas. Census data indicate that the urban population grew from 6 percent in 1967, to 14 percent in 1978, to 21 percent in 1988, and to 24 percent in 1996. Tanzania's rapid urbanization rate is among the highest rates in the world. As a result, considerable pressure is placed on the capacity of urban service amenities and on the growth of opportunities for gainful employment in and around urban centers.

An analysis of the 1978 census showed that 16 percent of the mainland's total population had their birth places outside their regions of residence. This proportion of migrant population varied greatly from one region to another, ranging from 65 percent for Dar es Salaam to 4 percent for Iringa. The population exchange between mainland Tanzania and Zanzibar accounted for only 0.2 percent of the total population. The immigrants to the mainland constituted about 3.2 percent of the total population. The analysis of the 1978 census further noted that, with the exception of Dar es Salaam, most regions that had shown immigration proportions above the national average of 16 percent—Rukwa, Kagera, Pwani, and Tabora—were also high recipients of immigrants. A substantial proportion of the immigrants were either refugees from across the international borders, or peasant farmers who had settled in neighboring regions. In the case of Dar es Salaam, the immigrant population is more heterogeneous in origin.

Labor Force and Employment

Because of the high proportion of young people in Tanzania, the labor force is growing rapidly and outstrips growth in employment opportunities. Fifty percent of the labor force is under 30 years old. The urban labor force is 16.8 percent of the total, and the rural areas host 83.2 percent of the total labor force. The proportion of women in the labor force is 50.2 percent, close to their share in the total population. The rate of growth of the labor force is 3 percent. The number of new entrants into the labor market has been increasing more rapidly than the population growth rate, and the average age of workers has been declining. About 50 percent of the labor force is currently under 30 years old. Tanzania has about 400,000 to 600,000 new job seekers each year (World Bank 1996). The labor force is mostly unskilled and has a low level of education attainment. Only 67 percent of the labor force is functionally literate, 32.1 percent never had any formal education, 21.4 percent went to primary school but never finished, 43.1 percent finished primary education, and 3.2 percent went to secondary school and above.

The statistics given by the Tanzania government (URT 1993) and the World Bank (1996) on unemployment and underemployment differ greatly. Using the same data, the World Bank adopted a rigorous definition of employment status. The unemployment rate ranges between 4 and 10.7 percent, depending on the source of analysis. The Tanzanian government has the total unemployment rate for the population aged 10 years and above at 3.6 percent, with the rate for men at 2.9 percent and for women at 4.2 percent. The government has the overall underemployment rate at 4.1 percent, 4.3 percent for men and 3.9 percent for women. The World Bank reports the unemployment rate at 10.7 percent, with men at 9.2 percent and women at 12.3 percent. According to this source, the underemployment rate is 2.7 percent overall, with men at 2.72 percent and women at 2.68 percent. Underemployment is most prevalent in rural areas, where labor demand declines seasonally.

Sources indicate that employment grew by between 2 and 3.2 percent during the 1980s and 1990s, respectively. The World Bank (1996) reports total employment grew at an annual average rate of 3.2 percent between 1978 and 1988, and continued to grow at the same rate or even faster in the early 1990s. Bol (1995), in contrast, reports employment growing at 2–2.5 percent during the 1980s, with the growth rate slowing to 2 percent in the 1990s. In both cases, the bulk of employment growth was observed to come from traditional agriculture and, increasingly, from the informal sector.

Formal engagement in the civil service, parastatal organizations, and private firms accounts for about 10 percent of the total employment. The Tanzania government estimates that about 0.81 million people are employed in the formal sector as their main activity, of whom about 60 percent are in the public sector (URT 1993). Private sector employment is becoming more important and has been growing at a faster rate of 10 percent. The number of people employed in the formal private sector more than doubled between 1984 and 1991.

More than 80 percent of the employed, working-age population is engaged in agriculture. Most of them work on smallholdings as self-employed or unpaid family workers. Those working primarily as paid employees are few, but involvement in occasional wage work is common, especially for youths, women, and members of lower-income households. More and more family members are refusing to work as unpaid family workers and are instead opting to join the wage-earning employment group of the agriculture sector (Mbilinyi 1993). The informal sector expanded quickly with economic reforms and is considered a growing source of employment, accounting for about 16 percent of the labor force. The Tanzanian government reports that about 1 million people are currently engaged in the informal sector as a main activity, and 1.8 million as a secondary activity (URT 1993). The survey found that one out of four households in mainland Tanzania has at least one person self-employed in the informal sector during the year.

Structure and Potential of Tanzania's Economy

Results from the study by Kenny and Syrquin (1999) indicate that structural transformation in Tanzania, as elsewhere in East Africa, is extremely limited (see table 1.2). The shares of agriculture in total output and employment, and of primary exports in total exports, have shown the expected downward trend but remain dominant in total production and exports. For the past four decades, the share of investment in Tanzania seems to have risen marginally, from 15 percent in the 1960s to an average of 20 percent in the last five years. The share of food consumption in total consumption has likewise remained stagnant at approximately 70 percent of total household expenditure. Comparative structural change indicators for East Africa (Kenny and Syrquin 1999) also indicate that only limited structural transformation has occurred in Tanzania. It shows that primary exports as a percentage of total exports declined only marginally, from 87 percent in 1965 to 82 percent in 1987. The corresponding ratio for South Asia declined from 63 percent to 36 percent over the same period. Similarly, the share of the labor force in agriculture decreased from 90 to 84 percent over the same period. Exports as a percentage of gross domestic product (GDP) also declined, from 26 percent in 1965 to 22 percent in 1997.

Table 1.2. *Structural Change, Selected Locations and Years, 1965–97*

Structural change	Period	Tanzania	Kenya	Uganda	Sub-Saharan Africa	South Asia
Per capita income	1987	180	330	260	330	290
Growth of per capita income	1965–1973	2.0	4.7	0.7	2.9	1.5
	1973–1987	−1.3	0.2	−4.3	−1.4	2.3
	1985–1995	1.0	0.1	2.7	−1.1	2.9
Investment (percentage of GDP)	1965	15	14	11	14	18
	1987	17	25	12	16	22
	1997	20	19	15	18	23
Exports (percentage of GDP)	1965	26	31	26	22	6
	1987	13	21	10	26	8
	1997	22	29	13	32	13
Primary exports (percentage of merchandise exports)	1965	87	94	100	92	63
	1987	82	83	100	86	36
Resource balance (percentage of GNP)	1965	1	1	1	−5	−3
	1995	−38	−6	−9	−3	−3
Value added in manufacturing	1965	8	11	8	9	14
	1987	5	11	5	10	18
	1997	7	10	8	17	19
Value added in agriculture	1965	46	35	52	43	46
	1987	61	31	76	34	31
	1997	47	29	44	18	25
Labor force in agriculture	1965	90	86	91	77	73
	1987	84	81	86	71	68
Urban population (percentage of total population)	1965	5	9	7	14	18
	1987	24	22	10	27	25

Source: World Bank data.

Agriculture and industry are the mainstays of the economy. Tanzania's economy is basically agrarian. The economy depends on agriculture, which is predominantly smallholder and subsistence in nature, marked by backward technology and low use of modern inputs, and has significant linkages to other domestic sectors. Agriculture accounts for about 50 percent of GDP, provides 85 percent of merchandise exports (raw and processed), and is directly or indirectly a source of employment and livelihood for 90 percent of the total work force and the majority of Tanzanians. Industry is dominated by the manufacturing sector, which currently accounts for about 8 percent of GDP and concentrates on agricultural processing and the manufacture of light consumer goods. However, Tanzania has limited production of equipment and machinery. Industrial development has mainly been pursued in the form of import substitution, until recently has been dominated by public enterprises, and is marked by low technological adaptation and absorption. As competition and the privatization of manufacturing enterprises that formerly were publicly owned gather momentum, signs are appearing of gains in efficiency and greater use of new technology. Recently, even as inefficient firms folded and the industrial base shrank, the manufacturing sector has maintained growth rates of between 5 and 8 percent. Both industry and commercial agriculture are considered the main bases for modernizing the economy.

Minerals and tourism are the new pacemakers for growth. Given the natural and mineral endowments of Tanzania, tourism and mining are envisaged to offer a big push toward economic growth. In 1998 tourism contributed 7.6 percent of GDP, up from a paltry 1.5 percent in the early 1990s. The sector's annual growth rate has averaged 22 percent over the past three years. The number of tourists visiting Tanzania has increased by 34 percent, from 360,000 in 1997 to 482,000 in 1998. This increase in tourism boosted foreign exchange earnings from the sector by 45 percent, from US$392 million in 1997 to US$570 million in 1998. Unlike the prereform period, when the sector was dominated by government institutions and lacked a coordinated tourism policy, the core of the tourism business is now market oriented and guided by the National Tourism Policy. As much as 25 percent of the land area in Tanzania has been set aside as wildlife and botanical sanctuaries. The country aims to attract more than 1 million tourists per year by 2010 and raise the tourist sector's contribution to GDP to more than 25 percent. However, for this ambitious target to be realized, more investment will be needed in market research, infrastructure, publicity, promotion, and improvement of service skills.

As regards mining, the opening of the sector to private investment is already showing positive responses, with Tanzania for the past two years being among the top destinations for mineral prospecting investment in the whole of Sub-Saharan Africa, particularly for gold. The government has abolished its monopoly in the sector and adopted the Mineral Policy of Tanzania to guide and spearhead the development of the sector in the market-oriented approach. This response is also expected to help overcome problems of poor technology and widespread smuggling of minerals. Already there are large entries of foreign direct investment (FDI) in the sector, which hitherto was dominated by artisan and small-scale miners, most of whom used crude mining technology and operated informally. In 1998 the mining sector contributed 1.8 percent of GDP and grew 27.4 percent. The target is to raise the contribution by the sector to GDP to 10 percent as new mining operations come on line and a more robust formal market for minerals develops.

Infrastructure remains a key constraint to exploiting Tanzania's potential. To achieve the growth and modernization targets described above, Tanzania must pay closer attention to its infrastructure network to enable improved accessibility to productive locations. The transport network is geared toward serving an economy dependent on the outside world for output markets and imported inputs, leaving gaps for a cohesive network that would help develop the domestic market. The vastness of the country and the wide geographical distribution of its economic activities, partly following the location of natural endowments, have posed enormous pressures on the rather undeveloped communication and transport systems. Statistics show that Tanzania has a road network consisting of only 85,000 kilometers of roads, of which 10,300 kilometers (12 percent) are trunk roads, 24,700 kilometers (29 percent) are regional roads, and 50,000 kilometers (59 percent) are district roads. District roads include 27,550 kilometers of feeder roads, 20,000 kilometers of district-to-district roads, and 2,450 kilometers of urban roads. Out of the total road network, only about 5 percent are paved and 95 percent are unpaved (10 percent are gravel and 85 percent are earth). Of the unpaved roads, only about 14 percent are in good condition, 25 percent are in fair condition, and the remaining 61 percent are in poor condition. The challenge is therefore to upgrade, rehabilitate, and maintain the road network.

The railway system covers about 3,570 kilometers, with Tanzania-Zambia Railways Authority (TAZARA) railway lines covering 970 kilometers and Tanzania Railways Corporation lines covering 2,600 kilometers. Water transport in lakes Tanganyika, Victoria, and Nyasa is not well developed and depends on old vessels. Tanzania has about 123 airports, of which only 11 have paved runways. These include the three international airports in Dar es Salaam, Kilimanjaro, and Zanzibar.

The communication systems, especially the telephone system, are fairly well developed, but have low coverage across the country and are mainly concentrated in urban centers. This shortfall is partly offset by greater use of radios. At 278 radios per 1,000 people, the use of radios in Tanzania is significantly above the Sub-Saharan African average of 196. Television recently has spread fairly rapidly on the basis of private sector initiative but, again, is largely concentrated in the five most important urban centers: Dar es Salaam, Mwanza, Arusha, Dodoma, and Moshi.

Tanzania has not as yet exploited its large potential for power generation. Although its hydroelectric power system is relatively well developed by African standards, the cost of power is relatively high. Cost inefficiencies in the distribution system and low revenue collection are the main sources of the relatively high unit cost of power in the country. The electricity supply is predominantly hydroelectric, with fairly good coverage by the National Grid distribution system, which supplies about 85 percent of total electricity. The remainder of the supply is thermal. A prospective switch from diesel-based to gas-based (using Songo Songo gas reserves) generation of electricity for heating should further lower the overall unit cost of power generation. Currently the power generation capacity stands at 350 megawatts and is set to increase by another 180 megawatts after the commissioning of the Kihansi hydropower project. In 1996 electricity consumption per capita was estimated at 59 kilowatts. However, power service is concentrated in urban centers and rural electrification is still relatively undeveloped. Solar power is not well tapped, and areas with no electricity depend on other sources of power, mainly firewood and charcoal and, to a lesser extent, biogas.

Tanzania is also well endowed with abundant water sources, but the harnessing of this water for irrigation is still inadequate. The installed capacity of water schemes, rated at 1,156,607 cubic meters per day, is still low. Out of this, only about 69.8 percent is fully used. While the overall objective is to provide clean, safe, and adequate water for all by 2002, the current water supply covers only 46 percent of rural areas and about 68 percent of urban centers. Out of the rural coverage, 30 percent is erratic or completely inoperative, while 52 percent of the urban coverage is eroded by technical and commercial losses. In an attempt to improve supply conditions, urban and rural water schemes are being reorganized into autonomous systems. Urban water authorities are aimed at being self-financing, while rural water schemes will still depend on the government budget to a large extent.

Trade is dominated by traditional exports and imports, but is diversifying. Although significant developments in nontraditional exports have occurred in recent years, Tanzania's exports remain dominated by primary agricultural commodities. Seven commodities—coffee, cotton, cashew nuts, cloves, tea, tobacco, and sisal—have traditionally constituted more than half of the value of total exports. Given the still large share of primary commodity exports, Tanzania's export sector remains highly vulnerable to the vagaries of weather and to fluctuations in world market prices. Nontraditional exports that have good potential in Tanzania include manufactured goods, minerals, services (especially tourism), and horticulture. Noncompetitive imports dominated in the past, but competitive imports have increasingly become prominent, creating competitive pressure for more efficient domestic production. This change has brought with it rising cries of protectionism from some local manufacturers.

Institutional reforms focus on supporting a transition to a market economy. Tanzania is governed by its 1977 constitution, as revised in 1984 and 1999. The country is a signatory to the International Human Rights Charter, and its legal system is based on English common law, with judicial review of legislative acts being limited to matters of interpretation. Power is separated into three branches of government: executive, legislative, and judicial. The country is democratic and adopted a multiparty system in 1995. More than a dozen political parties are registered, five of which are represented in the unicameral National Assembly (which governs the union of Tanzania and Zanzibar) and two in Zanzibar's House of Representatives. Elections are held every five years to elect the president and members of the National Assembly of Tanzania and the president and members of the House of Representatives of Zanzibar. The presidents' tenure in office is limited by the constitution to two five-year periods. Politically, Tanzania has been stable. The country owes its stability, in part, to a cohesive national identity that is built around a common language, Swahili, despite the country's multiplicity of ethnic groups. The government recently adopted a decentralized governance structure, but is still predominantly centralized in operation and has weak capacity in terms of public service delivery. To effectively implement market-based economic policies, the government has decided to leave most of the economic activities in the hands of the private sector and concentrate on the core functions of the government. These core functions include law and order, defense and security, the regulatory framework, and the provision of infrastructure.

Over the past four years, the government has embarked on institutionalizing market-oriented economic systems after nearly three decades of a socialist approach to economic and social development. For nearly a decade, economic reforms took place against the backdrop of the inertia of the government's control mentality, as well as property rights and legal systems that were designed to facilitate a socialist economy. This disjuncture accounted partly for the lack of a robust private sector response, as possible reversals were feared. Changes in the perceptions of the credibility of reforms needed to be grounded by binding legal and institutional reforms. Recent public service reforms target changes in attitudes and enhanced efficiency in the delivery of public services. Supportive institutions and changes in the legal provisions are needed to buttress the development of the private sector in the economy and remain the main challenges in enabling the economy to move to a higher level of supply response, growth, and poverty reduction.

2. Review of Recent Macroeconomic Performance

Since 1986 the Tanzanian government has implemented macroeconomic reforms with the objective of sustaining a stable macroeconomic environment and higher growth. This chapter takes stock of the macroeconomic developments in Tanzania over the period 1986 to the present. The broad objective of the chapter is to characterize trends and to draw out specific policy episodes and analyze their impact on growth and welfare. The chapter is organized into six major sections. The first section reviews macroeconomic reform programs pursued since 1986, identifies the impetus for change, and describes the sequence of actions from the first through the second generation of reforms. The discussion then follows the sequence of the reforms, starting with the first Economic Recovery Program (ERP I) and moving to the current broader macroeconomic and structural reforms. Subsequently, economic performance in response to such reforms is reviewed, focusing on results and challenges. The second section explores the extent to which various policy measures have contributed to achieving the reform objectives. The third section reviews recent developments in the external sector, concentrating on the structure and contribution of exports to growth, the composition of imports and trends, capital account liberalization, and developments in the balance of payments. The section also discusses issues related to economic integration, globalization, and patterns of markets. Special attention is given to export constraints inhibiting export growth and diversification. The fourth section reviews the state of the financial sector before and after the financial sector reforms initiated in 1991, with the objective of assessing the achievements of the reform and the challenges for the future. The following section analyzes Tanzania's debt burden, both domestic and foreign. The main focus is on the impact of both categories of debt as well as the high debt-service requirement, particularly as they affect the budget and balance of payments position. The section also proposes strategies to deal with the debt problem and appraises current initiatives for dealing with the problem. The last section briefly concludes the chapter, highlighting the major issues.

The Genesis and Overview of Macroeconomic Reforms

Tanzania experienced severe economic strains starting in the late 1970s. By the mid-1980s the Tanzanian economy was in deep macroeconomic crisis, with overall economic performance having declined to the lowest levels since independence. The decline in economic performance, which started in the mid-1970s, was manifested in a number of aspects, including the following:

- Insufficient and declining overall GDP growth, averaging only 1 percent growth per year during 1980–85, which translates into negative per capita growth given the annual population growth of 2.8 percent
- Poor performance of the agriculture sector, resulting in the emergence of food deficits and declining export volumes of traditional export crops
- Currency overvaluation and severe problems with balance of payments caused by declining export volumes and commodity export prices; rising import prices; and rising debt-service obligations, as both domestic and foreign debts accumulated
- A widespread shortage of foreign exchange and goods
- An accelerating rate of inflation, which seriously eroded the already low levels of real incomes

- An increasing and unsustainable budget deficit, caused by decreasing tax revenues as the government's revenue base (GDP) eroded and leading to excessive government bank borrowing and increased dependence on external sources of finance
- A general deterioration of both social and physical infrastructure
- Negative real interest rates.

Causes of the crisis have been a subject of considerable debate. At the start of the 1980s, the crisis was associated with and explained in terms of exogenous factors that affected the economy during the 1970s. Such factors included drought, the large increase in petroleum prices, the collapse of the East African Community, the war with Uganda under Idi Amin, and volatility in the terms of trade. However, these shocks, despite their severity, clearly could not alone have accounted for the magnitude and persistence of economic decline. They exacerbated a situation that had already begun to deteriorate. The stringent macroeconomic environment, manifested through central control of economic activity was, in essence, the core factor for the deterioration of the economy.

To deal with the macroeconomic crisis, the government launched two successive "home-grown" stabilization programs: the two-year National Economic Survival Program (NESP) in FY81 followed by the three-year Structural Adjustment Program (SAP) in FY82. Generally, NESP and SAP measures were aimed at restoring economic growth and sustaining it through increasing the output of food and cash crops. The methods employed included using appropriate incentives, increasing foreign exchange earnings and improving their utilization, increasing capacity utilization in industries, increasing industrial exports, reducing the import content of industrial production, and controlling government expenditure.

Given its hasty preparation, the NESP was more of a program of targets and exhortation than an operational program serving as a guide on how to achieve those targets. For example, foreign exchange could not be used more effectively because the government lacked a prioritized list of enterprises to which to allocate the available meager foreign exchange. At the same time, capacity expansions continued instead of concentrating on increasing capacity utilization in existing projects (Wangwe 1988). Although the SAP further elaborated the objectives of NESP, the success of the SAP, like that of the NESP, largely depended on foreign resource inflows, which were never realized. In general, the implementation of NESP and SAP measures achieved limited success for two main reasons. First, some of the economic problems that were being tackled were structural in nature, and thus required not only stabilization, but also complete structural transformation. Second, to deal with most of the problems relating to increasing production, a significant amount of foreign exchange was needed—more than what could be realized in the two programs.

After extensive discussions with the World Bank and the International Monetary Fund (IMF), the government adopted ERP-I in June 1986. The program reflected a renewed effort to overcome the economic crisis. The program, which was to cover three years (FY86 through FY88), was designed basically to deal with problems similar to those the SAP was intended to address, but was supported by Tanzania's major donors. The main objectives of the ERP-I were to increase efficiency and restore economic growth to at least 5 percent per year, reestablish macroeconomic stability by reducing inflation and fiscal deficits, realign the exchange rate, and improve the balance of payments by increasing exports and foreign exchange earnings. Other objectives were to rehabilitate the country's physical infrastructure, especially in the transport and communication, energy, and water sectors, so as to support directly productive activities; to improve capacity utilization in industries from 20–30 percent to 60–70 percent through the allocation of scarce foreign exchange to key priority sectors, programs, and firms; and to improve the quality of social services delivered by existing facilities, as opposed to expanding facilities. Unlike earlier adjustment programs, ERP-I was bold in that it suggested policy measures that challenged and aimed at dismantling, the existing state-controlled economic setup; stated plainly that increased external assistance in the medium term was a precondition for a recovery that would lead to renewed economic growth; and has rigorously implemented most of the measures since June 1986. Given the size of the economy, the number of sectors within the economy, and the gap between resource requirements and their availability, a frontal approach for the whole economy could not be sustained. Instead, the government identified a few sectors—agriculture, transport, industry, energy, and social services—for resource concentration.

Specific measures taken to achieve the objectives of ERP-I included substantial increases in agricultural producer prices and improvements in marketing structures to provide incentives for increased production of food and export crops; devaluation of the local currency; reactivation of interest rate policy to attain positive interest rates and thus encourage savings mobilization and their efficient deployment; rehabilitation of the worn-out physical infrastructure of the country in support of directly productive activities; increase in capacity utilization in industry through the allocation of scarce foreign exchange to priority sectors and firms; and reduction of the inflation rate with the aim of bringing it from above 30 percent to less than 10 percent.

By the end of the three years of ERP-I (June 1989), some encouraging, positive signs of achievements emerged. First, GDP grew at an average annual growth rate of about 4 percent (albeit below the target of 5 percent) over the program period, from an average of about 1 percent during 1980–85. Agriculture contributed most of the growth recovery. Other major contributions to such growth came from increased industrial output and increased retail and wholesale trade, following a deepening of trade liberalization and progressive price decontrol that started in 1984. Second, the inflation rate (national consumer price index) declined marginally from about 32.5 percent in 1986 to about 30 percent by end of the program period. This inability to contain inflation was mainly due to excess expansion of domestic credit (particularly to specified institutions, including some parastatals, cooperative unions, and crop marketing authorities), which led to expansion of the money supply beyond planned levels. Third, manufacturing capacity utilization for some firms increased substantially. This was particularly true for those firms that benefited from the increased inflow of external resources (through import support and open general license arrangements) in support of ERP-I. Fourth, exports, particularly of nontraditional products, increased. Reforms introduced in the external sector (including the exchange rate adjustment and the export retention scheme), coupled with external support, helped stimulate the export sector. Fifth, foreign exchange earnings increased slightly. Finally, the exchange rate was steeply depreciated during FY87 (through devaluing the local currency), by 338 percent in nominal terms and 111 percent in real terms (Sahn and Younger 1997).

Despite the foregoing achievements, economic growth continued to be limited by a number of factors, namely:
- Domestic savings and investments in physical infrastructure—notably transport, marketing, and processing—was inadequate.
- The rate of inflation was still high, having declined only slightly during the program period (mainly because of a failure to control domestic credit, as well as unsatisfactory supply response and distribution bottlenecks).
- The position of the balance of payments was still weak because of a decline in export commodity prices; rising import prices, which became increasingly burdensome; a rise in debt-service obligations; and slow recovery of the export sector.
- Weaknesses in the agricultural marketing systems and processing and transportation problems persisted.
- A worsening trend in the provision of social services—particularly education, health, water, and nutrition—continued. Besides continuing to cause hardships to the people, this trend posed a long-term threat to the whole economy. This was partly a consequence of ERP-I focusing on

sectors that were expected to bring about fast recovery so that some sectors, such as social services, became disadvantaged in resource allocation.

ERP-I was followed by another three-year program launched in FY89, referred to as ERP-II or the Economic and Social Action Program. Like its predecessor, ERP-II covered three years (FY89 through FY91). However, apart from implementing and fostering wider market reforms started under ERP-I, ERP-II was broadened to include consideration of the social aspects of adjustment, with the aim of cushioning the most vulnerable groups from the burden of adjustment. The program focused on ensuring the existence of a stable macroeconomic environment, efficient resource allocation, and improvement in the provision of incentives so as to stimulate supply responses. In particular, government efforts were focused on improving fiscal management and on comprehensively reforming the public sector, including privatizing state-owned enterprises and reforming the civil service. The incentive structures were also realigned toward export growth and conservation of scarce foreign exchange (IMF 1999a; Ndulu 1994; Ndulu and Wangwe 1997).

Specific objectives of ERP-II were to increase the domestic production of food and export crops; rehabilitate the physical infrastructure, in particular, transport and communications; reduce the rate of domestic inflation to below 10 percent within the program period; revamp the industrial sector; restore efficiency in the mobilization and utilization of domestic resources; restore internal and external balances by pursuing appropriate fiscal, monetary, and trade policies; and rehabilitate the social services through appropriate strategies and programs that would enhance people's participation in the operation and management of such services.

After three years of implementing ERP-II and some aspects of ERP-I, achievements were mixed. Implementation of the social action programs under ERP-II could not be realized during the program period. The formulation and design of such programs took substantial time, and their implementation required even more time. In fact, the objectives of the social action programs are still being pursued under another, wider program called the Social Dimension of Adjustment. Specific results of ERP-II included the following. First, improvements in the growth of the economy recorded under ERP-I could not be maintained, although 1990 showed a big rise following good agricultural performance, which rose by 5.5 percent that year. Nonetheless, on average, agricultural performance during ERP-II slackened compared with ERP-I. Second, the procurement and marketing of agricultural crops (in particular, food crops) was liberalized, coupled with restructuring of the National Milling Corporation and crop authorities. Third, performance of the industrial sector in general slackened slightly, although a number of industries managed to perform above 50 percent of capacity. With the objective of enhancing efficiency in this parastatal-dominated sector, the government embarked on a restructuring program that would include privatization, starting with the shoe and leather subsector. Fourth, in 1992 the Investment Promotion Center was established and the National Investment Promotion Act was enacted to promote private investment in the national economy by providing attractive incentives to prospective investors, both local and foreign. Fifth, the rate of inflation declined significantly to about 21.8 percent by the end of 1992, to some extent caused by the increased availability of consumer goods following further trade liberalization.

Overall, during ERP-I and ERP-II a wide range of market reforms were implemented. These reforms included liberalizing food and some cash-crop marketing; liberalizing agricultural input distribution; deregulating prices, exchange rates, wages, and interest rates; rationalizing the tariff structure; adopting a national investment policy to protect and promote private investment; initiating fiscal and monetary reforms; reforming the civil service reform with the aim downsizing the government; restructuring the parastatals; and allowing private banking. The main emphasis of the reforms was on the need for greater reliance on market institutions and forces and the need for increased private sector participation in the development process.

After ERP-II, further efforts to make the economy recover and stabilize on a sustained growth path continued to be made under the auspices of IMF's Enhanced Structural Adjustment Facility (ESAF) beginning in FY95, after a slow-down due to inappropriate policies during FY92 and FY94. The major focus of ESAF was on consolidating earlier recovery efforts, particularly those aimed at ensuring a stable macroeconomic environment; efficient resource allocation; increased production, growth, and poverty reduction; and more private sector participation in economic activities.

Reform efforts after ERP-II also focused on transforming the public sector to serve a market-oriented economy led by the private sector. This was particularly aimed at aligning policy reform programs with the institutional orientation (which was then predominantly parastatal or public). As a result, price incentives intended to motivate producers were absorbed by public marketing institutions, dampening the impact of such well-intended policies. In addition, the government's role in the economy as a whole had to be reviewed accordingly, taking into account the changing economic environment. Thus, the public sector reform program—encompassing the parastatal sector, the financial sector, the civil service, and the planning and budgeting system—carried over the reform program of the ERPs to distinct sectoral reform programs. As some aspects of the public sector reform program started during the ERPs, in essence the objectives of the reform agenda continued to be the attainment of sustainable economic growth, with each sector expected to play its respective role in the process.

Reforms in the public sector, which are still ongoing, may be looked at as composed of two distinct aspects: macroeconomic stabilization measures (as set out in fiscal, monetary, and trade policies), and the respective institutional reforms (in, for example, the parastatal sector, financial sector, civil service, and budget). While details of macroeconomic reforms are covered in subsequent sections, the next few paragraphs focus on institutional reforms, because the preceding discussion of macroeconomic stabilization measures cannot be complete without linking it to institutional reforms.

Institutional or structural reforms have been undertaken to provide the requisite environment for implementation of adopted macroeconomic and sectoral policies. In this context, therefore, the public sector had to be reexamined with a view to making its institutions adapt to the new policy environment, where central direction and control of economic activity gives way to a liberalized economy. In the same vein, the government has redefined its role and functions accordingly. These reforms, which are still ongoing at various stages, have been more difficult and challenging to implement.

Institutional reforms in the financial sector have been undertaken progressively, including strengthening the supervisory role of the Bank of Tanzania (as provided for in Parliamentary acts of 1991 and 1995) in managing monetary policy. Other measures have included licensing both local and foreign private financial institutions (for example, banks, *bureaux de change*, stock market exchange, and insurance) and restructuring public institutions in the sector—the Cooperative and Rural Development Bank (CRDB);, the Post Office Savings Bank, the Tanzania Housing Bank; and the National Bank of Commerce (1997) Ltd., or NBC (1997). These measures have introduced competition in the previously publicly dominated financial sector, in effect enhancing efficiency in the mobilization of financial resources and their allocation to economic activities.

With the objective of strengthening tax administration, the government established, through an act of Parliament, the autonomous Tanzania Revenue Authority (TRA) which started operating in July 1996 out of the former tax departments of the Ministry of Finance. The value added tax (VAT) was also introduced and became operational from July 1998.

In 1992 the government established the Parastatal Sector Reform Commission to supervise the reform of the parastatal sector, which comprised a multitude of state-owned firms and companies with a dominating influence on the economy. Measures taken during this process have included divestiture (whole or partial privatization) and disbanding those parastatals no longer considered useful, particularly those that had become inefficient and a major drain on public resources. These measures were intended to reduce the public sector's dominance of economic activity and to pave the way for private sector development, while at the same time alleviating fiscal and efficiency problems in government associated with the overly large parastatal sector.

Institutional reforms in the agriculture sector mainly focused on three aspects: streamlining crop marketing, rationalizing agricultural input distribution, and restructuring cooperative unions. Measures taken in these reforms, have included the following:

- Restrictions on farmers selling their produce through specified marketing channels were progressively eliminated, thereby improving their profit margins on sales, and hence their income. Farmers are no longer bound to sell their produce through the burdensome cooperative unions.
- The monopoly of the state-owned enterprises in agricultural input distribution (for example, the Tanzania Fertilizer Company and the Tanzania Seed Company) were eliminated, as were their financing arrangements through cooperative unions. These reforms have been among the most challenging in the sector and have enhanced the role of the private sector.
- The Cooperative Act of 1991 was adopted. The act redefined criteria for membership in, equity requirements for, control of, and management of cooperatives. Subsequently, commercial viability of cooperative unions became paramount for their sustainability, with the result that only the strong and well-managed unions have survived.

Overall, notwithstanding the hitches faced, reforms in the agriculture sector have had a marginally positive impact on the sector's output and its contribution to overall GDP. Downswings in agricultural performance have mostly been attributed to bad weather (droughts and floods), over which the rain-fed sector has no control. Important institutional and infrastructural bottlenecks, however, remain to be tackled.

The main objective of reforms in government, through the Civil Service Reform Program has been to enhance the government's efficiency. Thus, consistent with liberalization and other reforms outlined earlier, the government, on its part, has had to undertake structural reforms. These included downsizing its staff numbers and operations to alleviate undue pressures on the government budget, as well as to enhance its efficiency. While staff numbers have been considerably reduced (77,000 workers were retrenched between 1992 and 1998, reducing the work force to around 270,000), the envisaged efficiency has yet to be realized because of the government's inability to enhance the pay of its remaining staff sufficiently and inculcate a merit-based and performance-based culture.

Output Performance during the Reform Period

The performance of Tanzania's economy, in terms of real GDP growth over the past 10 years, and in particular in recent years, appears to be stabilizing and hence poised for higher levels of growth in the long term. Notwithstanding weather that is adverse to agricultural output, the country has managed to maintain positive GDP growth rates, averaging 4 percent per year in the second half of the 1990s (table 2.1). The main driving force behind the improved economic performance has been the various economic reforms the country has pursued consistently over the past 10 years. In fact, looking at the performance of some immediate neighbors and the Africa in general, Tanzania compares quite well. Nonetheless, Tanzania's economic performance during the 1990s (except for 1998) was below the world average growth rates (table 2.2).

Notwithstanding overall GDP performance over the past 10 years (figure 2.1), the structure of the economy does not appear to have changed much (figures 2.2 and 2.3). Agriculture continues to be the predominant sector, contributing more than 46 percent to overall real GDP and employing about 80 percent of the total population. Thus agricultural performance significantly influences overall annual economic performance. This situation makes the economy highly susceptible to adverse changes in weather that affect agriculture, as happened in 1997 and 1998, when drought and the El Niño rains, respectively, hit the economy hard. Yet the fact that the economy could withstand such shocks and managed to register positive growth rates averaging more than 3 percent per year indicates that the economy is now stabilizing and poised for higher levels of growth.

Table 2.1. *Tanzania's GDP Growth Rates, 1988–98*
(percent)

Indicator	1988	1989	1990	1991	1992	1993	1994	1995	1996	1997	1998
Economic activity											
Agriculture	2.2	3.9	5.5	3.6	1.2	3.1	2.1	5.8	3.9	2.4	1.9
Crops	2.0	4.3	6.4	3.9	0.7	3.1	2.0	6.8	4.2	2.3	1.8
Livestock	2.8	2.7	3.0	2.7	2.7	2.7	1.4	2.7	2.7	2.7	1.9
Forestry and hunting	2.7	2.7	2.8	2.7	2.7	2.9	2.7	2.7	2.7	2.7	1.2
Fishing	3.0	3.1	2.9	2.9	3.0	4.4	3.9	4.0	4.1	3.7	3.5
Mining and quarrying	−1.3	13.0	16.5	11.7	7.7	8.2	15.0	11.7	9.6	17.1	27.4
Manufacturing	3.1	5.2	4.1	1.9	−4.0	0.6	−0.2	1.6	4.8	5.0	8.0
Electricity and water	9.3	9.1	7.9	11.1	−1.3	0.9	2.0	6.1	11.1	2.2	5.5
Electricity	12.5	12.1	9.9	12.6	−1.8	0.7	2.0	6.8	12.4	2.3	6.0
Water	−3.8	−5.2	−3.1	1.1	2.5	2.0	1.8	1.6	1.6	1.7	1.8
Construction	23.1	−14.0	30.5	−7.1	5.8	−14.4	1.4	−14.7	7.6	8.2	9.9
Trade, hotels, and restaurants	2.7	2.1	7.4	2.5	−0.7	−0.4	1.1	3.5	3.5	5.0	4.7
Transport and communication	3.2	2.2	0.5	2.7	14.2	0.1	0.9	5.9	1.1	4.9	6.2
Financial and business services	5.7	9.4	1.7	1.4	3.8	4.8	2.7	0.6	0.4	7.7	5.6
Finance and insurance	9.8	19.7	1.1	−3.6	3.2	8.0	4.6	−5.2	−5.4	16.5	9.0
Real estate	3.7	3.8	2.1	4.6	4.2	2.9	1.4	4.1	3.5	3.3	3.4
Business services	2.5	3.0	3.2	3.3	3.5	3.5	4.5	5.0	6.0	1.2	6.0
Public admin. and other services	9.8	3.8	3.0	5.0	5.6	−3.9	−0.1	−2.7	1.6	3.2	2.7
Public administration	12.2	3.1	2.1	5.3	5.7	−7.3	−2.2	−6.3	0.0	2.0	1.5
Education	3.9	6.3	6.4	3.2	7.0	3.5	4.7	3.6	3.8	3.7	6.6
Health	4.4	4.7	4.7	4.3	3.3	3.8	3.6	3.7	3.7	5.1	2.4
Other services	4.8	4.9	4.3	5.2	5.1	4.7	4.2	5.1	4.9	6.3	4.0
Total GDP (factor cost) growth	4.4	2.6	6.2	2.8	1.8	0.4	1.4	3.6	4.2	3.3	4.0
Per capita real GDP growth	1.3	−0.3	3.3	−0.1	−1.0	−2.4	−1.4	0.7	1.3	0.2	0.9
Inflation—consumer price index											
(1994 = 100)	31.8	30.3	35.6	28.7	21.8	24.0	35.5	27.4	21.0	16.1	12.9
GDP deflator	27.0	26.4	24.8	24.2	23.7	23.6	23.3	22.5	21.6	20.9	20.1

Source: URT (1999b).

Table 2.2. *Comparative GDP Growth Rates, 1988–98*
(percent)

Country	1988	1989	1990	1991	1992	1993	1994	1995	1996	1997	1998
Tanzania	4.4	2.6	6.2	2.8	1.8	0.4	1.4	3.6	4.2	3.3	4.0
Kenya	5.1	5.0	4.3	2.3	0.4	2.6	4.4	4.1	2.1	2.3	2.7
Uganda	7.1	6.4	5.5	5.2	4.5	6.3	10.1	8.4	5.0	5.5	4.0
Africa	2.1	3.3	2.6	3.3	1.8	0.2	2.6	2.9	4.0	2.9	3.3
Major industrial countries	3.7	8.4	2.8	2.2	1.9	1.2	3.2	2.5	3.0	3.1	2.0
World	4.3	3.3	2.5	1.8	2.7	2.7	3.9	3.7	4.2	4.1	2.0

Sources: URT (1999b); Uganda–Background to the Budget (FY98); *Kenya Economic Survey* (1993), World Bank (1999a); ADB (1998); ECA (1999); IMF and World Bank (1999).

Figure 2.1. *Growth of Main Production Sectors, 1988–98*

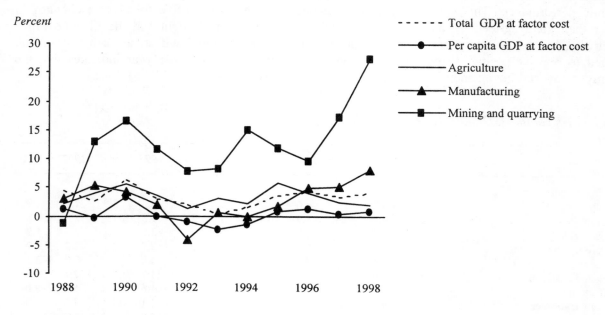

Figure 2.2. *Sector Contribution to Overall GDP in 1988*

Figure 2.3. *Sector Contribution to Overall GDP in 1998*

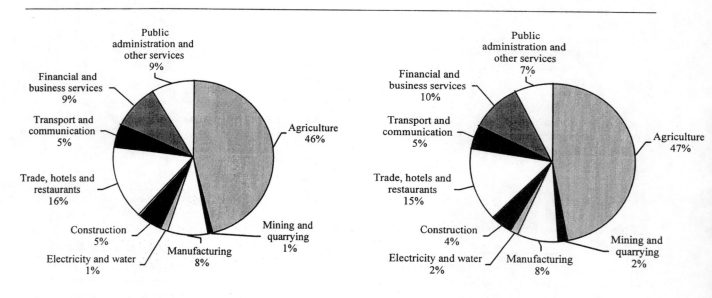

The performance of the industrial sector (including manufacturing, mining and quarrying, and construction) starting from the second half of the 1990s shows an upward swing after years of declining growth before 1994. On the one hand, the restructuring and privatization process in the manufacturing subsector in many cases entailed curtailing and stopping production pending conclusion of the transactions involved. This adversely affected the subsector's output, with its contribution to overall GDP declining from 8.4 percent in 1988 to 8 percent in 1998. On the other hand, the restructuring process has started to pay off, as may be noted from the upswing in the subsector's growth beginning in 1995. Increased growth in manufacturing has been recorded, and this trend is expected to be maintained as privatization revives defunct public enterprises. Enhanced competition following the economic liberalization process will help spur increased efficiency. Mining, which has over the years contributed around 1 percent to overall GDP, is poised to be one of the most important subsectors, as investments continue to increase in the mostly unexploited vast mineral deposits, including gold, diamonds, and various precious gemstones. Growth in this sector is higher than in other economic sectors, reaching 27.4 percent in 1998.

In the services sector, tourism—whose data is captured under the trade, hotels, and restaurants subsector—stands out as another promising, sustainable contributor to GDP, given its vast potential, for example, extremely large game reserves, sandy beaches, the Ngorongoro crater, and Mount Kilimanjaro. Tourism accounts for more than 50 percent of the sectoral GDP of trade, hotels, and restaurants. The tourism subsector is expected to maintain its recent impressive three-year average growth of more than 16 percent per year. Tourism alone earned the country an estimated US$470 million in 1998, making it the country's number one foreign exchange earner. This subsector still has potential for even higher levels of contribution to the economy: an estimated US$600 million by 2002. The optimism for higher future growth of the subsector is attributed to increasing active participation of the private sector, motivated by the intensification of international tourism marketing and promotional campaigns overseas. The government, for its part, has improved existing road infrastructure in the tourist zones and rationalized tariffs applicable to tourist services.

The Government of Tanzania has articulated the long-term development perspective of the country in *Development Vision 2025* (URT 1998b). While taking account of lessons learned from past and ongoing economic reforms, the government has charted the future outlook of Tanzania in terms of explicit objectives and the respective strategies for reaching the identified destination of a sustainable and better Tanzania by 2025. Challenges to be surmounted along the journey of implementation have accordingly been identified by the government, so that meeting the goals and targets set out is contingent on appropriately setting priorities and exerting effort in the process. In broad terms, overall goals and targets for *Development Vision 2025* are the attainment of high-quality livelihoods, a strong and competitive economy, good governance, and the rule of law.

To realize those goals, the macroeconomic environment will need to be corrected by minimizing price distortions, ensuring price stability, and managing macroeconomic balances in such a way that Tanzania does not live beyond its means. This will also call for mobilizing higher levels of domestic savings and investment, broadly based human resource development, and sustainable economic growth.

Over the period of *Development Vision 2025*, the government envisages that real GDP growth will increase from the current average of 3–4 percent per year to an annual average of 8–9 percent by 2025. The economy is to be diversified and semi-industrialized, with combined contributions from mining, manufacturing, construction, and power rising from the current level of 14 percent GDP to 40 percent, and with a modernized agriculture sector. Tanzania is expected to attain the human development level of the current middle-income countries, which implies attaining an average real GDP per capita of US$3,000. Abject poverty is also expected to have been eradicated by 2025. Specific policy interventions are reviewed next in greater detail.

Policy Developments and Macroeconomic Management

Monetary Policy, Fiscal Policy, and Inflation

The government's strategy for reducing inflation in Tanzania has, since 1986, focused on tight monetary policy and increased output production. This focus has been determined by the fact that Tanzania's inflation has been both a monetary and a structural phenomenon (Kilindo 1992; Ndulu and Hyuha 1989). The task of slowing down inflation proved difficult, both under ERP-I, ERP-II, and in the first half of the 1990s. This difficulty was due to structural problems that hindered efficient production (for example, dependence on the weather) and to inflationary financing of persistent fiscal deficits caused by a combination of high government expenditure and poor domestic revenue collection. Inflation remained high during these periods, although at a slightly lower level than the prereform level of 32.3 percent in 1985. Inflation averaged 31.1 percent during ERP-I, 28.8 percent during ERP-II, and 29 percent during 1993–95 (table 2.3).

The fall in inflation to 21.8 percent in 1992 was a result of ERP-II's modest success in controlling government expenditure and improving revenue collection, thereby narrowing the gap between the two. Expenditure as a percentage of GDP declined from 24.8 percent in FY85 to 15.3 percent in FY91, while revenue declined from 16 percent in FY85 to 9.9 percent in FY87 before picking up again after tax rationalization efforts in FY88 to attain a 13.6 percent level in FY91. During the same period, the level of overall fiscal deficit as a percentage of GDP declined from 8.9 percent (before grants) in FY86 to 1.7 percent (before grants) and a surplus of 0.9 percent (after grants) in FY92. ERP-II's fiscal measures made it possible for the government to reduce rapidly the inflationary financing of its budget and to make a net repayment to the banking system in FY91. To a large extent, the narrowing of the fiscal deficit during this early period of reforms was enabled by a sharp rise in the noninflationary external financing of the budget. This is evident from the fact that the fiscal deficit before grants as a proportion of GDP remained high at an average of 4.5 percent.

Fiscal and inflation reduction measures under ERP-II were, however, short-lived. Toward the end of 1992, the government's commitment to implementing economic reforms was virtually abandoned, partly as a result of fears, real or not, that the adjustment programs were hurting the poor disproportionately. By this time the governments' financial discipline had also begun to dissipate and corruption was becoming deep-rooted (Ballali 1999). Revenue collection declined following massive discretionary exemptions on import duties and taxes. Revenue collection recorded a low level of only 10.2 percent of GDP in FY92 before rising slightly to 11.8 percent of GDP in FY94 in response to donors' alarm about the abuse of exemptions and their decision to cut aid. Despite the fall in revenue, government expenditure increased from 15.3 percent of GDP in FY91 to 19 percent in FY92 before declining slightly to 17.5 percent and 14.1 percent in FY93 and FY94, respectively.

The combination of a collapse in revenue and increase in expenditure resulted in a huge overall fiscal deficit (before grants) of 8.8 percent of GDP in FY92. Despite a decrease in expenditure in the following two fiscal years, the budget continued to sustain large deficits equal to 6 percent of GDP in FY93 and 2.3 percent of GDP in FY94 (table 2.3 and figure 2.4), mainly because of a slow recovery in revenue in the face of continued discretionary exemptions. The deficits were largely financed through borrowing from the banking system. Government borrowing from the banking system as a percentage of GDP was as high as 2.1 percent in FY94 and 2.7 percent in FY95, thus fueling inflation from 21.8 percent in FY92, to 35.5 in FY94, to 27.4 percent in 1995. Figure 2.5 shows the relationship between the budget deficit, government bank borrowing, the money supply, and inflation. Other factors that contributed to the inflationary process during this period were high import prices; inadequate supplies, especially of food items; and overall poor economic growth.

Table 2.3. *Important Macroeconomic Indicators, 1985–98* [a]

Indicator	1985	1986	1987	1988	1989	1990	1991	1992	1993	1994	1995	1996	1997	1998
Real GDP growth, calendar year (percent)	—	—	—	4.4	2.6	6.2	2.8	1.8	0.4	1.4	3.6	4.2	3.3	4.0
Money supply (M3) growth (percent)[b]	—	—	20.2	34.8	37.3	45.4	26.9	40.5	43.9	46.3	36.1	16.3	18.2	7.7
Public sector share of domestic credit (percent)[c]	—	100.0	100.0	100.0	83.4	83.2	77.5	70.7	71.2	57.8	63.8	76.1	73.4	58.4
Government share of domestic credit (percent)	—	65.0	53.5	53.9	44.2	38.2	26.9	27.7	34.3	36.5	44.7	70.3	68.9	56.2
Change in government credit (as percent of previous M3)	—	—	4.3	38.9	8.6	3.3	-9.1	0.9	19.3	18.0	13.0	14.6	-2.5	-3.7
Expenditure as a percentage of GDP	26.3	24.8	15.7	15.7	16.1	16.6	15.3	15.3	19.0	17.5	14.1	12.2	12.0	11.1
Revenue as a percentage of GDP	18.5	16.0	10.3	9.9	12.3	12.5	13.5	13.6	10.2	11.4	11.8	13.0	13.4	12.1
Fiscal deficit—before grants (percent of GDP)	—	-8.9	-5.4	-5.8	-3.8	-4.2	-1.9	-1.7	-8.8	-6.0	-2.3	0.8	1.1	1.0
Fiscal deficit—after grants (percent of GDP)	—	—	-1.6	-2.4	-0.2	-0.5	0.4	0.9	-5.1	-2.4	1.5	2.2	3.2	1.9
Inflation—year average (percent)	32.3	32.6	29.8	31.8	30.3	35.8	28.7	21.8	24.0	35.5	27.4	21.0	16.1	12.9
Savings deposit rate—average[d] (percent)	10.0	10.0	21.5	21.5	26.0	26.0	26.0	26.0	24.0	25.0	21.1	16.7	15.1	7.00
Real saving rate (percent)[e]	-22.3	-22.6	-8.3	-10.3	-4.3	-9.8	-2.7	4.2	0	-10.5	-6.3	-4.3	-1.0	-5.9
Lending rate—average[d] (percent)	13.5	13.5	24.0	24.0	26.0	26.0	26.0	30.0	30.0	31.5	35.5	33.5	26.5	26.0
Real lending rate (percent)[e]	-18.8	-19.1	-5.8	-7.8	-4.3	-9.8	-2.7	8.2	6.0	-4.0	8.1	12.5	10.4	13.1
Wedge between lending rate and savings rate (percent)	25.9	25.9	10.4	10.4	0	0	0	13.3	20.0	20.6	40.6	50.1	43.0	73.1
Official exchange rate—average (Tanzanian shillings per U.S. dollars)	17.5	32.7	64.3	99.3	143.4	195.1	219.2	297.7	405.0	509.6	574.8	580.0	612.1	669.8
Effective REER index (1990 = 100)	22.0	36.8	63.1	79.8	91.0	100.0	89.6	106.5	103.7	102.2	98.0	82.5	73.2	69.4

—Not available.
a. Fiscal years, unless stated.
b. M2 = M3 before 1993.
c. Includes credit to the private sector before 1988.
d. Based on the lowest and highest rates within the calendar year.
e. Calculated as the difference between the average nominal interest rate and inflation.
Sources: Appendix tables, various; Bank of Tanzania, Planning Commission, and Treasury data.

21

Figure 2.4. *Revenue, Expenditure, and Fiscal Deficits, 1986–98*

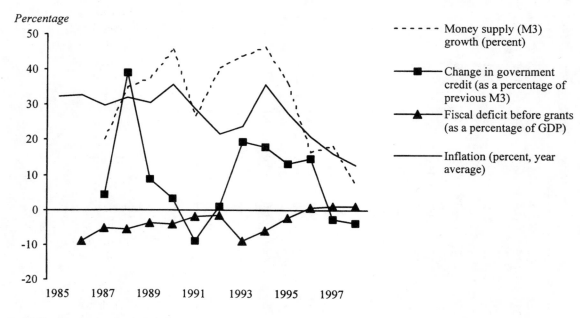

Sources: URT (various years); authors' calculations.

Figure 2.5. *Relationship Between Fiscal Deficit, Government Credit, Money Supply and Inflation, 1986–98*

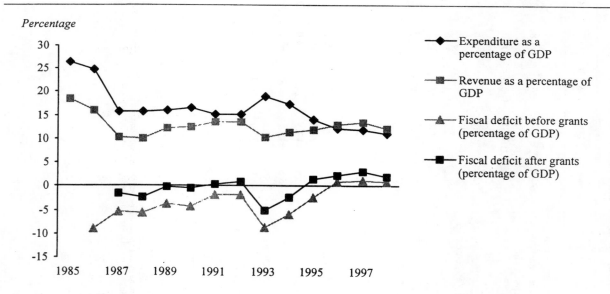

Sources: URT (various years); authors' calculations.

Although the budgetary position improved slightly in early 1996, it was only after the country adopted a monthly cash budget system in the second half of 1996 that discipline was instilled in government expenditure and any reversion to minibudgets and inflationary financing was rendered unnecessary. The cash budget system, which matches expenditure obligations with available resources, has, by and large, managed to curb budget deficits (both before and after grants) and generated surpluses during its period of implementation (table 2.3 and figure 2.5). This success has made it possible for the government to repay its liabilities rather than borrow from the banking system beginning in FY96, and to reduce growth in the broadly defined money supply (M3) from 36.1 percent in FY94 to 7.7 percent in FY97. Reduction in money supply growth, in turn, helped to reduce inflation to 12.9 percent in FY98 (table 2.3) and to 6 percent by March 2000. Apart from government borrowing, earlier attempts to reduce the supply of money were frustrated by the state-owned banks' poor credit policies. This resulted in massive bank borrowing by public institutions, especially agricultural marketing parastatals, government guaranteed cooperative unions, and other insolvent borrowers.

In addition to the cash budget system, the improvement in the government budgetary position has also been made possible by an increase in revenue collection following the creation of the TRA in July 1996 and the introduction of a VAT in July 1998. Moreover, the privatization and divestiture of the majority of ailing parastatals, the liberalization of crop marketing activities, and the collapse of cooperative unions has substantially reduced government obligations in terms of transfer payments, which had increased from 1 percent of GDP in FY85 to 4 percent of GDP in FY92. From about T Sh 20 billion in FY92, government transfers to parastatals fell to T Sh 2.2 billion in FY96 (IMF 1999a). Except for strategic grain reserve management and assistance to state banks awaiting privatization, the government has made no more transfers to crop authorities and other public enterprises since FY96. The privatization strategy, which was adopted in the early 1990s, aims at facilitating government withdrawal from majority ownership of commercial enterprises and the promotion of the private sector by creating a framework conducive to private investment. Private sector participation in ownership of former public enterprises is expected to improve access to capital, technology, and external markets and to sustain employment. At the same time, government withdrawal from majority ownership is also expected to reduce budgetary subventions to them, increase the efficiency of the productive sector, and raise growth rates. Privatization has progressed considerably, with about 60 percent of the 400 parastatal entities earmarked at the beginning of the privatization process being divested by mid-1998 (IMF 1999a).

The success of the cash budget system in reducing fiscal deficits has not been without consequences. As a result of massive expenditure cuts made in trying to match revenue availability, most government obligations, apart from wage bill and debt service, have had to be cut substantially. In the process, service delivery in all sectors have been affected although priority activities within priority social sectors (education, health, water, roads, and agriculture) have now been protected. Under the cash budget, expenditures on other charges and counterpart funds for donor-funded projects have acted as residuals, while the protection of the priority sectors has been done by locking in the sectors through the Government of Tanzania's Policy Framework Paper, the ESAF, the Structural Adjustment Credit I, and more recently under the multilateral debt fund (MDF). Moreover, to mitigate some of the negative effects of cash budgeting, in July 1998 the government introduced an expenditure commitment monitoring system that allows 10 key ministries to operate with three-month commitments instead of monthly commitments. As a result of this protection, expenditure to social sectors as a percentage of discretionary expenditure has shown an upward trend in recent years, rising from 17.1 percent in FY95 to 22.2 percent and 24.7 percent in FY96 and FY97, respectively. However, the long-lasting solution to the problem of underfunding of government operations lies not in aid dependence, but in increased mobilization and efficient use of domestic resources. Tanzania's revenue mobilization effort, currently at about 11.5 percent of GDP, is low when compared with other countries in Sub-Saharan Africa, such as Kenya (29.6 percent) and Zimbabwe (30 percent). Reductions in tax exemptions, tax rates, and the multiplicity of taxes and an improvement in tax administration to curb tax evasion are some of the important measures that could help broaden the tax base and increase tax revenue collection.

The cut in government expenditure, especially development expenditure, has at times been necessitated not only by unpredictability of counterpart funds, but also by unpredictability of donor finances, particularly those that went directly to the projects without passing through the budget or being recorded by the government. The extent of integration of donor resources into the budget, for example, was 19 percent in FY94, 12 percent in FY95, 28 percent in FY96, and 33 percent in FY97 (URT 1999d). Moreover, actual releases of resources as compared with those budgeted have shown a large variance for the development budget. Between FY94 and FY97, for example, the shortfall of donor disbursements ranged between 42 and 79 percent of budget projections, while local counterpart funding shortfalls ranged between 16 and 76 percent. The problem of unpredictability of the budget—caused by shortfalls in local counterpart funds, nonadherence to conditions for donor disbursement, inaccurate projections, or unrecorded donor support—is among the issues that are at the core of the debate on how to strengthen the government–donor partnership in development.

The management system for the cash budget has been fairly successful in imposing fiscal discipline on the spending units, restoring macroeconomic equilibrium, and boosting confidence in the Tanzanian economy. However, accountability or the extent of compliance to prudential budget management procedures and regulation by the government is still a problem that needs to be tackled. As evidenced by reports of the controller and auditor general for the past few years, embezzlement of government resources and nonaccountability for them are still rampant, pointing to the need for increased effort to rectify the situation. Between 1994 and 1997, for example, on average, 76 percent of audited statements received either a qualified or adverse opinion from the controller and auditor general. These opinions stemmed primarily from undercollection of revenue, divergence of spending from budgets, and failure to maintain or to provide timely supporting documents to the auditors. Improper vouching of expenditures and of cash and store losses also remains a major problem, with the share of nonvouched and improperly vouched expenditures rising from 5.5 percent of the total in FY94 to 8.4 percent in 1997 (URT 1999d). The main causes of poor audit opinions include weaknesses in technical capacity for maintaining proper accounts and ineffective superstructure for reporting and for applying the necessary sanctions. The introduction of the Platinum system of financial management and the Performance Budgeting system, though still in their infancy, are some of the most promising measures that the government has taken toward strengthening the accounting system and accountability of the government and enhancing the efficiency of resource use. Measures that remain to be taken are those that would apply sanctions to responsible officers in the case of irregularities and losses, and those that would address decisively the problem of extrabudgetary spending and lack of coordination of accounting and audit systems between the government and donors.

Interest Rate Policy

Changes in the price level have had an impact on the level of real interest rates, with the decline in inflation making real interest rates positive or less negative. Before the reform program, real interest rates were substantially negative. In 1985, for example, average real interest rates were −22.3 percent for savings deposits and −18.8 percent for lending (table 2.3 and figure 2.6). The rates were, however, increased progressively, becoming less negative or positive as inflation declined during ERP-I and ERP-II. In 1991 interest rates were liberalized as the Banking and Financial Institutions Act was enacted. The act legalized the establishment of private financial institutions and gave the Bank of Tanzania the responsibility of licensing, regulating, and supervising banks and nonbank financial institutions. By July 1991 only the maximum lending rate continued to be controlled. However, two years later all the remaining ceilings were abolished ,and in August 1993 treasury bills and a more active Bank of Tanzania discount rate were introduced, making credit markets more flexible.

Figure 2.6. *Inflation and Real Interest Rates, 1986–98*

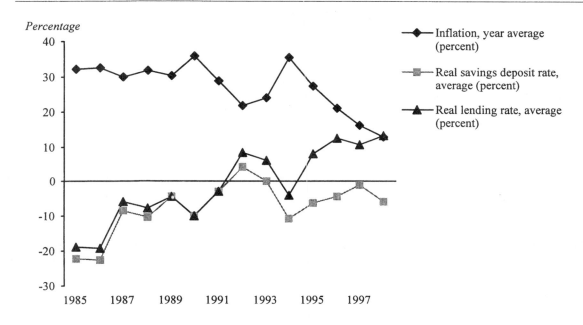

Sources: URT (various years); authors' calculations.

The liberalization of interest rates, however, led to a decline in deposit rates, even when inflation was rising. As a result, average savings deposit rates have been negative in real terms sincethe early 1990s—except in 1992 and 1993, when inflation went down—and the wedge between deposit rates and lending rates increased, as lending rates increased or declined at a slower rate than deposit rates (table 2.3 and figure 2.6). Only recently has the prospect of real deposit rates becoming positive increased, as inflation fell to a single-digit level. The decline in deposit rates and the increase in the wedge between deposit and lending rates have occurred for two main reasons. The first is operating state-owned banks inefficiently and according to noncommercial criteria that focus on protecting the banks' clients—mostly parastatals and the government—from interest rate rises. The second reason is a lack of competition, because private banks, in particular, large foreign banks, are mostly involved in foreign trade finance and limit their customer base to a handful of low-risk, high-value customers. By June 1998 the financial sector consisted of 19 licensed (17 operating) commercial banks, 9 nonbank financial institutions, 105 foreign exchange bureaus, and a number of informal intermediaries. However, state-controlled banks—NBC (1997), the National Microfinance Bank (NMB), and the People's Bank of Zanzibar —controlled 40 percent of domestic credit and 55 percent of deposits. At the same time, the six largest banks—NBC (1997), NMB, CRDB, Standard Chartered, Citibank, and Stanbic—held 90 percent of all assets (IMF 1999a).

The hesitation of the large, private, foreign banks to expand their lending activity to areas other than trade financing and to a handful of high-value customers is attributable to difficulties in collecting debts from defaulting customers, as evidenced from the experience of state-owned banks; and to risk aversion due to lack of information on borrowers' past performance (IMF 1996a). Repayment delays and difficulties in loan enforcement are attributable to the weak judicial system. All these factors plus other regulatory factors, such as a high minimum reserve requirement, impose costs that limit investment opportunities for banks. Consequently, the lending rates and the wedge between them and deposit rates are still high despite interest rate liberalization.

Exchange Rate Policy

The exchange rate, which at the beginning of ERP I was overvalued and misaligned, is among the variables that have responded well to various policy actions meant to correct its value and realign it. As empirical studies have shown, the exchange rate, together with trade reforms, formed the centerpiece of ERP-I and its successors, with the result that the country moved toward a unified exchange rate market gradually, but determinedly, over the next eight years (Kaufmann and O'Connell 1999). From 800 percent at the end of 1985 and early 1986, the parallel exchange rate premium fell to about 50 percent in 1990 and about 10 percent (against the *bureau de change* rate) by August 1993, when the foreign exchange market was unified.

The unification of the foreign exchange market followed the introduction of foreign exchange bureaus in 1992, which were allowed to transact in foreign exchange at freely determined exchange rates for current account transactions, and the liberalization in 1993 of nearly all remaining foreign exchange transactions for current account purposes. Although the parallel foreign exchange market is still in existence, its premium is small, reflecting mainly the operation of residual capital controls, the financing of illegal activities, and the evasion of taxes. The virtual disappearance of a parallel exchange rate premium also reflects the extent to which the adoption of the crawling peg at the start of ERP-I in 1986 has realigned the real exchange rate to its long-run path. Currently the exchange rate is determined freely at the interbank foreign exchange market. This market was introduced in June 1994 to replace weekly foreign exchange auctions that were started in July 1993, shortly before the foreign exchange market was unified. As the rate of domestic inflation declines and becomes consistent with inflation in Tanzania's major trading partners, the real value of the exchange rate is expected to become more stable. As at the end of 1998, the real exchange rate was slightly overvalued when compared with its 1990–94 effective rate (table 2.3). In general, the liberalization of the exchange rate has boosted exports and foreign exchange inflows, making it possible for the country to accumulate foreign exchange reserves equivalent to four months' worth of imports.

To the extent that domestic prices were determined at the margin largely by the parallel exchange rate rather than the official exchange rate, the direct cost-push effects of nominal devaluations were minimized after the unification of the exchange rates. The relatively favorable outcome of inflation during the unification process indicates the possibility that the long-run fiscal effect of the parallel exchange rate premium was negative, so that the reduction in the premium avoided any tradeoff between inflation and the premium during the move toward unification of the exchange rate market (Kaufmann and O'Connell 1999). This is in contrast to what has been argued in the literature (see Pinto 1989, 1991) and observed in Sierra Leone and Zambia: that if the government is a net seller of foreign exchange to the private sector at an overvalued official exchange rate, then exchange rate unification imposes a fiscal shock that will raise money supply growth and inflation in the long run unless the policy package includes contractionary fiscal measures. In the case of Tanzania, both variables—the parallel exchange premium and inflation— enjoyed a simultaneous reduction during the second half of the 1980s (Kaufmann and O'Connell 1999).

Policy Guidance for the Future

After over a decade (1986–2000) that witnessed the implementation of the ERPs and the subsequent ESAF initiatives, Tanzania's macroeconomic environment has, to a large extent, stabilized. Macroeconomic reforms have yielded good results, which need to be further consolidated and sustained. Inflation, which for more than two decades proved to be difficult to bring down, was at a single-digit level of 7.7 percent in June 1999 and decreased further to 6 percent in March 2000. Although this level of inflation falls short of the 5 percent target for June 2000, it nevertheless reflects a serious commitment on the part of the government to ensure that it attains its set objectives. It also reflects the importance of the interplay between various policies that determine the price level, and therefore a need for an inflation reduction approach that recognizes this interplay as the government gears toward attaining low inflation that is consistent with the level of inflation prevailing in Tanzania's major trading partners. Thus tight monetary and fiscal stances will need to be maintained, coupled with increased output production, especially of food items, if excess demand and inflationary pressures are to be avoided. Excess money supply can be avoided if the government balances the money supply with real output and observes monetary targets, does not operate and finance its deficits by borrowing from the banking system, and controls its expenditures to levels consistent with available resources.

Although it has been criticized for its stringency, which has negatively affected service delivery, the management system for cash budget management has to a great extent instilled discipline in government expenditure and overall budget management. A move away from monthly expenditure commitment to a three-month commitment, which has been introduced in 10 ministries, ought to be extended to other ministries if resource predictability and flexibility in planning are to be enhanced. However, this requires increasing resource availability through increased revenue collection from conventional taxes and mainstreaming the government so as to enhance its efficiency. Some of the important measures that could help broaden the tax base and increase tax revenue collection are reductions in tax exemptions, tax rates, and the multiplicity of taxes and improvement in tax administration to, among other things, clamp down on tax evasion.

Despite instilling discipline in government expenditure and overall budget management, the cash budget and Tanzania's overall fiscal stance has raised two concerns that need to be addressed. The first regards the coexistence of an overall fiscal surplus side-by-side with underfunding of priority sectors. The perception is that the government has been putting monies away (building up reserves) or making it available to the private sector through the domestic banking system (by reducing its stock of domestic debt with the banking system) while government expenditures and net lending declined sharply. The decline relative to the size of the economy was a sharp 4.1 percentage points, from 18.3 percent in FY94 to 14.2 percent in FY98. It may be argued that a shift of resources from the budget to the private sector may raise overall effectiveness in their utilization if, as presumed, the private sector is a more effective user of resources. However, given the slow movement of these resources from the banking system to the productive sector, as reflected by loan-to-deposit ratios ranging between 30 and 50 percent, the shift may not actually be happening. Moreover, a rise in gainful absorption of these resources by the private sector depends also on the absorptive capacity of the private sector, which can be enhanced only if supportive infrastructure and better public service delivery can be financed.

The second issue concerns determining the desirable level of domestic revenue mobilization and finding the appropriate balance between competing demands for higher revenue mobilization and lower taxation. Tanzania has a relatively low ratio of tax revenues to GDP, considerably below the Sub-Saharan Africa's average of 16.4 percent. Estimates indicate that the revenue potential of the Tanzanian economy might be 6 to 9 percentage points higher than what is currently achieved, that is, between 17 and 20 percent of GDP (URT 2001). However, it is also clearly understood that realizing this revenue potential is an extremely tedious and slow process that is likely to take a considerable number of years. The demand for higher revenue mobilization comes from the severe underfunding of basic social services, such as primary health care and primary education, and of physical infrastructure services, which have been identified as impediments to economic growth and progress in sustainable human development. On the one hand, the key arguments for increasing revenue would be that it would have high payoffs in terms of facilitating growth and reducing poverty. The argument for higher revenue is also closely intertwined with the provision of foreign aid by donors and the issue of aid dependency. A central assumption underlying most donor assistance is that their resources are additional to whatever funds can be mobilized efficiently domestically, rather than substituting for domestic revenue. On the other hand, the transfer of private resources to the government also has a cost.

The cost of higher revenue mobilization in this regard is twofold. First, taxation withdraws resources from the private sector and households, and thus has a significant opportunity cost. Second, taxation may introduce inefficiencies into the incentive system of an economy. The issue of the withdrawal of resources is accentuated by the fact that in Tanzania the easily accessible tax base is relatively small and tax evasion is widespread, which increases the marginal effective tax rate. This leads to private sector perceptions of an overly high tax burden. The key challenge in this area is thus to increase tax revenue without increasing the marginal effective tax rate. This implies a requirement to broaden the tax base and reduce tax evasion.

As regards distortions in the incentive regime that may be introduced by higher resource mobilization, it is understood that in the past, many structural adjustment efforts have aimed at reducing these inefficiencies, which have led to a decline in the ratio of tax revenue to GDP for many African economies. The focus of many of these reforms was clearly on efficiency rather than on the implications for revenue and public finance. Here the government assumed that either distortionary taxes would be replaced by nondistortionary taxes and thus reforms would be revenue neutral, or the Laffer-curve argument that reductions in tax rates could actually increase tax revenue. The final and most important assumption was that public spending is wasteful and has lower returns than private spending, making a reduction in the resource transfer to the public sector desirable. The key factor determining the desirability of domestic resource mobilization efforts has to be the effectiveness and efficiency of public spending. If efficiency is low, increasing resource flows to the public sector is clearly undesirable unless increased resource flows are truly necessary and will lead to increased efficiency in public service delivery. The other argument is that the willingness to pay taxes is closely related to the perceived quality and quantity of service delivery by the public sector. This further strengthens the argument for public sector efficiency as a precondition for increasing resource mobilization. However, it also cautions against using the budget excessively as an instrument for redistribution, because if the perceived service delivery to those who pay taxes goes down, their willingness to pay taxes may also decline.

The problem of the unpredictability of resources for the development budget—due to nonadherence to conditions for donor disbursement, inaccurate donor resource projections, or unrecorded donor support— is another issue that needs to be pursued further through the "government–donor partnership in development" dialogue. As regards further increasing expenditure discipline and accountability, measures that remain to be taken are those that would apply sanctions to responsible officers in the case of irregularities and losses, and those that would address decisively the problem of extrabudgetary spending and lack of coordination of accounting and audit systems between the government and donors.

Interest rates are important for savings mobilization and for channeling such savings into productive activities. The decline in deposit rates and increase in the wedge between deposit and lending rates that have occurred in Tanzania act contrary to this wisdom. This anomaly needs to be corrected through, first, ensuring that state-owned banks are privatized or are operating efficiently and according to commercial criteria, and second, enhancing competition between banks by reducing unnecessary regulatory costs and risks associated with lending to all types of customers. The latter entails putting in place a loan enforcement mechanism by enhancing the judicial system, such as developing well-functioning commercial courts, and reducing the costs associated with regulatory factors, such as a high minimum reserve requirement, that limit investment opportunities for banks.

As mentioned earlier, the exchange rate is one variable that has responded well to various policy actions in the long term, although as at the end of 1998 the real exchange rate was slightly overvalued when compared with its 1990–94 effective rate. As the rate of domestic inflation declines and becomes consistent with the rate of Tanzania's major trading partners, the real value of the exchange rate is expected to become more stable. However, deliberate efforts to correct for this overvaluation may also be undertaken by the government. This would include nonintervention and allowing for a free fall in the value of the exchange rate (as happened in July 1999) until it is back on a stable path.

Recent Developments in the External Sector

The narrative on developments in the external sector is divided into two parts: time trends in the pattern of trade and domestic policy issues. These are treated separately even though they are closely related, because diverse exogenous factors—including weather, trade policies of other countries, and historical linkages—all influence the pattern of trade, and domestic policy may not be able to counteract their effects.

Size of the External Sector and Trends in 1990

The participation of Tanzania in the world economy is shown in figure 2.7 as shares of Tanzania's GDP. The three solid lines show the various account balances as indicated, with the largest negative intercept being that of the balance of trade, followed by the current account. For 1990 and 1998 the balance of trade (deficit) was estimated as US$935.6 million and US$1058.4 million, respectively. These are Bank of Tanzania estimates and do not take into consideration estimates of unrecorded foreign trade, valued at about US$270 million, and exports exceeding imports by US$70 million. Because of weak administrative capacity and a dearth of resources for monitoring the porous borders, especially to the north, the assessment of the flow of goods and services continues to be difficult. The three lines in figure 2.7 represent various elements in the current account—net flow of goods, net flow of services, and net flow of income—with the first two constituting the balance of trade. The vertical distance between lines representing the balance of trade and the current account is the sum of net income flows plus current public and private transfers. As the net flow of income to Tanzania remained negative during the 1990s, large current grants bridged the gap between the balance of trade and the current account balance. Inflows of current grants are mostly public, with the private share only recently increasing from 9 percent in 1990 to 33 percent in 1998. The values for the current account deficit were US$558.9 million and US$846.6 million for 1990 and 1998, respectively.

Figure 2.7. *External Sector Performance*

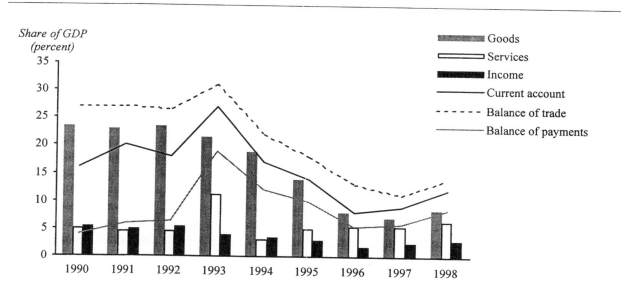

The time path of the balances of trade, the current account, and payments have been significantly influenced by the government's overall reform program aimed at achieving macroeconomic stability, restraining fiscal expenditure, and reducing aid dependency. Since the mid-1990s, as the country followed an active program of macroeconomic stability and liberalization, the three balances have moved in unison away from needs for short-term transfers to fill the payments gaps. All the deficits have declined significantly as a share of GDP. The deficits of trade and the current account were lowered to US$727.7 million and US$461.3 million by 1996, before the setbacks of the last two years.

The deterioration in 1997 and 1998 was largely due to the negative effects of El Niño. This climatic system brought erratic rains in FY96, drought in FY97, and floods in FY98, causing the production volumes of cash crops to decline sharply, marketing to be hampered by the severe disruption of transportation services, and production costs to rise because of an increase in the prices of inputs and basic commodities. The effect on export crops was far greater than on the food crops.

Generally, Tanzania's exports have been influenced to a greater extent by changes in volume rather than terms of trade changes. Empirical evidence (tables 2.4 and 2.5) shows that real exports declined between 1970 and 1998. The decline was attributable both to the decline in the quantity of output and the terms of trade. Of the decline in real exports, the decline in quantity contributed 70 percent, whereas the terms of trade contributed only about 30 percent.

The intercept between the current account and the balance of payments is composed of the balance of the capital account (which summarizes the capital transfers); net FDI; portfolio investment; and other financial flows, including trade credit and government loans (volume 3, table 3.1). There is no portfolio investment in Tanzania, and FDI picked up from US$12 million in 1992 to US$172 million in 1998, geared significantly toward mining and mineral extraction.

Tanzania has an abundance of unique, exotic destinations for regional, as well as European and American, tourists. As an agricultural economy with a small manufacturing base and a nascent extractive industry, the country needs to plan the development of this sector in a culturally responsible and environmentally sustainable way, with community participation, so that its potential foreign exchange earning capacity can be used to stimulate economic growth. The coordinated development of accommodations, roads, railways, airports, telecommunications, banking, and water supply has to be planned to give Tanzania a competitive edge over Ghana, Kenya, and the Seychelles, at least near the Northern Circuit, and the coastal region around Zanzibar and Dar es Salaam. Over the long run, the government must not only encourage private investment in the sector, but must also effectively coordinate and regulate the classification and standardization of services, the training of personnel for hotel management, the travel agencies, and the conservation of sanctuaries.

Over the short run, exports show signs of recovery beyond their pre-El Niño levels. The growth of imports is likely to be modest given the low world oil prices and a lesser need for food imports. The current account deficit was likely to decline slightly in relation to GDP in 1999. Aid flows are projected to increase if Tanzania succeeds in observing donor conditionality. However, to achieve the government's reform program objectives, financing gaps are likely to occur. Over the longer term, export-led growth is projected, with a strong recovery of export volumes. Exports are projected to grow more rapidly than the 6 percent growth in the target real GDP. With imports also growing faster than GDP because of the rise in investment needed for the growth, the current account deficit is initially likely to increase and then decline gradually in relation to GDP. Official grants and loans are projected to change little in real terms, showing a gradual reduction in aid dependency. Rapid increases in direct foreign investment and in portfolio investment can be expected if capital controls are eased judiciously. Export diversification will reduce the country's vulnerability to external shocks and the need to hold international reserves.

Table 2.4. *Impact of Quantum Growth and Terms of Trade on Real Export Growth, 1970–98*

Category	Real export growth	Quantum growth	Terms of trade growth
Coefficients (significant at 1%)	–0.057	–0.040	–0.017
Contribution to the decline (percent)	100	70.2	29.8

Source: Authors' calculations.

Table 2.5. *International and Regional Trade in Selected East African Countries, 1999*

Category	Kenya	Uganda	Tanzania
Imports (US$ millions)	3,263	1,231	1,338
Industrial countries (percent)	46.0	46.1	34.0
O/w European Union (percent)	34.1	34.5	24.2
O/w United States of America (percent)	3.2	2.6	3.1
O/w Japan (percent)	5.5	6.0	4.8
Developing countries (percent)	53.9	53.9	62.5
O/w Asia, excluding Japan (percent)	25.9	13.4	20.0
O/w Middle East (percent)	14.8	3.0	12.5
O/w Europe (percent)	1.1	0.5	0.7
O/w Africa (percent)	11.0	36.8	28.7
O/w COMESA (percent)	1.7	32.6	14.8
O/w Kenya (percent)	—	29.4	9.9
O/w Uganda (percent)	0.25	—	0.11
O/w Tanzania (percent)	0.39	1.5	—
O/w South Africa (percent)	9.3	4.2	12.6
Exports (US$ millions)	2026	622	721
Industrial countries (percent)	46.3	82.1	38.9
O/w European Union (percent)	38.5	72.6	27.8
O/w United States of America (percent)	4.6	2.7	2.2
O/w Japan (percent)	1.1	1.8	7.3
Developing countries (percent)	48.3	17.9	52.7
O/w Asia, excluding Japan (percent)	8.9	2.9	30.3
O/w Middle East (percent)	6.5	2.0	5.0
O/w Europe (percent)	0.6	10.7	2.6
O/w Africa (percent)	32.1	2.3	14.8
O/w COMESA (percent)	25.8	2.2	12.0
O/w Kenya (percent)	—	1.6	1.6
O/w Uganda (percent)	9.0	—	1.2
O/w Tanzania (percent)	7.3	0.4	—
O/w South Africa (percent)	1.6	0.2	0.6
Gross international reserves (1997)	603	633	622
Trade share of GNP (1997)	57	28	36
Exports (percent)	22	9	11
Imports (percent)	35	19	25

— Not available.
COMESA Common Market for Eastern and Southern Africa.
Source: Rajaram and others (1999).

Diversification of Markets

Although exports to Japan and the United States have expanded significantly, the pattern of export sales remains concentrated on the European Union, India, and neighboring countries. The European Union was the market for only some 30 percent of Tanzania's exports in 1998, compared with 55 percent at the beginning of the decade. The pattern is similar in the case of imports. Around 10 percent of Tanzanian exports are sold in India, which also provides an increasing share of imports, up from 3 percent in 1990 to 8 percent in 1998. Imports from the United States remained steady in the 1990s at an average of 3.7 percent, and those from Japan declined from 10 percent to 5 percent. The destinations of exports and the origin of imports for Tanzania are slowly but steadily becoming more diversified, with "other countries" increasing their share from 17–19 percent to 37–40 percent of the totals during the last decade.

Current Account Liberalization

One of the major constraints to trade liberalization for a developing country are the fiscal implications of reforms. Given the traditionally weak tax assessment, the inefficient collection mechanisms, and the absence of a broadly based tax system because of numerous exemptions within the domestic economy, the revenue-related costs of trade liberalization are often significant. Even though export and import volumes increase with trade liberalization, the revenues from these sources often fall as export taxes are eliminated and imports are taxed less heavily. Moreover, while international trade and transactions are relatively easy to tax, taxing income and domestic consumption requires a sophisticated accounting system that may be lacking.

During the period of liberalization, Tanzania has progressed significantly in removing impediments to both exports and imports. These have, for the most part, been measures aimed at adapting the tax system to a market-based economy with low, broadly based taxes coupled with a strong and independent administration. In the export sector the replacement of agricultural parastatals with cooperatives introduced some flexibility in pricing, but the most important step was in 1994, when the government granted permission to the private sector to compete in the processing and marketing of cash crops. By FY94 the system of export licensing even for traditional crops was abolished, the requirement that export companies be registered was eliminated, and the requirement that export proceeds be surrendered was no longer imposed. As mentioned before, the remaining restrictions—a 2 percent tax on traditional exports, including minerals, and the ban on exports of scrap metal—were abolished by 1998.

On the import side, the reduction in the tariff burden (to a trade-weighted level of 23 percent) through rationalization of the rates was supported by the introduction of the open system of general licensing and the creation of the Own Funds Facility in the use of own foreign exchange resources for imports in 1988–90. However, the benefits of liberalization became visible only during 1991–93 as the foreign exchange market was completely liberalized and all import licenses were abolished. By FY94 the negative list of luxury import items was abolished. However, during FY94 and FY95 the liberalization of imports slowed significantly as the government increased customs duty rates to compensate for shortfalls in domestic tax revenues. Figure 2.8 shows the share of total taxes on international transactions, specifically, import duties and sales tax on imports in total government revenue over FY86–99.

The sweeping liberalization measures affect the level and composition of budgetary revenues. On the one hand, productive resources shifted from the public sector to farmers, small enterprises, and the informal sector, which are not covered by the narrow tax base and weak tax administration. This has led to a steep decline in the ratio of tax revenue to GDP. On the other hand, the trade and foreign exchange liberalization led to a rapid growth in imports, and hence in custom duties, despite the weak customs administration and the large number of exemptions. Thus the share of taxes in international transactions in total revenue reversed its earlier decline, rising to approximately 30 percent in recent years.

Figure 2.8. *Contribution of the External Sector to Government Revenues, FY86–99*

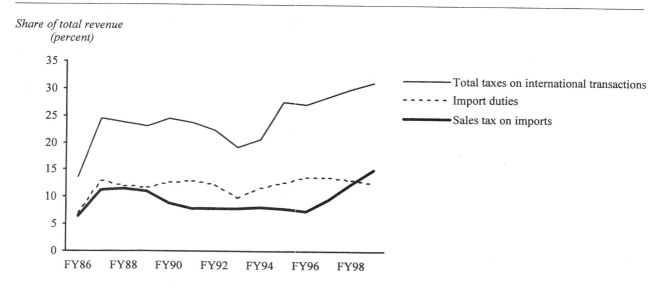

Share of total revenue (percent)

Sources: URT (various years); authors' calculations.

In the last two years the government, following technical assistance in developing options with respect to reform of the customs duty and exemptions regime, agreed to introduce reforms. These would reduce customs duties in line with Tanzania's Cross-Border Initiative and eliminate all duty exemptions or remissions other than those required under international agreements. The initiative calls for participating countries to lower the maximum duty rates to no more than 20–25 percent and the trade-weighted average duty to no more than 15 percent, and to adopt no more than three nonzero duty rates. The timetable had a target date of June 1998; the reduction of trade duties and actions to move toward the initiative standards were included in the FY00 budget for Tanzania. The government has not eliminated exemptions completely, although it has taken significant steps to reduce the misuse of exemptions through increased control by the TRA and preparations to amend the Import Duty Act to centralize certification of exemption status.

In the government's FY00 budget, the tax structure has been reviewed to emphasize incentives to investors and further reduction of barriers to international trade, with some accommodation for various pressure groups and the need to minimize revenue loss. On the international trade side, the maximum tariff rate has been reduced from 30 to 25 percent and nonzero-rate categories from five to four bands (5,10, 20, and 25 percent). This is an apparent accommodation of the protectionist pressure from the growing private industrial sector. In support of investment and production, tariffs on capital goods, raw materials, and replacement parts are either 0 or 5 percent, and the preferential treatment of investors has been harmonized between those enjoyed by holders and nonholders of Tanzania Investment Center (TIC) certificates. Common Market for Eastern and Southern Africa rates apply for all traded goods except beer. Excise duties for domestic and imported goods have been harmonized—albeit at a higher rate than originally planned to compensate for revenue loss from lowering the lowest nonzero rate to 5 percent—to avoid hidden discrimination against imports. The government has also decided to postpone the elimination of a large number of smaller excise taxes and other "nuisance" taxes until the revenue base is strengthened.

Other specific measures relating to the trade sector include reducing the tariff on computers and accessories from 20 percent to 5 percent to encourage international connectivity and technology development and providing cost relief to initiatives dealing with the Y2K problem. The 5 percent import duty on tractors has also been abolished. Tourist air charters were exempted from the VAT, as were approved pharmaceuticals. Allowable depreciation for buildings has been raised from 4 to 5 percent.

The overall policy reform challenge for the government is to raise the overall tax to GDP ratio and reduce the weight of trade taxes in total taxes. In the external sector the tradeoff mandates balancing the slow pace of reduction of remaining tariff rates with the tax and customs administration improvement, the reduced scope of exemptions, and the broadened domestic tax base.

Capital Account Liberalization

Whatever the controversies that have arisen in recent years about capital account liberalization, there is little disagreement on the potential benefits of foreign equity investment in an economy such as Tanzania's, which is characterized by a chronic shortage of resources for investment. At the same time, there is little doubt that any plan for such opening up the economy would have to be cautious, with due consideration given to safeguarding macroeconomic stability and Tanzania's aspirations for local participation in capital markets.

Since May 1997 the government has been carrying out weekly auctions of two-year bonds to replace long-term high interest bonds held by the Bank of Tanzania. The thinness of Tanzania's markets has limited the demand for bonds, thereby subjecting sales to rising interest rates at a time when inflation has been coming down. In addition, short-term rates have been fluctuating, with no clear trend. Permitting foreigners to invest in these long-term securities could help mobilize foreign savings to deepen capital markets and support investment in Tanzania. The government had plans to supplement the previous liberalization of direct investment by permitting some foreign portfolio investment in privatized companies as they were listed on the stock exchange; however, in response to experience with recent international financial crises, the government adopted a cautious policy of complete exclusion of foreign portfolio investment in such companies.

Financial Sector Reform Developments

The argument for financial liberalization is rooted in the works of McKinnon (1973) and Shaw (1973), who assert that while finance could act as a catalyst to development, it could become an obstacle if the financial sector is repressed, a phenomenon common in many Sub-Saharan African countries in the early 1980s. Financial liberalization decries the use of repressive financial policies through measures such as ceilings on interest rates, selective credit policies, exchange controls, and restrictions on entry into the banking industry. In many countries the situation is also characterized by excessive political interference in the operations of banking firms, most of which are normally state owned. Such policies damage the economies by reducing savings and encouraging unproductive investment.

A common prescription for countries undertaking reforms places emphasizes removing repressive policies and enhancing competition in the financial sector. Measures may include introducing or improving the functioning of financial markets, increasing the transparency of financial transactions, and strengthening the standards of banking supervision. This is expected to enable savers and investors to see the true scarcity of capital and thereby improve savings mobilization, promote efficient investment, and accelerate economic growth. Countries that have undertaken financial reforms, however, have had different experiences depending on the country-specific social, political, and economic environment; the level of repression of the financial sector; and the approach used to implement reforms.

Since 1991 Tanzania has been implementing financial sector reforms that form part of wider macroeconomic reforms that began in 1986. Although by 1991, when the financial sector reforms began, the real sector had undergone some reform, but general macroeconomic stability had not yet been achieved. Inflation and the money supply were still growing by 25 percent per year.

Overview of the Financial Sector

Tanzania adopted centrally planned economic management after the 1967 Arusha Declaration, which proclaimed that Tanzania was a socialist state. This announcement was followed by the nationalization of major activities in all sectors of the economy regarded to be the chief sources of income. In the financial sector all private commercial banks were nationalized and their assets and liabilities put under the former National Bank of Commerce, which became the sole commercial bank in Tanzania.[3] In contrast, the Bank of Tanzania, besides its central banking role, assumed developmental roles and applied direct control to interest, credit, and exchange rates. In other words, the bank used direct instruments of monetary policy.

Throughout the 1970s the National Bank of Commerce remained the only commercial bank operating in mainland Tanzania. A few other financial institutions were established in the 1970s, namely, the Tanzania Investment Bank, and the Tanzania Rural Development Bank. In 1984 the Tanzania Rural Development Bank was transformed into the CRDB and also started offering checking accounts, bringing the number of commercial banks in Tanzania to two. With the exception of the Diamond Trust Fund and Tanzania Development Finance, Limited, all financial institutions were state owned. The government intervened in their day-to-day operations in a bid to ensure that their operations accommodated the government's political objectives.

Because of the specialized nature of the publicly-owned banks and their monopoly positions, they became less innovative and more insensitive to the opportunities and constraints in the market, as they no longer faced competitive pressures. This, coupled with the government interference in their day-to-day operations and widespread managerial weaknesses, undermined the performance of the financial institutions. Financial markets, particularly capital markets, were also absent, a factor that led to insufficient deposit mobilization efforts because few financial instruments existed through which private savers could lend to potential investors. The Bank of Tanzania's direct instruments—the Annual Finance and Credit Plan and the Foreign Exchange Plan, both of which directed lending and administered interest rates—failed to function efficiently because of inherent weaknesses. These weaknesses included government intervention that often overruled the judgment of managers of the financial institutions. Moreover, the financial institutions were established by acts of Parliament, thereby limiting the role of the central bank as supervisor of the financial sector.

The private sector, which was small, was discriminated against in credit allocation through a system of directed lending and preferential interest rates. The state-owned commercial enterprises and the cooperative unions enjoyed preferential treatment from the formal financial sector, obliging the private sector to resort to the informal financial sector for loans. Most of the loans that went to both these institutions, however, were not repaid. This not only led to a misallocation of resources, but also to a high proportion of nonperforming loans among the commercial banks. These institutions expanded in size through the supply-led approach to financial services, leading to the opening of commercially nonviable bank branches, especially in rural areas. This imprudent banking was also characterized by the misuse of depositors' funds, often to finance the National Bank of Commerce's expansion projects. This forced the bank to borrow from the Bank of Tanzania to lend to its customers, especially the publicly-owned commercial enterprises. A considerable amount of the credit given to these firms was not repaid, thereby forcing the National Bank of Commerce to borrow even more funds from the Bank of Tanzania for

---

[3] "Bank" means a financial institution authorized to receive money on current account subject to withdrawal by check.

continued on-lending. This process led to quick growth in the money supply, followed by high rates of inflation.

Just before the financial sector reforms in 1990, the extended broad money supply (M3)—the monetary aggregate most closely related to the rate of inflation—grew by a high 43 percent per year, with a rate of inflation of 35.9 percent. Similarly, during the same year, while credit to the government from the banking system was only 15.4 percent of total domestic credit, credit to other domestic sectors (which consisted mainly of publicly-owned parastatals) constituted 84.6 percent of total domestic credit. Net domestic credit as a percentage of GDP was also high, at 31.1 percent.[4]

Financial Sector Reforms

REFORM OBJECTIVES. The reform efforts were aimed at the following:
- Increasing the autonomy of banks in making decisions based on commercial principles
- Allowing the entry of privately-owned banks and financial institutions to increase competition and stimulate efficiency in the financial sector
- Creating a financial system that would adequately carry out the Bank of Tanzania's monetary policy and provide the economy with an efficient and reliable means of payment
- Creating an environment that would facilitate the development financial markets so as to increase efficiency in the mobilization and allocation of financial resources.

THE REFORM PROCESS. As a first step in the reform process, in 1991 Parliament passed the Banking and Financial Institutions Act. This provided for a more liberalized financial sector and strengthened the monetary policy role of the Bank of Tanzania, including supervision of the financial system.

The second step was to prepare the publicly-owned financial institutions for operations in a competitive environment, and ultimately for privatization. To address the large portfolio of nonperforming loans, Parliament passed a law in 1991, that led to the establishment of the Loans and Advances Realization Trust. The law gave the trust the mandate to assume and subsequently realize nonperforming loans of the national Bank of Commerce and the CRDB. To this effect, the trust's bonds were issued to the National Bank of Commerce and the CRDB in 1992 and 1993 in place of nonperforming loans. Publicly-owned banks were restructured and recapitalized in phases, with the CRDB being fully restructured and privatized in 1996. The Tanzania Housing Bank was closed in 1995, following huge losses, while the National Bank of Commerce was split into two banks—the NBC (1997) and the NMB—in 1997 to improve its efficiency. Recapitalization of the National Bank of Commerce and the NMB also took place in 1997.

The third step involved putting in place a mechanism that would enable the conduct of monetary policy within the context of a liberalized financial sector framework. The government introduced public auctioning of treasury bills in 1993 to provided a means for noninflationary deficit financing and a basis for market-determined interest rates. The requirement for minimum deposits was removed, and the maximum lending rate was abolished. In 1994, therefore, interest rates were fully liberalized, with the rediscount rate being tied to the weighted average yield of treasury bills of all maturities plus a penal 5 percentage points to reflect the tight monetary policy stance.

The Capital Markets and Securities Act (1994) put in place the enabling environment for the establishment of a stock market to provide long-term capital. The Bank of Tanzania Act was amended and the bank's prudential guidelines revised in 1995 to increase the autonomy of the central bank and to redefine its primary mission as the maintenance of price stability. Liberalization of the insurance business

---

[4] GDP in 1990 is taken as T Sh 830.7 billion.

was achieved in 1997, when the Insurance Act was passed. Eight private insurance companies have already been licensed, bringing the total of insurance companies licensed to operate in Tanzania to 10.

Outcome of the Reforms

INSTITUTIONAL SETUP OF THE CURRENT FINANCIAL SECTOR. As of the end of May 1999, the financial system comprised 43 institutions, including the Bank of Tanzania. There were 20 licensed commercial banks in Tanzania at the time, of which 17 were operational, with 9 of the operational ones being foreign owned. Of the remaining 11, 6 are joint ventures and 5 are locally owned. There are 11 nonbank financial institutions and 12 other financial institutions. During the reform period all banks and licensed nonbanks are not specialized. The Bank of Tanzania currently relies on indirect instruments to achieve its monetary policy objectives as stated in the Bank of Tanzania Act (1995). The 91-day treasury bill is used solely as a liquidity management instrument. The Bank of Tanzania also uses other methods of indirect liquidity control, including issuing deposit certificates and repurchase agreements and participating in the interbank foreign exchange market. A competitive and efficient banking system is already emerging: new banks are licensed, and the process of restructuring publicly-owned banks is reaching advanced stages. The banks have been operating in a relatively competitive environment, especially after the National Bank of Commerce was split up in 1997. The NBC (1997)'s share of total deposits has now declined substantially to only 35 percent of total deposits, compared with a share of 79 percent held by the former National Bank of Commerce.

MONEY SUPPLY DEVELOPMENTS. During the postreform period, the main preoccupation of the Bank of Tanzania has been lowering money supply growth to levels consistent with a low and stable rate of inflation. M3 declined from an annual growth rate of 43 percent in 1990 to 35.5 percent in 1994 and to 10.8 percent in 1998. Broad money supply (M2) growth, in contrast, declined from an annual growth rate of 45.4 percent in 1990 to a rate of 32.5 percent in 1994 and of 11.1 percent in 1998. The rapid decline in money supply growth led to a rapid decline in inflation, from 35.9 percent in 1990 to 12.8 percent in 1998 and only 7.7 percent in June 1999, just 0.2 percent percentage points above the targeted 7.5 percent. The decline in the inflation rate has contributed positively toward the stability of the exchange rate.

As a percentage of GDP, however, quasi-money increased to 18.6 percent of GDP in 1993, but declined to 14.9 percent of GDP in 1997. At the same time, M3 increased to 26.2 percent of GDP in 1993 and to 26.9 percent of GDP in 1995, before declining to 21.7 percent of GDP in 1997. Although the decline points to demonetization, it can be categorized as a temporary problem associated with the restructuring of the state-owned NBC (1997) and NMB. The two banks still control more than 70 percent of the market, but are currently not actively involved in lending or deposit mobilization. The situation is expected to improve with the completion of the restructuring and privatization of these banks.

Liquidity is currently parked in the banking system, where low loan to deposit ratios are prevalent. With lending by the NBC (1997) and NMB frozen under a memorandum of understanding with the treasury, except for holding treasury bills, excess liquidity in the banking system has risen at a time when the private sector is starved of credit. This characterizes the process of disintermediation referred to earlier. As the returns to treasury bills have fallen from their giddy heights of more than 45 percent before 1995 (to their current range of 8–15 percent, commercial banks are hard-pressed to look for more profitable outlets, having squeezed saving deposit rates as far down as possible to reduce the cost of funds. Therefore the banking system is likely to shoot a strong dose of liquidity into the economy as lending activities pick up. To the extent the prospective rise in credit is matched immediately with higher output, inflation will not ensue. However, a transitional period of a lagged output response is likely to occur as the gestation period of investment takes its course. This may be a temporary problem, but needs to be well managed to avoid building up inflationary pressures.

INTEREST RATE DEVELOPMENT. At the inception of the treasury bills market in August 1993, treasury bill rates rose rapidly, reaching an average yield of 48 percent during the first month. Although the discount rate that was tied to the treasury bill rate jumped from 27 to 50 percent in February 1994, savings deposit rates rose only moderately, reaching a maximum of 27 percent in December 1995 before declining to between 11.1 and 22.3 percent in 1996 and between 2 and 12.0 percent in 1998. The fall in the savings rate, however, was not matched by a fall in lending rates. Medium- and long-term lending rates ranged between 31 and 40 percent in 1995, declining to a range of 29–38 percent in 1996 and 20–32 percent in 1998. The high margin between deposit and lending rates indicates that competitiveness in banking is yet to be achieved as the restructuring and privatization of the major commercial bank—NBC (1997)—continues.

DEPOSIT MOBILIZATION. Little achievement has been recorded with regard to deposit mobilization. As can be seen in figure 2.9, real monetary liabilities of banks (demand deposits, savings deposits, and time deposits) have not shown any upward trend following financial sector liberalization.

Figure 2.9. *Total Deposits as a Percentage of GDP, 1967–97*

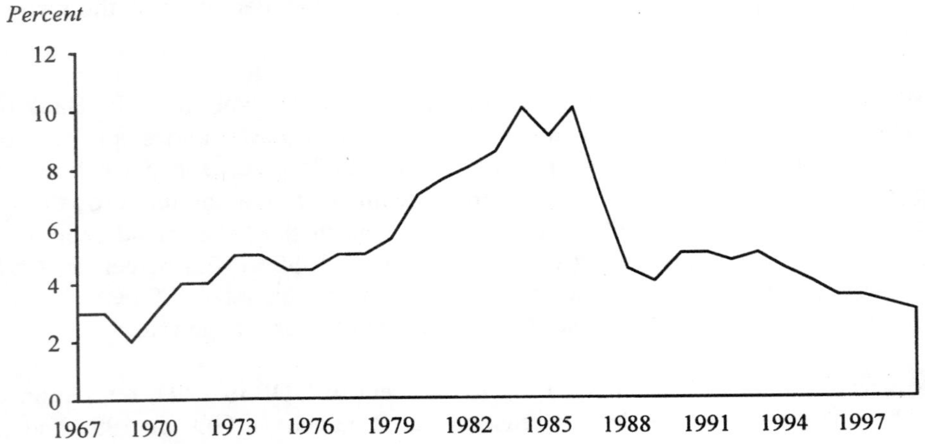

Sources: Authors' calculations.

While the fall in deposits may be explained by the current restructuring, as pointed out earlier, it is notable that the slow response to the increase in deposit rates to take advantage of the declining inflation has considerably reduced real gains to depositors, and hence created a disincentive to save. Nevertheless, the failure of lending rates to respond fully to the falling inflation rate indicates rigidities in the cost structure of commercial banks, specifically the dominant banks whose operating costs have been too high.

CREDIT DEVELOPMENTS. The performance of credit growth after liberalization, particularly of credit to the productive sector, has not been impressive. As shown in table 2.6 and figure 2.10, although lending to the private sector increased briefly from a total of T Sh 156.9 billion in 1990 to T Sh 310.9 billion in 1994, it declined sharply to T Sh 185.1 billion in 1997 before rising to T Sh 251.8 billion in 1998. A close view at the lending-to-deposit ratio shows clearly that this ratio has declined consistently, from 141.4 percent in 1990 to a low 33.8 percent in 1998.

Table 2.6. *Commercial Bank Lending and Holding of Securities, 1990–98*

Year	Total lending (T Sh billions)	Lending-to-deposit ratio	Holding of government securities (T Sh billions)
1990	156.9	141.4	3.6
1991	208.9	154.3	3.5
1992	199.5	109.0	14.0
1993	272.3	102.2	102.5
1994	289.9	88.5	114.5
1995	260.8	48.8	168.1
1996	147.3	25.5	255.9
1997	184.8	27.7	245.5
1998	251.1	33.8	309.9

Source: Bank of Tanzania.

Figure 2.10. *Lending Rate and Loan/Saving Ratio*

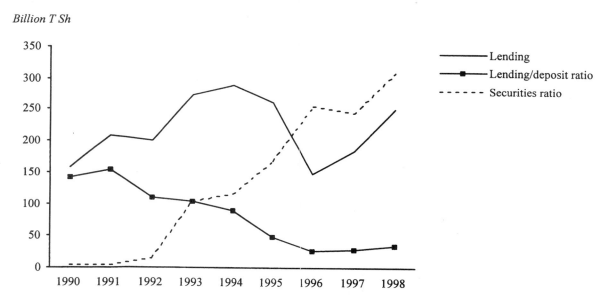

Sources: Authors' calculations.

Commercial banks also manifested increasing risk aversion in lending, as their preference for holding risk-free government paper increased from a total of T Sh 3.6 billion in 1990 to T Sh 251.1 billion in 1998. This shift may have been partly due to three factors: a high-risk component in lending emanating from the structure of the economy, structural rigidities that have made it difficult for commercial banks to assess the creditworthiness of private borrowers, and problems associated with the handling of commercial disputes. Note also that at high lending rates some investors would be motivated to invest in more risky projects—a manifestation of adverse incentive—which would make banks even more cautious when deciding to lend.

The sectoral allocation of credit has also been biased. The rural sector is deprived of financial services, and agriculture has experienced the steepest decline in the sectoral share of credit. The collapse of the input credit system and rural credit schemes have resulted in a major gap in the provision of rural credit. The concentration of new banks in major urban centers and the closure of remote branches of the National Bank of Commerce has left the gap in financial services to rural areas unfilled. This demands a deliberate strategy to intensify microfinance services and pursue new initiatives for providing such services.

REGULATORY AND SUPERVISORY ISSUES. The Bank of Tanzania Act (1995) spells out clearly that the Bank of Tanzania is responsible for ensuring that commercial banks and other financial institutions conduct their business on a sound basis, as laid down by banking regulations and other prudential requirements. The objective of this stance is to ensure that the financial system is stable and efficient in extending its services, which are so important to the growth of the economy.

During FY98, the financial sector witnessed temporary closure of the Trust Bank (Tanzania), Ltd. The bank was put under statutory management by the Bank of Tanzania, but was reopened after measures to improve its viability were successfully undertaken. In April 1999, Greenland Bank (Tanzania), Ltd. was also put under statutory management; its viability was still being assessed at the time this report was written.

The Bank of Tanzania continues to take measures to ensure that stability in the banking system is attained. Along these lines, for the last four years the bank has concentrated on strengthening its banking supervision. On-site and off-site inspection have been strengthened, and an early warning system has been established. This will enable the bank to determine problems in the banking industry before they get out of hand. Prudential guidelines governing capital adequacy, liquidity, and concentration of credit and risk diversification have been put in place to ensure that banks are adequately capitalized and that their lending activities are prudent. The Bank of Tanzania has also tightened its licensing requirements to ensure that only adequately capitalized banks are licensed to do business in Tanzania.

THE WAY FORWARD. Financial sector reform has been implemented as part of wider macroeconomic reforms. The financial reforms have focused on creating an environment where the true price of capital will be determined, and hence increase savings mobilization, promote efficient investment, and eventually accelerate growth. The measures have started to bear fruit, but the benefits of reforms may take a long time to be fully realized. This is partly because of the information gap between banks and borrowers, and partly because of rigidities in the cost structure of the banks, which hinder timely adjustment of the lending rate to reflect changes in the fundamentals.

The Bank of Tanzania is currently undertaking measures to promote the establishment of a credit information bureau. This is expected to provide information on creditworthiness to prospective borrowers from commercial banks. The Bank of Tanzania is also spearheading the establishment of commercial courts to speed up the resolution of commercial disputes. Such courts will increase assurance to the lending institutions, as justice will be enforced at reduced time cost. The closure of remote branches of the National Bank of Commerce and the concentration of new banks in major cities heads in the direction of depriving the rural sector of financial services. This calls for a deliberate strategy to provide the rural sector with microfinance services. The Bank of Tanzania is already working on a policy framework to guide the operations of microfinance institutions in the country, including a regulatory framework for these institutions to ensure their viability.

Finally, while newly licensed private banks are fully operational, the process of privatizing the National Bank of Commerce is ongoing. The process needs to be expedited to enhance the implementation of monetary policy and competitiveness in the financial sector, and thus realize more benefits from the reform.

Debt

Tanzania has traditionally relied on official bilateral and multilateral donors for financing its development projects and balance of payments requirements. As in other low-income countries, Tanzania's debt problems have been caused by a combination of faulty domestic policies and adverse external shocks. From 1975 through 1985, a series of domestic and external shocks hit the country. Notable are the first and second oil price shocks that contributed to serious budget and balance of payments deficits. This necessitated borrowing not only from external, but also from domestic sources to finance it's the deficits. The debt crisis worsened following slumps in commodity prices, the breakup of the East African Community, and rising real interest rates in global financial markets. On the domestic front, expansionary fiscal and monetary policies contributed to the worsening debt problem. Between 1970 and 1998 total external debt stock grew from US$1,445 million to US$7,972.7 million.

For more than a decade Tanzania has struggled to reduce its outstanding debt through various debt programs designed in collaboration with donors and international financial institutions. Since 1986 the government has been implementing various programs aimed at revamping the economy, with support from the World Bank, the IMF, and other multilateral and bilateral agencies. The economic recovery programs implemented since 1986 had a debt reduction component embedded in them, but despite these efforts, divergence between debt service demands and debt service capacity has been growing, leading to a relentless build-up of arrears and an increasingly unsustainable debt stock. Under the Paris Club arrangements, between September 1986 and January 1997 total debts worth US$2,453.5 million were set for rescheduling and US$594.9 million for cancellation. Until June 1998 bilateral creditors—both Paris Club and non–Paris Club—had canceled a total of US$1,616.1 million.

As at the end of June 1999, Tanzania's medium- and long-term external debt stock stood at 100.6 percent of GDP, which is unsustainable. If Tanzania were to pay all the outstanding debt arrears and thereafter remain current, the implied debt service ratio would have been about 285 percent.[5] Thus the existing stock of debt will clearly continue to grow even if no new lending is taking place, thereby scaring away foreign investors and leading to a paucity of foreign investment in Tanzania.

Debt Profile

CREDITOR CATEGORY. The share of multilateral debt has been increasing in recent years. By 1986, multilateral debt consisted of only 27 percent of the total debt stock.[6] By the end of FY98 its share had reached 56.2 percent. By contrast, the share of bilateral debt has been falling, recording a 36.2 percent share during the same period. The main bilateral creditors are Japan (28 percent), Russia (20 percent), the United Kingdom (10 percent), and Italy (6 percent). Collectively, this group accounts for more than half of the total bilateral debt. The shift from bilateral to multilateral debt was mainly due to increasing assistance provided by the multilateral institutions to the government, the relatively low levels of new loans approved by bilateral creditors, and the writing-off of some bilateral debt under the Paris Club arrangements. This can be supported by the national debt statistics, which indicate that between 1986 and 1998 the share of concessional loans increased from 60.5 percent to 76 percent.[7] In contrast, the share of nonconcessional debt decreased from 39.5 percent to 24 percent.

The share of multilateral debt service in actual debt service has also been on the increase, rising from 21 percent in 1992 to 41 percent by 1998. Multilateral debt stock was expected to represent more than three-

---

[5] The debt service ratio is total debt service/exports of goods and services.

[6] Major multilateral creditors include the International Development Association and the African Development Bank's African Development Fund.

[7] A loan is considered to be concessional if the grant element is 25 percent or more of the loan.

quarters of the total stock by 2000, with the World Bank's concessional arm, the International Development Association (IDA), dominating. Note, however, that the multilateral debt, although substantial in magnitude, is normally serviced on due dates, as defaulting calls for suspension of future disbursements from multilateral financial institutions.

BORROWER CATEGORY. In 1986 the government accounted for 89 percent of the disbursed outstanding debt, while public corporations accounted for 10 percent and the private sector for 2 percent. However, by the end of June 1999 the government accounted for 93 percent of the disbursed outstanding debt, public corporations for 2.8 percent, and the private sector for 4.2 percent. The decline in public corporations' share and the increase in private sector debt is attributed to the ongoing privatization of parastatal organizations.

WORSENING OF THE DEBT. The worsening debt problem became evident by the early 1980s, when the level of debt rose dramatically from about US$2,000 million in 1980 to US$4,917 million in 1986. Between 1986 and 1998 total external debt stock grew by about 62.2 percent, with the aggregate ratio of debt service to exports estimated at 27.4 percent at the end of 1998. This implied that more than 20 percent of Tanzania's export earnings were required just to service its foreign debt. The total of the principal and interest owed by Tanzania as of the end of June 1999 was US$7,312.5 million.

IMPACT OF THE DEBT. Tanzania's debt repayments have grown rapidly over time. In 1986 the stock of arrears was recorded at US$635.7 million, but by the end of June 1999 it had reached US$2,664.9 million, equivalent to 319.2 percent growth over just 14 years. Actual debt service increased from US$15 million in 1986 to US$204.6 million by June 1998, an increase of 1,264 percent, before dropping by 8.2 percent to US$187.9 million by June 1999. Actual debt payments during the first half of the 1990s averaged between 40 and 70 percent of scheduled payments, with an attendant accumulation of arrears. Beginning in 1994, bilateral debt has accounted for more than 70 percent of all arrears, followed by commercial and private debt. Non–Paris Club creditors account for the bulk of the bilateral debt arrears.

By the end of FY98 debt service as a percentage of exports was recorded at around 16.8 percent, up from 16.2 percent during FY97. The persistent increase in the stock of arrears reflects the country's low debt service capacity. Repayments to the Paris Club over 1999–2001 were expected to significantly exceed average payments for FY90–95, with a major hump in payments during 1999. Projections show that future debt servicing is expected to increase to an average of US$368.9 million per year in the early part of the next decade.

Sustainability of the Debt

A country is simply considered to have an unsustainable external debt position if it cannot meet its current and future external debt obligations in full without recourse to debt relief measures or without compromising growth. However, various other definitions are based on more quantitative criteria.

The introduction of the Heavily Indebted Poor Countries (HIPC) initiative has been intended to address the problems of debt overhang and the growing profile of multilateral creditors. The established debt sustainability indicators under the initiative are linked to the ability to pay and to extend debt relief to categories of debt—including multilateral debt—previously deemed ineligible for rescheduling or reduction. The first step taken by the government has been to ensure proper management of its current debt by establishing an accurate and reliable debt database, while ensuring that new loans are directed to resource-generating projects that contribute toward enhancing the country's payment capability.

The HIPC framework has three main criteria for assessing debt sustainability: the ratios of the present value of debt stock to exports, of debt servicing to exports, and of the present value of debt stock to budget revenues. Additional requirements include an export-to-GDP ratio of above 30 percent and a revenue-to-GDP ratio of above 15 percent. As data in table 2.7 show, Tanzania's debt burden is unsustainable on each count.

Table 2.7. *Unsustainability of Tanzania's Debt*
(percent)

Criteria	HIPC's sustainable level	Tanzania's current level
Debt stock/exports	150 (fixed net present value)	311
Debt service/exports	20–25	26.5
Debt stock/budget revenue	250 (net present value)	673
Exports/GDP (percent)	More than 30	15
Budget revenue/GDP	More than 15	13
Debt stock/GDP	40	106

Source: Bank of Tanzania.

In addition, the unsustainability of Tanzania's debt position is not fully captured by the HIPC criteria. As shown in table 2.8, Tanzania also has a high ratio of debt service to revenue, a factor that makes the country's debt even more unsustainable. A large proportion of government revenue is actually spent on debt repayment.

Table 2.8. *Debt Service and Government Revenues, 1997–2000*
(percent)

Category	1997	1998	1999	2000
Debt service/revenue	33	27	25	24
External debt	24	18	17	18
Domestic debt	9	9	8	6

Source: Bank of Tanzania.

In view of its high indebtedness, Tanzania was initially declared eligible for assistance under the HIPC initiative in September 1999. The other main consideration was its track record of reforms. Subsequently, Tanzania qualified for the enhanced HIPC initiative in April 2000 because of its 14-year steady implementation of macroeconomic, structural, and poverty reduction policy reforms, including bringing inflation down to 6 percent as of March 2000, its lowest level in at least 25 years, and the government's repayment of domestic debt after many years of borrowing an equivalent of more than 3 percent of GDP annually. Total relief from all of Tanzania's creditors is worth more than US$2 billion, which is equivalent to more than half of the net present value of total debt outstanding after full use of the traditional debt mechanisms. The debt reduction operation will translate into debt service relief over time of US$3 billion, or half of Tanzania's debt service obligations during FY01–03 and about one-third of the country's debt service obligations thereafter. Funds that would have been used to service external debt would now be freed up to fund poverty reduction programs in critical sectors such as health and education. The assistance of US$152 million committed by the IMF will be delivered over a 10-year period and will cover, on average, 58 percent of debt service obligations to the IMF, while the debt relief provided by the IDA of US$1.2 billion will be spread over 20 years and will cover 69.1 percent of Tanzania's debt service obligations to IDA.

Strategies for Debt Reduction

EXTERNAL DEBT. Over the past decade, a number of debt reduction initiatives have been designed for Tanzania in collaboration with donors. Although some relief has been realized, more comprehensive programs need to be put in place. These could include, for example, measures for the alleviation or cancellation of sizable volumes of the country's external debt, debt-equity swaps, and various types of debt-to-development swaps. The government intends to give priority to settling internal debts as well, especially those owed to productive enterprises. This would help maintain productive activities, safeguard employment, and promote investment.

The government intends to continue requesting bilateral creditors to cancel official loans. Until June 1998, total debts worth US$1,616.1 million were canceled. Also between September 1986 and January 1997 Tanzania had been to the Paris Club creditors five times for debt relief, and was able to get US$594.9 million worth of debt canceled and US$2,105.5 million rescheduled. Although under the Paris Club V arrangement of January 1997 a total amount of US$700 million was set for rescheduling and US$1,000 million for cancellation, as of March 1999 only US$371.1 million had been canceled, US$584.4 million rescheduled, and US$9.6 million deferred. The Paris Club V arrangement expired in November 1999. Tanzania signed the Paris Club VI agreement in April 2000 on Cologne terms.

Between 1990 and 1993 debts worth US$182 million were converted and the proceeds were reinvested in 82 selected projects. However, the program was suspended in 1994 because of its inflationary impact. This was followed by the Debt Buyback Scheme for eliminating arrears of commercial debts at the cutoff date of January 1, 1990, as Tanzania is one of the countries eligible for the IDA Debt Reduction Facility (which gives grants to buy back commercial, nonguaranteed debts at notable discounts). The project was launched in October 1999. As of June 2000 debts worth US$155 million had been extinguished using resources from the facility.

In April 1998, the the government established the MDF in collaboration with donors. Under the program, resources contributed by donors will be used to repay multilateral debt, while the same amount of domestic resources is directed to the social sector. The intent is to release more budgetary resources to the social sector, which has been depleted of budgetary allocations because of the tight budget. The proposed MDF offers an important opportunity to address the problem of poverty while preventing the build-up of arrears to multilateral creditors. Following the launching of the MDF in FY98, the government has signed agreements with six donor countries, including Denmark, Finland, Ireland, the Netherlands, Norway, Sweden, and the United Kingdom. Pledges for FY98 amounted to US$80.8 million.

Between July 1998 and March 1999, total disbursements made to the MDF Account opened at the Federal Reserve Bank of New York amounted to US$85.4 million. Through the Netherlands Trust Fund, the government received DGL 30 million, equivalent to US$15.4 million, which was paid directly to the World Bank to service IDA debts due January–December 1998. By the end of March 1999, the MDF Account had a balance of approximately US$19.9 million after using US$51.9 million for debt obligations due to IDA, IMF, and the African Development Bank's African Development Fund. The important point, however, is for the government to use the resources from the enhanced HIPC, the MDF, and other initiatives judiciously.

DOMESTIC DEBT. Public domestic debt stood at US$1,324.2 million (T Sh 918.9 billion) by the end of March 1999. Government securities (treasury bills, stocks, bonds, promissory notes, and tax certificates) were worth US$932.9 million (T Sh 692.7 billion), or 85.3 percent of total debt. Contingent liabilities (government guarantees, the revaluation account, and other instruments) accounted for US$162.9 million (T Sh 119.5 billion), or 14.7 percent of total debt. Domestic debt servicing has consumed a substantial part of government revenue, accounting for about 8–15 percent of annual recurrent expenditure for FY95–98.

The government has adopted a strategy of being actively involved in domestic securities markets. It has been restructuring the debt and securities portfolio to lower the cost of existing and future debts. The continuing efforts to adopt policies to bring inflation down to a sustainable level have started to bear fruit, as for the first time Tanzania recorded single-digit inflation of 9.1 percent in January 1999. By June 1999 headline inflation had reached 7.7 percent and went down further to 6 percent by March 2000. This has facilitated a decline in yields on treasury bills, bonds, and stocks. The government is also working to reduce debt service charges by lengthening the maturity structure of domestic debt. The government now ensures that pending bills will be within its servicing capacity through various methods such as cutting down expenditures to reduce government borrowing. In its efforts to protect and develop a financial market, the Bank of Tanzania is working to advise the government on instituting measures that will avoid delays in settling government securities dues. Settlement priority has been extended to the two-year treasury bonds because of their newness in the market as their holders are typically commercial and always claim penalties on late settlements.

Conclusion

The review of recent macroeconomic performance points to a number of important lessons and outstanding issues. First, the analysis clearly shows that the recent recovery of growth performance has been robust and driven mainly by macroeconomic and structural reforms aimed at dismantling state control of economic activities and at achieving strong macroeconomic fundamentals. An important lesson to be drawn from this experience is that consolidating and sustaining benign macroeconomic fundamentals is essential for maintaining the vitality of growth. However, despite the encouraging up-turn in GDP growth, it remains inadequate to have any significant impact on reducing abject poverty. This implies that the achievement of higher and sustained growth is also imperative for Tanzania. It will require improving agricultural performance, privatizing and restructuring the industrial sector further to spur increased efficiency, and realizing the full growth potential of the mining and tourism sectors through further improvements in the investment climate.

Second, this chapter has also demonstrated that the government's tight fiscal policy stance has been rewarding, as shown by the decline in the overall fiscal deficit—from almost 9 percent of GDP in 1986 to about 2 percent of GDP in 1991, and further to a surplus of 1 percent of GDP in 1997 through 1999—with the operation of the cash budgeting system. Nevertheless, concerns are growing that fiscal stability has been achieved largely at the expense of compressing public expenditure at a time when public services are deteriorating and key welfare indicators are declining. In addition, in recent years budget surpluses have been recorded side by side with underfunding of priority sectors. Resources for the development budget also remain highly unpredictable because of nonadherence to conditions for donor disbursement, inaccurate donor resource projections, or unrecorded donor support. This is despite attempts being made under the Public Expenditure Review process and the Tanzania Assistance Strategy within the overall framework of the government–donor partnership dialogue. The challenge is therefore for the government to continue to infuse fiscal discipline through cash budgeting, but simultaneously to spur greater efficiency in the delivery of public services. Continued government–donor dialogue is also the key to improving the integration of donor resources into the budget.

The third issue is the question of finding the appropriate balance between competing demands for higher revenue mobilization in view of the severe underfunding of basic social services as they relate to demands for lower taxation. These demands derive from private sector perceptions of an overly high tax burden, which in turn induce tax evasion. The key challenge here is thus to increase tax revenue without increasing marginal effective tax rates. This requires the complicated task of broadening the tax base, further rationalizing the tax policy regime, and increasing the efficiency of tax administration to reduce tax evasion. This chapter also points out that the key factors determining the desirability of increasing domestic resource mobilization has to be the effectiveness and efficiency of public spending and the perceived quality and quantity of service delivery by the public sector. If efficiency is low, increasing resource flows to the public sector are clearly undesirable. Analogously, the higher the quality and quantity of public service delivery, the higher the willingness to pay taxes.

Fourth, the review of recent macroeconomic performance also indicates clearly that Tanzania's high indebtedness (US$7,312 as of the end of June 1999, with external debt service due amounting to 29.2 percent of the exports of goods and nonfactor services) is a drag on the delivery of public services and on poverty reduction. Thus, the inclusion of Tanzania among the first beneficiaries of the enhanced HIPC initiative after the Cologne Summit, as well as the continuation of the MDF, are opportunities for a sustainable exit from the debt overhang problem. The critical issue emphasized in this report is for the government to use the resources judiciously.

Fifth, this chapter has pointed out that the government's tight monetary policy stance pursued over the reform period paid off substantially. This is evidenced by the record decline in inflation from almost 36 percent in 1995 to 6 percent in March 2000. In addition, financial repression has been eliminated by raising interest rates to positive real levels and by allowing the free determination of interest rates in the financial market. However, the margin between deposit and lending rates is high and growing, which limits the potential for lowering the cost of finance for investment and deters higher financial savings. This points to the existence of rigidities in the cost structure of the major commercial banks, the NBC (1997) and the NMB; high credit risks based on past high default rates; and a lack of robust competition in the banking sector. To correct this problem, the government must expedite the privatization of state-owned banks and enhance competition among the private banks. Related actions would be to institute commercial courts that can enforce loan repayment mechanisms and thereby reduce the risks that deter bank lending to all types of customers. The setting up of a credit rating bureau will also help reduce the banks' costs of screening potential borrowers.

The sixth important issue relates to the recent increase in overvaluation of the real effective exchange rate. The problem is that this appreciation of the real value of the Tanzanian shilling has eroded the profitability of exports and lowered relative prices, particularly for cash crops. The long-term solution to this problem lies in lowering inflation further to be at par with Tanzania's trading partners and in developing effective mechanisms for sterilizing the effects of surges in capital flows. In addition, repoliticizing the exchange rate by returning to the practice of setting its value would be a mistake. To the extent that monetary authorities have the resource capacity for smoothing fluctuations in the exchange rate within a reasonable band, judicious open-market interventions could be pursued. The authorities can also look into measures tp further enhance the efficiency of the foreign exchange market by removing the residual capital account controls.

Finally, this chapter also restates that Tanzania's high dependence on the export of primary agricultural commodities, which exposes it to the vagaries of weather and the volatility of world market prices. Thus further diversification of the merchandise export base, especially into export of services, is suggested here as the single most effective avenue for reducing exposure to economic shocks induced by the international economy or changes in weather conditions. However, the chapter also shows that 70 percent of the decline in real exports between 1970 and 1998 was due to the decline in quantity of output, and the remaining 30 percent was due to a decline in the terms of trade. This in turn suggests that Tanzania stands to realize more export earnings by also increasing the quantity of exports.

3. What Matters Most for Growth?

During the four decades since attaining independence in 1961, Tanzania has gone through three main phases of growth performance. After a period of relatively robust growth of income per capita during the 1960s, it experienced nearly two decades of decelerating growth during the 1970s and 1980s before embarking on a modest but sustained recovery in the 1990s. Tanzania's "golden era" of growth of the 1960s has yet to be reattained. When measured in constant dollars at international prices, by 1998 per capita income was US$534, only 71 percent above its 1960 level of US$319. In contrast, Botswana, which in 1960 had an income per capita of US$535 in constant dollars, had achieved a per capita income of US$2,790 by 1998 (figure 3.1). Measured in international prices, Botswana has persistently maintained a high growth rate of per capita income of 4.4 percent since 1960, while Tanzania's growth rate has averaged a much more modest 1.4 percent over the same period. Measured in domestic prices, Tanzania's real per capita income grew at an even smaller average rate of only 0.7 percent per year.

Figure 3.1. *Real GDP Per Capita in Constant Dollars, International Prices, Botswana and Tanzania, 1960–98*

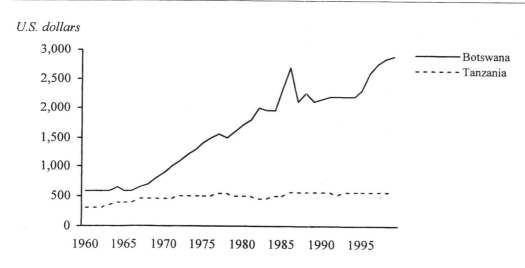

Sources: World Bank (2000f); URT (various years).

Industrial countries have sustained a remarkably steady per capita growth of approximately 2 percent for about 100 years. The newly industrializing countries have maintained income growth rates of more than 3 percent for nearly three decades, enabling them to gain significant ground on the industrial countries. A good understanding of the causes of slow and punctuated growth and the pattern of responses provides the necessary analytical basis for developing a strategy aimed at achieving a sustainable increase in the rate of economic growth in Tanzania.

In addition to fluctuations in economic growth over time, significant imbalances in Tanzania's growth performance have occurred across sectors and regions. The relatively high growth rates of electricity and water, construction, and transport and communications would indicate a significant expansion of infrastructure services. However, poor maintenance of infrastructure has severely restricted the actual availability of infrastructure services. Regional incomes have persistently converged over the past 40 years, indicating that poorer and disadvantaged regions were able to catch up with more prosperous regions. Nonetheless, regional disparities still exist, with per capita income in Dar es Salaam being almost four times the per capita income of Kagera.

This chapter analyzes the magnitude, pattern, and quality of growth achieved in the Tanzanian economy, as well as the determinants of growth. This general assessment of the various dimensions of economic growth will provide the basis for a detailed assessment of the prospects for economic growth in Tanzania presented in chapter 6.

Tanzania's Growth Record

Overall Growth Performance

Since independence in 1961, Tanzania's real GDP has grown annually, on average, by 3.8 percent (table 3.1). With an annual population growth rate of 3.1 percent, per capita GDP increased, on average, only by 0.7 percent per year between 1962 and 1998, and at the end of this period was only about 30 percent higher than it was in 1961. If Tanzania's future growth performance were to be the same as in the past, it will take another 60 years for per capita GDP to double from its level at the time of independence.

Table 3.1. *GDP and Population Growth, 1960–98*
(percent)

Category	1962–98	1962–77	1978–83	1984–91	1992–94	1995–98
Real GDP	3.8	5.4	0.5	3.8	1.6	3.8
Population	3.1	3.1	3.2	3.2	3.1	2.8
Per capita GDP	0.7	2.2	− 2.6	0.6	− 1.5	0.9

Source: URT (various years).

Tanzania's growth performance during the past four decades has by no means been uniform. In addition to short-term fluctuations caused by climatic conditions and other factors underlying the business cycle, its growth performance shows several major shifts. The first major break in Tanzania's economic growth occurred in 1978 (figure 3.2) and was triggered by the military conflict with Uganda; the breakup of the East African Community; and the subsequent foreign exchange shortages, which severely constrained imports of raw materials and intermediate goods and led to a prolonged period of economic stagnation. Recovery started in 1984 and lasted until 1991, when Tanzania entered a second period of low growth from 1991–94. Underlying this second period of reduced growth were a prolonged drought, which led to a fall in agricultural output; and economic restructuring, which resulted in contraction of the public sector.

At the time of independence in 1961, Tanzania (then Tanganyika) was one of the poorest countries in the world, almost solely dependent on subsistence agriculture and a few estate crops, with a small industrial base. During the first six years after independence, the government pursued market-based policies with the main objective of increasing per capita income. Growth during these six years (1961–67) averaged 6.2 percent per year, which is in line with estimates of real growth during the 1950s.

Figure 3.2. *Growth Rates of Real GDP at Factor Cost and Population, 1960–98*

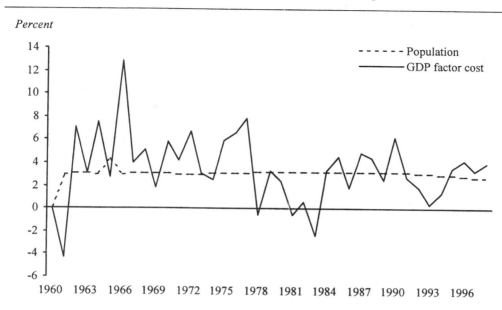

Percent

- - - - - Population
——— GDP factor cost

Sources: URT (various years).

In 1967, Tanzania switched from a market-based system to a policy of socialism and self-reliance, announced in the Arusha Declaration in February 1967. The implementation of these policies between 1967 and 1977 included the nationalization of all commercial banks, insurance companies, and commercial buildings and the formation of parastatal enterprises. The parastatal enterprises included the National Milling Corporation, which consisted of most of the major nationalized food processing industries; and the State Trading Company, responsible for domestic and external trade. Under the "villagization" campaign, massive relocations of the rural population took place to achieve the objective of having the entire rural population live in permanent villages by the end of 1976 to facilitate and rationalize the provision of basic services to the rural economy. Economic growth slowed down from 6.2 percent per year in the years preceding the Arusha Declaration to 5 percent in the 10 years following it. In comparison Kenya, which maintained market-based policies throughout, continued to grow at a rate of 7.1 percent during 1968–77, with no apparent change compared with the previous period. A severe drought and sharp increases in oil prices led to a decline in economic growth in 1973 and 1974. The coffee boom in the subsequent three years, during which the price of coffee tripled because of frost in Brazil, fueled an economic recovery.

The period 1978–84 saw a dramatic decline in economic growth, which averaged only 0.5 percent per year. The factors underlying this economic stagnation included the costly conflict with Uganda, the second oil price shock, and the breakup of the East African Community. While Tanzania saw its growth rate drop by about 4.5 percentage points, the growth rate for Kenya dropped only by 2.7 percent. One of the main causes for the larger drop in GDP for Tanzania, aside from the conflict with Uganda, can be found in the absence of market mechanisms, which would have allowed quick adjustments to take place and could have thus mitigated somewhat the impact of external shocks.

In the face of the economic crisis, in 1979 the government entered into consultations with the IMF to negotiate a standby loan arrangement. However, this loan arrangement ended in disagreement. In 1981 the government adopted a national emergency program—the NESP—followed by a three-year structural adjustment program in June 1982. A partial import liberalization program was put in place beginning July

1984, through which private imports were allowed using foreign exchange held by the importer, the source of which had to be declared. This move was combined with dismantling the price control regime and significantly reduced the dire scarcity of essential commodities and of transport and equipment. As a result, the economic situation improved in 1984, with an average annual rate of growth of 3.5 percent, which was slightly above the population growth rate of 3.2 percent.

In 1986, the three-year ERP-I introduced some measure of economic liberalization, including enhanced incentives to work, save, and invest; liberalization of key resource prices and interest rates; and an adjustment of the exchange rate. These reform efforts were supported by the IMF, the World Bank, and other donors. Between 1991 and 1994, adverse climatic conditions led to a prolonged drought, which in turn led to another economic setback, with economic growth again falling below the rate of population expansion. Finally, economic growth accelerated again during 1995–98 to 3.7 percent per year. (For details on Tanzania's national accounts see box 3.1.)

International Comparisons

During the past four decades, real growth of per capita income was slightly above the average growth rate for Sub-Saharan Africa. While Tanzania grew at 0.7 percent during 1960–98, the average for the whole of Sub-Saharan Africa was 0.5 percent. The slowdown in economic growth experienced by Tanzania since the late 1970s also closely mirrors the decline witnessed by the rest of Sub-Saharan Africa. As the average growth rate for Sub-Saharan Africa is negatively affected by the performance of countries that experienced civil strive and conflict, comparing Tanzania with African economies that experienced a degree of political stability similar to that of Tanzania is more revealing. Thus, comparing Tanzania's performance with that of Kenya, which grew at 1.5 percent annually, reveals what Tanzania might have been achieved. Had Tanzania grown at the same rate as Kenya, its GDP per capita would have doubled over the past four decades instead of only increasing by less than 30 percent. Note that once Tanzania introduced economic reforms and liberalizing markets, its economy performed slightly better than that of Kenya, while during the years of state control, Tanzania's growth persistently lagged behind that of Kenya.

A look at developing countries shows that those in East Asia and the Pacific experienced the highest per capita growth rates in the past four decades, averaging 4.9 percent per year (table 3.2). While growth in Tanzania showed a declining trend since independence, growth in these countries accelerated, reaching 6.8 percent in the period 1990–97, before the onset of the Asian crisis. Had Tanzania grown at that rate, its per capita GDP would have quadrupled since independence and it would have joined the rank of middle-income countries instead of remaining one of the poorest and least-developed countries. Performance in Latin American, Caribbean, and South Asian countries was less spectacular than that of East Asian countries, but still above that of Tanzania.

Sectoral Growth Patterns

Tanzania's economy is dominated by agriculture, which in 1998 contributed 45 percent of value added (figure 3.3). In the same year, the service sector contributed 40 percent and industry 15 percent. Compared with other African economies, Tanzania's dependence on agriculture is high. In only seven other African countries does agriculture play a greater role than in Tanzania. While the share of agriculture in an economy tends to decline with increasing income, a number of other African economies have income levels similar to that of Tanzania, but less dependence on agriculture. For example, in 1997 agriculture accounted for 43.8 percent of GDP in Uganda, 36.3 percent in Malawi, 31 percent in Mozambique, and 28.8 percent in Kenya.

Box 3.1. *National Accounts Revisions*

National accounts data for Tanzania are compiled and published by the National Bureau of Statistics. In recent years the bureau has undertaken major efforts to improve the quality of national accounts data, resulting in the publication of revised data in 1995 and 1997. The 1995 revision produced a new set of national accounts data in current prices for 1976–94, with no matching revisions of the constant price data. The data set published in 1997 provided a completely revised set of data for 1987–97 in constant and current prices. The base year for constant price data was moved from 1976 to 1992.

These revisions were necessitated by the significant structural changes the economy had undergone since the last major revision of the national accounts methodology in 1976. Data from a number of recent surveys, including the FY92 Household Budget Survey; the 1991 Informal Sector Survey; agriculture surveys; and economic surveys of the construction, trade, and transport industries, served to strengthen the statistical base for the estimation of national accounts data.

The revisions led to a significant increase in the level of estimated GDP. For example, the revised estimate for GDP at factor cost at current prices for 1990 is 90 percent higher than the original estimate. The re-estimated value added of the manufacturing, construction, and finance and insurance sectors is three to four times as high as the original estimates. Consequently, the revised estimates also provide a completely different picture of the economic structure of the Tanzanian economy than do the original estimates. For example, while the original estimates suggested that the share of agriculture in GDP had increased from 52 to 57 percent during 1987–94, the revised estimates show that the share of agricultural production in GDP actually fell from 51 percent in 1987 to 45 percent in 1994.

As shown in the following table, the revision of the estimates of GDP in constant prices yielded an estimated average annual growth rate of 4 percent for 1987–91, slightly higher than the previous estimate of 3.7 percent for the same period. The revised estimates also yielded significantly different growth rates for some sectors. For example, while previous estimates of activity in electricity and water supply and the construction sector showed an annual real decline of more than 2 percent, the revised estimates show robust growth of these sectors by 9.4 and 6.5 percent, respectively. By contrast, the revisions lowered the estimates for agriculture sector growth from 5.1 to 3.8 percent.

Sectoral Shares—Original Data Compared with Revised Data
(percent)

Sector	Sectoral shares, 1990[a]		Change between original and revised data, 1990[a]	Average annual change in real GDP, 1987–91	
	Original data	Revised data		Original data	Revised data
Agriculture, forestry, and fishing	58	46	49	5.1	3.8
Mining and quarrying	1	1	36	12.7	9.7
Manufacturing	5	9	285	4.0	3.6
Electricity and water supply	2	2	57	−2.2	9.4
Construction	3	6	259	−2.2	6.5
Wholesale and retail trade, restaurants and hotels	14	16	113	4.2	3.7
Transport and communications	9	5	13	2.4	2.2
Finance and insurance services	6	13	308	2.8	4.5
Public Administration and other services	8	8	100	2.8	5.4
Imputed bank charges	−6	−6	87	7.2	7.2
Total	100	100	90	3.7	4.0

a. Based on data in current prices.
Source: URT (various years).

In 1987, the first year for which revised national accounts data exist, GDP at factor cost in current prices was underestimated by 34 percent, as shown in the following table. If GDP is assumed to have been estimated more accurately in some previous year, growth rates for the years before 1987 would have to be adjusted to compensate for the apparent underestimation of GDP. If GDP is assumed to have been estimated accurately in 1976, the year of the last major revision of national accounts data, annual nominal growth rates would have been, on average, 3.8 percentage points higher than estimated by the Bureau of Statistics. An alternative would be to assume that GDP was estimated relatively precisely until the early 1980s. The justification for this assumption is that market reforms were introduced starting from 1981, and that many emerging private sector activities were consequently not adequately captured by the statistical system, leading to a significant underestimation of GDP. Under this assumption, the average nominal annual growth rate for 1982–87 could have been 8.6 percentage points higher than that reported by the Statistical Bureau.

Underestimations of Sectoral Shares, 1982–87
(percent)

Sector	Underestimation of 1987 GDP	Potential underestimation of annual growth	
		1982–87	1976–87
Agriculture, forestry, and fishing	23	5.4	2.4
Mining and quarrying	82	40.4	16.7
Manufacturing	45	12.6	5.6
Electricity and water supply	−49	−7.7	−3.6
Construction	53	16.1	7.0
Wholesale and retail trade, restaurants, and hotels	42	11.5	5.1
Transport and communications	4	0.7	0.3
Finance and insurance services	69	26.8	11.4
Public administration and other services	43	12.1	5.3
Imputed bank charges	56	17.6	7.7
Total	34	8.6	3.8

Source: URT (various years).

Drawing conclusions about the possible underestimation of real growth rates requires information as to whether this underestimation is due to shortcomings in the estimation of GDP deflators or to incomplete coverage of real economic activity. If most of the underestimation can be attributed to an underestimation of real economic activities, the average real growth rate for 1976–87 could have been as high as 6.1 percent per year instead of the reported 2.3 percent. If it were assumed that the severe underestimation of GDP only started in 1982, GDP growth could have been as high as 12.1 percent per year instead of the recorded 2.5 percent per year, thus indicating a much speedier recovery after the years of economic stagnation, that is, 1977–82.

Structural changes appear to have taken place in Tanzania mainly during the first decade following independence, when the share of agriculture declined sharply from 59 percent in 1960 to only 41 percent in 1970. The service sector expanded from 24 percent to 42 percent of GDP between 1960 and 1970. The share of industry remained stagnant during the 1960s at around 17 percent of GDP.

During the 1970s, Tanzania's industrialization efforts resulted in an increase in the share of value added by industry from 17 percent in 1970 to 19 percent in 1980. However, as capacity utilization and productivity in the newly founded state-owned industrial enterprises was low, the contribution of industry to GDP had again declined to 18 percent by 1990 and, after the closing of many uneconomical parastatal enterprises during the 1990s, to only 15 percent in 1998, a lower share than at the time of independence.

Table 3.2. *Real Per Capita GNP Growth, Selected Countries and Regions, 1960–98 (percent)*

Country and region	1960–98	1960–69	1970–79	1980–89	1990–98
Countries					
Tanzania[a]	0.7	2.5	1.4	− 0.8	0.1
Kenya	1.5	2.4	3.4	0.6	−0.3
Ghana	− 0.3	− 0.4	− 0.5	− 1.4	1.4
Côte d'Ivoire	0.8	4.1	3.2	−4.4	0.8
Regions					
Sub-Saharan Africa	0.5	2.3	1.0	− 0.8	− 0.6
East Asia and Pacific	4.9	2.7	5.3	5.8	5.7
South Asia	2.5	—	0.5	3.4	3.4
Latin America and Caribbean	1.7	2.5	3.4	− 0.2	1.3

— Not available.
a. Data for Tanzania refer to per capita GDP growth rates.
Source: URT (various years); World Bank (various).

Figure 3.3. *GDP by Sector, Selected Years*

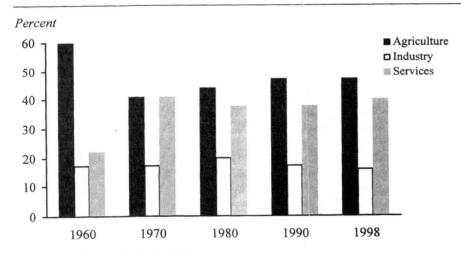

Source: URT (various years); authors' calculations.

The period 1970–90 also saw a reversal in the structural shift from agriculture to the service sector (tables 3.3 and 3.4). By 1990 the share of agriculture had again increased to 46 percent from 41 percent in 1970, while the share of the service sector had fallen from 42 percent in 1970 to 36 percent in 1990.

Table 3.5 shows the contributions of the agriculture, industry, and service sectors to overall growth. During 1962–98 the service sector contributed 2.3 percentage points to overall growth, agriculture contributed 1.6, and industry contributed 0.5. While the contribution of agriculture to overall GDP growth was fairly stable across subperiods, output growth of the industry and service sectors showed much larger variations. In particular, most of the economic stagnation witnessed during 1978–83 and 1991–94 was attributable to problems in the industry and service sectors, rather than in the agriculture sector, although growth in agriculture had also slowed down during these two periods. Periods of high growth were mainly the result of accelerated growth in the nonagriculture sectors (figure 3.4).

Table 3.3. *Sectoral Shares, Selected Years*
(percent)

Sector	1960	1970	1980	1990	1998
Agriculture, forestry, and fishing	59	41	44	46	45
Mining and quarrying	4	1	1	1	1
Manufacturing	7	10	12	9	7
Electricity and water supply	1	1	1	2	2
Construction	6	5	5	6	5
Wholesale and retail trade, restaurants and hotels	5	13	13	16	12
Transport and communications	7	9	8	5	5
Finance and insurance services	5	10	10	13	14
Public administration and other services	7	11	10	8	11
Imputed bank charges	0	−1	−3	−6	−3

Source: URT (various years).

Table 3.4 *Sectoral Growth Rates, 1962–98*
(percent)

Sector	1962–67	1968–77	1978–83	1984–90	1991–94	1995–98	1962–98
GDP at factor cost	6.2	5.0	0.5	4.0	1.6	3.8	3.8
Agriculture, forestry, and fishing	5.5	3.4	1.9	4.5	2.5	3.5	3.6
Mining and Quarrying	7.0	−2.7	−6.2	2.0	10.6	16.5	2.7
Manufacturing	10.5	7.4	−7.6	1.7	−0.4	4.9	3.3
Electricity and Water	7.4	8.4	7.1	9.0	3.2	6.3	7.3
Construction	10.7	2.8	−2.3	16.8	−3.6	2.7	5.2
Wholesale and retail trade, restaurants and hotels	8.2	3.8	−3.3	5.0	0.6	4.2	3.3
Transport and communications	10.4	8.2	−1.6	2.0	4.5	4.5	5.0
Finance and insurance services	5.4	3.5	4.0	4.9	3.2	3.6	4.1
Public administration and other services	4.5	10.3	5.0	1.2	1.7	1.2	4.9

Source: URT (various years).

Table 3.5. *Sectoral Growth Contributions, 1962–98*
(percent)

Sector	1962–67	1968–77	1978–83	1984–90	1991–94	1995–98	1962–98
Agriculture	2.6	1.3	0.7	1.8	1.2	1.8	1.6
Nonagriculture	3.6	3.6	−0.3	2.5	0.4	2.0	2.3
Industry	1.2	0.8	−0.9	0.9	−0.1	0.8	0.5
Services	2.4	2.9	0.6	1.6	0.5	1.2	1.7
Total	6.2	5.0	0.5	4.3	1.6	3.8	3.8

Source: URT (various years).

Figure 3.4. *Sectoral Growth Rates, 1960–98*

Manufacturing

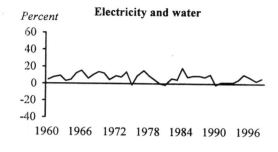

Electricity and water

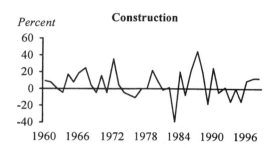

Construction

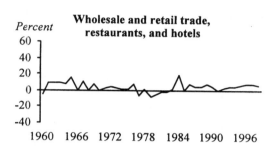

Wholesale and retail trade, restaurants, and hotels

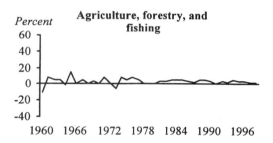

Agriculture, forestry, and fishing

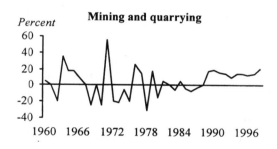

Mining and quarrying

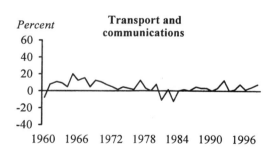

Transport and communications

Finance and insurance services

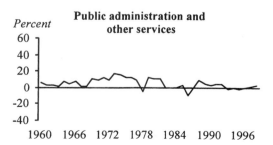

Public administration and other services

Source: URT (various years).

Volatility of Growth Performance

The welfare of households and individuals is affected not only by average levels of overall and sectoral growth rates, but also by their variability. The extent to which variability affects welfare depends on whether households are able to smooth consumption through saving, insurance, or other safety net mechanisms that can cushion temporary falls in income. In addition, high variability of output also implies economic costs, because it may lead to uneven capacity utilization and complicates planning by the government, firms, and households.

When the standard deviation of annual growth rates is applied as the measure of variability of growth, Tanzania has the lowest variability of 34 African countries for which sufficiently long time series data are available. While for many African countries high variability of growth rates is the result of political upheaval and civil conflict, even countries that have a similar degree of political and social stability, such as Kenya and Côte d'Ivoire, display a significantly higher variability of output growth than Tanzania. While the standard deviation of GDP growth rates for Tanzania for 1962–98 is 2.8, it is 5.3 percent for Kenya and 5.8 percent for Côte d'Ivoire. Among the possible explanations for Tanzania's comparatively low output variability are deliberate attempts by the government to reduce exposure to economic shocks, which at the same time, however, might have led to reduced average growth. Substantial amounts of foreign aid may also have contributed to smoothing output volatility for two reasons. First, to the extent that aid flows to Tanzania are not related to other shocks affecting the economy, a high share of foreign assistance in GDP leads automatically to less volatility. Second, donors may have actively pursued aid policies aimed at smoothening out external shocks, thereby lowering the volatility of overall GDP.

In Tanzania, the variability of the growth of GDP at factor cost has declined steadily since independence. One important factor contributing to this decline in variability is the diversification of the economy that has taken place since independence. With respect to sectoral growth rates, agriculture and finance show the lowest variability (table 3.6). The relatively small variability of growth rates in the agriculture sector is quite remarkable, given the sector's exposure to variations in climate and in world prices for cash crops. The variability of agricultural growth has also declined over the past four decades, reflecting the diversification of the agriculture sector. While at independence the production of cash crops was mainly limited to sisal, coffee, and cotton, during the past 40 years tobacco, tea, pyrethrum, and cashew nuts have been added.

Table 3.6. *Standard Deviations of Real Growth Rates, 1962–98*
(percent)

Sector	1962–98	1962–69	1970–79	1980–89	1990–98
GDP at factor cost	2.8	3.2	2.6	2.2	1.6
Agriculture, forestry, and fishing	3.5	5.1	4.1	2.0	1.5
Mining and quarrying	18.6	18.2	27.6	7.9	5.8
Manufacturing	7.2	3.5	6.1	7.1	3.3
Electricity and water	7.3	8.4	9.1	6.8	5.1
Construction	5.2	8.2	4.7	5.3	3.0
Wholesale and retail trade, restaurants, and hotels	5.4	5.4	4.0	6.5	2.5
Transport and communications	6.3	5.4	4.7	6.1	4.2
Finance and insurance services	3.1	4.7	1.6	2.8	2.3
Public administration and other services	6.1	2.1	6.2	6.4	3.1

Source: URT (various years); authors' calculations,

The mining and quarrying sector and the construction sector show the highest variability in growth rates. While variability of growth in the mining sector was high during the first two decades after independence and much lower during the last two decades, variability of growth in the construction sector was high throughout. The variability of growth rates of the manufacturing sector, public administration, and other services was high during the 1970s and 1980s, but relatively low during the 1960s and 1990s. With respect to the manufacturing sector, the high variability reflects Tanzania's changing policy stance toward industrialization as well as the problems experienced with the adoption of the government-led industrialization strategy. Growth rates in the sector were low during the first half of the 1970s, when the government focused on agriculture and neglected manufacturing. Once the industrialization policy was adopted in 1976, growth in manufacturing accelerated for a short period, but with the onset of the economic crisis in 1978, growth rates in the sector turned negative and a slight recovery only took place during the 1980s. The relatively high variability in the growth rate of public administration and other services reflects Tanzania's socialist experiments, which fostered rapid expansion of the public sector. However, this rapid expansion of the public sector was not sustainable. While the economic crisis between 1978 and 1983 forced a temporary halt of government expansion, serious public sector restructuring started in the second half of the 1980s.

Monetary and Nonmonetary GDP

Tanzania's subsistence sector—comprising nonmonetary agricultural activities, construction, and owner-occupied dwellings—accounts for about 27 percent of total GDP. During the past four decades, the growth rate of monetary GDP was, on average, above the growth rate of nonmonetary GDP. This led to a decline in the share of nonmonetary GDP in overall GDP, from 34 percent in 1960 to 27 percent in 1998. As can be seen from figure 3.5, no consistent relationship exists between monetary and nonmonetary GDP growth rates. The subsistence sector growth rates do not move in parallel to monetary sector growth

Table 3.7. *Growth Rates and Standard Deviations of Monetary and Nonmonetary GDP, 1961–98 (percent)*

Category	1961–97	1961–69	1970–79	1980–89	1990–98
Monetary GDP					
Average	4.1	5.5	4.5	2.6	3.1
Standard deviation	3.6	4.2	4.1	3.5	2.3
Nonmonetary GDP					
Average	3.2	2.2	4.1	2.2	3.0
Standard deviation	4.9	5.8	5.9	5.8	0.9
Total GDP					
Average	3.5	4.5	4.4	2.1	3.1
Standard deviation	3.2	4.6	2.8	3.2	1.7

Source: URT (various years); authors' calculations.

rates neither does the subsistence sector act as a shock absorber to shocks suffered by the monetary sector. However, growth of nonmonetary GDP appears to be much more stable after 1987 than in previous years, when the volatility of nonmonetary GDP was greater than that of monetary GDP. However, the relatively high volatility before 1987 could be due to different GDP estimation methods, as the post-1987 figures are from the revised data set.

Subsistence agriculture accounts for 80 percent of nonmonetary GDP, which could explain the higher variability of nonmonetary GDP compared with monetary GDP, given that agricultural output depends on climatic conditions. Nonmonetary subsistence agriculture grew considerably faster than total agriculture, while construction grew relatively more slowly than total construction (table 3.8).

Figure 3.5. *Growth of Monetary and Nonmonetary GDP, 1960–98*

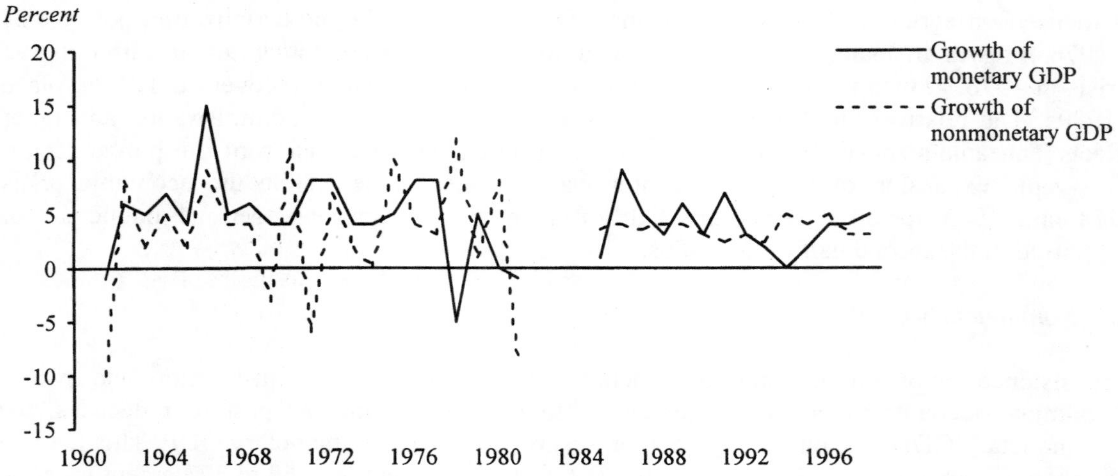

Source: URT (various years); authors' calculations.

Table 3.8. *Sectoral Composition and Growth of Nonmonetary GDP, 1962–98 (percent)*

Sector	1962–98	1962–69	1970–79	1980–89	1990–98
Share in total GDP					
Nonmonetary GDP	29	32	28	28	27
Share in nonmonetary GDP					
Agriculture	77	75	76	79	80
Construction	3	3	2	3	3
Owner-occupied dwellings	20	23	22	17	16
Growth of nonmonetary GDP					
Agriculture	4.3	3.7	5.5	5.7	3.0
Construction	2.6	3.5	2.6	2.4	2.0
Owner-occupied dwellings	3.1	3.5	2.9	3.0	3.1
Nonmonetary GDP	4.0	3.6	4.8	5.1	3.0

Source: URT (various years); authors' calculations.

Regional Incomes and Growth Patterns

Per capita incomes in Tanzania vary significantly across regions. In 1997 the per capita income in Dar es Salaam was about four times higher than the per capita income in Kagera, the poorest region of Tanzania. Arusha, Rukwa, Iringa, Ruvuma, and Shinyanga also had per capita incomes of up to 20 percent higher than the national average, which stood at T Sh 147,026 in 1997. However, most regions have per capita incomes that are between 10 and 20 percent lower than the national average, including the regions of Mwanza, Singida, Tabora, Mbeya, Lindi, Mtwara, Morogoro, the Coast region, and Mara. Kilimanjaro, Dodoma, Kigoma, and Kagera are the regions with the lowest per capita GDPs, 30 to 35 percent below the national average.

A measure commonly used to assess the dispersion of regional per capita income is the coefficient of variation, that is, the standard deviation of per capita income across regions divided by the national mean. To remove the arbitrariness introduced by political definitions of regions, the coefficient of variation can be recalculated using the shares of regional population as weights, thereby giving relatively more importance to the more populous regions. Regional dispersion is generally much higher in developing countries than in industrial ones.

In 1997 the weighted and unweighted coefficient of variation for Tanzania were 0.433 and 0.399, respectively (table 3.9). Income dispersion in Tanzania is thus larger than in industrial countries. For example, income dispersion measured by the weighted coefficient of variance for France, the United Kingdom, and the United States is 0.255, 0.120, and 0.159, respectively. Compared with other developing countries, Tanzania's income inequalities across regions appear to be similar to those observed in many Latin American economies. Regional income disparities in Asia are generally considerably higher. Relatively little evidence is available on regional income disparities in Sub-Saharan Africa, but income distribution across regions appears to be more equal in Tanzania than in South Africa or Kenya.

Table 3.9. *Dispersion of Regional Per Capita GDP, Selected Countries and Years*

Country	Year	Vw	Vu	Number of regions
Tanzania	1997	0.433	0.399	20
Industrial countries				
France	1993	0.255	0.182	22
United Kingdom.	1993	0.120	0.109	11
United States	1990	0.159	0.194	48
Developing countries				
China	1995	0.496	0.694	27
Indonesia	1995	0.673	0.718	27
Brazil	1994	0.409	0.424	26
Columbia	1989	—	0.358	25
Kenya	1994	0.439	0.596	8
South Africa	1994	0.644	0.557	—

— Not available.
Vw Coefficient of variation using regional populations as weights.
Source: For Tanzania and Kenya, staff calculations; for other countries, Fallon (1998).

An important question in relation to income dispersion is whether the per capita income of poorer subnational regions tends to catch up with those of more prosperous regions. Such a convergence would be expected if barriers to goods and factor mobility were low within a country and returns to capital were diminishing. Convergence can also occur through the redistribution of incomes from relatively rich regions to relatively poorer ones by the central government.

For Tanzania, regional disparities have clearly been narrowing over the past 20 years. Figure 3.6 shows the unweighted coefficients of variation of per capita income for the years 1980–97. Underlying the narrowing dispersion of income across regions are different regional growth rates, but also migration from poorer to high income areas, in particular to the Dar es Salaam region. While in 1980 the per capita income of this region was almost five times the national average, in 1997 the average per capita income in this region was only 2.5 times as high as the national average and its population had increased by more than 50 percent. Other regions that registered slower per capita growth than the national average are Arusha, Morogoro, Tanga, Kilimanjaro, and Kagera. All the other regions saw improvements in their relative per capita income positions, with Rukwa, the Coast region, Lindi, Shinyanga, and Singida experiencing the largest increases in per capita incomes during 1980–97.

Figure 3.6. *Dispersion of Regional GDP, 1980–97*

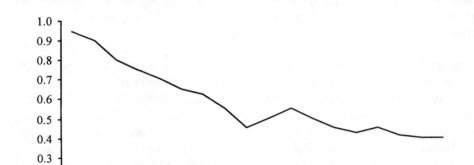

Source: Authors' calculations.

Convergence of regional per capita incomes seems to have progressed much faster in Tanzania than in other industrial and developing countries. During 1980–97 income dispersion in Tanzania changed dramatically from being one of the highest in 1980 to being one of the lowest in 1997. Most other countries for which data are available show relatively little change in income dispersion during this period.

Explaining Tanzania's Growth Performance

This section undertakes an analysis of the determinants of Tanzania's growth performance. The focus is on understanding long-term trends in economic growth, and in particular, identifying the causes of Tanzania's poor growth performance. The analysis is undertaken at three levels.

At the first level, the aggregate production function is analyzed, with growth being the outcome of investments in human and physical capital as well as of enhancements of total factor productivity (TFP). In conjunction with this, a closer look is taken at economic policies and institutions, which are key factors determining the incentive regime that drives investment in human and physical capital and factor productivity.

At the second level, the analysis focuses on the external environment within which growth takes place, looking at the influence of economic growth of Tanzania's trading partners and neighbors.

Finally, the impact of governance systems on economic growth is examined. Governance provides the framework within which economic policies and institutions are designed and shaped. This analysis is of particular importance in the assessment of Tanzania's growth prospects, given the significant changes in governance that have taken place during the past decade and that are still evolving.

Sources of Economic Growth

Foreign economic developments and the system of governance provide the environment within which economic production and growth take place. In this and subsequent sections, the immediate determinants of production—that is, human and physical capital and TFP—are analyzed.

The first step in the analysis is to examine whether Tanzania's growth performance was mainly driven by the accumulation of human and physical capital or by gains in TFP. The analysis is conducted by using an economic method called growth accounting, which separates the contribution of physical capital, human capital, and TFP to overall growth.

During 1960–98, average annual growth of output per worker was 0.7 percent (table 3.10). Increases in physical capital per worker contributed 0.4 percentage points to increases in output per worker. The contribution of education per worker was even smaller, averaging only 0.1 percentage points, with the remaining 0.3 percentage points of annual growth being attributed to increases in TFP.

Table 3.10. *Sources of Growth, Selected Country and Regional Comparisons, 1960–94 (percent)*

| Country/region | Output per worker | Contribution of | | |
		Physical capital	Education	TFP
Country				
Tanzania	0.7	0.4	0.1	0.3
Uganda	−0.3	0.3	0.2	−0.8
Kenya	1.5	−0.3	0.3	1.4
Ghana	−0.2	0.4	0.5	−1.1
Côte d'Ivoire	1.6	1.3	0.3	0.1
Region				
East Asia	4.2	2.5	0.6	1.1
South Asia	2.3	1.4	0.3	0.1
Africa	0.3	0.8	0.2	−0.6
Middle East	1.6	1.5	0.5	−0.3
Latin America	1.5	0.9	0.4	0.2
Industrial countries	2.3	1.1	0.3	0.8

Source: Collins and Bosworth (1996).

Table 3.10 compares the results obtained for Tanzania with a sample of regional comparators and the performance of other regions around the world. The contribution of TFP to output growth for Tanzania lies well above the African average: only East Asia and the industrial countries average higher increases in TFP than Tanzania. However, the contribution of education to output growth in Tanzania is below the African average, and also below the average values of all other regions. Similarly, the contribution of physical capital to growth in Tanzania is below the average for Africa and all other regions.

Table 3.11 shows the decomposition of output growth per worker for each decade of the postindependence era. The most striking aspect of the growth accounting results is the huge decline in TFP between 1960 and 1990. During the first decade after independence, increases in TFP were the driving force underlying economic growth, contributing 1.2 percentage points to an overall annual growth rate per worker of 1.9 percent. The 1970s saw a decline in TFP to 0.3 percent, and during the 1980s

Tanzania experienced a further decline in TFP, which turned negative, reducing growth of output per worker by 0.4 percent annually.[8] Underlying the decline in TFP were poor incentives for productivity under a socialist economy; poor macroeconomic policies that led to foreign exchange shortages and insufficient availability of inputs into the production process; and poor investment decisions by parastatal enterprises, which resulted in overcapacities. The economic reforms initiated in the 1990s reversed the declining trend of TFP. However, with an average contribution of 0 percent, TFP was still low. This indicates the scope for relatively large gains in TFP in the future, both through enhancing the productivity of the existing capital stock as well as though introducing new technologies. Agriculture provides a good example for possible increases in factor productivity, considering that yields per hectare on farmed land are often only 25–30 percent of the land's potential.

Table 3.11. *Decomposition of Tanzania's Growth, 1960–98*
(percent)

| Year | Output per worker | Contribution of | | |
		Physical capital	Education	TFP
1960–70	1.9	0.4	0.3	1.2
1970–80	1.3	1.0	0.1	0.3
1980–90	−0.3	0.2	−0.1	−0.4
1990–98	−0.2	−0.2	0.0	0.0
1960–98	0.7	0.4	0.1	0.3

Source: Authors' calculations.

Figure 3.7 provides an indication of the output loss caused by low TFP. With an average increase of 1 percent annually instead of the realized increase of only 0.3 percent, per capita income in 1998 would have been 30 percent higher, that is, US$275 instead of US$210.

The contribution of physical capital accumulation to growth has fluctuated significantly during the past four decades. It peaked during the 1970s, when the government introduced a new industrialization strategy and invested heavily to establish key industries. However, the contribution of these new investments was severely hampered by low productivity, resulting in an overall decline in output per worker instead of the expected accelerated economic growth. During the 1980s the contribution of capital accumulation to economic growth was only 0.2 percent, and declining investment during the 1990s led to a negative contribution of physical capital accumulation to growth.

The contribution of human capital to growth declined from 0.3 percent during the 1960s to 0.1 percent during the 1980s, despite the government's efforts to strengthen human resources and to increase access to school education. Although progress was made in expanding primary school enrollments, Tanzania's secondary school enrollment ratios are the lowest in Africa, which explains the marginal role education appears to play in the determination of economic growth in Tanzania.

---

[8] Pritchett (1999) argues that low rates of TFP could also indicate problems in measuring the value of the capital stock. In particular, corruption, lack of government efficiency in investment, patronage, and a variety of other factors may lead to costs of investment that overstate the actual contribution of investment to capital accumulation. Consequently, the results of growth accounting would overestimate the contribution of capital accumulation to growth and underestimate the contribution of TFP.

The following sections provide a more detailed analysis of investment in human and physical capital. As low TFP is one of the main elements contributing to the poor growth performance, considerable attention is also devoted to identifying the underlying causes for poor productivity in Tanzania.

Figure 3.7. *Potential and Actual Output per Worker, 1961–98*

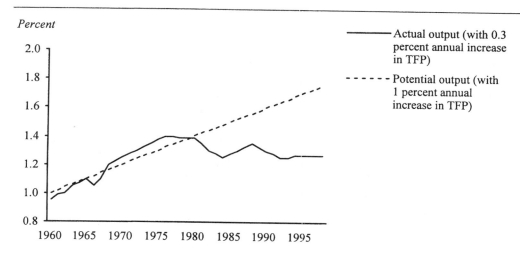

Source: Authors' calculations.

Human Capital

Investing in human capital in the form of education, training, health care, or improved nutrition is recognized as being a key element of the development process. Our growth-accounting exercise indicates that the contribution of enhancements to human capital was relatively modest in the past, accounting for a mere 0.1 percentage points of GDP growth per worker annually. Although recent research (Easterly and Levine 2000; Pritchett 1999) has questioned whether investment in human capital leads in the short term to increased economic growth, there is little doubt that investment in human capital is a precondition for sustained, long-term economic growth. Investment in human capital takes a particularly significant role in an environment of private sector-driven development as it affects the development of entrepreneurial, managerial, and organizational skills, as well as innovation, learning, and adaptation of new technology and modern practices. In addition to contributing to and supporting economic growth, most human capital investment also directly improves the quality of life of the beneficiaries.

This section provides a brief overview of changes in human capital that have taken place since 1960. The most commonly used indicator of human capital is the level of educational attainment of a country's population. Table 3.12 shows educational attainment in Tanzania, which is divided into seven groups according to the highest level of educational attainment:
- No formal education
- Primary education (completed and not completed)
- Primary education completed
- Secondary education (completed and not completed)
- Secondary education completed
- Higher education (completed and not completed)
- Completed higher education.

In the interpretation of the data, the quality of education is as important as the quantity of education, an aspect that is not appropriately captured in available statistics.

Table 3.12 provides a clear picture of Tanzania's achievements and shortcomings with respect to improving the level of education among its population. The strong focus of successive governments on enhancing access to primary education is clearly reflected in the sharp decline of the share of the population with no formal education, which at independence stood at more than 80 percent, but by 1996 had declined to about 23 percent. However, while Tanzania was successful in expanding access to primary education, high dropout rates[9] and high failure rates at the Primary School Leavers Exam[10] result in a high share of the population that has not acquired the necessary skills and knowledge to be able to pass the exam. This implies a relatively low level of human capital formation, despite Tanzania's efforts to achieve universal primary education. Recent declines in the gross enrollment ratio for primary education further threaten the sustainability of whatever progress has been made at the primary level over the past forty years.

Table 3.12. *Educational Attainment in Tanzania, Selected Years*
(highest educational attainment, percentage of the population age 15 and older)

Year	No formal education.	Primary education	Primary education completed	Secondary education	Secondary education completed	Higher education	Higher education completed
1960	81.91	13.21	3.66	1.21	0.25	3.67	2.87
1965	65.07	30.89	8.47	1.16	0.22	2.88	2.25
1970	60.64	35.76	9.50	1.32	0.21	2.28	1.78
1975	62.65	34.10	8.28	1.43	0.17	1.82	1.43
1980	48.60	48.10	8.70	1.70	0.10	1.50	1.17
1985	52.24	44.60	8.71	1.89	0.13	1.27	0.99
1991	27.41	69.39	14.21	2.20	0.10	1.00	0.80
1996	23.19	73.61	15.38	—	—	—	—

—Not available.
Source: 1960–85, Barro and Lee (1993); 1991–96, staff estimates based on Filmer (1999).

With respect to secondary and higher education, Tanzania's attainment rates are among the lowest in Sub-Saharan Africa. The data indicate that the share of the population that has at least some formal postprimary education had declined from almost 5 percent at independence to about 3.2 percent by 1990. Postprimary education has clearly not been able to keep pace with the expansion of the population, and even less with the demands of a modern economy. The emigration of skilled labor further accentuates the problem. A major cause of low enrollment levels in postprimary education is the high cost of secondary and tertiary education relative to income levels. The low student–teacher ratio, high overheads (for example, because of boarding and related subsidies, which are disproportionately enjoyed by the better-off), and low utilization of facilities combine to raise unit costs. Only since the middle of the 1980s has access to secondary education expanded more rapidly, mainly through the opening up of the sector to private sector participation.

---

[9] Entry rates are relatively high (nearly 90 percent), but survival rates at the end of the cycle are low (54 percent). The problem is more acute for children from poorer and female-headed households.
[10] In 1998 about 70 percent of pupils taking this examination did not receive a passing grade.

Data on the gross enrollment ratio for both secondary and tertiary education confirms that Tanzania does not rank well when compared with the performance of strongly performing economies in the region (table 3.13).

Table 3.13. *Gross Enrollment Ratios, Secondary and Tertiary, Selected Years*
(percentage of total)

Enrollment level, by country	1980	1985	1990	1991	1992	1993	1994	1995	1996
Secondary enrollment									
Tanzania	3.3	3.3	4.9	5.3	5.3	5.3	5.3	5.4	5.3
Botswana	18.8	29.0	42.7	52.2	51.9	56.6	55.4	62.6	64.6
Côte d'Ivoire	18.6	19.7	22.0	22.9	22.9	23.0	22.8	23.0	24.1
Kenya	19.6	21.3	24.1	27.9	27.3	25.7	24.8	24.4	—
Uganda	5.0	10.0	13.2	12.1	11.8	11.4	11.7	12.0	—
Tertiary enrollment									
Tanzania	0.3	0.3	0.3	0.3	0.3	0.4	0.4	0.5	0.5
Botswana	1.2	1.8	3.1	4.2	4.6	5.1	5.6	5.3	5.8
Côte d'Ivoire	2.8	2.6	3.2	3.1	3.6	4.4	4.5	4.6	4.6
Kenya	0.9	1.2	1.6	1.5	1.5	1.5	1.5	1.5	1.5
Uganda	0.5	0.8	1.2	1.4	1.3	1.4	1.6	1.7	1.8

— Not available.
Source: World Bank (1999b).

Estimates of economic rates of return enable an assessment of the attractiveness of investing in education. Table 3.14 shows both private and quasi-social returns to education in Tanzania. The private rate of return to any level of education can be computed by comparing the present value of the earnings differentials in the population between two levels of education with the economic (out-of-pocket and opportunity) costs incurred in obtaining the higher education. While the calculation of private returns is based on the cost of education incurred by the household, quasi-social returns are based on the cost of education covered by government. The calculation of the social return to education would require information on nonmonetary returns to education that occur to the individual, as well as on externalities arising from education, that is, benefits such as improved social cohesion, political participation, or accelerated economic growth beyond what is captured in earning differentials.

Private rates of return increase with education levels, especially for men, with the rates of return to university education and vocational and technical training being the highest. This implies that individuals are deriving significant earnings gains from higher education and training. However, the net returns to society are negligible because of excessive and inefficient spending on public tertiary education. The high private rates of return create a situation of high private demand for slots in secondary, technical, and higher education. In Tanzania's system, this translates into pressure for the government to allocate more funds for postprimary education at the expense of the primary level. The extent to which measured returns translate into economic growth depends on whether these returns simply reflect rents to be earned in public sector jobs or whether they are compensation for higher productivity.

While the analysis of quasi-social returns could suggest that resources should be shifted to primary education, these rates are distorted by inefficiencies in service delivery. While pupil–teacher ratios in primary education are relatively high, postprimary education suffers from significant inefficiencies. Pupil–teacher ratios in secondary schools are low, and the unit cost of educating a university student are high. For example, compared with Ghana, which has a strong higher education tradition, the Tanzanian government spends, on average, T Sh 1 million more on training a university student. The first measure thus needs to be to increase the efficiency of service delivery at the postprimary level, which would lead to an increase in the calculated quasi-social returns for postprimary education. In addition, given the public sector's severe financial constraints, private provision and financing at the secondary and tertiary level should be facilitated and encouraged.

Table 3.14. *Annual Rates of Return to Education and Training*
(percent)

Group	Education level			Training	
	Primary	Secondary	University	Vocational and technical	On the job
Private rates					
All	3.6	6.9	9.0	19.4	35.2
	(2,113)	(609)	(41)	(814)	(514)
Male	1.9	6.6	9.9	17.8	33.0
	(1,612)	(360)	(28)	(523)	(416)
Female	10.8	9.0	11.4	20.2	35.0
	(501)	(249)	(13)	(291)	(98)
Quasi-social rates					
All	3.6	1.5	0.0	0.0	

Note: Numbers in parentheses are the number of observations.
Source: World Bank (1997).

The relevance and quality of education is an important determinant of economic growth and returns to education. Given the relative scarcity of Tanzanians with a postprimary education, the estimated returns to education appear low in international comparison. This is likely to reflect the poor quality and relevance of formal postprimary education in Tanzania. Another consequence of poor quality and limited relevance of education to the requirements of the economy are relatively high levels of unemployment among graduates from secondary schools, universities, and technical and vocational training institutes. While much of this unemployment is the direct consequence of civil service restructuring and greatly reduced hiring by the public sector, many of these people apparently do not have the necessary skills and qualifications to be absorbed by the private sector. However, the relatively weak private sector response to economic reforms must also be taken into account. Once private sector activities start to expand more rapidly, the demand for educated employees, the returns to education, and the demand for education are bound to increase.

The preceding analysis suggests that for Tanzania to realize and sustain higher growth will continue to be difficult unless significant investment in education, particularly in technical and managerial skills, is forthcoming. To this end, a number of interventions will be necessary. Key among such interventions will be to increase the efficiency of service delivery and to foster opportunities for the development of a growing cadre of well-trained engineers and applied scientists and well-educated public and private sector managers. Because the benefits of such education accrue mainly to the students in the form of increased future income, much of this training should be financed and provided privately, with public financing limited to supporting students from poor households. However, if the private sector is to play a proactive role in supporting higher investment in human capital development, revising college curricula to reflect the demands of the private sector will be pertinent as the market for graduates in the government bureaucracy shrinks.

Investment in physical capital is another essential element needed to stimulate accelerated economic growth. However, there is no automatic link between the quantity of investment (as measured in the national accounts) and economic growth. Recent research clearly shows that the quality of investment determines whether investment will be productive and result in economic growth. In particular, the public investment process is prone to inefficiencies that result in investment that has little or no impact on economic growth. Such inefficiencies may be in the form of poor investment choices, where political and rent-seeking considerations can outweigh economic consideration. In addition, public investment often suffers from poor maintenance, which leads to a fast erosion of the public capital stock. Private investment is generally less prone to these inefficiencies, insofar as investment is constrained by a shortage of capital. Higher domestic savings and foreign resource inflows are, in turn, indispensable imperatives for realizing higher growth.

INVESTMENT TRENDS. Gross domestic capital formation in Tanzania increased from about 13 percent of GDP in 1964 to 30 percent in 1991 (figure 3.8). During the 1990s, the share of capital formation in GDP declined from a peak of about 30 percent in 1991 to only 18 percent in 1997. Most of the increases in fixed domestic capital formation that occurred until 1990 were the result of growing private investment. The decline in investment after 1992 reflects mainly a fall in public investment as a result of cutting down overall government spending and privatization.

Figure 3.8. *Share of Gross Fixed Capital Formation in GDP at Factor Cost, 1964–98*

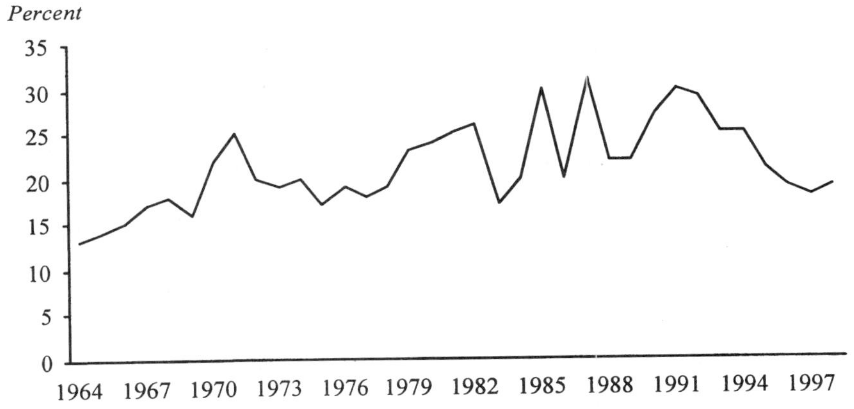

Source: Authors' calculations.

Private investment did not respond quickly to the reform measures undertaken since the late 1980s and did not compensate for the decline in public investment. The slow investment response may indicate problems of policy credibility. A fragile economic and policy environment increases the perceived riskiness of investments, leading to a wait-and-see attitude by the private sector. The weak response of private investment to economic reforms may also reflect a positive link between public and private investment, where private investment depends to a certain extent on public investment in the form of the provision of basic infrastructure and of human and institutional capital.

Table 3.15 shows the shares of public and private investment in overall gross domestic fixed capital formation. Investment patterns have changed considerably since the 1970s. While during the first half of the 1970s public investment still accounted for 58 percent of total investment, its share declined in the subsequent two decades and currently stands at around 20 percent of total investment. Part of this decline could be due to an underestimation of central government investment. The reason for this potential underestimation is that most government investment in Tanzania is financed by donors. As several recent public expenditure reviews have shown (for example, URT 1999d), a significant share of donor development funds is disbursed outside the government budget. In addition to the inefficiencies and poor incentives for good budget management created by off-budget financing, this also makes it difficult for the Tanzanian Bureau of Statistics to capture government investment adequately. Aside from this possible underestimation, the decline in government investment is a consequence of the government's fiscal austerity, which led to a fall in total government expenditures from 35 percent of GDP in 1981 to less than 13 percent in 1998.

Table 3.15. *Public and Private Investment as a Share of Total Fixed Capital Formation, 1970–98 (percent)*

Category	1970–74	1975–79	1980–84	1985–89	1990–94	1995–98
Gross fixed capital formation	100	100	100	100	100	100
Private sector	42	56	61	55	67	80
Public sector	58	44	39	45	33	20
Central government	18	22	20	8	8	3
Institutions	7	4	1	0	0	1
Parastatal enterprises	34	18	18	36	24	15

Source: URT (various years).

Public sector investment consists of investment by the central government, by parastatals, and by other public institutions. The investment shares of all three subsectors have declined substantially since 1970. The decline in investment by parastatals is closely linked to the government's privatization program during the 1990s. However, as the decline in parastatal investment during the 1990s was not offset by increased private sector investment, it led to a matching decline in the share of overall investment in GDP. The first year in which the decline in the share of investment in GDP was reversed and private investment as a share of GDP increased by more than parastatal investment fell was 1998. Since the parastatal sector was highly inefficient and many of its investments uneconomical, the decline in parastatal investment is unlikely to have negative economic consequences.

An evaluation of the potential consequences of the decline in central government investment is less straightforward. While central government investment accounted for about 20 percent of total investment until the mid-1980s, during the past four years the share of government investment in total investment has fallen to 3 percent. Even if gains were made in the efficiency of the public investment process, this drastic fall in central government investment implies that severe shortages in physical and social infrastructure persist, creating bottlenecks for overall development and economic growth.

The bulk of investment has been in transport, storage, and communications, which together account for 30 to 35 percent of total annual investment (figure 3.9). Investment in manufacturing comes second and accounts for between 20 and 25 percent of total investment per year. Investment in electricity and water supply accounts for about 15 percent of the total. The share of investment in construction has been in the range of 10 to 15 percent until 1998, when it jumped up to about 28 percent. Investment in the remainder of the sectors each account for less than 7 percent of the total.

Figure 3.9. *Investment Type of Economic Activity*
(percentage of total)

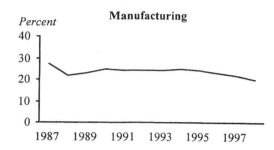

Manufacturing

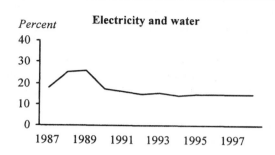

Electricity and water

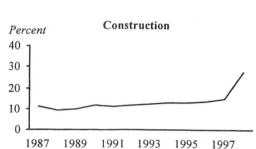

Construction

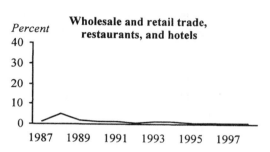

Wholesale and retail trade, restaurants, and hotels

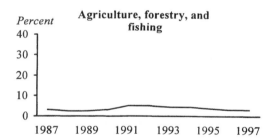

Agriculture, forestry, and fishing

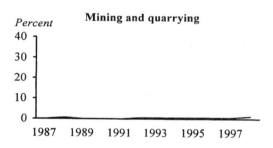

Mining and quarrying

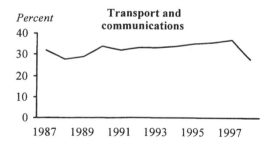

Transport and communications

Finance and insurance services

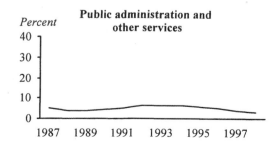

Public administration and other services

Source: URT (various years): authors' calculations.

Although gross fixed capital formation (GFCF) has declined markedly since 1992 in most of the sectors, the decline was significantly more pronounced in public administration and other services; finance insurance, real estate, and business services; and agriculture, forestry, fishing, and hunting. Sectors that have witnessed growth in investment in the recent past include mining and quarrying and construction. However, data on investment in mining seem not to capture the huge investments that have been made in the sector in the last few years that could account for the huge and rapid increase in the growth rate for the sector from − 1.3 percent in 1988 to 27.4 percent in 1998. In the case of agriculture, investment in the sector (which accounts for about half of GDP) has been not only low, but was declining throughout the 1990s. Correspondingly, the growth of the agriculture sector has also generally been on the decline. As asserted earlier, agriculture dominates total real GDP growth. This picture raises the fundamental point that if Tanzania is to achieve and sustain higher GDP growth, it must increase both the level and efficiency of investment in this key sector.

The other observation is that a large share of investment has been directed to sectors such as transport and communications, electricity, and water. Much of these infrastructure investments were financed from foreign aid without taking local capacity to operate and maintain these investments into account. Subsequently, poor maintenance has severely limited the effective provision of infrastructure services. Recent measures aimed at addressing these problems include the establishment of the Roads Fund to finance the maintenance of the roads network, the introduction of user fees in the health sector, and the increasing provision of general budget support by donors that can be used to finance maintenance and operation expenditures. In addition, the government is also restructuring public finances with the aim of providing more resources for operations and maintenance.

FOREIGN DIRECT INVESTMENT. FDI has increased in recent years, but remains small as a proportion of total resource flows to Tanzania. The tremendous surge in this form of investment, which flows globally (World Bank 1999c), has largely bypassed Tanzania, along with most other African countries. Net FDI in Tanzania for 1990–98 averaged about 1.3 percent of GDP, an amount that is nevertheless higher than the average for the whole of Sub-Saharan Africa (table 3.16).

Table 3.16. *Net Foreign Direct Investment, Selected Countries in Sub-Saharan Africa, 1990–98 (percentage of GDP)*

Country	1990	1991	1992	1993	1994	1995	1996	1997	1998
Tanzania	0.0	0.2	0.3	1.4	1.5	2.1	2.3	2.1	2.1
Uganda	0.1	0.0	0.1	0.1	0.1	0.0	1.8	2.5	2.8
Kenya	0.3	0.2	0.1	0.0	0.1	0.1	0.4	0.4	0.2
Botswana	2.4	−0.4	−0.3	−6.5	−0.5	0.6	1.6	0.9	0.9
Ghana	0.3	0.3	0.3	1.8	3.8	4.0	1.0	0.8	−0.1
Sub-Saharan Africa	—	—	—	0.1	0.4	0.6	0.8	1.1	—

— Not available.
Source: World Bank (1999b).

A key determinant of foreign investment is the attractiveness of the political, economical, and financial environment in a particular country. Country ratings undertaken by various organizations provide useful information about the assessment of these factors by investors. Figure 3.10 shows the ratings undertaken by *Institutional Investor Magazine*[11] for Tanzania, Kenya, and Uganda for 1979–99. Tanzania's perceived

[11] *Institutional Investor Magazine* credit ratings are based on a survey of leading international bankers who are asked to rate each country on a scale from zero to 100 (where 100 presents maximum creditworthiness). *Institutional*

creditworthiness dropped rapidly at the beginning at the 1980s and remained at that low level for the rest of the decade. However, investor confidence has started to recover since the beginning of the 1990s, reflecting successful policy reforms undertaken by Tanzania. This improvement in the economic, financial, and policy environment also explains the increase in direct foreign investment that has taken place since the beginning of the 1990s.

Figure 3.10. *Institutional Investor Country Ratings for Tanzania, Kenya, and Uganda, 1979–99*

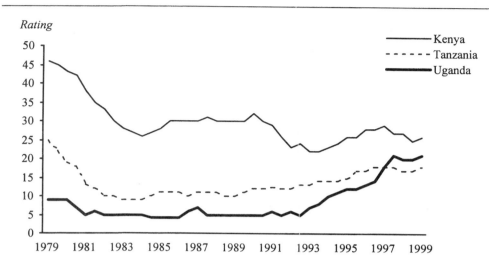

Source: Institutional Investor (various issues)

These improvements in the country rating have also led to an improvement in Tanzania's relative ranking compared with other countries. Figure 3.11 shows the ranking of Tanzania compared with all other countries ranked.[12] While during the 1990s only 10 percent of the countries received poorer rankings than Tanzania, during the 1990s Tanzania's ranking improved, and Tanzania is now ranked higher than 20 percent of the other countries covered by the survey. Indeed, the rankings of Kenya and Tanzania now differ little. While in 1979 Kenya was ranked 20 places above Tanzania, in 1999 Kenya was only 9 places above Tanzania.

In terms of the future outlook, Tanzania still has a large potential for attracting increased foreign investment flows, particularly in the mining and tourism sectors. However, for this potential to be exploited, investor confidence will need to be strengthened by sustaining the economic and institutional reform drive toward stable macroeconomic fundamentals, developing an efficient and well-functioning legal and regulatory framework, lowering the costs of and improving the conditions for doing business, and undertaking vigorous promotion of the country's rich resource base.

FINANCING OF INVESTMENT. Investment is financed from both domestic and foreign savings by the public and private sector. Figure 3.12 shows national savings (which is the sum of domestic savings, net factor receipt, and net transfer receipts from abroad) and GFCF. The difference between investment and national savings represents foreign savings that enter the country, either in the form of direct foreign investment;

Investor averages these ratings, attaching greater weights to respondents with greater worldwide exposure and a more sophisticated system for analyzing countries' economies.
[12] As the number of countries covered has increased from 93 in 1979 to 136 in 1999, the graph shows a normalized ranking on a scale from 100/*n* –100, where 100 is the last-ranked country.

short-, medium-, and long-term capital flows; or changes in Tanzania's international reserve position. Apparently, the recent decline in investment is associated with a decline in foreign savings entering the country. Because national savings did not decline to the same extent as investment, this indicates that Tanzania became less attractive for foreign investors or that investment opportunities for foreign investors were less than before.

Figure 3.11. *Institutional Investor Country Rankings for Tanzania, Kenya, and Uganda, 1979–99*

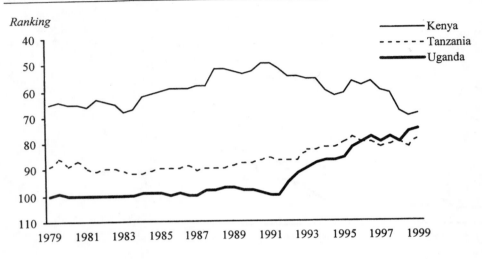

Source: Institutional Investor (various issues)

Figure 3.12. *Government and Private Savings, 1990–97 (percentage of GDP)*

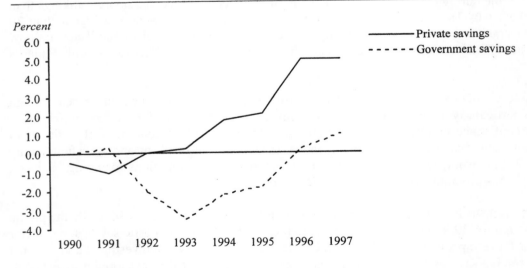

Source: Authors' calculations.

The period 1987–91 was characterized by an increase in gross national savings, averaging about 12 percent of GDP during 1987–92. However, national savings declined in 1993 to below 5 percent. This sharp drop in national savings was related to the worsening of the recurrent budget position and cutbacks in donor assistance to Tanzania following the revelation of massive tax evasion and corruption cases. The decline in national savings performance turned around beginning in 1996 to about 9.5 percent of GDP, partly because of the recovery of domestic private savings since 1993 and the achievement of positive government savings starting in 1996 (figure 3.13).

Figure 3.13. *Domestic Savings, Selected Countries, 1988–97 (percentage of GDP)*

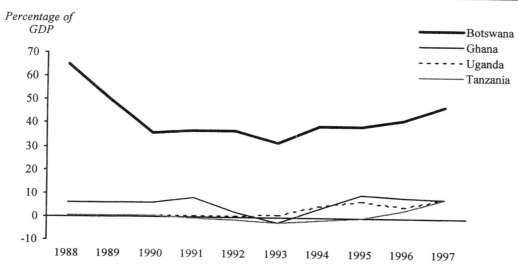

Source: World Bank data.

DETERMINANTS OF SAVINGS. Savings performance is influenced by both domestic policy and nonpolicy factors as well as by foreign factors. These include the level of development of financial markets; per capita income; inflation; real interest rates; social security arrangements; demographics; fiscal policy, especially taxation; and government savings. External factors include terms of trade shocks and the current account balance (Dayal-Gulati and Thirmann 1997; Schmidt-Hebbel and Serven 1997).

A close look at Tanzanian data suggests that a number of factors constrain savings mobilization. Some of these constraints started to be addressed in 1991 in the context of the financial sector reform program prompted by the report of the Presidential Banking Commission (the Nyirabu Commission). However, Tanzania still has a long way to go to achieve a competitive and market-based financial system. Perhaps the biggest constraint relates to the low level of development of the financial market. The number of financial intermediaries is small and their geographical distribution is largely limited to a few urban centers.

As of mid-1998 Tanzania had only 17 operating banks, 9 nonfinancial institutions, 105 foreign exchange bureaus, and a number of informal intermediaries. The NBC (1997) and the NMB together account for 55 percent of deposits and are the only banks that have a countrywide branch network. The NBC (1997) was successfully privatized in early 2000 and sold to Amalgamated Banks of South Africa. The NMB is under management contract. Other private banks operate almost exclusively in Dar es Salaam, although a few also have branches in Arusha and Mwanza municipalities. Moreover, these private banks maintain high minimum deposit balances and lend primarily for short-term trade finance, thereby limiting their customer base to a handful of low-risk, high-value customers (donors, international or big local companies, and high income earners).

Small and medium urban enterprises, as well as the rural population, continue to have limited access to banking services (IMF 1999a). The range of available savings instruments is limited and a wide spread exists between lending rates (a base lending rate of 18 percent) and deposit rates (a maximum deposit rate of 10 percent). This interest rate spread is attributable to the lack of investment opportunities for banks, costly loan processing and collection, and the minimum reserve requirement of 10 percent.

Tanzania has a number of collective savings and investment institutions. These include the National Insurance Corporation, the National Social Security Fund, the Parastatal Pension Fund, the Government Employees Provident Fund, and the Local Authorities Pension Fund. However, all four pension funds and the National Insurance Corporation are state owned, are therefore not subject to competition, and thus have few incentives to introduce innovation to attract more savings. It is only as recently as 1998 that private insurance funds began operating, although deregulation of the industry began in October 1996. The capital market in Tanzania is still in its infancy, as the Capital Market and Securities Authority only started operating in 1995. The Dar es Salaam Stock Exchange also started operating in April 1998, trading shares of three listed companies: Tanzania Oxygen Limited, Tanzania Tea Packers Limited, and Tanzania Breweries Limited. Foreign investors are not yet allowed to participate in the stock exchange, and the mobilization of savings through these channels for investment is also limited.

ECONOMIC POLICY AND INVESTMENT. Since the mid-1980s Tanzania has undertaken serious policy and institutional reforms that have a direct bearing on investment. These reforms have included the following:

- An anti-inflationary stance.
- Elimination of price distortions by discarding the use of direct price controls.
- Pursuit of higher economic growth and stable and sustainable macroeconomic fundamentals.
- Financial sector reforms.
- Tax reforms.
- The establishment of the Investment Promotion Center and the National Investment Promotion and Protection Act of 1992 specifically to promote investment by providing investment incentives. Such incentives include tax holidays, accelerated depreciation of rehabilitation and expansion investments, and refunds of withholding taxes on interest payments, dividends, and royalties.

However, numerous factors continue to inhibit productive investment in Tanzania. Among them are a poorly functioning legal framework, administrative and regulatory complexities, poor infrastructure (roads and the power and water supply), and inefficient and unreliable transport and telecommunications. For example, even though the government has gone a long way toward reducing price distortions, considerable distortions remain in areas such as power, where prices and tariffs are yet to be freed. Considerable economic uncertainty also remains. The persistence of substantial capital flight indicates that domestic investors continue to perceive that they are better off investing their financial resources abroad. This uncertainty is partly motivated by the complexity of and ambiguities in the tax regime and in the legal and regulatory framework, which remains ineffective. The lack of clear and enforceable property rights and contractual and other commercial relations further reduces the attractiveness of Tanzania as an investment destination.

The Tragedy of Poor Productivity Growth

A striking feature of the Tanzanian growth experience is that when the growth trend is juxtaposed with that of the investment rate, as in figure 3.14, investment and growth hardly seem to correlate. The period of the steepest deceleration of growth (1976–84) coincides with that of the highest investment rates. The growth impact of high investment during 1992–94 appears to have been rather weak, even after the influence of exogenous factors is taken into account. Investment rates (five-year, moving, average ratio of fixed capital formation to GDP) averaged nearly 23 percent during 1976–83, when the growth rate decelerated persistently from 6.6 percent in 1976 to –2.4 percent in 1983. This meant that the productivity of investment must have been declining steeply over the same period, as confirmed by the results of the growth accounting exercise presented earlier. To the extent the "wasted" investment was financed through debt without corresponding growth returns, it would have impaired the country's ability to service its debt obligations.

Figure 3.14. *Real GDP and Investment, 1966–96*

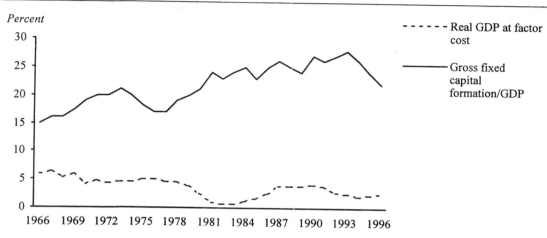

Sources: URT (various years); authors' calculations.

A comparison with a sample of other African countries is also revealing. While Tanzania's investment level was higher than that of the strongly performing economies of Uganda and Ghana (figure3.15), Tanzania did not grow any faster. Thus Tanzania can achieve a higher GDP growth even with the existing investment-to-GDP ratio as long as investment productivity is increased.

Figure 3.15. *Investment as a Share of GDP, Selected African Countries, 1988–97*

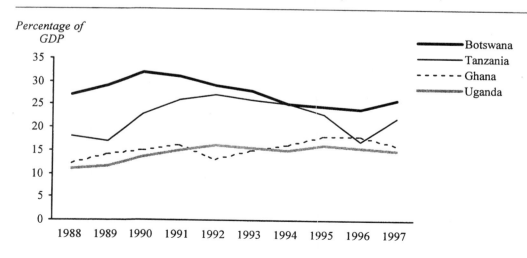

Sources: URT (various years); authors' calculations.

Various factors contributed to the investment productivity tragedy. One was a lack of complementary human skills needed to use more complex capital gainfully. The deepening of import substitution during the second half of the 1970s entailed investment in more complex processes requiring higher skills. This was typically pursued in advance of building the requisite human competence. Evidence exists to show that the productivity of FDI is higher in countries with a higher educational attainment (Elbadawi, Ndulu, and Ndung'u 1997; Jaspersen and others 1995). Both the studies cited show that the interaction between FDI and secondary educational attainment is statistically significant in explaining growth, while interaction with primary education is insignificant. Given that Tanzania has the lowest level of secondary education in the world (5 percent of the relevant school-age population), this may be one good explanation for slower productivity growth in industry as Tanzania attempted to build more complex industries (see box 3.2).

Box 3.2. Productivity in the Manufacturing Sector

A recent World Bank study (Devarajan, Easterly, and Pack 1999) examines productivity in the Tanzanian manufacturing sector. Value added and value added per worker in manufacturing rose from 1964 to 1975. However, thereafter a sustained decline in value added per worker started, leading to a 39 percent fall between 1975 and 1990. At the same time, Tanzania experienced a significant decline in the wage–rental ratio. The user cost of capital rose as the cost of imported equipment increased because of devaluations, and local building costs also rose.. While this would be expected to lead to a decline in the capital–labor ratio, that ratio increased during this period.

This implies that firms were not minimizing costs, a result not surprising in an environment in which large numbers of government interventions assured that inefficient firms survived. The absence of competitive pressures in product markets and the presence of policies to maintain employment for political purposes can probably explain the low levels of both value added per worker and TFP. About one-third of the decline in factor productivity in manufacturing can be explained by declining capacity utilization.

As much of the investment in manufacturing is undertaken by private firms, the socialist orientation of the Nyerere period cannot be blamed directly, although policies that may have discouraged the effective use of capital may well have played a role. The study also claims that there is little evidence that productivity in the parastatal sector is lower than in the private sector. Favored access to imported inputs and the resultant higher rates of capacity utilization probably explain this.

The study concludes that "unless the sources of declining productivity are better understood, advocacy of more investment as a source of growth is premature. Improving utilization rates, for example, offer a much less expensive and more certain path to sustained growth in production."

The second likely reason is the quality of investment choices. Part of the evidence here is the long death trail of white elephants, the majority most of which either lay incomplete or never became operational. A significant proportion of that that did become operational were extremely underused or collapsed once subsidies were stopped as the fiscal crisis began in the early 1980s. Apart from normal wear and tear of capital assets, loss of productive capacity has also occurred because of rapid deterioration caused by a lack of maintenance, or simply because of the closing down of plants that could not withstand competition as the economy opened up and subsidies to unprofitable public enterprises were scaled down or discontinued. An interesting issue therefore arises: whether unusable capacity should be included in the measurement of investment productivity, much as white elephants appear in the productive capital stock through application of the perpetual inventory method in computing the capital stock, even if the stock is lying idle and may never be used.

A third factor contributing to the decline in investment productivity during the decade of the deep economic crisis was a steep decline in capacity utilization as a result of either poor investment choices, import strangulation caused by a severe foreign exchange crisis experienced during this period, or poor infrastructure services for operating the installed capacity. Figure 3.16 indicates that overall import capacity declined sharply during the crisis period. In particular, export performance faltered badly because of distortions in the foreign exchange market and production incentives. The export-to-GDP ratio declined sharply by 1985 to nearly a third of its 1977 level, and net foreign inflows could not compensate for this sharp fall. Closure of the trade gap was therefore a major constraint to foreign exchange availability. What was perhaps more important was that a good part of the net flow of aid was tied up in capital projects and could not be used for importing intermediate goods needed to operate at capacity. Furthermore, such project finance also tied up counterpart finance in capital expenditure, part of it in foreign exchange. The evidence in figure 3.16 is also suggestive of directing available foreign exchange to finance the high import content of the apparent investment boom during the same period. This inflexibility of aid resource allocation changed in the mid-1980s as the import support modality was introduced with a strong emphasis on supporting better utilization of capacity. The blip in investment productivity during 1987 and 1988 is probably explained by this change. (For the specific case of Tanzania see, for example, Devarajan, Easterly, and Pack 1999; Ndulu 1986; also see box 3.3.)

Figure 3.16. *Investment Productivity, Imports Strangulation, and Buildup of Debt Overhang, 1972–96*

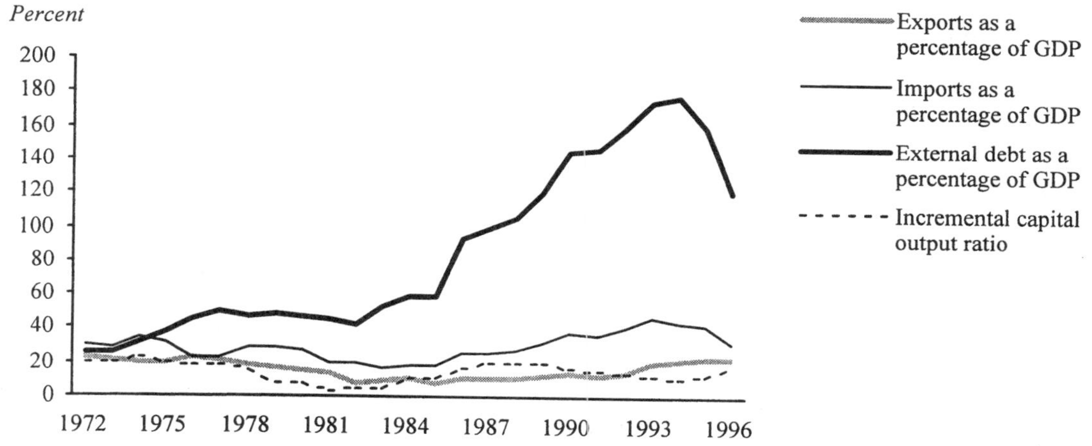

Sources: URT (various years); authors' calculations.

The prevalence of distortions in policies and markets also contributed significantly to the steep decline in the productivity of investment. Devarajan, Easterly, and Pack (1999) argue that poor incentives created by foreign exchange market distortions and high budget deficits could explain why investment is not productive in Africa. The rapid improvement in investment productivity and growth performance in the 1990s may be attributed to the considerable improvements in the policy environment.

Monopoly rights in factor markets that are protected by government also lead to low factor productivity. These monopoly rights prevent the adoption of new and more efficient technologies or work processes and cause the inefficient use of already inefficient technologies. Eliminating these protected monopoly arrangements could well increase output by roughly a factor of three without any increase in inputs (Parente and Prescott 1999). Evidence is ample that such protected monopoly rights in factor markets, in particular the labor market, play an important role in Tanzania. Restrictive labor laws and practices coupled with the protection of domestic firms from outside competition through tariffs and nontariff barriers to trade are among the prime factors that help create these protected monopoly rights in factor markets. Such protected monopoly rights are also consistent with the inefficient capital–labor ratio observable in Tanzania's manufacturing sector. In addition to lowering productivity, these distortions in factor markets also lead to a lack of incentives to invest in physical and human capital.

Box 3.3. *Investment and Capacity Utilization, 1976–80*

Investment productivity deteriorated sharply during 1978–83. Underlying this deterioration were both an expansion of production capacities beyond market demand and problems in securing the necessary inputs to make productive use of existing capacities. Most of the manufacturing sector expansion took place through parastatals, often with the support of bilateral and multilateral donors. Donor financing also enabled government and parastatal enterprises to increase investment until 1982, despite the foreign exchange shortage, which had severely restrained the importation of raw materials and spare parts since 1978, and had therefore led to the stagnation in production of the manufacturing sector.

Investment Productivity Deterioration, 1976–80
(percent)

| Sector | 1976–80 increase in | | Capacity utilization | |
	Capacity	Output	1976	1980
Textiles	122	13	92	47
Cement	76	25	72	51
Beer	8	–4	84	75
Cigarettes	15	29	77	86
Paints	12	–54	59	24
Fertilizer	28	21	40	38
Shoes	133	12	62	30
Tires and tubes	23	15	86	80
Bicycles	—	—	—	30
Leather	175	113	66	51
Hoes and plows	150	15	141	65
Corrugated iron sheet	—	–33	50	—
Blankets	0	–15	14	12
Garments	—	—	—	19
Dry cells	0	37	60	83
Rolled steel	0	75	35	61
Bags	0	43	37	53
Sugar	53	—	—	68
Bottles	209	6	121	42
Petroleum refining	0	– 48	99	52

— Not available.
Source: Kahama and others (1986).

A significant part of investment in Tanzania is financed by official development assistance. In the past, several factors have limited the productivity of official development assistance in general, and donor-financed investments in particular. Aid-financed investment coupled with limited absorptive capacity leads to capacity expansion without adequate growth of budgetary resources and exports needed to operate or maintain the larger capacity. The problem arises essentially because the investment and utilization of ensuing expanded capacity face two different levels of stringency of resource constraints. The constraint for development expenditure financed mostly through aid is less stringent, and the constraint on operative requirements (recurrent expenditures), which largely depends on much more scarce own resources, is more stringent. Large aid financing of investment at a time when policy distortions abound also significantly lowers the cost of scarce capital, and hence encourages the tendency to overinvest relative to absorptive capacity and ignores the discipline of the appropriate investment choices.

Inadequate attention to the institutional capacity for effective and efficient delivery of public services is one of the greatest weaknesses affecting the effectiveness of aid. In the 1970s a greater emphasis was placed on supporting the expansion of the facilities for social services, particularly under the Basic Needs Program, without paying sufficient attention to the institutional requirements for more effective delivery of these services and budgetary limitations for sustained operation and maintenance of these facilities. Constraints on project implementation capacity were dealt with using enclave management units through technical assistance. Efficiency in the delivery of services received little emphasis as concerns were focused on ascertaining whether monies were being used for the intended purpose rather than on what value was obtained from the expended resources. In the earlier phase, civil service reforms were driven by the primary objective of downsizing the government to reduce the fiscal deficit. Much more recently attention has turned toward strengthening the government's capability and efficiency to deliver public services effectively. Apart from capacity-building initiatives, these efforts have also begun to address the low motivation of the civil service and problems in attracting and retaining high-caliber personnel.

Until recently accountability systems were fragmented and revolved around a dialogue between the government and the multitude of donors. The emphasis has been on external restraint to imprudent behavior by the main intermediary of aid—the government—and seldom on internal mechanisms for restraint. This arrangement was consistent with the prevalence of autocracy, but is now facing serious challenges as open polities and inclusiveness in the system of governance are being widely adopted and intolerance toward corruption by donors, as well as domestic stakeholders, is much greater. The problem of dual accountability has been recognized, and efforts are being made to resolve it through an integrated approach. The much more sanguine conclusions regarding the ineffectiveness of external conditionality in begetting change and reforms buttress the shift toward greater reliance on domestic constituencies to motivate and sustain change, and toward promoting the role of citizens' voices in begetting accountable behavior by those responsible for managing the development process.

Growth Spillovers from Trading Partners and Neighbors

For a small, open economy such as Tanzania's, economic developments in neighboring countries and its trading partners are important determinants of economic growth. The key transmission channels are economic linkages through trade and investment. A recent World Bank study (Easterly 1999) argues that the poor growth performance of most developing countries during 1980–98 was attributable to the slowdown in growth in the industrial countries rather than poor policies or policy ineffectiveness in the developing countries.

In addition to the transmission of growth impulses through trade and investment, neighborhood effects and spillovers also occur among neighboring countries (Easterly and Levine 2000). Such contagion effects can occur for a number of reasons. The first is the possibility of policy imitation, that is, successful policies adopted in one country are copied in other countries. The second is the possibility of spillovers from FDI. Once foreign investors have established a successful base in one country, have become familiar with local conditions, and have adopted their technologies to local conditions, they are likely to expand their activities in neighboring countries. The transmission of growth effects may also occur through migration to and from neighboring countries or through benefits from improvements in infrastructure in neighboring countries.

In addition to such spillover effects, which imply some degree of causality, external shocks that affect both Tanzania and its neighbors and trading partners may also play an important role. Among regional shocks would be climatic variations that affect the economy, political unrest, wars that affect the region, and so on. Among external shocks that may affect both developing and industrial countries are variations in prices for resources such as oil.

This section examines to what extent such growth spillovers are important in explaining Tanzania's growth experience. The relationship between growth in Tanzania and that of its main trading partners is analyzed, followed by an analysis of spillover effects between Tanzania and its neighbors.

Table 3.17 shows the correlation between Tanzania's real rate of GDP growth and that of neighboring countries. In addition, the correlation with the weighted average growth rate for Tanzania's trading partners among Organisation for Economic Co-operation and Development (OECD) countries is shown.[13] As with many other African countries, most of Tanzania's international trading partners are located in Europe or Asia. Over the past 40 years, trade with its neighbors accounted, on average, for less than 10 percent of Tanzania's trade. With the exception of Mozambique and Uganda, the analysis is based on data for 1961–98. For Mozambique and Uganda, time-series data on economic growth are only available from 1981 and 1982 onward, respectively.

Table 3.17. *Correlation of Tanzania's Real Rate of GDP Growth with that of Its Neighbors, 1961–98*

Data used	Burundi	Congo, Dem. Rep.	Kenya	Malawi	Rwanda	Mozambique	Uganda	Zambia	Trading Partners
Annual	0.39	0.32	0.48	0.17	0.13	0.50	− 0.14	− 0.02	0.34
Five-year moving average	0.41	0.35	0.62	0.76	0.14	0.79	− 0.22	0.64	0.83

Note: For Uganda and Zambia, the figures are for FY81–98.
Source: Staff calculations using data from World Bank (1999a).

In the medium term (based on five-year moving average growth rates), the correlation between growth in Tanzania and that of its OECD trading partners is stronger than the correlation with neighboring countries. This indicates that the impact of the growth performance of Tanzania's OECD trading partners may have a stronger impact on growth in Tanzania than growth impulses originating from neighboring countries. Among neighboring countries, Kenya, Malawi, Mozambique, and Zambia show the strongest correlation with growth in Tanzania in the medium term.

In the short run (on the basis of annual data), the growth correlation between Tanzania and its trading partners is significantly smaller than the medium-term correlation. In the short run the correlation is higher for Kenya and Mozambique than for OECD trade partners. This points toward the possibility that in the short run exogenous shocks, such as climatic variations, play an important role in determining regional growth rates, while in the medium term, contagion effects emanating from Tanzania's trade partners seem to dominate.

---

[13] We use Easterly's (1999) data on the average growth rates of developing countries' OECD trading partners, which are calculated as the trade-weighted average growth rate of countries' OECD trading partners.

DEMAND-SIDE IMPULSES FROM TANZANIA'S TRADING PARTNERS. Figure 3.17 shows annual data and five-year averages of the trade-weighted growth rate of Tanzania's main OECD trade partners as well as the real GDP growth for Tanzania. From the graph it is apparent that in the medium term, Tanzania's GDP growth follows the major movements of economic growth of its trade partners quite closely. In particular, the two periods of persistent low growth at the beginning of the 1980s and 1990s coincide exactly with the slowdown observed in industrial countries.

Figure 3.17. *Economic Growth Patterns in Tanzania and Its Trading Partners*

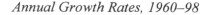

Annual Growth Rates, 1960–98

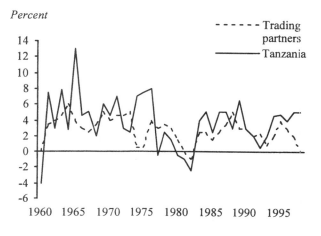

Five-Year Average Growth Rates, 1960–98

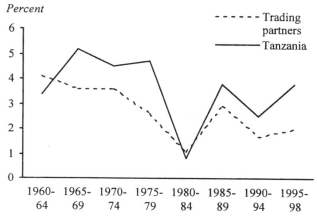

Sources: Easterly (1999); URT (various years); authors' calculations.

What is particularly interesting is that Tanzania did not experience the same slowdown in economic growth during the second half of the 1970s as its trading partners did. While its trading partners went into recession, partly as a consequence of the first oil shock, Tanzania benefited from the coffee boom and associated high coffee prices in 1976–78. However, these temporary windfall gains from high coffee prices only delayed Tanzania's adjustment to the international recession, and the decline following the years of the coffee boom was then even more pronounced.

The fact that Tanzania's growth rate was in general above that of its trading partners is accounted for by Tanzania's higher population growth. In per capita terms, Tanzania's growth was actually less than the average growth rate of its trading partners.

The econometric analysis presented in table 3.18 confirms the close relationship between growth in OECD countries and in Tanzania. In the short run, a 1 percent increase in GDP in Tanzania's OECD trade partners leads to a 0.7 percent increase in Tanzania's GDP. In the medium term, the relationship appears even stronger: a 1 percent increase in the GDP of Tanzania's trading partners leads to an increase in Tanzania's growth rate by 1.37 percentage points. Of course, this also implies that a recession in OECD countries will have a strong negative effect on growth in Tanzania. The regression results obtained for Tanzania match quite closely the results Easterly (1999) obtained. He found that for a cross-section of developing countries, 1 less percentage point of OECD trading partner growth is associated with 1.2 percentage points less of home country growth.

Table 3.18. *Real GDP Growth in Tanzania Regressed on Real Average GDP Growth of Tanzania's Trading Partners*

Item	Annual observation				Five-year moving average			
	Coefficients	Standard error	t statistic	P-value	Coefficients	Standard error	t statistic	P-value
Intercept	1.73	0.98	1.78	0.08	0.05	0.45	0.10	0.92
Trading partners	0.70	0.33	2.14	0.04	1.37	0.16	8.44	0.00
Regression statistics								
Multiple R		0.34				0.83		
R square		0.11				0.69		
Adjusted R square		0.09				0.68		
Standard error		2.92				0.91		
Observations		38.00				34.00		

Source: Staff calculations.

Although the link between domestic and foreign growth in Tanzania is clear, whether both Tanzania's and its trading partners' growth performance were affected by common external shocks or whether and how shocks were directly transmitted from the country's trading partners to Tanzania is not clear.

NEIGHBORHOOD EFFECTS. To investigate whether regional spillovers play a role in the case of Tanzania, the link between Tanzania's growth rate and that of its neighbors is examined. A regression of Tanzania's growth rate on that of its neighbors shows that in addition to the growth rate of its trading partners, only the growth rates of Burundi and Malawi are related to that of Tanzania in a significant way in the medium term (using five-year, moving average growth rates). A 1 percentage point increase in the rate of growth of Burundi or Malawi leads to a 0.18 and 0.39 percentage point increase in GDP growth in Tanzania, respectively (table 3.19).

The use of annual data yields similar, though weaker, results. While in the medium term variations in foreign growth rates are able to explain 79 percent of the variation in Tanzania's growth rate, in the short term these variations are only able to explain 28 percent of changes in Tanzania's growth rate. Furthermore, while growth in Malawi is no longer significantly related to growth in Tanzania, Kenyan variations in growth now appear to be significantly related to Tanzanian growth. This might be explained by Kenya's dominant economic position in the region. In addition, Tanzania's principal agricultural areas border Kenya in the north and Malawi in the southwest, making it likely that climatic variations affect agricultural output and economic growth in these three countries in a similar way.

POLICY IMPLICATIONS. What does this strong relationship between growth abroad and growth in Tanzania imply for economic management in Tanzania? First of all, the links discussed in this memorandum refer primarily to changes in the growth rate, but not to the level of the growth rate. Thus the links are no reason for economic fatalism. Even if changes in growth abroad are transmitted to Tanzania, increasing per capita income depends mainly on the fundamental long-term growth rate of per capita incomes, which is determined by factors such as human and physical capital, factor productivity, and economic policies. Countries that were able to achieve and maintain high average growth rates during the past few decades were not immune to the slowdown in economic growth in OECD countries. However, with their relatively high fundamental growth rate, they were still able to maintain positive growth rates when faced with negative growth impulses from abroad. The government thus needs the prerogative of providing the appropriate policy environment for higher long-term growth, which necessarily must encompass a stable macroeconomic environment that includes low inflation, sustainable fiscal and monetary policies, and a market-determined exchange rate. Policy predictability, the provision of infrastructure and basic social services, as well as an enabling environment for the private sector are further requirements for sustainable long-term growth.

Table 3.19. *Real GDP Growth in Tanzania Regressed on Real Average GDP Growth of Tanzania's Trading Partners*

Item	Five-year moving average n				Annual observation			
	Coefficients	Standard error	t statistic	P-value	Coefficients	Standard error	t statistic	P-value
Intercept	−0.86	0.50	−1.72	0.10	0.74	0.99	0.75	0.46
Trading partners	0.92	0.28	3.32	0.00	0.35	0.34	1.03	0.31
Burundi	0.18	0.06	3.06	0.01	0.20	0.07	2.77	0.01
Congo, Dem. Rep.	−0.12	0.06	−1.95	0.06	−0.04	0.09	−0.41	0.69
Kenya	−0.03	0.10	−0.31	0.76	0.23	0.11	2.11	0.04
Malawi	0.39	0.11	3.44	0.00	0.09	0.10	0.92	0.36
Rwanda	−0.01	0.05	−0.15	0.88	0.00	0.04	−0.02	0.98
Zambia	0.01	0.12	0.10	0.92	−0.06	0.10	−0.61	0.54
Regression statistics								
Multiple R	0.91				0.64			
R square	0.83				0.42			
Adjusted R square	0.79				0.28			
Standard error	0.74				2.59			
Observations	34.00				38.00			

Source: Staff calculations.

Second, to allow Tanzania to benefit from positive growth impulses from abroad and to minimize the negative impact from an economic slowdown abroad, the incentive regime and economic policies need to provide the economy with the flexibility to adjust to foreign growth impulses. Attempts by the government to offset negative growth impulses from abroad are likely to be at best ineffective in the short run, and detrimental to growth in the long run. As experience in industrial and developing countries has amply shown, problems with the timely recognition of external economic shocks, with the timing of policy intervention, and with policy implementation and unpredictable policy effectiveness speak against government interventions. Letting the market mechanism work and allowing prices, in particular the exchange rate, adjust to shocks is more likely to maximize benefits and minimize the cost of economic shocks from abroad.

Finally, while Tanzania has relatively little scope for affecting the growth performance of its OECD trading partners, it has considerably more scope for influencing regional development in East Africa through cooperation with its neighbors. The key message here is that regional relationships among neighboring countries should not be considered as being a zero-sum game, where one country gains benefits from investment and trade at the expense of neighboring countries, thus giving rise to protectionist measures within the region. It is much more likely that measures for facilitating trade within the region, for improving regional infrastructure, and for creating an investor-friendly environment in all countries of the region will lead to enhanced growth in all countries in the long run, independent of who benefits first from trade and investment. Thus long-term gains from cooperation are likely to outweigh the short-term benefits from protectionism within the region.

After presenting the external influences on growth in Tanzania, which are large and significant, the following section examines the role of governance in Tanzania's growth and development.

The Role of Governance In Tanzania's Growth and Development

In a recent analysis of the relationship between governance and economic growth, Ndulu and O'Connell (1999) found a striking relationship between the typology of the political regimes and growth performance. Following the Bratton and van de Walle (1997) categorization, Ndulu and O'Connell distinguished three types of political regimes: multiparty systems, single-party systems (whether competitive or plebiscitory), and military oligarchies. At this level of aggregation, a striking feature of Africa's first generation of postindependence regimes emerges: the five countries that had multiparty systems throughout their postindependence history were richer, on average, in 1960 and at every subsequent point than countries with other types of regimes. Within the group of countries with authoritarian regimes, the military oligarchies in 1988 had, on average, been poorer at the outset and remained so throughout.

These observations are based on three factors. One is the relative youth of the political systems at independence, which had weak institutional constraints to predatory behavior and stringent limits on mass political participation. Such a system fails to raise the stakes of leaders in the future prosperity of their own countries. Under the neopatrimonial autocracies, which were the dominant form of governance, the ruling (unconstrained) elite tend to sacrifice the general interest of the nation to extract rents and retain power. Development policy was in the hands of these elite, who quickly moved to subordinate existing agencies of restraint to the executive powers. For example, currency boards were quickly dismantled and central banks subjected to the direction of the finance minister.

The second reason is the that the early preoccupation was with the laudable building of nationhood from fragmented subnational entities retained under colonial rule, which occurred quite often at the expense of a focus on growth. This is epitomized in the famous quote from Nkrumah: "Seek ye first the political kingdom, and all the rest shall be added unto ye." The Africanization campaigns, protective stances of local activities, and above all the distribution of rents to maintain delicate balances across interest groups preoccupied policy and resource allocation. Easterly and Levin's (1997) article links such balancing (particularly across ethnic groups) to limiting adoption of progrowth policies. This was probably stronger at the early phase after independence than later on.

The third reason is that neopatrimonial regimes have been authoritarian but weak in contrast with the bureaucratic–authoritarian regimes more prevalent in Asia and Latin America. There was less control on bureaucracies, which had an excess of discretion, leading to an overextension of patron-client networks. These networks made large claims on dwindling public resources and had control over other rent-earning avenues. This governance approach was of necessity not progrowth, as it led to a bias against the allocation of resources for productive use.

Much of the foregoing applies rather closely to Tanzania's experience with governance. For three and a half decades the political system operated along neopatrimonial and autocratic lines, with a weak institutional framework for restraint and for rewarding good performance. The state had an overwhelming role in resource allocation and control over the actions of economic agents. Although significant political participation was exercised under a populist regime, the effectiveness of restraining power or predatory behavior was rather weak, judging by the continued struggle with removing rent-seeking and corruption.

Going by these observations, Tanzania is now poised to exploit the benefits of the open political regime that it adopted in 1995. Democratization in the 1990s and increased contestability of power are expected to spur more accountable behavior among the leadership. The current focus is on strengthening institutions of restraint, promoting orderliness after a decade of efforts to dismantle the control regime, and strengthening the citizens' voices through democracy, decentralization, and a freer press.

So far, economic reform has been slow to deliver higher investment and growth. One of the reasons for this is the lack of powerful domestic political constituencies for the maintenance of market-oriented reforms. In addition, the institutional framework is still significantly oriented toward servicing the needs of the previous control regime. Furthermore, before pluralist domestic politics can constrain policy in useful ways, the government's capacity to determine the national agenda must be reconstituted and high taxes on success must be removed.

Governance matters for long-term growth, not only through its effects on policy distortions and uncertainty, but also through its capacity to handle external shocks. The institutional framework through which Tanzania encountered shocks to commodity markets in the 1970s and to world financial markets in the early 1980s had limited flexibility to allow the required difficult adjustments. This problem was exacerbated by the belief during the second oil crisis that such shocks are temporary and reversible, based on Tanzania coming through the first oil shock without much trauma. At the same time a tendency to overtax potentially dynamic sectors and a heavy reliance on revenues to service patron–client networks had created vulnerable balance of payments and fiscal positions. In the context of Tanzania's growth experience, the long stagnation period that followed the negative shocks of the late 1970s needs to be explained from the point of view of economic management. In this regard, Rodrik (1997) shows that deceleration in growth is determined by a combination of negative shocks to the economy and the inability to adjust to these shocks as influenced by the political calculus of adjustment effects across interest groups. In addition, there has been latent, though muffled, reaction by the grassroots entities and those whose interests were not served by the control economy. The preponderance of parallel markets and the growth of the underground economy during the 1970s and early 1980s indicates that exit options were widely used to avoid controls. The encouraging part is that this latent "uprising" has given rise to wide adoption of reform measures.

A typical example of the pattern of response to shocks constrained by inflexibility is that in relation to the commodity price boom followed by the second oil crisis. A prudent response to commodity price fluctuations requires financing temporary resource shortfalls and adjusting to permanent disturbances. Terms of trade movements are highly persistent ex ante. Together with the asymmetric costs of contraction, this suggests a policy of conservative response to booms and decisive response to busts, a pattern closely followed by Botswana. However, this requires fiscal flexibility and a willingness to devalue the exchange rate—and face real wage declines—when major deterioration in the terms of trade occurs. Tanzania weathered the first oil crisis by tightening import and exchange controls, as well as by drawing down automatic and quick-disbursing facilities, such as the oil facility operated by the IMF. The tropical beverage boom of FY76 seemed to validate this strategy, and even led to renewed expansion of spending (Bevan and others 1989, 1990). When the prices of export commodities collapsed and the second oil crisis erupted in 1979, governments expected a similar short-lived crisis and a quick reversal of fortunes. However, resource shortfalls worsened with the recession in the world economy and the debt crisis of the early 1980s. Fiscal adjustment and exchange rate unification were then delayed as attempts were made to maintain patron–client networks through monetary financing and exchange controls.

An important dimension of this issue is the influence of aid in promoting or hindering the emergence or nurturing of good governance. A view has emerged in empirical literature and case studies that aid has had little effect on policy outcomes in Africa, and that its contribution to growth has been heavily conditioned by pre-existing state capability (see, for example, World Bank 1998c). It has also been argued that aid was, on balance, undermining institutional capacity in Africa. Furthermore, bilateral aid is an instrument of foreign policy. In Africa, the geopolitical interests of major donors centered on the support of political or ideological clients rather than on rapid economic development, the implications of which, for donors, were remote. For these reasons, donor pressure was poorly suited to generate credible feedback from poor performance to better policy, much less from authoritarian rule to greater pluralism or institutional constraints.

The foregoing analysis indicates that a rise in fungible aid will increase transfers to political clients whenever they are already active. Moreover, unless the government is fully encompassing, there is some level of aid above which transfers will be initiated in preference to further tax cuts (Adam and O'Connell 1998). Aid does not directly reduce growth in these cases, but policy distortions will appear, ex post, to be robust to inflows. Indeed, to the degree that aid flows enhance the domestic competition for politically motivated transfers and the power to dispense them, they may reinforce the neopatrimonial patterns described earlier.

Adam and O'Connell limit their recommendations to implementing more selectivity in aid disbursement so as to reward those leaders who adopt progrowth policies and a more focused agenda on the policy undertakings deemed to be most potent for growth. An even more important aspect of the new approach to effective aid delivery is embedded in the new World Bank approach, the Comprehensive Development Framework. Among other important aspects, this approach emphasizes local ownership of policy and wider participation by local stakeholders in the process of policy formulation and implementation. Binding new approaches to economic management in strong institutional and legal frameworks is also emphasized. These are effective instruments for strengthening internal agencies of restraint and raising the credibility of the policy environment, all critically important for spurring investment and growth. Furthermore, they confer a sense of perpetuity more encompassing of interests and accountability.

"Visionary" national leadership makes an important difference in achieving sustainable growth, as evident from successful "heroes" of "strong bureaucratic-autocracies" in Asia and the policy reform elite (Harberger's influential technocrats) in Latin America. Further evidence can be gleaned from the Harvard Institute for International Development's investor surveys across 23 African countries, in which most respondents placed credible leadership as a top concern holding back the flow of investment into the region. An important question does arise from this change, however. Should Africa follow the Asian strong autocracy model built around heroes, or does the ongoing democratization process rule this out? In the latter case the heroes will be those leaders who set up effective systems of accountability and build an institutional framework for restraint against predatory behavior.

4. Combating Poverty, Ignorance, and Disease

At independence, President Julius Nyerere declared the three archenemies of development to be poverty, ignorance, and disease, and the development strategy adopted then focused on their elimination. Poverty as a central development concern received a sharper focus after the adoption of a socialist strategy in 1967 and dominated the central-government investment programs during the 1970s, with emphasis on expanding facilities for delivery of basic social services—education, health and water. The "basic-needs" approach to development programming, which was then high on the global development agenda, underpinned this strategy. Indeed, rather ambitious targets were adopted to achieve universal primary education, primary health, and water for all by the early 1980s, with major support from donor financing. The strategic emphasis during the first two decades of independence was thus placed on raising public consumption of basic services financed mainly through income redistribution and aid, and raising private consumption of basic goods through subsidies, price controls, or both. Less emphasis was placed on economic growth as a means for raising private incomes and public revenues needed for sustainable financing of the poverty-reduction programs.

Although overall human development is significantly higher currently than at independence, the rapid rate of improvement achieved until the early 1980s has slowed down. Retrogression in primary school enrollment and possibly in life expectancy as the spread of the AIDS pandemic threatens to erode past achievements in human development. Major and rapid improvements in the human development were achieved during the first two decades. Primary school enrollment rose rapidly from 25 percent of school-age children at independence to 93 percent in 1980. Adult illiteracy fell sharply from 80 percent at independence to 5 percent in 1985. Access to primary health facilities and medical personnel improved rapidly with the growth of dispensaries and health centers from a total of 1210 in 1961 to 2839 in 1980. Population coverage by medical personnel rose sharply from 1 physician for every 21,000 people in 1960 to one physician for every 15,000 people. Nursing staff increased from one for every 10,000 in 1960 to one for every 5,000 in 1997. The access to piped water also improved from about 750,000 Tanzanians in 1961 to at least 10,000,000 Tanzanians in 1980. For a country whose per capita income rate increased only by 30 percent between 1961 and 1985, these achievements were indeed spectacular.

The rapid deterioration of the facilities for delivery of social services since the early 1980s and indeed the inability to keep pace with the rapidly expanding population needs is mainly due to a mismatch between the pace of these achievements and deceleration of growth. The previous fast improvement in human development could not be sustained because of lack of growth necessary for underpinning such progress. To a very large extent, investment finance for the expansion of facilities depended on aid resources and was thus less constrained. Maintenance and operations, in contrast were mainly the responsibility of the government. With a declining tax base due to poor growth and a mushrooming underground economy (outside the tax net), the resource base for financing maintenance and operations was severely constrained. Austerity programs associated with macroeconomic stabilization and higher debt-servicing obligations during the subsequent period exacerbated this financing pressure.

Four decades after independence, between 15 million and 18 million Tanzanians still live below the poverty line of US$0.65 a day. Of these, nearly 12.5 million live in abject poverty, spending less than US$0.50 on consumption a day. This is despite the fact that for the past four decades, poverty reduction has been on Tanzania's policy agenda with significant variation in form and content. However, less emphasis was placed on economic growth as a means for raising private incomes and public revenues needed for sustainable financing of the poverty reduction programs.

Focus has now resumed on poverty reduction after a decade of preoccupation with reestablishing macroeconomic stability and structural reforms for creating an enabling environment for growth. Tanzania faces massive challenges to sustaining gains made in improving the human development status. This renewal is part of a global effort for a sustainable exit from the poverty trap. The global effort finds expression in the 1995 World Summit on Social Development, the United Nations Development Programme (UNDP) paper on Poverty Eradication (1997), the United Kingdom White Paper on international development (1997), the OECD's Development Assistance Committee targets for the 21st Century, the Second Tokyo International Conference on African Development 1998, and the Enhanced HIPC Initiative (1999). International development targets flowing from these focus on poverty reduction and are part of the renewed interest in addressing the poverty problem in a sustainable manner. They combine sustaining growth, redressing extreme inequalities, integrating public and private sector initiatives, and placing greater emphasis on effective service delivery as well as accountability.

Tanzania is party to these international initiatives and has committed itself to achieving the international targets. A National Poverty Eradication Strategy has been drawn up, and preparations for an effective poverty monitoring systems are underway. Through the Public Service Reform Program, an emphasis on improved public service delivery has been adopted. This is to be done through an orientation to performance improvement and results, rationalization of public service functions, and an enhanced meritocratic incentive system. The central government has undertaken to prepare a National Poverty Reduction Strategy, a crucial part of the HIPC development program. The adoption of a Medium-Term Expenditure Framework approach to allocating strategic-priority resources focused on poverty reduction in budgets that also ensure sustainable investment. This budget management system will be embedded in an overall development strategy that also coordinates external assistance (Tanzania Assistance Strategy). Prospectively, Tanzania will benefit from the poverty-focused Enhanced HIPC Initiative. Finally, the recent adoption of decentralized public service delivery is aimed at raising effectiveness, taking public choices closer to the stakeholders, and promoting improved accountability.

If the renewed effort at poverty reduction is to succeed, the strategic approaches have to incorporate lessons from past failure to sustain improvements in human development. Two questions arise from that experience even as growth resumes and aid flows improve. Had Tanzania embarked on an unsustainable rate of improvement in the quality of life relative to its income level? Is the current retrogression in some key indicators of human development a process of returning these achievements to a level commensurate with the country's income? The answers to these two questions will temper the ambition of regaining past achievements in a hurry even in the context of the recent renewed focus on poverty reduction. Analysis, which estimates expected status of human development indicators for Tanzania's income level based on international experience, concludes that Tanzania's achievements exceeds expectations.

There is now significant evidence that growth is essential for reducing poverty on a sustained basis. However, a growing economy offers opportunities for the poor to earn a decent income, if growth is also widely spread and occurs in those sectors on which the poor depend the most. Thus while the impact of growth on poverty reduction is four times more powerful than redistributional interventions in Tanzania, as the analysis by Eele and others (1999) shows, growth needs to be complemented by actions that redress gross inequalities in earning capacities and opportunities across geographical locations, socioeconomic groupings, and gender. Such actions should be informed of who the poor are and reasons for their being trapped in poverty. The design of effective safety nets for the most vulnerable depends also on such information. Furthermore the analysis in this chapter points to the need to pay attention to the high population dependency ratio, which places an unsustainable burden on the productive labor force to fend for minors and the elderly. An accelerated demographic transition enables higher savings and therefore investment and growth.

Thus the concern about poverty is not merely a welfare issue. It is also one of limiting the productive capacity of the economy. The poor are typically less educated, of ill health, and with large families. Evidence based on adjusted FY91 household budget survey (HBS) data indicates that, first, the incidence of poverty (basic needs) is highest among the households that their own farms (57 percent), followed by those that are economically inactive (53 percent), self-employed (27 percent), and employed (17 percent). Second, the incidence of poverty is highest for households with no formal education (61 percent) and falls with increases in educational attainment (for example, poverty incidence is only 8 percent of those with an education level of grade 5 or higher). Third, poverty incidence rises with dependency ratio—from 32 percent for a 0–0.25 dependency ratio to 56 percent for a 0.75–1.0 dependency ratio. Fourth, incidence of poverty rises with the size of household. It is only 6 percent for households with one member but 67 percent for households with 10 or more members. Fifth, poverty falls with a larger proportion of household members being employed. The incidence of poverty is high (58 percent) for household with no members employed but low (18 percent) for households with four or more members employed (URT 2000). These dimensions of poverty curtail the capacity of the poor to engage in income generation, throwing them into a vicious circle of a poverty trap. Reducing poverty and improving social conditions therefore ought to be viewed as part of a growth and development strategy.

The following sections review the dimensions of poverty, analyze its fundamental causes in Tanzania, and suggest strategic approaches to reducing its pervasiveness as well as achieving a sustainable exit from the poverty trap. Much of the analytical work on poverty to date has wide methodological variations, making consistent time trends difficult to discern. Recent efforts to reclaim consistency in tracking poverty status and new surveys to establish poverty lines and poverty monitoring indicators will form a good base for tracking the effectiveness of future measures to reduce poverty.

Trends in Poverty and Human Development

Analytic Problems of Poverty in Tanzania

A major problem with the analytic work on poverty in Tanzania is a lack of consistent and comparable poverty status to enable an assessment of changes over time. This is mainly due to differences in definitions of consumption baskets, population coverage, and sample sizes, as well as consistent valuation of expenditures. Recent techniques have been applied in Tanzania to quantify poverty so as to inform policymakers on the extent of the problem, its spatial dimensions, and differential incidence across social groups (for example, gender) and other characteristics of poverty. Quantification exercises have not been without controversy, especially those involving computation of the national poverty line and related indexes of poverty using survey data. Most survey studies are at pains to portray their results as nationally representative as possible. Table 4.1 shows some of the recent surveys in Tanzania. To this end, the National Master Sample has since 1984 been referred to by many studies. Whether they all succeed is not clear. However, it is not easy to dismiss offhand the spirit and intent of having a common reference sample, at least for possible analysis and tracing of changes in poverty over time. The problem is that the definitions, population coverage, and sample sizes do not always match; neither do the prices, especially when adjustments (for example, for price changes) have to be made.

The magnitudes derived by most studies, such as the poverty line, the head-count ratio, and other measures differ across studies. There is no obvious reason that they should coincide, considering the differences in coverage. As such, there is no single, official poverty line so far in Tanzania. Some of these factors are manifestations, while others are really causes of poverty. Nevertheless conclusions about the pervasiveness and depth of poverty are not controversial, and the determinants of poverty or factors are highly correlated (associated) with poverty where the different poverty lines have been used and cross-matched with the factors suspected to be related to poverty.

Table 4.1. *Some Recent Household Budget Surveys*

Survey	Coverage	Number of households
FY77 BOS	National	5,000
1983–BOS	4 regions, mainland, rural	498
FY92–BOS	Countrywide	5,328
FY92–Cornell/ERB	Mainland	1,046
1993 HRDS—World Bank	Countrywide	5,184
1995 PPA—World Bank	Mainland, rural	768
1998–REPOA	3 regions, mainland, rural	649
1999 Peri-urban (World Bank)	Dar es Salaam districts	148

BOS Bureau of Statistics (now National Bureau of Statistics).
HRDS Human Resources Development Survey.
PPA Participatory Poverty Assessment.
REPOA Research on Poverty Alleviation.
Source: Research on Poverty Alleviation (1998); World Bank (1993, 1996b).

Absolute poverty measures that focus on private consumption expenditure (also known as income poverty) include the headcount indexes based on the poverty line concept, supplemented by computations of the poverty gap and index of poverty severity. Apart from the measures based on the poverty line, the other approach to quantitative analysis of poverty in Tanzania that goes beyond the approach of private consumption expenditures uses the human development index as applied by, for example, UNDP. The index combines measures of literacy, life expectancy, and income into a single aggregate index.

These measures ought to be complemented by analyses of other subjective, not strictly economic, aspects—such as leisure, personal security and esteem, social rights, services from common property, and the like. Studies that use more anthropological and sociological methods collectively called "participatory poverty appraisal" try to capture these dimensions of livelihood. The debate is not carried too far as to which of the approaches—income and expenditure on poverty, the human development index, or participatory poverty appraisal—is more adequate than the other. However, it may be noted that, because of the underlying differences, the three approaches can sometimes generate conflicting results (Baulch 1995).

Poverty Lines: Diversity of Methods and Implications for Headcount Ratios

There have been a number of attempts to construct poverty lines (for example, ILO and JASPA 1982; Mkai and Mwisomba 1998; World Bank 1993), for the country as a whole or separately for rural and urban areas. However, because of differences in sample characteristics, definitions and prices used in the construction of the poverty lines, populations, survey methods and price-level adjustments, coming up with some headcount ratio (say 51 percent or 70 percent) as the right "global" number is difficult. As shown in table 4.2, different headcount ratios have been reported for different poverty lines. This, however, has not been totally in vain in terms of useful, albeit sometimes difficult, broad generalizations about prevalence of poverty. Comparisons across time have to be approached rather carefully when changes in the headcount ratios have to be used.

The International Labour Organisation measure covered the basic needs for food, topped up for other needs, such as shelter, clothing, fuel, rent, and water. The basic food basket was drawn on the basis of the assumption about the local eating habits and minimum nutritional requirements (calorie intake, then

Table 4.2. *Absolute Poverty Lines and Incidence of Poverty in Rural Tanzania*

Study/Citation	Year applying	Poverty line (Tanzanian shillings)	Headcount (percent)	Qualifications
ILO and JASPA 1982	1982	7,200	25	
World Bank 1996	1983		0.52 (rural)	
Tinios and others 1993	1991	27,303	58.4	Update of 1989, Sarris and others 1993
		25,613	50.1	Assuming expenditure at 1,900 calories
		27,721	54.1	Assuming expenditure at 2,100 calories
		29,831	58.2	Assuming expenditure at 2,200 calories
World Bank 1996	1991	31,000	44.1 (rural) 35.9 (mainland)	Update of ILO and JASPA poverty line
Mkai and Mwisomba 1998	1994	71426	65	Absolute
PPA (World Bank)	1995	—	58.6	
REPOA 1999	1998	105,449	46.2	Lower line
		138,831	61	Upper line
URT 1998	1995	73,877	>50% (all) (60% rural) (9 % urban)	

—Not available
ILO International Labour Organisation.
JASPA Jobs and Skills Programme for Africa.
PPA Participatory Poverty Assessment.
REPOA Research on Poverty Alleviation.
Source: IDC 1996; ILO and JASPA (1992); Research on Poverty Alleviation (1998); World Bank (1996).

converted into foodstuff quantities, subsequently valued at market prices). The poverty line of T Sh 7,200 per year (1981 prices) was obtained, approximating the income required to meet basic needs for sustaining a family of five. More recently, Mkai and Mwisomba (1998) constructed a poverty line based on the FY91 HBS data, by estimating the cost of a basic food-consumption basket featuring the consumption pattern of lower-income groups. The poverty line was computed in 1994 prices and the amount of T Sh 71,426 per adult equivalent per year was obtained. Subsequently, Research on Poverty Alleviation, using expenditure data from the rural survey, made inflation and adult-equivalence updates and adjustments to the rural poverty line. The parallel survey by World Bank (1996b) aimed at establishing poverty status in peri-urban Dar es Salaam. The two 1998 poverty lines were then used by Eele and others (1999) to derive a weighted average line for the whole mainland.

The differences in the levels of headcount ratios in table 4.2 are not trivial in that they confound interpretation of trends and tracing of changes in the incidence of poverty at the aggregate level. The World Bank (1996b) report notes that, relative to 1993, poverty seems to have increased by 1995, when the rural poverty index is reckoned to have reached 58.6 percent. Estimates based on the survey by REPOA (1998) show that poverty headcount ratio lies between 46 percent and 61.0 percent. This result suggests that poverty has worsened in the rural areas as of 1998 relative to 1995 in aggregate terms. These are comparable to current official estimates of aggregate poverty (URT 1998a). The poverty problem is amplified by the fact that, at the same time, the population has been growing (at approximately 2.8 percent per year), implying, indeed, that the number of the poor has actually been rising rapidly in absolute terms.

Human Development

Despite overall improvement in the human development index (HDI) between 1991 and 1999, relative to global achievements, Tanzania's rank has declined over the same period. The HDI combines life expectancy, the literacy rate, and income. HDI indexes have been used to rank countries, with indexes scaled between 0 and 1, where a value of 1 indicates better performance in terms of life expectancy, income, and literacy. Table 4.3 shows the indexes for Tanzania (second row) and its ranking on the world scale for 1991–99, while figure 4.1 compares Tanzania with neighboring countries, Sub-Saharan Africa, and industrial countries in terms of HDI in 1999. As shown in table 4.3, the index rose by 58 percent (an average of 5 percent per year relative to 1991), but the country slid 29 places down the global scale. Other countries have been making faster gains recently relative to Tanzania. Tanzania's index is just below the Sub-Saharan Africa average of 0.463. An index for all developing countries is 0.637. In 1998, Tanzania ranked 150th out of 174 countries, down from 126th in 1990.

Table 4.3. *Tanzania's HDI and Ranking*

Year	1991	1992	1993	1994	1995	1996	1997	1998	1999
HDI	0.266	0.268	0.270	0.306	0.364	0.364	0.357	0.358	0.421
Rank by HDI (out of 174 countries)	127[a]	126[a]	138[b]	148[b]	147	144	149	150	156
Per capita income (U.S. dollars)	180.7	167.0	149.2	156.2	176.9	210.3	235.6	257.0	270.0

[a]Out of 160 countries.
[b]Out of 173 countries.
Sources: United Nations Development Programme, Human Development Reports; Bank of Tanzania, *Economic Bulletin*

Figure 4.1. *Human Development Index: Comparison between Tanzania and Neighboring Countries, 1999*

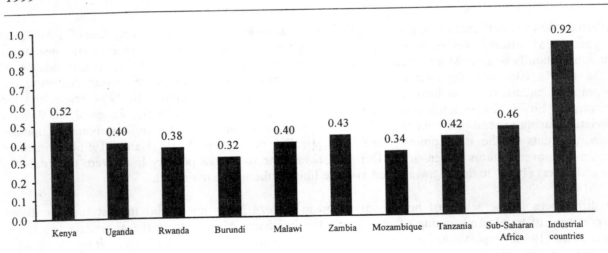

Sources: United Nations Development Program.

It is noteworthy, however, that relative to its income per capita rank of 5th from the poorest country globally, Tanzania's rank in HDI is far above expectation. Empirical evidence shows that, on average, countries' HDI rankings correspond to their income per capita ranking, making income the most dominant component in the index. Tanzania's better ranking in HDI relative to the country's income may be attributed to its more egalitarian policies of the past and the high aid dependence in financing social sector investments. The latter reason, however, raises the question of sustainability of this achievement in the absence of robust growth.

Inequality

Two ways of looking at inequality in Tanzania are employed in this memorandum. The first is the overall income inequality (as also manifested by differences in consumption expenditures). Gini coefficients are usually derived to indicate existence and level of inequality. However, other than income (expenditures), the Gini coefficients do not cover all possible sources of inequalities. A second approach has to seek explanations of inequality in the observed distribution of factors that are strongly correlated to income. These have to do with opportunities of income generating; differences in access and possession of education, physical assets, credit, and natural resources; and other income factors.

Table 4.4 shows the Gini coefficients from different studies. The same caveat that applies to the analysis of changes in poverty lines (surveys using different methodology and definitions, and covering different populations) applies here too. Besides, some coefficients have been based on income measure and others on expenditures. Inequality is reckoned to have increased between 1969 and 1991 as the Gini coefficient rose from 0.39 in FY69 to 0.44 in FY76 and 0.57 in FY91. The socialist-oriented income policies after the 1967 Arusha Declaration were responsible for the decline in the urban–rural ratio of income from 11.33 in 1969 to 2.76 in 1991. Rural inequality increased between 1967 and 1977, while urban inequality declined between 1969 and 1991). The data in the table suggest that overall inequality in Tanzania declined by 5 percent between 1991 and 1993, while rural inequality declined by about 6 percent.

Table 4.4. *Gini Coefficients from Different Surveys*

Year	Tanzania	Rural	Urban non–Dar es Salaam
1983	—	0.52[a]	—
1991(a)	0.57	0.62	0.46
1991(b)	0.432	0.372	0.416
1993	0.41	0.35	0.42
1995	—	0.52	—
1998	—	0.45	—

—Not available.

a. According to World Bank (1996). This figure is based on income and not on expenditure, as are other figures in the table.

Source: Data for 1991(a) are based on the Household Budget Survey FY92 and for 1991(b) on Tinios and others (1993); for 1993 and 1995, World Bank (1996b); for 1998, Eele and others (1999).

Inequality seems to have marginally declined in the period immediately following economic liberalization, even though impressions of inequality persisted. This apparent pessimistic perception was grounded on the continued significant differences in per capita expenditures between the poor and relatively well-to-do household. It emerges from the surveys (for example, World Bank 1993) that the average expenditure per capita and the per adult for the better-off household is 6 to 7 times higher than that of the poor and 8 to 10 times that of the "very poor." For the rural survey (REPOA 1998), it was found that the top 20 percent of the population surveyed account for 45 percent of the (mean) expenditures. The lowest quintile accounted for only 6 percent. Those in the highest quintile spend 7 times more than those in the lowest quintile. The socioeconomic groups face different hurdles, and so the gaps are still a reality.

The most apparent sources of income inequalities have their root in the differential access to productive assets—including education, and land and livestock ownership—which reflect inequalities, mostly intrarural. World Bank (1996b) reports measured Gini coefficients as high as 0.8. Data from the REPOA survey show that the poor generally hold less land in terms of acreage. Differences arise also with respect to the quality of the land, and acquisition of farm implements, inputs, and credit, which the poorer can ill afford. Data from the 1991 HBS suggests that in 1991, 54.3 percent of the rural poor were literate (could read and write) compared with 61 percent for the rural population as a whole. Between 1983 and 1991, illiteracy among the poor increased, while the proportion of illiterate women remained more or less the same but still higher than any other socioeconomic group. Data from the Human Resources Development Survey (HRDS) for FY93 suggest that gross enrollment rates among poor children aged 7–9 decreased from 82 percent in 1983 to 80 percent in 1993. Lack of access and inadequate resource endowments at the household level has not only led to income inequality but also to localized food insecurity and hunger. HBS data confirm increased incidence of malnutrition among the poorest children between 1991 and 1996 (table 4.5). Rates of infant mortality are also higher for the poor, particularly in rural areas, than for the general population. Infant mortality seems to have worsened between 1991 and 1996 for the poorest quintile (table 4.6). Mortality rates for children under age three have improved but remain high. The other type of inequality that does not necessarily reflect itself in the Gini coefficient is that relating to gender imbalance.

Table 4.5. *Percent of Children Malnourished by Asset Index Quintile*

	Height for age, stunting		Weight for age, wasting	
Quintile	1991	1996	1991	1996
First	43.14	46.02	8.12	8.18
Second	43.52	43.98	6.73	9.82
Third	42.97	41.79	5.27	9.02
Fourth	40.12	39.00	6.22	8.89
Fifth	26.06	28.42	6.83	6.24

Source: Sahn, Stifel, and Younger (1999).

Table 4.6. *Infant and Under Age Three Mortality by Asset Index Quintile*

	Infant mortality		Under-age-three mortality	
Quintile	1991	1996	1991	1996
First	113.7	116.2	155.6	144.1
Second	112.0	103.2	168.3	144.1
Third	97.4	88.5	152.4	138.0
Fourth	87.7	99.9	141.3	153.3
Fifth	75.9	66.1	126.6	91.2

Source: Sahn, Stifel, and Younger (1999).

Poverty Elasticities

Changes in poverty are likely to be influenced by mean income (or mean consumption expenditure) and changes in the distribution of the income reflected by Gini coefficients. Poverty is generally considered to be sensitive to economic growth (changes in GDP or mean income), but this impact depends also on the level of inequality. With constant distribution (a given state of inequality), an increase in mean income will lead to a reduction in poverty (based on the headcount ratio). The magnitude of this impact would vary from country to country, and there is no general agreement on this. However, according to Roemer and Gugerty (1997), the poor do better in countries that grow fast, "even if income distribution deteriorated slightly." Growth is more likely to reduce poverty when economic assets are distributed relatively equally or when growth is based on intensive employment of abundant factors of production, especially labor.

The absolute value of the elasticity of the headcount ratio with respect to mean expenditure for Sub-Saharan Africa is reported to be 1.05 compared with 2.02 for North Africa. The elasticity of poverty with respect to distribution is found to be 0.67 for Sub-Saharan Africa and 2.42 for North Africa (UNECA 1999). This means that economic growth is likely to lead to a higher reduction in poverty in North Africa than in Sub-Saharan Africa. However, the United Nations Economic Commission for Africa (UNECA 1998) finds that the elasticity of the headcount ratio with respect to growth in urban areas is slightly higher than that in rural areas, whereas elasticity with respect to the inequality measure is about three times higher for urban areas than for the rural areas.

The first poverty elasticities computed for Tanzania are those by Eele and others (1999). These are based on the approximated changes in the headcount ratios and Gini coefficients for the intervals 1983, 1991, and 1998. Recent REPOA data indicate the elasticities with respect to changes in mean income lie between 0.53 and 1.09; for changes in inequalities, the elasticity ranges between 0.05 and 0.24, all in absolute value, (table 4.7). It should be noted also that the elasticity measures are sensitive to the poverty line chosen. Lower values with respect to income distribution imply that changes in distribution have a lower impact on poverty reduction.

Table 4.7. *Poverty Elasticities and Required GDP Growth Rate*

Country/Area	Growth elasticity of poverty	Elasticity with respect to distribution	Population growth rate (percent)	Required per capita growth	Required. GDP growth rate
Tanzania	0.53–1.09	0.05–0.24	2.8	3.2	6.0
Eastern Africa (13 countries)	−0.64	—	2.7	6.25	8.95
North Africa (7 countries)	−0.95	—	2.0	4.21	6.21
West Africa (countries)	−0.70	—	2.9	5.71	8.61

— Not available.
Source: Eele and others (1999); UNECA 1999.

Implications for growth required to reduce poverty to some future target can be drawn from the elasticities of poverty incidence—and only approximations can be made, assuming "normal" years over the forecast period. The possibility of reducing poverty by half by 2015 depends on the assumed poverty line (and headcount ratio) and the elasticity of poverty with respect to changes in income (growth), holding distribution constant, or changes in the distribution with growth unchanging.

The study by Eele and others (1999) includes performance of a number of simulations. The overall result targeted reduction of poverty incidence to around 30 percent by 2015. Assuming the population will grow at the current rate of 2.8 percent, and if growth per capita income is set at between 1 percent and 2.5 percent per year, the minimum required growth for up to 2015 would have to be between 3.8 percent and 5.3 percent per year. Then the future possible exogenous shocks, which may (as often) slow down growth in any one year, should be factored in. These shocks include extreme weather and international market conditions beyond the power of the authorities. With all these taken into account, the economy should grow at the annual rate of 6 percent or above.

The UNECA report notes that the required rate of growth for the two poorest regions of the African continent, West and East (where Tanzania belongs), is 8.6 and 8.95 percent, respectively. However, the study cautions that, except for North Africa (which needs 6–7 percent growth to halve poverty by 2015), "the remaining required growth rates are fairly high and may prove to be beyond the region to attain and sustain specially given the initial conditions" (UNECA 1998, p. 28). This conclusion is important in view of Tanzania's Development Vision 2025, which targets a growth rate of 8 percent. The Vision 2025 takes a longer perspective compared with the year 2015 of the international development targets.

Selected Correlates of Poverty and Inequality

Using the poverty indexes and poverty groups computed from the household survey data, it has been possible, using statistical means, to associate levels of poverty (incidence) with a number of determinants of poverty. Here, a brief discussion is made on the results that have empirically established close associations between the level of poverty, and poverty (and inequality) attributes. The discussion also emphasizes the sources of inequality as yet another dimension of poverty.

Spatial Distribution of Poverty

By nearly all indicators, poverty is predominant in the rural areas. It can be inferred from the poverty indicators that the level of human development is relatively better in those areas that are endowed with an export crop and relatively worse in areas that do not have an export product. Incidentally, this reflects the agro-climatic pattern. The spatial distribution of poverty is also demonstrated by the World Bank (1993) ranking of regions and agro-climatic zones, using the Foster-Greer-Thorbecke measures. Poor regions have infertile soils, unreliable rains, remoteness, or all of these factors. Arid regions are forced to grow low-value, drought-resistant crops (cassava, millets) and livestock. Areas with better soils and reliable rainfall are less severely inflicted by poverty. Apart from the temporary deprivation inflicted by occasional weather extremes, the long-term antipoverty question is what can be done about these regions and districts, as surely they should not be permanently condemned to the dictates of nature and remoteness. Generally, poverty is less severe in urban areas than in rural areas partly because most amenities and infrastructure are located in towns. The business firms tend to locate in areas with a ready market both in terms of income and population.

Between these two "polar" cases, the peri-urban areas could be cited as a domain with interesting features. Thus, from the preliminary results of the World Bank (1999j) survey of the peri-urban areas of Dar es Salaam, it would appear that poverty incidence increases the farther way from the city (town) center and the more toward the rural areas. Peri-urban clusters and rural areas with relatively easier access to urban areas in terms of transport, especially to urban markets and many of the nongovernmental organizations that advance finance for small businesses, seem to do better than more remote areas. The REPOA (1998) survey included two clusters that would fit the description of the peri-urban area. They are Igombe in Mwanza (close to Mwanza town) and Lipaya (close to Songea town). In many respects, such as (annual) expenditure and access to and maximum level of education, they did far better than the truly rural clusters.

Socioeconomic Groups

FARMERS AND PEASANTS, AND URBANITES. Extreme poverty is found amongst the rural farm households. These have agriculture as their primary occupation. For reasons that include poor technology, lack of capital (credit), unsteady supply of inputs, lack of adequate extension, and changing marketing institutions, the returns to agricultural activities have been depressed. Remoteness separates the rural producers from markets for their produce. The institutions that deal with marketing of the agricultural produce have been changing a lot and most of them have been facing managerial and financial problems.

It is now questioned whether liberalization that brings in private crop buyers (and also supplies credit) will be a panacea in view of discontents in some areas (Banda 1997).

To supplement their farm earnings, most rural households engage in other activities. These activities are largely on a small, unsophisticated, and hardly commercial scale because of lack of capital, markets, and basic skills. They include poultry, charcoal making, retail shops, handicraft, sewing, and food and beer selling. Livestock keeping is combined with farming in semi-arid areas. Only in a few densely populated but relatively better off areas are cattle raised in more modern ways (for example, zero grazing) rather than in large, uneconomical numbers. A few households by the lakes, rivers, and dams, and along the coast engage in small-scale fishing as their primary source of income. Intrarural differentiation is largely due to the distribution of and access to income-generating assets, usually land and livestock (mostly passed by inheritance) and education (part of human capital). There are a few self-made, better-off entrepreneurs owning small shops, and general traders. These happen to be relatively more-educated people who have on a few occasions traveled to towns.

The second broad socioeconomic class may be located in the urban area, where most people are employed in the public formal employment, the informal sector, or private business, or are unemployed. Poverty afflicts the unemployed and those in the low-income brackets. Antipoverty strategies ought to be addressed foremost to this poor class, which is rated to be 36 percent of the urban population. The poor often will be found in residential areas that are unplanned in the outskirts of the towns and cities. Many live in slums. In 1995, 70 percent of the population in Dar es Salaam, Arusha, and Mbeya, and 40 percent in Mwanza lived in squatter settlements, with poor sanitation and waste-disposal facilities. Apart from low incomes for those in formal and informal employment, some urban dwellers have made recourse to agriculture activities rather as a "coping" mechanism and not as permanent solution. An increasing number of people have been buying up plots in the outskirts of the towns to cultivate all kinds of foods as a means to cushion falling real incomes, and for a possible retirement residence away from the hectic town life. This trend has also raised the value of land and the importance of peri-urban areas.

GENDER IMBALANCE. It has been widely held that women are poorer than men in Tanzania. Women were said to be poorer even though they are the major actors in production and reproductive activities—basically because they are inadequately remunerated. Earlier evidence based on the 1993 HRDS and 1995 Participatory Poverty Assessment perception surveys had concluded that households headed by women (especially in rural areas) were more likely to be poorer than male-headed households mainly because female-headed households own less assets (including land and livestock), have less years of schooling, and have higher dependency ratios. This is in contrast to evidence based on adjusted FY91 HBS data, which points to the opposite conclusion. The National Bureau of Statistics analysis of poverty based on these data indicates that male-headed households are typically poorer than female-headed households. Assuming that poverty profiles have not changed fundamentally since 1992, the proportion of male-headed households that are under the poverty line is 49 percent, while for female-headed households the proportion is 45 percent (URT 2000).

The bureau results are interesting and do actually point to an important policy implication regarding the context of the position of a woman in a society. This relates to the fact that where there is not formal discrimination against women, women tend to occupy a better position economically. However, since traditional and cultural barriers still assign the male the dominance role in day-to-day decisions of the majority of Tanzania families, the main concerns that have been echoed regarding the position of a woman in the society are still applicable.

Further ample reasons exist to call for a greater push for the women's cause. Up the schooling ladder, from primary school to the university level, the representation of female students as a percentage of total student population declines. Figure 4.2 presents the situation in 1990 and 1996 for female enrollment in public education facilities at the primary school level, enrollment in grade I and grade V, as well as in the university. Private schools have not been included. However, this would not alter the fact that female enrollment declined from primary school because of reasons that do not befall boys: for example, teenage pregnancies and forced early marriages and, in many areas, the disproportionate load of domestic chores assigned to girls.

Figure 4.2. *Female Enrollment as a Percentage of Total Enrollment, 1990 and 1996*

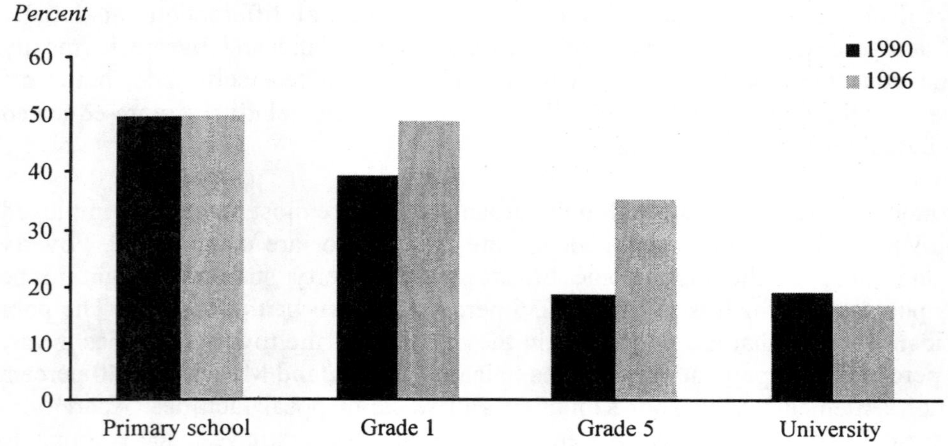

Source: UNDP.

Table 4.8 gives a snapshot of the gender gaps in other respects. Female adult literacy lags behind that of the males as does, generally, school enrollment. However, recent policy emphasis on increasing postprimary enrollment and gender equality in enrollment has raised the proportion of girls joining secondary schools to more than 45 percent (Semboja and Likwelile 1999), while efforts at the higher levels of education point to improvement in female student enrollment.[14]

Table 4.8. *Gender Gaps*

Quality	Male	Female
Life expectancy at birth 1994 (year)	48.9	51.7
Life expectancy at birth 1996 (year)	49.0	51.0
Adult literacy rate 1994 (percent)	78.8	54.3
School enrollment ratio 1994 (percent)	35.0	33.0

Source: UNDP (1997).

Policy initiatives by both government and nongovernmental bodies targeting reduction of gender imbalances are called for to seek and open up opportunities for the unemployed in the informal sector,

---

[14]Probably caution is being sounded that the question may not lie only with increasing the numbers. In their review of the 1998 grade 4 results, the authors found that that girls' performance remained poor, even where increased enrollment was supposed to improve their showing. Boys dominated in the best divisions and girls dominated in the poor divisions of performance in grade 4.

removing barriers to educational attainment and addressing the issue of property ownership and inheritance for women.

GROSS ENROLLMENT COMPARED WITH EDUCATIONAL ATTAINMENT. Generally, educational attainment of children in Tanzania is poor and has been deteriorating during the 1990s, basically because of three major problems with education in Tanzania (IDA and IMF 2000). First is the rapid deterioration in the enrollment rates during primary school: entry rates are relatively high (nearly 90 percent), but survival rates at the end of the cycle are low (54 percent). The problem is more acute for the children from poorer and female-headed households. The second major concern is Tanzania's low enrollment rate in secondary and tertiary education, compared with other countries with a similar level of income. A major reason for this is affordability: the cost of secondary and tertiary education is high relative to income levels in Tanzania. The low student–teacher ratio, high overheads (for example, because of boarding and related subsidies, which are disproportionately enjoyed by the better-off), and low use of facilities combine to raise unit costs. Third, although the overall budget provision for education in Tanzania (at about 2.5 percent of GNP) is comparable to other low-income countries, subsector allocations and cost-effectiveness in delivery remain major obstacles to reaching the poor.

Although much focus has been on assessing achievement in education based on gross enrollment, it is clear from the above that recently educational attainment is a bigger and more fundamental problem. It is also the case that the effect of education on growth is most commonly assessed in terms of attainment rather than enrollment.

Figure 4.3, from Filmer (1999), shows educational attainment for children aged 15–19 in Tanzania, using 1996 as a sample year. The pattern of educational attainment varies greatly across population, with different groups displaying a variety of profiles in attainment. Overall, about 90 percent of children aged 15–19 complete grade 1. The attainment ratio changes over time as a result of dropout. The ratio for grade 4 is 75 percent, while only about 50 percent complete grade 7 (figure 4.3a).

There are also interesting differences in educational attainment patterns, based on wealth status of various groups. For example, attainment of children from the richest 20 percent differ strikingly from that of the poorest 40 percent. About 80 percent of the poor complete grade 1, whereas almost 100 percent of the rich do so (figure 4.3e). These differences increase over time, with only 40 percent of the poor (and almost an equal proportion of the middle class) completing grade 7, compared with 75 percent of the rich. This indicates that shortfalls in universal primary completion are, for the most part, due to children from the poorest households not completing target levels of schooling.

Gender differences in educational attainment show an interesting but not striking pattern. Whereas the attainment ratio for grade 1 is about 95 percent for males and 85 for females, for grade 4 the ratio, though lower, is the same at 80 percent for both genders (figure 4.3b). For subsequent grades, the attainment ratio falls further down but remains higher for females (55 percent) compared with males (45 percent). This pattern does not seem to change even when the attainments are compared on the basis of a combination of gender and wealth status (figure 4.3f). Girls seem to be performing better up to grade 7, for both rich and poor groups. However, their dropout ratio rises sharply after grade 7.

Educational attainment also differs enormously between various groups on the basis of location. Educational attainment seems to be higher for urban children compared with rural children (figure 4.3c). The attainments for urban and rural areas are, respectively, about 95 percent and 85 percent for grade 1; 90 percent and 80 percent for grade 4; and about 70 percent and 55 percent for grade 7. Again, girls seem to be performing better than boys up to grade 7, for both urban and rural groups, although their dropout ratio rises sharply after grade 7.

Figures 4.3. *Tanzania: Educational Attainment for the 15–19 Age Group, 1996.*

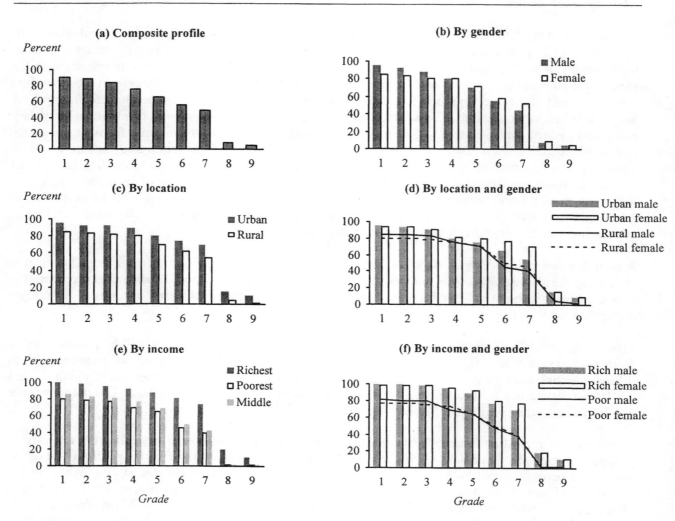

Figure 4.4 compares primary-level educational attainments for groups aged 20–29 and 30–39 in 1996. The former group attended primary school between the mid-1970s and early 1980s, while the latter group went to primary school between the mid-1960s and the mid-1970s. The educational attainment of the two groups is then compared with that of the 15–19 age group to gauge whether any significant change in educational attainment has occurred over the past 30–40 years. The following observations are clear: first, enrollment in grade 1 has increased over time from about 75 percent during the mid-1960s and early 1970s, to about 85 percent during the mid-1970s through early 1980s, and about 90 percent in the mid-1980s through late 1980s. Second, the educational attainment to the grade 7 level has fluctuated over time, with a decline (increase in dropouts) in recent years. It rose from about 60 percent in the mid-1960s through the early 1970s to 70 percent during the mid-1970s through early 1980s, but declined to about 50 percent in the mid-1980s through late 1980s. Third, the difference in educational attainment based on gender has declined substantially over time (Figs. 4.3b, 4.4b and 4.4d). The improvement is substantial and, as noted earlier, is marked by better performance by girls up to grade 7.

Figures 4.4. *Tanzania: Educational Attainment for the 20–29 and 30–39 Age Groups, 1996*

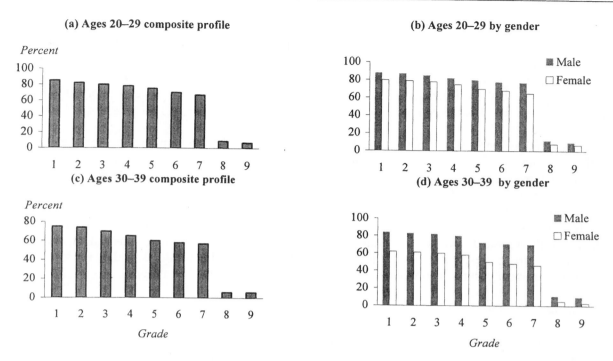

(a) Ages 20–29 composite profile

(b) Ages 20–29 by gender

(c) Ages 30–39 composite profile

(d) Ages 30–39 by gender

CHILDREN AND THE OLD. The other group afflicted by poverty includes children and the old. This is reflected in the high dependence ratios. Comparison of results among the various surveys, large and small, is fair. Nationally, on average, a little more than 45 percent of the population is below the age of 15 (table 4.9). Those aged 65 years or above make up a little more than 3 percent, although this proportion was lower (1.8 percent) in urban areas in the FY91 HBS.

Table 4.9. *Distribution of Age Group and Dependency Ratios Across Surveys (percent)*

	Age structure			
Name of the survey/study	0–14 years	15–64 years	65 and above	Dependence ratio
Population census 1988 (national)	46.9	48.4	4.7	1.01
1991/1992 HBS (national)	45.7	51.3	3.0	0.88
1998 RHBS (REPOA 1998) (rural)	48.8	47.6	3.6	1.10

HBS Household Budget Survey.
REPOA Research on Poverty Alleviation.
Source: URT Economic Survey (1996); Research on Poverty Alleviation (1998).

It would appear that the population-age structure does not show any marked shifts in recent years. Child dependency is greater than old-age dependency. The comparable figure for Sub-Saharan Africa is reported to be 0.94). Analysis of the REPOA (1998) rural survey data shows that, overall, 48.8 percent of the (surveyed) population was under 15 years of age, 47.6 percent were between 15 and 64 years, and 3.6 percent were 65 years or above. The average dependency ratio for the rural areas covered is as high as 1.1. This means that the few able-bodied (the effective labor force) have to support a majority dependent group of children and the old. In support of this, further analysis of REPOA data shows that poverty incidence is between 51 and 52 percent among the dependent age groups of those under 15 and those 65 years or older.

It is also widely observed that poorer households tend to be larger than richer households. The results from the REPOA survey indicate that the better-off group has a smaller household size of about 6 members while the *poor* group is larger, with the mean of 8 members. By way of comparison, the HRDS 1993 data indicate that, for Tanzania, households of 6–10 people were nearly twice as likely to be poor as households of between 1 and 5 people.

The direct relationship between poverty and size of the household has implications for the ability of households to have sufficient demand for education and health of the entire household. Apart from the household income, usually education and health of the children depend also on the level of education of the father and mother in the first place. For mothers, for instance, evidence shows that, with higher levels of education, demand for health as indicated by delivery in clinics and essential vaccinations increases, while fertility rates, premature pregnancies and infant mortality rates drop and nutritional standards improve. Furthermore, the higher the education, the higher the potential for higher income earnings. Higher-income groups (especially if educated) tend to be less vulnerable to diseases, they are aware of the need for preventive measures, and when they fall ill they can better afford treatment.

Environment Conditions

Poverty and degradation of natural resources seem to reinforce each other, especially where population grows rapidly. Exploitation of land and water resources, if not well planned, leads to rapid exhaustion of the resources and negative environmental consequences. For example, traditional farming practices using low technology, such as "slash and burn," lead to soil exposure and erosion apart from producing carbon dioxide, one of the principal agents responsible for global warming. Tree felling for cultivation, fuel wood, and other purposes without commensurate reforestation has led to shrinking of forest area at the rate estimated to be 350,000 hectares per year. Currently about 61 percent of Tanzania's land surface faces rapid degradation and a danger of desertification.

Overgrazing exposes the soil and exhausts pasture resources. In Tanzania, the natural pastures include savanna with varying tree strata. There are very small areas of "managed pasture," as well as places where these are supplemented by tendering of fodder crops. However, usually overgrazing is acute around water points and densely populated areas. The problem is critical in Dodoma, Singida and Shinyanga, and parts of Arusha. Pastoral communities have also gradually spread to Morogoro, Tabora, and Mbeya regions, where conflict between the "newcomers" and farmers have been reported. The urgent need for an optimal size of livestock required to avoid environmental destruction is difficult to instill among most pastoral and semipastoral communities. This is because most of these communities place importance in cattle as form of wealth, prestige, and in part, food security, at the expense of other basics, such as quality housing and living compounds, and education for their children.

In urban areas, problems arise from industrial pollution and unplanned, usually congested housing estates that are sparsely supplied with sewerage disposal infrastructure and water. It is estimated that 80 percent of urban dwellers use pit latrines and that up to 5 percent of others have no toilet facilities of any kind. It has been noted above that urban areas are better served with tap water compared with rural areas, but the quality of the services are overwhelmed by the growing size of the population and budgetary limitations in terms of maintenance requirements. Education and awareness programs are carried out in rural and urban areas, and, where necessary, the laws are applied.

As regards health, Tanzania faces three major challenges, which if addressed will have substantial impact on poverty reduction. The challenges relate to

- Increasing the impact of health services by focusing on the most cost-effective interventions, improving the efficiency in the allocation and use of available resources, and improving management and delivery mechanisms
- Broadening the resource base for financing health services
- Providing special attention to protecting the poor and the vulnerable (IDA and IMF 2000).

Economic Policies and Impact on Poverty Alleviation

The impact of public policies on poverty alleviation is one of the unsettled discussions, especially as regards adjustment and reforms carried out since the mid-1980s. Views differ and outcomes are mixed. Some views hold that adjustment policies had negative impact on welfare by eroding spending on social services (Wagao 1992). Other studies find positive outcomes for the poor associated with improved and growth (Demery and Squire 1996). Whichever the view, it is quite possible that some of the population gain and others lose. In the course of adjustment, fortunes keep changing. In addition, just as it takes time for the signals to reach through, the responses and results have varying speeds for different socioeconomic groups.

What is seen in Tanzania is that poverty has not relented, at least for the majority, and the reforms have not been perfected. Nevertheless some sense ought to be made out of the progress so far, even though the problem, as Lipton and Ravallion (1995) would note, lies in isolating the role of adjustment or lack of it, in the evolution of incomes and welfare. This is because macroeconomic and adjustment policies affect incomes and welfare indirectly through a number of channels, and it is not easy to predict the effects of a single policy action in isolation of other factors.[15] The main channels include factor and product markets; and economic infrastructure and social infrastructure, such as health, sanitation, and education. The impact would also depend on how the households perceive and respond to the incidence of these policies: Do they interpret them as incentives, deceitful impositions, or something else? Above all, being definitive on the precise time it takes for the transmission of signals and the outcome is difficult. Obviously, it should not be tryingly too long.

Adjustment policies since the mid-1980s have covered most aspects of economic management and have been reviewed in several forums. Here a cursory look is taken at the channels for impressions on the outcome or implications for poverty. First, at the macroeconomic level, one general outcome for the product and factor *markets* is inflation. The rate of inflation reflects fiscal and monetary policy performance, the growth of output, and the state of economic infrastructure, mainly transportation. The transport problem has contributed to high food prices, especially in urban areas, and high prices of manufactured, "incentive" goods in the rural areas. The lifting of both internal and external price and trade controls improved the availability of goods and services, although inflation in the post-1985 period persisted and only gradually came down. It is only in the last year or so that the inflation rate has been brought down to a single digit, and it is tempting to believe that this is more because of improvements in fiscal and monetary policy management than to a sustained improvement in production and economic infrastructure. Nevertheless, a longer period of a sustained, stable inflation rate will be needed for the public to perceive their welfare as improving.

With regard to agriculture, the reforms opened market access to wider agents, including those supplying inputs, credit, and extension, and those buying crops, as the government gradually withdrew from many

---

[15]In the absence of sufficient data and a comprehensive, computable model of general equilibrium that would make possible analysis of the counterfactuals, what remain are partial kinds of analyses focusing on specific policies and on the before-and-after analysis, despite the known weaknesses of this approach.

of these activities. At the time, the problems of income being concentrated in the marketing boards or cooperatives and unpaid or delayed cash concentrated among farmers seemed to be over. However, instead the farmers face new difficulties in the wake of the new form of competition in the rural markets. Agricultural inputs and credit supply are more expensive, in short or irregular supply, while the poor farmers are offered low producer prices. The remaining cooperatives have to put up with the private crop buyers, about whom numerous complaints have been raised.[16] How "transitional" these problems will be is not clear, but evidence suggests a welling fervor by farmers in some areas to reinvigorate their ailing cooperatives.[17] Lack of action would give an impression that the beneficiaries of reform policies are private traders, moneylenders, and a few commercial farmers (Bienefeld 1995). It is expected that the market may not, by its own volition, take care of the poor; some form of government corrective regulations seems to be desirable, for the sake of the rural producers.

The reforms have also brought dramatic changes in the labor market. In part because of declining economic growth, the growth of formal wage employment fell from a yearly average of about 5 percent during the 1970s to 2 percent between 1980 and 1988 (Wagao 1992). Nearly 95 percent of the entrants into the labor force were absorbed into the agricultural and urban informal sectors. Between 1986 and 1987 only 7,300 new jobs were created, compared with an estimated 200,000 individuals who were seeking wage employment. The restricted growth was attributed to SAP and ERP and to recession, which tended to erode real incomes (Wagao 1992). It is now estimated that about 600,000 join the labor market each year, when the formal sector can absorb not more than 22,000–25,000 each year (URT 1999a). This is not an encouraging trend. Official data (see for example, URT 1998a) put the unemployment rate at nearly 30 percent.

At the same time as the manufacturing sector has been either contracting or recovering slowly, the rural areas has not been offering gainful opportunities for the energetic youths, since returns to agriculture are simply low. Off-farm activities, including those in the informal sector, have not multiplied adequately despite the liberalization for lack of basic entrepreneurial skills and access to credit.

The financial sector reforms have seen the shrinking of banking services that used to be provided by a single national commercial bank (NBC). The reduction of NBC branches was not followed by any replacement. The new private banks, catering to the middle- and upper-income classes, mainly in the urban areas, do not give any indications of plans to serve rural areas, again for commercial reasons. To fill the vacuum, a number of nongovernmental organizations have come up with innovative financial strategies targeting the poor who are unable to raise collateral. The government has also formed "social funds" to cater for the income poor who are unable to get loans from the banks. The targets specifically are women, unemployed youth, and those in the informal sector. By and large, these have been limited to urban and peri-urban areas. Accessibility in terms of communications infrastructure is one of the reasons why the rural areas are not served.

As for the social infrastructure, it was mentioned in the discussion of HDI that resource constraints have adversely affected both health and education. Inadequacy and unequal access indicate and perpetuate poverty. Many facilities are largely concentrated in urban areas. Since the advent of the reforms, the introduction of user fees and greater private practice, in both health and education, have brought mixed outcomes for different socioeconomic groups. Many rural areas are served by government facilities that are not always well stocked, and often villagers have to travel long distances to the district or regional

---

[16]The reasons for the failure of the cooperatives have a longer history than can be covered here. For the role of government in the changing fortunes and prospects of the cooperatives during reforms, see, for example, Banda 1997.

[17]For evidence on the efforts by coffee growers and leaders in parts of Kilimanjaro Region and tobacco growers in Ruvuma Region to stand up for their cooperatives, and some complaints about private buyers practices, see, for example, Rutasitara 1997.

headquarters where most facilities are located. The question of the ability to pay lingers, since not all people are able to pay.

Several institutions give one or the other form of human capital development and not all are under one ministry.[18] At many levels, a number of factors adversely affect the delivery of education—shortages of teachers, staff accommodation, classrooms, desks, teaching aids, and textbooks. The problems are more acute in the rural areas, and many private schools have many unqualified staff compared with government schools. Higher education faces problems of rising operational costs, and a shortage of staff and learning materials—all reflecting budgetary limitations on the part of the government (URT 1998a). One of the major departures from the prereform period is the requirement that parents do contribute directly toward the education of their children.

A number of other utilities—including roads, communications, and the provision of safe water—largely affect both poor and nonpoor alike with differential access in broad categories, such as rural and urban. Telephones and television are almost exclusively for the better off, largely in urban areas, while access to newspapers and radio makes a difference in the rural areas. Therefore, information and the power it brings is largely absent. The quantity and quality of these infrastructures affect the process of production and distribution. Like investments in the health and education infrastructures, they require huge investment and maintenance resources. It is only recently that privatization of some aspects of them is being considered. As long as they remain in a poor state, neither the poor nor the nonpoor are likely to benefit from the opening up of economic opportunities.

The Pattern of Growth Against Poverty

Is Tanzania likely to attain poverty reduction targets by 2015? It was indicated earlier that this might require a growth rate of 6 percent or more per year, assuming the rate of population of 2.8 percent per year. The Vision 2025 sets the target growth of 8 percent to be reached in 2025. The pattern by which the growth rate is achieved is probably more important than the rate itself, however high it may be. There is little doubt about the government's commitment to poverty eradication. The National Poverty Eradication Strategy divides macroeconomic and sectoral policies that aim to eradicate poverty into those that create an enabling environment and those that build capacity and sector-specific policies and strategies. It further spells out basic requirements of good governance, responsibility, accountability, and transparency. The monitoring plan has been in place, specifying quantitative indicators. The strategy rallies all citizens, nonpoor and poor alike. Perhaps one of the first steps would be to get the antipoverty strategy well understood, with ample provision for the feedback channels so that the conceived socioeconomic programs may be fully supported and, where possible, conceived by the targeted poor.

For growth to have a maximum impact on poverty, the strategy should aim specifically at giving the poor access to income-generating or gainful employment and at improving the incentives and earning potentials. This may be referred to as redistribution at the production front. Inequalities can be reduced by a growth strategy that increases access of the genuinely poor to income-generating possibilities. For rural economies based on small-scale farming, poverty-reducing growth would entail growth in agricultural exports and in food and raw materials. In Tanzania, currently this sector is dismally provided in terms of supplies of inputs, credit, extension services, marketing, and infrastructure. Setting the improvement of rural roads as a priority, for example, would go a long way to reducing urban–rural inequalities. Where

---

[18] The focus here is on formal education, including primary, secondary, and even tertiary. Formal education is now under three institutions: primary education, under the Ministry of Regional and Local Government; secondary and teacher education, under the Ministry of Education and Culture; and tertiary education, under the Ministry of Higher Education, Science, and Technology, and other parent ministries.

there is evidence of self-help—rural, community-based initiatives to contribute to the roads, water supply, schools, dispensaries, and the like—the government should avail its backing in every way possible.

Opportunities exist also for growth based on the nonfarm activities and "informal" activities in urban and rural areas. At policy or administration levels, actions and attitudes such as long licensing procedures, complicated tax systems, road blocks in rural areas, and open or unopen demand for bribes create an inimical environment for legitimate economic effort of the poor that is centered mainly around small businesses in the informal and formal sectors. Moreover, a better investment environment for local and foreign capital should be expected to increase employment and national output. More than enough has been said about removing the red tape and corruption that, together with poor communications and uncompetitive power tariffs, tend to deflect away much-needed foreign investment.

Rural and urban self-help groups require technical and financial support. There are social fund,[19] established by government or with donor support, which target the informal sector groups, women, and youths. They offer access to entrepreneurial skill; training; and, above all, credit finance with relatively less difficult conditions. The National Income Generating Programme aims to create employment by using the private sector and nongovernmental organizations. Of the 17 "poverty alleviation projects" compiled in 1994 by the Economic and Social Research Foundation, which is based in Dar es Salaam, 7 or about 50 percent exclusively targeted women. However, the support tends to locate more in urban and peri-urban areas than in rural areas. Probably this is because of the high visibility and location near the center of policymaking. However, because of the less than tight "screening of potential recipients," resources find their way into the hands of a few middle and upper classes or the relatives of those who have influence and power. Although this anomaly does not apply to many of the programs all the time, it cannot be ignored. It slows down the closing in of the gap already within the urban areas, not to speak of the rural poor who are far away.[20]

As hinted above, government needs to pay attention to the poor and the most vulnerable at the same time as it is allowing the private sector to take part in the provision of education and health. There is no elaborate social security system, and the traditional "extended family" and local "informal security networks" cannot cope with the speed and demands of the modern sector. Provisioning for those that are genuinely unable to pay for health and basic education implies targeting the old, children, and women—especially those who are expecting and cannot afford medical services. This is not supposed to be an easy exercise, though. In addition, in both areas of education and health, the government may have to stay close in matters of supervising adherence to the quality of services delivered. All these require resources. The objectives of the Basic Education Master Plan for 1998–02 are elaborate, as are the Health Sector Reforms that are underway. The public expenditure reviews have a difficult task of protecting shares that go into the social sectors and economic infrastructure, especially rural roads.

Lastly, it may be noted improvements in macroeconomic performance take time to be felt in terms of welfare. Sometimes the macroeconomic statistics—such as inflation rate, exchange rate, and money supply—may mean little to the income earners. To have their meaning thoroughly understood, sustained

---

[19] Different objectives have been attributed to the "social fund." The main ones include channeling external funds to local groups, compensating those who suffered because of adjustment policies, protecting the poor and vulnerable during adjustment, "buying" political support for the adjustment programs, and generating employment (Steward and van der Geest 1994).

[20] Stock may need to be taken of the impact of the social funds with particular focus on their targeting and output efficiency. Evaluation can also be done for other "poverty alleviation projects". It would entail an examination of the administration of the resources of the schemes, targeted population or socioeconomic group(s), eligibility criteria, screening criteria (applicable) and, needless-to-say, poverty indexes before and after some specific time of participation in the scheme(s).

good macroeconomic performance is required. Furthermore, a constant check on how the people are faring in the proposed poverty monitoring and evaluation will be essential.

Imperatives for the Strategic Action to Reduce Poverty in Tanzania.

In light of the pervasive nature of poverty and its multidimensional character, the action program needs to be frontal in approach, with the predominance of improving income opportunities as the most sustainable way toward the Vision 2025 targets. The starting point is to recognize that, given the breadth of poverty, action would need to focus on creating and expanding opportunities for the poor to earn a decent income and thus enable their access to the essentials of life. It is based on the belief that reducing poverty on a sustained basis, when it is both broad and deep, pivots around enabling the poor to earn a decent income rather than solely on public transfers, important as they may be in the interim period and for addressing the needs of the vulnerable groups. This does not necessarily mean that programs targeted at the most vulnerable of the poor are not essential. It is to accept the fact that, with slightly more than half of the population being below the poverty line in Tanzania, adoption of a broad strategy is needed. In the Tanzanian context, safety nets are organized around informal private networks. Public-financed safety nets ought to focus on the old and orphans not supported under such networks as well as on consequences of disasters, which typically affect whole geographic zones. Identification of zones most highly at risk climatically would be particularly useful in the latter case. Moreover, measures to improve income opportunities for the poor would need to be anchored in macroeconomic policies aimed at maintaining a low inflation rate and overall fiscal discipline; at improving incentive framework for private investment, particularly in agriculture; and at providing the supportive infrastructure to small-scale enterprises in the informal sector in both rural and urban areas.

Capabilities for designing operational programs for poverty reduction and for monitoring implementation are key for success. One of the major impediments to the design and execution of poverty-reducing programs has been a lack of supportive analytical capacity and good data, in easily usable form, at the country level. The presence of this capacity, and of organized information on poverty profiles and the structure of poverty, is necessary not only for careful selective targeting in line with resource constraints but also for performance monitoring. The Tanzania government has a good "feel" of the problem and periodically studies are carried out by outsiders on the issues to give sense to magnitudes and profiles. It is heartening to note that the government has appreciated the breadth of the problem and is poised to adopt measures that focus not only promoting high growth but also on addressing other fundamentals behind the pervasiveness of poverty. The government prepared and approved the National Poverty Eradication Strategy on the basis of inputs from a rural participatory poverty assessment. The strategy was published in 1998, after widespread consultation with civil society and endorsement by Parliament. The government has also set up a monitoring system and data bank managed by the vice president's office. The strategy includes an endorsement of and commitment to targets agreed on at World Social Summit. The location of the program in the vice president's office helps to give credence to the high priority accorded this problem and to mainstream poverty-reducing programs.

A lack of local technical support for the programs has meant that advice is sporadic, when available from the outside; monitoring is not continuous; and design is largely based on guess work. Investment in this competence locally is key to sustained action, particularly where the more demanding targeted programs are concerned.

Three broad areas of needed action are identified. The first is strengthening local capacity for research and policy analysis in support of the formulation of appropriate interventions and policies for reducing poverty. Even where data pertaining to poverty exists, these have largely remained unused because of a lack of skills and knowledge to analyze them. Such skills are needed for analyzing poverty profiles and their changes over time, for monitoring and targeting purposes; for explaining the major causes of poverty in the specific context so as to enable prioritization of action; and for assessing options for action in terms of potential effectiveness for given resource envelopes. Such knowledge will benefit both public entities and nongovernmental organizations (including local communities) in designing effective interventions. A large range of these skills can be obtained through specialized training programs, maintenance of local research network for exchange of information, and availing opportunities for research to enable learning by doing. It is highly unlikely that such capacity will reside in the institutions housing the main actors. A networking approach between research and other academic institutions where most analysts reside, on the one hand, and professionals in concerned public policy institutions and activist groups, on the other, will provide the necessary framework for division of roles. Competence in absorbing and applying knowledge to programs and interventions should be strengthened in the using institutions.

The second area is rationalizing the operations of state institutions responsible for collecting information pertinent to analyzing and monitoring poverty. The bureau of statistics regularly collects and organizes information on, for example, the status of living conditions, household budget surveys, and population census. These contain valuable information for required analysis of poverty and its determinants. An important improvement would be to anticipate data needs for such analysis in the design of surveys in close consultation with analysts and researchers. However, even more important would be the removal of impediments to the timely access of information collected so as to avail the same for policy analytical purposes and to inform the design and impact assessment of appropriate interventions. Most urgent is the need to undertake a fresh household budget survey to set up a base for the poverty reduction programs and for monitoring implementation. This is also necessary for the design and monitoring of a poverty-focused HIPC initiative.

The third area pertains to setting up mechanisms for the effective transfer of knowledge from experts availed through technical assistance to local experts. To this end, monitorable mechanisms for such transfers under technical assistance packages need to be provided, with assessment at the point of conclusion of support. Careful selection of understudies with the ability to absorb the knowledge is crucial for success, and so is the selection of experts involved in the technical assistance, where ability and willingness to teach others should be important criteria for selection. This mechanism for transfer of knowledge could be linked to the wider network of researchers and analysts, so as to broaden benefits from it and raise the scope of retaining skills availed.

Investment in a healthy and educated work force holds an important key not only to overall growth of the economy but also enhances the capacity of the poor to earn a decent income. Greater priority of public spending on social sectors and more efficient delivery of these services is crucial for enhancing human capital of the poor and their welfare. Improved human capabilities and their wide spread are crucial for raising the productivity and hence incomes of the poor. Improvements in education, health, and nutrition are not simply definitions of welfare status, but also crucial human capital for sustaining this status through growth. They constitute important inputs into human assets for earning an income.

Public spending in education and health has been inadequate, as reflected by declining real expenditure per head until recently and needs now to be given the highest priority. The problem has been due to both the small size of the discretionary resource envelope after servicing debt obligations and lack of prioritization in the expenditure allocation in favor of the social sectors. While consistency of social sector objectives with macroeconomic realities is ensured, the share of the budget destined for social sectors needs to be scaled up and efforts to integrate government and donor funds more fully into the poverty strategy need to be increased. Furthermore, strengthened budget management would ensure that funds earmarked for poverty programs actually are spent on them. Within the sectors, existing data show a bias toward tertiary services rather than primary services. The former benefit largely the wealthier groups with urban concentration (Appleton and Mackinon 1996). Prioritization should be toward services with high social returns. Tertiary services typically can be better financed privately, since the benefits are largely private. However, perhaps what is more crucial now is pursuing cost-effectiveness in achieving well-defined goals.

The involvement of the state in poverty-reducing programs is not limited to public expenditure programs or provision of public services. To a large extent the effectiveness of the central government's contribution hinges on creating an enabling environment for other actors and promoting a sense of urgency in dealing with the problem of poverty. Its own commitment to raising the welfare of the poor is an important signal to the rest of the society and should be reflected partly by the extent of priority it gives in its budget and the efficiency of its application of resources toward eradicating poverty. The effectiveness of the central government's contribution should also reflected by the vigor with which it pursues promotion of market efficiency in support of poverty-reducing private expenditures and regulates providers against exploiting information failures to the detriment of the welfare status of the country.

Closer to its own functions, the central government should promote the culture of evaluation of its own programs to assess effectiveness of action. In this regard, raising the profile of expenditure reviews into the public domain is crucial for engendering the discipline of self-evaluation. Such reviews ought to go beyond ascertaining whether or not the money was used for the purpose, to include, as a very important aspect of the assessment, whether the monies achieved the intended purpose. The recent introduction of performance budgeting and the Performance Improvement Programme under the Public Sector Reform program supplements the comprehensive initiative for improving budget management under the annual Public Expenditure Review process. Parliaments review budgetary expenditures for ascertaining authorized expenditures and virtually do not dwell on assessing impact. Expenditure reviews that incorporate assessment of cost-effectiveness and impact of previous budgets should form an important basis for approving new budgets in support of poverty reduction. Similarly, policy framework papers and the proposed Tanzania Assistance Strategy are the most important instruments for directing development in the country, and ought also to be key items of parliamentary business. It is there where the broad interests of the poor, as opposed to the more influential lobbies of the wealthy, can best be protected.

The main adjustments to current public policy practice include restructuring budgets in favor of primary and secondary education, improving the flow of health information that is considered most effective for improving public health, raising the quality of education by providing more inputs in the form of textbooks and other learning devices, and soliciting additional resources through user charges provided they do not crowd out allocations from budgets. Moreover, the recent trends toward decentralization of management of these services augurs well not only for enhanced accountability and hence cost-effectiveness but also for encouraging local initiatives. Decentralization will also assist in reducing the bias toward urban centers and enhance provision of these services to the rural areas, where the majority of the poor reside. Focus of public provision to the rural areas complements the existing concentration of private services in urban centers.

The contribution of local communities as a framework for providing inexpensive education and, to a limited extent, primary health services has grown in many countries. Harambee schools in Kenya provide a good example of mobilizing resources at community levels for provision of education. Harambee (community fund raising) has also been used for collective financing of costs for tertiary education and expensive treatment when deemed necessary. Other forms of community support are organized under parental associations and women's organizations. Tanzania had aimed at promoting such arrangements of community involvement and ought now to raise their profile politically and in reality. These are worthwhile self-help traditions that ought to be promoted, and they provide a useful framework for assistance by governments and nongovernmental organizations.

Public health education has proved effective in achieving impressive results in reducing mortality in countries such as China and Vietnam, where income levels remain low and comparable to many African countries. This information function remains quite weak in the prioritization of government spending in Tanzania. In light of tight budget constraints, this approach will enhance the effectiveness of public resources in raising the health status of the majority of citizens. Successes of public awareness campaigns against the spread of communicable diseases, such as AIDS, have been reported in countries where such campaigns have been vigorously promoted. Health codes enforced by local governments and rapid expansion of primary health care had played a pivotal role in the pre-independence periods, and in the first decade after independence, in achieving phenomenal reduction in mortality. Reappearance of some of the communicable diseases, long thought to have been eliminated, is partly due to relaxation of these efforts during the 1980s. It is therefore necessary that the government and nongovernmental organizations reinvigorate health education and promote hygiene to avoid reversals of achievements from past effort in this area and to consolidate gains made to date.

Poverty reduction is likely to be achieved faster if the poor are empowered—given voice in designing, implementing, and monitoring poverty-alleviation measures. Good governance and accountability are also important in ensuring that earmarked funds reach the poor. Measures for improving governance include tracking public expenditure at all levels of government, setting and monitoring priority indicators, strengthening the regulatory framework in key markets to improve transparency and competition, and implementing programs for promoting the welfare of women and other groups that for various reasons (for example, racial or ethnic) do not fully participate in society (URT 1999d).

Priority needs to be given to areas of locational and socioeconomic concentration of poverty. An important point to bear in mind in designing poverty-reduction strategies is the fact that the majority of the poor reside in the rural areas and are primarily engaged in agriculture. In the case of the urban poor, the majority are engaged in the informal economy. The growth strategies to be adopted necessarily then have to place high priority on addressing the locational concentration of poverty and on uplifting productivity in these two critical sectors. The related investment in infrastructure to support production and market integration needs to be consistent with these locational and sectoral priorities.

The renewal of growth has to start at the countryside for it to effectively begin making a dent in poverty. Previous attempts at agricultural transformation were frustrated by problems of poor design and implementation. State involvement substituted for grassroots initiatives; and committed resources were inadequate, while policies heavily taxed agriculture in favor of failed import substitution industrialization. The past decade has seen a significant shift away from these problems as market orientation took root. Some encouraging results in the upturn of the growth of the sector and productivity growth have been achieved (Delgado 1996). The focus now should be on pursuit of investment in new sources of productivity growth. This entails reducing transaction costs related to transport costs; facilitating the adoption of technological innovations to enhance supply responsiveness; and creating schemes aimed at reducing risks, to enable specialization according to ecological comparative advantages. Opening and rationalizing the scope of the private sector participation in supplying inputs and other agricultural services will complement more focused government action in this sector. Much more on the imperatives for renewing agricultural growth in Tanzania is dealt with in the next chapter of this memorandum.

The informal sector in Tanzania is probably the most dynamic and most important source of livelihood for the poor urban dwellers. The urban informal sector has been most noteworthy in grassroots efforts to cushion against declines in real incomes even for those employed in the formal sector at the lower end of the pay scale. It is considered to be the most dynamic in terms of employment generation and productivity growth), and it has thrived in spite of government restrictions. Tanzania ought to harness the dynamism and enthusiasm of this sector by removing impediments to its growth and providing a framework for availing credit and supportive infrastructure to small-scale enterprises and trading activities. This sector's contributions to the public coffers can be elicited through less hostile means than curtailment of its activities. Indirect taxes have captured this source of income. Nongovernmental organizations have played an important role in the organizational improvements and business orientation of this sector, and more needs to be done by these entities in sharpening skills and enhancing the capacity of the sector to thrive.

Improved access to the productive assets by the poor is crucial for expanding their income-earning opportunities. Access by the poor to productive physical assets is fundamental to their engagement in productive activities. Given the dominance of agriculture in the provision of livelihood to the poor, access to land is pivotal. This raises two further issues. First, it may entail reforms in land tenure such that the poor are availed this crucial means of production. Politically sensitive as it may be, redistribution of land in cases of high concentration of this asset in a few hands may be a necessary first step. Although fears of reduced productivity due to small parceling of large units abound, several studies have confirmed higher productivity of small holdings particularly with improved husbandry. Second, top priority must be given to the conservation of this productive resource, particularly when its scarcity is rising with population pressures. The fight against environmental degradation is for the survival of the poor.

Speeding up the demographic transition is necessary for reducing pressure on domestic resource constraint for supporting poverty-reduction programs. The pressure of rapid expansion of demands on the limited means of the economy occasioned by the high population growth in the country and its high dependency structure is a major drawback to growth and poverty reduction. While in a few countries demographic transition to lower population growth and a more mature age structure has begun, Tanzania, like the majority of African countries, has not embarked on a demographic transition. The problem of rapid population growth in Tanzania remains intact. Population policies and programs for encouraging low fertility (in the demographic sense) sprang up several years back but continue to be constrained by limited resources. Higher growth of the economy and education are important elements in the effort to stem rapid growth of the population. The large contribution of population growth inertia to this problem in spite of the above actions means, however, that for the foreseeable future the country will have to contend with this problem from the side of higher economic growth and productivity to meet growing needs.

Combating HIV/AIDS

One measure of economic development in a country is the well-being of its population. At the same time, the well-being of the population influences economic development; that is, a healthy workforce is one of the prerequisites of any nation's development. As noted earlier, major and rapid improvements in human development were achieved during the first two decades. Access to primary health facilities and medical personnel improved rapidly with the growth of dispensaries and health centers between 1961 and 1980. Population coverage by medical personnel rose sharply during this time and subsequent years. However, the facilities for delivery of health and other social services have deteriorated rapidly since the early 1980s as population continued to expand rapidly and economic growth decelerated. The problem has further been exacerbated by the outbreak of the killer disease HIV/AIDS beginning in the mid-1980s, but with intensifying in the 1990s.

Epidemiology of HIV/AIDS

The spread of the HIV/AIDS epidemic in Tanzania has been fast. HIV infection already ranks at the top of health problems in Tanzania's urban populations. As of December 1997, Tanzania was estimated to have 1.5 million productive adults infected with the deadly virus, with infection spreading at a high rate (URT 1998c). The infection rate in urban centers is estimated to exceed 24 percent, and up to 10 percent in rural areas. The impact of the HIV/AIDS epidemic is devastating, given that it strikes adults in their prime years—including the elite and professionals, which implies that it kills workers of much greater than average productivity. Furthermore, it is estimated that by 2015, more people living in rural areas who are infected with HIV than in urban areas, with a serious effect of reducing the agricultural labor force and therefore production. Worse, more women than men are infected with HIV, a ratio of 1.5:1. This is important considering that women spend more time in production and reproduction activities than men. Thus, HIV/AIDS is not just a health problem but a grave development problem. Virtually all sectors are experiencing a loss of experienced and trained professionals. Given the mortality rate increases, life expectancy is estimated to decline by almost a decade, and the population structure will shift toward the younger age. The country has also witnessed a large increase of AIDS orphans in the last few years. The estimated number of orphans since the beginning of the epidemic is 730,000.

HIV/AIDS is first and foremost a consequence of sexual behavior. As such, AIDS is completely preventable. Some effective interventions are the effective diagnosis and treatment of sexually transmitted diseases; the reduction of the number of sexual partners; promotion of condom use; information, education, and communication about the epidemic and its prevention; counseling and testing; messages and media; and abstinence. Key factors that cause susceptibility and vulnerability to the spread of the epidemic need to be determined. The purpose of the concept of vulnerability is to enable identifying of the factors that make certain population groups more vulnerable to HIV/AIDS and thus enable addressing them. Variables that have been identified as the key factors of vulnerability to HIV/AIDS transmission are poverty, economic inequality, gender inequality, migration, and poor health.

Poverty and AIDS

HIV/AIDS has become a fast-spreading epidemic in Tanzania primarily because of poverty and gender inequality. Poverty makes HIV/AIDS education difficult because of high levels of illiteracy and little access to mass media, health, and educational services. Poverty directly exacerbates HIV transmission through prostitution and inferior health care. Poverty indirectly exacerbates HIV transmission by increasing migrant labor, family dissolution, and homelessness, all of which lead to a greater risk of someone's having multiple partners. Poor people are also less likely to take seriously an infection that takes years to kill its victims while they focus on trying to survive day-to-day. The incubation period of the disease is shortened because of poor standards of nutrition, repeated infections, and limited access to medical care. A loss of an adult in a poor household drives the family into greater poverty. Poverty affects women most, their economic dependence on a man in a marriage, or in sexual relations that are commercial and less formal, is thereby increased.

Gender and AIDS

Women are particularly vulnerable to HIV because of biological and socioeconomic factors. Biologically, a woman can more easily get infected from each sexual encounter than a man can. Having gender-biased social roles also increases the vulnerability of women to HIV infection. Gender inequality in culture, wealth, power, and politics tends to keep women oppressed. Women are not able to force their partners to wear condoms, nor are they able to refuse to have conjugal relations with them. Reducing women's and men's risk of infection demands gender-based responses that focus on how the different social expectations, roles, status, and economic power of men and women affect, and are affected by, the epidemic.

Economic Impact of AIDS

Countries severely affected by HIV/AIDS will experience a large impact on their health sectors. Total national expenditure on health care will rise. Each adult HIV/AIDS case treated in the health care system absorbs about US$290 (about T Sh 232,000) in nursing and drug costs, and the cost for pediatric AIDS is about US$195 (about T Sh 156,000). Lower-income households will be less able to cope with medical expenses and loss of income, which will lead to increased poverty and inequality. In economies in which the public sector bears a large proportion of medical costs, the government must make difficult decisions about how to finance medical expenditure as HIV/AIDS-related spending rises. Three types of care are available for AIDS patients: relief of symptoms, prevention of opportunistic illnesses, and antiretroviral treatments. Each of these different types of care bear a different cost, with antiretroviral treatments being prohibitively expensive. Evidence shows home-based care to be more cost-effective than hospital care in Tanzania (URT 1999h). The epidemic has indirect costs:

- Costs of funerals and mourning
- Lower nutrition status and poor health of children
- Reduced schooling of children as income declines and demand for child labor increases
- Reallocation of labor across household members to treat the terminally ill and to compensate for their lost labor
- Sale of land or other assets
- Dissolution or migration of the household
- Burdens placed on relatives to help finance medical and funeral costs.

HIV/AIDS was the leading cause of death among adults aged 15–59 in Dar es Salaam, Hai, and Morogoro Rural) in 1992–95 (URT 1997c). Currently AIDS, combined with tuberculosis, is the leading cause of death in all areas covered by the project, causing 50 percent of the death in both men and women for the 35–59 age group in Ilala and Temeke. Ill health and death due to AIDS were reported to have reduced the agricultural labor force, productivity, and disposable incomes in many families and rural communities. A trend of declining GDP has been observed in the Kagera and Tanga regions, associating reduced agricultural production to the increase in number of AIDS cases.

The impact of the HIV/AIDS epidemic is devastating and poses a serious threat to productivity and growth in the future. It kills adults in the prime of their working and parenting lives, thus reducing the labor force, impoverishing families, orphaning children, and destroying communities. The impact of the epidemic is through its effect on two key inputs—labor and capital, and the size and quality of the labor force and through changes in productivity. The effects of HIV/AIDS can be grouped into those associated with rising morbidity rates and those associated with rising mortality rates. With morbidity, the effect on labor productivity is negative—loss of labor from the sick and their caretakers. Health care expenditures increase, causing a negative savings effect and a decline in human capital investments. The population growth rate has declined because of the epidemic. While decreasing the birth rate may ease pressure on economic resources, the death of experienced workers, as is the case in the HIV/AIDS epidemic, change the labor-force composition to younger, less-experienced workers. This causes declines in human capital stock and thus in national output.

Without decisive policy action, HIV/AIDS may reduce Tanzania's GDP in 2010 by an estimated 15–25 percent in relation to a no-HIV/AIDS scenario, according to Cuddington (1993). The presence of AIDS is estimated to reduce the average real GDP growth rate in 1985–2010 from 3.9 percent to a range of 2.8–3.3 percent. Per capita income levels are expected to fall by between 0 percent and 10 percent. Per capita GDP is expected to be moderately affected because of the decrease in population growth rate. Bloom and Sachs (1998) show that the factors contributing to Africa's poor economic performances, that is, low life expectancies and extremely youth-heavy age distributions, are exacerbated by the HIV/AIDS epidemic.

Prevention and Control of AIDS

HIV/AIDS control activities need to become an integral part of development policy and practice. The adverse impact of the disease on development calls for widening the response outside of the health sector and supplementing the health intervention with interventions that address the socioeconomic determinants and consequences of HIV/AIDS. Therefore, HIV/AIDS needs to be featured in the context of other cross-sectoral topics, such as poverty alleviation, gender, youth, and population. With the negative consequences of AIDS on the labor force, policy initiatives to restore productivity and maintain the stock of human capital will be critical for achieving economic growth.

The National AIDS Control Program is in its third Medium-Term Plan (1998–2002). The objectives of this third plan is to prevent transmission of HIV/AIDS and other sexually transmitted diseases; to protect and support vulnerable groups; to mitigate the socioeconomic impacts of HIV/AIDS; and to strengthen the capacity of institutions, communities, and individuals to arrest the spread of the epidemic and mitigate its impact. The program's strategy focuses on 11 priority areas for providing a framework for an expanded, multisectoral response to the HIV/AIDS epidemic in Tanzania:

- Reduce the number of cases of sexually transmitted diseases
- Reduce unsafe sexual behavior among highly mobile population groups
- Reduce transmission of HIV and other sexually transmitted diseases among commercial sex workers
- Reduce unsafe sexual behavior among the armed and security forces
- Reduce the vulnerability of youth to HIV/AIDS and other sexually transmitted diseases
- Maintain safe blood-transfusion services
- Assist women commercial sex workers in poverty develop alternative means of income
- Improve the well-being of people living with HIV/AIDS
- Reduce unprotected sex among men with multiple partners
- Improve educational opportunities, especially for girls
- Reduce vulnerability of women in an adverse cultural environment.

Use of the participatory appraisal technique is important in enabling the communities to express their needs and concerns about the HIV/AIDS epidemic. A community will embrace what it considers important, so analysts should be informed on what the community perceives as vital and incorporate this into the strategies laid out above. Also, with the participatory rural appraisal technique, the communities can be informed on sensitive issues that might be harder to discuss openly. Many nongovernmental organizations are doing excellent work in prevention and mitigation of the HIV/AIDS epidemic. Their approach may vary: working with high-risk groups or with youths (in and out of school); assisting orphans and needy families; counseling on the impact of HIV/AIDS, including the legal rights of those left behind; or conducting research and instructional activities. However, government needs to show a strong political will and commitment such that policy and sensitization of HIV/AIDS issues at all levels of the political structure is adequate.

5. Unleashing the Private Sector's Potential for Tanzania's Development

This chapter focuses on the role and contribution of the private sector to sustained growth and poverty alleviation in Tanzania. The role of the private sector as the principal agent for sustained growth takes precedence as the Tanzanian economy shifts away from a control regime and public sector dominance to a market orientation and a reinvigoration of the private sector.

The private sector is loosely defined here to encompass all agents in the economy not formally classified as part of the public domain. This definition therefore excludes government ministries and departments, public or state-owned enterprises or parastatals, independent public agencies, and those voluntary associations that depend on government subventions for their operations, for example, community secondary schools. To focus on that part of the private sector envisaged to constitute the principal engine of economic growth, we narrow the usual definition of the private sector—which includes all private enterprises, farmers, the self-employed in the informal sector, nongovernmental agencies, and community organizations not dependent on government subventions—to include only formal enterprises and those engaged in agriculture.

Throughout the postindependence period the private sector has been the most dominant contributor to people's livelihoods and to the growth and dynamism of the economy. On average, the sector has accounted for more than 70 percent of GDP and more than 60 percent of fixed investment. In recent years the private sector has dominated the rehabilitation of the ailing state industry mainly via the privatization program and the expansion of the export base, in addition to the rapid expansion of its share in the fast-growing mining and tourism sectors. With the liberalization of trade and the rolling back of public sector involvement in commerce, the private sector has also consolidated its dominant role in commerce. The private sector has been increasingly strengthening its participation in the provision of social services—education and especially health—since the second half of the 1980s. Previously these services were the preserve of the government. There appears to be a distinct move toward private sector dominance in supplying social services at the secondary and tertiary levels, while the public sector plays an overwhelmingly dominant role in the provision of these services at the primary level. Finally, with a contribution of more than 50 percent to overall GDP and as an employer of over 25 million Tanzanians, agriculture has traditionally been a private sector bastion.

Notwithstanding the private sector's growing presence in the economy, one of the less impressive outcomes of reforms has been the less than wholehearted response of private investment to the measures taken so far. Private investment as a proportion of GDP remains at 12 percent, which is low even by African standards. Without a robust investment response, the economy's productive capacity will remain stagnant and growth levels cannot be accelerated, or even sustained. Much of the recorded private investment during the past decade has been rehabilitative in nature, and has barely kept pace with the continued decommissioning of public enterprise capacity, as public enterprises are weaned off budgetary subventions. A good part of the foreign investment outside mining and tourism has financed transfer of ownership in the privatization process rather than added new capacity.

Furthermore, efficiency of investment remains low despite recent improvements, and certainly cannot compensate for the inadequate expansion of productive capacity in the long run. The overall rate of return to investment is estimated at 20 percent (converse of an incremental capital output ratio of 5), which is far below the 33 percent level maintained in the East Asian economies for nearly three decades of high growth, and also less than Tanzania's historical peak of nearly 40 percent during the 1960s. Two of the major reasons for Tanzania's low investment efficiency are the poor quality of investment choices made in the past and the high protective walls that shielded enterprises from efficiency-enhancing competition. Part of the evidence here, particularly among public enterprises, is the long death trail of white elephants, most of which were never completed or never became operational. A significant proportion of those that did become operational were extremely underutilized or collapsed once subsidies were stopped, as the fiscal crisis set in, or when protection from international competition was scaled back. In addition distortions in the policy environment and a weak human skill base militated against gains in efficiency and technological learning. The severe import strangulation in the late 1970s and early 1980s caused by the foreign exchange shortage accentuated the deleterious impact of policy distortions.

As Tanzania stands at the brink of the new millennium, it is imperative that measures be taken to encourage a more robust private investment response and increased productivity of investment. Such an investment response also needs to be broadly distributed across different economic sectors in contrast to the recent concentration in the enclave sectors of mining and tourism. Spreading income-earning opportunities so that they reach the poor entails encouraging investment in smallholder agriculture as well as in microenterprises and in small and medium enterprises. Thus efforts must be directed not only at raising the overall level of private investment, but also at paying closer attention to its poverty-reducing aspects.

The Government's Stance toward Competition and the Private Sector's Response

The changes in the public policy regime in the decades since independence and the government's and the private sector's respective stances are fundamental to explaining the dynamics of the private sector's performance and its role in the economy. The following paragraphs describe the key policy phases in relation to the room created for private sector initiative, the incentive structure affecting the profitability of private ventures, the openness and competitiveness of the operating environment, and the institutional framework governing risk perceptions and security of property.

The private sector's history has been checkered, and has depended predominantly on the government's stance toward its own role in the economy relative to that of the private sector. We can identify three main phases during which the private sector's role has declined sharply from a dominant position at independence to a survival phase for the next two decades before subsequent slow but sure revival in the 1990s. In the process, Tanzania missed out on two decades of private sector development and the sector's potential contribution to the country's overall growth and development was lost. This loss is clearly illustrated by the current operational and commercial immaturity of indigenous businesses, and, more broadly, weaknesses in institutions charged with governing the execution of private business and property rights.

Phase 1 (1961–68): Complementary Role

In the early postindependence period, 1961–68, the government played a supportive role to the private sector. This phase, characterized by macroeconomic stability and a capital-friendly environment, was conducive to private sector development. Much as the institutional structure was nascent and fragile, the stance the government adopted toward the private sector was relatively nonintrusive and broadly favored foreign participation in a wide range of sectors, although agriculture and agro-industry were clearly the most dominant. The protective walls for domestic industry were still diminutive.

The government sought to transform smallholder agriculture through two approaches to develop and augment agricultural production. The first was to improve basic farming and marketing practices by providing community development staff and extension services to change individual farmer behavior and encourage commercialization. The second was to encourage farmers to adopt modern agricultural production techniques. To facilitate the adoption of these techniques the government also sought to regroup and resettle of farmers in village settlements and voluntary cooperatives, as well as to develop irrigation schemes in the river basins.

Furthermore, to encourage the expansion of foreign-owned private estates, the government offered land concessions to private estates, which at that time accounted for 40 percent of total agricultural exports. However, these concessions were offered on the condition that the foreign owners of estates support the establishment of indigenous estates through the provision of financial and technical assistance. This caveat was in response to the pressure for Africanization, a carry over from the political campaigns for independence.

In industry, expectations were for the private sector to contribute 75 percent of investment. The government encouraged this through a range of incentives, including the provision of government guarantees for private investment and repatriation of profits; the development of industrial sites with public resources; the granting of tax concessions and investment allowances, including accelerated depreciation; and the provision of information on investment opportunities to potential investors in the form of economic surveys and feasibility studies. It also helped some enterprises secure financing from the government-owned Tanganyika Development Corporation.

The drive for better education and skill formation was emphasized to support the modernization process across all sectors. The expansion of education was also one of the main priorities in the First Five-Year Plan. The government expected that a well-developed education sector would be the main vehicle for building a large cohort of trained manpower with the skills and knowledge needed to further Tanzania's development process. The expansion of education was not limited to formal education at the secondary and technical levels, but also included adult education. Indeed, investment in education was not only for the benefit of the individual, but was viewed to benefit the economy as a whole, serving both the public and private sectors. The involvement of nongovernmental agencies in this endeavor was particularly notable.

Aware of the importance of other development actors in the implementation of the First Five-Year Plan, the government institutionalized two main consultative bodies: the Sectoral Relations Committee and the National Economic and Social Council. The committee comprised representatives from the private sector and relevant sectoral ministries. It facilitated communication between the private sector representatives and the government on development issues and various problems facing the sector. The council was a forum for interaction between the government and representatives of various professional and civic groups on various aspects of the First Five-Year Plan. These two bodies provided an apposite forum for the various stakeholders in the development process to interact with the government on the plan's achievements, constraints, and prospects.

The private sector responded positively to the amenable and largely supportive environment created by the government. The contribution of the private sector, broadly defined, to income generation (GDP) between 1962 and 1967 averaged 90 percent. Private investment grew by 70 percent between 1963 and 1975, while investment by the public sector grew by 24 percent. The share of private fixed investment averaged slightly below 60 percent between 1962 and 1967. During this early period, the quasi-public sector was relatively small. It was composed mainly of three institutions: the National Cooperative and Development Bank, the Tanganyika Agricultural Corporation, and the Tanganyika Development Corporation. The latter was the only public corporation empowered by the government, either alone or in partnership with private capital, to engage in industrial and agricultural production on a commercial basis. Indeed, the private sector not only complemented the government's investment plans, but also supplemented them significantly during this period.

Phase 2 (1968–85): Restraining Role

The second phase saw a major shift by the government toward a dirigist and socialist strategy. The main objective was to establish the dominance of the public sector on the basis of socialist principles. In addition to the traditional functions of providing economic and social infrastructure and maintaining law and order, the public sector plunged into production and commerce functions. The policy thrust of the 1967 Arusha Declaration squarely placed the responsibility for investment in the productive sectors on the government as a way to catalyze rapid development. Thus in the Second Five-Year Plan, and later the Third Five-Year Plan, the government development budget was to be the main source of investment, including subventions to parastatals and cooperative society investment programs. Private sector investment was envisaged to grow at a much slower rate, corresponding to the deliberate strategy of reducing its importance in the economy.

The watershed in implementing this shift in strategy came in 1968 with the nationalization campaign and trade and other elements of commerce being placed in public hands in earnest. The hallmark of this shift in policy was the nationalization of banks, insurance companies, mills, import and export business, and real estate businesses. Public sector involvement was subsequently broadened by acquiring majority shares in mining and agricultural and industrial enterprises, and essentially limiting the formation of new industrial enterprises to the parastatal sector. However, the 1976–78 commodity price boom in the international markets and the concomitant relaxation of Tanzania's foreign exchange constraint resulted in the partial liberalization of licensing of private enterprises in 1977.

On the whole, the government adopted a systematic approach through the 1970s, favoring the development of the public sector and stifling the growth of the private sector. During 1970–85 a combination of policy restrictions to private sector expansion, combined with a deliberate drive to expand public participation in production and trade, led to an incentive structure loaded against private sector development, and furthermore limited its access to financial resources through the formal financial system. Explicit limits to and control on the access to credit and foreign exchange and the mandatory surrender of foreign exchange proceeds from exports to the central bank were put in place. A licensing system was set up to restrict private sector entry into industry and trade, as well as to grant exclusive trading rights in most commodities and products to public monopolies. Policy and bureaucratic attitudes generally became inimical toward the private sector and have entrenched themselves since.

The Second Five-Year Plan placed priority on rural development, industrialization, transport and communications, commerce, and education. The most drastic policy change was in agriculture and rural development, which shifted from the earlier transformation approach through village settlements to rural transformation primarily through the adoption of Ujamaa villagization programs. The government justified its abandonment of the earlier approach through its inability to meet the relatively high costs of establishing the village settlements. The shift in policy towards Ujamaa villagization entailed increased mobilization of Tanzanians by the government to undertake cooperative production. For its part, the government would provide them with social services, training, credit, and extension and marketing services. With respect to large-scale farming and livestock husbandry, the government undertook to establish state farms and ranches through parastatals and subsidiary companies, such as crop and livestock authorities, corporations, and marketing boards.

In accordance with the strategic stance of the Arusha Declaration, the public sector was given the main responsibility for industrialization, leaving the private sector to play a residual role. However, the policy allowed the establishment of joint enterprises between the public sector as the majority shareholder and foreign, private, minority investors. With hindsight, this was apparently just as a vehicle for facilitating the transfer of technology and training. These joint venture arrangements were supplemented with management contracts that were strictly under the control of the parent industries and were largely ineffective.

The bulk of industrial investment—84 percent of the total—was to be implemented by the parastatal sector, with another 4 percent destined for the workers' and cooperative organizations, and the remaining 12 percent for the private sector. The central institution for implementing industrial projects was the National Development Corporation, which was to develop managerial talent for all projects and for subsidiary companies. Protective measures for shielding nascent industries were established, including preferential customs tariffs, transfer taxes, government purchasing policy, import licensing, and refunds of duties paid on imported raw materials used to produce industrial exports.

The major policy objective in the transport and communications sector was to improve existing services to the most rapidly growing areas and to open up new areas to provide incremental development opportunities. It involved improving the existing road network and developing both an adequate trunk road network and feeder roads to open up previously inaccessible areas and strengthen cross-country links across regions, facilitate agricultural production and marketing, develop urban centers, and encourage internal and external trade. In addition to improving and expanding the road network, government and EAC investments were made to develop various modes of transport, that is, air and marine transport, railways, and roads.

To be consistent with the new thrust on rural development, the focus in education shifted from secondary education to primary education. Primary education was viewed as providing the basic training required for functioning in a rural economy. Adult education was also emphasized, but the focus was on promoting rural development by providing rudimentary training in agricultural techniques, craftsmanship, health education, and accounting. The government took on the principal responsibility for developing the education sector, which included constructing the infrastructure and literally running all schools, including those that were formerly owned by nongovernmental institutions such as religious entities.

In internal and external commerce and trade, the focus was on institutional changes to accommodate the socialist philosophy. The government emphasized the diversification of export commodities and export markets, and gave the numerous parastatals and marketing boards the central role in internal and external trade. The State Trading Corporation, and subsequently public entities under the Board of Internal Trade, assumed the key role in wholesale and retail trade in the domestic market and import trade in most commodities. The Board of External Trade and commodities trade monopolies controlled external trade. This arrangement was buttressed by extensive price controls managed by the Price Commission. The government thereby assumed the central role in virtually all commercial and trading operations and related activities, especially financing, transportation, and shipping.

During this period, private investment was to be largely confined to a narrow range of activities, for example, residential and large-scale construction, supply of transport equipment, and the production of miscellaneous manufacturing and agricultural equipment. Private sector investment was forecast to grow at a lower rate of 7 percent, in view of the deliberate strategy of diminishing its importance in the economy. As was to be expected, in the face of the initial shock resulting from the nationalization and self-reliance programs unleashed by the government, the private sector shriveled. Its contribution to GFCF had dropped to just over 27 percent by 1971, from more than 52 percent only three years earlier. However, during 1970–85, and more so in 1980–85, even though the share of public investment remained high, the public GFCF rate declined dramatically as public revenues were diverted to finance oil imports following the oil shock of 1973/74 and FY80 and the drastic scaling down of donor support, notably, by the International Monetary Fund and the World Bank. Conversely, the private sector GFCF rate picked up, averaging around 50 percent during 1980–85. However, despite this resurgence, not only did the marginalization by the public sector stifle the development of private sector entrepreneurial capacities, overall, the import substitution policies and generally protectionist stance of the government led to an enfeebled private sector that viewed subsidies, subventions, and defense against external competitive forces as a matter of right.

Phase 3 (1986 to Date): Supportive Role

Following partial liberalization of the import regime in 1984 (through the Own Funded Imports Scheme) and significant rollback of price controls, internal and external commerce was opened up to greater participation by the private sector. As discussed in chapter 2, in 1986 the government launched the ERP, and in 1989 broadened it to encompass action on poverty alleviation and renamed it the Economic and Social Action Program. This marked a dramatic departure from the earlier policy stance anchored in the principles of a staunch socialist ideology. The control regime had been undermined by a thriving parallel market and other forms of exit options. It was in the context of this environment that the government initiated a wide-ranging reform process aimed at restructuring the economy from its previous reliance on control mechanisms toward a predominantly market-oriented system.

Thus the second half of the 1980s saw a rapid dismantling of price controls and an initiation of the first steps toward liberalization of trade and financial and foreign exchange markets. However, it was not until the second half of the 1990s that these measures began to be grounded in appropriate institutional and legal frameworks. The foreign exchange market was liberalized, exchange controls were dismantled, the financial market was opened up to private sector participation, and the privatization process was formally launched. During this period the government accelerated the pace of reforms thereby further freeing up markets, sustained improvements in macroeconomic stability, stepped up the pace of privatization, and took proactive measures to encourage foreign investment in Tanzania.

During the 1990s the government also made several institutional changes with a bearing on private sector development. First, consistent with its reform program, the government has been taking steps to redefine its role to include the core functions of formulating policy, managing the economy, providing basic social and economic infrastructure and legal and regulatory frameworks, and maintaining law and order. The government now considers the creation of an enabling environment for the private sector and other economic agents to allow investment in productive and commercial activities for the acceleration of growth and development paramount.

Second, the government promulgated the national investment promotion policy and enacted the National Investment (Promotion and Protection) Act of 1990. It established the Investment Promotion Center, spelled out priority sectors for investment by local and foreign investors, and guaranteed investment protection. In the act, the government explicitly recognized that private foreign and local investments have played, and will continue to play, an important role in the development of the economy. Realizing the inherent deficiencies in that act, in 1997 the government enacted the Tanzania Investment Act to make the Tanzania Investment Center (TIC) a one-stop center for investors in coordinating, encouraging, promoting, and facilitating investment in Tanzania.

Third, through the 1995 Bank of Tanzania Act the central bank was given an enhanced role; ensured autonomy; and adequately empowered to license private and foreign banks, set regulations, and undertake prudential supervision of other banks and financial institutions. Moreover, the Foreign Exchange Act of 1992 enabled the liberalization of foreign exchange transactions, which has greatly facilitated investments and other commercial activities. In addition, the liberalization of the current account went a long way toward reducing transfer risks for foreign investors. The institutionalization of capital market operations through the Capital Market and Securities Act of 1994 has opened up another avenue for enhancing private sector participation in investment operations.

Fourth, the government has sought to strengthen the legal and institutional framework in support of its privatization program by establishing the Parastatal Sector Reform Commission and the Loans and Assets Realization Trust, and in 1999 set up a commercial court. Furthermore, it has placed greater emphasis on developing transparent and more effective procedures for the liquidation and divestiture of parastatals and state-owned enterprises. Both local and foreign private investors are now more actively participating in different sectors and in activities earlier exclusively or largely under government purview. However, the process remains cumbersome and prone to delays in the face of vested interests, in particular, in the privatization process. However, the government has been focusing on tackling some of these issues.

In supporting the private sector's contribution to accelerating socioeconomic development, the government is developing methods to re-institutionalize the currently ad hoc consultative processes with the private sector in developing appropriate and effective macroeconomic and sectoral policies. Similarly, the private sector is the process of establishing institutional mechanisms to permit better interaction and consultation with the government. While there has been a resurgence in the private sector presence (the private sector's share in GFCF has averaged around 68 percent), the effects on the general populace of some two decades of an anti-private sector stance have been deleterious. A strong attitudinal bias against profit making and individual enterprise has largely sapped the commercial spirit, resulting in the Tanzanian business community being relatively small and underdeveloped. The commercial sector is dominated by the Tanzanian Asians, who are primarily traders (importers, retailers, and exporters of goods) owning holding companies with numerous subsidiaries. The indigenous firms that are in business remain, for the most part, less diversified and less sophisticated in their activities. The general expectation of government-led support still remains as a major challenge in developing a competitive private sector.

Tanzania's Private Sector: A Profile

The private sector's response to the developments described has been cautious, but positive on the whole, as evident from the rise of its share in total investment and share of output levels.

Private Sector's Contribution to GDP

The contribution of the private sector to GDP at current prices is analyzed in terms of its share in overall GDP. The analysis also includes a brief review of the share of private sector output by major economic activity, including agriculture, mining, and manufacturing; trade and tourism, including hotels and restaurants; transport and communications; construction; and utilities, including electricity and water.

Table 5.1 summarizes the private sector's contribution to GDP. The overall picture that emerges is one of private sector predominance, albeit declining. Table 5.1 indicates that, while fluctuating in some cases (for example, manufacturing and transport and communications), private sector output both at the aggregate level and by major economic activity has constituted the larger part of GDP. At the aggregate level the relative share of private sector output has averaged around 80 percent. At the sectoral level the relative share averaged around 99 percent for agriculture, forestry, fishing, and hunting; 84 percent for mining and quarrying; 66 percent for manufacturing; 78 percent for trade, hotels, and restaurants; and 52 percent for transport and communications. The lowest share, 44 percent, was for electricity and water, rent, and public services. This reflects the government's dominance in the provision of public services and utilities.

Several other noteworthy features emerge from the table. First, with the exception of agriculture, transport and communications, and construction and utilities, the relative share of private output was higher in 1962 than in 1980. This reveals the negative effects of socialist policies, which made initiatives and investments in certain areas, such as health, mining, electricity, and water off-limits to the private sector. The sustained dominance of private sector output in agriculture, forestry, fishing, and hunting is striking, and reflects the overwhelming presence of private operators in this sector, including in the socialist years. A second notable feature is the steady growth of the relative share of private sector output in mining and quarrying, starting with the liberalization of the sector in the early 1980s. This growth has been sustained because of recent changes in the policy framework that have promoted greater private sector involvement in mining activities.

Table 5.1. *Share of Key Sectors in GDP (Current Prices), Selected Years 1962–95*

Sector	1962	1980	1985	1990	1991	1993	1994	1995
Overall (T Sh millions)	1,966.4	37,454	99,676	663,771	834,730	1,701,969	2,243,031	2,909,828
Public sector	163.4	7,649	20,579	94,572	134,139	373,841	482,124	619,601
Private sector	1,803	29,805	79,097	569,199	700,591	1,328,128	1,760,907	2,290,227
Share of private sector (%)	91.69	79.58	79.35	85.75	83.93	78.03	78.51	78.71
Agriculture, forestry, fishing, hunting (T Sh millions)	1,009	16,636	51,634	364,849	480,500	773,469	955,983	1,318,459
Public sector	47	240	437	2128	3946	5108	4082	5647
Private sector	962	16,396	51,197	362,721	476,554	768,361	951,901	1,312,812
Share of private sector (%)	95.34	98.56	99.15	99.42	99.18	99.34	99.57	99.57
Mining and quarrying (T Sh millions)	101.5	329	334	6,424	11,809	19,062	26,170	35,190
Public sector	1.5	179	66	919	1801	307	277	1387
Private sector	100	150	268	5,505	10,008	18,755	25,893	33,803
Share of private sector (%)	98.52	45.59	80.24	85.69	84.75	98.39	98.94	96.06
Manufacturing (T Sh millions)	156.9	4,097	7,763	59,961	65,600	120,479	157,445	200,525
Public sector	6.9	1,513	3,553	30,598	24,834	47,226	61,262	76,724
Private sector	150	2,584	4,210	29,363	40,766	73,253	96,183	123,801
Share of private sector (%)	95.60	63.07	54.23	48.97	62.14	60.80	61.09	61.74
Trade, hotels, restaurants (T Sh millions)	510	4,713	14,195	103,376	124,800	244,644	318,940	417,626
Public sector	0	700	3,208	18,590	12,992	41,053	71,674	125,262
Private sector	510	4,013	10,987	84,786	111,808	203,591	247,266	292,364
Share of private sector (%)	100.00	85.15	77.40	82.02	89.59	83.22	77.53	70.01
Transport and communications (T Sh millions)	189	3,019	7,021	39,722	50,440	98,207	131,670	159,771
Public sector	108	1,305	2,769	18,442	24,248	40,502	46,442	57,783
Private sector	81	1,714	4,252	21,280	26,192	57,705	85,228	101,988
Share of private sector (%)	42.86	56.77	60.56	53.57	51.93	58.76	64.73	63.83
Construction, electricity, water, rent, public services (T Sh millions)	38,278	10,639	20,535	114,556	129,803	446,108	652,823	778,257
Public sector	21,816	4,676	12,352	49,012	94,540	239,645	298,387	352,798
Private sector	16,462	5,963	8,183	65,544	35,263	206,463	354,436	425,459
Share of private sector (%)	43.00	56.05	39.85	57.21	27.17	46.28	54.29	54.67

Source: National Bureau of Statistics, *National Accounts of Tanzania.*

122

Value Added in Key Private Sectors

The focus here is on performance by broad economic areas in respect of value added. Value added (at factor cost) in the mostly private agriculture sector, ranged from US$1.7 billion in 1989 (in constant 1995 prices) to some US$2.3 billion in 1998, or an increase of 35 percent over the decade (figure 5.1). Agriculture has clearly been contributing the lion's share to Tanzania's real GDP, averaging 45 percent. During the same period private value added in industry grew but at a lower rate of about 2.5 percent per year, while the private component of the service sector grew, at an average rate of some 2.2 percent per year. Value added in private services contributed around 30 percent of real GDP during 1989–98, amounting to US$1.4 billion in 1998. Figure 5.1 shows the relative contributions of the private component of agriculture, industry, and the service sectors to overall growth.

Figure 5.1. *Value Added by Key Private Sectors, 1989–98*

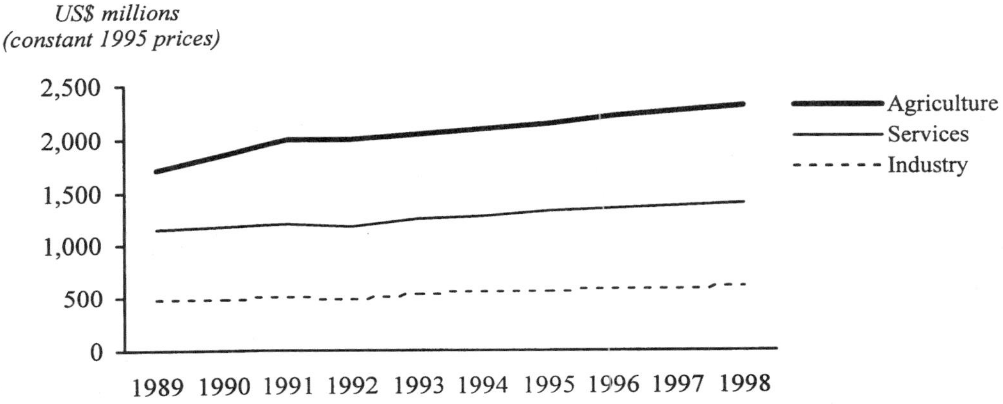

Source: World Bank (2000f); authors' calculations.

Private Sector's Contribution to Gross Domestic Investment

Gross private investment for Tanzania compare favorably with levels in Kenya and Uganda, but since the mid-1990s has been falling below the levels achieved by some other Sub-Saharan countries, including Gabon, Mauritius, the Seychelles, Swaziland, and Zimbabwe. The declining trend is more worrisome than the level, as it has also meant that gross domestic investments have consistently remained below the 25 percent of GDP suggested as a requirement for sustained growth (figure 5.2). This points to the need for concerted efforts to mobilize more domestic and foreign resources for investment in private productive activity. As a proportion of total gross domestic investment (defined as domestic GFCF plus changes in the level of inventories), gross private investment has ranged between a high of 92 percent in 1991 and a low of 75 percent in 1998, averaging some 83 percent in the period since 1989.

However, in this regard it is important to assess the real extent of the response by the private sector as far as investment levels are concerned. First, privatization has often involved a combination of a premium on the sale of a going concern (reflected in the budget as privatization proceeds) and re-capitalization by investors, often for financing rehabilitation and plant retooling. FDI data combine both. Only the resources directed toward rehabilitation, replacement, or additions to productive capacity should be counted as part of the new or incremental investment in a given year. Therefore proceeds related to the pure transfer of ownership (in instances of privatization of productive assets) should be excluded from the calculation of the level of FDI. Second, the usable productive base being transferred in the privatization process is typically much lower than assumed under the perpetual inventory methods of computing the size of capital stock, because some of this capacity is completely dysfunctional. The capital stock of the private sector may therefore be overstated, or conversely, the inefficiency of usable capacity may be understated.

Figure 5.2. *Gross Private and Public (Domestic) Investment, 1989–98*

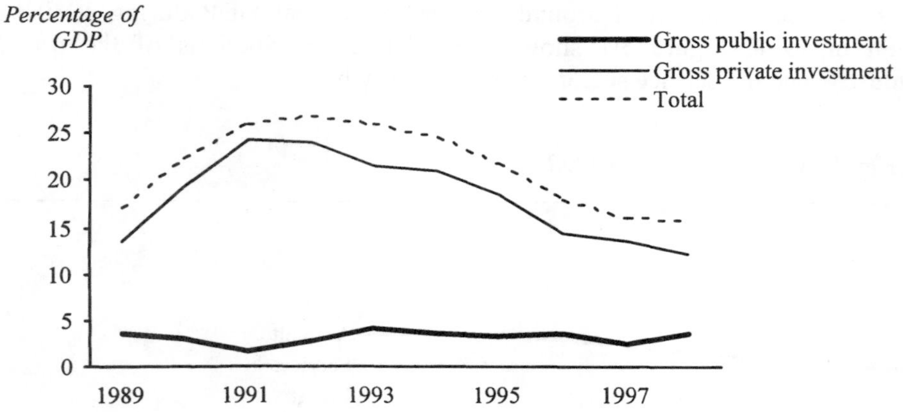

Source: World Bank (2000f); authors' calculations.

Relative Contribution in Gross Fixed Capital Formation

Data pertaining to the relative contributions by the private and public sectors to capital formation is based on economic surveys for the years under review. The analysis is limited to data related to GFCF and does not include changes in inventory. Table 5.2 summarizes the relative contributions and shares in GFCF during 1961–98. The table shows clearly that growth of both public and private gross fixed capital over the period under review exhibited a fluctuating pattern that mirrors distinct policy phases and major economic and social events in the Tanzanian economy and in the world economy. Between 1962 and 1966, the annual rate of increase of public fixed capital was a nominal 1.7 percent, with the private sector also keeping pace during this "complementary phase," growing at about 1.2 percent per year.

The highest spurt in terms of the public share of fixed investment emerged during the subsequent restraining phase and shortly thereafter through 1989. The public contribution to GFCF jumped by 33.5 percent in 1970 alone, growing another 13.5 percent over the next two years. This performance was repeated in 1979—81, when GFCF averaged growth of 8 percent per year, and again in 1988, when the public intervention rate grew by a huge 73 percent, albeit from a low base the year before. However, overall the rate of change in public GFCF was negligible, and indeed even declined somewhat during 1970–85, and fell more dramatically between 1980 and 1985. This reflects the effects of three factors: the oil shock of 1973/74, the partial relaxation of private enterprise licensing in 1977 in the wake of the commodity boom, and the subsequent withdrawal of donor support that helped create greater room for the private sector to intervene. The rate of increase of private GFCF picked up, increasing by more than 14 percent per year during 1971–76 and by some 4 percent per year during 1977–86. Nevertheless, the net effect of the restrictive policies adopted by the government was to markedly subdue the private sector response, such that between 1967 and 1986 the growth rate of the share of private GFCF averaged only some 2.5 percent per year.

Table 5.2. *Fixed Capital Formation by the Public and Private Sectors, 1961–98*
(percentage of total)

| Year | Public sector | | | | Private sector |
	Central government	Nonprofit bodies	Parastatals	Total public sector	
1961	41.7	—	3.7	45.4	54.6
1965	18.9	8.4	4.3	31.6	68.4
1970	22.4	7.0	34.5	63.8	36.2
1975	23.8	7.2	31.0	62.0	38.0
1980	23.7	0.5	15.2	39.5	60.5
1985	11.4	0.8	22.8	34.9	65.1
1989	3.9	0.3	55.1	60.2	39.8
1990	3.4	0.2	36.9	40.6	59.4
1995	4.0	12.8	0.5	17.2	82.8
1996	2.6	18.0	0.5	21.1	78.9
1997	3.7	15.6	0.5	19.9	80.1
1998	15.5	3.4	3.5	22.4	77.6

— Not available.
Source: National Bureau of Statistics, *National Accounts of Tanzania;* authors' computations.

The resumption of donor support in 1986 appears to have had positive impact on public GFCF, as reflected by the jump in government-funded investments during FY89. Concomitantly, the private share levels sank. However, in line with the government's encouraging stance, which had just started to take root in the late 1980s, the rate of increase of public GFCF decelerated, and has continued to do so since 1989. The deceleration during 1993–95 may also partly reflect the suspension of fund disbursement by key creditors following donor concerns regarding transparency in the use of public resources. As table 5.2 shows, in general the relative share of private fixed capital continues to grow with time, reflecting the effects of government policy to promote private investment while restricting government investment to core public sector functions. The private sector's share in fixed capital investments has thus been mostly increasing since 1990 and has grown to account for nearly 80 percent of total GFCF over the past five years.

Foreign Direct Investment

Net FDI grew from US$10 million in 1991 to US$165 million in 1998, a more than sixteenfold increase (table 5.3). The annual average level of FDI in Tanzania during 1990–98 was close to US$80 million (in current prices). The public monopoly of the financial sector has been eliminated, and more than 20 private banks now account for nearly 80 percent of total assets in the banking system. The insurance market has been opened up to private and foreign participation, and a stock exchange is now operational, as is a commercial court. The infrastructure sector is increasingly coming under private sector management through privatization, concessioning of assets for private operation, and new entry. This cuts across railways, power, telecommunications, and shipping services. The most robust response has been in mining and tourism, the sectors attracting the bulk of foreign investment. A number of multinationals, including Coca Cola, R. J. Reynolds (now Japanese Tobacco Company), De Beers, Samax Gold of Canada, and South African Breweries, have invested significantly over the past few years in a resurgence of investor confidence in Tanzania's future prospects. Highly successful privatizations are Tanzania Breweries, Limited in 1993 and the sale of NBC (1997) in December 1999 to the South African financial group, Amalgamated Banks of South Africa. Other notable cases involving major international investors include the sale of a 51 percent stake in the Tanzania Cigarette Company to R. J. Reynolds, the sale of 60 percent shares of the Tanga Cement Company to Holderbank, the sale of 60 percent shares of Tanganyika

Portland to Scancem and Swedfund, and the transfer of two-thirds ownership of Kilombero Sugar to investors from the United Kingdom and South Africa. A US$35 million Coca Cola bottling plant has also been set up in Dar es Salaam.

Table 5.3. *Net Foreign Direct Investment, Selected East African Countries, 1991–98*

Country	1991	1992	1993	1994	1995	1996	1997	1998
Amount of investment (US$ millions)								
Tanzania	10	15	62	63	104	134	150	165
Kenya	19	6	2	4	33	13	40	40
Uganda	1	2	4	5	2	113	160	190
Growth rates (%)								
Tanzania		50.0	313.3	1.6	65.1	28.8	11.9	10.0
Kenya		− 68.4	− 66.7	100.0	725.0	− 60.6	207.7	0.0
Uganda		100.0	100.0	25.0	− 60.0	5,550.0	41.6	18.8

Source: World Bank (2000f).

During the 1990s net capital inflows to the developing countries increased sizably. In 1990 private capital flows were about US$50 billion; within six years this had increased to a little under US$200 billion. Most of the surge was concentrated in Asia and Latin America, with no more than a dozen countries accounting for three-quarters of the total resource flow. While Africa had been receiving more than 16 percent of all FDI flowing to developing countries (amounting to nearly US$700 million per year) in the 1970s, its share fell below 3 percent in the 1990s, although in absolute terms the average annual volume grew to US$3.7 billion. FDI in Africa is concentrated in few countries and is primarily directed to industries engaged in mineral and oil extraction. Although FDI resource inflows in Tanzania, albeit above or comparable with those in selected other African countries, maintained a consistent upward trend over the past decade, in general they remained low at about only 1.3 percent of GDP (figure 5.3). Better capitalization of foreign financial resources by Tanzania could come about if improvements in the policy and business environment were sustained.

Sectoral Distribution of Investments

Table 5.4 sheds further light on the magnitude and sectoral distribution of private investments over the past four years on the basis of the investment certificates issued by the TIC. Another source of information is the debt conversion instrument operated by the central bank between 1993 and 1996. Table 5.5 presents the magnitude and sectoral structure of the private investment response through this facility. Both sources of information indicate that the mining, tourism, and manufacturing industries received the highest level of applications, and concomitantly the greatest level of investment flows.

Postscript

The private sector survived a difficult period of controls during the 1970s and much of the 1980s, to a large extent through use of the informal financial system and the growth of parallel markets in contravention to these restrictions. The collapse of private investment during this period from an average share of more than 60 percent of total investment in the early 1960s to an average of less than 40 percent through the 1980s manifested the difficulties the sector faced under this restrictive system. Private ventures developed during this period did so under a pervasive rent-seeking environment, and were

Figure 5.3. *Net Foreign Direct Investments, Selected Countries, 1990–98*

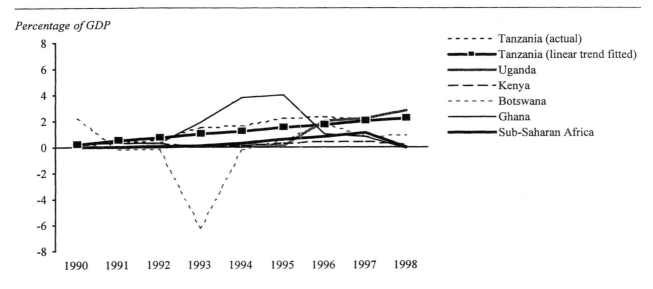

Percentage of GDP

Tanzania (actual)
Tanzania (linear trend fitted)
Uganda
Kenya
Botswana
Ghana
Sub-Saharan Africa

Source: World Bank (2000f).

Table 5.4. *Investment Certificates Issued by the Tanzania Investment Center by Sector, 1994–99 (March)*
(percentage of total)

Sector	1994	1995	1996	1997	1998	Jan.—March 1999	Sept. 1990 to March 1999
Agriculture and livestock development	0.84	3.57	1.12	2.71	26.41	14.12	3.36
Natural resources	7.73	6.89	3.43	20.59	3.94	0.30	11.30
Tourism	1.30	3.57	5.34	6.81	9.67	3.88	8.68
Manufacturing	70.40	38.25	48.97	29.97	35.34	26.75	4.67
Petroleum and mining	0.00	0.00	1.24	28.77	5.62	5.15	8.87
Construction	3.76	40.63	2.00	3.44	3.75	6.14	35.85
Transport	1.04	2.56	2.39	2.11	6.14	1.68	3.30
Service	0.47	0.66	5.74	5.35	3.13	0.77	3.56
Computers and information technology	0.00	0.00	0.00	0.00	0.00	0.00	0.01
Financial	8.17	0.37	1.69	0.25	0.11	0.25	3.52
Telecommunications	2.49	3.51	2.14	0.00	5.45	2.57	3.39
Human resources	0.00	0.00	0.00	0.00	0.47	38.40	1.35
Energy	0.00	0.00	25.94	0.00	0.00	0.00	1.30
Total	100.00	100.00	100.00	100.00	100.00	100.00	100.00

Source: TIC data.

largely dependent on protection by the state and on preferential access to state controlled resources. People's mindsets were therefore attuned to the need for connections with those in control to get ahead and survive. As a consequence, the incentive structure was loaded against the development of an efficient private sector and spawned a rent-seeking environment that the country is still struggling to undo. Business capabilities and the supportive and technical skills of the labor force remained undeveloped. However, as the private sector revived in the last decade, a number of important transitional issues have emerged. On the one hand, many old businesses that were established with the public sector as the primary client or source of subsidized resources may prove to be unsustainable if they do not undertake significant structural reforms. On the other hand, the new generation of firms established under the new dispensation have had to contend with market realities right from the start. While both sets of enterprises continue to contend with a series of structural, institutional, and administrative constraints, the obligation to face up to market-dictated forces should establish the basis for a much more efficient and robust private sector over the medium term.

Table 5.5. *Sectoral Distribution of Investment through the Debt Conversion Facility by 1997*

Sector	Amount (T Sh millions)	Percentage of total
Industrial	2,802.9	21.91
Tourism	6,852.2	53.57
Agriculture	1,433.4	11.21
Social	1,348.1	10.54
Transport	52.0	0.41
Fisheries	84.8	0.66
Mining	217.8	1.70
Trade	0.9	0.01
Total	12,792.1	100.00

Source: Bank of Tanzania.

How Competitive Is Tanzania?

The promotion of a well-functioning marketplace and a robust private sector is now deemed to be the most effective way of fostering sustainable economic growth and poverty reduction in Tanzania. However, the market relies on a core set of amenities that need to be provided within a broader public framework that may or may not be subordinate to a profit motive or paradigm based on monetary returns. A conducive business environment offering a consistent policy framework is a key example of such a public good. Sound macroeconomic policies, deregulation, and privatization are no longer considered sufficient for building a genuine free market economy. The government must also promote market-supporting institutions such as fair and transparent laws, efficient courts, and active competition authorities.

The private sector investment response depends to a large extent on perceptions about the quality of government and leadership as they influence the stability of the policy regime, the transparency of the framework for regulating business, and the availability and quality of supportive infrastructure. This proposition is underpinned by investor perceptions of the cost of doing business (transactions costs) and the fact that investors can exercise the option to wait until such time as these costs are front-loaded, otherwise they can vote with their feet in choosing other locations for their investment or flight capital in the case of potential local investors. With the increasing integration of the world economy, countries are less able to protect capital within their borders and a capital-friendly environment matters a lot more in attracting foreign investment and retaining domestic capital.

A number of reliable sources of information, many drawing from private investors' assessments of Tanzania, confirm the importance of these factors. Tanzania is still haunted by investor perceptions about numerous business risks and uncertainties, which retard growth of the private sector. Addressing these risks and uncertainties is key to stimulating a private sector response. The main risks relate to sovereign risk, including dangers of expropriation or default; low sustainable development; and policy risks in terms of sustainability, possible reversals, and political risks. Indeed, a number of respected international, country-specific risk ratings do not paint a good picture of Tanzania.

The findings from recent key reviews are discussed here, including the World Economic Forum and the Harvard Institute for International Development (1998, 2000) surveys of private investor perceptions of competitiveness; a World Bank survey of investor perceptions in 22 African countries; the Economist Intelligence Unit's (1999) risk rating for Tanzania; a series of *Investor Roadmap* reports funded by the USAID; two private sector assessment surveys carried out in 1998, one by Foreign Investment Advisory Services in relation to reforming the operations of the TIC, and another by a consultant funded by the Netherlands in 1998; the *Tanzania Investment Guide* prepared by Price Waterhouse Coopers and Lybrand (1999a); and a FY97 survey of business executives worldwide carried out in the context of the World Bank's (1997b) *World Development Report*.

Results from the 1998 survey conducted by the World Economic Forum and Harvard Institute for International Development, which covered 23 African countries, ranked Tanzania's competitiveness in the lower and in the middle group (16th), indicating that the country is reforming, but is still saddled by its past reputation. The same survey incorporated two new indexes of investors' perceptions about changes in the business environment: the "improvement" and "optimism" indexes. Reforms of greatest interest to investors were identified to be those that enhance political and policy stability, openness to trade, transparency in the relationship between business and government, and improved infrastructure. Here Tanzania did quite well, ranking third on the improvement index for 1992–97 and second in the investor optimism index. In both cases investors showed strong expectations of continued improvement and little worry about reversals. Note, however, that perceptions about corruption and transparency showed limited improvement, as supported by the Transparency International 1999 survey. In the overall World Bank country assessment index (2000) combining transparency, accountability, and corruption in the public sector Tanzania is ranked among the middle group of African countries. In another study by the World Bank (1997b) on investor perceptions across 22 African countries four key indexes were generated following similar surveys. These were arbitrariness in bureaucratic practice (affecting transparency), regulatory hassles, regulatory obstacles, and service quality. Tanzania scored poorly in arbitrariness and regulatory hassles, ranking 19th and 14th respectively. However, in the World Economic Forum and the Harvard Institute for International Development (2000) survey Tanzania had improved its overall rank to 14th place (out of 24 countries), moving squarely to 1st place in the improvement index for 1996–99, while maintaining 2nd place in the optimism index. These observations are corroborated by the *Investor Roadmap* reports for Tanzania and the two private sector assessment surveys.

The *Tanzania Investment Roadmap* (Price Waterhouse Coopers and Lybrand 1999) notes that "there is still a legacy of old attitudes and approaches across much of the civil service and other Government institutions." The report goes on to state that these constraints cause delays, increase uncertainty, and reduce the confidence of investors. Clearly this translates into additional transaction costs for investors. In a precursor to the guide, the *Investor Roadmap to Tanzania*, (Price Waterhouse Coopers and Lybrand 1997) the consulting firm concludes that of the four countries where the exercise was undertaken, Tanzania offered the most difficult environment for establishing a new business. An average delay of 18 to 36 months to commence operations in Tanzania compares with 6 to 12 months for Namibia and 12 to 24 months in both Ghana and Uganda. The start-up process is viewed as being more ambiguous and less transparent in Tanzania than elsewhere.

Although Tanzania's scores in the *Institutional Investor* survey have improved in recent years, they remain significantly below those considered to be attractive to investors (table 5.6). *Institutional Investor* country risk ratings for 1998, whereby leading international banks grade countries on a scale of zero to 100, with 100 representing countries with the strongest business environment (or the least chance of sovereign default), ranked Tanzania as 20th out of 35 African countries. Tanzania comes out looking unfavorable against many regional contenders for private resources, its ratings consistently below even the average for Sub-Saharan Africa. Indeed, Tanzania's ranking slipped slightly from 106th out of 133 countries in 1998 to 109th out of 136 countries in early 1999. Among its peers, Kenya's performance during this same period mirrored that of Tanzania's, slipping marginally from 95th to 97th position, while Uganda improved its relative rank from 107th to 103rd. The 1998 *Institutional Investor* sustainability index, which measures a country's potential to attain rapid and sustainable long-term development, also gives Tanzania a low rating.

Table 5.6. *Comparison of Institutional Investor's Country Credit Ratings, Selected Countries, 1993– March 1999*

Country	1993	1995	1997	November 1998	March 1999
Botswana	41.1	48.5	51.2	51.9	—
Kenya	24.7	24.9	28.6	25.9	24.1
Mauritius	38.4	45.4	51.9	53.0	—
Swaziland	22.2	28.5	33.3	32.0	—
Tanzania	12.9	15.5	18.7	19.9	18.3
Uganda	7.3	12.8	20.1	19.9	20.3
Sub-Saharan Africa	18.7	19.9	21.9	23.3	—

— Not available.
Note: Rankings run from 0 to 100, with 100 representing countries with the strongest business environment.
Source : Institutional Investor 1993 and 1999.

The Economist Intelligence Unit's 1999 risk rating also gives Tanzania a low (D) rating on sovereign debt risk (table 5.7). It also notes concerns that the government may loosen its policy stance with regard to incurring further external borrowing and maintaining low levels of international reserves. Indeed, the liquidity risk remains low and the D rating reflects the low reserve levels and the stringency of monetary austerity measures, which have prompted a liquidity squeeze, short-circuiting increases in output and efficiency gains in the productive sectors. The Economist Intelligence Unit's overall investment risk rating for Tanzania has also remained almost unchanged at a poor overall D rating, notwithstanding the improvement in the score for currency risk as a result of reasonable stability of the Tanzanian shilling and downward pressure on the currency associated with buoyant demand for increasingly scarce foreign exchange.

Table 5.7. *Country Risk Ratings, Tanzania, Third Quarter of 1999*

Period	Overall rating	Overall score	Political risk	Economic policy risk	Economic structure risk	Liquidity risk
Current	D	61	D	C	C	D
Previous	D	61	D	C	C	D

Source: Economist Intelligence Unit.

The Heritage Foundation's scale for economic freedom runs from 1 to 5 (table 5.8). A score of 1 signifies a regime that is the most conducive to an economy without checks and restraints, while a score of 5 is least conducive. In 1999 Tanzania ranked 90th out of 160 countries with a score of 3.2. In 2001 Tanzania slipped to 110th position with a score of 3.5.

In 1998 Transparency International equated Tanzania with Nigeria in terms of the pervasiveness of official graft. While deemed a harsh, and even unfair, comparison by some, the reality is that since the mid-1980s the level of known rent-seeking by public employees has risen to unprecedented proportions. Both foreign and Tanzanian investors' perceptions about corruption and transparency coincide, and have showed limited improvement in recent years. This is confirmed by the most recent assessment by Transparency International, in which Tanzania ranked among the worst cases as far as investor perceptions are concerned: 81st of 85 countries reviewed (table 5.9).

Table 5.8. *Index of Economic Freedom, 1999 and 2001*

Country	1999 rank	1999 score	2001 rank	Score
Uganda	54	2.5	75	3.0
Tanzania	90	3.2	110	3.5
Kenya	75	3.1	87	3.1

Note: Scores run from 1 to 5, with 1 being the most conducive to economic development.
Source: Index of Economic Freedom: Heritage Foundation/*Wall Street Journal.*

Table 5.9. *Comparison of Transparency International's 1998 Corruption Index Rankings, Selected African Countries, 1998*

Country	Ranking (1= least corrupt)	Corruption perception index (1= most corrupt)
Botswana	23	6.1
Kenya	74	2.5
Mauritius	33	5.0
South Africa	32	5.2
Tanzania	81	1.9
Uganda	73	2.6
Zimbabwe	43	4.2

Note: Total number of countries ranked was 85.
Source: Transparency International.

These lingering perceptions of Tanzania's investment climate being unfriendly despite recent improvements partly reflect the longevity of the control and command heritage of the past and continued unsustainable debt overhang, which poses a risk of reversing the recent move toward budgetary discipline. It appears that while investors recognize the significant recent improvements in the policy environment, they still harbor doubts about Tanzania's ability and willingness to stay on course. Sustained implementation of macroeconomic and structural reforms is the key to firmly grounding investors' confidence in the country as a long-term destination for their resources. Creditors' recent decision to offer substantial debt relief to Tanzania under the enhanced HIPC initiative augurs well for future improvements in the perception of investors. As for corruption, it is not simply a matter of rooting out corrupt individuals, but also of plugging systemic weaknesses that offer opportunities for malfeasance as the Warioba report (URT 1997d) emphasizes. The government's recent efforts to develop a strategy for dealing with corruption and showing commitment to dealing with graft are steps in the right direction. However, full credibility will only come once serious implementation of the strategy has been carried out.

Major Challenges Confronting Private Sector Development

In FY97 a survey of business executives worldwide that focused on obstacles to doing business was carried out in the context of the World Bank's 1997 *World Development Report* (World Bank 1997b).Additional data on selected countries was gathered by researchers at the University of Basle, and the results of this work were synthesized in an International Finance Corporation paper (Pfeffermann, Kisunko, and Sumlinski 1999). The survey covered nearly 4,000 firms in 74 countries (an average of 55 firms per country), mostly in manufacturing and services, as well as some agri-businesses. The findings demonstrated the importance to private investment decisions of a few critical factors, including the rule of law, the predictability of judiciary systems, the real exchange rate, and the availability of financial resources for doing business. The last line of table 5.10 indicates the number of areas that 50 percent or more of the respondents in the respective country considered to be serious ("strong" and "very strong") obstacles. For Tanzania the top five constraints listed by managers in order of priority were nontransparent tax regulations and/or high taxes, followed by an inadequate supply of infrastructure (including financial infrastructure), corruption, and inflation. The only two areas identified as problem free by the Tanzanian respondents included the absence of terrorism followed by the absence of price controls. While offering a more conducive environment than such African countries as Madagascar and Nigeria, Tanzania must vie for attracting and keeping private investments with Malawi, Mauritius, Uganda, and other African countries viewed as having relatively fewer obstacles to doing business. While comparisons across countries must keep in mind the subjective nature of the survey results, the assessment points out that the average number of serious obstacles to doing business is 3.7 in the developing and transition countries and 1.5 in the advanced industrial countries.

Table 5.10. *Reported Obstacles to Doing Business in Selected Sub-Saharan Africa Countries (total number and ranking)*

Obstacle	Kenya	Tanzania	Uganda	Malawi	Mauritius	Madagascar
Unpredictability of the judiciary	—	—	—	—	—	1
Regulations for starting business/new operations	—	—	—	—	—	—
Price controls	—	—	—	—	—	—
Regulations on foreign trade (exports, imports)	—	—	—	—	—	—
Financing	5	3	3	—	—	8
Labor regulations	—	—	—	—	—	—
Foreign currency regulations	—	—	—	—	—	—
Tax regulations and/or high taxes	4	1	1	—	—	1
Inadequate supply of infrastructure	1	2	—	1	—	5
Policy instability	—	—	—	—	—	4
Safety or environmental regulations	—	—	—	—	—	—
Inflation	—	5	—	3	—	6
General uncertainty about costs of regulations	—	—	—	—	—	—
Crime and theft	2	—	—	2	—	7
Corruption	2	4	2	—	—	3
Terrorism	—	—	—	—	—	—
Other	—	—	—	—	—	—
Total number of serious obstacles per country	5	5	3	3	0	8

— Not available.
Source: Pfeffermann, Kisunko, and Sumlinski (1999).

Results from a 1994 survey of potential foreign investors for Eastern Africa and the findings of the more recent *Investor Roadmap* surveys and other consultations with the private sector undertaken in the context of various World Bank activities (including the Country Assistance Strategy; the first Programmatic

Structural Adjustment Credit, which focuses on private sector development; and this Country Economic Memorandum) corroborate the constraints identified by Tanzanian executives, with the exception of the concern about inflation. While inflation was an issue through the mid-1990s, prudent macroeconomic management by the government has brought inflation levels down from nearly 40 percent in 1993 to single digits since early 1999. Recent findings underscore the business community's discontent with a range of administrative or bureaucratic constraints that result in gratuitous delays and lower productive efficacy, thereby multiplying the operating costs of businesses. Tanzanian businesses are not highly competitive, and their relatively low quality of products and services has kept price levels subdued, while the high cost of credit, low labor productivity, inequitable utility rates, and multiplicity of taxes, including nuisance taxes, have led to shrinking profit margins. The Price Waterhouse Coopers and Lybrand (1997) study showed that Tanzanian business costs are almost 20 percent higher, on average, than their East and South African peers, while regulatory costs in Tanzania are some 15 percent above those in the rest of the region. The 1999 *Investment Roadmap* survey (Price Waterhouse Coopers and Lybrand 1999b) did not find any significant change in the relative costs of doing business in Tanzania.

Given the remarkable consensus across different categories of respondents on the most important constraints limiting the expansion and efficiency of the private sector in Tanzania, the discussion will focus on each of the key challenges in turn: the tax regime, the poor quality of infrastructure, the lack of microfinance and high transaction costs related to commercial finance, the administrative impediments toward doing business, the absence of a well-defined legal and judicial framework, and the pervasiveness of corruption.

High Costs of Doing Business: The Tax Regime

Since the mid-1980s the government has been increasingly concerned about its budgetary deficit, which has arisen partly out of its inability to collect sufficient tax revenue. Following the passage of legislation by Parliament in April 1995 and presidential assent in July 1995, the government established the TRA as an independent corporate body under the Ministry of Finance responsible for, among other things, administering the revenue laws and assessing, collecting, and accounting for revenues. The government also undertook other important measures, such as introducing the VAT in July 1998 and enacting the Investment Act in October 1997. In addition, because both the central and local governments impose taxes, the government appointed a task force to identify, rationalize, and harmonize these taxes. Notwithstanding these improvements, further measures, especially with respect to simplifying and rationalizing certain aspects of the direct and indirect taxes, have been identified and will form an agenda for action in the near future. Table 5.11 summarizes key problems of the tax regime, recent actions taken to address them, and areas for future action.

In addition, with the ongoing decentralization of fiscal operations to local levels, coordination of taxation between the center and local governments becomes critical to avoid double taxation and the proliferation of tax regimes. Harmonization of tax regimes with Tanzania's neighbors in the context of subregional arrangements has also been targeted as a way to attract investors on a wider scale. All these measures will also help broaden the tax base for the government to ameliorate the disproportionate burden falling on the narrow base of current major taxpayers and to increase revenues. The level of bureaucracy stemming from three different sets of administrative procedures and requirements of the three departments within the TRA (Customs and Excise, VAT, and Income Tax) have also been identified for action, and will target reducing unproductive, cascading taxes and the lack of transparency in the overall tax administration system.

COMPLEX TAX POLICY, HIGH TAX RATES, AND BUREAUCRACY. The central plank of the personal income tax regime is the Income Tax Act of 1973 as amended in 1994. The government has taken steps to reduce the complexity of the personal income tax structure by reducing the number of tax bands from 11 to 4 in

Table 5.11. *Specific Tax Regimes Constraints that Increase the Costs of Doing Business for the Private Sector*

Objectives [assumptions]	Measurable indicators	Proposed actions	Status	Pending actions
Removed major policy-related and institutional impediments to private investment and efficient business operations [*Sustained positive government disposition toward liberalization of markets and continued implementation of the reform program to rationalize functions and change attitudes toward the private sector; continue drive toward simplification and lowering of taxes*]	Reviewed tax policy to reduce trade taxes, remove nuisance taxes at various levels of government; removed bureaucratic barriers to export; operationalized tax appeals system; harmonized tariff system within East Africa and COMESA zone; contained tax evasion through porous borders to ensure fair competition, e.g., Zanzibar route; reduced the coverage of tax exemptions for transparency and raising the revenue base	Amend tax laws to Reduce the marginal income tax rates from 11% to 6 %	More transparent, rate categories reduced from 11 to 4 in PAYE (17.5%, 20%, 25%, 30%) based on fixed multiples of GDP per capita	Maintain the progressive, transparent PAYE system; develop auditing program
		Raise threshold and eliminate additional levies on payroll taxes	--threshold raised to TSh 45,000 from TSh 20,000	Eliminate VETA levy at 2% and housing levy at 4% (consolidate into nonearmarked levy in transition period)
		Simplify personal income tax for noncorporate businesses.	Maximum marginal rate reduced from 35%and matched with corporate tax at 30%; interest income at 30%; Treasury bill interest at 15%	Remove existing collection discrimination, which favors self-employed professional practitioners
		Take specific measures to encourage private investment	Depreciation of buildings raised from 4% to 5%; capital gains tax applied at 10%; stamp duties minimized; export tax on scrap metals abolished; harmonized TIC and non-TIC investors with full capital allowance; tariff on computers reduced from 20% to 5%	Rationalize capital gains tax; for businesses not under VAT introduce 3 fixed liability bands on business turnover using stamp duty assessment as basis for band
		Harmonize VAT and minimize exemptions	Harmonized and adopted in Zanzibar Jan. 1999; exemption to tourist air charter and approved drugs	Minimize exemptions and establish transparent criteria
		Minimize differential treatment in application of import duties of similar commodities	COMESA tariffs for all consumer goods, except beer; rate on capital goods, raw materials and replacement parts 0 or 5%	Minimize surtaxes and consolidate them into tariff bands for enhanced transparency of tariff regime.

Objectives [assumptions]	Measurable indicators	Proposed actions	Status	Pending actions
		Adopt 3 basic categories of products subject to tariffs	From 5 adopted 4 basic categories; reduced maximum rate to 25%	Reduce to 3 basic categories: final consumer goods, full processed inputs, raw materials and capital goods
		Equalize treatment of excise tax for domestic and imported goods	Done	
		Reduce the number of excisable commodities to only products that account for bulk of excise duty revenue		Eliminate all low-yield excisable items; reduce excisable goods to 6 that currently account for 99% of excise revenue; harmonize excise tax rate for these items
		Consolidate all taxes on petroleum to only VAT and excise duty to minimize administrative costs and leakage		Consolidate road toll and excise duty on petroleum, followed by other taxes on petroleum
		Carry out investor surveys to verify reduction in barriers to improved business along with regular supervision reports		Institutionalize annual independent surveys for monitoring the efficacy of implementation
Increased private investment in agriculture across small and large producers and marketing agents [Continued positive disposition of the government toward the liberalization of the sector and amendment of local government law]	Streamlined and rationalized agricultural taxation at local government level and rationalized central and local government taxation	Reduce pressure for proliferation and ad hoc taxes at the local government level and establish reasonable uniformity of taxation across localities to improve predictability. Official gazette for amendments of acts; supervision reports	1999/2000 budget harmonized jurisdiction of local and central tax authorities; raised share of revenue retained by local governments; shifted tax handles from center to local government; Tariff on tractor imports reduced from 5% to 0	Restrict ad hoc taxation; establish reasonable uniformity; remove double taxation across localities.

PAYE Pay as your earn
COMESA Common Market for Eastern and Southern Africa.
Source: Authors.

the current budget. This has lowered concerns with respect to equity and monitoring. The progressive income tax system allows for deductions of fringe benefits, which have contributed to further distorting the system while propagating loopholes and inequity. With respect to corporate taxes, Tanzania is likely to face significant and increasing revenue risks, primarily with respect to the corporate income tax, on account of the investment incentive regime. These incentives are provided at low investment thresholds, cover a broad class of investors, and provide long tax holidays. The preferential treatment of the mining sector is a case in point. Table 5.12 breaks down the direct taxes currently applicable to businesses and individuals.

Table 5.12. *Revenue Shares of Direct Taxes in Tanzania*

Type of tax	Percentage of direct taxes
Corporate tax	43
Pay as you earn (PAYE)	29
Withholding tax	10
Individual income tax	6
Other taxes (19 others)	12
Total	100
Direct taxes as a percentage of total TRA revenues	23-25

Source: TRA date; Price Waterhouse Coopers and Lybrand (1999b).

The absence of a streamlined tax administration system and the attendant level of bureaucracy are further compounded by the relatively high taxes being applied to various areas of private enterprise. Various interview reports (based on discussions with, among others, a number of Tanzanian entrepreneurs and representatives of private sector associations, financial institutions, and government bodies dealing with the private sector) relating to the 1999 private sector assessment indicate this as an issue. In particular, the taxes levied on small enterprises were viewed as being at prohibitive levels. Analysis carried out by Price Waterhouse Coopers and Lybrand indicates that about 25 different taxes and levies are imposed on the hotel and catering businesses, and that taxes make up the bulk of the costs of certain businesses. In the steel industry tax-related costs are put at the untenable level of 88 percent.

The corporate income tax rate for both resident and nonresident enterprises is 30 percent. The maximum VAT rate is 20 percent, compared with 17.5 percent in Uganda and 15 percent in Kenya. There are a number of withholding taxes, ranging from taxes on rent and interest income to dividends and pension or retirement annuities. Residents pay lower withholding taxes than nonresidents in some instances. The level of bureaucracy and related red tape while declining, needs further curtailing. In an interview report from the 1999 private sector assessment, a private sector respondent noted the level of harassment from the TRA. He pointed out that even if business owners are not cheating, the tax inspectors treat them like criminals. The value of imports is raised for tax purposes based on the assumption that they have been undervalued. The procedures for assessment and payment are extremely lengthy, and enable the inspectors to offer to take bribes to speed up the process. He noted further that importing items is particularly difficult.

LACK OF HARMONIZATION. As pointed out by the government task force appointed to look into the issue of local and central tax regimes, there is no clear jurisdiction between the agencies at these two levels. This leads to both agencies targeting the same sources for revenue, which results in double taxation in some cases. Revenue considerations lead local authorities to impose a variety of levies, but their revenue yields are questionable. Examples of the wide range of levies and fees include business license fees, property taxes, development levies, city service levies, parking levies, garbage collection levies, professional levies, motor vehicle licenses and fees, and crop and livestock cesses. This is complicated by the fact that most local governments have a weak tax administration infrastructure. As noted in the report of the task force, a reconsideration is needed of, among other things, the delegation of functions and responsibilities to local governments on the one hand, and the fiscal relations between the central and local governments on the other. This is particularly important in enforcing various measures promulgated via the Finance Acts.

THE TRADE REGIME. Tanzania has made good progress in reducing the anti-export bias of the past. The maximum tariff rate has been reduced to 25 percent from peaks in excess of 300 percent, as have the number of positive tariff bands, which are now down to 4. However, Tanzania still some way to go in removing barriers to trade, particularly within regional arrangements. Tables 5.13–5.16 compare Tanzania's position in relation to its peers.

Poor Quality and Inadequacy of Infrastructure

The poor state of Tanzania's physical infrastructure is a major detriment to private sector takeoff, as efficacious infrastructure is a key to "crowding in" domestic and foreign investments. The provision of basic infrastructure and utilities in Tanzania is in public hands, and the poor quality of infrastructure continues to be a major deterrent both to growth in investment levels and to improvements in productivity rates. The often inefficient parastatals and other government agencies responsible for providing utilities and transport services face major financial and operational problems. As a result the coverage and/or depth of facilities is extremely limited and service quality is poor. Lengthy delays in providing connection, high connection charges and tariffs, unreliable service, and generally low-grade service have been the bane of Tanzania's infrastructure (table 5.17).

Table 5.13. *Tariff Structures, Selected African Countries*

Country	Maximum/mini- mum import tariff tates (%)	Number of nonzero rates	Incorporate other duties or charges into tariff	Preference margin (%)	Trade-weighted average tariff rate (%)
Kenya, October 1999	0/25	3	No	80	12.3
Tanzania, April 2000	0/25	4	Yes	80	13.6
Uganda, October 1999	0/15	2	No	80	10.7
Zambia, October 1999	0/25	3	Yes	60	11.4

Source: Cross-Border Initiative (2000).

Table 5.14. *Tariff Exemptions, Selected African Countries, End of 1998*

	Category of exemptions					
Country	Government	Parastatals	Investment code or general convention	Recognized NGOs	Goods for foreign-financed projects	Other (includes discretionary waivers/exemptions)
Kenya	Yes	No	Yes	Yes	Yes	Yes
Tanzania	Yes	Yes	Yes	Yes	Yes	No
Uganda[a]	No	No	No	No	No	No
Zambia	No	No	Yes	Yes	Yes	Yes

a. Although no exemptions are shown, there are limited exemptions on goods for the president's use, for diplomats, and by statutory instruments.
Source: Cross-Border Initiative (2000).

Table 5.15. *Import Nontariff Barriers, Selected African Countries, End of 1998*

Country	Quantitative restrictions		Licensing requirements		State trading monopolies	Discriminatory taxes (excise/VAT)	Other (countervailing duties, dumping)
	Bans	Quotas	All products	Certain products			
Kenya	No	No	No	No	No	Yes	No
Tanzania	No	No	No	No	No	Yes	No
Uganda	Yes	No	No	No	No	Yes	No
Zambia	No	No	No	No	No	Yes	No

Source: Cross-Border Initiative (2000).

Table 5.16. *Export Trade Regime, Selected African Countries, End of 1998*

Country	Quantitative bans	Quantitative restrictions	Restrictive licensing	Duties	Marketing monopolies
Kenya	No	No	Yes	No	No
Tanzania	No	No	No	No	No
Uganda	No	No	No	No	No
Zambia	Yes	No	No	No	No

Source: Cross-Border Initiative (2000).

Table 5.17. *Time Taken for Utility Connections in Eight Towns*
(days)

Service	Median delays	Maximum delay	Minimum delay
Telephone	27	202	8
Electricity	26	364	39
Water	5	82	1

Source: Economic and Social Research Foundation (ESRF), Tanzania: USAID-ESRF Roadmap Survey on Customers; Survey Benchmarks (April 1998).

The government is taking steps to address some of the issues in roads and railways (internal transportation), ports and shipping, power, telecommunications, and water, mainly by privatizing the state-owned utilities and by establishing autonomous regulatory and administrative agencies. The poor quality of services offered has meant inadequate and low-grade facilities, combined with relatively high costs per unit, for example, from power tariffs and days lost in shipping. These issues are likely to continue to impinge on productivity and new investment levels for several years (see table 5.18 for comparative costs across East Africa). Despite some improvements since the mid-1990s, Tanzania's indicators for infrastructure services are considerably below the averages for Africa.

The utility and transport sectors are also plagued by the absence of a well-defined regulatory environment; the existing legislative structure is not deemed to be supportive of future expansion by the productive sectors. The proposed creation of a multisectoral regulator for utilities and another regulating agency for the transport sector with clear mandates, decisionmaking capacity, and adequate resources to carry out their functions would greatly assist in ameliorating the situation. However, further work on the external factors that may negatively affect the decisionmaking process of such agencies and the related approval procedures is necessary to ensure the design of a system that is largely impervious to exogenous pressures or lobbying.

Table 5.18. *Comparative Utility Costs across Selected East African Countries (US$)*

Service	Kenya	Tanzania	Uganda
Electricity (kwh)	0.035	0.073	0.075
Water (cubic meters)	0.56	0.104	0.0014
Industrial fuel (liter)	0.373	0.353	0.489
Telecommunications (per minute)			
To the United States	3.36	5.63	4.30
To COMESA	1.64	5.52	1.61

COMESA Common Market for Eastern and Southern Africa.
Source: Economic Research Bureau, University of Dar-es-Salaam.

The erratic, inadequate, and expensive power supply is among the top complaints by the private sector (coverage is estimated at a little over 5 percent of the population in mainly urban areas). Electricity costs are some 215 percent higher in Tanzania than in Kenya and nearly sevenfold the charges in South Africa. Furthermore, the tariffs applied by the Tanzania Electric Supply Company (TANESCO) have been rising, while the quality of service remains relatively substandard. Since 1996 the tariffs for residential, small-scale commercial and industrial usage (average monthly consumption below 7,500 kilowatt hours) have jumped by a massive 44 percent. For low voltage supply (400 volts) and average monthly consumption of less than 7,500 kilowatt hours, the tariff has increased by 23 percent. A 32 percent price hike has been applied to the primarily industrial users requiring high voltage supply, and public lighting and Zanzibar supply charges have been increased by 31 and 19 percent, respectively.

Notwithstanding the foregoing, the financial and operational viability of the state utility, TANESCO, has been severely strained by low billings and poor collection rates over several years. Indeed, a poor payment record by the public sector has been a key source of TANESCO's problems. While energy production by TANESCO, which accounts for more than three-fifths of the total power supply, grew by some 15 percent between FY95 and FY97, the available supply level is estimated at being well below total demand for production and consumption purposes, and most businesses have backup generators and capacity banks as antidotes to load shedding (albeit this is improving), voltage fluctuations, and burn-outs.

Another principal area of concern has been the lack of an adequate and well-maintained road network. The road network of about 80,000 kilometers in a country with a total area of 945,000 kilometers and a population of about 32 million provides meager coverage. This situation is compounded by poor road conditions due to the state of serious disrepair into which a large percentage of the existing road network has fallen. Almost 70,000 kilometers are regional and rural roads, mostly unpaved, and the balances consists of trunk roads. Notwithstanding the Road Fund (funded mostly via fuel taxes) established in 1998 in an attempt to ensure the availability of funds to maintain roads, only minimal maintenance work has been undertaken. The result has been wide-scale degradation of the road network, with many roads, especially the local networks, practically impassable during the rainy seasons and attendant implications for backward and forward linkages with markets and urban centers. Cargo and passenger transport facilities are offered by the Air Tanzania Corporation; the Tanzania Railways Corporation, which serves the northern and central areas; and Tanzania Zambia Railways, which serves the south and offers a link to southern Africa via Zambia. Both the air and rail parastatals have been affected by low traffic volumes and financial difficulties. The Tanzania Harbors Authority, which runs the four major mainland ports on the Indian Ocean, is currently undergoing a major rehabilitation and expansion program, and its container terminal in Dar es Salaam has recently been leased out to private operators. The Dar es Salaam port's annual handling capacity for dry cargo is expected to increase by more than 25 percent to 2.5 million tons (in addition to a 4.5 million ton capacity for liquid cargo).

Tanzania has been making some progress in expanding its telecommunications services, although it still has a long way to go. The mobile telephone network is growing rapidly, with a number of private companies now competing in the Tanzanian market, which was once the sole preserve of the Tanzania Telecommunications Company, Limited. Notwithstanding the issuance of mobile and cellular licenses to private operators such as Mobitel and TriTel, as well as the entry of radio paging and data communication operators, the private presence in the sector is still inadequate to foster the much needed competition for lower costs. Telephone density in Tanzania is one of the lowest in the world, at 0.32 sets per 100 inhabitants, and costs are relatively high. The telephone density levels in Kenya are nearly triple those in Tanzania and tariffs are considerably lower.

Similar issues obstruct the provision of water for productive purposes. There is no regular and adequate water supply for private sector usage (or for domestic consumption for that matter) in Dar es Salaam. The last Price Waterhouse Coopers and Lybrand *Investor Roadmap* notes that in other urban areas the water supply is more regular, albeit the pressure (throughout the main system) is abnormal, ranging from 0 to 30 pounds per square inch. Theft and leakage from the water system are responsible for close to a third of the total water supply being lost. Average installation costs for businesses near a main water line are put at about US$1,500. Smaller businesses are assessed at a flat monthly rate, ranging from about US$15 per month to about US$90 per month (for instance, for brickmakers or irrigation purposes). Metered rates of US$1.7 per 1,000 gallons apply to water usage by larger industrial concerns.

Inadequate Micro, Rural, and Corporate Financial Services

Although Tanzania has made some progress in reforming and liberalizing the financial sector, a number of weaknesses and deficiencies still remain in the provision of financial services. The financial market is still fragmented and relatively shallow. Competition in the sector remains weak, as reflected by the wide spread between banks' borrowing and lending rates: real deposit rates currently average 3 percent, while real lending rates are nearly 13 percent. There are large buildups of overdrafts or nonperforming commercial bank assets, which endanger the solvency of the banking system. Commercial banking activities continue to be highly concentrated in urban centers mainly financing trade-related activities, while agriculture remains starved of credit, hampering the development of the sector. Payment and clearing systems remain inefficient. On average it takes three or four days to clear a check within the city of Dar es Salaam and up to two weeks in rural areas. An assessment of the sector's efficacy is now necessary to chart out a strategy for deepening the reform and liberalization process to spur greater efficiency. Furthermore, significant gaps that have emerged in the provision of rural finance services following the folding up of development banks have not been addressed by the private sector. Credit to agriculture has seen a particularly sharp drop from 20 percent of total credit to 6 percent over the last decade. The contractual savings subsector now comprises 10 insurance companies (up significantly from the original 2) and the state-run pension plans (the National Social Security Fund and the Parastatal Pension Fund), but markets remain underdeveloped and are dominated by one or two larger players, contributing to continued inefficiencies in these sectors. Tanzania's capital market has yet to mature; it remains shallow and weak with low liquidity levels. These weaknesses will have to be addressed if a robust response from private investors is to be expected. The deepening of the reforms and continued privatization in the sector is expected to foster higher competition and efficiency; however, the road ahead is long and fraught with complexities.

RURAL AND MICROFINANCE SERVICES. With the collapse of the cooperatives and the CRDB and the splitting up of the NBC essentially along commercial-rural and microfinance lines into the NBC (97) and the National Microfinance Bank (NMB), the key traditional channels for rural and microfinance credit have dried up. Initiatives are currently under way to strengthen the microfinance system, and the policy governing its operation has been approved. The process of setting up microfinance banks to cater to small rural investors has benefited from lessons of successful experiences in Asia, for example, the Grameen Bank. To fill this vacuum rural cash crop producers and others are forming savings and credit cooperative organizations. The system remains unregulated, however, and the cooperatives often suffer from the lack of even basic accounting and financial skills.

THE BANKING SECTOR. While to a large extent inefficiencies in the operation of the largest commercial banks, the NBC (97) and the NMB, have influenced the overall high cost of credit to producers and traders, there is a need to begin addressing the low competitiveness in the financial sector as a whole more vigorously. In this respect, even though significant progress has been made since liberalization efforts began in 1991 with the passage of the Banking and Financial Institutions Act, the country's banking sector remains weak. Among the issues facing the sector are urban concentration, low deposit mobilization, "sticky" lending, and high interest rate spreads that cast doubts on the competitiveness and efficiency of the banking sector. Despite the existence of 17 commercial banks, 10 nonbank financial institutions, and 105 foreign exchange bureaus, 3 banks continue to account for about 85 percent of the deposit market, which is geographically concentrated mainly in Dar es Salaam, with a total balance sheet of about US $2 billion equivalent. Real monetary liabilities have continued to decline despite the liberalization, with the fall in deposits due to the restructuring of the former NBC and the slow response of deposit rates to decreasing inflation, thereby reducing the real gains to investors. Savings rates range from 2 to 12 percent, while in 1998 total deposits were only about 3 percent of GDP.

Credit growth, especially to the productive sector, has been lackluster. Private banks continue to maintain high minimum deposit balances and to lend to a small group of low-risk, high-value customers. Small and medium urban enterprises and the rural population continue to have limited access to banking services. In addition, most lending is short term, largely because of the difficulties the banks face in mobilizing term deposits to match their assets and liabilities. Lending to deposit ratios have declined considerably from more than 150 percent in 1991 to less than 35 percent in 1998. Concomitant with this, the commercial banks' investment in risk-free government paper increased almost 100 times from T Sh 3.5 billion in 1991 to more than T Sh 300 billion in 1998. The lending rates have remained unresponsive, not moving in line with inflation. This is in part explained by the perceived high-risk structure of the economy (including protracted dispute resolution), and structural rigidities also make it difficult for commercial banks to assess the creditworthiness of private borrowers. In addition, the banks are likely to be passing on some of their own high transaction costs to borrowers. An indication of banks' own operating cost levels is that they are required to submit more than 200 formal reports per year to the Bank of Tanzania. Another constraint to bank lending thus far has been the significant level of restrictions on the provision of collateral. In particular, the inability to use land as collateral has proved to be a major impediment in this regard. As discussed further later, effective implementation of the recently amended Land Law would be necessary to address this problem.

CONTRACTUAL SAVINGS INSTITUTIONS. The deregulation of the insurance industry commenced with the enactment of the Insurance Act in October 1996, which led to the creation of the National Insurance Board in 1998. The insurance industry mainly suffers from the predominance of the National Insurance Corporation of Tanzania, Limited (NIC) and the lack of local or regional insurers. Insurance and pension funds provide the only major collective investment schemes. The NIC, which has functioned as a state monopoly since 1967, still accounts for 55 percent of the general insurance market, mainly from public sector clients, and 98 percent of that for life insurance. It has a large asset base and is significantly overstaffed. Jubilee Insurance, one of the first competitors to enter the industry, holds 12 percent of the general insurance market, with the rest divided among another eight companies.

Although the government has embarked on transforming pension funds from their exclusive focus on retirement into social security arrangements with pensions organized around a defined benefit principle, the implementation of these reforms remains incomplete. While there are currently four pension funds (of which three are private), the market is dominated by the Parastatal Pension Fund created in 1987. Nevertheless, only a small percentage of the labor force, 5.1 percent in 1990, has pension coverage. In 1998 the National Provident Fund was legally converted into a social security arrangement covering pensions and other benefits. As the parastatals are privatized, the Parastatal Pension Fund has made some efforts to extend its coverage to include the private sector.

The high contribution rates to the public pension system compared with other countries, 20 percent of salaries, hinders the development of private funds. The issues facing these funds are manifold, most of them related to management. The difficulties in managing the pension reserve funds have been aggravated by limited investment opportunities in the economy. A weak collection and enforcement mechanism, as well as the lack of appropriate investment guidelines, are perhaps the most obvious problems of the pension funds. The result is poor customer service orientation, including low benefit levels and long lead times to process claims; high administrative costs; lower than potential returns on the portfolio; and limited participation in supporting economic growth.

CAPITAL MARKETS. At the onset of financial sector reforms in 1991 there were no capital or money markets, and foreign exchange controls limited current and capital account transactions. Government bonds and treasury bills were the only securities issued, and these were held by the state-owned insurance company (NIC), the National Provident Fund, and the Parastatal Pension Fund. The Bank of Tanzania introduced treasury bill auctions in 1993, and currently sells treasury bills of 91-, 182-, and 364-day maturities in the primary market through weekly auctions. Since May 1996 the bank has issued the 91-day repurchase bill as its own paper, using it for open market operations, and the government uses the 182- and 364-day treasury bills to finance its deficit. Despite the appointment of primary dealers, secondary markets are nonexistent and the role of these dealers as market makers is in question.

The Foreign Exchange Act was enacted in 1992, providing for the establishment of currency bureaus and allowing residents to hold foreign currency deposits in domestic banks. Controls on the exchange auctions have also been eased, and the currency is now allowed to float freely, with the Bank of Tanzania intervening periodically to reduce excessive fluctuations and to increase official international reserves. This measure was enacted to provide incentives for inflows of foreign investment. The Capital Markets and Securities Act was enacted in 1994 to encourage greater private sector participation in the development of capital markets, which facilitated the formulation of the regulatory framework for capital market institutions and the stock exchange. The Dar es Salaam Stock Exchange was officially opened for business in April 1998. At the time of writing, the exchange has had three equity and one debt listings. The stock exchange is regulated by the Tanzanian Capital Markets Authority, which was developed along the lines of Kenya's Capital Markets Authority. In this respect, even though Tanzania has seen significant inflows of funds recorded as net private transfers, the potential remains far greater. This potential is related to a large extent to the repatriation of proceeds associated with unrecorded exports.

Major Administrative Barriers to Private Investment.

Since the early 1990s government programs have focused on addressing institutional constraints hampering private sector development; however, further improvements are required. One important area is to change the attitudes of personnel in public institutions that are part of the chain of doing business, including the TRA, the Tanzania Licensing Authority, the Immigration Department, the Labor Department, and sectoral ministries to become more responsive to inquiries from the private sector and to improve service delivery. The legacy of public servants as controllers rather than as facilitators of private sector activity is still prevalent and needs to be reversed. Institutions at the front line of private sector support need to be geared up to respond quickly and positively to exigencies and to work with in partnership the private sector. This may require reorientation or educational programs for public servants focusing on how the private sector operates and the suitable public response mechanisms. It also requires a re-examination of the structure and procedures of such government institutions as the Investment Promotion Center and the TIC with dualistic or overlapping, complex, and at times unclear mandates. Equally important is the sustained reform of the regulatory and administrative system, which is critical to reducing the cost of doing business and ensuring that the procedures in use are applied consistently and efficiently.

As noted earlier, a series of private sector roadmap surveys (supported by the USAID) have been carried out in the past four years. These surveys focused on identifying the major administrative barriers to investment in Tanzania. These were grouped under the broad rubrics of employment issues, business location issues, reporting to the government, and constraints to business operation. The six areas identified as deserving priority attention due to poor relations with customers and procedural problems were (a) import clearance, (b) business and trade licensing, (c) expatriate permits, (d) investor immigration permits, (e) land acquisition, and (f) planning approvals. Subsequently, a survey on access to services at the local government level (municipalities and towns) was carried out. Maximum delays of 250 days (median of 18 days) in issuing business licenses (schedule II and III) and maximum delays of 80 days (median delays of 14 days) in issuing building permits by local authorities in eight cities were recorded. The minimum delay was one day in either case. The problems arise not simply from Tanzanian public servants' fears of "foreignization" or a return to economic colonization, but also from the proliferation of government agencies and the multiplicity of "applicable" procedures. Table 5.19 provides a vivid illustration of the host of administrative procedures (several of these comprising a number of steps each) to be completed by a foreign investor gearing up to do business in Tanzania. A system to monitor improvements has been established through repeat surveys. Table 5.19 also provides information on progress in each of these areas.

The government set up the TIC to enable it to respond better to the needs of the private sector. Notwithstanding its good intentions, and despite some improvements, a number of areas requiring action remain unattended since the enactment of the 1997 Investment Act, which emphasizes the facilitative role of the TIC. Even though the TIC's focus is supposed to be business promotion and facilitation and not granting fiscal incentives, the TIC remains mired in its old ways. Investment procedures remain largely unchanged and the TIC's activities are still centered on project screening and approval. Of the roughly 40 employees of the TIC, fewer than a quarter are professionals, and to add to the problem most of these are seconded from various ministries and have little knowledge of the private sector. There are no incentives for the employees to follow-through on their new role. Monitoring remains based on the issuance of certificates rather than on new investments. The considerable time and effort that must be expended to obtain TIC certificates as well as licenses and permits from other government bodies translate into high opportunity costs and considerable frustration to investors. The investors obviously value these certificates as they provide substantial fiscal incentives. Unfortunately, the incentives are provided on an ad hoc basis and are extremely generous in many cases. Stories of corruption are rampant. In addition, frequent disagreements with the TRA on the validity of the tax exemptions adds to investors' frustrations even after they have invested substantial sums within the country. Given that existing investors are an important mouthpiece for future, potential investors, this is of serious concern.

Deficiencies in the Legal and Judicial Framework

The absence of a transparent and supportive legal and regulatory framework has clearly been an issue affecting private sector operations. A key deficiency in the legal framework is in the area of enforceable property rights. The process of legal reforms has lagged behind such that in its current state it cannot support the operations of a market-oriented economy. Banks operating in Tanzania still face not only the problem of nonrepayment of credit extended to individual borrowers, but also fail to realize collateral on overdue debts. The time needed to process the recovery of debts through the courts remains excessively long, and the outcome of the legal process is unpredictable, leading to a general lack of confidence in the judicial system. This lack of confidence has tended to have a negative effect on the ability of private firms to raise capital through credits. At the same time, Tanzania is only now embarking on the process of establishing commercial courts. A genuine commercial orientation of the existing judicial system (in line with the shift to a market-based economy) has yet to come about, including the required change in attitudes of the judiciary. The task of dealing with entrenched vested interests requires a strong resolve for credible action. Clearly there are also problems of capacity within the judicial system in terms of resources, manpower, and facilities, which need to be addressed expeditiously.

Table 5.19. *Major Administrative Barriers to Investment*

Issues	Status
Employment issues • Residency permits • Labor relations (flexibility in hiring and firing)	• Right to 5 expatriate employees without extensive scrutiny; improved Department of Immigration procedures via "green channel" for TIC certified investors; reduced delays • Labor laws under review by the government
Location issues • Land purchase • Transferring deeds • Developing land • Utility hookups	• Land laws revised; effective implementation necessary to address issues of purchase and title • Procedural/regulatory simplifications introduced by Dar es Salaam, Mwanza governments, Registrar of Companies, Internal Trade Section, Industrial Licensing Board, and others • Privatization and regulatory framework being introduced for key utilities
Reporting to the government • Business registration • Incentives • Environmental compliance • Tax registration and reporting	• Increased procedural/regulatory simplifications and improvement in communications under way now in the TIC, Registrar of Companies, Ministry of Lands, TRA, National Environmental Management Council, and others leading to improvements
Constraints to business operation • Importing • Exporting • Profit repatriation	• Import/export procedures have improved; single bill of entry, reduced number of goods requiring preshipment inspection, random inspection system (an automated system for customs duties administration) adopted; computerization of some customs functions; capital goods tariff rates lowered and qualifying system simplified • Capital account liberalized; 1997 Investment Act guarantees unconditional transferability of net profits; dividends; servicing payments for foreign loans; royalties; fees; technology transfer charges; liquidation proceeds remittance; emoluments; other benefits paid to foreign personnel employed in Tanzania for businesses to which the act applies

Source: Price Waterhouse Coopers and Lybrand (1997, 1999b).

The existing ordinances, particularly those that have a bearing on private sector development, are weak and need to be revised. The main areas where redrafting of the laws are urgently needed include corporate law, contract law, bankruptcy law, and labor law to eliminate the vestiges of the past control regime. Reforms would target creating a level playing field for private investment and doing business. The revision of the various laws has to be accompanied by legal reforms to ensure that the laws are applied properly and to ensure legal support for claims for payment and for property rights. In the same vein it will be important to revisit the new Land Law to include provisions that will enable or provide for the use of land as collateral to obtain credit from banks. An overhaul of outdated laws is vital, for instance, the provisions concerning limited companies are contained in the Tanzania Companies Ordinance Cap 212, which is modeled closely on the U.K. Companies Act of 1948. The new Land Act still refers to the 1922 British law on the procedures for using land as collateral. Labor markets in Tanzania are not entirely free of policy-induced distortions. This is especially visible in the archaic laws for firing workers, which limit the options available to employers for removing poor performers or for changing the profile of the work force in response to changing market requirements.

Corruption

Widespread corruption in the public sector has led to massive economic losses in terms of reduced income from taxes, revenues, and other fiscal charges; loss of income from natural resources; and losses through misappropriation of government assets. The deteriorating and inadequate quality of physical and social services delivered by the government bears witness to the paucity of resources, – as often due to the diversion or abuse of resources as to inadequate levels of funding.

In addition to the usual crime prevention and law enforcement agencies, Tanzania has four other agencies combating corruption: the Prevention of Corruption Bureau, the Permanent Commission of Enquiry, now the Commission of Human Rights and Administrative Justice; the Ethics Secretariat for top political and administrative leaders; and the Inspectorate of Ethics within the Civil Service Department for all other public servants. In view of the lack of coordination among government agencies (as well as the donor community) in this regard, there is great potential for overlap of mandates and duplication of functions among these agencies. The agencies have relatively little impact both individually or collectively, and are generally perceived as lacking teeth. At the same time, there also remains much room for interagency rivalry and conflict. Much needs to be done to rationalize the agencies' functions, establish clear linkages, and strengthen their capacity.

Government Actions to Promote Sustainable Private Sector Growth

This section focuses on actions that the government is undertaking to support increased private sector productivity through making better use of existing capacity and fostering fresh private investment. First, the most critical factors for ensuring a robust private investment response and greater efficiency in the allocation of private resources include the stability of the macroeconomic environment and the efficiency of markets as they influence business expectations and operative costs. While not direct line item contributors to business costs, macroeconomic uncertainty (including the risk of policy reversals), sovereign risk (expropriation, default), and risks associated with political instability (safety of property), these risks can be paramount in creating a pejorative environment for private operators. A key concern is the lingering inhospitable attitudes in the public service toward the private sector and apathy toward private initiative born of the control economy ideology. However, equally damaging are the vested interests or protectionist stances of those elements in the private sector that cannot effectively make the transition to the more open and increasingly competitive business environment. While the government has made significant progress in stabilizing the economy and removing most gross policy distortions, the emphasis here is on how to sustain this positive environment and ensure the removal of underlying pressures for possible reversals.

Second are those factors with a direct bearing on the competitiveness of the business sector and greater contestability in markets that are needed to spur efficiency in business through competition and ensure a level playing field. These affect profit margins and/or the operational efficiency of businesses and have muffled a private sector resurgence in Tanzania. They include the trade barriers that raise the cost of imports to local businesses, the elevated costs of financial resources, the high taxation, and the poor availability and high costs of infrastructure services. The institutional impediments to investment and business operation, including deficiencies in the legal framework, weak enforcement of property rights, and corruption, are key areas requiring strong resolve, institutional restructuring, and an overhaul of staff competencies and attitudes. The key areas of government "intervention" include policy and structural actions for enhanced corporate competitiveness and performance through the establishment of a structured public/private sector dialogue mechanism. The dialogue mechanism would allow the government and the private sector to work collaboratively and in close partnership to put in place the basic prerequisites for a dynamic and competitive private sector. Such prerequisites include

- Secure and flexible transactions, with private sector operators possessing the liberty, flexibility, and security to acquire, use, and leverage property rights (real, tangible, and intellectual)
- Nonintrusive, efficient, and credible public administration that sets widely understood rules for economic activity, enforces them objectively across the board in a predictable fashion, and when necessary changes them in a transparent manner
- Competitive markets that promote mobility of products, capital, labor, and knowledge through simple, transparent, and objectively applied incentive and regulatory systems
- Efficient and responsive social, physical, and technological infrastructure, including investments in information infrastructure to ensure availability and easy access to quality data, that increases the economy's long-term competitiveness and reduces transaction costs.

Stable Policy Environment

Over the past five years the government has deepened the implementation of its macroeconomic policy reform program with the objective of creating a more stable macroeconomic environment. This overarching target was pursued with the understanding that such stability was a necessary condition for achieving sustained growth, which itself is essential for reducing the pervasive poverty in the country. As a result, Tanzania has made significant progress toward reestablishing macroeconomic stability. It is now imperative to ensure that such stability is sustained in order to firmly root the confidence of investors and other economic agents. At the same time greater effort needs to be directed at deepening complementary structural reforms and strengthening institutional structures to elicit a supply response from the private sector.

Macroeconomic stability and growth have re-emerged, providing evidence of sensible policies now taking root. Tanzania has registered a significant improvement in macroeconomic performance, with real GDP growth reaching 3.8 percent in 1995–98, and inflation fell from nearly 40 percent earlier in the 1990s to 7.4 percent in late 1999, its lowest level in 25 years. The economic resilience of Tanzania is demonstrated by its capacity to grow even when affected by the El Niĝo-induced adverse weather conditions. The fiscal situation improved from a 5 percent deficit in FY95 to a surplus of 0.8 percent in FY99. The brunt of adjustment was initially on government expenditure, but in the past two years the government has given priority—in the context of the Medium-Term Expenditure Framework and the annual public expenditure reviews—to the sectors that have a larger impact on poverty, such as education, health, water, rural roads, and agriculture. This process has been reinforced by the conditions of the Multilateral Debt Fund,[21] and more recently under the HIPC initiative, which seek to protect expenditures earmarked for these priority sectors. On the revenue side, Tanzania's tax revenue has reached an average of 13 percent of GDP over the past four years, which nevertheless is still below the African average of 15 percent. In additional, the exchange rate remained reasonably stable for the 8 months prior to the recent nearly 15

---

[21] The aim of the Multilateral Debt Fund, supported by bilateral donors, is to help the government meet multilateral debt service obligations. The relief, tied to the budget, is conditional on the government's commitment to sustain budgetary allocations to the priority sectors: education, health, water, and roads.

percent depreciation, and the foreign reserves position has climbed from about 6 weeks of merchandise imports in 1995 to the current level of 18 weeks.

What is perhaps more noteworthy in these achievements is the steady decline in inflation over the past five years, including the years when drought and floods adversely affected growth and revenue collection. This augurs well for the positive perceptions of credible and tenacious macroeconomic management among consumers and investors. If this trend is maintained, Tanzania should be able to reduce its inflation rate to that obtaining in the economies of its major trading partners, and hence considerably reduce the pressures of maintaining the international competitiveness of its export and tourism business. Furthermore, such an achievement would also enhance the stability of the shilling's exchange rate.

There have been dualistic concerns regarding the movement of the exchange rate from exporters (when it appreciates) and importers (when it depreciates). The government has typically desisted from intervening to influence the level of exchange rate, given that Tanzania has chosen the path of a monetary approach to stabilization and has left the exchange rate to be market determined. This choice is probably the best given the limitations of various interventionist options. Intervention through open market operations in the market for foreign exchange is hardly tenable given the limited size of the reserves under the Bank of Tanzania. Experience from other countries with greater reserves (Kenya and Zimbabwe) has shown that this option was unworkable against currency slides prompted by changes in fundamentals and proved to be disastrous to the reserve position. The option that the Bank of Tanzania has so far pursued is to bring down inflation to the level in Tanzania's major trading partners. This approach has two advantages. First, it ensures that there is no appreciation of exchange rate on the basis of purchasing power parity; and second, it eliminates or minimizes government intervention, and thereby political pressures on the exchange rate. The approach must be supplemented by judicious sterilization of capital flows and booms in export earnings, which generate pressure on the local currency, pushing it to appreciate.

In parallel to the macroeconomic reforms, the government also embarked on structural reforms focusing on realigning the incentive structure toward increased exports, making more efficient use of the scarce foreign exchange, liberalizing markets for goods and services, and reducing the involvement of the public sector in commercial activities. Many of the gross economic distortions have been dealt with effectively. Though still fragile and shallow, markets are relatively freer; the parastatal sector is considerably smaller; and a significant improvement in fiscal discipline has been registered, particularly through enforcing cash budgets. In addition, more than half of the 400 public enterprise have been privatized, and the banking system has been opened up to private sector participation, which now accounts for nearly half of the sector's presence.[22] In keeping with the rolling back of government's participation in various productive sectors, the civil service is being reduced and rationalized and civil service salaries are being brought in line with market levels. The critical legislative reform of the Land Act was undertaken in February 1999 to strengthen transparency in ownership and facilitate its administration.

International country risk rating agencies are noticing this positive track record. The 1999 country policy and institutional assessment index for less developed countries places Tanzania squarely with the cohort of the better African performers in terms of economic management, structural policies, and policies for social inclusion and equity (table 5.20).[23]

Comparisons with the benchmark countries like Côte d'Ivoire and Malawi demonstrate that Tanzania's overall rating of 3.6 indicates that the country is moving in the right direction, and is considerably stronger than the average for Sub-Saharan Africa in all these areas (3.0). However, Tanzania's

---

[22] In 1997 the NBC was restructured into the NMB and the NBC. The NBC was privatized in December 1999, and the NMB was put under private management in August 1999.
[23] Assessment carried out annual on a regional basis by the World Bank Group.

Table 5.20. *Country Policy and Institutional Assessments for Africa, 1999*

Assessment	Botswana	Kenya	Mauritius	Mozambique	Tanzania	Uganda	Avg SSA
				Country			
Economic management							
Management of inflation policy and currency	5.0	3.5	4.0	4.0	4.0	4.5	3.3
Fiscal policy	4.5	3.5	4.0	4.5	4.5	5.0	3.2
Management of external debt	6.0	4.5	5.0	4.5	4.0	5.0	3.4
Management and sustainability of development program	4.5	3.0	4.5	3.5	4.0	4.0	2.9
Average	5.0	3.6	4.4	4.1	4.1	4.6	3.2
Structural policies							
Trade policy and foreign exchange regime	4.0	4.5	4.5	4.0	4.0	4.5	3.6
Financial stability and depth	4.0	2.0	2.5	3.0	2.5	2.5	2.7
Banking sector efficiency and resource mobilization	4.0	3.0	4.5	3.0	3.0	3.5	3.0
Competitive environment for private sector	4.0	3.0	5.0	3.5	3.0	5.0	3.1
Factor and product markets	4.0	3.5	4.0	3.5	4.0	5.0	3.2
Policies and institutions for environmental sustainability	4.0	2.5	4.5	3.0	3.0	3.5	2.8
Average	4.0	3.1	4.5	3.3	3.3	4.0	3.1
Policies for social inclusion and equity							
Equality of economic opportunity	4.0	3.0	3.5	3.5	4.0	4.0	3.0
Equality of public resource use	4.0	3.0	3.5	3.5	3.5	4.0	2.9
Building human resource	4.0	3.5	3.5	3.5	3.5	4.0	2.9
Safety nets	4.0	3.0	4.0	3.0	4.0	3.0	2.9
Poverty monitoring and analysis	4.0	4.0	4.0	3.5	5.5	4.5	2.9
Average	4.0	3.3	3.7	3.4	3.7	3.9	2.9
Public sector management and institutions							
Property rights and government	4.5	2.0	4.0	3.0	3.0	3.0	2.7
Quality of budget and financial management	5.0	3.0	4.0	3.0	3.5	3.5	2.8
Efficiency of revenue mobilization	4.0	4.0	4.0	3.5	3.5	3.5	3.1
Efficiency of public ext	4.5	2.5	4.0	3.5	2.5	3.5	2.8
Transparency account and corruption in public sector	4.5	2.0	4.0	3.0	2.0	3.5	2.7
Average	4.5	2.7	4.0	3.2	3.3	3.4	2.8
Overall ratings	4.3	3.2	4.2	3.5	3.6	4.0	3.0

SSA Sub-Saharan Africa.
Source: World Bank calculations.

performance in the criteria related to public sector management and institutional depth indicates room for improvement, particularly in the spheres of property rights; governance; and transparency, accountability, and corruption in government.

The government has repeatedly avowed that maintaining a sound macroeconomic framework and overall fiscal discipline are central to its program. The government aims at reducing the inflation rate to less than 5 percent, consistent with the inflation level in Tanzania's major trading partners. Modernization of tax administration, effective containment of smuggling and tax evasion, reduction of exemptions, and tax simplification form the core challenges for improving revenue collection efforts. The government will maintain expenditure control, which will be facilitated by full implementation of the Integrated Financial Management System,[24] and will continue strategic prioritization of public expenditures, with a focus on poverty,. Furthermore, any additional resources generated by the HIPC debt relief would be allocated to the priority sectors.

With respect to the sustainability of Tanzania's reform program, since being elected in 1995 and re-elected in October 2000, the government has embarked on institutionalizing the large range of reform measures implemented previously so as to bind them legally and provide a transparent institutional framework for operating under a liberalized economy. This process is still at an early stage and is fraught with obstacles related to difficulties in changing mind sets, vested interests, the political hurdles to proceed expeditiously and resolutely, and capacity constraints for designing and implementing the required changes. The government urgently needs to assess the consistency between the new operative environment and the laws and executive orders governing it to reduce any room for opportunistic policy reversals. Concerns about the risks of policy reversals can only be dealt with if measures are taken to bind the various positive policy changes in legal provisions and institutional arrangements that cannot be easily reversed.

Transparent, Streamlined Tax Policy

In an environment where the partnership between the government and key stakeholders is of increasing importance in forging growth, complementary institutional and administrative changes in the tax structure are crucial for firmly rooting investor confidence. The establishment of the TRA has been key in simplifying and consolidating the government's revenue efforts and in increasing tax compliance. It has gone a long way toward increasing the stability and administrative efficiency of the tax regime to provide the foundation for a predictable incentives regime, especially for foreign investment. The TRA has submitted a proposal for further simplification of the tax structure as part of its ongoing efforts to remove or suspend any taxes that have low yields in the current stage of economic development and high administrative costs of collection, for example, the excise regime.

The budget for FY2001 is supportive of growth and poverty reduction. The tax structure has been reviewed to emphasize incentives to investors, further reduce barriers to international trade, lower the tax burden of the lowest income-earning categories, reduce the prevalence of double and nuisance taxation, enhance the transparency of the tax system, and encourage voluntary compliance. The budget for the past three fiscal years has increasingly reflected an effort to harmonize the jurisdictions of the central and local tax authorities, tilting the revenue sharing arrangement in favor of the latter. Some taxes that were previously collected centrally have moved under the purview of local authorities, for instance, locational service charges, thereby expanding their tax base. This is in addition to an increase in the revenue share of centrally collected taxes going to the local authorities from taxes and charges such as those levied on land and parks.

As the private sector and the range of economic activities expand, a key government responsibility will be to both simplify tax administration and make it more effective. The revamped judicial system must provide for an effective commercial court and expeditious tax appeals process. The government's capacity to assess the specific nature of each industrial segment with respect to prospects, nature of

---

[24] This system includes all budgetary units and accounts in the central government. The system will produce monthly commitment monitoring and expenditure controls. It includes a new classification of government financial statistics that from now on will represent the single government accounting and financial information system. The integrated financial management system will be introduced in all districts, and introduction of the software underlying the system was recently completed in the pilot districts.

investment, gestation period, debt financing, and the effect of these on generation of real profit and the resultant tax revenue effort must be strengthened. It must guard against the temptation to compensate for its incapacity to do so through ad hoc tax measures. Concerns have been raised regarding the current cap of five years on the allowance for company losses in tax returns for all sectors other than mining. This is perceived to discriminate against tourism, industry, agriculture, and infrastructure in which investment may have longer gestation periods. Currently, many of these sectors have not attracted much investment even though they are extremely important in terms job creation and technology transfer, and are therefore crucial for poverty reduction. Moreover, such allowances are far more generous in Kenya and Uganda, which may repel potential investors. However, caution must be exercised to clarify the definitions in the tax laws to minimize discretionary interpretational powers, scope for negotiation, and a possible rise in bureaucratic intervention and corruption.

The trade tax regime is being reformed with a view to harmonizing taxes for the country's economic integration with its neighbors. Starting with the liberalization in Zanzibar, the union has initiated and consolidated considerable changes. Tariff categories and levels have been compressed culminating in the current four positive rate categories and maximum import duty of 25 percent. Further lowering of tax barriers to international and internal trade will result in a temporary decline in revenues unless exemptions that currently account for a 50 percent loss of revenue are reduced and collection leakages plugged, especially given that tariff rates have been compressed to a level where further cuts will probably result in a temporary negative effect on revenue.

At the same time it is important to ensure that the tax regime does not create any disincentives to investment in comparison to Kenya and Uganda, which have a longer history of attracting foreign investment. The income tax rates are at par in all the countries. The maximum import duty in Kenya is equal, but there are only three positive rate bands of 25 10, and 5 percent. Uganda supports a lower band of tariffs, starting at 15 percent, but effectively the supplementary charges in that country add another 10 percent effective tax. With the exclusion of interest deductions from the tax obligation for local investors, there is concern that they are being discriminated against by the provisions of existing law on assessment of company income. This is because foreign investors will have the option to raise loans abroad and introduce the funds as equity in Tanzania.

To encourage a more robust response of private investment in Tanzania, the incentives need to be broadly distributed across sectors, in contrast to the recent concentration in the enclave sectors of mining and tourism. As more than 95 percent of agriculture is privately managed and this sector accounts for about half of GDP and contributes up to 70 percent of foreign exchange earnings, a major part of the effort to encourage private sector investment should target this sector. Reducing tax and nontax controls and the opaqueness of agricultural taxation, which raise the costs of business operations, will encourage greater participation by agri-business and increase the productivity of investment in agriculture. A broader distribution of income-earning opportunities to reach the poor entails promoting investment in smallholder agriculture as well as in small and medium enterprises in rural areas. It is therefore necessary to pay attention to the poverty-reducing quality—employment creation, skill development, regional location, market access, removal of artificial shortages—of the investment response. The government took some preliminary steps at the local government level by amending the Local Government Act in 1999 and the budget for FY00, and is initiating reforms in two major areas. The first area is the removal of controls and taxes on the internal movement of agricultural commodities to enable greater marketing efficiency. The second is to consolidate taxes and other charges levied on agriculture, rationalize their implementation, encourage reasonable uniformity of treatment across localities, and remove multiple taxation at different levels of government to foster greater transparency.

With respect to the larger corporate entities, in the longer term the government should aim to promote investment not by granting unsustainable, generous tax incentives, but by providing a stable corporate income tax regime with a moderate rate and a reasonably attractive system of depreciation. Areas with glaring weaknesses in the corporate tax regime include the tax treatment of financial incomes (interest, dividends, capital gains, and so on) and the rules for depreciation of capital equipment. In addition to restructuring the system of depreciation allowances, reforms need to be instituted to rationalize the corporate income tax structure with respect to withholding taxes for interest and dividends and to close loopholes. Indirect taxes would benefit from a general simplification of the excise tax system, limiting its scope to few major excisable products and recovering the small revenue loss from minor adjustments to the excise rates on the products, including petroleum.

In this regard the government is considering eliminating 46 of the 52 items subject to excise tax from the list, retaining excise tax on the 6 items that currently account for 96 percent of excise tax revenue. The other performance improvement measure focuses on expediting the payment of VAT refunds. For businesses not in the income tax net, it is proposed that three fixed liability bands on business turnover using stamp duty assessment as the basis for each band be introduced. Over the next couple of years, the government is considering abolishing withholding taxes on goods and services and rationalizing the differential rates of withholding taxes in sectors other than mining and infrastructure and for the stock exchange. Over the longer term the government is planning to minimize surcharges and consolidate them into tariff bands to enhance the transparency of the tariff regime. A comprehensive review of the tax policy may also be in order with a view to lowering trade taxes in the long run.

The government envisages that following the implementation of the recommendations made by its task force appointed to look into rationalizing local and central tax regimes, many of the shortcomings and inefficiencies identified will be addressed. This is imperative, as is no clear mechanism is available to ensure that the cascading system of taxes does not crush, or at least, provide disincentives to, investment and growth. The government is to review options for establishing a system to rationalize the overall tax regime and to initiate a unified tax appeals system to guard against unfair treatment.

An Apposite Legal and Judicial Framework

To facilitate investment the government has embarked on a program to review and implement legal reform measures in critical areas to remove the inconsistencies and impediments to private sector development. As noted earlier, the key areas requiring action are corporate and contract law, bankruptcy law, labor law, and property and land rights. In Tanzania businesses engaged in litigation can face frustrating delays, and at times there is a lack of impartial adjudication. Access by small and microenterprises to the formal legal system is fraught with complexity. There is a need for transparent, expedient, and cost-effective companies acts and conflict resolution mechanisms, including effective recourse against government decisions, that would help boost private sector confidence in the system.

LEGAL SECTOR REFORM PROGRAM. With support from the World Bank the government carried out a comprehensive study of the legal sector some three years ago. The study clearly identified the range of problems affecting performance, set up a legal sector task force, and proposed a series of recommendations to improve the performance of the legal sector. While the Cabinet approved most of these recommendations, only limited progress has been made in implementing them. The sector receives few resources from the government, and also from donors, who have been waiting for an action plan to which they could subscribe. Donors financed the studies that provided the basis for the task force's report. After many attempts, the Ministry of Justice and Constitutional Affairs and other stakeholders have finally produced and agreed on a strategy and an action plan for a broad reform program for the legal sector. This program was launched recently. The hope is that this will demonstrate the government's intentions and commitment to reforming the legal sector. To succeed, this reform program will need to be closely coordinated with the other major reforms initiatives under way, namely, decentralization and local government reform and the public service reform programs. Donors, the private sector, and other key stakeholders have identified the reform of the legal sector as key to good governance, improved transparency, and accountability. However, skepticism prevails about the seriousness of the Ministry of Justice and Constitutional Affairs' commitment to reforming the legal sector. Donors, including the World Bank and the Danish International Development Agency, are supporting the activities of the Law Reform Commission, the launch of commercial courts, the establishment of the Commission of Human Rights and Administrative Justice, and the provision of legal aid through a network of NGOs.

Progress in this area, albeit still limited, is now visible. The Fair Trade Practices Act, which regulates trade practices, came into effect recently. A commissioner for fair trade practices has been appointed, but has yet to constitute the commission to which complaints of unfair trade practices may be channeled. The legislation also regulates monopolies, acquisitions, and takeovers of businesses. A statutory Capital Markets Authority regulates issues related to the securities listed on the Dar es Salaam Stock Exchange. Effective implementation of the revised Land Law would strengthen property rights and enhance access to business credit.

As noted, progress to update laws has been made, but much remain to be done to (a) modernize a bureaucratic and outdated legal and regulatory framework, (b) create citizens' awareness of their rights, and (c) restore faith in a credible judicial system. To improve governance, the government will need to commit more resources to law and order, with a focus on prevention rather than on ex post sanctions and punitive measures. Other issues that must be addressed include the seemingly overlapping mandates of institutions such as the Commission of Human Rights and Administrative Justice, the Prevention of Corruption Bureau, the Ethics Commission, and others. There is a need to review their mandates and ensure closer collaboration. All interlocutors identified the judiciary as one of the weakest links in the transparency and accountability framework. It is seen as corrupt, unethical, and inefficient and should feature prominently in an improved transparency and accountability agenda. Donors have indicated, in general, their willingness to support this specific area.

A brief review of some of the key areas of legal and judicial reform being undertaken by the government that have a specific bearing on private sector activities follows below.

COMPANIES LEGISLATION. While the actual process for incorporating and registering companies, including trademark registration, with the Registrar of Companies has witnessed improvements in recent years such that it compares favorably with other developing countries, the agency has no regional outreach and all companies must be registered in Dar es Salaam. Furthermore, businesses continue to be hampered by other cumbersome procedures and onerous, and at times opaque, requirements for their day-to-day operations in areas relating to obtaining business and sectoral licenses, investment certificates, tax and social security fund registration, import and export clearances and for reporting requirements. Specified businesses like banks, insurance companies, contractors, tour operators, hotels, and professionals must have specific licenses in addition to their business license. The following finding of the Price Waterhouse Coopers and Lybrand 1997 *Roadmap* is indicative of the extent of the problem. Firms based in Dar es Salaam are expected to submit a minimum of 89 separate filings (not including import or export documentation, repatriation of funds, utility payments, or sectoral forms) per year, compared with 21 in Ghana, 29 in Namibia, and 48 in Uganda. Tanzanian banks and hotels are respectively required to make 285 and 545 or more separate submissions per year. The government is aware of the multiplicity of its requirements and the multitude of public sector employees engaged in overseeing private sector activities. To address this issue, the government has carried out an extensive review of the legal regime relating to the incorporation and functioning of private sector companies and has decided to introduce a completely revised legislative framework. The preparation of the new legislation is now under way (with World Bank support) and is expected to be completed by the end of 2001.

BANKRUPTCY LAWS. Revisions to the country's bankruptcy laws are under preparation to meet the demands of a free market economy. At present the courts are still using antiquated British laws and regulations dating back to 1891.

SETTLEMENT OF COMMERCIAL DISPUTES. In an attempt to speed up the settlement of commercial disputes the government has established the Commercial Court as a division of the High Court. The newly established Commercial Court, based in Dar es Salaam, adjudicates commercial cases as defined in the High Court regulations. Three judges have been assigned to the court. The next steps envisaged include opening commercial courts in five regional centers and expanding the court in Dar es Salaam. To streamline and facilitate its operations, the court is seeking to computerize its activities, including the court's registries. To this effect, the government is preparing a commercial court project plan and will establish an automatic filing and registry system through computerization. A system would thus be established to monitor the volume of cases adjudicated by the court in a given period.

Tanzania has arbitration legislation that allows the settlement of disputes outside the courts. Tanzania is a signatory to the Convention on Recognition and Enforcement of Foreign Arbitral Awards (the New York Convention of 1958), which it ratified in 1964. Even though Tanzania has not adopted any provisions based on the United Nations Commission on International Trade Law model, the Investment Act allows investors to adopt the model's rules and procedures. There is also legislation providing for reciprocal enforcement of foreign judgments. However, the applicability of the foregoing remedies remains limited because of inherent complexities and the associated high costs of implementation.

LAND LAW. A new Land Act, was enacted in February 1999, is a major improvement in the area of land law and the administration of land matters. In particular, it has codified, unified and simplified the law relating to mortgages, which is paramount for private sector growth, as the ability to mortgage land is a preferred and effective form of security worldwide. This modification to the Land Act should provide the impetus to encourage bankers and other financiers to lend to businesses more readily. However, concerns about the use of land as collateral for bank credit have also re-emerged, even though Article S 3(1)f and S.112(1) of the Land Act stipulates that land can be used as collateral for purposes of borrowing from financial institutions.

There are also continuing concerns regarding procedural matters and regulations, particularly with respect to foreign acquisition of usage rights. Section 20(1) of the Land Act extends a right of occupancy to noncitizens for the purpose of investment, which is aimed at attracting investors. However, a serious disincentive stems from the problems related to land titling. While the process of land allocation is provided for in the legislation (Section 12[3] of the Land Act states that land allocation committees shall be established at central, urban, and district authorities), the Land Act does not go far enough in specifying the time frame in which one can obtain a fully registered land title. The government is working toward ensuring that the time frame is reduced to a reasonable period of say 180 days, and to this end is planning to develop an effective system for issuing land titles. This provision is envisaged to be made in the regulations for implementing the new Land Law. In addition, to assist in effective implementation of the law, the government is planning wide dissemination of the regulations and the Land Law.

LABOR LAWS. Tanzania's labor laws date from the 1960s and have not kept pace with changes in the economic environment. In particular, the procedures for dismissing and retrenching employees, albeit intended to protect them against unjust treatment, are viewed by investors as unduly cumbersome. In addition to businesses having to keep nonperformers on the company's payroll indefinitely (with few legal alternatives by way of disciplinary action), employers' options for changing the skill mix of their employees are also restricted. The government is undertaking a review of Tanzania's labor laws at this time, and based on the findings may promulgate amendments to facilitate performance-related separation of staff.

IMMIGRATION PROCEDURES. Red tape and burdensome immigration procedures remain one of the problems that continue to hinder private sector development. Excessively bureaucratic procedures and corruption are common. There is therefore a need to review immigration policy and amend the laws, particularly as they affect investors, and also to streamline procedures and accelerate the clamp down on corruption. Opportunities to extract rent for public services rendered, such as issuing work permits and visas, must be eliminated by refocusing staff performance measures, including the adoption of transparent output and/or service indicators.

CONTROL OF CROP MOVEMENTS. Although in principle Tanzanian law allows for free movement of crops within the country, this has not been the case in practice. A number of permits have been required for transporting food from one point to another, and road blocks exert physical control over crop movements. Exports bans have also been instituted from time to time, impinging on profitability and limiting access to closer and more lucrative markets. Given the ongoing decentralization process, there is a further risk that districts and local authorities may intensify these controls for revenue generation purpose. The government is, however, planning to abolish controls constraining crop movements within and across borders and to subject such movements to the existing broader trade regulations.

Building a Better Business Environment

THE TANZANIA INVESTMENT CENTER. In 1997 the government enacted a new investment law, the Tanzania Investment Act, that replaced the previous investment law of 1990. The thrust of the new legislation was to unify all investment incentives under the general financial system. The legislation provides the basis for a dynamic investment promotion agency to help achieve the government's goal of increased private investment. Furthermore, in response to the persistent criticism of the country's investment environment, the government also converted the old investment agency, the Investment Promotion Center, to the TIC. The new TIC was expected to be the primary agency to coordinate, encourage, promote, and facilitate investment in Tanzania and to advise the government on investment policy and related matters.

In 1999 the board of the TIC commissioned a study by the Foreign Investment Advisory Service. The objective of the study was to recommend a strategy and a specific action plan to implement the changes envisaged under the new act. The study addresses immediate functional and organizational changes for the TIC and recommends a series of steps to enable it to become a truly client-oriented and effective promotion agency. Almost a year after the completion of the study, TIC's management has prepared a business plan based on the study.

In view of the persisting issues and to complete the transformation of the TIC, a complete overhaul of the organization is necessary. The government has some experience with overhauling organizations, and given the size of the TIC could achieve this fairly quickly. However, it is critical that the recruitment of staff be based on qualifications, experience, and integrity. The introduction of clear performance targets for staff, along with a clarification of the TIC's mandate, will help ensure that the TIC makes progress on promotion and facilitation as opposed to regulation. Over the medium term it is also necessary to eliminate the distinction between TIC certificate holders and noncertificate holders, making the same tax benefits available to all investors engaged in the same activities. This could be done by amending the finance acts.

CREDIT INFORMATION BUREAU. The establishment of a credit information bureau will also reduce commercial risk by providing historical information to lenders. These risks have been a major constraining factor in the expansion of credit, even when the government's debt retirement initiative has raised loanable funds. The government has prepared a study on this issue. The Tanzania Banker's Association has actively supported the idea, and a credit rating bureau will be established under the auspices of this association. Ideally the private sector should own and operate such an information bureau. Sustainability of the bureau's services could be guaranteed by recovering the cost of services and sharing information among lending institutions.

In practical terms it is important that the Bank of Tanzania, in collaboration with the Tanzania Banker's Association, develop and implement a business plan to establish and operationalize a credit information bureau, including the methods to be used for cost sharing and information reporting and a user fee structure.

Strengthening Public-Private Relationships and Dialogue

Since 1995 private sector institutions in Tanzania have invested significant efforts and resources in successive consultations among themselves and with the government to identify and establish the most appropriate framework for consultation that will optimize the benefits of partnership between the public and private sectors for the process of social –and economic development. In this endeavor the private sector institutions have been supported by the government as well as by bilateral donors and multilateral institutions. While the private sector has more than 50 formally established representative bodies or umbrella organizations, such as the Tanzania Chamber of Commerce, Industry, and Agriculture; the Confederation of Tanzania Industries; and the Tanzania Business Council, the private sector's representation is still not as organized as that in Kenya. A few strong advocacy groups are emerging, such as the Confederation of Tanzania Industries, which have started increasingly to engage in dialogue with the government. These private sector lobbyists have been playing a progressively more visible role over the last few years, and in part because of their persistent efforts, the government is beginning to pay increasing attention to the sector's concerns. However, the need to establish an informed and organized body capable of influencing the direction of important policy changes is now clear.

A consensus view in Tanzania is that to improve the environment for private investment and to establish a closer working relationship between the public and private sectors to foster more efficient business operations, an institutionalized and well-functioning public-private sector consultative mechanism is vital. For a successful, close working partnership between the government and the private sector, it is necessary to develop competent and agile institutions that will support and respond rapidly to the needs of dynamic firms making business decisions in reaction to changing market conditions in a competitive framework. The institutions necessary for the success of the public-private sector partnership include government institutions responsible for macro-level management, for example, institutions responsible for legal and regulatory systems; public finance, especially the tax and customs administration institutions whose functions connote close interactions with the private sector; and trade and investment institutions, as well as institutions that support technological development and advancement, for instance, universities, standards and metrological agencies, productivity centers, agricultural extension services, research and development institutions, and labor training institutes. In the current context in Tanzania this will entail major structural changes and the provision of support to existing institutions like the TIC, the TRA, licensing authorities (such as the Business Registration and Licensing Agency), industrial and agricultural research institutions, policy research institutions, universities, the Institute of Financial Management, and other similar institutions that support production and trade activities.

Despite different views on the form of the consultative mechanism, a promising coalition and broad agreement on the way forward have been formed. The Tanzania Private Sector Foundation is in place and has been registered since 1995. It boasts a broad membership of 92 cross-cutting private sector associations. Even though the foundation is not an apex organization for the private sector, it is popularly recognized as a focal point for private sector institutions. Its mission is to promote private sector-led social and economic development by coordinating with other private sector institutions and providing its member associations with services they need and value, representing their interests, and engaging in effective advocacy with the government. The foundation's aim is to champion private sector interests by influencing government policies and regulations through regular consultations with the government. In one such relatively recent consultation meeting, organized jointly by the Civil Service Department and the Tanzania Private Sector Foundation, the government reiterated its firm commitment and support to the development of a culture and a policy framework that, through a transparent consultative mechanism, will encourage the private sector to be fully integrated into the economic development process. To this end the government reached agreement with the business community to form the Tanzania National Business Council. A task force under the auspices of the Ministry of Industries and Commerce comprising representatives from ministries, academia, research institutions, and the private sector is proposing an appropriate institutional framework for the council and is working toward its establishment.

The Tanzania Private Sector Foundation is a young institution that must function in a challenging environment characterized by conflicts of interest between different private sector institutions and some distrust between the private sector and the government. Currently some perceive the foundation as a weak, and therefore, ineffective body; however, currently it is the only private sector coordinating body with a broadly based affiliation, and therefore has the potential to lead the private sector toward the establishment of an institutionalized public-private sector consultative mechanism, that is, a national business council.

Improved Infrastructure Services

High utility costs and an underdeveloped transportation system erode profit margins and have undermined the development of a vibrant private sector. In view of the foregoing, the government has embarked on a dual-pronged approach to improving the provision of key infrastructure services. The key elements of the government's strategy include undertaking a comprehensive divestiture program with a focus on early privatization of the larger utilities and strengthening the regulatory framework governing the major utilities and other basic infrastructure with a view to enhancing performance in terms of improved service delivery and lower costs.

PRIVATIZATION. The government adopted a privatization strategy in the mid-1980s within the context of a broader macroeconomic and structural reform program. Objectives of the privatization policy have included the government's withdrawal from majority ownership of commercial enterprises and the promotion of the private sector by creating a framework conducive to private investment. Improved access to capital, technology, and external markets and the development of a local capital market were additional objectives. The divestiture of parastatals was expected to reduce the budgetary burden, increase the efficiency of the productive sectors, and raise growth and employment levels. Initially the government had planned to retain its ownership of major utility companies, but in 1997 decided to privatize these as well. In the next few years the government intends to make decisive progress toward completing the privatization process (box 5.1).

At the present time, the finalization and application of a cogent policy framework in the areas of parastatal debt restructuring and retrenchment is critical for underpinning the government's ability to achieve its privatization targets rapidly and effectively. The government commissioned a series of studies on the treatment of excess debt on the balance sheet of privatization candidates and the retrenchment of parastatal employees. These studies are currently being analyzed to decide whether existing government policies need to be amended. Current policies on debt provide for minimal debt forgiveness for privatization candidates. On retrenchment, the policy limits payoffs to statutory payments unless the company can afford to do more. An issue with respect to the latter has been the lack of consistency in applying the retrenchment policy. Furthermore, the current policy on debt has resulted in significant delays in the privatization program, sometimes even preventing the concluding of transactions.

Box 5.1. *Efforts to Foster Private Sector Development through Privatization*

In 1986 the government embarked on an adjustment program to dismantle the system of pervasive economic controls and encourage more active participation by the private sector in the production of goods and services. Successful implementation of its privatization program is the cornerstone of Tanzania's economic reform program intended to stem the substantial fiscal drain resulting from ineffective parastatals and to improve the performance of inefficient state-owned utilities and infrastructure. To date the government has privatized about 52 percent of parastatals and state-owned enterprises. However, about 48 percent parastatals, mostly in areas such as utilities and agriculture, remain to be privatized.

As part of its continued privatization efforts, by the end of 2002 the government is planning to
- Privatize 80 percent of parastatals (by total employment and turnover)
- Privatize 20 strategic and /or large enterprises
- Privatize 180 small and medium enterprises, of which at least 2 utilities, 1 large entity, 40 small/medium entities
- Adopt a comprehensive policy on public enterprise retrenchment compensation
- Adopt a comprehensive policy on public enterprise debt treatment and resolve the indebtedness of parastatals.

Two examples of successful privatizations undertaken by the government involve Tanzania Breweries, Limited, one of Tanzania's first major privatizations, and the more recent NBC (97).
The privatization of Tanzania Breweries was one of the first major privatizations to be undertaken by the Tanzania Parastatal Sector Reform Commission created to oversee the transition of some 250 state-owned enterprise to private ownership. The program to remove Tanzania Breweries from government ownership and management involved privatization, rehabilitation, and modernization of the existing breweries and expansion through the construction of a greenfield brewery at a total cost of US$87.2 million. South African Breweries became the majority shareholder after international bidding. The International Finance Corporation (IFC) helped cement the relationship between the government and a new foreign investor and to structure the financing necessary to carry out the project.

This represents the most successful privatization effort to date, with the company's production levels, product quality, market share, and financial performance all showing significant improvement. Tanzania Breweries operates breweries in Dar es Salaam, Arusha, and Mwanza. The Mwanza brewery was constructed in late 1995 as part of the expansion program. IFC approved loans totaling US$18.4 million, including a "B" loan of US$7.4 million and US$6 million in equity for its own account. The "B" loan was syndicated to financial institutions including Proparco and Dresdner. Dresdner made an equity investment of US$2.6 million for its own account. The project performed better than expected. Tanzania Breweries canceled IFC's loan, including the "B" loan. Internally generated funds were higher than projected and more than sufficient to complete the expansion and rehabilitation. IFC has an equity position of 9.6 percent of common shares. The IFC equity investment initially diluted the government's ownership in Tanzania Breweries to less than the 50 percent level. The government reduced its ownership even further through a public offering in 1998, and currently owns about 28 percent. Tanzania Breweries was one of the first companies to be listed on the newly established Dar es Salaam Stock Exchange. The company made a public offering of 20 percent of its shares in 1998 to local investors. The offer was 75 percent subscribed and the balance was canceled. IFC was considering warehousing part of the government's remaining 28 percent ownership in the company, as the overhang of shares on the market has depressed the company's share price on the Dar es Salaam Stock Exchange.

The company tripled capacity to 2.2 million hls under a US$75 million expansion program that was financed from equity from South African Breweries and internally generated funds. Tanzania Breweries has 85 percent of the clear beer market, with imports and other producers supplying about 15 percent. Local demand exceeded the company's ability to produce until a capacity increase in 1998. Turnover increased by more than 400 percent between 1994 and 1998, and the company reported after tax profits of US$36 million for FY98. Since the rehabilitation was completed, IFC has received cumulative dividends of more than US$6.5 million on its US$6 million equity investment. South African Breweries opened a new brewery in Kenya in 1998 to compete against Kenya Breweries, Limited, and Tanzania Breweries has stopped exporting to Kenya This was one of the first major privatizations and its success has had a positive demonstration effect. The project should achieve better use of asset, ensure continued long-term employment, and relieve the government budget. Incremental tax revenues are estimated at US$245 million over the life of the project. Total additional economic benefits have been estimated at about US$29 million per year.

At the time of writing, the privatization transactions relating to the Tanzania Telecommunications Company and the Dar es Salaam Water and Sewage Authority were at various stages of the bidding process, and the lease agreement for the container terminal of the Tanzania Harbors Authority had been signed. The privatization of the Tanzania Telecommunications Company is at an advanced stage. The information memorandum has been sent out to potential investors and the prequalification has been completed. The bids for the company have been received and evaluated and the highest bidder identified. The offers exceed expectations both in terms of prices and the roll out plans for the services.

With respect to TANESCO's privatization options, a Cabinet paper was submitted to the government in October 1999. The government endorsed the general strategy of vertical and horizontal separation or unbundling of TANESCO's functions and the privatization of the resulting parts. The next step of assembling the divestiture transaction team in line with the privatization guidelines endorsed by the Cabinet has been completed. The next major step is to prepare a detailed strategy and help implement the restructuring and privatization of TANESCO. The strategy and other critical decisions will be prepared by the divestiture transaction team under the leadership of the Parastatal Sector Reform Commission and submitted for approval. The strategy will set out the broad timetable for phasing in competition and moving from monopoly to retail competition.

Once the government approves the strategy for reorganizing TANESCO and restructuring the electricity sector, TANESCO's legislative framework will be drafted and presented to Parliament. This is envisaged to be completed in 2002. After Parliament has ratified the legislation, divestiture and legal advisors will be recruited. The government is expected to endorse a final Cabinet paper to outline the divestiture strategy within the next year. The first phase of divestiture should start by 2003, with the process expected to be completed by late 2005.

Consultants retained for preparing a transaction strategy for the Tanzania Railways Corporation made a presentation in December 1999, and submitted their recommendations for privatizing the corporation. The approach suggested is an exclusive concession of 25 years of a vertically integrated Tanzania Railways Corporation, such that the infrastructure is separated from operations and placed into an asset holding company. Opinions seem to be converging on the vertically integrated option, and once there is a final agreement on the privatization modalities, a strategy paper will prepared and submitted for approval to the Cabinet.

INFRASTRUCTURE REGULATORY AGENCIES. As the liberalization process gathers momentum, there is an immense need for strengthening the regulatory framework in key markets to enhance transparency and foster competition to achieve greater accessibility to services and improved quality. This line of action needs to be pursued to reduce inefficiencies and establish an enabling environment for private sector activity by enacting appropriate laws to establish a transparent regulatory framework for the key supportive sectors such as utilities, the transport and petroleum sectors, the financial sector, and other infrastructure services; setting up institutions for administering the regulatory frameworks; and providing appropriate adjudication machinery within the Commercial Court to deal with disputes that may arise in connection with applying the relevant laws. A broad consultative process is to help the government select the most appropriate regulatory framework to be applied, including rationalization across sectors to minimize costs and multiply cross-cutting efficiencies of scale. Expeditious adoption of the agreed frameworks for implementation and full operationalization of the regulatory bodies is key to redressing such issues as the deterioration in service delivery and the absence of standardized treatment of clients.

The government has been deliberating on the options with regard to the appropriate scope and mandate of the multisectoral (or dedicated) regulatory institutions to be created. The two broad areas that would be under the regulatory oversight of these institutions include public utilities (energy electricity and natural gas, telecommunications, and water and post) and transportation (maritime and ports, road, rail, and aviation sectors). The government recognizes that great thought and careful planning need to go into the relationships between these industry regulators and other concerned public agencies and bodies and the exact nature and role of each. The creation of the regulatory institutions, appointment of commissions to these new institutions, and their full staffing are planned to be carried out over the next couple of years.

LEGISLATIVE FRAMEWORK. Each of the infrastructure sectors is preparing to re-examine and amend the relevant sectoral legislation to ensure a coherent, modern, pro-competitive legislative framework to underpin its operations. The preparation of detailed sectoral regulations by the regulator will be the key agenda item for the respective regulatory institutions, following their commencement. It is envisaged that the legislative changes to be proposed to Parliament for railways, power, water, ports, and maritime activities will be prepared as soon as the government agrees on the divestiture strategies for the respective sectoral parastatals. Over the long term, the government recognizes the need to pass directives governing the national regulatory framework, which would provide for the possibility of private sector participation and the resultant increased competition in power, water, ports and shipping, and the telecommunications sectors.

Liberalization of the petroleum sector is an important part of the efforts to increase the efficiency of the economy. While the government has taken various measures, such as liberalizing petroleum prices and adopting a three-option strategy for the divestiture of the refinery, further discussion is needed on the type of regulation required in the sector. Initial discussions with the government on the nature and location of the agency to handle quality and to monitor safety and health standards suggest that a small monitoring unit within the Ministry of Energy and Minerals would be more appropriate than a unit or division within the multisectoral regulator. Following a study to determine the appropriate regulatory framework for the petroleum sector, work relating to the amendment of the Petroleum Conservation Act (1981) is under way. The amendment provides for overseeing fair play in the market, quality, and safety and health standards.

PROGRESS IN IMPROVING KEY INFRASTRUCTURE SERVICES. Long periods of neglect in maintenance and the curtailment of development budgets led to a serious deterioration of transport networks. In turn, poor mobility has hampered efficiency in production, supply responsiveness, and market integration. Infrastructure is one area where external assistance can play an effective role in promoting growth and alleviating poverty. However, unlike in the past, such support should be tied to clear commitments in the budgetary provision for recurrent maintenance costs. Such earmarking approaches have been developed by targeting revenue from user charges for maintenance of the infrastructure. The protection of the Road Fund in the annual budget since 1998 was a step in this direction. An independent road agency is currently being established. Some key appointments have been made, for example, the chief executive officer, and the agency is expected to be fully operational by June 2003. Most critical in this regard is the need to strengthen the government's capability to prioritize investment and develop an effective maintenance system that pays greater attention to cost-effectiveness. To this end the government is engaged in a dialogue with the donor community for developing a comprehensive, long-term transport strategic framework, and the Ten-Year Road Sector Development Program is now in preparation.

Initiatives have been set up to make greater use of private contractors for road maintenance in place of the traditional approach, whereby the public agency in charge of works undertakes repairs and/or rehabilitation. The training of small contractors has been part of this worthwhile initiative, and a national association with regional chapters has been set up to help galvanize this initiative and strengthen the capacity of local contractors. Another worthwhile initiative is the Village Travel and Transport Project, which is aimed at rationalizing travel based on local initiatives. It combines redesigning the location of essential service points within villages to minimize distances and improve access; improving travel modes, predominantly by using intermediate technology; and improving access to services outside the village through a feeder roads program. Expansion of the feeder road networks to improve the accessibility of rural areas is therefore an important complement to this initiative. The contribution of rural community efforts to the upkeep of these networks is an important financing avenue worth exploring. These experimental initiatives are worth paying attention to for possible scaling up, should these pilots prove successful. They augur well for sustainable approaches to improving the transport system at the local level.

A recent starting point for rehabilitating road networks has been the major arteries connecting the countryside and the major consumption centers and export points. This is essential for ensuring the basic minimum connectivity for moving produce over long distances. Upgrading these strategic links will reduce marketing costs and improve accessibility. The next phase should be developing feeder roads to and from these arteries to reach the production points in rural areas. A clear strategy under the Integrated Roads Program needs to be developed to focus on a cost-effective and sustainable feeder roads program. Such a strategy should also explore the possibility of engaging local contractors to make effective use of the trained capacity from the initiative described above, as well as schemes such as food for work, which have proved successful in several countries. Cost considerations are important, but if feasible, such schemes pay a double dividend by providing opportunities for the poor to raise their consumption while at the same time improving road networks. Given that such schemes have often used rural labor in the off-season, they have helped to expand opportunities for rural employment to supplement agricultural activities.

Improved access to a low-cost and stable power supply is critical for private sector investment and efficient business operations. The focus in the past two decades has been on expanding the power supply and developing the national grid system for arterial distribution countrywide. With the commissioning of Kihansi and Songosongo, the power supply capacity will increase significantly. A key issue is a cost-effective distribution system. The privatization process for the distribution system is now quite advanced and will lead to substantial cost reduction, which if passed on to users will significantly reduce the costs to businesses. The distribution of power through rural electrification and other forms of energy has lagged behind other developments in the power sector. The majority of the rural population and low-income urban dwellers depend on forest resources for energy. Thus deforestation and land degradation are major concerns in connection with sustainable development. Desertification—caused primarily by fuelwood consumption—is increasing, destroying the very resource on which most of Africa's poor depend. . Rural electrification and the promotion of alternative fuels is thus important not only for bettering the quality of life and providing needed energy sources for production, but to ensure the sustainability of Tanzania's forests, soil quality, and wildlife resources. Environmental protection initiatives will gain considerably from the development and distribution of energy sources other than fuelwood.

Financial Sector Reform

The government began implementing a series of financial sector reforms in 1991. It liberalized interest rates, removed credit controls, revised the Banking and Financial Institutions Act, allowed private banks to enter the market, and vested the central bank (Bank of Tanzania) with supervisory and regulatory controls for both banks and nonbank financial institutions. It also began the restructuring of the most troubled banks and privatized others. To facilitate the recovery of nonperforming assets of the state-owned banks, these assets were transferred to the newly established Loans and Assets Realization Trust, which overcame the legislative hurdles by establishing (legally) its own tribunal, and therefore avoiding the courts altogether, which were widely seen as the bottleneck. Finally, the government also liberalized the insurance sector. The impact of these changes has been dramatic, and as noted earlier has led to a respectable increase in the number of privately-owned institutions across various subsectors: banking, insurance, pension funds, and so on.

Tanzania has three major financial regulatory authorities. The Bank of Tanzania has the licensing and supervisory powers to guide the development of the financial sector; the Capital Markets Authority regulates the Dar es Salaam Stock Exchange; and the National Supervisory Department, established in 1998, supervises the insurance sector. Not surprisingly the rapid growth of the financial sector has created new challenges for the Bank of Tanzania. Recently the bank has had to take preemptive actions three times, first in 1998, when it closed down the Trust Bank; then in April 1999 when the Greenland Bank was put under statutory management; and again in May 2000, when the Bank of Tanzania put the First Adili Bank under its direct management. At the same time the speedy liberalization of the insurance subsector has not been supported by increased capacity to regulate and supervise this rapidly growing industry. The recent embezzling of funds from an insurance company raises many concerns, especially about the adequacy of the regulator. In addition, the pension system remains largely unregulated, and therefore potentially open to misuse. The principal areas where the government is leading the charge in encouraging development of the financial sector are discussed in the following paragraphs, as are some areas requiring further action.

REGULATION AND SUPERVISION. While the banking crises were well managed and the Bank of Tanzania successfully prevented any systemic failure, these near misses taxed the central bank's capacity and resources. In this regard, the bank should carefully review existing licensing requirements, prudential regulations, and enforcement systems and capacity for both off-site and on-site supervision. It is imperative that a system of oversight for the entire sector be promulgated after the government carefully considers its options for instituting appropriate regulations and investment guidelines in the contractual savings subsectors. This will minimize further mismanagement of assets and help improve transparency, thereby curtailing opportunities for corruption, and most important, protecting beneficiaries' rights. Such options should include the establishment of one regulatory agency for all contractual savings institutions with different departments for overseeing insurance and pensions. The government should also undertake an options study for pensions regulation in the longer term to ensure that the insurance companies observe due process in conducting their business. In addition, there is a need to institute cogent investment guidelines for all contractual savings institutions (within the framework of the broader Bank of Tanzania's financial sector guidelines), and subject these institutions to a supervision process undertaken by the central regulator.

COMPLETING THE MICROFINANCE AGENDA. The NMB is a unique institution that will need significant preparations for divestiture, given the first unsuccessful attempt to attract strategic investors. In 1998, under the rationalization program for the NBC, the government issued an investment memorandum for this newly established microfinance bank. In view of a lack of interest from serious buyers, the government has entered into a management contract with Development Alternatives, Incorporated as an interim solution to improve the NMB's performance and attract strategic investors the second time around. Subsequently, the NMB's business plan was endorsed by its board of directors. The government established a task force—including members from the Bank of Tanzania, the World Bank, and the International Finance Corporation under the stewardship of the Parastatal Sector Reform Commission—to agree on a provisional strategy and explore the options for privatization. The findings of the task force and consultations with potential investors are the basis for recommendations on the strategy for finalizing the divestiture of NMB.

It would also be advisable to bind the recently approved microfinance policy by revising the Financial Institutions Act to stimulate coordinated growth in microfinance. Such amendments to the legislative framework are essential for ensuring prudential operations of microfinance institutions. An agenda item for the central bank, over the short term, is a review of its banking supervision policy to include microfinance institutions with a view to ensuring integrity of the system. Sound development of the microfinance sector would meet a genuine need in the credit-starved agriculture and small and medium enterprise sectors.

CONTRACTUAL SAVINGS INSTITUTIONS. The NIC continues to dominate the insurance segment: 55 percent of the general insurance market and 98 percent of the life insurance market. As part of its financial sector reform program, the government is planning to divest the NIC. Studies to review and formulate an apposite privatization strategy have been undertaken. The two studies focus on an audit and actuarial analysis of NIC and on the NIC's market and business operations. It is key that the privatization program for NIC carefully develops the options for outstanding claims in relation to assets, retrenchment of staff, closure of nonviable branches, and choice of a strategic management partner.

The pensions industry is plagued by high contribution rates to the public pension system compared with other countries, low coverage of the work force, perceived weaknesses in the investment management of pension funds, and inferior customer service. As noted earlier, a weak collection and enforcement mechanism and the lack of appropriate investment opportunities and guidelines are central to the problems besetting the sector. These issues need to be analyzed carefully, with practical options leading to the development of an appropriate framework for the funds' operations. In the near term, the government is reviewing the possibility of opening up the pension funds to private and public companies as a first step toward improving the extremely low coverage of the work force.

CAPITAL MARKET. The lack of maturity of primary and secondary capital market in Tanzania plays a vital role in constraining the development of a vibrant private sector. The absence of much needed supplies of long-term capital (debt, quasi-equity, and cofinancing) is a function of the relatively diminutive size of the formal corporate sector. The government has been moving in the right direction to allow the development of a sound financial sector and an efficient payments system for goods, services, and capital transactions by liberalizing the sector to private activity. The development of an adequately strong prudential and supervisory mechanism, for example, the development of transparent means of ensuring that the primary dealers fulfill their expected roles as market makers, is also critical to allowing Tanzania to compete in the global marketplace for resources. To expand the scope of open market operations and enhance the effectiveness of monetary policy, Tanzania's secondary markets must be strengthened.

Since opening its doors in April 1998, the Dar es Salaam Stock Exchange has not seen much action. The potential for greater inflow of net private transfers remains high and is largely related to the repatriation of proceeds associated with unrecorded exports. To help enhance the liquidity of the stock exchange and to attract foreign equity investments, the government is reviewing actions necessary to open up the floor to foreign participation, while instituting appropriate safeguards against the negative effects of volatility in share trading and prevention of "hot" money. In addition, it is important to examine the current framework for listing companies and provide adequate incentives for listing. Over the coming year, critical steps aimed at strengthening the functioning of Tanzania's capital market would include the development of a medium-term policy on capital account liberalization, including measures to improve transparency; to develop and implement a comprehensive capital flows monitoring system; and to assess the capacity of the financial system to handle capital flows, including the creation of a supervisory system, as well as the capacity to reduce risks associated with opening up the banking system to cross-border and foreign currency transactions. Over the longer term Tanzania aims to develop and implement a proposal to relax restrictions on foreign portfolio investment in equity instruments with appropriate safeguards.

Combating Corruption

Good governance is a key determinant of economic growth and a precondition for sustainable private sector development. The government is planning to undertake measures to strengthen economic governance and enhance the effectiveness, efficiency, and quality of public service delivery to provide a solid foundation for sustainable development and poverty eradication. The proposed measures include actions in the following areas: (a) anticorruption measures, (b) improved management of public finances,

(c) enhanced financial accountability, and (d) increased efficiency and effectiveness in the delivery of public services.

Reestablishing a credible budget process, in which overall fiscal discipline is accompanied by allocative and operational efficiency, is key to the government's efforts to promote growth and fight poverty. The improvement and expansion of systems for improved budget management at all levels, with a focus on the priority sectors, is central to poverty alleviation. Measurable indicators include continuing and deepening the Public Expenditure Review/Medium-Term Expenditure Framework process adopted by the government, leading to enhanced allocative and operational efficiency; roll-out of the computerized integrated financial management system to all ministries and regions; introduction and application of performance budgeting across all priority areas; improved performance of the audit process by the controller and auditor general in a credible and timely manner, respecting the timetable stipulated by law for the performance of audits and the publication of reports; and the finalization and implementation of a strategy for reducing corruption in all key sectors (tax, law and order, public works, judiciary and social sectors).

ANTICORRUPTION MEASURES. A central constraint to attracting investment resources to Tanzania is the widespread corruption in the public sector. To curb corruption the government has developed its National Anticorruption Strategy and Action Plan, which was published in 1999. As a result, the Prevention of Corruption Bureau is now seeking technical support to develop a coherent national action program. The need to reform the judiciary and to strengthen the Office of the Controller and Auditor General (OCAG) are often mentioned as key areas for support. The action plan proposes measures that cut across all levels of government as well as ministry- and agency-specific measures. Actions being considered for implementation by the government include (a) carrying out diagnostic surveys on specific areas most prone to corruption, including the judiciary, the ministries of Works, Education, Health, Rural Administration and Local Government, and Home Affairs, the TRA, and the OCAG; (b) passing new procurement laws and regulations; (c) publicizing all contracts with significant pecuniary implications; (d) making tender results public; (e) disseminating the annual report of the Permanent Commission of Enquiry to a wider audience; and (f) amending the Public Leadership Code of Ethics Act to include currently nondeclarable assets in disclosure requirements.

PUBLIC FINANCIAL MANAGEMENT. Since the introduction of the cash budget system, the government's budget management has been dominated by the objective of achieving fiscal discipline and macroeconomic stability. While this objective remains extremely important in providing an enabling environment for private sector activities, there is also an urgent need to give similar weight to strategic prioritization of public expenditures and improving the efficiency of implementing expenditure programs in the public sector.

Performance budgeting and the Medium-Term Expenditure Framework are important tools for achieving all three objectives of the government's fiscal strategy. Piloting of both systems started in 1998, and it is now important to extend the coverage and quality of the Medium-Term Expenditure Framework and Performance Budgeting Initiative and to ensure that both approaches are integrated in order to streamline the budgeting system and make the best use of scarce human resources in both the Ministry of Finance and the spending units.

To improve financial control and management, the government is currently implementing the Government Accounts Development Project, which encompasses the introduction of a computerized integrated financial management system and the reclassification of the government chart of accounts. The integrated financial management system has been introduced to all central budgetary voteholders, including Defense and the Office of the President, as well as to a number of subtreasuries. As part of the Local Government Reform Program, the system was also introduced to 28 of the 35 phase I local authorities. To ensure the effectiveness of the system, it is crucial that the system covers all votes and that key financial information is published in a timely and accessible manner. This is key if the system is ultimately to function as the only instrument for accounting and controlling expenditure and revenue.

FINANCIAL ACCOUNTABILITY. The OCAG plays a crucial role in ensuring the proper use of public funds. Even though the OCAG suffers from human resource constraints that affect the quality and timeliness of its reporting, the office has made substantial progress in improving the timeliness of its reporting, both at the central and the local level. To fully capitalize on the work of the OCAG, improving publicity and follow-up to the auditor general's report is essential. A precondition for follow-up is that reports are prepared and submitted within the time stipulated by law, which requires adequate funding for the OCAG. In this connection the actions the government has considered for implementation include (a) increasing the budgetary allocation to the OCAG to at least at the same rate as nominal GDP growth and ensuring full release of budgeted funds to the OCAG, (b) bringing OCAG reports increasingly into the public domain, (c) ensuring more deliberate and effective follow-up to the reports' recommendations, and (d) disseminating the Ministry of Finance's and the Treasury's minutes on follow-up to the OCAG reports.

EFFECTIVENESS AND EFFICIENCY OF PUBLIC SECTOR SERVICE DELIVERY. Improving service delivery in the public sector plays an important role in providing an enabling environment for the private sector. Physical infrastructure and basic social and regulatory services are key inputs to the production process. Due to the positive externalities from quality services on the overall performance of the economy, the government has an important role to play in providing or financing these services. While the government has made significant progress in enhancing fiscal discipline and strategic resource allocation, it has done relatively less to enhance efficiency in the use of public resources. It is therefore considering various measures that aim directly at enhancing the efficiency and quality of public services provision. Central to these efforts is the introduction of performance management systems in key areas of public service delivery, as well as the establishment of an executive agency for greater financing autonomy, including for the roads sector. Actions being considered for implementation by the government include (a) developing and approving the framework for the introduction of performance improvement systems in the give priority sectors (education, health, water, agriculture, and roads), (b) implementing performance improvement modules in the five priority sectors, (c) introducing output accountability in service delivery for the five priority sectors, and (d) establishing an independent road agency.

As the government is moving to performance budgeting and management to make public service accountable for the delivery of better services to citizens, it will be important to have mechanisms to measure the performance of the public sector in place. The regular measurement of public sector performance has the potential to help create a performance culture and is an essential institution of good governance. As the government is also moving toward implementing an assistance strategy for improved coordination and more effective use of external aid, it will need to seriously evaluate the performance of those responsible for implementing its development programs and assessing the impact of resources allocated to these programs. It will therefore need adequate capacity to establish and monitor credible performance and impact indicators.

Scrutiny by Citizens

PARLIAMENT AND ITS COMMITTEES. The need for Parliament to play a more proactive role in ensuring the government's prudential performance has been identified as key to transparency and accountability. In this regard, while some perceive the Public Accounts Committee as having improved its functioning, the overall opinion is that the committee system could do much better. The hearings of the Public Accounts Committee are not public and no change is envisaged in the near future. The rotation of members (6 of the 12 members change every 6 months) makes it building any long-lasting capacity and functional memory difficult. Interventions to strengthen the capacity of Parliament and key committees remain ad hoc and small, and are not part of an overall strategy to strengthen these institutions. Financial constraints, including unattractive pay and inadequate information, impair the proper functioning of Parliament. Furthermore, members of Parliament tend to have a limited understanding of budgetary and policy processes and their implications. As mentioned earlier, certain limited interventions are trying to address some of these problems, but require a more in-depth needs analysis. There is also no follow-up at present on how policies are implemented; a critical shortcoming that needs to be addressed.

MEDIA AND COMMUNICATIONS. In general, there is still much uneasiness with respect to the press in Tanzania. The press is seen as young and with limited experience. Therefore, there is reluctance to give it more power and access. A common view is that the media are weak on appreciating and monitoring the policy process, and are therefore unable to serve the public effectively.

The value of consistent information flows and reliable communication channels for raising productivity and improving the population's education and health status cannot be overstated. The critical consideration here is availing affordable means of communications. Until the 1990s the government had a total monopoly of the communication systems and legislated against other conveyors of information and private media. This curtailed the expansion of means of communication and sustained high levels of inefficiency due to the lack of competition. Encouraging changes have now taken place, which have altered the situation impressively: an open governance system and political pluralism are challenging this monopoly in information, and legislation has been amended to permit private providers. The response has been tremendous, with a mushrooming of daily papers and radio and television stations. The telephone system has also greatly benefited from opening the service to competition, which has reduced both costs and waiting time to obtain service. As the Tanzania Telecommunications Company is poised for privatization, if handled appropriately, the process would contribute to a bright future for telecommunications service. These changes have broadened the scope of information and means of conveyance available to the public. Improvements in education can now be better exploited for innovation and social interaction. The effectiveness of education and agricultural extension services can also be improved with increased literature and information through better communication means. This trend should be encouraged, and providers of education services, extension services, and health education should make better use of improved means for the flow of information.

NATIONAL BOARD OF ACCOUNTANTS AND AUDITORS. With donor assistance the National Board of Accountants and Auditors is becoming a stronger regulatory body for the accounting and auditing profession, but further improvements are still required. The board has been active in preparing accounting and auditing guidelines for Tanzania, and correctly takes the view that the reporting structure needs to be reinforced as the private sector is opening up. A series of studies are to provide crucial information on the status of the accounting and auditing profession in Tanzania. These studies cover the following areas: (a) the introduction of quality reviews, (b) the status of the accounting profession and harmonization with regional and international standards, (c) the board's examination system, (d) the board's work methods and computerization, (e) the effectiveness of board graduates, and (f) a review of the OCAG. With respect to public sector accounting, the National Board of Accountants and Auditors is working closely with the Public Sector Accounting Committee to develop appropriate standards. Overall, Tanzania appears to be ahead of other countries in the region when it comes to its regulating body. However, there is still a long way to go before the board develops sufficient "muscle" to supervise the profession and enforce ethical and professional standards. The issue of retaining quality staff remains linked to the question of adequate incentives and pay.

Areas of Potential and Promise for Private Sector Development

Clearly the provision of an enabling environment for the private sector is central to making the Tanzanian economy competitive. Across-the-board institutional reforms to further improve the administrative and regulatory framework should go a long way toward attracting higher levels of domestic and foreign investment. Tanzania has made substantive progress in introducing broadly based macroeconomic reforms and is pursuing an impressive structural reform agenda. In view of Tanzania having successfully implemented a series of reforms conducive to fostering private sector development, it is useful here to identify here a select number of "entry points" or areas of competitive advantage where invested resources could earn meaningful returns and in turn contribute to Tanzania's socioeconomic growth. Figure 5.4 provides an integrated perspective of the essentials for fostering private sector development and of the entry points of greatest relevance to Tanzania, given its specific natural, human, and other economic endowments and incentives, political, and institutional conditions.

Figure 5.4. *Integrated Perspective of the Essentials for Fostering Private Sector Development*

Incentives and politics/institutions	Sources of growth	Private sector development tools	Outcomes
ANALYSIS	SECTORS	ACTIONS	LEARNING
Macro (fiscal, monetary, exchange) 6 Adjustment Public 7 Reformers and laggards Endowments 8 Natural, human and infrastructural Microeconomic 9 Trade and market liberalization (services, labor, finance) Private 10 Industrial structure (small and medium enterprises, public enterprises, etc.) 11 Institutional structure (chambers of commerce, trade associations)	12 Agriculture and agribusiness 13 Mining 14 Tourism 15 Private participation in infrastructure 16 Social services 17 E-commerce	18 Roll-back government 19 Strengthen financial, legal, judicial and regulatory underpinnings 20 Transform domestic perceptions 21 Mitigate risks 22 Develop sound infrastructure 23 Attract foreign investment 24 Strengthen regional linkages 25 Develop robust export performance 26 Nurture small and medium enterprises 27 Foster enterprise learning	28 Develop broad-based growth 29 Implement feedback, monitoring and evaluation systems 30 Strengthen strategic underpinnings

Source: Adapted from World Bank (1998).

The areas where Tanzanian private sector potential can be viably unleashed over the next few years thus include, but are by no means limited to, the following:
- The agriculture and agri-business sector, which by sheer force of its size and presence in the country is an economic segment that cannot be ignored
- Mining and tourism are areas where Tanzania has a demonstrated advantage and has already had a head start
- Infrastructure is another growth area with considerable room for greater private sector participation, because the government is placing a large number of publicly held utility and infrastructure entities on the block for sale

- Private users have indicated their willingness to pay for quality education (and Tanzania already has significant private provision of education) and health services, largely in urban areas
- Changes being introduced at a rapid pace by developments in information and communication technologies could help Tanzania take a giant leap toward meeting its growth and development objectives.

Promoting a Profitable Agriculture Sector

Agriculture hosts the largest share of private sector activities in the economy, spanning individual smallholders and large commercial farmers, but little attention has been paid to the imperatives for a robust private sector involvement in this sector. The environment for investment, commercial production, and processing is still nascent and measures are needed to bring about a more open and fair trade environment to reduce the costs of doing business.

Agriculture has been severely discriminated against in the past by urban-oriented policies. It is only now beginning to regain some vitality in the key export sectors, despite heavy taxation, high transport costs, and unfavorable movements in the real exchange rate. More important, agriculture has a proven comparative advantage, strong links with other sectors, and employs the bulk of the poor. To a large extent the basic constraints both smallholders and commercial farmers face are similar in nature. The main differences between the two are related to marketing issues based on international trade and taxation bottlenecks. While export agriculture has the potential for major growth linkages with the nonfarm sector, backward linkages are currently negligible as most inputs are imported.

Broadly speaking, six key areas of action are proposed to improve the business environment in this sector:
- Remove controls over the internal movement of agricultural produce to enable greater marketing efficiency and eliminate artificial shortages
- Reduce the number of taxes and charges levied on agriculture.
- Encourage reasonable uniformity of treatment across localities to improve predictability for potential investors and remove multiple taxation at different levels of government to foster greater transparency
- Convert the crop boards into genuine stakeholder entities, with the justification for their existence being closely linked to the benefits accruing to farmers who finance the crop board activities through cesses
- Develop and clearly articulate action plans for a unified voice for the private sector interests across small and large farmers, resolve any conflicts of interest across these two groups, and strengthen dialogue between the government and the private sector.
- Decide on the appropriate regulatory framework for more liberal operation of the sector following the conclusion of studies and consultations on this matter.

Although decisions to institute some of these measures have been made in principle, there is a need to galvanize action in these areas.

Pursuit of productivity growth in agriculture is critical for raising returns to committed resources and effort, and requires four critical interventions in addition to consolidating the realignment of price incentives, which have been implemented for the past decade and a half, and reducing the burdensome taxation of agriculture. The first intervention is to create conditions that are conducive to long-term investment for improving the productivity of the main agricultural resources, land and labor. Existing land tenure arrangements do not attract long-term commitments of resources for improving the productivity of land through such means as drainage and irrigation. The 1999 Land Law has laid the foundation for more transparent execution of land-based transactions and property rights; however, problems in the administrative procedures and in the use of land as collateral for obtaining credit still need to be addressed. Typically the pace of providing permanent occupancy titles has been slow and the system of allocation is still fraught with corrupt practices. The weak administrative capacity of village governments to apply the law within the decentralized system of land administration is also worrisome. This situation introduces significant uncertainties that militate against long-term investment and encourage land mining. Raising the capacity of the concerned institutions for surveying land and issuing titles to holders is an first important step. The preservation of these rights against risk of expropriation and the ability to settle disputes fairly and expeditiously are important components of establishing firm property rights.

The second intervention is to build credit markets for financing investment. The bulk of the rural economy depends on informal credit arrangements. These are typically small and segmented and cannot meet investment financing needs. In the past public credit schemes and development banks attempted to fill this gap, but following the termination of the cooperatives, of the Cooperatives and Rural Development Bank, and of input credit schemes, which were the main channels for rural credit, all such avenues for rural credit have now ceased. The existing banking system, which is increasingly privatized, caters to short-term credit and focuses on large clients. Only the NMB is expected to provide credit through microfinance programs. Nongovernmental agencies such as PRIDE have been channeling resources from donors, and the government has set up specific funds to offer credit to communities and individuals. However, there is still a serious shortage of long-term microfinance for smallholders seeking resources for investment. Initiatives are under way to strengthen the microfinance system and the policy governing its operation has been approved. The process of setting up the microfinance bank to cater to small rural investors has benefited from lessons of successful experiences in Asia, for example, the Grameen Bank. Contract farming arrangements, whereby input credit is provided in advance of harvests, partly fill the gaps, but are dogged by problems in enforcing repayment. Self-selecting groups within villages have also organized themselves as credit unions and guarantee members' credit applications. The success of these schemes is crucial for supporting agricultural investment. Their success is not just a matter of mobilizing financial resources, but of having the know-how that will ensure minimal defaults by good selection of investment projects and of mechanisms for enforcing repayment. These would supplement existing social networks engaged in informal credit arrangements that operate on the basis of social trust and sanctions against defaulters.

The third intervention is facilitating the adoption of technological innovations for improving the productivity of both land and labor. Agricultural research for adapting imported technology and improved seeds to local conditions as well as developing new varieties and technology is one part of this effort. To this end there is a need to reverse the decline in agricultural research support and rationalize research on a regional scale for similar ecological conditions. National and regional research infrastructure exists, but is underfunded. A related issue is creating an effective system for conveying new technological information. The agricultural extension system has not been spared the budgetary crunch of the last decade and a half, which has affected the quality of extension agents and the geographic coverage of their services. Strengthening capacity for extension services therefore requires better training of agents, improved access to new information on available technology and husbandry, and the provision of facilities to reach farmers on a more regular and demand-driven basis.

Closer links between research systems and extension services will improve the flow of information between the two agents of innovation. Thus another aspect of technological innovation is to raise farmers' capacity to absorb and apply new technologies made available through the extension system. Education is an important part of this capability. Evidence indicates that farm productivity improves with education through enhanced ability to access information on innovations and to apply it correctly. The largest impact has been from primary education (Appleton and Balihuta 1996), which points to the need for refocusing budgetary support toward primary education.

The fourth intervention is improvements in marketing infrastructure, which complement the foregoing measures to increase productivity by permitting a more efficient flow of larger volumes of produce and raising the profitability of agriculture through reduced marketing costs. With the dismantling of public monopolies in agricultural marketing, the excessive margins exacted from producers have declined, and transport costs are now the single largest cost element in marketing. Private marketing agents are emerging, but rather slowly, and are confining themselves to more accessible areas. Thus the transport infrastructure needs to be improved to ensure wide coverage of marketing services. There is also a need to ensure that marketing agents are not starved of the credit required for their operations.

In view of the dominant position of the agriculture sector in private economic activity, focusing efforts on the sector's potential to produce directly exportable items, lowering the costs of producing value added tradables, and creating large spin-off effects through intersectoral linkages are all important.

Broadening the Returns from an Enclave Industry: Mining

Given its rich mineral deposits of precious (gold, diamonds, tanzanite, and rubies) and industrial (tin, nickel, copper, iron, phosphate, gypsum, graphite, salt, and limestone) minerals and fuels (coal and natural gas) and the government's liberalization policies in the sector, Tanzania saw an upsurge in international interest in exploration in the 1990s. More money was spent on nonferrous minerals exploration in Tanzania in 1998 than in any other African country. The first commercial gold mine started operations in November 1999, with good prospects of several more projects coming on-stream. Tanzania's mining sector grew by almost 28 percent in 1998, up from 17 percent growth the previous year. The government expects this performance to continue at a level of 10 percent per year through 2005. The mining policy enacted in 1997 continues to guide sectoral development, although the government has been introducing further changes to the Mining Act with a view to improving investment performance. Exploration spending in 1999 was expected to drop below the US$60 million of 1998 to around US$45 million, but mine development spending could soar from around US$50 million in 1998 to US$400 million over FY00 (*Financial Times* 1999).

Diamonds and gold contribute just under 65 percent of the value of mineral exports, with other gemstones accounting for more than 35 percent of sales receipts and industrial minerals and coal amounting to a mere 0.1 percent. While contributing only some 2 percent of GDP (in 1992 prices), the volume of mineral exports increased by 11 percent in 1998, compared with a 7.4 percent increase the year before. In terms of value, mineral exports grew from US$93 million in 1997 to US$103 million in 1998, notwithstanding the seemingly terminal decline of gold prices to around US$285 per ounce and the flooding of mining sites as a result of the El Niĝo phenomenon. Tanzania expects mining to boost foreign exchange earnings by 50 percent by 2003, as the sector is starting to account for an important share of total export earnings: 17 percent in 1998 compared with 6 percent in 1990.

The number of mining rights licenses has increased sharply over the past decade, rising from about 30 licenses issued between 1985 and 1991 to nearly 400 licenses by 1997. The extractive sector has been attracting significant levels of private foreign investment and prospects for gold mining in Tanzania are considered to be sound. The *Financial Times* (1999) special feature on Tanzania noted that total estimated gold deposits now stand at around 30 million ounces, with another 8 million ounces discovered last year. Indeed, the attractive geology of the region holds the promise of a significantly higher gold resource base that may be revealed through further exploration. Feasibility studies are under way for diamonds, gemstones, and base metals like nickel and cobalt. Exploration for industrial minerals—soda ash, kaolin, and silicon—is also planned.

In October 1997 the first gold mining project started operations. Golden Pride, operated by Australia's Resolute in joint venture with Ashanti (which bought out Samax Resources in 1998), boasts an estimated resource of 2.4 million ounces and is expected to produce 180,000 troy ounces per year. The Bulyankulu gold mine, owned by Barrick, is a world-class deposit with 9 million ounces, and is believed to be the largest gold mine in East Africa. It has the potential of producing a highly attractive grade of 12–13 grams per tonne, and should become fully operational in the near future. The Kahama Mine, owned by Barrick, is expected to produce around 300,000 ounces of gold annually, adding more than 30 tonnes of gold output per year by next year and adding close to US$300 million to annual export revenues. Ashanti Goldfields, East Africa Mines, and Anglo-American companies are all exploring and developing other areas containing an estimated 9 million ounces of resources around the Geita and Ramagaza Greenstone belts, and Afrika Mashariki is expected to make progress on the Tarime gold project in northern Tanzania, with well over a million troy ounces. Estimates indicated that Tanzania would be able to produce a total of 800,000 ounces of gold by the end of 1999. Roman International and Sutton Resources of Canada are exploring nickel deposits in Kagera, while Anglo-American's nickel project in Kabanga, which also contains copper and cobalt, is expected to start operations within the next year, reflecting a general move toward diversification. Furthermore, Williamson Diamonds have been divested to De Beers; diamond production increased from less than 73,000 carats in 1997 to more than 95,000 carats in 1998.

Notwithstanding the high level of investment since 1996, the sector's performance has been constrained by inadequate capacity, poor technology, and lack of capital on the one hand, and high production costs on the other. These constraints aside, the mining sector's medium-term prospects appear promising. The incentives afforded by the government, which include the repatriation of profits and duty free and VAT free imports of equipment, have created a favorable operating environment that is competitive by international standards. Local governments are also seeking to benefit more significantly from mining activity in their regions. The government currently takes royalties of 3 percent once production comes on line, plus 35 percent corporation tax after a 100 percent capital write-off allowance.

However, opening up new mines will only lead to sustained and broader dissemination of benefits in the long term if Tanzania's mineral sector policy is finalized to ensure sensible management of mineral resources, greater overall transparency, and enhanced clarity with respect to health and safety issues. The government must guard against poor management of revenues flowing from the sector, corruption, and negative environmental and social consequences, which could negate the envisaged benefits of larger mineral exports, increased employment, and higher tax revenues. At the same time relevant public institutions, for example, the Ministry of Energy and Minerals, must be strengthened to promote, administer, and regulate private investment in industrial mining ventures; establish and maintain investor confidence through consistent and transparent legislation for competitive participation in mining; and formulate appropriate rules for mineral rights registration, mine safety, environmental regulations and monitoring, and revenue collection from the sector.

Another critical element of a strategy that would allow broader sharing of the outcomes of this enclave sector entails the development and execution of a policy and infrastructural framework to promote an effective and sustainable small-scale mining industry. Measures to promote organized artisanal mining and to strengthen partnerships and links with large-scale investors (to facilitate technology transfer and the optimization of mineral resource exploration) and with mineral dealers will encourage formal mineral marketing and thereby help curb mineral smuggling.

Developing World-Class Tourism

With 15 percent of Tanzania's total land mass reserved for tourism, the industry is one whose time is come. Neglected and constrained by poor infrastructure for decades, Tanzania is now becoming increasingly popular as a tourist location in Africa. The *Financial Times* (1999) notes unequivocally that: "From the spectacular game reserves of the Serengeti Park and Ngorongoro crater to the peaks of Kilimanjaro and the crumbling island charm of Zanzibar, Tanzania's tourism industry does not need to lie when it claims to offers one of the world's most complete holiday destinations." Tanzania's relative political stability, the general absence of internal strife and violence, the wide choice of beaches and game parks, and the relatively uncrowded destinations have all helped enhance Tanzania's attractiveness.

Currently some 142,000 square kilometers have been earmarked for national parks and protected areas, triple the total tourism area identified in Kenya. The Northern Circuit with its well-known destinations is much more developed than the equally promising Southern Circuit. Tanzania also boasts an 800-kilometer coastline and island tourism opportunities on Zanzibar and elsewhere. As noted in chapter 6, foreign exchange earnings from tourism remained low through 1985, with an especially steep decline in activity during 1977–84, when the border with Kenya was closed. While the industry's performance has been improving since the mid-1980s, it was only with the adoption of the national tourism policy in 1991 along with economic liberalization in the 1990s that growth in the sector accelerated.

During 1989–99 the estimated number of tourists quadrupled to some 560,000 per year. During the same period total foreign exchange earnings increased nearly ninefold to about US$750 million, reflecting a significant increase in spending per head. Zanzibar has also witnessed tourist visits increasing at an average of 10 percent a year for the past 10 years, with the exception of a small dip in 1998. Nearly 70 percent of all tourists are on vacation, with some 18 percent being business travelers. While the bombings of the American embassies in Kenya and Tanzania and the El Niño-related adverse weather conditions dampened the sector's performance in 1998, the longer-term picture is positive and, alongside the mining industry, offers one of the most outstanding instances of rewards from the past 10 years of liberalization and structural reforms. Estimates indicate that more than 135,000 people are either directly or indirectly employed in tourism, up from 110,000 in 1997. The number of international tourist hotels stood at 215 in 1998, offering a total of 7,500 rooms.

The significant increases in tourism revenues and tourist presence are attributed to strengthened publicity and promotion of Tanzanian tourist facilities, including increased participation by private sector operators and by the Tanzania Tourist Board staff in various international tourism and trade promotion fairs, along with improved efforts undertaken by the government in collaboration with donors to both improve tourism services and enhance technical capacity in the sector. The government aims to sustain visitor levels at around half a million and to focus on diversifying the product and developing newer products like cultural tourism. In broad terms, the government's future strategy for the sector is geared toward promoting low–volume, high-yield tourism. A related objective is to improve the tourism infrastructure and facilities, particularly in the Southern Circuit game reserves of Selous and Ruaha, so that the current average of 7.6 days spent in-country by each tourist increases substantively. The government also recognizes the importance of environmental protection as key to the sector's long-term future of the sector, in addition to peace and security.

There is clear evidence that Tanzanian tourism stands to benefit from being offered as part of an East African package that combines beaches and animals. The Tanzanian tourist industry depends closely on that sector in Kenya, with 66 percent of tourists arriving by road from Kenya to the northern wildlife area. While earlier efforts to create an East African identity for tourism have not met with success because of bureaucratic disagreements and philosophical differences, the private sector confirms that combinations of Kenyan and Tanzanian itineraries have performed well. However, unless the EAC's strategic action plan with respect to tourism coordination is implemented adequately, the full extent of rewards is not likely to ensue, and glitches such as the closed borders between Masai Mara and Serengeti will continue to affect returns to the sector.

The government and the private sector are now recognizing the importance of the tourism sector's enormous potential in contributing further to GDP, creating additional employment opportunities, boosting foreign exchange receipts, and driving the development of ancillary services. With its abundance of unique, exotic destinations, Tanzania should move ahead to develop its tourist industry in a culturally sensitive and environmentally sustainable way. It is critical that the coordinated development and continued maintenance of transport, telecommunications, and banking infrastructure and water supply be carried out, at the very least near the Northern Circui, and the coastal region around Zanzibar and Dar es Salaam. Over the longer run the government must not only encourage private investment in the sector, but also coordinate and regulate the sector effectively. It is also imperative that private enterprises focus on improving the level, reliability, and quality of services to bring Tanzania into the ranks of world-class destinations.

Promoting Private Investment in Infrastructure

Starting in North America and Europe, the share of private sector provision of infrastructure has been growing worldwide during the past two decades. Governments, particularly in Africa, are finding that financing the operations, maintenance, and capital investments needed to upgrade and expand infrastructure facilities is increasingly difficult. Inadequate management and operational capacity constraints have also overwhelmed governments. Having effectively launched the privatization of its commercial, agricultural, and industrial public enterprises during 1994–98, Tanzania has now embarked on an ambitious and far-reaching program to divest its major infrastructure public enterprises during 2000–04. The process of divestiture is more than 50 percent complete, with some 250 of a total of more than 400 public enterprises privatized, including most large commercial entities, but the tough agenda of divesting large infrastructure public enterprises has just begun.

The completion of the privatization program with respect to the main strategic public enterprises, particularly in infrastructure services, will have a significant bearing not just on lowering the cost of doing business in Tanzania, but also in terms of increasing the operational efficiency of the private sector and stemming the significant drain of public resources expended to keep inefficient utilities and other infrastructure parastatals afloat. The government envisages the key outstanding actions to entail unbundling the power company, TANESCO, and bringing its distribution system to the point of sale; concessioning the railways for private operation; leasing the Dar es Salaam Water and Sewage Authority to private operator(s); divesting the NMB and the NIC; and implementing the strategy for further concessioning of port services. Of the remaining public enterprises in agriculture, the government intends to divest the cashew nut processing factories, ranches, and farms through sale or liquidation.

The divestiture programs and community-based initiatives now under implementation or preparation in supplying utilities and infrastructure services augur well for greater efficiency in their provision. In particular, water, power, telecommunications, and roads services should benefit from private sector inputs. A decisive and well-managed approach to these programs would go a long way toward cost-effective expansion of these services to the public. The government's strategy for improving efficiency in the provision of utilities is to introduce competition through various forms of private participation in infrastructure. Key elements of effective private participation in infrastructure include privatization of the incumbent utilities and clear rules for bidding procedures for public procurement plus an appropriate regulatory regime. Private participation in infrastructure is widely viewed as a key entry point, in that it supports virtuous cumulative spirals in the real economy by providing more reliable and efficient services, easing fiscal constraints on the government, and supporting increased private sector activity. It is also seen as a key entry point in terms of institutional development, that is, the emphasis on legal, an regulatory, and judicial issues leads to strengthened national capacity and awareness and the transfer of technology and management and administrative skills. In this regard it is important to ensure that the private participation in infrastructure fits well within Tanzania's overall sectoral reform and development strategy and contributes toward the country's investment and performance goals.

To provide an effective enabling environment for attracting increased private participation in these key sectors in the medium to longer run, Tanzania is now focusing on the creation of new sectoral regulatory laws and independent cross-sectoral regulatory institutions to progressively build modern economic regulatory capacity. The establishment of effective infrastructure regulatory capacity and the preparation and implementation of Tanzania's privatization program in infrastructure, banking and insurance, and agriculture are critical both to the development of a robust private sector and enhanced economic growth. Regulatory reforms will be sequenced to create pro-competitive regulatory environments prior to the divestiture of public enterprises in the sectors concerned by building clear, transparent regulatory rules into concession contracts and enhancing regulatory capacity.

The regulatory frameworks for industries such as telecommunications, energy, water, ports, and railways will play a critical role in successful privatization. Wherever possible, reforms should focus on encouraging competition to minimize the need for regulatory intervention. Where regulation is required to provide the necessary investor confidence, most of the rules for regulating price and service conditions must ensure that there is little room for regulatory discretion; transactions must be embodied in binding contracts backed up by international arbitration. Effective regulatory institutions will be required in this environment to monitor and enforce these rules, and so that in the longer term, when investor confidence in these institutions has been established, sectoral rules can be developed that provide more flexibility to adjust to changing economic circumstances and stronger incentives for efficiency. The government intends to focus on developing sector-specific frameworks sufficient for privatization to proceed and on establishing the basic institutional arrangements. Full consolidation and harmonization within and between sectoral frameworks and institutions is essential.

The regulatory institutions must be fully staffed, and cohesive, detailed regulations for each sector must be completed. Reforms would (a) provide for increased competition and private sector participation, (b) ensure a clear and consistent cross-sectoral approach to the allocation of regulatory responsibilities, and (c) ensure consistent approaches to regulation across sectors and issues of common interest. Principal issues of common interest include accounting principles, regulators' decisionmaking processes, appeals mechanisms, resolution of disputes among competing operators seeking access to shared facilities, and processes for dealing with unsolicited investment proposals requiring concessions from the government.

Private Sector Participation in the Provision of Social Services

The rationale for governments' continued pivotal role in providing and catalyzing the provision of education and health by others derives from three considerations. First is the failure of markets to provide adequate credit for investment in education and a lack or narrowness of insurance markets for health services. Credit market failures arise from difficulties in collecting information about individuals whose return to education will be high, the lack of collateral, and difficulties in ensuring repayment. These problems curtail lending for investment in education even though returns to education have been shown to be as high as in other sectors (Glen and Sumlinksi 1995). In the case of the insurance market, failures arise because of the high costs of monitoring and fears of adverse selection. Although health insurance markets do exist, in many African countries they are confined largely to urban areas and mainly serve the wealthier groups in these areas. The second reason is the existence of significant externalities from health and education expenditures. The social returns from such expenditures include the reduction in the spread of communicable diseases by treating known cases and through awareness campaigns, and the beneficial spread of preventive action. Education externalities include a rise in social interaction facilitated by literacy, numeracy, and knowledge of the national language and skills that have higher social than private returns. Third are social justice and distribution objectives, particularly for those in need who cannot afford these services. For these reasons, without public action, investments in human resources are likely to be inequitable, inadequate, and inefficient (Appleton and Mackinon 1996).

Nevertheless, public action is not confined to provision of these services. It includes encouraging other providers and setting up an effective regulatory framework to guard against malpractice and to counter information failures. Public provision of education has faced problems related to underfunding of essential services and cost-effectiveness. Underfunding resulted from budgetary constraints and allocations of limited budgetary resources that did not give priority to these sectors historically. The problem of low cost-effectiveness has resulted from a lack of prioritization of services with high social returns and information failures, which raise the cost of services and waste resources.

The challenge of meeting the requirements for providing an adequate quantity and quality of social services is immense, especially if the government has to largely undertake this challenge alone. Even if done with donor support, the challenge is huge. Private sector participation and contributions by users to financing the costs of providing these services are necessary to improve the sustainability and quality of services over the long term. The private sector has demonstrated its interest in supplying education services at the postprimary level. For example, the private sector runs nearly half the secondary schools in the country. It is much less involved in primary education, which the public sector continues to dominate. Similarly, private dispensaries and hospitals have mushroomed in urban centers, while public services still dominate in rural districts and villages. A natural divide is therefore emerging that can be exploited to concentrate and rationalize the involvement of the public and private sectors in the provision of social services. There is also increasing evidence of users' willingness to contribute to the costs of these services provided they are of acceptable quality. The examples here include parental contributions toward education and the introduction of the drug revolving fund and user fees in hospitals. The scope for budgetary relief is therefore quite wide. The government should seize this opportunity by eliminating entry barriers to private sector participation while ensuring adherence to required standards and regulatory and safety measures.

The Economy

It is now widely accepted that well-developed and widely applicable information and communication technology is a critical resource and the basis for the competitiveness of today's economies. Increased use of these technologies can lead to improved information flows and reduced uncertainty to improve the performance and productivity of both private enterprises and public sector organizations. It allows businesses to access national and international markets for traditional and new products and inputs more readily and enhances the financial, economic, and strategic planning capacity of both private and public entities. A revised definition of market dynamics informs that supply chain management is "the planning and control of flow of goods and services, information, and money electronically back and forth through the supply chain." The potential of information and communication technology for improved service delivery and provision of education- and health-related services is immense. Furthermore, the use of modern information technology "has the potential to increase the efficiency, transparency and accountability of governments" (Bedi 1999). The most pervasive of these Internet-based "push" technologies are emerging as e-commerce and e-communications.

The development and use of these technologies should be viewed as an integral element of any country's development strategy and they are increasingly expected to help bridge the North-South divide. Bedi notes that at a macro level, the use of information and communication technologies may be expected to enhance the productivity of the various factors of production and should be associated with increases in aggregate output. At a micro level, the use of these technologies should be associated with increases in productivity and a variety of infrastructure alternatives. The growth potential of e-commerce for financial and other products and services and inter- and intra-business applications appears to be unlimited. In rural Costa Rica and Côte d'Ivoire small farmers use telecommunications to obtain information about international coffee and cocoa prices from the city. In Sri Lanka small farmers can use information acquired through the telephone to sell their crops at 80 to 90 percent of the price obtained in Colombo,

174

substantially more than the 50 to 60 percent they were able to achieve before the service become available (World Bank 1998b).

The so-called digital divide or knowledge gap can no longer be ignored, and will be a serious development constraint to countries that lag behind. What is more worrying is that the divide is growing exponentially. With respect to the private sector, Internet-based business applications are no longer simply a wave of the future, but are here to stay and are flourishing. The advantages and cost savings from carrying out business on the Internet have caused e-commerce to mushroom, notes the *Economist* (February 26, 2000), adding that, governments, tax authorities, and the "unwired" all risk being left behind in this phenomenon. The revolution is already fueling high levels of employment and profits in the United States and other countries. While the implications for private sector development are abundantly clear, governments across the world are starting to think of how best to regulate this burgeoning commercial force. The bearing on areas such as business licensing, taxation, and quality or standard of goods and services traded over the Internet is potentially huge. Experience in countries at the vanguard of this revolution is proving that existing rules applied to this new business order prove to be confusing, cumbersome, and the product of a different time.

Indeed, the Internet as an information and communication technology medium is extremely dynamic and fast-paced, even when measured against the rapid changes that increasingly characterize the communications sector. One school of thought holds the view that Internet governance best lends itself to self-regulatory models, and as such the private sector should take the lead in developing self-regulatory approaches suited to the new environment. This is critical to the orderly growth and development of electronic-based commercial and public sector applications. However, regulatory leniency on the part of governments in this regard does not obviate the need for policymakers to better understand how the industry is evolving and to assess its policy and practical implications. Ready access to available indicators in areas such as infrastructure development is fundamental to a better understanding of the networks that enable electronic commerce. From a policy perspective such indicators are also important. Recent examples where indicators have been used to inform issues include the management and administration of the domain name system, as well as trying to assess the impact of mergers on the level of competition in Internet backbone markets. Internet indicators may also help to inform issues related to convergence between different communication platforms as the Internet develops more multimedia capabilities.

Realizing the depth of the trough emerging between the new binary "haves" and "have nots," the International Finance Corporation has joined hands with SOFTBANK, a global Internet company based in Japan, to found SOFTBANK Emerging Markets to incubate Internet-related businesses in developing countries. The company is nurturing new Internet enterprises both by investing seed money and by providing an array of technological, legal, and management support to quickly turn ideas into solid businesses. SOFTBANK Emerging Markets will accelerate the creation of Internet-anchored enterprises in developing countries by working with a network of global industry leaders and local partners. It will also help entrepreneurs in developing countries use established business models to start up locally adapted versions of some of the world's leading Internet companies. A global incubation center to facilitate the transfer of the latest Internet technologies and business models from industrial countries to emerging markets is also being launched. This technology company will ensure the availability of adequate technical resources for the incubated companies and foster the development of a mature technological base in the target countries. Tanzania should not let opportunities such as this pass it by.

While over the medium to long term a mature information and communication technology infrastructure can lower costs and time frames of doing business, enhance efficiency, and encourage the spread of markets in developing countries like Tanzania, access to the new technologies is also dependent on the education and skill base and level of wealth in a particular country. The inability to access information because of limited education or inappropriate language skills and the prevalence of inequalities in access exacerbates the digital gaps and increases income inequality in developing countries. Given the relatively narrow skill base of Tanzania's labor force, an escalation in demand for information technology-related functions could strain other segments of the economy over the medium term. Just as critical in this respect is Tanzania's limited financial resources, which have to be shared among a number of competing, and perhaps more pressing investment priorities. Devoting constrained resources to information and communication technologies would be difficult to justify, especially if the evidence of investment returns is scanty.

Thus while these technologies are becoming increasingly pervasive, Tanzanian businesses have, not surprisingly, been constrained in their access to them. Indeed, the technology used by a broad swathe of private sector entities, especially small and medium enterprises, is generally outmoded, creating issues of quality and standards, especially in regard to external markets. Constraints to adopting modern technology range from the high cost of acquisition to the low profit margins that do not justify additional technology-related costs. Equally important is the low skill base of the general work force, which makes technology adoption and use even more complex. While the Internet and other information and communication technology usage is skewed toward the better-off segments within the better-off economies, the Web is an instrument that, if made widely available and accessible, could in the long run help reduce knowledge and economic inequities.

That said, there is confirmation that the information and communication technology revolution is slowly but steadily taking root across the country. Following the government's call for tenders for international data carriers in 1996, the national regulator issued licenses to three locally registered companies with international ownership. These licenses have a period of 10 years (subject to review after 5 years). In addition, some six Internet providers are based in Dar es Salaam. Their services encompass distribution, publishing, Internet media platforms, and a broad range of e-commerce business-related support functions. A few Internet providers are now servicing Zanzibar as well. Furthermore, protocols for public key infrastructure (cryptography) are being refined and expanded. The government is joining in as well: the Parastatal Reform Commission, the Government of Tanzania's privatization agency, recently launched its own Web site, which provides information about the privatization process in Tanzania; updates on divestitures currently under way; and data on companies to be privatized, labor standards, environmental regulations, and implementation of Uruguay Round agreements. Various other public agencies and ministries, for example, the Tanzania Tourism Board and the Ministry of Energy and Minerals, have their own Web sites. Indeed, the number of Tanzanian Internet host sites has jumped from zero in 1995 to almost 150. The number of Internet subscribers was put at 2,500 in 1998.

English-speaking nations with relatively low labor costs and high skills, such as India and the Philippines, are cashing in on the global dispersion of business, attracting international jobs and substantial revenues. The government must move rapidly to promote sound primary and secondary education to build a skilled labor force (the state of Tamil Nadu, India, alone spends US$10 million a year on computer literacy in local schools). This must be buttressed by boosting investments in infrastructure, especially power and telecommunications networks. Again taking the example of India, the government there has facilitated rapid information and communication technology sector development by endorsing information and software technology parks, and recently agreed to an increased Internet bandwidth, providing global-class infrastructure. Eliminating red tape and instituting an encouraging, state-of-the-art policy agenda, including a transparent, cohesive tax regime for the information and communication technology industry will be conducive to its growth, as will government action to develop a well-thought through and integrated strategic framework.

Tanzania now stands at a cross-roads, where missing the right direction will have incalculable costs for the country amounting to fairly comprehensive economic isolation. By the same token going, even if somewhat belatedly, the way the rest of the world is headed could lead to massive economic growth and resultant poverty alleviation. The high-speed developments in online business technology—defying geographical boundaries and time constraints—are transforming the economic face of the world. This transformation is no less critical than the industrial revolution of the 1900s and is to be taken seriously. As various classified advertisements proclaim with one voice: "It is either E-business or out of business." For Tanzania, bridging the information gap via appropriate information and communication technologies can contribute to accelerated growth, increased industrial productivity, and enhanced agricultural potential from improved efficacy of the private and public sectors. Civil society empowerment; the promulgation of an effective, democratic system of government; an improved quality of life; and enriched development of media, culture, and community are some of the other contributions of an Internet revolution that is pervading every facet of the global society and economy.

Conclusion

Political and macroeconomic stability, liberalized markets, and improved governance are the cornerstones of an attractive investment climate. The attention of private investors has been turning toward Tanzania in the last five years because of improvements in these areas. Tanzania's adjustment efforts regained momentum after the election of the current government at the end of 1995. Under its economic program, macroeconomic stabilization has largely been achieved; trade liberalization and financial sector reform programs have been launched; budget deficits have been contained; inflation has declined, and since the beginning of 1999 has consistently been in single digits for the first time in over two decades; and privatization and civil service reform are gaining momentum. Indeed, notwithstanding adverse weather conditions during the last few years, annual GDP growth has averaged some 4 percent. However, much more needs to be done if Tanzania wishes to establish its reputation as a serious contender for private resources.

While the stabilization component of Tanzania's reform program has been largely successful, the structural reform agenda has yet to be completed, making the gains to date somewhat fragile. In this respect, judicious public investments in social and physical infrastructure that complement private sector inputs and sustained good governance are also key ingredients. The challenge for Tanzania today is to continue to address these constraints with a view to promoting private sector development as the fulcrum of growth and poverty alleviation. This should promote resource flows, not simply for the obvious candidates—mining and tourism—but also for other important sectors, including agriculture, infrastructure, and industry. Indeed, domestic resource mobilization would also receive the requisite impetus from these positive developments in the business climate. In addition, Tanzania needs to pursue a multipronged approach to foster a robust and vibrant private sector that would focus on strengthening regional linkages for broadening its markets and investment base, attracting broadly based foreign investments, and developing and diversifying its export performance.

As discussed in detail in chapter 6, regional integration and economic cooperation is an integral step toward offering a serious, united presence in global markets. Genuine trade integration with the attendant benefits of opening up a larger marketing block at a regional level and providing a more competitive and cohesive supply and investment base on an extraregional basis is a challenge that Tanzania should explore seriously. Not only would the combined regional population provide a larger outlet for the products and services of each of the member states, but it would also provide a broader resource mobilization base. Beyond this, regional integration's strengths are viewed to emanate from the "growth triangles" concept, spatial development initiatives, and transport and development corridors. Differences in factor endowments and increased scope for specialization should be used to drive the formulation of economic development strategies for well-defined, cross-border areas, which should lead to the promotion of private trade and direct investment. Strengthening of infrastructure and development corridors is complementary to the development of cross-border areas, resulting in important economic benefits, particularly through increasing private investment over time in areas such as transport and communications infrastructure. The other extrinsic benefits of regional integration include the likelihood of greater political cooperation, stability, and security in the member states, which are critical to investment and steady growth. That said, regional integration is a complex and time-consuming process that would benefit from a phased approach over the medium term.

The significant growth in the levels of private investment flows to many low- and middle-income countries is an opportunity that Tanzania must take advantage of by creating an investment destination with long-term appeal for investors. FDI represents not just a strengthening of the capital and resource base and production facilities, but is also important for transferring up-to-date technology and know-how, developing stronger entrepreneurial and planning skills, and improving management and operational capacity. In this regard, evolving wisdom in this field suggests that foreign corporations are now increasingly taking state-of-the-art FDI and business facilitation policy frameworks as given. What transnationals are now seeking is a combination of cost reduction from information and communication and other technologies, increased clustering of economic activities and infrastructure, and a marketing nexus to hone their competitive edge. Government must thus move to create the conditions to foster the development of information and communication technology and to promote regional integration, which leads to larger markets on the one hand, and competitive pricing of resources and facilities on the other.

Over the last few years, the Tanzanian economy has witnessed three encouraging developments in the area of export growth: the development of mining, an increase in tourism, and an expansion of horticulture exports. The promising performance of gold, the game parks, cashew nuts, and tropical cut flowers can and must be replicated across other sectors, products, and services through a joint public-private effort. The emerging trade environment is laying the groundwork for Tanzania to increase its export competitiveness. Indeed, the untapped potential in this regard is huge, and exports can be expected to rebound in the traditional areas in the medium term. The goal for the government would be to create conditions conducive to further increasing the range, depth, destinations, and thus the growth rate of Tanzania's net export production. The formulation and implementation of a cohesive strategy for promoting greater efficiency and diversification of the economy to enhance its export orientation and to successfully face the challenges of the changing external environment would also be important. Over the medium to longer term, export performance can be boosted through a concerted drive by the private sector (facilitated by government policy and institutional actions) on three fronts. First, improved productivity levels within traditional agricultural commodities and manufacturing (total merchandise exports currently account for only about 10 percent of total GDP). Second, diversification of exports away from traditional products to nontraditional horticultural products and manufacturing exports. In this respect tremendous scope exists for enhancing Tanzania's agroprocessing capabilities to improve the value added of its products and to generate greater employment. Finally, an improved quality and image of Tanzanian tourism combined with more aggressive marketing offer safari, beach, and eco-tourism packages as viable alternatives to the standard tour destinations across Europe and Asia.

In general, Tanzania's efforts at sustaining a stable macroeconomic policy framework, adopting outward-looking policies, improving the administrative and regulatory environment for businesses, and creating the requisite physical and human infrastructure are all essential building blocks for creating an investment destination with a long-term appeal for investors. Conjoint and sustained action on these fronts will make the difference in Tanzania's pursuit of private investments.

6. Pacemakers for Sustainable Economic Growth

The Impetus and Urgency for Higher Sustainable Growth

Four decades after independence, Tanzania remains one of the 10 poorest countries in the world. Poverty is manifested not only in low per capita income, but also in the low human development indicators defining the welfare of its citizens. About half the population cannot acquire the daily consumption necessities of life (in relation to international standards), their vital statistics in health are somewhat low, and their capabilities for self-sustenance undeveloped. This situation persists even though Tanzania is endowed with a rich natural resource base, has easy access to the international market, and has had a peaceful and politically stable environment since its independence. Notwithstanding its large ethnic diversity, Tanzania has managed to forge a cohesive national identity around a common language.

Despite the encouraging recent upturn in GDP growth, the challenge for Tanzania remains that real income growth is still too low to make any significant impact on poverty. Today Tanzania's income per capita is only 30 percent higher than four decades ago, and the average annual growth rate during the period has been a paltry 3.8 percent.. Meanwhile, some Asian countries, for example, Indonesia and the Republic of Korea, which were at a more or less similar level of per capita income at the time of Tanzania's independence, have been able to increase their incomes per capita more than tenfold during the same period. Tanzania's per capita GDP is also low relative to the high-performing economies in the region such as Botswana, Côte d'Ivoire, Ghana, Mauritius, and Uganda. The achievement of higher and sustained growth is therefore imperative for Tanzania.

Tanzania's Development Vision 2025 is a statement of hope for the future and a desire to break with the past. Its ambitious target is to achieve in a quarter of a century what Tanzania could not do in four decades: to halve abject poverty; create a base for sustained development of the economy; and fashion a diversified, middle-income, market economy. This it intends to achieve through managing sustained, export-led growth at a rate of 8 percent per year, judiciously exploiting the country's natural resource base, unleashing dormant private sector potential, and paying particular attention to poverty reduction programs.

The objective of this chapter is to assess the viability of this ambitious vision in several ways. We start by using policy-based growth projections to evaluate the magnitude of economic growth that can be expected from consolidating reforms and further improving policies and institutional arrangements. Next we analyze what the achievement of higher growth would require in terms of enhancing productivity and investments in human and physical capital, including discussion of policy measures needed in each of these areas.

After this macro-economic assessment of Tanzania's growth potential and factor input requirements, we present the implications of enhanced growth coupled with structural transformation on the sectoral distribution of growth. We conclude by examining the growth potential of three areas that promise to contribute significantly to growth in the short and medium term. In the long term, growth can only be sustained if growth impulses originating from the exploitation of natural resources are accompanied by a process of structural transformation, in which the contribution of the secondary and tertiary sectors to GDP increases significantly.

In addition to domestic supply conditions, foreign economic growth and international demand conditions also play an important role in Tanzania's development. The chapter thus closes with an examination of opportunities to benefit from regional integration.

Policy-Based Growth Projections

Policies and institutions are important determinants of growth. This section uses the estimated relationship between economic growth and various indicators of the quality of policies and institutions to assess Tanzania's growth potential.

These projections are based on recent World Bank work that links assessments of policies and institutions to economic growth. This research indicates that policy-based predictions are generally closer to eventual outcomes than traditional projections based on assumptions about investment and investment productivity. In addition to the policy indicator, a variety of conditioning variables, including initial per capita GDP, telephones per capita (a measure of infrastructure), primary school enrollment (a measure of human capital), and lagged per capita GDP growth, are used to predict future growth.

The underlying model is estimated from cross-country regressions of per capita GDP growth in 1990–97 for 75–90 countries, depending on data availability. As assessments of country policy and institutions may differ depending on which criteria are used, we estimate the model using four different assessments of policies and institutions:

- The World Bank's Country Policy and Institutional Assessment[25]
- The Institutional Investor assessment[26]
- The International Country Risk Guide assessment[27]
- The Euromoney assessment.[28]

The original quantitative assessments of each of these four institutions are rescaled so as to measure the quality of institutions and policies on a range from 1–6, where 1 indicates poor quality and 6 indicates high quality. Table 6.1 presents projections of per capita growth using the four different policy indicators.

---

[25] The World Bank's Country Policy and Institutional Assessment is based on Bank economists' and sector specialists' rating of 20 items in the areas of management of inflation and the current account, structural policies, policies for social inclusion and equity, and public sector management and institutions.

[26] Institutional Investor credit ratings are based on a survey of leading international bankers who are asked to rate each country on a scale from 0 to 100, where 100 presents maximum creditworthiness. The Institutional Investor averages these ratings, attaching greater weights to respondents with greater worldwide exposure and more sophisticated country analysis systems.

[27] The International Country Risk Guide compiles monthly data on a variety of political, financial, and economic risk factors to calculate risk indexes in each of these categories, as well as a composite risk index. Five financial, 13 political, and 6 economic factors are used. Political risk assessment scores are based on subjective staff analysis of available information, economic risk assessment scores are based on objective analysis of quantitative data, and financial risk assessment scores are based on analysis of a mix of quantitative and qualitative information. The political risk measure is given twice the weight of financial and economic risk.

[28] Euromoney country risk scores are based on the weighted average of quantitative indicators in nine categories: political risk (25 percent), economic performance (25 percent), debt indicators (10 percent), debt in default or rescheduled (10 percent), credit ratings (10 percent), access to bank finance (5 percent), access to short-term financing (5 percent), access to capital markets (5 percent), and discount on forfeiting (5 percent). For items for which no data are available, the rating is zero, which might introduce a downward bias for countries like Tanzania, for which data availability is often poor.

We provide projections for three scenarios. The first scenario assumes that policies and institutions remain unchanged, while the other two scenarios assume that policies and institutions improve, reflected in an increase in ratings of 0.5 and 1 point, respectively. In addition to the individual projections, we also provide the average of these four projections, on which the following discussion is based.

Table 6.1. *Policy Based Growth Projections*

Policy indicator	Projected GDP growth per capita (percent)			
	1999 rating	Constant policy	Improve +0.5	Improve +1.0
World Bank Country Policy and Institutional Assessment	3.55	1.80	2.88	3.95
Euromoney	2.22	1.67	2.31	2.95
International Country Risk Guide	3.38	1.39	1.90	2.41
Institutional	1.97	1.85	3.07	4.30
Average	2.77	1.68	2.54	3.40

Source: Authors' calculations.

With no improvement in institutions and policies, Tanzania's projected average per capita growth is 1.68 percent, implying a considerable improvement over past growth performance. This positive growth outlook for Tanzania reflects improvements in policies and institutions that took place during the past decade and that are expected to pay off in terms of significantly enhanced future growth.

Further improvements in policies and institutions, including the consistent pursuit of these policies, are projected to lead to significant enhancements in growth performance. For example, if Tanzania's performance rating increased by 0.5 points, per capita growth would increase to 2.54 percent. Many countries, including Mauritius, Sri Lanka, and Vietnam (based on the Euromoney rating) have already achieved such ratings of policies and institutions. An increase in the quality of policies and institutions by about 1 point, putting Tanzania at the same level as countries such as Brazil, India, and Namibia, would lead to a further upward revision of projected per capita growth to 3.4 percent. According to the policy and institutional assessments underlying these projections, the greatest weaknesses constraining economic growth can be found in the areas of the financial sector, governance, and public sector management.

However, these policy-based growth projections do not take into account the effect of HIV/AIDS. While earlier estimates indicated that the impact of HIV/AIDS on per capita GDP growth would be small, more recent work demonstrates that the impact of HIV/AIDS on economic growth will pose a significant obstacle to raising per capita incomes. At Tanzania's present level of HIV/AIDS prevalence, HIV/AIDS is estimated to reduce economic growth by almost 1 percentage point, compared to a situation without HIV/AIDS (see box 6.1).

These policy-based growth projections provide a useful assessment of Tanzania's growth prospects and indicate what rates of growth can realistically be expected. Clearly, the stronger the institutional and policy framework, the higher economic growth. While the policy improvements considered for the purpose of these projections are achievable in the short to medium term, in the long term further policy improvements, and thus higher growth than projected, are conceivable. This brings Vision 2025's growth target of 8 percent within the realm of possibility.

The Path Toward Sustained Growth: A Macroeconomic Scenario

To spur and sustain a rate of growth sufficient to have a significant impact on poverty will require increased investments in human and physical capital. Even more important, ensuring higher productivity and efficiency of both existing and new investment will be absolutely necessary.

Box 6.1. *HIV/AIDS Reduces Projected Per Capita GDP*

Recent work by Bonnel (2000) indicates that the impact of HIV/AIDS on per capita incomes will be severe, as HIV/AIDS erodes some of the main determinants of economic growth, such as social capital, domestic savings, and human capital.

HIV/AIDS has dramatically reduced life expectancy in many African countries, including Tanzania, which leads to a shortened payoff period for investment in human capital through education. HIV/AIDS thus directly reduces the rate at which human capital is accumulated.

The second channel through which HIV/AIDS affects per capita income growth is reduced savings. First, HIV/AIDS raises expenditures on health care, and thus reduces available funds for consumption or saving. Second, with the reduced life expectancy, saving becomes less attractive and a greater share of income is likely to be devoted to consumption. HIV/AIDS is also likely to have a negative impact on macroeconomic policy, which is an important determinant of growth. The diversion of private and public resources from investment to the treatment and care of those with HIV/AIDS can bring about a decline in domestic savings and an increase in fiscal deficits. In addition, the loss of human capital might adversely affect the macroeconomic management capacity of governments.

A third channel is through the impact of HIV/AIDS on private sector development. HIV/AIDS can lead to higher costs because of increased staff turnover, greater attrition, and higher wages for skilled staff, which in turn may affect firms' investment decisions. In addition, private sector development would suffer to the extent that HIV/AIDS would erode the quality of regulation and of the legal environment.

Finally, HIV/AIDS also affects social capital by eroding existing social networks and traditional support mechanisms. The result might be a generation of AIDS-related orphans who have to grow up without the support and guidance of adults.

Bonnel (2000) finds that all four channels are significant and can lead to a significant reduction of per capita income growth. In the case of Tanzania, at the current prevalence rate of 13.7 percent, HIV/AIDS is estimated to reduce the rate of growth of GDP per capita by almost 1 percentage point per year.

Source: Bonnel (2000).

Looking forward, two stages in Tanzania's quest for higher growth are clearly discernable. In the initial phase, the main source of growth is an increase in productivity through more efficient use of resources. By necessity, this also includes the enhanced use of foreign aid, which represents an important source of financing of the public sector's support for development. During this phase, Tanzania will move closer to the production frontier.

As Tanzania moves closer to its production frontier, growth will have to be sustained by higher levels of investment, financed from both domestic and foreign sources. While public investment has an important role to play in the areas of infrastructure and human resource development, growth will come mainly from market-driven increases in private investment. In addition to providing an investment-friendly policy and institutional framework, key elements for achieving increased investment rates are functioning financial markets, access to foreign financing, and openness to foreign investors.

In terms of policy this implies that despite the low level of income, higher investment rates will have to be generated from more zealous domestic savings mobilization and continued opening up of the economy to private investment. The issue then boils down to figuring out how to (a) devise the most effective policies and vehicles for achieving higher savings rates; (b) provide an investment-friendly environment; (c) ensure that existing and new capital stock is utilized fully and efficiently; and (d) take the sectoral pattern of output growth fully into account when formulating investment programs, and also considering the complementarity or substitutability between public and private investment in targeting poverty reduction.

The previous section indicated that based on continued progress in improving the policy and institutional framework, long-term growth rates of up to 6.7 percent could be within reach. What would such enhanced growth require in terms of investment in human and physical capital and enhancements in total factor productivity? The analysis of Tanzania's past growth performance has used the method of growth accounting to identify the contribution of investment in human and physical capital and changes in TFP to economic growth. This section employs the same method to identify the human and physical investment requirements, as well as productivity, enhancements necessary to meet Tanzania's growth targets.

Investment in Human Capital

A strengthened focus on human capital development is a precondition for achieving higher economic growth. Investment in human capital includes not only formal education, on-the-job training, and adult education, but also health care and various other activities to enhance the productivity of the labor force. Investment in human capital is also extremely important for Tanzania's poverty reduction efforts. In addition to raising the income earning potential of the poor, many activities associated with investments in human capital also contribute directly to human development and well-being.

Numerous studies have demonstrated the importance of investment in human capital for economic growth. For most Asian countries, improvements in education have contributed 0.4–0.9 percentage points to growth in output per worker. To assess whether such gains would also be possible for Tanzania, this section analyses what improvements would be necessary in the educational status of Tanzania's labor force and whether such improvements are attainable.

Educational attainment serves as the principal indicator for the quality of human capital in Tanzania. Table 6.2 shows the shares of Tanzania's population according to highest educational achievement. In 1996, 23.2 percent of the population had no formal education, 15.4 percent had completed primary school, 0.1 percent had completed their secondary education, and 0.8 percent had completed their higher education.

Based on the current status of educational attainment, table 6.2 presents three scenarios showing improved educational attainment by 2025. Assuming a 7 percent rate of return to education and a labor share of 65 percent in Tanzania's output, the annual effect on output per worker is calculated for each scenario.

The first scenario is characterized by relatively modest improvements in the status of educational attainment. The population share with only a primary education, both completed and not completed, increases from 73.6 percent to 77 percent, but with 27 percent of the population completing primary education, compared with only 15.4 percent in 1996. The population share with no formal education declines correspondingly from 23.2 percent to 20 percent, with no improvements in postprimary attainment. The impact of these improvements on output per worker is modest: they would add only 0.08 percentage points to annual economic growth.

The second scenario assumes that in addition to progress in primary education, a greater share of the population is able to progress to and complete secondary education. These additional improvements in secondary school attainment would lead to an annual growth contribution of 0.33 percentage points per year.

Table 6.2. *Scenarios for Investment in Human Capital and Economic Growth (percentage of the labor force)*

		Scenarios for 2025		
Highest educational achievement	*1996 actual*	*Low*	*Medium*	*High*
No formal education	23.2	20	10	10
Primary, not completed	58.2	50	40	17
Primary, completed	15.4	27	36	48
Secondary, not completed	2.1	2.1	8	7
Secondary, completed	0.1	0.1	5	15
Higher education, not completed	0.2	0.2	0.2	1
Higher education, completed	0.8	0.8	0.8	2
Annual effect on output per worker (%)		0.08	0.33	0.60

Source: Author's calculations.

The last scenario is the most ambitious one, showing significant improvements in primary, secondary, and higher education. By 2025, only 10 percent of the population would not have received any formal education, 65 percent would have received at least have some primary education, 25 percent would have at least some secondary education, and 3 percent would have some higher education. In this case, the contribution of education to economic growth would be 0.60 percentage points per year. Such improvements in educational attainment would require massive investments in education, in particular, in primary and secondary education, and require significant increases in gross enrollment ratios at the primary and secondary level.

To assess whether these improvements in educational attainment are feasible, let us examine other countries' experience with improvements in educational attainment. Table 6.3 shows the change in educational attainment for three Asian countries—Indonesia, the Republic of Korea, and Malaysia—between 1960 and 1985. All three countries made significant progress during that period.

Indonesia reduced the share of its population without any formal education from 68 percent in 1960 to 23.6 percent in 1985. In Korea and Malaysia, the share of population without any formal education dropped from more than 40 percent in 1960 to an impressive 10.9 percent in Korea and 23 percent in Malaysia. Reducing the share of Tanzania's population without any formal education from the current figure of around 23 percent to 10 percent by the year 2025 would only be feasible if within the next few years if 100 percent of children attended primary school.

Increasing the population share that has at least completed primary education from the current 15.4 percent to 48 percent is a bigger challenge. Between 1960 and 1985, Indonesia increased its share of population with at least primary education by 23.1 percentage points, Korea by 28.5 percentage points, and Malaysia by 29.6 percentage points. Although the task of achieving an increase from 15.4 percent to 48 percent, that is, an increase of about 33 percentage points is greater than what Indonesia, Korea, and

Malaysia achieved, a fairly large percentage of Tanzania's children at least enter primary school. The challenge is thus to increase completion rates in primary school if ambitious targets are to be achieved.

Table 6.3. *Educational Attainment in Indonesia, Korea, Malaysia, 1960 and 1985 (percentage of the population)*

	Indonesia		Korea		Malaysia	
Highest educational attainment	1960	1985	1960	1985	1960	1985
No formal education	68.0	23.6	43.8	10.9	49.7	23.0
Primary, not completed	16.8	37.9	3.8	7.2	25.0	22.2
Primary, completed	11.8	25.6	32.4	13.7	13.6	23.4
Secondary, not completed	2.7	7.3	9.7	31.3	6.9	18.7
Secondary, completed	0.7	5	7.7	23.4	3.2	10.0
Higher education, not completed	0.1	0.4	1.2	7.3	0.4	1.3
Higher education, completed	0	0.1	1.4	6.2	1.1	1.4

Source: Barro and Lee (1996).

With respect to secondary education, Tanzania's target under the high human capital investment scenario is similar to what Malaysia achieved between 1960 and 1985. Indonesia's record with respect to improving the share of its population with secondary education is weaker, while Korea was able to raise its population share with at least secondary education from less than 10 percent in 1960 to more than 20 percent in 1985.

Finally, with respect to higher education, the target under the high human capital investment scenario is relatively unambitious and appears easily achievable. It has deliberately been kept low, as increasing primary and secondary education should be a clear policy priority.

Policies for Increasing Investment in Human Capital

Investment in human capital covers a wide range of activities, such as formal education at all levels, on-the job training, life-long learning, preventive and curative health care, and nutrition. The actual investment in human capital is determined by a multiplicity of factors that affect the cost of and returns to human capital investment. Because many forms of investment in human capital also entail significant externalities, public support for specific forms of human capital investments has an import role to play, particularly in the financing of education and health services. Unfortunately, the past two decades saw a diminishing capacity of the public sector to support human capital investments, while at the same time low growth and widespread poverty limited households' capacity to contribute sufficiently to human capital investments. Labor market constraints, a compressed wage and salary structure, and low economic growth coupled with poor labor market prospects also contributed to low investment in human capital by reducing the expected returns to such investments.

Enhancing human capital investment therefore requires measures in various areas. These include measures to enhance overall economic growth, and thus the demand for labor; to liberalize the labor market; and to increase public support for basic education and health care, coupled with increased public sector efficiency in the delivery of these services.

Improving the level of educational attainment is a key element of enhancing human capital investment. One of the major constraints in this area is the poor quality of primary education and the lack of opportunities to obtain secondary education. The government will have to play a significant role in ensuring broad access to primary education and expanded access to secondary education. With respect to technical and vocational training and postsecondary training, increased emphasis needs to be put on private sector provision and financing by beneficiaries to ensure that demand is met.

International experience provides guidance on key elements of a successful strategy to strengthen a country's educational system as follows:

- The government's contribution to education must be in line with clear priorities, both in terms of financing and provision, to achieve the maximum impact from extremely scarce public and private resources.
- Government provision and financing should focus on a limited set of core subjects in primary education. However, for this limited set of core subjects, the government would assume primary responsibility for providing key inputs such as teachers and teaching materials.
- The overriding objective should be to provide good quality education to ensure full mastery of literacy and numeracy skills.
- The main source of expansion of education at the postprimary level should be the private sector.
- Nongovernmental providers of education services can play an important role at all levels, and the government should support their activities rather than hinder them through various obstacles.
- The limited availability of resources requires particular attention to efficiency measures, such as avoiding low pupil to teacher ratios and using double shifts or grouping multiple grades in the same classroom.
- Centralization of the educational system should be avoided by locating most decisions at the school level, unless there is a clear rationale and justification for locating them at a higher level.
- Parental and community-level participation in educational decisions is key to ensuring the quality of service delivery.

When all these elements are in place, the re-allocation of government resources toward the education sector, along with donor support, is likely to lead to improved educational outcomes. In close cooperation with stakeholders and development partners, the government is developing a program that will provide a coherent framework for the development of the education sector. In addition, accelerated economic growth and improved job market prospects are also likely to increase the demand for education and households' willingness and ability to contribute more to the financing of their children's education.

The analysis of returns to education showed that employer-provided training and on-the-job training yields the highest rates of return. Consequently, employer-based training should be encouraged. Employers are aware of their skill requirements and can either train employees themselves or purchase training services. Fiscal incentives such as properly design public subsidies, tax deductions, or rebates on training expenses will increase firm training.

Enhancing Total Factor Productivity

Enhancing factor productivity refers to the ability to obtain more output from a given amount of resources, be they human or physical capital. In the long run, there are essentially two types of constraints to productivity: policy-imposed constraints and distortions and knowledge constraints. In the short run, productivity can be constrained by demand, leading to the underutilization of resources. However, in the absence of other constraints, such demand constraints would be either temporary or the economy would adjust appropriately. Policy-imposed constraints and distortions were the main factors retarding productivity growth in Tanzania during the past four decades. Ongoing reform efforts are removing many of these constraints and distortions, which can be expected to lead to substantial productivity gains in the short term.

A rough idea of the potential for increasing output by using existing capital more efficiently can be obtained by looking at the difference between actual and potential GDP (figure 6.1). With an average annual increase of 1 percent instead of the actual increase of only 0.3 percent in 1998, per capita income that year would have been 30 percent higher than what it actually was. Thus closing the productivity gap that has opened up since the late 1970s could yield a substantial increase in output from more efficient use of capital. However, much past investment is no longer available for productive use. Aside from general depreciation, the reasons for this include technical obsolescence, poor maintenance and repair, and investments that never led to a matching increase in the capital stock because of factors such as overpricing, corruption, or poor investment choices.

Figure 6.1. *Potential and Actual Output per Worker, 1961–98*

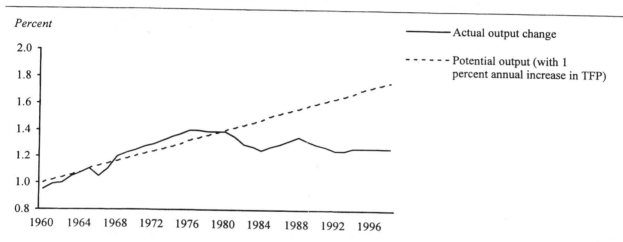

Source: Authors' calculations.

Theoretical and empirical studies for other countries indicate the possibility of efficiency gains from removing policy and institutional constraints. For example, a study by Parente and Prescott (1999) indicates that such measures could triple output through the more efficient use of existing capital and the adoption of new technologies.

Once policy and institutional constraints have been removed and the associated gains in productivity harvested, Tanzania could only achieve additional productivity gains by expanding its knowledge frontier. The World Bank (1998b) identifies two sorts of knowledge that are critical for developing countries, namely:

- Knowledge about technology, that is, technical knowledge or know-how. In the context of economic growth, examples would be knowledge about manufacturing processes, agricultural methods, and organizational methods. Developing countries typically have less of this know-how and the poor have less than the nonpoor.
- Knowledge about attributes, such as the quality of a product, the diligence of a worker, or the creditworthiness of a firm, which are all crucial for effective markets. Mechanisms to alleviate information problems, such as product standards, training certificates, and credit reports, are generally fewer and weaker in developing countries than in industrial countries. Information problems and the resulting market failures especially hurt the poor. In the context of Tanzania, an

particularly apparent information problem is banks' costs to obtain credit information, which has resulted in the almost complete absence of credit markets for small and medium enterprises.

Consequently, expansion of the knowledge base has to be another key element in Tanzania's growth strategy. Direct foreign investment and joint ventures provide an important source for enhancing the knowledge base of the economy and the importance of these to ensure dynamic growth through learning cannot be overemphasized. Enhancing the knowledge base of the economy also depends critically on the information and communications infrastructure. As experience elsewhere has shown, liberalized markets for providers of such services are generally the precondition for efficient and affordable communication services.

Cross-country studies on factor productivity provide an indication of possible productivity growth rates for Tanzania in the long run. Looking at the experience of Southeast Asian countries (table 6.4), some studies suggest that about half of their rapid growth is attributable to productivity gains. More conservative estimates still attribute between 0.8 and 2 percentage points of these countries' growth of output per capita to increases in TFP. In assessing Tanzania's growth potential, it thus appears possible that about 1 percentage point of growth per worker could come from productivity gains. As mentioned before, in the immediate future the contribution of productivity gains to output growth is likely to be even higher, given the potential for more productive use of the existing capital stock.

Table 6.4. *Growth and Total Factor Productivity in Selected East Asian Countries, 1960–94 (percent)*

	Indonesia	Korea	Malaysia	Thailand	Taiwan (China)
Growth of output per worker	3.4	5.7	5.7	5.0	5.8
Contribution of TFP	0.8	1.5	1.5	1.8	2.0

Source: Bosworth and Collins (1996).

Policy Actions to Increase Total Factor Productivity

The first set of actions to increase TFP should be the continued pursuit and consolidation of policy and institutional reforms that will create an enabling environment for growth. Such actions are outlined throughout this report.

The second set of actions concern the area of knowledge and information. As the World Bank (1998b) points out, governments and international institutions have an important role to play in supporting the creation, adoption, absorption, dissemination, and utilization of knowledge. Because the market for knowledge often fails, there is a strong rationale for public action. The state is in a unique position to narrow knowledge gaps, for example, by adopting an open trade regime, supporting life-long learning, and establishing a sound regulatory environment for a competitive telecommunications industry.

In the context of knowledge about new technologies, it is useful to distinguish between technologies that complement existing technology and those that substitute for existing technology. To facilitate the adoption of the former, activities such as those described in the previous paragraph are adequate. However, with respect to introducing new technologies that replace existing ones, the government also needs to ensure that market structures are flexible enough to allow existing technologies to disappear (exit of some firms) while new technologies are created. For example, how inflexibility in the labor market has both prevented the introduction of new technologies and the efficient utilization of existing technologies is well documented. Similarly, the distortion of market signals through subsidies or market protection through tariffs or quotas may allow firms that use inefficient technologies to remain in the market and thereby prevent the adoption of more efficient technologies.

Although information is crucial to the functioning of markets, they do not always provide enough of it on their own, because those who generate information cannot always appropriate the returns to information. Public action is thus required to provide information to verify quality, monitor performance, and regulate transactions to provide the foundation for successful market-based development. Of course, as in any other area for potential government intervention, the likely gains from government intervention have to be weighed carefully against the potential for government failure. In particular, in designing interventions in this area, the severe institutional and human capacity constraints that exist in Tanzania need to be taken into account.

The third area concerns the better use of foreign aid, which plays a significant role in Tanzania. As noted in chapter 3, one of the main problems affecting the effectiveness of foreign aid was insufficient attention to the recurrent cost implications of aid-financed investments. Recent years have witnessed a gradual change in the relationship between donors and the government. This includes efforts to bring donor assistance within the government's planning and budgeting framework through mechanisms such as broad donor involvement in the Public Expenditure Review process and the formulation of the Medium-Term Expenditure Framework. However, it also includes measures to strengthen the government's own financial management and accountability mechanisms to increase donor confidence in government systems. The initial aim is to strengthen the information flow between the government and donors, with the medium-term goal being to make greater use of government systems to manage and deliver donor assistance. Parallel to this is the ongoing shift from narrow, donor-controlled projects to more encompassing approaches, such as sector programs and general budget support.

Investment in Physical Capital

Using the same growth accounting framework as in the section on human capital, in this section we derive the required growth in the physical capital stock under the assumption of annual depreciation of the capital stock by 4 percent and a share of capital in output of 35 percent.

Table 6.5 presents the quantitative input requirements for achieving the range of growth outcomes obtained from the policy-based growth projections. Clearly the higher the contribution from investment in human capital and enhanced productivity, the less the requirement for physical investment. For example, to achieve a growth in output per worker of 4.3 percent would require an initial investment of 23 percent of GDP, declining over time to 20 percent, if parallel investments in human capital and enhancing productivity were undertaken. By contrast, if achieving a growth rate of 4.3 percent were to be attempted without any improvements in human capital or productivity, the required investment would initially be 28 percent of GDP, increasing to 36 percent by 2025.

The results also indicate the possibility of virtuous and vicious investment cycles. In those cases where investment in human capital and enhancements in TFP contribute significantly to the achievement of the growth target, the physical capital stock required to achieve the growth target can grow at a rate below output growth. This in turn implies that replacement investment grows at a smaller rate than output, and the share of investment in GDP can actually decline for a given growth target. Put slightly differently, if the share of investment in GDP is kept constant, the growth contribution of that investment will increase and thus fuel further growth. In the case of Tanzania, achieving the growth target of 4.3 percent per year would initially require investment of around 23 percent of GDP. However, by 2025 this capital requirement would decline to 20 percent. This would be a virtuous investment cycle.

By contrast, a vicious investment cycle occurs if growth is generated exclusively from investment in physical capital, with little investment in human capital or enhancements in TFP. In such a case, to achieve a particular growth target, the share of investment in GDP would have to increase continuously. For example, if Tanzania were to achieve the growth target of 4.3 percent based purely on physical capital accumulation, the share of investment in GDP would have to increase from 28 percent initially to 36 percent by 2025, a situation that is clearly unsustainable in the long run.

Table 6.5. *Sources of Growth*
(percent)

| Growth scenario | Growth of output per worker | Contribution by component | | | Required investment as a share of GDP |
		Education per worker	Total factor productivity	Physical capital per worker	
High growth	4.3	0.6	1.0	2.7	23–20
	4.3	0.6	0.5	3.2	25–24
	4.3	0.4	0.5	3.4	26
	4.3	0.0	0.0	4.3	28–36
Medium growth	2.6	0.6	1.0	1.0	19–16
	2.6	0.6	0.5	1.5	20
	2.6	0.4	0.5	1.7	21
	2.6	0.0	0.0	2.6	24–30
Low growth	1.4	0.6	0.5	0.3	17–16
	1.4	0.2	0.3	0.9	18–19
	1.4	0.0	0.0	1.4	20–25

Source: Author's calculations.

Policy Actions to Raise Investment and Improve Savings Performance

INVESTMENT. In terms of policy, the simple analysis performed earlier implies that the more potent policy in the short to medium term is for Tanzania to reduce the level of inefficient utilization of existing and new investments. To accelerate growth to 6.7 percent, raising the current investment rate will also be imperative. Because the share of public investment in total investment has been declining, this implies that more private sector investment will have to be mobilized. Unfortunately, the situation regarding private investment during the reform period has not been encouraging, especially since 1994. Given this gloomy picture, Tanzania has no option but to embark on reforming its economic and political environment affecting private investment decisions. These areas of reform include government leadership; corruption; rule of law; racial and ethnic tensions; quality of the bureaucracy, including the degree of independence from political pressure and red tape; risk of repudiation of contracts; security of property and persons; risk of expropriation by the government and policy reversals; political rights; civil liberties; external conflict risk (social and political stability); high costs and unreliability of transportation and telecommunications; and unstable macroeconomic fundamentals. The recent increase in TFP suggests that structural reforms have had beneficiary effects, especially through the privatization of low capital efficiency investment, and enhanced the efficiency of investment at least modestly from 1996. However, TFP remains below that achieved by high performers in Africa. This in turn implies that if Tanzania is to attract private capital, the government must focus on improving the rate of return to investment, physical infrastructure, and human capital.

In the medium to long term, Tanzania will face high competition for foreign direct investment from the emerging economies of Eastern Europe. The challenge is therefore for Tanzania to implement domestic policies to spur higher savings and investment and to attract both foreign direct investment and official development assistance resources. This implies that Tanzania should continue to implement financial sector reforms, sustain a positive fiscal balance, and create a conducive environment to attract foreign capital and arrest massive capital flight.

SAVINGS. Given the low level of development of the financial infrastructure, attempts to increase savings substantially will require a number of bold and pragmatic policy actions. Key among these is to accelerate and sustain the reform of the financial sector and institutions to address the limitations cited earlier, solidify the stability of macroeconomic fundamentals, and increase per capita income. Comprehensive pension reform would be an important step toward realizing the potential of contractual saving institutions to encourage private saving. Such reforms should free pension funds from government control to foster efficiency, competition, and extension of the coverage of the pension system to enhance the performance of compulsory social security savings. Strengthening microfinance and supporting informal financial intermediation are important instruments for providing access to saving instruments and credit in rural areas and to the informal sector Finally, tax-driven saving instruments, such as five-year tax free deposits, have helped increase savings in other countries such as the Philippines, and their potential to raise savings in Tanzania should be examined.

In addition to encouraging private saving, increasing public saving to support public sector investment and to limit public sector deficit financing requirements is desirable. During the past three years, the government was able to achieve recurrent budget surpluses and reduce its stock of outstanding domestic debt. However, it is essential to ensure that increased public savings do not reduce the public sector's capacity for service delivery in such essential areas as basic education and primary health care. Thus efforts to increase public saving need to be clearly focused on curtailing unproductive expenditures, fraud, and waste; limiting public financing to those areas where there is a clear rationale for public sector participation; and enhancing the efficiency of the taxation system.

The Path Toward Sustained Growth: A Sectoral Scenario

Tanzania's own development experience, as well as that of countries further ahead on the development road, provide clear lessons about the relative importance of various sectors as engines of growth. The following are among these lessons:

- A well-performing agriculture sector provides the basis for growth.
- Exploitation of natural resources helps to fuel growth, but exclusive reliance on natural resource exploitation is rarely sustainable, necessitating the need for broadly based growth in manufacturing and services.
- Sustained growth is accompanied by structural transformation, that is, the manufacturing and service sector will grow faster than the agriculture sector.
- The factors that contributed to the failure of Tanzania's industrialization efforts during the 1970s were clearly policy related, implying that industrialization driven by the private sector can succeed if Tanzania avoids repeating its mistakes of the past and creates preconditions for expansion of the manufacturing sector, including a sound macroeconomic environment, an enabling policy and regulatory framework, efficient public service delivery, and sound institutions.

This section provides a scenario for sectoral growth that might underpin Tanzania's overall growth targets. The starting point for the discussion is an analysis of the link between sectoral transformation and economic growth. Table 6.6 shows the shares of agriculture, industry, manufacturing, and services in total value added for various countries in 1980 and 1998. The table illustrates two important points that are well established in the economic literature. The first is that progress in economic development is accompanied by substantial structural transformation of the economy. In particular, the industrial and service sectors generally become more significant in terms of their contribution to total GDP, while the contribution of agriculture to total GDP tends to decline significantly over time. Second, in a period of 20 years, substantial structural transformation is possible. This holds for countries with exceptional growth performance such as Indonesia and Thailand, but also for slower-growing countries, such as Ghana. However, faster economic growth generally also leads to faster economic transformation.

Table 6.6. *Structural Transformation, Selected Countries 1980 and 1998 (percentage share of GDP)*

Country	Agriculture		Industry		Manufacturing		Services	
	1980	1998	1980	1998	1980	1998	1980	1998
Ghana	58	37	12	25	8	8	30	38
India	38	25	24	30	16	19	39	45
Indonesia	24	16	42	43	13	26	34	41
Kenya	33	29	21	16	13	10	47	55
Thailand	23	11	29	40	22	29	48	49
Tanzania	45	46	18	14	12	7	37	40

Source: World Bank (1999i).

Thus if Tanzania can achieve accelerated, sustained economic growth over the next 25 years, that growth is likely to be accompanied by significant structural change. Drawing on the experience of other countries, the share of industry can be expected to increase from the current 14 percent to somewhere between 20 and 30 percent of GDP, depending on the pace of economic growth. At the same time, the share of agriculture is likely to fall from its current 46 percent of GDP to somewhere between 20 and 30 percent of GDP. The impact of economic growth on the relative size of the service sector is more difficult to predict, given that Tanzania's service sector already accounts for 40 percent of the economy, a share that is comparable to that of countries that have already undergone significant structural transformation from agriculture to industry, such as Indonesia. However, given Tanzania's tourism potential, the need to develop supporting business and financial services, as well as the need to expand social service delivery, the share of the service sector is likely to increase during the next 25 years.

We now examine in more detail the implications of an acceleration in economic growth and structural transformation. The starting point is the policy-based growth projections that, depending on the pace of consolidation and further improvements in policies and institutional reforms, predict overall real economic growth in the range of 3.8 to 6.7 percent (assuming an average population growth rate of 2.4 percent during 1998–2025). Table 6.7 presents three scenarios of economic growth and structural transformation.

The slow growth scenario assumes average real economic growth of 3.8 percent during 1998—2025 and a slow pace of structural transformation, resulting in shares in GDP of agriculture, industry, and services of 40 percent, 18 percent, and 42 percent, respectively, in 2025. The implicit real growth rates for the individual sectors are 3.2 percent for agriculture, 4.8 percent for industry, and 4 percent for services.

The medium growth scenario assumes real economic growth of 5 percent during 1998–2025 and a faster pace of structural transformation, resulting in shares in GDP of agriculture, industry, and services of 30 percent, 20 percent, and 50 percent, respectively, in 2025. The implicit real growth rates for the individual sectors are 3.2 percent for agriculture, 6.5 percent for industry, and 5.9 percent for services.

Table 6.7. *Scenarios for Economic Growth and Structural Transformation (percent)*

		Slow growth		Medium growth		Fast growth	
Sector	Share in GDP, 1998	Average real growth rate, 1998-2005	Share in GDP, 2025	Average real growth rate, 1998-2005	Share in GDP, 2025	Average real growth rate, 1998-2005	Share in GDP, 2025
Agriculture	46	3.2	40	3.2	30	3.2	20
Industry	14	4.8	18	6.5	20	10.0	30
Services	40	4.0	42	5.9	50	7.7	50
Total	100	3.8	100	5.0	100	6.7	100

Source: Authors' calculations.

The fast growth scenario assumes real economic growth of 6.7 percent during 1998–2025 and a faster pace of structural transformation, resulting in shares in GDP of agriculture, industry, and services of 20 percent, 30 percent, and 50 percent, respectively, in 2025. The implicit real growth rates for the individual sectors are 3.2 percent for agriculture, 10 percent for industry, and 7.7 percent for services.

An interesting result of this analysis is that all three sets of assumptions regarding overall economic growth and structural transformation yield virtually the same implied long-run rate of growth of the agricultural sector: 3.2 percent. This is a result of the empirical regularity that faster economic growth is also linked to faster economic transformation. Given that the long-run growth rate of agriculture appears to be fairly invariant to the overall rate of growth, higher growth in Tanzania has to be mainly a result of faster growth of industry and services. To achieve the overall growth target of 5 percent, industry and services will have to grow at 6.5 percent and 5.9 percent per year, respectively. To achieve the growth target of 6.7 percent, industry will have to grow by 10 percent and services by 7.7 percent per year.

Toward Structural Transformation: A Second Try

Early industrialization efforts in postindependence Tanzania aimed at addressing the unfavorable balance inherited from the colonial era. At independence there were only 220 firms involved in smithing, weaving, woodworking, and pottery (Rweyemamu 1973). The industrial strategy was to spearhead structural transformation into a self-sustaining process, promote technological innovation, create employment, and foster links in the economy. The pre-independence era pursued an inward looking, import substitution industrial policy. During 1961–76, the industrial sector grew at an impressive annual rate of 9 percent (figure 6.2). However, from 1977–86, the sector recorded negative growth rates in all years except in 1978, 1979, and 1984. The reforms implemented since 1986 were, among other things, expected to restore the sector's growth, employment, and competitiveness. The sector's growth rate increased from zero in 1986 to a high of 4 percent in 1990 before plummeting to a low of negative 4 percent and gradually picking up again to reach its current peak of 6 percent.

In the pre-reform period—especially during the 1980–85 crisis—the sector was characterized by gross inefficiencies as reflected by low output growth, low capacity utilization, low productivity, and low export performance. The World Bank (1996b) has referred to this as a period of de-industrialization in Tanzania. Capacity utilization, which was as high as 75 percent in 1975, fell drastically to an average of

20–30 percent during the crisis. Despite efforts to revive the sector, Tanzania was no more industrialized in the 1990s than it was two decades before. The sector's poor performance was attributed mainly to internal factors, such as the highly regulated environment, poor investment decisions, and poor macroeconomic policies that resulted in foreign exchange rationing and a shortage of critically needed inputs, while at the same time the international environment was less benign than it had been. The sector's development was also hampered by an unreliable and insufficient supply of utilities, resulting in frequent power cuts and rationing. To exacerbate the problem, Tanzania's electricity tariffs are the highest in the region. Other utilities, the road network, and the water supply are also insufficient. Whereas during the era of government control the undercapitalization of public firms was a severe problem, with private ownership the main complaints have been the high tax tariff structure and the unavailability of bank credit. Tanzania's industrial tariffs are higher than in a number of other countries in the region. The result of these constraints is a high average cost per unit of output, which has rendered Tanzanian manufacturing firms uncompetitive.

Figure 6.2. *Real Growth in the Manufacturing Sector, 1960–95*

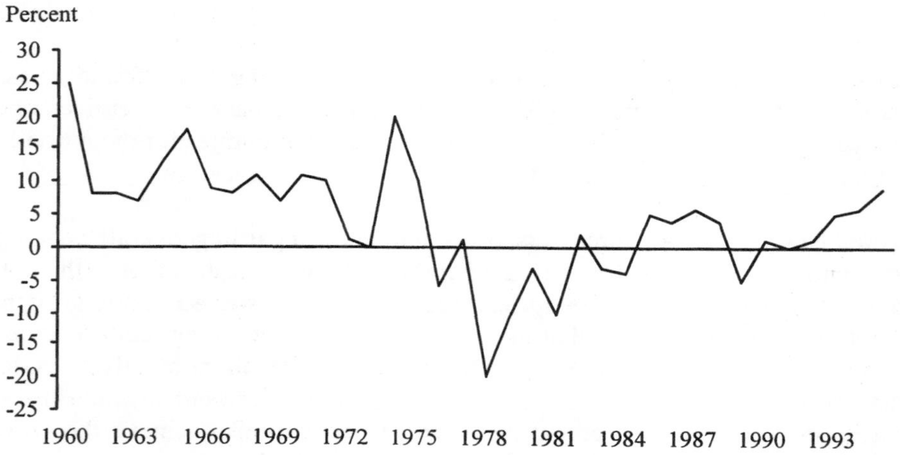

Sources: URT (various years); authors' calculations.

Current economic reforms are addressing many of the factors that have led to the dismal performance of the manufacturing sector in the past, with the objective of creating an enabling environment for private sector activities. While macroeconomic stabilization has been achieved, the focus is now on completing the privatization process and developing an appropriate regulatory and incentive framework. At the same time, reforms in public expenditure management aim at increasing the public sector's capacity to provide supporting services for private sector activities, such as an improved road network and a functioning commercial courts system.

As these reforms progress, Tanzania will gain attractiveness as a location for basic manufacturing. Several factors contribute to Tanzania's potential attractiveness for manufacturers. First are Tanzania's three sea ports, which provide those involved in international trade with easy access to markets. Second, wages are relatively low, although this partly reflects low educational attainment and labor force productivity. Third, Tanzania's huge and productive hinterland provides a strong basis for agricultural inputs to agro-processing industries. Fourth, Tanzania has significant potential for hydroelectric generation. Effective power generating capacity is currently 377 megawatts from hydroelectric sources and 147 megawatts from thermal sources. The completion of the Lower Kihansi and IPTL power plants will increase this capacity to 714 megawatts, and further expansion of generating capacity is planned. Finally, significant iron, coal, and mineral deposits, along with large deposits of natural gas in the Songo Songo delta that are currently being developed, also contribute to Tanzania's manufacturing potential.

The first step in realizing the sector's growth potential is to exploit existing structures. In that connection, the rehabilitation and consolidation of current industrial capacity through financial, capital, and management restructuring will have to play an important role in conjunction with the ongoing privatization process. The main aim is to upgrade commercial efficiency, resulting in improved competitiveness and better capacity utilization. During the prereform era, Tanzania had more than 400 state-owned enterprises, but about half of them have already been divested. About 30 percent of the remaining ones are manufacturing based and could relatively easily be rehabilitated and increase their productivity.

The informal small-scale artisanship sector is quite large and contributes significantly to the manufacturing sector. With an appropriate business environment, including access to credit, some informal sector activities could make the transition into the formal sector.

To sustain high growth rates, more efficient utilization of existing production capacities will need to be accompanied by the creation of new capacities. The biggest potential for value added, employment generation, growth, and poverty reduction lies in agro-allied industries. Agroprocessing leading to increased export of manufactured goods has a considerable multiplier effect on the economy. Basic industries such as food processing, leather working, and textiles play a crucial role in Tanzania's economy.

Given the relatively small size of the economy, expansion of the manufacturing sector will need to be export led and will depend on firms' ability to become competitive internationally and to make full use of various preferential market access arrangements. Schemes such export processing zones (EPZs) and export credit guarantee schemes can be useful tools to support export-led expansion of the manufacturing sector. The deepening of regional integration under existing arrangements, such as the East African Cooperation (EAC) or the Southern African Development Cooperation, could also provide a way to expand market access, benefit from policy and technology spillovers, and become more attractive as a place for foreign investors to establish regional manufacturing bases.

A 1996 study (World Bank 1996b) indicated that Tanzania could benefit from establishing an EPZ and recommended the establishment of the Tanzania Export Processing Zone Authority. However, to date no actions have been taken in this area. Box 6.2 summarizes the findings of a recent study on international experience with EPZs.

Another strategy to promote exports is the establishment of an export credit guarantee scheme, because export financing has been one of the major constraints for potential exporters. The central bank can support such a scheme through the commercial banks by extending credit to exporters and recovering the loans as export proceeds start to flow in. Tanzania established such a scheme in 1989, but suspended it in 1994 after experiencing a number of implementation problems. However, with better accountability and follow-up by the commercial banks, export credit guarantee schemes still have a role to play in Tanzania's economy.

Exploiting the Natural Resource Potential for Export-Led Growth

As argued in the previous sections, sustained high growth will depend on the consolidation and deepening of economic reforms, which provide the basis for enhanced productivity and increased investment in all sectors and pave the way for structural transformation of the economy. However, given Tanzania's substantial endowment of natural resources, exploitation of the natural resource potential could give rise to additional growth. This section discusses three areas likely to boost the economy's growth rate.

Box 6.2. *International Experience with Export Processing Zones*

Many countries have established EPZs to encourage the expansion of manufacturing activities. However, the record of these zones is mixed and depends critically on the design of the EPZ and the environment for manufacturing activities in the particular country. Contrary to many people's expectations, an EPZ is not an automatic panacea for export problems. Studies have also indicated that an EPZ is not the best policy choice (Madani 1998). Nonetheless, EPZs can play a dynamic, long-term role if they are appropriately set-up, well managed, and used as an integrated part of a national reform and liberalization program.

EPZs generally achieve the two basic goals of increasing foreign exchange earnings and creating employment, especially nontraditional employment and income earning opportunities for women. However, some people argue that net foreign exchange earnings may not be large enough to warrant the investments undertaken to establish the EPZs.

EPZs are sensitive to the national economic environment. They will perform better when the host country pursues sound macroeconomic and realistic exchange rate policies (Alter 1991; Romer 1993) For instance, the creation of backward linkages seems largely conditional on the industrial base of the host economy. In countries that did not already enjoy a solid industrial base and that adopted an EPZ, some linkages occurred, although the process was spotty and inconsistent (Rhee and others 1990). However, a number of countries, including Mauritius and some South Asian countries, have benefited immensely from setting up EPZs. In economies where a solid industrial base existed prior to the establishment of the EPZ, for example, Taiwan (China) and Korea, linkages have occurred.

Export Potential of Agricultural Commodities

The bulk of Tanzania's export sector remains traditional agricultural commodities, although in the last five years nontraditional exports have increased as a share of total exports. Seven commodities—coffee, cotton, cashew nuts, cloves, tea, tobacco, and sisal—have traditionally constituted more than half of the value of total exports. Their share in total export value rose from an average of 65 percent in 1980–83 to an average of 75 percent in 1984–86, and then fell to an average of 57 percent until 1996. Tanzania's share as a supplier to the world market of any one of these commodities has not been large enough to influence the price. Thus the largest portion of the export bundle remains vulnerable not only to external factors like climatic vagaries, but also to the decline in world commodity prices. Internally, the export of commodities is affected not only by their output, but by the government's accelerated efforts to liberalize production, prices, transport and marketing structures, and the foreign exchange regime since FY94.

In 1997 and 1998 the negative impact of El Niño counteracted some of the positive effects of the reforms in the agriculture sector on the production of cotton, tobacco, cashews, tea, and coffee. The share of commodity exports in total export value was 45 and 42 percent, respectively, for these years because of the heavy rains. As noted before, the value of total exports also declined during this period because of disruption in power generation and transportation caused by El Niño.

In general, the removal of subsidies has resulted in more efficient allocation of agricultural inputs. However, the collapse of the inputs credit system and the minimal presence of commercial banks in rural areas has resulted in a steep decline in the use of inputs. At the same time, even though property rights remain unclear, large-scale production of cotton, cashew nuts, and coffee based on foreign investment is increasing. Productivity in the rest of the agriculture sector remains low. The privatization of processing factories and changes in marketing methods caused disruptions during the initial years of reform. Since

1994 marketing boards for cash crops have assumed exclusively regulatory functions. The role of the cooperative unions in marketing is still significant and focuses on procuring crops from individual farmers, helping with initial processing, and negotiating prices with buyers. While the number of private buyers is large, there are only 10–15 export companies. The 2 percent tax on agricultural exports constituted a disincentive to exporters until it was abolished in July 998.

Figure 6.3 presents scatter diagrams of the value of exports of each of the seven commodities listed before during1980–98. To look beyond the short-term fluctuations in value of these commodity exports, polynomial trends were estimated for each time series and shown by the respective trend lines. Remarkably, the trends in all the commodities are positive in the recent past, even though the rate of growth various considerably.

Cashew nuts, starting in 1986, and coffee, as of 1992, showed the steepest recovery in value exported. The value of cotton exports has exhibited a steady rise since the early 1980s. The trends in the value of tea and tobacco exports were relatively flat until the mid-1980s and exhibited a small upward trend thereafter. The values of sisal and cloves exports, which have been declining for most of the last two decades, have also begun to recover, sisal since 1993 and cloves since 1995.

To isolate the upturn in the trend of export values from the trend in world prices for commodities over the years, we also look at the volume of commodity exports in the last two decades. Figure 6.3 is a scatter diagram of the volume of commodity exports during 1980-98, with polynomial trend lines for each of the seven commodities as before. The volume of cloves exported continues to show a declining trend, although the recovery in the volume of sisal exported is stronger than the value of exports indicates. The trends in tea, tobacco, and cotton are similar to their trends in values. The most significant recovery in the volume of exports is that for cashew nuts, whereas for coffee the rise in value of exports is mostly due to world prices and not to significant increases in the volume exported.

Though some efforts to expand exports of horticultural, forestry, livestock, and fishery products have been attempted, these have been piecemeal and without any lasting effect on the overall export pattern.

Exports of Minerals

According to independent mining analysts, the prospects for gold mining are brighter in Tanzania than in any other Sub-Saharan country with the exception of Ghana. Even though Tanzania's mineral development potential has been known for decades, the production and export performance of this sector remained poor in the 1970s and 1980s when state enterprises were major actors in the sector. Mineral trade liberalization in 1990, followed by macroeconomic stability and the removal of restrictions on foreign exchange, led to an expansion of artisanal and small-scale mining (see box 6.3). The sector produced gemstones and an estimated US$10 million to US$20 million of gold per year. In the early 1990s the financial institutions' inability to offer a competitive price for gold and the mismanagement of gold buying schemes pushed small-scale producers toward the parallel market, and production remained understated in official records because of extensive smuggling. Small-scale mining activities by individual prospectors are further constrained by poor technology and a lack of capital.

In 1993 the government started formulating the Mineral Sector Policy Framework to provide an enabling environment for private participation in the mining sector, and in 1998 passed the Mining Act to promote additional investment. The Mining Act provides significant tax exemptions for new investors in the sector and has been able to attract considerable FDI required to exploit the full potential of the deposits. However, the salient question remains whether the mining operators will manage to reduce production costs. In October 1997 the first gold mine, Golden Pride Project, a joint venture between Canadian and

Australian Companies in Lusu, was opened. It was followed by Ashanti Goldfields, a Ghanaian mining conglomerate, in Geita. The number of prospecting licenses issued per year was ten times higher in the second half of the 1990s than in the first half of the 1990s. Feasibility studies are under way for diamonds, gemstones, and base metals like nickel and cobalt. Exploration for industrial minerals—soda ash, kaolin, and silicone—is also planned.

Figure 6.3. *Export Performance of Various Commodities, Trend in Value of Commodity Exports, 1980–98*

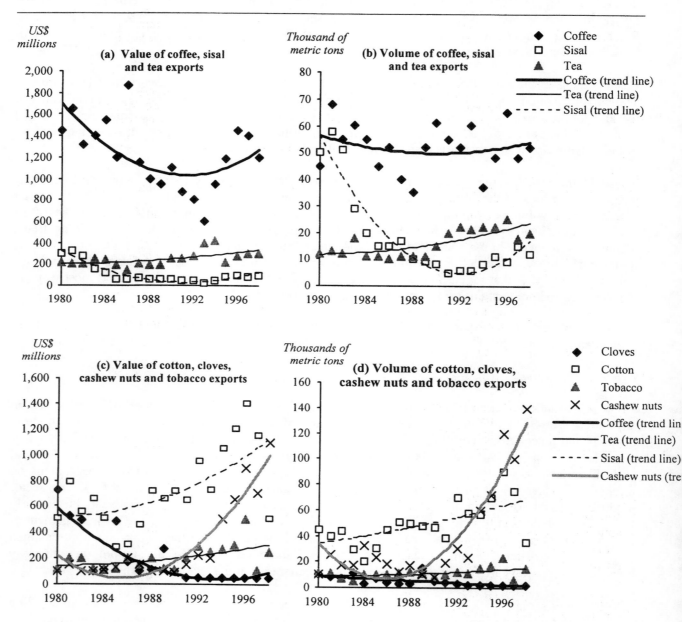

Source: Authors' calculations.

Box 6.3. *Fiscal Incentives in the Mining Sector*

Input Taxes

- Import duty, sales tax, and excise duty exemptions for mining equipment and supplies directly related to the operations of the project granted up to one year after the start of production. A cap limit of 5 percent import duty and 5 percent sales tax on imports of equipment and supplies shall apply thereafter.
- Full VAT exemption for purchases of inputs and supplies (where the product is exported).
- Mineral rights holders shall be exempt from domestic withholding tax on goods and services they supply. However, they shall be obliged to pay withholding tax on domestic goods or services they purchase.
- Withholding tax or technical tax on technical service payments to subcontractors, both resident and nonresident, and management fees will be 3 percent of gross payment (unless management fees exceed 2 percent of operating costs, when tax will be 20 percent), the tax withheld will satisfy the income tax liability of the subcontractor in respect of the technical service.

Output Taxes

- Royalty: 3 percent on netback value at the mine of the minerals sold (5 percent for diamonds). Gemstones: 3 percent on exports of rough stones (to discourage exports of rough stones). Nil for cut and polished stones (to promote value adding and mitigate smuggling). The aim is to develop Tanzania as a gemstone center.
- No export tax or stamp duty on receipts apply to the sales of minerals.

Profit Taxes

- The "specified minerals" provision in the Income Tax Act is to be abolished and all minerals extracted under the Mining Act treated alike.
- Corporation tax on income from mining activities at the standard rate determined for all types of investments in Tanzania in the context of any revision of the Investment Act.
- The expenditure on a taxpayer's interest in one mine may be deducted from that taxpayer's income from an interest in another mine, but mining expenditure may not be deducted from income from other kinds of business (and vice versa).
- Depreciation allowances of 100 percent will be available on all mining capital expenditure. All types of assets will be pooled and depreciated at the same rate.
- At the end of each tax year the balance of unrecovered capital expenditure in respect of a mining license (or other right to develop a mine) will receive an addition of 15 percent capital allowance each year. No other investment allowance is to apply.
- Losses may be carried forward for recovery without limit.
- Accounts for tax purposes may be kept in U.S. dollars.
- Withholding tax on paid out dividends and tax on distribution of branch profits to nonresidents will be 10 percent.
- Interest withholding tax will not apply to interest payments by mining rights holders on foreign borrowings at arm's length.
- The state will not seek concessional state participation.

While tax incentives provided under the Mining Act of 1998 are effective in attracting investors to the sector, at the same time they also significantly reduce the government's tax revenues. Given also that mining is to a large extent an enclave activity with only weak links to the rest of the economy, the overall benefits for the economy and the impact of the expansion of mining activities on poverty reduction are likely to be limited in the near future.

Figure 6.4 shows the investment levels in mining exploration and development and export earnings from the mineral sector during 1990–98. Investment in the sector was negligible in 1990 and 1991. Starting from a level of US$26.2 million in 1992, the investment boom in the sector averaged US$52.6 million per year up to 1998. The mining industry requires extremely large investments in equipment in the initial years, and analysts forecast that this investment will lead to a high growth rate of mineral exports earnings in the near future: 40 percent in 2000, 83 percent in 2001, and 74 percent in 2002. Annual export earnings from this sector have fluctuated from US$5.5 million in 1990 to US$22.6 million in 1998. The share of mineral exports in total exports rose from 1.4 percent in 1990, to 3.3 percent in 1998, with 4.1 percent as the average for the nine years.

Figure 6.4. *Mining: Investment and Sector Growth, 1990–98*

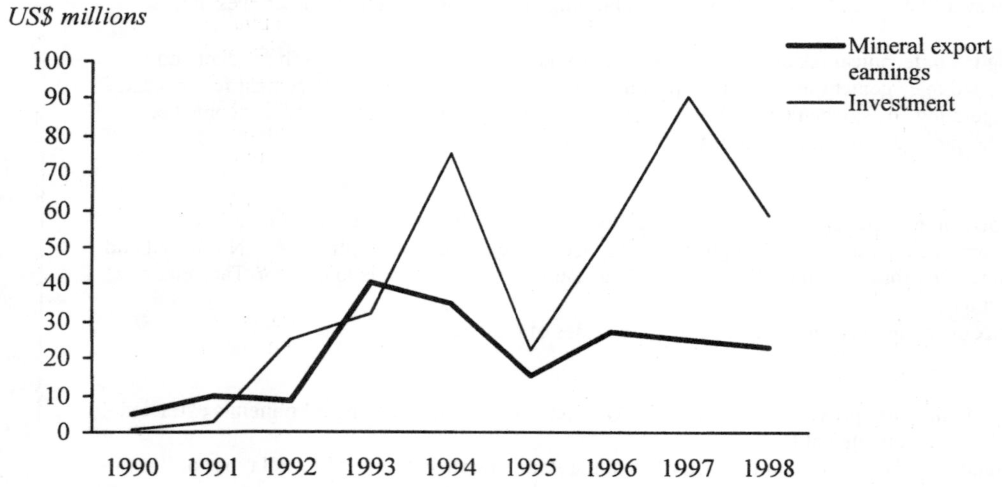

US$ millions

Sources: Authors' calculations.

Recent development experience in many countries has indicated that resource-rich countries tend to grow more slowly than less well-endowed countries. Only a few countries such as Botswana have been able to translate increased income from natural resource exploitation into sustained long-term growth.

A combination of several factors is responsible for the poor growth performance of resource-rich countries. First, there are often weak backward and forward linkages from the mineral sector to other sectors in the economy. This leads to a situation where income from natural resources is not evenly spread and little activity is stimulated in other sectors. Second, the discovery and exploitation of natural resources leads to a shift in relative prices, for example, an appreciation of the exchange rate that makes other sectors less competitive, referred to as the Dutch disease, or an increase in returns to unskilled labor, which makes investment in human capital less attractive in the short term, but may lead to reduced economic growth in the long term. Third, political pressures can lead to the inefficient use of resources, either in the form of overconsumption or investment in inefficient projects. Finally, significant dependence of a country on mineral exports increases its vulnerability to changes in international prices. Expenditure commitments that are undertaken while income from mineral exports is high, such as increased investment in infrastructure or social services or increased public sector employment, may not be easily reversed.

However, as the example of Botswana shows (see box 6.4), good economic policies can ensure that increased income from natural resources translates into sustained long-term growth.

The problems that hinder exploitation of the full potential of mineral exports by Tanzania are a scarcity of capital resources and management skills critical for mineral exploration, resource development, and technological innovation in this area. The inexperience of financial institutions in financing mining activities, along with inappropriate legislative and fiscal regimes, have also affected the investment climate through their influence on contractual relationships, taxation, and political risks. The global competition for investment resources and recent global financial crises have made finalization of the mineral sector policy and maintenance of the appropriate macroeconomic policies more urgent.

Box 6.4. *Botswana: Transforming Mineral Wealth into Economic Growth and Prosperity*

Botswana is one of a small group of countries that in the contemporary era has been able to transform mineral wealth into sustained economic growth. Over the past three decades, Botswana's real per capita income grew by more than 7 percent per year, which is comparable to rates of growth achieved by countries like Korea and Thailand. Remarkably, this growth led neither to isolated enclaves nor to profligate spending. It continued to be high as a result of structural change within the economy as growth in the mining and government sectors slackened. The growth of real incomes was spread throughout the economy. Although relative income inequality has not been reduced, it has not worsened, and the poor are better off than they were before.

The growth record is explained primarily by the economic policies that Botswana has pursued. In each of the major policy areas, growth-promoting policies have dominated.
- Minerals policy established mutually profitable arrangements with foreign investors and participation in one of the few successful international marketing arrangements.
- Minerals policy generated the rents that initiated the growth, but the government's long-term development planning was crucial in channeling funds into investments that promoted both growth and human development and in maintaining a modicum of fiscal discipline.
- Trade policy kept the economy open to competition from imports and maintained access to markets for some important nonmineral exports.
- Money and banking policies, while not always optimal, generally provided stability to the macroeconomy and to the financial sector.
- Exchange rate policy accorded stability to the tradables sector and avoided the perils of an overvalued currency commonly encountered following mineral discoveries.
- Fiscal policy, on the whole, has been disciplined. To a large extent this is attributable to the institution of national development plans, which have kept government expenditures from growing as fast as government revenues over the long term. The resultant accumulation of substantial government savings and foreign exchange reserves has provided an important cushion to enable the country to ride out the current downturns in the diamond market, while the careful management of those reserves has generated a significant return to the nation.
- Given the fiscal discipline adopted, the independent central bank could accumulate substantial foreign exchange reserves and pursue a conservative monetary policy.
- This combination of fiscal and monetary discipline, in turn, enabled trade policy to keep the economy open and exchange rate policy to encourage the emergence of nontraditional exports and import-competing production.
- Labor market policies avoided both the extremes of an exorbitant real minimum wage and a bidding war for scarce talent. The government pursed a policy where wage and salary levels in the private and parastatal sectors generally had to conform to those paid by the government to comparable grades of public employees.

Source: World Bank (2000d).

The projected growth in mineral output assumes that the Ministry of Energy and Minerals will develop effective capacity to promote, administer, and regulate private investment in industrial mining ventures; establish and maintain investor confidence through consistent and transparent legislation for competitive participation in mining; and formulate appropriate rules for mineral rights registration, mine safety, the environment, and monitoring and revenue collection. Over the longer term Tanzania will have to develop an appropriate manpower base with the necessary technical and managerial skills for this sector, devise effective marketing strategies for minerals in the international markets that will discourage illegal exports, establish downstream manufacturing to provide direct services to the mineral sector, and formulate an efficient and sustainable small-scale mining program.

Foreign Exchange Earnings from Tourism

Like for the mining sector, the foreign exchange earning capacity of the tourism sector has been recognized since independence, but little of its potential had been realized until recently. Tanzania's huge potential in natural and historic resources could make it a hub of tourist activity. As much as 25 percent of the land area—12 national parks, 17 game reserves, 50 controlled game areas, a conservation area, and a marine park—has been set aside as wildlife and botanical sanctuaries. The country also has Africa's highest mountain, access to three great lakes—Victoria, Tanganyika, and Nyasa—and 6 percent of the total land area is a coastal zone of pristine beaches. Historical sites on the island of Zanzibar, located on the major trade routes of the last two centuries, are based on strong commercial and cultural ties with the Far East and Middle East. Archeological sites from the Stone Age and Iron Age abound in northern Tanzania.

Foreign exchange earnings from tourism were low until 1985. The number of tourists showed distinct periods of decline and growth in the early 1970s, with a steep decline during 1977–84, when the border with Kenya was closed. Both the number of tourists and foreign exchange earnings improved in the second half of 1980s. It is only with economic liberalization in the 1990s and following adoption of the National Tourism Policy in 1991 that growth in the sector accelerated. In the 1990s the number of tourists who visited Tanzania increased from approximately 153,000 in 1990 to 482,000 in 1998, while during the same period tourism receipts increased from US$65 million to US$570 million (figure 6.5). Estimates indicate that 30,000 people are directly employed in tourism and that another 43,000 benefit from ancillary activities.

Figure 6.5. *Tourism Sector Performance, 1990–98*

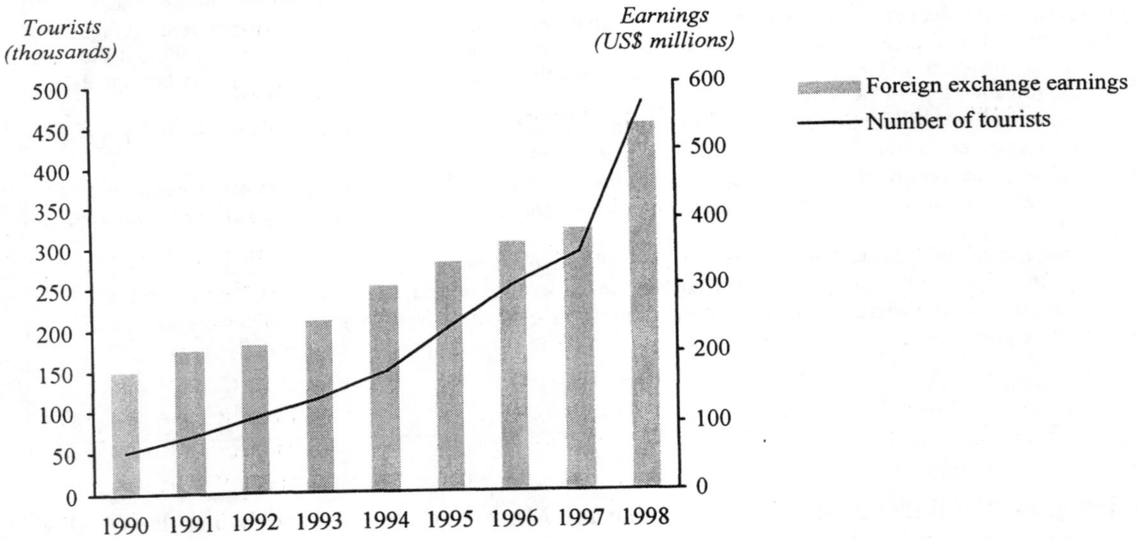

Sources: Authors' calculations.

The tourist industry is small and fragmented, without any coordinated policy or product development. The basic infrastructure facilities and services to support the industry are still rudimentary. Investment in market research, publicity and promotion, and improvement of service skills has been minimal. With the economic liberalization, private investors have taken the first steps to provide capital for new hotels or to rehabilitate older state-owned and state-operated hotels. Investment in the coastal region of Tanzania following the ethnic riots along the Kenyan coast in the early 1990s. Even now tourism in Tanzania depends closely on Kenya's tourism sector, with 66 percent of tourists arriving by road from Kenya to the Northern Wildlife area. Tourism has suffered from the lack of a multisectoral approach in government policies toward its development. Most laws that regulate this industry date from the 1960s and early 1970s, and are therefore outdated and inadequate for conservation and environmental sustainability, revenue collection, and consumer protection.

Tanzania has an abundance of unique, exotic destinations for regional, as well as European and American, tourists. As an agricultural economy with a small manufacturing base and a nascent extractive industry, the country needs to plan the development of this sector in a culturally responsible and environmentally sustainable way with community participation, so that its potential capacity to earn foreign exchange can be used to stimulate economic growth. The coordinated development of accommodations, roads, railways, airports, telecommunications, banking, and water supplies has to be planned to give Tanzania a competitive edge over Ghana, Kenya, and the Seychelles. At the very least these should be accomplished near the northern circuit and the coastal region around Zanzibar and Dar es Salaam. In the long run the government must not only encourage private investment in the sector, but also effectively coordinate and regulate the classification and standardization of services, the training of personnel for hotel management, the functioning of travel agencies, and the conservation of sanctuaries.

Regional Integration and Cooperation as an Engine Of Growth

Chapter 3 showed that growth in Tanzania is closely linked to growth in neighboring countries, indicating potential benefits from regional coordination and cooperation. This section describes in more detail areas for strengthening regional integration and cooperation, in particular within the framework provided by the Southern African Development Community (SADC) and the ECA.
Historically, regional integration efforts in Africa have resulted in relatively little trade creation and large trade diversion. The dominance of political considerations in the continent's regional integration experiences is not an exception to experience elsewhere. However, multicountry agreements often provide a strong springboard for governments to sell difficult policy reforms to the domestic polity. In integration efforts worldwide the differences in external policy have been foremost on the list of policy coordination issues requiring resolution, to be followed by other sectoral integration issues.

Apart from the advantages imparted by the combined size of markets—which are small in Africa—the policy argument for regional integration among adjacent countries is often based on traditional concepts of growth triangles, spatial development initiatives, and transport and development corridors. According to the first point, strategies for the integrated development of well-defined cross-border areas must be based on the exploitation of differences in factor endowments. Driven by the private sector, these will succeed in promoting trade and direct investment. The promotion of transport and development corridors is complementary to the development of cross-border areas. It includes the rehabilitation and improvement of key transport-building infrastructure through public-private partnerships, consolidation of density along particular transport corridors, and reliance on transport to drive private sector development along the corridor. In spatial development initiatives the central government plays the key promotional role in the initial phase by providing basic infrastructure, identifying and "packaging" anchor projects for private investment, and launching the initiative through marketing and conferences with investors. However, such state-driven initiatives can foster growth only if role of the central government recedes after their launch.

In the past, Tanzania has liberalized its trade regime under the mandates of the Cross-Border Initiative, the Common Market for Eastern and Southern Africa, and other regional integration initiatives. Given the size of the combined markets in the region and the direction of trade flows, major benefits from future integration are likely to stem from mandated policy reforms under the regional initiatives Tanzania chooses to participate in, rather than from the increased size of markets.

The second important set of benefits is likely to derive from integrated spatial development of various cross-border corridors, particularly through investment in transport and communication infrastructure. The design and objective of the integration schemes should be driven by basic policy coordination and function-based collaboration in regional projects, rather than a preference for formal trade and factor market integration. The following sections examine opportunities for regional cooperation within the framework of the SADC and the EAC.

Cooperation within the Southern African Development Community

The SADC was established in 1992. Its precursor was the Southern African Development Coordination Conference, which was set up in May 1979 as an informal organization by the "frontline" countries for closer cooperation aimed at reducing economic dependence on South Africa. At its inception the SADC had nine members: Angola, Botswana, Lesotho, Malawi, Mozambique, Swaziland, Tanzania, Zambia, and Zimbabwe. Since then, the Democratic Republic of the Congo, Mauritius, Namibia, the Seychelles, and South Africa have joined the community. The treaty establishing the SADC called for broadening cooperation among member states in 20 sectors, including transport, health, tourism, mining, and water.

The SADC Trade and Development Protocol, signed in August 1996, seeks to establish a free trade area eight years after ratification and the gradual elimination of tariffs and nontariff barriers to trade in the interim. Only five member states have ratified the protocol. Others agree on a tariff liberalization program, currently being negotiated by the 11 original signatories of the trade protocol. Current proposals call for removing all intraregional tariffs within eight years, but do not cover the liberalization of trade with non-SADC countries. Also, unlike agreements under the Cross-Border Initiative, proposals regarding trade liberalization among SADC countries allow for special treatment of so-called sensitive products (in agriculture, agro-industry, and manufacturing), involving a slower phase-in for import tariff reductions. Moreover, some of the proposals being considered leave open the possibility of entirely excluding some goods and sectors from the trade liberalization exercise. South Africa, on behalf of its partners in the South African Customs Union (between the Union of South Africa and Botswana, Lesotho, and Swaziland, first established in 1910) has offered to reduce its tariffs at a faster pace than non-South African Customs Union and SADC countries, although a number of sensitive goods—dairy products, wheat, sugar, cotton, fabrics, leather footwear, and vehicles—will be subject to a slower liberalization process.

In the postapartheid era South Africa is increasingly playing a pivotal role in the economic development of southern Africa. It is becoming the most important investor in the region and its financial markets are poised for important contributions. Within the SADC development is extremely disparate, with GDP per capita ranging between US$3,300 and US$3,800 for Botswana, Mauritius, and South Africa and between US$100 and US$220 for Malawi, Mozambique, and Tanzania. South Africa's total GDP is nearly 80 percent of the GDP of the SADC as a whole, and its freight share amounts to half of intraregional exports and 22 percent of imports. However, South Africa is increasingly becoming aware that its own growth depends on its neighbors' growth and development.

Multilateral and bilateral aid and capacity building initiatives can support Tanzania's effective participation within the SADC. To ensure that Tanzania can benefit from opportunities arising under the SADC, areas of critical importance range from conceptual and strategy work, classic public sector projects, restructuring assistance, reform of the legal and regulatory framework, and institutional reform to preparation for private sector entry into the economy and direct support of private sector projects through equity, partial guarantees, and insurance.

For the potential growth initiative of the TAZARA corridor (figure 6.6),[29] the current steps being taken with respect to the Maputo corridor between South Africa and Mozambique, based on a 1995 bilateral agreement, can provide important guidance. The initiative is a clear result of the democratization of both countries and the latter's transition to a market-based economy, with a corresponding opening up for private local and foreign investment. The corridor stands a good chance of success, because it connects South Africa's industrial heartland to a nearby sea port. The current initiative includes Swaziland, with provision to expand to Botswana and Namibia. Interministerial committees and consultations at the presidential level are being undertaken to revitalize rail, road, and port links and to promote the development of industry and services. The aim is to foster social progress while achieving environmental sustainability (World Bank 1999g).

In addition to development corridors within the SADC, expansion of the northern corridor that connects Dar es Salaam to Burundi, the Democratic Republic of Congo, Rwanda, and Uganda may be an important target for development, especially as it passes through the area in which most new mining development is currently taking place.

Figure 6.6. Possible Development Corridors of the Southern African Development Community

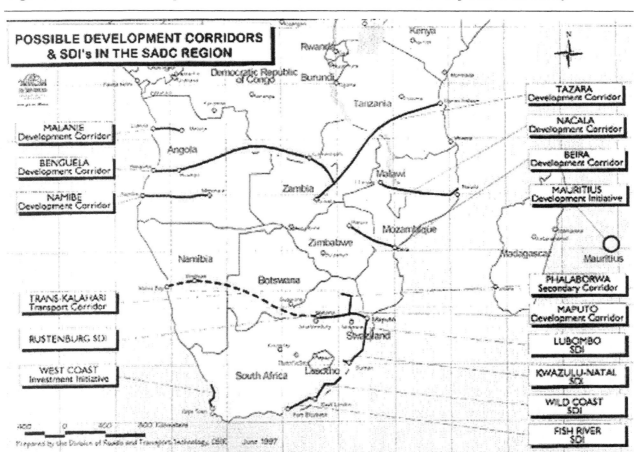

---

[29] The geographic belt around the railway line from Dar es Salaam, Tanzania, to Lusaka, Zambia, via Morogoro, Iringa, and Mbeya.

Cooperation within the East African Cooperation

The EAC between Kenya, Tanzania, and Uganda was established in November 1993 and is the most recent in a long line of regional integration arrangements between these three countries (East African High Commission, 1948–61; East African Common Services Organization, 1961–67; East African Community, 1967–77). The heads of state signed a treaty to upgrade the cooperation agreement into a sustainable regional integration scheme in 1999. The main policy organs of the EAC are the Summit of the Heads of State, the Permanent Tripartite Commission, the Coordination Commission, and the Secretariat.

Through regional cooperation, the EAC's objective include (a) strengthening and consolidating cooperation in agreed fields to engender equitable development in member states, (b) establishing a single market and investment area in the region, and (c) promoting sustainable utilization of the region's natural resources and effective protection of the environment. The activities listed on the EAC's ambitious agenda are to achieve full convertibility of the currencies; accomplish full liberalization of the external current account and make progress toward liberalizing the capital account; hold pre- and postbudget consultations to harmonize monetary and fiscal policies; develop a macroeconomic framework to guide the region's countries toward economic convergence; develop guidelines for economic and social development; facilitate the establishment of an East African stock exchange and cross-listing of stocks; set up an East African business council consisting of private sector organizations to promote cross-border trade and investment; and execute tripartite agreements to avoid double taxation along road and inland waterways. In addition, efforts are under way to eliminate internal tariffs, to launch an East African passport, and to identify an EAC-maintained transport network.

The first stage of regional integration with neighboring countries has been phased tariff reductions and synchronization of tariffs. The three partner states have indicated their broad commitment to lifting trade barriers, including eliminating tariff and nontariff barriers over time. A 1999 World Bank study on the appropriate transition to an East African customs union recommended adoption of a harmonized tariff structure of 0 percent for primary inputs and capital goods, 7 percent for intermediate goods, and 15 percent for final goods. Uganda is the only country currently adhering to this tariff structure.

Trade imbalances among the EAC's members are hindering the application of a common tariff. Kenya clearly enjoys a dominant trading position in relation to its neighbors (supplying some 30 percent of Uganda's imports and 10 percent of Tanzania's imports). The share of Kenya's imports was 0.23 percent from Uganda and 0.35 percent from Tanzania. Kenya has a relatively diversified export base, well-developed infrastructure, and favorable export incentives framework, enabling it to export significant amounts of manufactured goods to its EAC partners. As a result, business in the two countries fear the flooding of Tanzanian and Ugandan markets with Kenyan products.

A 1998 EAC study assessed the strengths and weaknesses of the region's private sector organization in promoting regional integration. The study collated the private sector's views through a series of interviews with business associations in the three member countries and a number of focus group discussions. Their views with respect to the benefits of regional integration varied by country. Kenyan enterprises viewed regional integration as an opportunity both in the short and long term, while the Tanzanian and Ugandan firms were worried about the short-term impact given Kenya's relative industrialization and dominance in regional trade, although even they were cognizant of economic rewards over the longer term. Some respondents also saw the potential for specialization, resulting in economies of scale. The heightened competition between cross-border regional enterprises could lead to improvements in product quality, efficiency gains, and enhanced international competitiveness. Integration could enable the region as a group to receive preferential trade access under the establishment of a regional economic partnership arrangement as proposed by the European Union. A larger economic block offering streamlined procedures to facilitate the movement of capital and other factors of production across Eastern Africa would also be more appealing to foreign investors looking at Africa as a potential destination for their funds.

Estimates indicate that fiscal revenue losses resulting from the introduction of internal free trade would amount to between 3 and 4 percent of total revenue for Uganda and between 1.5 and 2 percent for Tanzania firms, given Kenya's competitive advantage within the regional block. The impact on Kenya would be negligible (Maasdorp and Hess 1999). In Tanzania, tax and nontax revenues collectively accounts for about 14 percent of GDP (table 6.8). Taxes on imports, which include the import tariff and all applicable sales and excise taxes, together contributed more than 28 percent of total revenues, with about half derived from import tariffs. The reliance on import taxes is clear. During 1991–97 the share of total revenues due to taxation of imports has increased by more than 6 percentage points, with most of the increase resulting from increased collections of excise duties on imports. However, the decline of import duties as a percentage of total revenue from their highest level of 42.3 percent in 1968 to about 14 percent in FY97 is indicative both of the process of trade liberalization and the gradual broadening of the tax base in Tanzania. Other contributing factors include low collection efforts and tax evasion and avoidance (Rajaram and others 1999).

Table 6.8. *Sources of Government Revenues, Selected Countries, FY97*
(percentage of total revenues)

Uganda		Kenya		Tanzania	
International trade taxes	10.2	Taxes on international trade	15.3	Taxes on imports	28.5
Import taxes	9.9	Import duties	15.3	Customs duties	13.7
Export taxes	0.3	Export duties	0.0	Sales taxes	9.6
Excise taxes	41.2	Taxes on goods & services	37.0	Excise duties	5.2
Petroleum products	27.0	Taxes on income and profit	33.0	Domestic indirect tax	24.1
Other	14.2	Other taxes	1.3	Income taxes	21.8
Income taxes	14.0	Nontax revenue	13.4	Payroll and property tax	1.6
VAT/Sales taxes	28.7	Total revenue/GDP	26.3	Other taxes	13.9
Other taxes	0.0			Nontax revenue	10.0
Total revenue/GDP	11.6			Total revenue/GDP	13.9

Source: IMF.

The experiences of other regional cooperation mechanisms, for example, the European Community, indicate that funds may be set up to address social and economic disparities between their members, and to overcome this divide, compensatory mechanisms are suggested during the transition period. However, given the economic realities in the EAC countries, this is not feasible without external assistance. Thus under the EAC treaty, the member governments have agreed to create a customs union in a phased manner over the next four years. The harmonization of external tariffs before aligning internal tariffs may be considered as another mechanism for giving Tanzania and Uganda more time to strengthen their individual positions. Other actions to safeguard revenue levels in the EAC countries would include rationalizing exemption regimes, strengthening customs cooperation to prevent smuggling and diversion of transit goods, widening the tax base, and improving tax collection. Joint action on these fronts could help mitigate the envisaged fiscal losses for Tanzania and Uganda brought about by tariff harmonization with Kenya.

With respect to the external regime and exchange restrictions of the three EAC countries, while all are well on their way to achieving liberalization of the current account, Tanzania needs to institute complementary measures to stimulate investment, stabilize production, and simplify capital account transactions (see annex 6.1). The first two items include building up an effective and noncorrupt tax administration, an honest customs administration, functioning commercial courts, reliable infrastructure, and a functioning financial sector (World Bank 2000e). The EAC could provide the framework for undertaking and consolidating credible reforms in these areas.

Summary

The key to significant poverty reduction in Tanzania is accelerated growth. Policy-based projections that take recent improvements in the policy and institutional framework into account indicate that per capita GDP could grow between 1.4 and 1.9 percent per year. Further improvements in the policy and institutional framework raise the predicted annual rate of growth of per capita GDP to 2.4 to 4.3 percent. Estimates of poverty elasticities indicate that such accelerated growth could reduce the share of the population living below the poverty line from the current approximately 50 percent to 30 percent by 2015. However, the presence of HIV/AIDS makes the attainment of these objectives difficult. HIV/AIDS is estimated to reduce the annual growth rate by up to 1 percent, in addition to the pandemic's huge effects on overall human development. The relatively high incidence of HIV/AIDS has led to a drastic decline in some indicators related to human development and eliminated gains in life expectancy that had been painstakingly achieved during the past four decades.

Achieving the target of accelerated growth will require significant efforts to enhance productivity and increase investment in both human and physical capital. The removal of institutional and policy constraints under the ongoing reforms is an important element in closing the productivity gap that has opened up over the past 20 years. As this gap closes, higher rates of growth can be generated from the more efficient use of existing capacities. However, further increases in productivity will only be possible if close attention is paid to the acquisition, adoption, and use of various forms of knowledge, including technical know-how. FDI, an appropriate communications and information infrastructure, and an improved level of educational attainment are key elements to facilitate productivity gains through knowledge.

Increasing human capital investment requires measures to increase the incentives and returns for undertaking such investments, but also needs increased public support in areas where externalities are large, such as primary education and preventive health care. Increased public resource allocations to these areas have to be accompanied by increases in the efficiency of service delivery if the desired increase in the stock of human capital is to be achieved. Particular attention needs to be paid to the quality of education and its relevance to the demands of the labor market. Given the rapidly changing demands of the labor market, the emphasis should be on the acquisition of strong numeracy and literacy skills and the ability to acquire new knowledge through lifelong learning.

One of the key lessons of Tanzania's postindependence experience is the importance of a clear separation between public and private investment. The principal source of investment must be the private sector. However, public investment has an important role to play in providing certain infrastructure services that complement private investment and that the private sector is unlikely to provide in sufficient quantities. Another important role for the government in this area is to provide an appropriate legal and regulatory framework for private sector investment and to ensure property rights and legal contracts. Thus one of the imperatives for the immediate future is to continue reforms to improve the environment for private sector investment. Equally important is developing financial markets. At present, financial intermediation is barely working. This constrains both the rate of saving and the flow of savings to the most productive uses. In addition to domestic savings from both the private and public sectors, foreign savings can also be an important source of finance for domestic investment. While significant resource transfers currently take place in the form of official development assistance, these will need to be supplemented by increased inflows of private capital to finance increased investment levels in the private sector.

Structural transformation, that is, an increase in the share of value added by industry and services with a matching relative decline in the importance of agriculture, can be expected to occur alongside accelerated growth. Although the secondary and tertiary sectors will probably grow at significantly higher rates than agriculture, this does not imply that this growth should come at the expense of agriculture. Rather the opposite is true. Agriculture will, for the foreseeable future, remain the backbone of the economy, and only a prospering agriculture sector can provide the basis for sustainable poverty reduction and accelerated growth in the other sectors. A potential expansion of manufacturing activities will have to take advantage of various factors specific to Tanzania. These include easy access to international trade through Tanzania's three sea ports, whose efficiency is being improved through privatization measures; a significantly increased effective power supply from hydroelectric and thermal sources; significant, though not yet fully developed, iron, coal, mineral, and gas deposits; as well as a stable macroeconomic and political environment. The main constraints in the medium to long term are likely to be the low level of skills and educational attainment among Tanzania's population and a rudimentary system of financial intermediation. As progress in these two areas is extremely time-consuming, serious efforts to achieve improvements in these areas must remain high on the policy agenda and be vigorously pursued.

More intensive exploitation of Tanzania's rich resource endowment offers the opportunity for additional growth. Exports of agricultural commodities, increased activity in the mining sector, and expansion of tourism are three areas that have already registered relatively high growth rates in recent years, but which still have substantial potential for additional growth in the near future. However, some of these activities have an enclave character with weak links to the rest of the economy, which limits their potential to contribute significantly to poverty reduction. Measures that increase links with the rest of the economy are therefore imperative, for example, creating incentives to re-invest proceeds from these sectors in other parts of the Tanzanian economy and focusing on broadly based private sector development rather than making growth dependent on developments in these sectors only.

Given the small size of Tanzania's economy, growth will only be sustainable if it is firmly rooted in international competitiveness and the aggressive pursuit of export opportunities. While the strategic pursuit of preferential market access opportunities is also important, these opportunities are bound to become less with the phasing in of the new World Trade Organization rules and regulations, putting an even greater premium on measures to enhance international competitiveness. The deepening of regional integration within existing arrangements such as the EAC and the SADC also has an important role to play in this area. While the enlarging of markets is an important aspect of regional integration, equally important benefits are likely to arise from positive neighborhood effects and spillovers, such as policy and growth spillovers, network externalities from infrastructure, or increased attractiveness of the region as a manufacturing location for multinational corporations.

Annex 6.1: Exchange Rate Arrangements and Exchange Restrictions in the EAC Countries

The source for this annex was IMF (1999b, pp. 463-66, 854-59, 903-905).

Exchange arrangement: An unitary exchange rate structure prevails in all the countries, with independent floats in Tanzania and Uganda and a managed float with no prior announced path in Kenya. There are no exchange taxes or subsidies. Authorized banks may deal with customers in the forward exchange markets (in Tanzania only to facilitate export and import transactions).

Arrangements for payments and receipts: Kenya has the fewest prescriptions for arranging payments and receipts. By law, the power to license and regulate foreign exchange transactions is in the hands of the central bank. There are no international security restrictions, prescriptions for currency requirements, or controls on trade in gold coins or bullion and the export or import of banknotes. In Kenya payment arrangements are regional under Common Market for Eastern and Southern Africa and payment arrears are official. Tanzania has various operative and inoperative bilateral payment arrangements, regional arrangements, and clearing agreements. The Ministry of Finance delegates the authority to administer and manage foreign exchange transaction to the central bank and customs, which in turn delegate such authority to all licensed banks for payments abroad. Only those authorized can deal in gold coins and bullion. In the case of exports or imports of banknotes, payment in domestic currency to a nonresident requires Bank of Tanzania approval, except payments made under currency convertibility agreements with Kenya and Uganda .

Foreign exchange accounts, resident and nonresident: In Kenya and Uganda both residents and nonresidents are permitted to hold foreign exchange accounts domestically and abroad, with full convertibility of domestic currency to foreign currency. However, in Uganda an account for nonresidents could be blocked if the law required it. Tanzania has no limitations on foreign exchange amounts held domestically by residents, but the convertibility of currency in domestic accounts is reserved for United Nations organizations. The operation of offshore foreign currency accounts by individual residents is still subject to restrictions, unless the money is acquired outside Tanzania. Similar restrictions do not apply to resident banks, financial institutions, or authorized dealer banks operating accounts abroad in their name on behalf of their customers. Residents' foreign accounts have to be reported to the Bank of Tanzania. Nonresidents can maintain convertible domestic currency accounts, to be closed upon departure, while temporarily residing in Tanzania. Approval of the authorized bank is required when crediting any sum to nonresidents. Such a bank may direct the sum to a blocked account that does not pay interest.

Imports and import payments: Each country operates with negative list import licenses and other nontariff measures, applicable on grounds of health, security, and environmental reasons. Import taxes and/or tariffs are being brought to comparable levels under various regional and unilateral initiatives, though the pace is slowest in Tanzania. None of the countries have a state import monopoly or a foreign exchange budget. There are no financing requirements for imports in Kenya and Uganda , while in Tanzanian advance payments are permitted through authorized dealers. Uganda has no documentation requirements for the release of foreign exchange for imports, while a variety of documents—import declaration, final invoice, customs entry, clean report of findings—is required in the other two countries (in Tanzania only beyond a threshold of US$5,000). The preshipment inspection of goods imported worth more than US$5,000 is applicable in both Kenya and Tanzania , though only Tanzania requires domicilization and letters of credit.

Exports and export proceeds: There are no export quotas or taxes in any of the countries. The last export tax in Tanzania—2 percent on scrap metal—was removed in July 1998. Kenya and Uganda also have no requirements for repatriation, financing, and documentation. In addition, Uganda does not have any export licensing requirements, making its export sector completely free of regulations. In Kenya sales contracts for coffee, tea, and horticultural products are subject to registration by the respective boards. Certain agricultural products require special licensing certifying adequacy in the domestic market. Exports of minerals, precious stones, and other "strategic" materials are subject to special licensing. In Tanzania similar licenses are required from the respective ministries for exportation from the mainland of items covered under the health, sanitary, or national heritage lists. There are no financing requirements for exports from Tanzania, but letters of credit and domicilization are required. Requirements are still in place for the repatriations of export proceeds in foreign currency by exporters and the mandatory reporting of exporters delinquent beyond the time the Bank of Tanzania gives to banking institutions.

Invisible transactions and current transfers, payments and proceeds: None of the three countries imposes repatriation requirements on proceeds from invisible transactions and current transfers, neither do they have any restrictions on the use of such funds. Kenya and Uganda still have no controls on payments for these categories. Tanzania still maintains several bureaucratic controls with respect to indicative limits and bona fide tests. The Bank of Tanzania requires the presentation of relevant documentary evidence—invoices, shipping documents, report of an authorized inspection firm, audited reports, authenticated tax clearances from the TRA, and certification of duration of travel—at the time of buying foreign exchange. The list varies for trade-related, investment-related, and travel-related (beyond US$10,000) payments. For personal payments documentation from the relevant educational or medical institution is required, while foreign workers are obliged to document the transfer of their wages with contracts, permits, and reasons for remittance. Payments based on consultancy, management, and royalty agreements have their own list of required documentation.

Capital transactions: Currently Uganda has the simplest regime governing capital transactions. There are no controls on capital and money market instruments, derivatives and other instruments, credit operations, direct investment and liquidation thereof, personal capital movements, nor are any controls imposed by security laws. Real estate transactions are controlled, with nonresident foreign citizens only granted a lease not exceeding 99 years. There are no specific provisions for institutional investors. Commercial banks and other credit institutions must hold 20 percent of foreign deposits in reserve on their own account, in addition to cash deposits of 8 percent of time deposits and 9 percent of demand deposits with the central bank. These are in addition to the liquidation requirements based on total deposits, regardless of the currency denomination.

In Kenya there are no controls on credit operations, direct investment and liquidation thereof, personal capital movements, nor are any controls imposed by security laws. Transactions in derivatives and other instruments require the central bank's approval. There are a variety of controls and prior approval requirements on capital market securities, money markets instruments, and collective investment securities, especially for nonresidents. Real estate transactions by nonresidents need government approval. There are no specific provisions for institutional investors. In general, foreign currency deposits in commercial banks and other credit institutions are not subject to reserve requirements. There is a reserve requirement for accounts held by nonresidents.

Rules applicable to capital transactions in Tanzania clearly show that the government has not yet committed to liberalizing this account. Only for specific provisions for institutional investors and controls imposed by security laws are there no controls. Capital transfers to all countries are subject to approval by commercial banks, and all transfers of foreign currency funds from residents to nonresidents and foreign-controlled resident bodies require specific approval by the Bank of Tanzania. Participation in the domestic money and capital markets by nonresidents is restricted; participation by residents is subject to reporting. All transactions in derivatives and other instruments are subject to controls. A variety of controls apply to commercial credit, financial credit, guarantees, sureties, and financial backup facilities. A priori approval by the Bank of Tanzania, the TIC, and the TRA are required for outward and inward direct investments and the repatriation of capital and other associated income. Under the general category of personal capital movement specific rules apply, and these rules discriminate between residents and nonresidents. Thus, there are specific rules for loans; gifts, endowments, inheritances, and legacies; the transfer of assets, gambling and prize earnings; and the settlement of debts abroad by immigrants. For commercial banks and other credit institutions borrowing abroad is subject to external debt management regulations. Since 1998 the Bank of Tanzania has required that all statutory reserves be held in local currency. Banks are allowed to average their daily positions and count half of their vault cash toward meeting the requirements.

7. Performance of Zanzibar's Economy

Zanzibar is part of the United Republic of Tanzania and consists of two main islands: Unguja (also called Zanzibar) and Pemba. To avoid confusion we shall restrict the use of the name Zanzibar to refer to only the two islands of Unguja and Pemba and a few other smaller islands, which together with Mainland Tanzania make up the United Republic of Tanzania.

Unguja and Pemba enjoy a warm climate throughout the year with temperatures ranging between 20–40° C. The swampy loam soils in Pemba are more fertile than the land in Unguja, which is characterized by broad, sandy ridges in places and sandy loam soils in other places. The swampy loam soils are suitable for producing rice, bananas, and cassava. The difference in fertility between the two islands is reflected in the fact that 74 percent of the land in Pemba is under cultivation, while only 46 percent of the land in Unguja is regularly cultivated. Pemba also produces 70 percent of Zanzibar's clove output (ERB 1993, p. 6).

Under Tanzania's constitution Zanzibar has its own constitution, which provides for the Zanzibar presidency, a council of ministers (the cabinet), a legislature, and a judiciary. These are the main institutions of the Zanzibar Revolutionary Government, which was formed after the sultan's overthrow in 1964. At that time the Revolutionary Council was the supreme organ of the state, but over the years most of its power has been taken over by the cabinet and the legislature: the House of Representatives. The Zanzibar Revolutionary Government is fully responsible for running most socioeconomic government activities in Zanzibar. The Union Government is responsible for foreign affairs, international development, and security.

The main source of published data for the Zanzibar economy is the Department of Statistics of the Ministry of State Planning and Investments. The department is short of both financial and trained manpower, which has affected its performance as a reliable and timely source of economic and social statistics. Thus for 1976–97 we have used data from Mtatifikolo, Mabele, and Kilindo (1993); the *Statistical Abstract* (1999, various years); and other Government of Zanzibar sources (including direct retrieval of data from senior officials in various ministries). We tried to reconcile the data we already had with those from Bank of Tanzania publications (1996, 1999). In the case of differences, we used the bank's figures. More recently the Department of Statistics has started updating the national accounts, including changing the base year for GDP in constant prices from 1976 to 1980. This work is still ongoing and the results, at best, are still very preliminary. We therefore decided to retain 1976 as the base year for all national account data used in this report.

Population and Employment

In 1999 the islands of Unguja and Pemba were estimated to have a population of 800,000, with a population density of 340 people per kilometer. Like in the Mainland a population census is taken every 10 years. The last one was supposed to have been carried out in 1998, but did not take place because of budgetary problems

Table 7.1 shows the population of Zanzibar at the time of the last three censuses (1967, 1977, and 1988) and projected population for 2000 based on the 1988 census. The growth rates between censuses were 2.7

percent between 1967 and 1977 and 3 percent between 1977 and 1988. Between 1967 and 1978 the urban centers—the town of Zanzibar, Chakechake, Mkoani, and Wete—experienced growth rates of 4.4 percent, 4.6 percent, 6.2 percent, and 3.8 percent, respectively. During 1977–88 the town of Zanzibar recorded the biggest absolute growth, and its population reached 32.5 percent of the total population as a result of a 3.8 percent growth rate (Mtatifikolo, Mabele, and Kilindo 1993, p. 12). Zanzibar's population is predominantly young. By the 1988 census more than 65 percent of the population was younger than 20.

Table 7.1. *Population Density by Region, 1967, 1978, and 1988*

Region	Area (square km)	1967		1978		1988		2000[a]		Growth rate (percent per year)
		Population	Density	Population	Density	Population	Density	Population	Density	
Unguja	1,464	19,014	130	270,807	185	375,339	257	512,925	30.8	3..3
North Unguja	426	56,360	132	77,017	181	97,028	228	128,111	301	2.1
South Unguja	814	39,087	48	51,749	64	70,184	86	104,298	128.1	3.1
Urban/West	224	95,047	424	142,041	634	208,327	930	334,076	149	3.9
Pemba	868	164,321	189	205,304	237	265,039	305	354,547	359	2.5
North Pemba	459	72,015	157	106,290	232	137,399	299	181,006	394	2.6
South Pemba	409	92,306	226	99,014	242	127,640	312	173,541	424	2.6
Unguja and Pemba	2,332	354,815	152	476,111	204	640,578	275	867,473	327	3.6

a. Projected figures.
Source: Population censuses.

These demographic trends imply decreasing availability of land for farming and increased unemployment unless employment grows at a higher rate than population, which is impossible given the narrow economic base. Furthermore, the rates imply increasing pressure on available social services like education and health facilities. However, at present Zanzibar has no clear population policy.

Formal Employment

Table 7.2 shows trends in the growth and sectoral composition of employment for 1978–95. Note that about 50 percent of the population, estimated at 320,289 in 1988 (Mtatifikolo, Mabele, and Kilindo 1993, p. 12), is of working age (15–64). Assuming that 25 percent of the working-age group chooses not to participate in the labor force as is estimated in neighboring countries, this would put the active labor force at 240,216, divided between 156,140 in rural areas and 84,075 in urban areas (Mtatifikolo, Mabele, and Kilindo 1993). Formal sector employment has been declining for some time, from 39,500 in 1985 to 34,000 in 1989, a 13 percent decline. Employment in the public sector declined even more precipitously, from 9,350 to 7,750, during the same period. With the labor force of about 240,000 growing at 3 percent per year, about 8,000 new jobs must be created annually to avoid growing unemployment. Even with the Zanzibar Industrial Promotion Agency's (ZIPA's) commendable efforts to create new 19,603 jobs, of which only 2,951 have been created so far, the formal sector, given its growth trend, cannot save Zanzibar from massive unemployment (Mtatifikolo, Mabele, and Kilindo 1993, p. 13).

During the 1980s real wages fell sharply even though nominal wages in public enterprises increased more than 2.7 times between 1985 and 1989, because inflation increased by 52 percent during the same period. In 1985 wages in the public sector were 53 percent below their real value in 1980.

Table 7.2. *Employment Shares by Sector: 1978–95*

	Agriculture		Industry		Electricity and water		Commerce		Transport and communication		Finance, insurance, public administration and other services	
Year	Total	Percent	Total	Percent	Total	Percent	Total	Percent	Total	Percent	Total	Percent
1978	3,983	12.2	10,742	33.0	1,433	4.4	1,988	6.1	1,241	3.7	13,211	40.5
1979	7,499	22.4	5,572	16.8	1,244	3.6	1,936	5.8	4,211	12.6	13,006	38.9
1980	7,401	22.3	8,188	25.1	1,317	4.0	1,942	5.8	1,245	3.7	13,114	39.5
1981	7,640	24.2	9,024	28.5	1,084	3.4	1,913	6.1	1,052	3.3	10,879	33.8
1982	6,050	21.1	6,753	23.3	1,894	3.1	1,944	6.1	1,258	4.4	12,057	41.9
1983	12,088	32.31	6,762	18.9	720	1.9	1,429	3.38	1,584	4.2	14,533	39.9
1984	11,794	30.22	5,929	15.19	999	2.56	2,117	5.43	1,659	4.3	16,515	42.35
1985	8,026	20.32	7,831	19.8	1,093	2.8	2,149	5.4	3,033	7.7	17,366	43.9
1986	5,897	16.47	6,136	17.1	1,034	2.9	2,437	6.8	3,759	10.5	16,584	46.1
1987	6,935	18.71	6,612	17.7	1,043	2.8	2,114	5.7	27,723	7.3	17,648	47.6
1988	7,099	20.8	5,590	16.4	1,015	3.0	2,021	5.9	1,551	4.6	16,787	49.1
1989	8,255	24.1	5,556	17.1	782	2.5	2,405	7.0	1,570	4.6	15,667	45.5
1990	6,511	19.54	3,459	10.38	830	2.49	2,117	6.35	1,434	4.3	16,388	48.17
1991	7,817	21.49	1,568	9.81	836	2.30	2,195	6.03	1,641	4.51	17,601	48.38
1992												
1993	5,028	19.38	1,258	4.85	790	3.04	44	0.17	366	1.41	16,491	63.56
1994	3,854	14.70	718	2.74	675	2.57	79	0.30	409	1.56	17,748	67.69
1995	4,144	19.28	715	2.32	376	1.75	67	0.31	460	2.14	14,227	66.19

Source: Mtatifikolo, Mabele, and Kilindo 1993, appendix table 2).

Informal Sector Employment

Partly as a result of the poor trends in employment and wages in the formal sector, a vibrant informal sector has developed. Table 7.3 presents the results of a 1990 survey. The table shows that the island of Unguja has more than 70 percent of Zanzibar's informal sector enterprises, providing almost 70 percent of the employment in the sector. Employment per establishment is highest in livestock keeping (1.7) otherwise it averages 1.5 (Mtatifikolo, Mabele, and Kilindo 1993, p. 13). Trade and hotels have the biggest number of enterprises and the largest number of employees. As the survey was carried out in 1990 when liberalization had just started, the informal sector must now be playing a more dominant role in the economy.

Table 7.3. *Informal Sector Enterprises and Employment*

	Unguja			Pemba			Total		
Item	Urban	Rural	Total	Urban	Rural	Total	Urban	Rural	Total
Number of establishments	24,403	46,552	70,955	5,032	20,262	25,294	29,435	66,816	96,249
Percentage of total	25.3	48.4	73.7	5.2	21.1	26.3	30.6	69.4	100.0
Total employment	29,709	56,915	86,624	7,233	30,231	37,464	36,942	87,146	124,088
Percentage of total	23.9	45.9	69.8	5.8	24.4	30.2	29.8	70.2	100.0

Source: Economic Survey (1990).

Poverty, Food Security, and Nutritional Status

As food consumption is basic for survival and human welfare, the measurement of poverty is first and foremost connected with the measurement of the value of food consumed. At the national level, food security refers to a country's ability to meet the required food needs of all its citizens at all times. In Zanzibar, because of poor yields, food production has not kept pace with population growth, and imports of the most preferred foods—sugar, rice, and wheat—have increased. While continued production and imports assure national food security, this may not be enough for household food security.

Special surveys can provide the data needed to analyze household food security and nutritional status across different locations and income groups. To this end Tanzania has used household budget, demographics and health, and others surveys. Tanzania has carried out household budget surveys since colonial times, beginning with individual urban areas and now using year-long national surveys (Kapunda 1988). The regression coefficients obtained from household budget survey data show the relative importance of factors determining total food consumption and the consumption of individual food items across income groups and localities. The response of consumption levels to changes in total expenditure (that is, income) is obtained by computing the expenditure elasticity of demand.

The findings confirm Engel's Law, that is, the share of expenditure on food in total expenditure is inversely related to income levels: low-income groups spend a higher proportion of their incomes on food. When food is disaggregated, the consumption of some items decreases with increased income while the consumption of other foods increases with higher incomes. This is the distinction between inferior goods and luxury goods (meat and other sources of animal protein) (Kapunda 1988; Towo 1989). With regard to location, people in urban areas spend less of their incomes on food than those in rural areas.

The variables used in studies based on household budget surveys vary by author. Generally the earlier studies were simpler and used only a few variables, like total expenditure and household size. Towo (1989) looked at total expenditure, household size, educational level of the head of household, sex of the head of household, and urban or rural location. Kapunda (1988) used total expenditure, adjusted household size, regional average prices, literacy levels, and urban or rural location. Total expenditure was a common dependent variable in all the studies, and in most cases was the most significant variable (at the 1 percent level).

The change in the quantity of a commodity demanded resulting from a change in total expenditure is the expenditure elasticity for that item. Generally elasticities for rural areas in both Zanzibar and the Mainland were higher than in urban areas. Across commodities, expenditure elasticities for inferior goods had low elasticities, while those for normal goods had higher elasticities.

Nutritional status is related to the quality of food consumed. Often children and their mothers are the most vulnerable to deficiencies in essential nutrients. Thus the nutritional status of households is best captured by looking at the nutritional status of women and children. A rough comparison based on health and demographics surveys shows that children in Mainland Tanzania may have a better nutritional status than children in Zanzibar, especially on the basis of weight-for-height and weight-for-age criteria. Mothers on the Mainland may also be better nourished.

In addition to food security and good nutrition, other indicators of well-being are also important, as discussed in the following paragraphs.

Tanzania has seem a significant decline in infant mortality. The 1997 Demographic and Health Survey estimated that infant mortality declined by 14 percent in 1985–2000, perhaps because of the increased availability of prenatal, delivery, and postnatal care. In the five years before the survey, in the Mainland

47 percent of births took place in a health facility and 48 percent took place at home, compared with 31.2 of births in a health facility and 67.4 percent at home in Zanzibar. In Dar es Salaam almost 87 percent of births took place in a health facility.

Another area of child health where Tanzania has achieved remarkable success is child vaccination. The survey shows that 75.4 percent of children to receive vaccinations in Zanzibar had received all the required vaccinations, compared with 70.3 percent for the Mainland, 79.1 for Dar es Salaam, and 80.2 percent for other urban areas on the Mainland.

Tanzania had almost achieved universal primary schooling in the 1980s; however, that achievement was not maintained. Truancy abounds and many people complain about the quality of education. Some 43 percent of those in Zanzibar age six and older have no education whatsoever, compared with 22 percent for Dar es Salaam. However, Zanzibar's record is better for higher levels of education.

In an agricultural country like Tanzania, everyone can work on their own farm or work for others on the land. Few people are landless. Incomes in agriculture, however, are much lower than in other sectors, thus a number of people seek employment outside agriculture. The 1997 Demographic and Health Survey found that 19 percent of all men in Zanzibar were unemployed and were actively seeking work in sectors other than agriculture.

While the household budget surveys for the Mainland and Zanzibar are now done using the same methodology, as they are not done at the same time, and as the Mainland and Zanzibar use different cost of living indexes, making direct comparisons is difficult. However, given the high level of cooperation between the two departments of statistics, carrying out the surveys at the same time and making other changes to improve comparison, for example, supplementing the data with macroeconomic statistics from the Bank of Tanzania, should be possible.

The World Bank (1996b) notes that Zanzibaris are better off than their counterparts in the Mainland based on the observation that people in Zanzibar spend a smaller share of their total expenditure on food; however, more detailed work is needed before coming to a firm conclusion.

Land Tenure and Distribution

Zanzibar has a total area of 2,654 square kilometers. Unguja is 1,666 square kilometers in area and Pemba is 666 square kilometers in area Mtatifikolo, Mabele, and Kilindo (1993). According to a 1990 agricultural survey, the total cultivated area was 122, 436 acres. With an estimated agricultural population of 645,555, the cultivated land per capita was 0.19 acres or 0.07 hectares. This area increases to 0.4 acres or 0.16 hectares if we only consider the 309,087 family workers and exclude dependents. A land holding is defined as the total land owned or allocated for use by one family. This holding is often divided into parcels for cultivating individual crops or individual combinations of crops. In 1990 there were 10,547 holdings divided into 352,004 parcels, which means that each holding had about 3 parcels averaging 0.35 acres. The extent of land fragmentation is considerable.

Table 7.4 presents the overall land use picture in 1990, showing the division of total land into cultivated land, grazing land, forests and woodland, and land for other uses. Fifty-four percent of the total land available is cultivated. Expansion can only take place by converting grazing areas or forests and woodlands; however, the agricultural production potential for these areas is low, and extending agricultural production to these lands also involves considerable environmental hazards.

Of all rural households in Zanzibar, 5.4 percent are landless. As table 7.5 shows, the distribution of land is unequal. In Unguja, 14 percent of the holdings are under 2.5 acres each and account for only 2 percent of total cultivated land, while 1 percent of the holdings are 5 acres or more and account for 7 percent of the land area. In Pemba only 11,08 holdings are smaller than 0.25 acres, compared with 7,367 in Unguja. Also the 5 acres and above category accounts for only 1.7 percent of the holdings, but 6.3 percent of the land. Because more land is available in Pemba than in Unguja, the land holdings are bigger and more equally distributed.

Table 7.4. *Land Use Pattern, 1990*

Land category	Area (hectares)	Percentage of total
Cultivated land		
Sugarcane	1,850	1
Rain-fed rice	13,780	6
Irrigated rice	405	0
Other cropland in continual rotation	20,795	8
Pure-stand tree crops	33,520	14
Complex crop associations		
Associations of tree crops	41,835	17
Associations of tree and food crops	18,715	8
Other associations	670	0
Total cultivated area	13,1570	54
Grazing land		
Ranches and dairy farms	2,140	1
Unimproved grazing	77,560	32
Forests and woodland	30,595	12
Other land uses		
Settlements	2,995	1
Other	310	0
Total	245,170	100

Source: Ministry of Agriculture, Livestock Development, and Natural Resources, Government of Zanzibar.

Table 7.5. *Distribution of Land Holdings by Size*

Size of holding (acres)	Number of holdings	Percentage of total holdings	Area of all holdings in size category (acres)	Percentage of total area
Rural Unguja				
Less than 0.25	7,367	14	1,132	2
0.25–0.50	11,627	22	4,305	9
0.50–1.25	20,377	39	16,362	33
1.25–2.50	9,906	19	16,924	34
2.50–5.00	2,505	5	7,172	15
5.00 and above	581	1	3,236	7
Total	52,363	100	49,131	100
Rural Pemba				
Less than 0.25	1,108	2.1	214	0.3
0.25-0.50	3,127	5.9	1,209	1.6
0.50-1.25	2,5773	48.5	22,362	30.5
1.25-2.50	18,192	34.3	31,933	43.6
2.50-5.00	4,017	7.6	12,984	17.7
5.00 and over	877	1.7	4,603	6.3
Total	53,094	100.0	73,305	100.0

Source: Ministry of Agriculture Livestock Development, and Natural Resources, Government of Zanzibar.

To understand the current complicated land tenure system in Zanzibar, one must go back to before the 1964 revolution, when essentially two-land tenure systems existed simultaneously as follows:

- Individually-owned plantations, originally planted by Arabs, but some later sold to the Shirazi and Indians. Plantations were held under freehold and could be inherited according to Muslim law. The land could be sold, mortgaged, rented, loaned, or disposed off in any way the landlord deemed fit. Sharecroppers or squatters on these plantations had no say in their disposition. The sale of plantations between members of different races—Arabs, Indians, and Shiraz—had to be registered with the administrator general, but sales between members of the same race did not have to be registered.

- Along the coral rag where there are many indigenous settlements, land tenure was governed by a combination of communal and Muslim laws.

While slavery had been abolished in Zanzibar by the 19th century, landlords allowed former slaves or free immigrants from the Mainland to settle on their land and grow nonpermanent crops on their plantations so as to have their own crops weeded for free. These so-called squatters also provided a labor reserve for the labor-intensive work of clove harvesting. With the political awakening of the 1950s the relationship between landlords and squatters deteriorated rapidly, and the tranquil symbiotic relationship no longer existed. Decrees issued in 1921 and 1954 established the basis for land ownership. The 1921 decree essentially gave "natives" permission to cultivate public land without first seeking permission from the government. The rural squatters were one of the major pillars of the 1964 revolution. Following this revolution, land was declared to be state property. Subsequently some of the land was redistributed to the landless in three-acre (two-hectare) plots under the Land Redistribution Decree. About 26,000 hectares were redistributed between 1964 and 1974, 66,000 acres were distributed to 13,364 people in Unguja and 8,898 people in Pemba. This land was to be held on the basis of temporary rights, which could be revoked if the cultivators did not adhere to the underlying conditions. The main condition was that the land could not be left idle or fragmented Mtatifikolo, Mabele, and Kilindo (1993).

The land tenure system that emerged after the revolution lacked coherence and security, partly because it emerged from hurried decrees that did not pass through systematic legislative procedures. To bring land tenure in line with changing socioeconomic realities, in the 1980s and 1990s the following laws were passed by the Zanzibar House of Representatives and assented to by the president Mtatifikolo, Mabele, and Kilindo (1993):

- The Land Adjudication Act of 1989, which set up the administrative process for ascertaining land rights and empowered the adjudication officer to decide on land distribution issues
- The Land Surveys Act of 1989, which deals with the licensing and professional conduct of surveyors
- The Registered Land Act of 1989, which established the legal framework for registered land rights
- The Land Tenure Act Number 12 of 1992, which defined the law in relation to occupying, owning, or leasing land and owning or leasing trees and the boundaries of public and confiscated lands
- The Land Tribunal Act of 1994, which created the special land tribunal (court) that handles land disputes, which deals only with minor legal technical problems, and whose decisions can be challenged in higher courts
- The Land Transfer Act of 1994, which sets up land transfer committees to adjudicate in cases involving land sales and long-term leases.

Despite this legislation, land tenure and land use are still problematic. The basic problem is that many people are not aware of this legislation. Moreover, conflicts have arisen among various land users, for example, crop farmers versus livestock farmers, and those arising from agricultural and environmental considerations. The new agricultural policy has proposed policies and strategies aimed at resolving these problems and conflicts.

Recent Macroeconomic Performance

Like the Mainland, Zanzibar experienced economic decline during the mid-1970s to the mid-1980s. GDP declined in real terms from T Sh 978.8 million in 1976 to T Sh 854 million in 1991, a 12.1 percent decline over the decade, or an average of 0.8 percent per year. The decline was a result of adverse external shocks caused mainly by the drastic fall in the world price of cloves, Zanzibar's primary export commodity, and the rise in the price of oil imports. The other causal factor was the macroeconomic imbalances that distorted incentives, particularly in the agriculture sector.

In the mid-1980s some macroeconomic reforms were instituted, resulting in improved overall output, with real GDP rising gradually from T Sh 180 million in 1985 to T Sh 789 million in 1991 (which was still below the 1976 level). Indeed, annual real GDP grew by 3 percent in 1991 mainly because of a 200 percent increase in construction, a 66 percent growth in public administration, a 57.8 percent increase in trade and tourism, and a 45.5 percent growth in electricity and water output. However, manufacturing and transport and communication experienced declines of 2.4 and 17.6 percent, respectively.

We examine the performance of Zanzibar's economy during 1976–98 by looking at trends during the following subperiods:
- 1976–83, the prereform period, when the economic crisis was harshest
- 1984–88, the initial reform period, when reforms were gradually introduced
- 1989–94, the main reform period, when reforms were strengthened and the reform agenda was largely completed
- 1995–98, the postreform period, when most reforms were completed except for a few refinements.

Table 7.6 summarizes the economy's performance by major sectors. Note that real GDP and real per capital GDP fell by more than 5 percent during 1978–83. With the population increasing by more than 3 percent during the same period, GDP per capita fell more sharply than GDP.

Table 7.6. *Real GDP Growth, 1978–97*

Category	1978–83		1984–88		1989–94		1995–97	
In 1976 prices								
GDP(T Sh millions)	689	(− 5.4%)	743	(3.9%)	865	(3.4%)	1,308.2	(4.8%)
GDP per capita (T Sh)	1,348	(− 8.2%)	1,212	(1.0%)	1,211	(− 6.6%)	1,276	(2.9%)
Sectoral share (percentage of GDP)								
Agriculture	48.8	(− 6.2%)	58.4	(7.9%)	44.7	(1.0%)	33.6	(0.3%)
Manufacturing	3.5	(30.6%)	5.0	(− 8.6%)	2.3	(− 5.4%)	2.1	(11.1%)
Trade	18.0	(0.5%)	17.3	(3.1%)	26.5	(12.7%)	16.9	(8.0%)
Public administration	17.2	(1.5%)	14.5	(− 1.0%)	12.5	(5.5%)	9.8	(1.3%)
Construction	4.2	(− 5.4%)	2.8	(9.3%)	8.4	(34.9%)	16.6	(9.9%)

Note: Figures in parentheses are average annual growth rates.
Source: Mtatifikolo, Mabele, and Kilindo (1993, appendix table 8); World Bank (1996b, vol. III).

Sectoral Performance: Changes in Sectoral Contributions

Table 7.6 shows that the reform program did not have the same impact on all sectors. Some sectors continued to stagnate, or even declined. Consequently, the sectoral composition of output changed considerably. While agriculture accounted for 48.8 percent of real GDP during the prereform period, and actually benefited from the initial reforms, the sector could not maintain its growth momentum, declined in the second subperiod, and grew only marginally in the last subperiod.

Agriculture

Agriculture, the mainstay of Zanzibar's economy, accounts, on average, for 70 percent employment of the labor force, and in 1991 contributed 51 percent of total real GDP. The dominance of cloves in Zanzibar's agriculture explains not only the performance of the agriculture sector, but the performance of the economy as a whole. Agriculture's relatively poor performance is discussed in greater detail later.

Manufacturing

Manufacturing represented only 3.5 percent of GDP during 1978–83 (table 7.6). In relative terms it shrank even further in importance during the later subperiods shown. In 1993 output in the main industrial enterprises, including electricity distribution, amounted to only T Sh 3.02 billion, increasing to T Sh 7.2 billion by 1997.

Trade

Zanzibar ventured into trade liberalization much earlier than Mainland Tanzania. As a result Zanzibar's imports soon found a lucrative market on the Mainland. The Mainland began to complain about revenue losses caused by these imports, which found their way to the Mainland "duty free." The two governments moved to harmonize their external tariffs to deal with the problem of revenue loss by the Mainland. While some in Zanzibar now complain that this harmonization has resulted in fewer imports into Zanzibar and a loss of revenue to the government, others (even in Zanzibar) disagree with this contention. Continued harmonization of external tariffs is needed to ensure that trade between the two parts of the country flow without impediment, while at the same time ensuring that the interests of both parts of the Union are protected.

Tourism

Trade and tourism grew rapidly. After growing at an average 0.5 percent annually during the prereform period, the sector grew by 3.1, 12.7, and 8.0 percent in the following subperiods (table 7.6). Tourism is discussed further later.

Construction

This has been one of the economy's fastest growing sectors.

Public Finance

In discharging its responsibility to oversee and promote Zanzibar's socioeconomic development, the government performs the following main tasks (Mtatifikolo and Kilindo 1993):
- Socioeconomic development planning
- Resource mobilization and budget management
- External trade and foreign reserves management

- Debt and aid management
- Balance of payments management.

In a situation where the central bank is primarily responsible to the Union government and monetary issues are actually a Union matter, some of the above tasks are likely to be a source of conflict between the two governments in the absence of close coordination and harmonization of the two governments' policies and programs.

Mtatifikolo and Kilindo (1993) studied Zanzibar's public revenue and expenditure system for FY77–90. They note that while on the Mainland the government's budget estimates are published in four volumes, in Zanzibar everything is consolidated into a single volume that shows data for the current year as "estimates," data for the previous year appear as "approved," and the data for the year before that as "actual." Total government expenditure comprises recurrent and development expenditure. Development expenditure comes from the surplus of recurrent expenditure, domestic and foreign borrowing, and grants (Mtatifikolo and Kilindo 1993, pp. 54–56).

While the budget was in deficit during only 3 of the 14 years reviewed, Mtatifikolo and Kilindo (1993) observe that it was only in one of these years that the surplus from recurrent expenditure was enough to meet the needs of development expenditure. In that year, as well as in most other years, the government borrowed heavily from the banking system. The authors conclude that the budgeting process was not well executed and was based on poor records. They also note that total revenue as a proportion of GDP varied erratically. Thus between FY77 and FY81 government expenditure was, on average, 45 percent of GDP. In FY80 the ratio jumped to 60.7 percent, but by FY83 had declined to 37.9 percent, and to even lower ratios in the following three years, reaching 23.8 percent by FY85.

Government revenue appears both in absolute terms and as a proportion of GDP to have risen dramatically during the period reviewed by Mtatifikolo and Kilindo (1993).

Recurrent Expenditure

Like the total budget, recurrent expenditure was erratic, although it did exhibit a generally rising trend. It rose from T Sh 203.7 million in 1976 to T Sh 542.4 million in 1980, that is, it doubled over four years. In the next three fiscal years it declined, followed by a constant increase during the rest of the period reviewed by Mtatifikolo and Kilindo. By FY90 recurrent government expenditure had reached T Sh 2,383.5 million.

As a proportion of total government expenditure, recurrent expenditure behaved even more erratically. In FY77 it was about 50 percent of total expenditure. It rose to more than 60 percent in the next two fiscal years, but declined to 54 percent in FY80 before rising sharply to more than 70 percent in FY83. It dropped dramatically to 60 percent, but rose steadily in the next three years to reach 87 percent in FY90. The increase in recurrent expenditure in the late 1980s resulted from the government's attempt to compensate government workers for the large decline in real wages caused by high inflation rates (Mtatifikolo and Kilindo1993, p. 57).

When analyzed by purpose, the share of consolidated fund services increased slightly relative to ministerial services from 4.7 percent in FY80 to more than 100 percent in FY89 and FY91 (Mtatifikolo and Kilindo1993). A detailed examination of the ministerial share reveals that personal emoluments (salaries and fringe benefits) gained relative to grants and other charges, such as purchases of materials and services.

Development Expenditure

Development expenditure increased dramatically in real terms over the period reviewed by Mtatifikolo and Kilindo (1993, pp. 58–67). Again the increase was not consistent throughout the period: it declined from T Sh 195.4 million in FY77 to T Sh 131.7 million in FY79, but rose to T Sh 333.8 million in FY80. It peaked at T Sh 574.5 million in FY83, and the following year decreased to T Sh 156.3 million.

Development revenue comes from domestic and foreign sources. No foreign resources were received in FY79, and all development expenditure came from domestic sources. During the latter part of the period foreign resources were the main sources of development expenditure, contributing as much as 85.1 to 93 percent of the total. Most of the aid money was in the form of grants, although occasionally loans exceeded grants.

Regarding sectoral allocation, emphasis shifted markedly from the other sectors to economic services: communication, water, tourism, energy, trade, and forestry. Communication and public works received 53.4 percent of total development expenditure in FY89. Social services more or less maintained their share of total development expenditure at about 18 percent. The losers were the directly productive sectors and general and other services, which included finance and planning, administration, and sports.

Government Revenue: Composition and Structure

During FY85 tax revenues contributed 60 percent of total government revenue. Income tax was the main direct tax, although there were a few others that were relatively insignificant in terms of government revenue. Indirect taxes included duties on imported goods, sales taxes on both imported and locally produced goods, and special levies on some goods and services. The latter included excise duties levied on goods to either discourage consumption or simply to earn more revenue. Sales taxes on both local and imported goods have now been replaced by the VAT.

Imports increased along with trade liberalization, as did government revenue from foreign trade. The only tax levied on exports is that on cloves, which averaged 8 percent of recurrent revenue between FY84 and FY90. With the decline of the clove industry, little revenue has been accruing from this crop (Mtatifikolo and Kilindo, 1993, p. 5). Contributions from parastatals are the main form of nontax revenue. Parastatals pay what they are assessed irrespective of the outcome of their operations.

The increased revenue from foreign trade has been further enhanced by exchange rate policy. While taxes from parastatals brought in T Sh 145.5 million in FY90, the highest contribution of the four sources indicated, given Zanzibar's privatization policy, parastatals are unlikely to continue to be a significant source of government revenue. However, privatization, if successful, will attract more investment and boost employment, thereby increasing income and sales tax revenues.

ASSESSING THE TAX EFFORT. Mtatifikolo and Kilindo (1993) assessed the Government of Zanzibar's tax effort by using both simple revenue to GDP ratios and by calculating buoyancies and elasticities. In the latter case they measured effort as the difference between buoyancy and elasticity. Both methods revealed that the government's tax effort has generally increased, especially following the implementation of structural adjustment measures. By further analyzing individual taxes the authors found that the tax effort was greatest in relation to import duties. However, by comparing the tax-to-base responsiveness with base-to-GDP responsiveness, they found that only manufacturing (sales tax) had been taxed higher than its responsiveness. Import duties, income taxes, and special levies were all taxed below their responsiveness. As the special levy was resorted to only as a stopgap measure, which in any case should not be resorted to if the import duties and sales taxes were appropriately managed, the problem of levying this tax below its responsiveness could be ignored. As for income taxes, the lower effort appeared to have been a deliberate policy to try to maintain the value of take home pay after many years of falling real wages. By and large there was room to raise more revenue from imports. Those interviewed hinted that more revenue could be collected from import duties by tightening collection procedures.

As Zanzibar relies heavily on indirect taxes, the tax system is likely to be regressive. This is a problem many developing countries face (Due and Meyer 1989). Overtaxing some tax bases like value added on local production and undertaxing others, for instance, imports, violated the principle of neutrality, while the volatility of most taxes undermined sufficiency.

The foregoing general observations generally apply even when we extend the period covered by Mtatifikolo and Kilindo (1993) to more recent periods. The problem of volatility is still apparent as shown in figures 7.1 and 7.2.

Figure 7.1. *Growth Rates of Total Tax Revenues in Nominal and Real Terms, FY91–98*

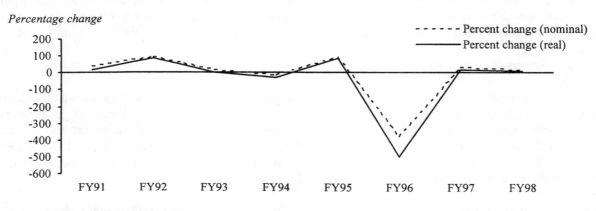

Sources: Mtatifikolo and Kilindo (1993).

Figure 7.2. *Growth Rates of Total Government Expenditures in Nominal and Real Terms, FY91–98*

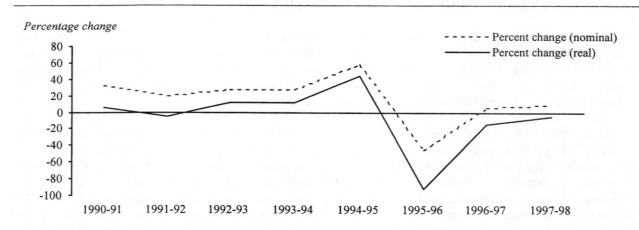

Sources: Mtatifikolo and Kilindo (1993).

GOVERNMENT REVENUE. Taxes are an important source of revenue (table 7.7). The trend of indirect taxes generally contributing slightly more than 90 percent of all tax revenue persists.

Table 7.7. *Zanzibar's Tax Structure, FY88–99*
(percentage of total tax revenues)

Tax	FY88	FY89	FY90	FY91	FY92	FY93	FY94	FY95	FY96	FY97	FY98	FY99
Import duty	30.44	30.46	40.35	28.66	38.46	34.52	5.17	50.59	33.51	37.53	40.11	36.76
Sales tax	52.59	49.75	35.52	0.20	0	43.96	66.13	31.79	32.37	33.19	33.95	24.48
Excise tax	0	0	7.01	12.30	14.41	16.36	20.58	10.47	8.33	14.07	0.25	3.32
VAT	0	0	0	0	0	0	0	0	0	0	0	4.02
Income tax	8.09	7.21	6.32	6.85	4.26	5.14	7.40	2.17	2.76	3.25	4.69	5.01
Special levy	7.35	1.57	1.73	45.03	0.16	0	0.70	1.76	2.58	1.79	6.56	9.25
Guest house tax	0	0	0	0	0	0	0	0.08	0.05	0	0	0
Transport tax	0	0	0.41	0.79	0	0	0	0.69	15.77	0.84	0.73	3.11
Stamp revenue	1.27	1.33	2.65	2.85	2.85	0	0	0	2.92	3.59	4.48	2.19
Sales tax/import duty (old)	0	0	0	0	39.83	0	0	0	0	0	0	0
Miscellaneous customs duty	0	0	0	0	0	0	0	0	0.16	2.39	0.02	0
Other earnings	0.24	9.65	5.97	3.29	0	0	0	2.41	0.16	0.02	0.67	3.44
Price stabilization	0	0	0	0	0	0	0	0	0	0	0.35	0.90
Price difference on petroleum	0	0	0	0	0	0	0	0	0	2.18	5.56	4.27
Fuel Sector Development Fund	0	0	0	0	0	0	0	0	0	0	1.17	1.02
Road Development Fund	0	0	0	0	0	0	0	0	0	0	1.41	1.77
Sea transport charges	0	0	0	0	0	0	0	0	1.32	1.12	0	0.38
Total	100	100	100	100	100	100	100	100	100	100	100	100

Source: Mtatifikolo, Mabele, and Kilindo (1993, appendix table 8).

With regard to the distinction between taxes on domestic goods as against taxes on imports and taxes on trade as against other sources such as incomes, we begin by classifying all government revenue by origin for FY94–98 as shown in table 7.8. In this classifications import duties on imports are added to sales taxes and excise duties on imports. All these taxes are levied on the same tax base, that is, imports. Similarly, sales taxes on locally-manufactured goods plus excise taxes on manufactured goods add up to taxes on domestic goods. The taxes on trade play a significant role in Zanzibar's revenue system.

INTRODUCTION OF THE VAT. The Union government had intended to introduce the VAT on the Mainland and in Zanzibar simultaneously to replace some taxes, especially sales taxes on specified goods and services. The study commissioned to advise on the feasibility of introducing VAT in Zanzibar (Mabele and Mwinyimvua 1998) was done and was approved by the Government of Zanzibar. However, the Government of Zanzibar decided not to introduce the VAT simultaneously with its introduction in the Mainland in January 1999, but instead did so six months later. It is too early to evaluate the results of the VAT.

Evolving Financing Problem

Government expenditure depends on government revenue. Tax and nontax government revenue should, as far as possible, meet recurrent expenditure needs. Tax revenue depends on the respective tax bases, for instance, foreign trade taxes depend on imports, taxes based on local goods depend on the production performance of local industries. Macroeconomic policies, some of which are determined by the Union, also influence the amount of taxes collected in Zanzibar. While some macroeconomic variables are market determined, and the Union government and its agencies may not be directly responsible, the two governments should work together closely in the area of fiscal and monetary policies to ensure the harmonization of macroeconomic fundamentals in the two parts of the country.

Table 7.8. *Sources of Government Revenue, FY94–98*
(T Sh millions and percent)

	FY94	FY95	FY96	FY97	FY98
By name					
Import taxes	3,194.08 (39.6%)	5,038.88 (35.0%)	7,837.68 (32.9%)	7533.(30.5%)	8,570.09 (48.1%)
Sales taxes	2,440.6 (30.2%)	3,256.19 (22.6%)	5,882.38 (24.8%)	5,297.36 (21.7%)	4,791.14 (2.9%)
Excise on domestic goods	659.92 (8.2%)	1,019.1 (17.0%)	2,213.89 (9.3%)	2,717.48 (11.0%)	466.76 (2.6%)
Excise on foreign goods	5,630.81 (69.8%)	8,960.78 (61.9%)	8,069.12 (63.6%)	4,703.17 (59.3%)	13,306.94 (74.6%)
By origin					
Tax on foreign goods	5,630.81 (69.8%)	8,960.78 (61.9%)	8,069.12 (63.6%)	14,703.17 (59.3%)	13,306.94 (74.6%)
Tax on domestic goods	664,79 (8.2%)	398.39 (2.7%)	814.83 (3.4%)	844.77 (3.4%)	521.05 (2.9%)
Income tax	587.19 (7.3%)	692.17 (5.0%)	535.48 (2.3%)	847.02 (3.4%)	1,011.56 (5.7%)
Non-tax revenue	584.90 (7.2%)	2,616.4 (18.0%)	2,912.32 (12.3%)	3,176.63 (13.0%)	145.18 (0.8%)

Note: Figures in parentheses are average annual growth rates.
Source: Government of Zanzibar.

Table 7.9 shows the Government of Zanzibar's financial operations for FY97 to FY99 The table shows that actual revenues constantly fell short of budget forecasts, whereas actual expenditures always exceeded estimates.

Table 7.9. *Zanzibar's Central Government Operations, FY97–99*
(T Sh millions)

	Actual FY97	Budget estimates FY98	Actual FY98	Actual FY98 as a percentage of estimates	Budget estimates FY99	Actual FY99	Actual FY99 as a percentage of estimates	Actual FY99 as a percentage of GDP
Total revenue:	19,808.0	44,013.7	37,285.7	84.7	44,780.0	37,691.0	84.2	29.6
Total expenditure:	19,833.0	55,496.5	38,393.8	69.2	46,150.0	38,206.0	82.8	30.0
Recurrent deficit	735.0	1,400.2	472.9	33.8	1,930.0	− 155.0	-8.0	-0.1
Development expenditure	760.0	12,883.0	635.2	4.9	3,300.0	360.0	10.9	0.3
Overall deficit before grants	735.0	11,482.9	1,108.1	9.7	1,370.0	515.0	37.6	-0.4
Grants (cash)	0.0	0.0	0.0	0.0	0.0	1.0	—	0.0
Overall deficit after grants:	735.0	11,482.9	1,081.1	9.7	1,370.0	514.0	37.5	-0.4
Adjustment to cash and other items	8,836.0	259.8	5,887.9	2,266.3	15,595	1,637.0	10.5	-1.3
Overall deficit checks issued	8,101.0	11,223.0	6,996.0	62.3	14,225.0	1,123.0	7.9	-0.9
Financing	8,101.0	11,223.0	6,996.0	62.3	14,225.0	1,123.0	7.9	
Program loans and import-support (cash)	0.0	11,223.0	0.0	0.0	—	4,498.0	—	0.9
Domestic (net)	8,101.0	0.0	6,996.0	0.0	—	-3,375	—	0.9
Bank	387.0	0.0	1,823.0	0.0	—	—	—	3.5
Non-bank	7,714.0	0.0	8,819.0	0.0	—	—	—	-2.7

— Not available.
Source: Bank of Tanzania (various years).

The revenue-expenditure gap needs to be financed from internal or external sources. Table 7.9 shows that Zanzibar relies heavily on internal financing from banks and nonbank sources, while external sources are meager or nonexistent.

The wide divergence between planned budgeted revenue and revenue actually collected is shown in table 7.10. Clearly the Government of Zanzibar needs to strengthen its ability to correctly forecast expected revenue and to manage the overall budget. Development expenditure is financed from the surplus from recurrent expenditure, bank and nonbank borrowing, and foreign loans and grants. As there is often little money left from recurrent expenditure, borrowing and aid has to finance most development expenditure. In recent years most donors, especially bilateral donors, have stopped giving aid to Zanzibar because of the political impasse that followed the 1995 general elections. While an accord has recently been concluded, most donors have yet to resume providing aid to Zanzibar.

Table 7.10. *Estimates Versus Actual Government Revenue and Expenditure, FY98–99*

Revenue	Import duty	Board of Income Tax	Revenue	Zanzibar	Total
Estimates FY98 (T Sh millions)	23,426	1,770	15,918	—	41,114
Percentage of total	57.0	4.3	38.7	—	100.0
Estimates July/March FY98 (T Sh millions)	17,569	1,328	11,939	—	30,835
Total collection (T Sh millions)	14,690	776	9,049	—	24,469
Collection estimate (%)	83.6	58.5	75.8	—	79.4
Expenditure FY99 (T Sh millions)	27,527	1,800	15,552	—	44,879
Percentage of total	61.3	4.0	34.7	—	100.0
Estimates July/March FY99 (T Sh millions)	20,645	1,350	11,894	—	33,889
Total collection (T Sh millions)	18,031	1,291	11,389	—	30,711
Collection estimate (%)	87.0	96.0	96.0	—	91.0

Expenditure	Recurrent				Development			All expenditure
	Personnel emoluments	National debt	Other expenditure	Total	Grants/ loans	Contribu- tion of SMZ	Total	
Estimates FY98	14,747	15,506	12,360	42,613	11,223	1,660	12,883	55,496
Percentage of total	34.6	36.4	29.0	100.0	87.1	12.9	100.0	100.0
Estimates July/March FY98 (T Sh millions)	11,060	11,630	9,270	31,960	8,417	1,245	9,662	41,622
Actual expenditure July/March (T Sh millions)	9,017	—	14,612	23,629	5,471	561	6,032	29,661
Percentage expenditure July/March	81.5	—	157.6	73.9	65.0	45.0	62.4	71.3
Estimates FY99 (T Sh millions)	16,000	2,000	24,850	42,850	14,225	3,300	17,525	60,375
Percentage of total	37.3	4.7	58.0	100.0	81.2	18.8	100.0	100.0
Expenditure estimates July/March FY99 (T Sh millions)	12,000	8,250	11,888	32,138	10,668	2,475	13,143	45,281
Actual expenditure July/March (T Sh millions)	10,004	175	19,851	30,030	6,934	504	74,380	34,336
Percentage expenditure July/March	83.0	2.0	167.0	93.0	65.0	20.0	85.0	76.0

Source: Government of Zanzibar.

Interstate Trade

Zanzibar maintains its own records for trade with the Mainland and with the rest of the world. As the transactions between Zanzibar and the Mainland are in local currency, we will distinguish between trade between the two parts of the Union by referring to it as interstate trade and refer to trade between Zanzibar and the rest of the world as external trade.

Zanzibar relies heavily on the Mainland as a destination for its exports. As table 7.11 shows, during 1990–94 Zanzibar's exports to the Mainland accounted for more than 50 percent of total exports. In 1991 exports to the Mainland reached 81.4 percent of total exports. This is explained by the fall in Zanzibar's external exports and the increase in re-exports from Zanzibar to the Mainland (table 7.12). For three of the four years shown in table 7.7 Zanzibar enjoyed a positive trade balance in its trade with the Mainland. As concerns imports, during 1988–94 Zanzibar's imports never exceeded 27 percent of total imports (table 7.13).

Table 7.11. *Interstate Trade Versus External Exports, 1988–94*

| Year | US$ millions | | | Percentage of total value | |
	Interstate exports	External exports	Total	Interstate exports	External exports
1988	6.22	7.39	13.62	45.69	54.30
1989	9.28	25.94	35.22	26.34	73.65
1990	8.21	8.00	16.21	50.64	49.35
1991	21.87	5.00	26.87	81.37	18.62
1992	21.42	5.47	26.87	79.62	20.37
1993	12.02	5.28	17.31	69.62	30.53
1994	9.73	3.45	13.18	73.78	26.21

Source: Mtatifikolo, Mabele, and Kilindo (1993, table 2).

Table 7.12. *Trends in Interstate Trade: Exports Versus Re-Exports and Trade Balance, 1995–98 (US$ millions)*

Year	Domestic exports	Re-exports	Total exports	Total imports	Trade balance
1995	796.98	15,064.88	15,861.86	8,385.61	7,476.25
1996	729.57	8,546.10	9,275.67	14,301.37	– 5,025.70
1997	2,804.49	21,687.11	24,491.60	13,236.69	11,254.91
1998	2,537.00	34,086.00	36,086.00	10,129.00	26,530.00

Source: President's Office and Ministry of Planning and Investments data.

Composition of Domestic Exports

Zanzibar's exports consist mainly of cloves and clove products, copra, and seaweed. Many commodities that are exported often appear grouped together as "other." in the official statistics. This category includes coconuts, copra, seaweed and other marine products, and tropical fruit. Despite the decline in output and value, clove exports still dominate Zanzibar's exports, though seaweed, one of the nontraditional exports, has considerably increased its share in total exports (table 7.14).

Table 7.13. *Interstate Versus Foreign Imports, 1988–94*

Year	US$ millions			Percentage of total value	
	Interstate imports	Foreign imports	Total	Interstate imports	Foreign imports
1988	6.46	20.68	27.15	23.82	76.17
1989	4.49	22.53	27.03	16.62	83.37
1990	4.15	11.60	15.75	26.90	73.64
1991	4.50	23.83	28.33	15.90	84.09
1992	12.33	66.75	78.98	15.48	84.51
1993	9.94	46.55	56.82	17.60	82.39
1994	8.61	55.21	63.82	13.49	86.50

Source: Mtatifikolo, Mabele, and Kilindo (1993, table 2).

Table 7.14. *Main Exports as a Percentage of the Value of Total Exports, Selected Years 1978–97*

Commodity	1978	1980	1984	1986	1988	1989	1990	1991	1992	1993	1994	1995	1996	1997
Cloves	6.71	79.92	80.49	70.94	52.84	0.00	47.60	13.74	76.50	69.71	43.96	62.33	31.85	56.50
Copra	2.02	6.64	19.42	2.00	0.00	—	—	1.35	0.52	29.29	6.24	2.41	63.50	0.00
Seaweed	0.23	0.22	0.00	0.01	0.00	—	—	0.25	15.95	0.80	27.33	9.78	32.02	6.80
Other	91.01[a]	13.21	0.08	27.02	47.15	0.27	52.39	84.64	7.01	0.18	9.49	25.46	26.50	36.70
Total	100.00	100.00	100.00	100.00	100.00	100.00	100.00	100.00	100.00	100.00	100.00	100.00	100.00	100.00

— Not available.
a. Boosted by coconut exports, which were worth about T Sh 69 million.
Source: Mtatifikolo, Mabele, and Kilindo (1993, table 2); Ministry of State, Planning, and Investment data.

In addition to seaweed, other nontraditional exports have also become important, but except for rubber, they have not shown a consistent increase (table 7.15). There appears to be some potential for increased exports of marine products and rubber.

Table 7.15. *Nontraditional Exports, 1992–96*
(metric tons)

Product	1992	1993	1994	1995	1996
Shark fins	1.5	0.2	0.6	0.3	—
Beachdemer	37.3	6.1	45.4	23.0	76.6
Skar	1.9	0.2	100.0	0.5	0.3
Shells	30.0	40.0	30.0	15.0	13.2
Lobsters	11.4	3.2	150.9	0.3	—
Fresh fish	7.2	1.0	77.2	2.7	70.0
Seaweed	2,343.0	2,095.0	2,542.0	4,287.0	5,285.0
Skin of grouper	0.3	8.4	—	—	—
Octopus	2.2	—	—	0.3	0.5
Rubber	94.3	208.0	137.0	59.0	60.0
Mangoes	58.0	41.9	76.5	27.0	82.0
Pineapples	—	1.1	—	—	2.3

— Not available.
Source: Government of Zanzibar.

Composition of Imports

Food imports are extremely important to Zanzibar (table 7.16). Imports of food and manufactured goods dominated imports during the period under review.

Table 7.16. *Main Imports, 1993–97*

Import	US$ millions					Percentage of total imports				
	1993	1994	1995	1996	1997	1993	1994	1995	1996	1997
Food	11.9	16.12	14.27	22.07	23.56	25.68	28.79	16.65	27.32	28.56
Beverages and tobacco	0.15	0.06	0.16	0.06	7.60	0.32	0.10	0.18	0.07	9.21
Raw materials	0.13	0.33	0.16	0.44	0.16	0.28	0.58	0.18	0.54	0.19
Mineral fuel	0.16	0.44	0.52	2.32	0.39	0.34	0.78	0.60	2.87	0.47
Chemicals	1.28	1.74	23.14	3.63	2.85	2.76	3.10	27.00	4.49	3.45
Textiles	4.66	4.02	2.18	6.78	11.46	10.05	7.18	2.54	8.39	13.89
Machinery	6.00	12.63	3.92	8.21	11.40	12.95	22.56	4.57	10.16	13.81
Transport equipment	8.00	5.32	14.12	7.39	9.05	17.26	9.50	16.47	9.14	10.97
Miscellaneous manufactured. articles	13.95	14.51	27.20	29.85	15.98	30.11	25.91	31.70	36.95	19.37
Total	46.33	55.98	85.70	80.78	82.49	100.00	100.00	100.00	100.00	100.00

Source: Ministry of Trade and Industries data.

Balance of Payments

Zanzibar's balance of trade was in deficit throughout 1986–98, except in 1992, when it registered a small surplus (figure 7.3). Since 1992 the balance of trade has generally been declining. Table 7.17 summarizes Zanzibar's balance of payments for the same period; however, because of the lack of complete data, it was not possible to give a full account of the balance of payments.

Private Sector Development

As noted earlier, Zanzibar ventured into privatization before the Mainland, and the private sector is strong in the areas of trade and tourism. Privatization started with the importation of consumer goods, their sale domestically, and quite often their re-exportation. The parastatal sector has virtually disappeared from trade except for trade in cloves, therefore the private sector can take the credit for this sector's good performance.

Government Strategies through ZIPA

One of the Government of Zanzibar's main strategies to engender higher economic growth and development is to diversify the economy to make it less dependent on agriculture in general, and cloves in particular. It is doing this partly by developing tourism, along with encouraging local and foreign investment.

The Government of Zanzibar has invested in export processing zones (EPZs) whose objective is to attract enterprises to undertake processing for export. It administers two industrial parks that provide basic infrastructure (water, electricity, and roads) to facilitate the establishment of processing factories. Currently one EPZ is operational, the Amaan Industrial Park, a well-developed industrial estate with adequate basic infrastructure, and another is at Micheweni, where investment in infrastructure is being undertaken prior to opening up. The government hopes to start up another industrial park at Fumba, for which it is trying to raise the financing. Since 1986 ZIPA has approved 234 investment projects worth US$420 million. The hotel and tourism sector attracted 107 projects, or 48 percent of all approved projects, illustrating the leading role this sector is playing in Zanzibar's efforts to diversify its economy and accelerate the pace of development.

Since its inception, the EPZ has made a very modest contribution toward job creation (table 7.18).

Figure 7.3. *Zanzibar Balance of Trade, 1986–98*

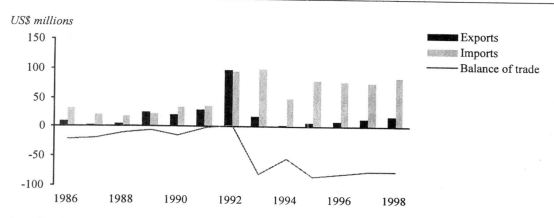

Source: Based on Tables 7.13 and 7.16.

Table 7.17. *Balance of Payments, 1986–98*
(US$ millions)

Category	1986	1987	1988	1989	1990	1991	1992	1993	1994	1995	1996	1997	1998
Exports	10	2.9	5.9	25.3	19.5	31.5	97.6	20.7	3.3	5.7	7.6	10.7	17.9
Imports	31.5	19.9	18.2	22.0	33.0	33.1	95.6	97.6	53.7	87.4	86.3	82.4	89.5
Balance of trade	− 21.5	− 17.0	− 12.3	− 3.3	− 13.5	− 1.6	+ 2	− 76.9	− 50.4	− 81.7	− 78.7	− 71.7	− 71.6
Service bureau	− 0.6	− 0.7	− 10.5	+ 13.2	—	—	—	—	− 0.9	+ 5.6	+ 7.2	+ 14.5	+ 14.4
Overall balance of payments	− 1.2	− 3.9	+ 0.9	+ 10.2	—	—	—	—	+ 13.0	− 8.3	+ 0.4	− 1.71	+ 0.6

— Not available.
Source: Mtatifikolo, Mabele, and Kilindo (1993, table 3).

Table 7.18. *Employment by the EPZ, FY96–00*

Year	Employment
FY96	869
FY97	563
FY98	211
FY99	390
FY00	445

Source: EPZ, Zanzibar.

During 1994–99 exports by the EPZ totaled almost US$6 million (almost T Sh 4 billion) and had a positive impact on Zanzibar's general external trade (table 7.19).

Table 7.19. *Value of EPZ Exports, 1994–99*

Year	US$	T Sh
1994	11,860	6,538,581
1995	158,246	89,502,074
1996	91,411	55,396,328
1997	1,426,495	875,162,498
1998	1,638,164	1,039,518,920
1999	2,578,122	1,858,987,990
Total	5,904,289	3,925,106,391

Source: EPZ, Zanzibar.

Table 7.20 breaks down all projects ZIPA has approved by sector and expected employment generated. Of the more than US$130 million of approved investment, only about 30 percent has been realized to date. The new investment is expected to result in the employment of more than 5,000 people. Table 7.21 classifies the projects by source of investment (local versus foreign) and indicates the proportion of operational and uncompleted projects.

Table 7.20. *Investment Projects by Sector and Expected Employment, 1999*

Sector	Number of projects	Proposed capital (US$ millions)	Approved investment (US$ millions)	Expected employment
Agriculture and fisheries	24	32.5	2.0	257
Business and services	34	1,257.7	2.2	322
Hotels and tourism	107	3,030.0	57.2	2,950
Industry	28	30.5	17.4	698
Tour operator	21	9.8	2.4	161
Air transport	7	10.4	0.8	67
Maritime transport	13	49.1	48.5	576
Total	234	4,420.0	130.5	5,031

Source: ZIPA data.

Table 7.21. *Status and Ownership of Approved Projects by Sector, 1999*

Sector	Total	Operating	Foreign owned	Domestically owned
Agrc/Fisheries	24	11	16	8
Business and Services	34	21	22	12
Hotel and Tourism	107	46	59	48
Industries	28	16	10	18
Tour Operator	21	14	13	8
Transport Air	7	4	6	1
Transport Sea	13	3	3	10
Total	234	115	129	105

Source: ZIPA data.

A written investment policy would help ensure that ZIPA can speed up procedural issues related to investment. Currently who is responsible for initiating investment programs and who is responsible for making critical decisions is sometimes unclear. In the absence of a clear investment policy ZIPA cannot successfully operate as a one-stop agency for clearing investment decisions.

Other Government Initiatives

The government is committed to developing the private sector and has reduced its role in production, trade (including tourism), and to a lesser extent service provision. To encourage the development of the private sector, the government has taken additional measures.

The ERP programs both in the Mainland and in Zanzibar ushered in the era of liberalization and privatization. The ERP II introduced the three-year system of a rolling plan and forward budgets, which includes annual development budgeting. In this document the government shows the programs intended to benefit the private sector. Development programs are divided into the following four sectors:

- Economic services: water, transport, and so forth
- Social services, for example, education and health
- Production sectors, such as agriculture and industry
- Public administration.

In all these sectors the aim is to increase people's capacity to increase production through improved economic infrastructure and social services. Some of the projects are tied directly to the development of infrastructure in the EPZ

Since FY90 the Government of Zanzibar has allocated money to help people implement development projects through self–employment programs. T Sh 50,000 million was set aside that year, and the amount has generally exhibited a rising trend (table 7.22). Not all the funds earmarked for self-reliance programs were made available. This was mainly because of an overall deficit in the money allocated to finance development expenditure (table 7.23).

Private Sector Institutions

This section draws heavily on a recent agricultural sector survey report completed by the Government of Zanzibar assisted by the Food and Agriculture Organization of the United Nations (Government of Zanzibar 1999c).

Zanzibar's equivalent of the Mainland's Tanzania Chamber of Commerce and Industries is the Zanzibar Chamber of Commerce, Industries, and Agriculture. The chamber depends considerably on donor funding to run its activities. It was established in 1909 and reorganized in 1992. Its main mission of is advising the government and discussing with representatives of the government and other public institutions issues related to business. The chamber collects, analyzes, and propagates private sector views on economic policies and acts as a pressure group for its members and the private sector in general. The chamber has plans to launch credit and saving schemes and to initiate small-scale agroprocessing enterprises in conjunction with foreign investors. The main problem is that the subscription fee the 1,000 members pay is too low to build up adequate operating funds. Moreover, the chamber is ill-equipped, with neither a library nor computer facilities to assist its members in the timely acquisition and analysis of information.

Zanzibar has an emerging nongovernmental organization (NGO) sector that consists mainly of small NGOs and community-based organizations. About 99 NGOs are registered, but only 33 are members of the NGO umbrella organization: the Association of Nongovernmental Organizations of Zanzibar. The

NGOs interested in economic development work in the area of poverty alleviation and focus on income-generating activities. The main problem facing the NGO movement is a lack of funds and working facilities. Many NGOs also lack well-trained staff:

Table 7.22. *Government of Zanzibar's Contributions to Self-Employment Activities, FY90–99*

Fiscal year	Budgeted (T Sh thousands)	Actual (T Sh thousands)	Percentage of budgeted funds actually allocated
FY90	50,000	18,421	37
FY91	80,000	69,523	87
FY92	50,000	30,000	60
FY93	150,000	54,500	36
FY94	150,000	39,000	26
FY95	254,000	159,220	63
FY96	77,000	38,000	49
FY97	100,000	22,500	23
FY98	100,000	28,650	29
FY99	100,000	18,757	19
Total	1,101,000	474,571	43

Source: Government of Zanzibar (1999a, table III).

Table 7.23. *Government of Zanzibar's Contributions to Development Expenditure, FY95–99 (T Sh millions)*

Fiscal year	Budgeted	Amount	Percentage of budgeted funds actually allocated
FY95	2,719.994	1,051.392	39
FY96	1,420.000	1,081.427	76
FY97	1,400.000	629.000	45
FY98	1,660.000	560.000	34
FY99	3,300.000	503.000[a]	15

a. July 1998–March 1999.
Source: Government of Zanzibar (1999a, table II).

The rice irrigation schemes have farmers' associations that help their members hire tractors and obtain subsidized inputs. The members work hand-in-hand with the government and other organizations to increase productivity. The main constraints facing the farmers' organizations are organizational and financial. While many women are members, they are not involved in managing these organizations.

Cooperatives do not seem to have played an important role in Zanzibar since their re-establishment in 1995. The agriculture sector alone has 303 registered cooperatives, of which 132 deal with crop production, 145 are in the fishing subsector, 11 are in forestry, and 15 deal with livestock keeping. Most of the registered cooperatives also run consumer retail shops. While the cooperatives could potentially play a significant role in stimulating and managing development activities, currently they are plagued with many problems, including embezzlement and mismanagement of funds, poorly trained staff, and organizational problems.

Pacemakers for Growth

The performance of Zanzibar's economy in recent years was described in earlier sections. This section identifies likely pacemakers for economic growth during the period under review.

Trends in Capital Formation

The available data do not distinguish capital formation by private and public sector, therefore we cannot discuss the relative contributions of each to economic growth. Nevertheless table 7.24 confirms what GDP figures had revealed about the performance of the various sectors of the economy: construction and trade, including tourism, have been the pacemakers of economic growth in Zanzibar. Construction of both residential and nonresidential buildings increased during 1989–94. However, by 1992 the trend in the buildings sector had already begun to decline.

Table 7.24. *Capital Formation, Current Years 1989–94*

Category	1989 Amount (T Sh millions)	1990 Amount (T Sh millions)	1990 Annual percent change	1991 Amount (T Sh millions)	1991 Annual percent change	1992 Amount (T Sh millions)	1992 Annual percent change	1993 Amount (T Sh millions)	1993 Annual percent change	1994 Amount (T Sh millions)	1994 Annual percent change
Buildings											
Urban residential	57.4	67.8	18.0	135.5	98.5	231.8	71.0	294.1	26.9	444.0	51.0
Nonresidential	56.0	69.3	23.7	162.3	134.3	278.0	71.3	332.5	19.6	502.0	50.6
Rural	13.5	14.8	10.0	16.3	10.0	18.0	10.2	19.8	− 10	30.0	51.8
Total	126.9	151.9	19.7	314.1	106.8	527.8	68.0	646.4	22.5	976.0	51.0
Construction											
Land improvement	69.6	82.1	18.0	254.5	209.8	427.6	68.0	537.1	25.6	814.0	51.6
Roads, bridges, etc.	200.5	236.5	18.0	634.6	168.3	1,066.3	68.0	1,406.7	31.9	2,133.0	51.6
Total	270.1	318.7	18.0	889.1	179.0	1,493.9	68.0	1,943.8	30.1	2,947.0	51.6
Equipment											
Transport equipment	416.9	2,706.1	549.1	1,303.9	− 51.81	4,088.0	213.5	3,218.1	− 21.28	2,768.0	− 14
Other	708.2	761.8	7.6	2,085.2	173.7	4,611.5	121.2	2,415.3	− 47.62	6,571.0	172.1
Total	1,125.0	3,467.9	190.5	3,389.1	-2.3	8,699.5	156.7	5,633.4	− 35.24	9,339.0	55.8
Other											
Increase in stocks	493.9	923.9	− 287.06	200.0	121.7	− 833.68	− 516.84	− 93.89	88.7	441.0	569.7
Total fixed capital formation	1,028.1	3,014.5	193.2	6,592.4	118.7	9,887.5	50.0	8,317.5	− 15.88	13,704.0	64.8
Subsistence	13.5	14.8	10.0	16.3	10.0	18.0	10.0	19.8	10.0	30.0	51.8
Monetary	1,014.6	2,999.7	195.6	6,576.0	119.2	9,869.5	50.0	8,297.7	− 15.93	13,674.0	64.8

Source: Government of Zanzibar.

Tourism

The warm weather throughout the year, coupled with the traditional hospitality, make Zanzibar a compelling tourist attraction Currently earnings from tourism, both directly and indirectly, amount to more than US$80 million per year. The average tourist stays in Zanzibar for seven days, up from three days in 1990–93 and four days in 1994. Part of this is due to the upgrading of a number of tourism facilities.

In terms of boarding facilities, Zanzibar has 4,981 beds in 168 accommodation units that include first-class hotels, resorts, villas, and guest houses. Some 500 more beds are expected to be added between 1999 and 2002. Table 7.25 categorizes the various accommodation units based on a 1997 Ministry of Tourism survey. Occupancy rates are between 45 and 55 percent except during March–May, the low season.

Table 7.25 *Classification and Capacity of Hotels, 1997*

Class of hotel	Number of beds	Percentage of total beds
No grade[a]	1,869	37
A[b]	304	6.1
AA[b]	76	1.5
One star	217	4.4
Two star	602	12
Three star	1,032	20.7
Four star	639	12.8
Five star	242	4.9
Total	4,981	100.0

a. Accommodations with less than the minimum requirements or quality for a star.
b. Accommodations that could qualify for a star with improvements.
Source: Ministry of Tourism, Government of Tanzania.

Investments in the tourism sector have been growing at a reasonable pace. For instance, between 1990 and 1997 more than 16 hotel projects were approved each year. Currently a total of 107 hotel projects have been approved, representing projected capital investment of more than US$3 billion. As concerns tour operators, a total of 13 companies were approved between 1990 and 1997. This constitutes 62 percent of all tourism projects approved, with a capital investment of approximately US$6 million.

Tourism offers employment opportunities, and 3,077 people have permanent employment in the industry. Many more are employed indirectly in the service sector that caters to the tourism industry.

Government revenue from tourism emanates from income taxes, corporate taxes, and VAT (which is applicable to some of the tourist units). Table 7.26 shows revenue collected from licenses and hotel levies from FY94–98. The amount of revenue generated from both sources is encouraging.

Table 7.26. *Revenue Collection from Hotels, FY94–98*

Fiscal year	Licenses (US$)	Hotel levies (T Sh)
FY94	48,224	59,136,345
FY95	33,277	207,689,182
FY96	75,000	381,982,945
FY97	126,000	650,700,000
FY98	147,000	840,700,000

Source: Ministry of Tourism, Government of Tanzania.

Fish and Marine Products

Zanzibar's fisheries are almost an entirely artisanal affair and are conducted in the shallow areas along the coast. The proportion of freshwater fisheries is negligible because of the lack of rivers and lakes. Fishing contributes 2.5 percent of GDP and 6.3 percent of total agricultural GDP. About 99 percent of the annual catch of 11,000 metric tons is sold locally, providing Zanzibaris with their main source of protein. Fish provides 100 percent of the protein needs of poor households and accounts for 22 percent of the average family's expenditure on food.

Zanzibar has 23,734 fishermen, of whom 11,965 are located in Unguja and the remainder live in Pemba. Only 9,443 fishermen in Unguja and 9,232 in Pemba use fishing vessels, which include dugout canoes, outrigger canoes, planked motorized boats, and wooden sailing boats. All these together make a total of 5,149 vessels.

The entire fishing grounds are about 4,000 square kilometers for Unguja and 2,720 square kilometers for Pemba. Much of this area has coral reefs and a variety of fauna and flora, making the region ideal for fishing. The types of fish available include pelagic fish, especially sardines, mackerel tuna, bill fish, and kingfish. Other types of fish include demersal species such as snappers, wrasses, parrot fish, and spine foots, along with marine water resources such as octopus, squid, lobsters, shrimp, and sea cucumber. Most of the fish is sold in domestic markets, though a small proportion is exported to Dar es Salaam and Kenya, while sea cucumber is solely for export.

Seaweed farming started in 1983 and became commercial in 1990. Currently about 12,000 households are engaged in this activity. The most commonly harvested seaweed is the red seaweed, especially *Eucheruma spinosium* and *Eucheruma cotton*. Table 7.27 presents the quantity and value of seaweed production. Quantity has exhibited a generally upward trend, although some years experienced a decline in production. In monetary terms, the value of seaweed production has exhibited a generally rising trend, with the highest value at almost T Sh 437 million in 1996.

Table 7.27. *Seaweed Production by Quantity and Value, 1990–98*

Year	1990	1991	1992	1993	1994	1995	1996	1997	1998
Quantity (tons)	261	1,298	2,487	1,768	2,542	4,434	5,607	3,667	4,305
Value (T Sh thousands)	11,146	70,974	142,075	106,118	183,861	312,759	436,865	329,622	434,570

Source: Ministry of Agriculture, Government of Zanzibar.

A comparison of year-to-year quantities and values of seaweed sales indicate that the price per unit of seaweed has remained constant. The market for seaweed is monopsonistic, that is, a few buyers control the commodity. To devise a marketing system that will encourage farmers to increase seaweed production, a detailed study of the structure, conduct, and performance of seaweed marketing in Zanzibar is needed.

Various fishery projects have been launched to boost fish production and raise fishermen's standard of living. In support of local fishery projects, the government provided fishing gear worth T Sh 134 million to groups and individual fishermen in FY91 and imported various fishing equipment worth T Sh 21 million through the Zanzibar Smallholder Support Project. In addition, fishing gear worth T Sh 2.5 million was loaned to fishermen in 1997, along with another T Sh 48 million of fishing gear through sources other than the Smallholder Support Project.

There is much scope for offshore and deep sea fishing, and the Government of Zanzibar is mobilizing resources to exploit this potential. Such activities are currently contracted to Japanese fishermen, and there is a need to check on the revenue generation element of this arrangement. Foreign fishermen often fail to declare the full extent of their catch to the customs authorities, thereby robbing the country of badly needed tax revenue.

Agriculture

Despite the government's various efforts to promote development, agricultural, and in particular clove, production is still the mainstay of the economy and is crucial for employment, food security, export earnings and poverty alleviation. This section examines the performance of agriculture and its role in the economy's development and growth. Agriculture is defined to include crop production, livestock husbandry, and the use of natural (marine and forestry) resources. Unlike on the Mainland, one Ministry—the Ministry of Agriculture, Livestock Development, and Natural Resources—administers all these activities.

Zanzibar's agriculture has two zones: the plantation zone found in the more fertile upland areas of both islands, and the more marginal coral rag. The cultivable area in the plantation zone is about 130,000 hectares in area, 85 percent of which are under permanent tree crops, which leaves little room for expansion. Furthermore, land holdings are small, about 1.2 hectares each. The average cultivated land holding of 1.6 hectares covers 70 percent of the total cultivated land. The remaining 30 percent consists of cultivated land holdings averaging less than 0.8 hectares. In a situation with almost no off-farm employment opportunities and where about 5.4 percent of rural households are landless, unemployment and poverty are serious issues in the rural areas.

Export crops, primarily cloves, occupy 40 percent of the total land cultivated. Chilies, coconuts, and a few other export crops are growing in importance, but are nowhere near cloves in importance. Until 1994, despite a stagnation in production and the uncertainty of demand in the world market, cloves accounted for 70 percent of Zanzibar's export earnings.

The remaining 60 percent of total cultivated land is used for food crop production to produce cassava, bananas, sweet potatoes, legumes, and maize. Cassava is the staple food for most rural households as a source of starch; however rice is the preferred starchy food and is grown wherever possible. Unlike the other food crops, which are grown in complex mixtures, rice is often grown alone.

Slightly more than 50 percent of households own livestock, 23 percent of whom own low-producing indigenous cattle. Livestock accounts for 12 percent of GDP. Per capita annual consumption of red meat and milk is estimated at 3 kilograms and 4 liters, respectively. In recent years 5,000 cattle and 4,000 goats per year have been slaughtered for the urban market. Some households also keep improved and/or unimproved poultry species.

CASH CROP PRODUCTION. The three most important agricultural exports are cloves and clove by-products, copra, and chilies. Table 7.28 shows the marketed quantities of the three main cash crops.

Although declining in output and value, cloves are still important as a source of foreign exchange and of income to many rural people. Almost all clove production is exported. While yields appear to be uneven from year to year, data to establish a long-term trend in yields are unavailable. Moreover, as cloves are often inter-planted with other crops in various combinations of plant densities, obtaining an accurate picture of yields is difficult. The yield is quite low, which is attributed to the old age of a large proportion of plants and the fact that replanting does not seem to have proceeded quickly enough to increase the

Table 7.28. *Marketed Production of Main Cash Crops, 1992–97*
(tons)

Year	Cloves	Copra	Chilies	Clove stems
1992	1,692	167	1.2	849
1993	1,843	1,304	2.1	38
1994	4,927	3,992	1.6	450
1995	1,576	67	1.1	251
1996	10,339	2,223	3.5	1,624
1997	2,111	767	0.2	755

Source: Bank of Tanzania and Zanzibar State Trading Corporation data.

proportion of young trees. Husbandry practices are also poor. The proposed agricultural policy is intended to improve extension services and create incentives for replanting.

Copra comes from processed coconuts. As with cloves, the age of the trees and slow replanting rates have contributed to low yields, in addition to poor husbandry, which is responsible for rampant pest and disease infestation of the coconut trees

FOOD CROPS. Before liberalization, the government was actively involved in purchasing and importing the main food crops. Food production decreased from 510,983 metric tons per year to 243,030 metric tons per year between FY85 and FY94 (note that rice is excluded for FY94, thus the figures shown here cannot be used for comparative purposes). Nevertheless, the decline appears to have been considerable, and yields appear to have dropped even further.

The major problem facing all food crops is the prevalence of low-yielding varieties and disease and pest infestation. Research and extension efforts need to be directed toward food production to attain higher levels of production. This will enable Zanzibar to achieve greater food security and self-sufficiency. As pointed out earlier, trade between Zanzibar and the Mainland is important as a source of food for Zanzibar, especially maize and rice. However, imports from other countries (made by the government) have also become important sources. Since liberalization the private sector has also been allowed to import food and has more or less taken over the importation of sugar and wheat. While no data are available, it is safe to state that sugar and wheat imports increased after liberalization and are now much larger than they were during 1980–92.

THE POLICY ENVIRONMENT. The Government of Zanzibar issued its first agricultural policy in 1984. The objective was to try to revamp the agriculture sector after some years of stagnation or deterioration. The policy emphasized and consolidated the state's role in a mechanization drive to rehabilitate and develop irrigation facilities. However, the policy lacked sectoral packages with detailed subsectoral policies and the institutional support mechanisms needed for effective implementation and monitoring. Furthermore, even as the government was promulgating this agricultural policy, Zanzibar had already started experimenting with economic liberalization measures, especially in the area of trade. In 1986 these experiments were consolidated and formalized into ERPI, which was followed by ERPII from 1991 to 1994. The ERP programs aimed at improving the production of food and cash and export crops, rehabilitating physical infrastructure, increasing capacity utilization in industry, and restoring external and internal balance through the pursuit of appropriate macroeconomic policies. Incentives to producers rather than central government directives were to be used to achieve the overall objective of increasing the production of goods and services.

No comprehensive review of the agricultural policy was undertaken to bring it in line with the new macroeconomic environment ushered in by the ERP. The Ministry of Agriculture, Livestock Development, and Natural Resources, with support from the FAO, finished such a review in 1999, and as a result has proposed a new agricultural policy. This new policy was submitted to the president and the cabinet for consideration and possible adoption (Government of Zanzibar 1999c).

Trade liberalization started earlier in Zanzibar than on the Mainland. The importation of most goods and domestic trade in imported goods were liberalized during the late 1980s. At that time imports of consumer and other goods were still rigidly controlled on the Mainland. Consequently the relatively small market for these imported goods in Zanzibar was quickly saturated, and a vigorous trade in these commodities developed between Zanzibar and the Mainland. When the ERP was introduced on the Mainland in 1995, Zanzibar had already established itself as a cheaper source of imported textiles, electronics, and other consumer goods.

Trade liberalization had a positive impact on the economy. It enabled Zanzibar to have shops fully stocked with consumer goods and to re-export a large share of these imports to the Mainland and to neighboring countries such as Kenya. This raised incomes in the trade sector, including the informal trade subsector, with resultant likely spillover effects on the incomes of rural people, directly through increased income by rural trading entities and indirectly through remittances from traders in urban and rural areas to nontraders in rural areas. The increased supply of consumer goods acted as an incentive for increased agricultural production.

The above hypothetical cause and effect is supported by GDP data presented earlier. Agriculture grew by 7.9 percent in real terms during the first four years of the economic reform programs; however, this growth could not be sustained, because the trade reforms in the agriculture sector were limited. While trade in food crops was liberalized, trade in export crops was not. This meant that the all-important clove subsector was left out of the liberalization.

Cloves are the only major source of export revenue. An export tax is levied on cloves, but details about this tax are unavailable. Clearly with the decline in production and exports, the importance of this source of revenue has decreased.

Detailed data about development expenditure on agriculture by subsector are unavailable. However, we have some information about the provision of subsidies to agriculture. Subsidies have been a major agricultural policy since the revolution, but it has been clear since the 1980s that subsidies were largely unsustainable. The plan was to do away with subsidies as part of the introduction of the economic reforms, but eliminating them entirely has proven difficult. Table 7.29 shows recent trends in the provision of subsidies to agriculture. The share of government development expenditure going to subsidies is considerable. Although the level of resources available to the government has been declining, subsidies have been increasing in general. Given the agriculture sector's dismal performance, this high degree of subsidization is probably not the best way of allocating public resources.

Agricultural Marketing

Because of its location, Zanzibar has been involved in trading for centuries. Cloves have been a dominant export commodity for more than a century. At the time of the revolution prices on the world market were quite good, enabling the government to generate revenue and foreign exchange that allowed it to launch ambitious social programs, like free, universal schooling for 10 years and modern housing equipped with imported modern kitchen equipment for the average citizen. The government nationalized domestic and export trade in cloves and gave the Zanzibar State Trading Corporation (ZSTC) the monopoly on all trade

Table 7.29. *Provision of Subsidies to Agriculture, FY95–99*

Fiscal year	Total available development budget (T Sh thousands)	Agricultural subsidies (T Sh thousands)	Subsidies as a percentage of available development budget
FY95	1,051,392	40,489	3.9
FY96	1,081,427	49,904	4.6
FY97	627,000	32,860	5.2
FY98	560,000	54,110	9.7
FY99	503,000	31,867	6.3

Source: Ministry of Agriculture, Livestock Development, and Natural Resources data.

in cloves, chilies, and copra. Before the revolution cloves had been traded through the Cloves Growers Association (Government of Zanzibar 1999a).

MARKETING SYSTEMS. Agricultural marketing systems in Zanzibar differ from those on the Mainland in two main ways. First, the three main export crops—cloves, copra, and chilies—are still under state monopoly even following trade liberalization, –though the marketing of these crops is soon to be liberalized. For the spices whose marketing is not controlled—ginger, black pepper, turmeric, cinnamon, and so on—traders (shopkeepers and exporters) seek out producers, especially when such items are in short supply, or farmers bring their produce to the urban markets and bear all the risks involved.

Second is the difference in marketing across commodities destined for domestic use or for export. The traders can buy produce from farmers and take it to wholesale markets, where they are bought by retailers who sell it to consumers. Farmers may also sell their produce directly to retailers, or even to consumers. Fisherman can take their catches to auction markets, many of which are near landing sites, where retailers and consumers can buy them. Some itinerant fishmongers buy at auctions and sell directly to consumers from door to door. Livestock marketing involves both live animals and their products. Live animals are sold at wholesale auctions or traded between individual owners and individual traders or consumers. Livestock products are sold directly by producers to either dealers or consumers. The extension of trade liberalization to the agriculture sector stimulated production and trade both domestically and for the external market. Thus the sale of mangoes and other fruit to the Mainland, the Middle East, and Kenya has increased in recent years; however, liberalization needs to be extended to include cloves, copra, and chilies. In addition, quality control, market information, and physical infrastructure need to be improved.

A recent report (Government of Zanzibar 1999c) indicated that the government should improve market efficiency by upgrading the physical infrastructure and introducing regulations to encourage participation by the private sector in production, processing, and marketing. The report cited the following issues that need to be addressed:

- Disorganized marketing systems and inadequate infrastructure and facilities
- Complex procedures involving high transactions costs
- Inappropriate regulations applicable to the wholesale and retail markets
- Inadequate availability of inputs and services
- Poor enforcement of quality control measures for exports and imports
- Lack of market information
- The ZSTC's monopoly of the clove trade, which is not beneficial to the industry or to the country
- Weak marketing system for livestock and their products
- Lack of properly organized marketing channels for fishery products

- Insufficient profits for seaweed farmers, who account for only 10 percent of the export market because of foreign monopolies.

The report recommends actions for dealing with these issues, notably by creating a competitive environment that encourages the private sector to participate in all aspects of the agriculture sector. In this connection, the collection of statistics, the passage of legislation, and the enforcement of marketing rules are part of a competitive, efficient, and liberalized marketing system.

PRICES. For export crops, the prices domestic producers receive depend on prices in the world market. Thus a sharp change in the price of an export crop in the world market affects rural incomes and general welfare. If the government taxes the export, then its revenue-generating ability is also affected.

Adequate time series data on world market prices for cloves were not available. We therefore used the unit export value to derive information on the value of clove exports. As table 7.30 shows, the unit value of cloves in U.S. dollar terms dropped sharply for the whole period under review, except for a few years when the price shot up. If the exchange rate had remained fixed, as was the case before the economic reforms, the value in Tanzania shillings would have been much lower; nevertheless, the exchange rate could not fully compensate producers for the large drop in world market prices for cloves.

Table 7.30. *Clove Exports, Selected Years 1978–96*

Year	Value (US$ millions)	Quantity (tons)	Value (US$/ton)	Percentage change
1978	9.11	1,364	6,000	—
1980	61.89	7,977	7,000	14.3
1982	39.13	4,588	8,000	12.5
1984	129.21	2,073	6,000	86.7
1986	16.83	2,620	6,000	− 900.0
1988	72.01	2,638	20,000	70.0
1990	7.72	3,520	2,000	99.9
1991	3.69	2,411	1,000	− 100.0
1992	4.19	4,450	900	− 11.1
1993	3.74	6,026	600	− 50.0
1994	1.52	2,585	500	− 20.0
1995	3.48	4,427	700	28.6
1996	1.35	2,331	500	− 40.0

— Not available.
n.a. Not applicable.
Source: Mtatifikolo, Mabele, and Kilindo (1993, appendix table 5).

During 1983–94 world market prices for copra were unstable, but declined overall despite the occasional sharp rises. The price of copra on the world market declined by more than 80 percent between 1984 and 1985, and fell by another 95 percent in 1986 before rising by 36 percent in 1987.

The prospects for chilies in the world market were quite good at the beginning of the period under consideration, when prices rose —each year during 1984–86. Thereafter prices fell precipitously for five years, rising modestly for the subsequent three years.

While the price of imported oil also fluctuated (figure 7.4), these fluctuations were less extreme than those pertaining to clove, copra, and chili exports. Given the general declining trends in the prices of

Zanzibar's major exports, the modest declines in oil prices did not have much effect on Zanzibar's balance of trade (figure 7.3).

Food commodities feature prominently on Zanzibar's import bill. In terms of foreign exchange conservation, rice imports from the Mainland are useful. However, given fluctuations in rice production caused mainly by the weather, Zanzibar must also import rice from elsewhere to meet its needs for rice, which is the preferred food. Figure 7.5 shows how rice imports fluctuated during 1980—92, and figure 7.6 shows that the price of rice on the world market has been relatively more stable than those of cloves, chilies, and copra.

Figure 7.4. *World Market Prices of Crude Petroleum, FY94*

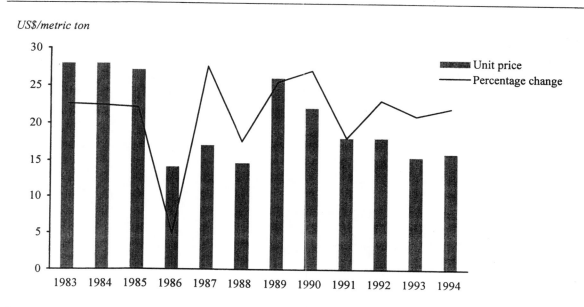

US$/metric ton

Source: World Bank data.

Figure 7.5. *Rice Imports, 1989–92*

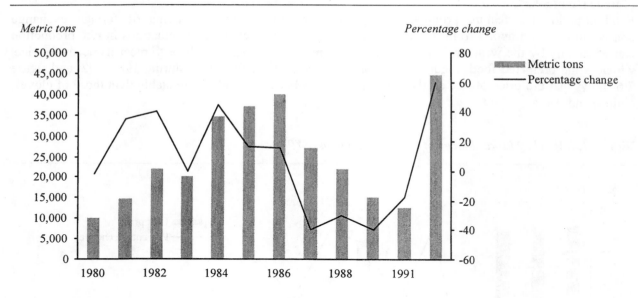

Source: Authors' calculations.

Figure 7.6. *World Market Price of Rice, 1983–94*

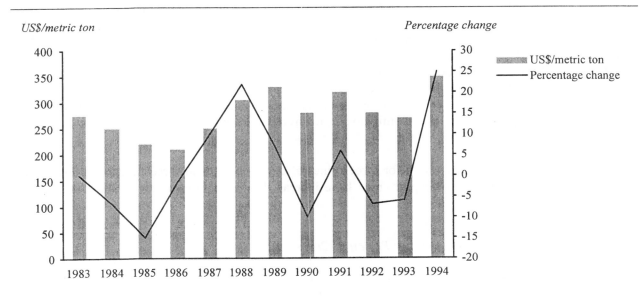

Source: Authors' calculations.

Wheat is relatively more important in people's diet in Zanzibar than on the Mainland. Figure 7.7 shows that wheat prices have been fairly stable in world markets, but given the large declines in the prices of export crops, any increases in wheat prices have a considerable impact on Zanzibar's capacity to meet its food import requirements.

Figure 7.7. *World Market Price of Wheat, 1983–94*

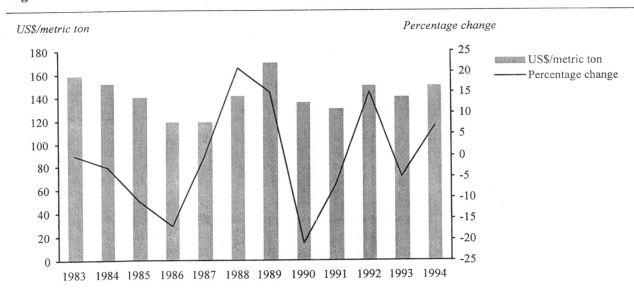

Source: Authors' calculations.

As noted earlier, the ZDTC still has a monopoly over cash crops. The prices for each season are fixed in advance based on the ZSTC's estimates of expected world prices and its marketing costs.

There are two criteria for judging whether producers have received a fair price for their produce. The first is to look at the extent to which the prices received affect producers' purchasing power to acquire other goods. Normally these prices are related to the consumer price index. In this case the most appropriate index would be the rural cost of living index. The second, appropriate for export goods, is to compare the producer price to the export price. Here we shall compare the producer price with the export price. We do not have the data for input prices, but this does not affect the results significantly because farmers in Zanzibar use few inputs.

Table 7.31 shows the producer prices for three principal export crops and three food crops in nominal prices. While nominal prices for export crops have increased significantly in recent years, these prices have stagnated in real terms.

Table 7.31. *Prices paid to Producers for Principal Crops, 1978–96*
(T Sh/kilogram)

Year	Cloves	Copra	Chilies	Maize	Sorghum	Rice (paddy)
1978	15.4	—	—	—	—	—
1979	15.4	—	—	—	—	—
1980	19.3	—	—	—	—	—
1981	19.3	2.8	13.3	3.4	4.4	3.9
1982	19.3	8.0	13.3	3.3	4.4	5.6
1983	25.0	8.0	13.3	3.3	4.4	5.6
1984	25.0	8.0	13.3	6.7	7.4	5.6
1985	25.0	8.0	13.3	6.7	7.4	5.6
1986	65.0	16.0	13.3	5.8	8.2	8.9
1987	65.0	16.0	13.3	20.0	30.0	11.7
1988	100.0	25.0	80.0	20.0	30.0	16.7
1989	100.0	25.0	80.0	38.0	52.0	22.2
1990	150.0	40.0	170.0	38.5	62.7	50.3
1991	170.0	40.0	320.0	43.0	68.0	50.3
1992	164.9	42.4	309.4	43.0	68.0	45.3
1993	158.6	99.6	331.5	52.0	75.0	45.3
1994	179.8	106.1	597.7	70.0	98.0	156.0
1995	198.4	126.6	631.8	91.0	127.4	187.2
1996	286.0	227.8	619.4	107.4	137.0	207.8

n.a. Not available.
Source: Government of Zanzibar.

A state monopoly like the ZSTC determines producer prices by taking the following into account:
- The expected world price of the commodity
- The expected exchange rate of the Tanzanian shilling, usually against the U.S. dollar
- The efficiency of the marketing parastatal
- The efficiency of producers.

In the absence of competition, the efficiency of the marketing agency can be examined by looking at the extent to which the agency contains its marketing costs. For example in FY93 the ZSTC estimated that it would spend T Sh 72,155 per ton in administrative and overhead costs, equivalent to 42.7 percent of its total marketing costs. This represented a 26.5 percent increase over the previous year (Government of Zanzibar 1992, p. 7).

Policy Recommendations for Agriculture

Zanzibar's agriculture sector has performed poorly in the last decade or so, especially with regard to food crop production. While liberalization was introduced in the trade, construction, and tourism sectors, which have made good gains, the agriculture sector has been left largely under state control. Even where marketing has been liberalized, production is hampered by other institutional issues, like land policy and land tenure. Under the new agricultural policy, the role of the Ministry of Agriculture, Livestock, and Natural Resources will be confined to public support, policy implementation, management, and the promotion of an enabling environment that will enable the private sector to play an active part in developing the agriculture sector.

Specifically, the policy will aim at (Government of Zanzibar 1999d, paragraph 1.3.1):
- Modernizing and commercializing the sector to achieve enhanced and sustainable productivity and incomes
- Attaining national food security and improving people's nutritional status
- Increasing agricultural exports to earn more foreign exchange
- Increasing the sector's contribution to national income and employment
- Enhancing the quantity and quality of those agricultural commodities in which Zanzibar has a comparative advantage
- Promoting primary processing and the production of raw materials for agroprocessing and industries based on agriculture.

Achievement of these objectives will be based on (Government of Zanzibar 1999d, paragraph 1.4):
- Liberalizing and rationalizing the production and processing of both traditional and nontraditional crops
- Encouraging private sector investment by means of specific incentives
- Encouraging increased production by the private sector, including commercial farmers and smallholders
- Improving the quality of commodity production, grading, and processing
- Making further reforms in agricultural marketing and pricing, especially with regard to export commodities.

Policy instruments to implement the policies will include
- Better execution of research, extension, and training
- Regular reviews of the impact of policies
- Promotion of small-scale irrigation
- Increased ministry capacity to acquire and analyze information relating to prices for inputs and inputs and other information and to disseminate the results to stakeholders in a timely fashion.

Appendix 7.1. *Growth of Total Tax Revenues in Real and Nominal Terms, FY81–98*
(1980 constant prices)

Fiscal year	Total revenue (nominal T Sh thousands)	Total revenue (real T Sh thousands)	Percentage change (nominal revenue)	Percentage change (real revenue)
FY81	850,265.0	850,265.0	—	—
FY82	971,226.0	849,716.5	12.45	−0.06
FY83	1,368,407.0	940,485.9	29.02	9.65
FY84	588,200.0	328,419.9	−132.64	−186.36
FY85	835,900.0	336,784.9	29.63	2.48
FY86	855,100.0	289,080.5	2.24	−16.50
FY87	1,600,900.0	410,382.0	46.58	29.55
FY88	1,705,500.0	327,037.4	6.13	−25.48
FY89	2,106,500.0	271,806.5	19.03	−20.31
FY90	3,714.3	336.1	−56,613.24	−80,762.10
FY91	5,404.7	354.8	31.27	5.26
FY92	6,448.4	332.2	16.18	−6.82
FY93	9,021.9	374.8	28.52	11.37
FY94	12,534.9	422.9	28.02	11.36
FY95	28,506.0	782.3	56.02	45.94
FY96	19,146.0	407.7	−48.88	−91.88
FY97	19,808.0	357.4	3.34	−14.07
FY98	21,012.1	336.3	5.73	−6.25

— Not available.
Source: Mtatifikolo, Mabele, and Kilindo (1993, appendix table 4).

Appendix 7.2. *Balance of Payments, 1996–98*
(T Sh millions)

Category	1996	1997	1998
Goods			
Exports	25,939.82	26,574.55	12,041.25
Imports	55,411.38	52,053.17	59,983.22
Trade balance	—	—	− 47,941.97
Trade Credit	29,471.56	25,478.62	34,114.15
Import support	− 3,245.13	3,963.24	1,200.00
Payments through banks	0.00	0.00	− 12,627.82
Services			
Total receipts	7,277.58	14,609.59	14,148.91
Total payments	2,845.14	5,415.28	4,436.08
Services balance	4,432.44	9,194.31	9,712.83
Current transfers			
Total Inflows	4,460.18	2,739.26	3,746.08
Total outflows	0.00	0.00	146.72
Transfer balances	4,460.18	2,739.26	3,599.36
Balance of good, services, and transfers	23,824.07	− 9,581.81	684.37
Capital account			
Total inflows	30,252.00	27,500.00	15,986.05
Total outflows	0.00	0.00	0.00
Balance on capital account	30,252.00	27,500.00	15,986.05
Errors and omissions	− 6,167.05	18,997.96	− 16,241.70
Total balance	260.88	-1,079.77	428.72
Changes in foreign reserves	− 260.88	1,079.77	− 428.72

— Not available.
Source: President's office, Ministry of State for Economic Planning and Investment data.

STATISTICAL APPENDIX

Population Statistics

Table 1.1. Population Characteristics of Tanzania

	Mainland Census-1988	Zanzibar Census-1988	Tanzania Census-1988	Tanzania WPI-1997
Number of population (in thousands)	22486	641	23127	31300
Population under 15-year old (%)	45.7	47.1	45.8	-
Sex ratio (males per 100 female)	94.2	94.6	94.2	98.02
Male (in thousands)	10907	311	11218	15494
Female (in thousands)	11580	329	11909	15806
Infant mortality rate (per 1000 live births)	115	120	115	85
Crude death rate (per 1000 population)	15	15	15	16
Life expectancy at birth	49	48	49	48
Crude birth rate (per 1000 population)	46	49	46	41
Total fertility rate	6.2	7.1	6.5	5.5

Note: The 1988 Census results show a smaller population size than those of the UN estimates.
Source: Bureau of Statistics, Planning Commission, *Statistical Abstract* (1992); World Bank, *World Development Indicators* (1999).

Table 1.2. *Population Size by Region, 1967, 1978, 1988 and 1998* (thousands)

	1967	1978	1988	1998
Mainland	11958.7	17036.5	22533.8	30019.5
Dodoma	709.4	972	1237.8	1551.0
Arusha	610.5	926.2	1351.7	1908.3
Kilimanjaro	652.7	902.4	1108.7	1857.2
Tanga	771.1	1037.8	1283.6	1602.0
Morogoro	682.7	939.3	1222.7	1607.5
Coast	428.0	516.6	638.0	780.0
Dar es Salaam	356.3	843.1	1360.9	2102.2
Lindi	419.9	527.6	646.6	783.3
Mtwara	621.3	771.8	889.5	1021.0
Ruvuma	395.4	561.6	783.3	1066.8
Iringa	689.9	925.0	1208.9	1559.9
Mbeya	753.8	1079.9	1476.2	1974.6
Singida	457.9	613.9	791.8	1003.5
Tabora	502.1	817.9	1036.3	1301.5
Rukwa	276.1	451.9	695	1026.4
Kigoma	473.4	648.9	854.8	1109.5
Shinyanga	899.5	1323.5	1772.5	2329.1
Kagera	658.7	1009.8	1326.2	1757.5
Mwanza	1055.9	1443.4	1878.3	2402.6
Mara	544.1	723.8	970.9	1275.6
Zanzibar	354.8	476.1	640.6	888.8
Total	12313.5	17512.6	23174.3	30908.3

Note: The 1988 Census results show a smaller population size than those of the UN estimates.
Source: Bureau of Statistics, Planning Commission, *Statistical Abstract* (1992); Bureau of Statistics, Planning Commission, *Economic Survey* (1998).

Table 1.3. Dependency Ratios, 1967-96

Age Group	1967 Census	1978 Census	1988 Census	1991-92 TDHS	1994 TKAPS	1996 TDHS
<15	43.9	46.1	45.8	46.8	49.3	47.2
15-64	50.5	49.9	49.9	49.3	46.4	48.5
64+	5.6	4.0	4.3	3.9	4.3	4.3
Total	100.0	100.0	100.0	100.0	100.0	100.0
Median Age	U	U	U	16.4	15.4	16.4
Dependency Ratio	98.0	100.0	100.0	103.0	115.0	106.0

U Unknown.
TDHS Tanzania Demographic and Health Survey.
TKAPS Tanzania Knowledge, Attitudes and Practice Survey.
Source: Bureau of Statistics, Tanzania Demographic and Health Survey (1996).

National Income Accounts

Table 2.1. Gross Domestic Product by Sector at Current Prices, 1987-98

	1987	1988	1989	1990	1991	1992	1993	1994	1995	1996	1997	1998
Agriculture, Forestry, Fishing & Hunting	153336	255726	295009	349281	476387	612402	773469	955983	1318459	1658275	2003763	2292747
Mining and Quarrying	3524	3956	5103	6525	8840	13503	19062	26170	35190	38511	53515	74386
Manufacturing	26812	35923	49202	70472	88720	104589	120479	157445	200525	254326	295272	380901
Electricity and Water	3345	3644	7600	11701	17509	19766	36770	39304	60347	65800	74599	79832
Construction	13718	21247	25049	45448	52087	68860	74049	98791	109429	132248	188123	255330
Trade, Hotels and Restaurants	44727	67341	85936	120793	153468	202207	244644	318940	417626	493572	562760	635305
Transport and Communication	12024	17464	29205	40775	49272	66191	98207	131670	159771	193946	219393	244492
Finance, Insurance, Real Estate	36201	53150	72947	98464	107506	127971	176027	310014	353080	451962	471067	736748
Public Admin. And Other Services	23497	35484	48185	63826	80479	117419	159262	204714	255401	300876	451733	564779
Imputed Bank Services	-14501	-25836	-36072	-47279	-44675	-56992	-94207	-117706	-113187	-136957	-138244	-141009
GDP at factor cost	302683	468099	582164	760006	989593	1275916	1607762	2125325	2796641	3452559	4281600	5125311
Indirect Taxes less Subsidies	26803	38328	51589	70687	96680	93958	117774	173542	223859	315083	421859	445830
GDP at market prices	329486	506427	633753	830693	1086273	1369874	1725536	2299867	3020500	3767642	4703459	5571140
Memo Items:												
Agriculture	153336	255726	295009	349281	476387	612402	773469	955983	1318459	1658275	2003763	2292747
Industry	47399	128155	86954	134146	167156	206718	250360	321710	405491	490885	611509	790449
Services	101948	530897	200201	276579	346050	254589	583933	847632	1072691	1303399	1666328	1621905
Indirect Taxes	27975	40125	53778	73463	99529	107089	131409	187554	247745	340999	446673	446673
Subsidies	1172	1796	2189	2776	2848	13131	13635	14012	23886	25916	24814	24814
GDP at m.p. (US$ million)	5127.388733	5100.483432	4420.093458	4258.653748	4956.529476	4601.370461	4510.854934	5255.236968	6496.158488	7530.715532	8381.435234	

Note: In calendar years.

Source: Bureau of Statistics, Planning Commission, *National Accounts of Tanzania, 1987-97* (1999) and *The Economic Survey* (1998).

Table 2.1a. Gross Domestic Product by Sector at Current Prices, 1987-98
(percentage share of GDP at market prices)

	1987	1988	1989	1990	1991	1992	1993	1994	1995	1996	1997	1998
Agriculture, Forestry, Fishing & Hunting	46.5	50.5	46.5	42.0	43.9	44.7	44.8	41.6	43.7	44.0	42.6	41.2
Mining and Quarrying	1.1	7.1	0.8	0.8	0.8	1.0	1.1	1.1	1.2	1.0	1.1	1.3
Manufacturing	8.1	0.7	7.8	8.5	8.2	7.6	7.0	6.8	6.6	6.8	6.3	6.8
Electricity and Water	1.0	4.2	1.2	1.4	1.6	1.4	2.1	1.7	2.0	1.7	1.6	1.4
Construction	4.2	13.3	4.0	5.5	4.8	5.0	4.3	4.3	3.6	3.5	4.0	4.6
Trade, Hotels and Restaurants	13.6	10.5	13.6	14.5	14.1	4.8	14.2	13.9	13.8	13.1	12.0	11.4
Transport and Communication	3.6	7.0	4.6	4.9	4.5	4.8	5.7	5.7	5.3	5.1	4.7	4.4
Finance, Insurance, Real Estate	11.0	10.5	11.5	11.9	9.9	9.3	10.2	13.5	11.7	12.0	12.1	13.2
Public Admin. and Other Services	7.1	0.0	7.6	7.7	7.4	8.6	9.2	8.9	8.5	8.0	9.6	10.1
Imputed Bank Services	-4.4	-5.1	-5.7	-5.7	-4.1	-4.2	-5.5	-5.1	-3.7	-3.6	-2.9	-2.5
GDP at factor cost	91.9	0.0	91.9	91.5	91.1	93.1	93.2	92.5	92.6	91.6	91.0	92.0
Indirect Taxes less Subsidies	8.1	7.6	8.1	8.5	8.9	6.9	6.8	7.5	7.4	8.4	9.0	8.0
GDP at market prices	100.0	100.0	100.0	100.0	100.0	100.0	100.0	100.0	100.0	100.0	100.0	100.0
Memo Items:												
Agriculture	46.5	50.5	46.5	42.0	43.9	44.7	44.8	41.6	43.7	44.0	42.6	41.2
Industry	14.4	25.3	13.7	16.1	15.4	15.1	14.5	14.0	13.4	13.0	13.0	14.2
Services	30.9	104.8	31.6	33.3	31.9	18.6	33.8	36.9	35.5	34.6	35.4	29.1
Indirect Taxes	8.5	7.9	8.5	8.8	9.2	7.8	7.6	8.2	8.2	9.1	9.5	8.0
Subsidies	0.4	0.4	0.3	0.3	0.3	1.0	0.8	0.6	0.8	0.7	0.5	0.4

Note: In calendar years.
Source: Table 2.1.

Table 2.1b. *Gross Domestic Product by Sector at Current Prices, 1987-98*
(percentage share of GDP at factor cost)

	1987	1988	1989	1990	1991	1992	1993	1994	1995	1996	1997	1998
Agriculture, Forestry, Fishing & Hunting	50.7	54.6	50.7	46.0	48.1	48.0	48.1	45.0	47.1	48.0	46.8	44.7
Mining and Quarrying	1.2	0.8	0.9	0.9	0.9	1.1	1.2	1.2	1.3	1.1	1.2	1.5
Manufacturing	8.9	7.7	8.5	9.3	9.0	8.2	7.5	7.4	7.2	7.4	6.9	7.4
Electricity and Water	1.1	0.8	1.3	1.5	1.8	1.5	2.3	1.8	2.2	1.9	1.7	1.6
Construction	4.5	4.5	4.3	6.0	5.3	5.4	4.6	4.6	3.9	3.8	4.4	5.0
Trade, Hotels and Restaurants	14.8	14.4	14.8	15.9	15.5	5.2	15.2	15.0	14.9	14.3	13.1	12.4
Transport and Communication	4.0	3.7	5.0	5.4	5.0	5.2	6.1	6.2	5.7	5.6	5.1	4.8
Finance, Insurance, Real Estate	12.0	11.4	12.5	13.0	10.9	10.0	10.9	14.6	12.6	13.1	13.3	6.2
Public Admin. and Other Services	7.8	7.6	8.3	8.4	8.1	9.2	9.9	9.6	9.1	8.7	10.6	11.0
Imputed Bank Services	-4.8	-5.5	-6.2	-6.2	-4.5	-4.5	-5.9	-5.5	-4.0	-4.0	-3.2	-2.8
GDP at factor cost	100.0	100.0	100.0	100.0	100.0	100.0	100.0	100.0	100.0	100.0	100.0	100.0
Indirect Taxes less Subsidies	8.9	8.2	8.9	9.3	9.8	7.4	7.3	8.2	8.0	9.1	9.9	8.7
GDP at market prices	108.9	108.2	108.9	109.3	109.8	107.4	107.3	108.2	108.0	109.1	109.9	108.7
Memo Items:												
Agriculture	50.7	54.6	50.7	46.0	48.1	48.0	48.1	45.0	47.1	48.0	46.8	44.7
Industry	15.7	27.4	14.9	17.7	16.9	16.2	15.6	15.1	14.5	14.2	14.3	15.4
Services	33.7	113.4	34.4	36.4	35.0	20.0	36.3	39.9	38.4	37.8	38.9	31.6

Note: In calendar years.
Source: Table 2.1.

Table 2.2. Gross Domestic Product by Sector at 1992 Constant Prices, 1987-98 (millions of Tanzania shillings)

	1987	1988	1989	1990	1991	1992	1993	1994	1995	1996	1997	1998
Agriculture, Forestry, Fishing & Hunting	521725	533184	553805	584070	604921	612402	631422	644718	682338	708741	726098	739942
Mining and Quarrying	8645	8529	9634	11226	12536	13503	14608	16803	18768	20579	24097	30700
Manufacturing	94781	97730	102814	107008	109002	104589	105244	105042	106750	111894	117489	126887
Electricity and Water	14005	15312	16707	18029	20026	19766	19937	20329	21578	23977	24514	25870
Construction	50660	62368	53660	70016	65064	68860	58955	59783	50983	54868	59341	65187
Trade, Hotels and Restaurants	176220	181040	184896	198611	203575	202207	201370	203684	210813	218105	229010	239830
Transport and Communication	53225	54935	56153	56453	57963	66191	66256	66875	70833	71597	75099	79755
Finance, Insurance, Real Estate	103324	109249	119494	121567	123300	127971	134103	137727	138510	139058	214781	158089
Public Admin. & Other Services	90225	99034	102805	105895	111176	117419	112879	112787	109763	111473	115007	118114
Imputed Bank Service Charge	-41270	-42365	-52223	-53639	-54431	-56992	-63767	-68805	-65090	-58581	-72327	-78547
GDP at factor cost	1071540	1119016	1147745	1219236	1253132	1275916	1281007	1298943	1345246	1401711	1448090	1505827
Indirect Taxes less Subsidies[1]	94886.3551	91625.15888	101708.4822	113399.2825	122426.8985	93958	93838.09197	106064.3272	107681.1161	127921.1469	130210	127995
GDP at market prices	1166426.355	1210641.159	1249453.482	1332635.283	1375558.898	1369874	1374845.092	1405007.327	1452927.116	1529632.147	1578300	1633822
Memo Items:												
Agriculture	521725	533184	553805	584070	604921	612402	631422	644718	682338	708741	726098	739942
Industry	168091	113042	182815	206279	206628	193215	198744	185154	179311	190739	201344	217944
Services	381724	401893	411125	428887	441583	456796	450841	452268	464829	481652	496551	517241
GDP per capita, at factor cost[2]	47351.72	47886.54	47559.74	48920.09	48812.52	48251.89	46961.16	46276.66	46575.58	47162.81	47350.15	47850.39

1 Deflator of GDP at factor cost is applied in deriving indirect taxes less subsidies at 1992 constant prices.
2 Excluding Zanzibar population; from FY94, population growth of 2.9% was assumed; GDP per capita is derived by dividing total GDP by the size of population.
Note: In calendar years.
Source: Bureau of Statistics, Planning Commission, *National Accounts of Tanzania, 1987-97* (1999) and *The Economic Survey* (1998).

Table 2.2a. Annual Growth of Gross Domestic Product at 1992 Constant Prices (percent)

	1987-88	1988-89	1989-90	1990-91	1991-92	1992-93	1993-94	1994-95	1995-96	1996-97	1997-98	1998-99
Agriculture, Forestry, Fishing & Hunting	2.2	2.2	3.9	5.5	3.6	1.2	3.1	2.1	5.8	3.9	2.4	1.9
Mining and Quarrying	-1.3	-1.3	13.0	16.5	11.7	7.7	8.2	15.0	11.7	9.6	17.1	27.4
Manufacturing	3.1	3.1	5.2	4.1	1.9	-4.0	0.6	-0.2	1.6	4.8	5.0	8.0
Electricity and Water	9.3	9.3	9.1	7.9	11.1	-1.3	0.9	2.0	6.1	11.1	2.2	5.5
Construction	23.1	23.1	-14.0	30.5	-7.1	5.8	-14.4	1.4	-14.7	7.6	8.2	9.9
Trade, Hotels and Restaurants	2.7	2.7	2.1	7.4	2.5	-0.7	-0.4	1.1	3.5	3.5	5.0	4.7
Transport and Communication	3.2	3.2	2.2	0.5	2.7	14.2	0.1	0.9	5.9	1.1	4.9	6.2
Finance, Insurance, Real Estate	5.7	5.7	9.4	1.7	1.4	3.8	4.8	2.7	0.6	0.4	54.5	-26.4
Public Admin. & Other Services	9.8	9.8	3.8	3.0	5.0	5.6	-3.9	-0.1	-2.7	1.6	3.2	2.7
Imputed Bank Service Charge	2.7	2.7	23.3	2.7	1.5	4.7	11.9	7.9	-5.4	-10.0	23.5	8.6
GDP at factor cost	4.4	4.4	2.6	6.2	2.8	1.8	0.4	1.4	3.6	4.2	3.3	4.0
Indirect Taxes less Subsidies	-3.4	-3.4	11.0	11.5	8.0	-23.3	-0.1	13.0	1.5	18.8	1.8	-1.7
GDP at market prices	3.8	3.8	3.2	6.7	3.2	-0.4	0.4	2.2	3.4	5.3	3.2	3.5
Memo Items:												
Agriculture	2.2	2.2	3.9	5.5	3.6	1.2	3.1	2.1	5.8	3.9	2.4	1.9
Industry	-32.7	-32.7	61.7	12.8	0.2	-6.5	2.9	-6.8	-3.2	6.4	5.6	8.2
Services	5.3	5.3	2.3	4.3	3.0	3.4	-1.3	0.3	2.8	3.6	3.1	4.2
GDP per capita, at factor cost[1]	1.1	1.1	-0.7	2.9	-0.2	-1.1	-2.7	-1.5	0.6	1.3	0.4	1.1

1 Excluding Zanzibar population; for FY94, population growth of 2.9% was assumed; GDP per capita is derived by dividing total GDP by the size of population.
Note: In calendar years.
Source: Table 2.2.

Table 2.3. *Gross National Product by Expenditure at Current Prices*
(millions of Tanzania shillings)

	1988	1989	1990	1991	1992	1993	1994	1995	1996	1997	1998**
GDP at factor cost	468099	582164	760006	989593	1275916	1607762	2125325	2796641	3452559	4286768	5125310
Indirect taxes	40125	53778	73463	99529	107089	131409	187554	247745	340999	446673	446330
Less subsidies	1796	2189	2776	2848	13131	13635	14012	23886	25916	24814	500
GDP at market prices	506428	633753	830693	1086274	1369874	1725536	2298867	3020500	3767642	4708627	5571140
Resource Gap	-92528	-136616	-206290	-253939	-368658	-512907	-528992	-526562	-452356	-466853	-469737
Exports, goods and NFS	48810	71925	104843	111474	170438	310305	473888	727177	751161	741443	1049355
Imports, goods and NFS	141338	208541	311133	365413	539096	823212	1002880	1253739	1203517	1208296	1519092
Gross Domestic Expenditures	506426	633752	830693	1086273	1369874	1725535	2298866	3020499	3767643	4708627	5571140
Consumption	500554	624596	835357	1092849	1402210	1779886	2325477	2995156	3565401	4381635	5074962
Private	416013	523191	687706	887123	1133194	1445366	1931976	2532841	3130072	3968072	4641176
Public	84541	101405	147651	205726	269016	334520	393501	462315	435329	413563	433786
Investment	83498	114563	216909	286073	373043	433947	566660	597791	627237	700803	837007
Gross fixed capital formation	81452	112207	213984	282428	369368	429945	561819	591935	620597	692400	827093
Private	30616	44651	127153	186576	243527	300280	424628	489915	489358	554762	641778
Public	50836	67556	86831	95852	125841	129665	137191	102020	131239	137638	185315
Central government	6642	5384	7357	16151	32904	52170	59682	23727	16313	25860	128079
Public enterprises	44194	62172	79474	79701	92937	77495	77509	78293	114926	111778	57236
Changes in stocks	2046	2356	2925	3645	3675	4002	4841	5856	6640	8403	9914
Gross National Product	487886	604376	790263	1045829	1299468	1665628	2229342	2957121	3730721	4632846	5466472
Gross Domestic Savings	40347	58702	78578	114120	131249	46686	-3625	75395	270988	347227	533941
Net factor income	-18542	-29377	-40430	-40445	-70406	-59908	-69525	-63379	-36921	-75781	-104668
Receipt	311	551	551	1735	2563	7934	8648	18258	24090	27452	30496
Payment	18853	29928	40981	42180	72969	67842	78173	81637	61011	103233	135164
Net current transfers	62371	93510	135270	180797	282812	291673	380518	194389	196342	208452	275690
Receipt	64549	97783	141122	187955	293750	303831	397080	212947	215086	249926	307127
Payment	2178	4273	5852	7158	10938	12158	16562	18558	18744	41474	31437
Gross National Savings	84176	122835	173418	254472	343655	278451	307368	206405	430409	479898	704963

** Provisional data.

Note: In calendar years.

Source: Bureau of Statistics, Planning Commission, *National Accounts of Tanzania, 1987-97* (1999) and *The Economic Survey* (1998).

Table 2.3a. *Gross National Product by Expenditure at Current Prices*
(percentage share of GDP at market prices)

	1988	1989	1990	1991	1992	1993	1994	1995	1996	1997	1998**
GDP at factor cost	92.4	91.9	91.5	91.1	93.1	93.2	92.5	92.6	91.6	91.0	92.0
Indirect taxes	7.9	8.5	8.8	9.2	7.8	7.6	8.2	8.2	9.1	9.5	8.0
Less subsidies	0.4	0.3	0.3	0.3	1.0	0.8	0.6	0.8	0.7	0.5	0.0
GDP at market prices	100.0	100.0	100.0	100.0	100.0	100.0	100.0	100.0	100.0	100.0	100.0
Resource Gap	-18.3	-21.6	-24.8	-23.4	-26.9	-29.7	-23.0	-17.4	-12.0	-9.9	-8.4
Exports, goods and NFS	9.6	11.3	12.6	10.3	12.4	18.0	20.6	24.1	19.9	15.7	18.8
Imports, goods and NFS	27.9	32.9	37.5	33.6	39.4	47.7	43.6	41.5	31.9	25.7	27.3
Gross Domestic Expenditures	100.0	100.0	100.0	100.0	100.0	100.0	100.0	100.0	100.0	100.0	100.0
Consumption	98.8	98.6	100.6	100.6	102.4	103.1	101.2	99.2	94.6	93.1	91.1
Private	82.1	82.6	82.8	81.7	82.7	83.8	84.0	83.9	83.1	84.3	83.3
Public	16.7	16.0	17.8	18.9	19.6	19.4	17.1	15.3	11.6	8.8	7.8
Investment	16.5	18.1	26.1	26.3	27.2	25.1	24.6	19.8	16.6	14.9	15.0
Gross fixed capital formation	16.1	17.7	25.8	26.0	27.0	24.9	24.4	19.6	16.5	14.7	14.8
Private	6.0	7.0	15.3	17.2	17.8	17.4	18.5	16.2	13.0	11.8	11.5
Public	10.0	10.7	10.5	8.8	9.2	7.5	6.0	3.4	3.5	2.9	3.3
Central government	1.3	0.8	0.9	1.5	2.4	3.0	2.6	0.8	0.4	0.5	2.3
Public enterprises	8.7	9.8	9.6	7.3	6.8	4.5	3.4	2.6	3.1	2.4	1.0
Changes in stocks	0.4	0.4	0.4	0.3	0.3	0.2	0.2	0.2	0.2	0.2	0.2
Gross National Product	96.3	95.4	95.1	96.3	94.9	96.5	97.0	97.9	99.0	98.4	98.1
Gross Domestic Savings	0.0	0.0	0.0	0.0	0.0	0.0	0.0	0.0	0.0	0.0	0.0
Net factor income	8.0	9.3	9.5	10.5	9.6	2.7	-0.2	2.5	7.2	7.4	9.6
Receipt	-3.7	-4.6	-4.9	-3.7	-5.1	-3.5	-3.0	-2.1	-1.0	-1.6	-1.9
Payment	0.1	0.1	0.1	0.2	0.2	0.5	0.4	0.6	0.6	0.6	0.5
Net current transfers	3.7	4.7	4.9	3.9	5.3	3.9	3.4	2.7	1.6	2.2	2.4
Receipt	12.3	14.8	16.3	16.6	20.6	16.9	16.6	6.4	5.2	4.4	4.9
Payment	12.7	15.4	17.0	17.3	21.4	17.6	17.3	7.1	5.7	5.3	5.5
Gross National Savings	0.4	0.7	0.7	0.7	0.8	0.7	0.7	0.6	0.5	0.9	0.6

** Provisional data.
Note: In calendar years.
Source: Table 2.3.

Table 2.4. GDP Deflators by Sector, 1987-98
(1992 = 100)

	1987	1988	1989	1990	1991	1992	1993	1994	1995	1996	1997	1998
Agriculture, Forestry, Fishing & Hunting	29.4	48.0	53.3	59.8	78.8	100.0	122.5	148.3	193.2	234.0	276.0	309.9
Mining and Quarrying	40.8	46.4	53.0	58.1	70.5	100.0	130.5	155.7	187.5	187.1	222.1	242.3
Manufacturing	28.3	36.8	47.9	65.9	81.4	100.0	114.5	149.9	187.8	227.3	251.3	300.2
Electricity and Water	23.9	23.8	45.5	64.9	87.4	100.0	184.4	193.3	279.7	274.4	304.3	308.6
Construction	27.1	34.1	46.7	64.9	80.1	100.0	125.6	165.2	214.6	241.0	317.0	391.7
Trade, Hotels and Restaurants	25.4	37.2	46.5	60.8	75.4	100.0	121.5	156.6	198.1	226.3	245.7	264.9
Transport and Communication	22.6	31.8	52.0	72.2	85.0	100.0	148.2	196.9	225.6	270.9	292.1	306.6
Finance, Insurance, Real Estate	35.0	48.7	61.0	81.0	87.2	100.0	131.3	225.1	254.9	325.0	219.3	466.0
Public Admin. And Other Services	26.0	35.8	46.9	60.3	72.4	100.0	141.1	181.5	232.7	269.9	392.8	478.2
Imputed Bank Services	35.1	61.0	69.1	88.1	82.1	100.0	147.7	171.1	173.9	233.8	191.1	179.5
GDP at factor cost	28.2	41.8	50.7	62.3	79.0	100.0	125.5	163.6	207.9	246.3	295.7	340.4
Indirect Taxes less Subsidies	28.2	41.8	50.7	62.3	79.0	100.0	125.5	163.6	207.9	246.3	324.0	348.3
GDP at market prices	28.2	41.8	50.7	62.3	79.0	100.0	125.5	163.6	207.9	246.3	298.0	341.0
Memo Items:												
Agriculture	29.4	48.0	53.3	59.8	78.8	100.0	122.5	148.3	193.2	234.0	276.0	309.9
Industry	28.2	113.4	47.6	65.0	80.9	100.0	126.0	173.8	226.1	257.4	303.7	362.7
Services	26.7	132.1	48.7	64.5	78.4	100.0	129.5	187.4	230.8	270.6	335.6	313.6

Note: In calendar years.
Source: Table 2.1 and 2.2.

Table 2.4a. Annual Changes in GDP Deflators by Sector, 1987-98

	1987-88	1988-89	1989-90	1990-91	1991-92	1992-93	1993-94	1994-95	1995-96	1996-97	1997-98	1998-99
Agriculture, Forestry, Fishing & Hunting	63.2	63.2	11.1	12.3	31.7	27.0	22.5	21.0	30.3	21.1	17.9	12.3
Mining and Quarrying	-9.8	13.8	14.2	9.7	21.3	41.8	30.5	19.4	20.4	-0.2	18.7	9.1
Manufacturing	-15.9	29.9	30.2	37.6	23.6	22.9	14.5	30.9	25.3	21.0	10.6	19.4
Electricity and Water	-0.4	-0.4	91.1	42.7	34.7	14.4	84.4	4.8	44.7	-1.9	10.9	1.4
Construction	25.8	25.8	37.0	39.1	23.3	24.9	25.6	31.6	29.9	12.3	31.5	23.6
Trade, Hotels and Restaurants	15.7	46.6	25.0	30.9	24.0	32.6	21.5	28.9	26.5	14.2	8.6	7.8
Transport and Communication	185.9	40.7	63.6	38.9	17.7	17.6	48.2	32.8	14.6	20.1	7.8	4.9
Finance, Insurance, Real Estate	33.8	38.9	25.5	32.7	7.6	14.7	31.3	71.5	13.2	27.5	-32.5	112.5
Public Admin. And Other Services	37.6	37.6	30.8	28.6	20.1	38.1	41.1	28.6	28.2	16.0	45.5	21.7
Imputed Bank Services	73.6	73.6	13.3	27.6	-6.9	21.8	47.7	15.8	1.6	34.4	-18.2	-6.1
GDP at factor cost	48.1	48.1	21.3	22.9	26.7	26.6	25.5	30.4	27.1	18.5	20.0	15.1
Indirect Taxes less Subsidies	48.1	48.1	21.3	22.9	26.7	26.6	25.5	30.4	27.1	18.5	31.5	7.5
GDP at market prices	48.1	48.1	21.3	22.9	26.7	26.6	25.5	30.4	27.1	18.5	21.0	14.4
Memo Item:												
Agriculture	63.2	63.2	11.1	12.3	31.7	27.0	22.5	21.0	30.3	21.1	17.9	12.3
Industry	302.0	302.0	-58.0	36.7	24.4	23.6	26.0	37.9	30.1	13.8	18.0	19.4
Services	394.6	394.6	-63.1	32.4	21.5	27.6	29.5	44.7	23.1	17.3	24.0	-6.6
Population: Total (000)	23245.24	24005.07	24789.7	25600.01	26369.35	27161.82	28019.01	28831.56	29667.68	30528.04	31413.35	32324.34
of which 97.35% are from Tanzania and 2.494% are	22629.38	23368.07	24132.7	24923.01	25672.35	26442.82	27278.01	28069.07	28883.08	29720.68	30582.58	31469.48
from Zanzibar	615.86	637	657	677	697	719	741	762.49	784.60	807.35	830.77	854.86

Note: In calendar years.
Source: Tables 2.1 and 2.2.

261

Table 2.5. *Investment at Current and at 1992 Constant Prices*
(millions of Tanzania shillings)

	1987	1988	1989	1990	1991	1992	1993	1994	1995	1996	1997	1998
At Current Prices:												
Gross Fixed Capital Formation	71058	81452	112207	213984	282428	369368	429945	561819	591935	620597	692400	827092
Increase in Stocks	1700	2046	2356	2925	3645	3675	4002	4841	5856	6640	8403	9914
Gross Capital Formation	72758	83498	114563	216909	286073	373043	433947	566660	597791	627237	700803	837006
As Share of GDP at Market Prices												
Gross Fixed Capital Formation	21.6	16.1	17.7	25.8	26.0	27.0	24.9	24.4	19.6	16.5	14.7	14.8
Increase in Stocks	0.5	0.4	0.4	0.4	0.3	0.3	0.2	0.2	0.2	0.2	0.2	0.2
Gross Capital Formation	22.1	16.5	18.1	26.1	26.3	27.2	25.1	24.6	19.8	16.6	14.9	15.0
At 1992 Constant Prices												
Gross Fixed Capital Formation	325546	250648	249610	336639	376461	369368	327090	331095	281793	268420	259690	297220
Increase in Stocks	3402	3468	3535	3617	3646	3675	3705	3734	3765	3795	3825	3855
Gross Capital Formation	328948	254116	253145	340256	380107	373043	330795	334829	285558	272215	263515	301075
Real Growth (%)												
Gross Fixed Capital Formation		-23.0	-0.4	34.9	11.8	-1.9	-11.4	1.2	-14.9	-4.7	-3.3	14.5
Increase in Stocks		1.9	1.9	2.3	0.8	0.8	0.8	0.8	0.8	0.8	0.8	0.8
Gross Capital Formation		-22.7	-0.4	34.4	11.7	-1.9	-11.3	1.2	-14.7	-4.7	-3.2	14.3
Investment Deflator (1992=100)												
Gross Fixed Capital Formation	21.8	32.5	45.0	63.6	75.0	100.0	131.4	169.7	210.1	231.2	266.6	278.3
Increase in Stocks	50.0	59.0	66.6	80.9	100.0	100.0	108.0	129.6	155.5	175.0	219.7	257.2
Gross Capital Formation	22.1	32.9	45.3	63.7	75.3	100.0	131.2	169.2	209.3	230.4	265.9	278.0

Note: In calendar years.
Source: Bureau of Statistics, Planning Commission, *National Accounts of Tanzania, 1987-97* (1999) and *The Economic Survey* (1998).

Table 2.6. *Fixed Capital Formation by Economic Activities*
(millions of Tanzania shillings)

	1987	1988	1989	1990	1991	1992	1993	1994	1995	1996	1997	1998
Agriculture, Forestry, Fishing & Hunting	2119	2146	2849	6851	13438	17020	17552	24367	22511	20609	19545	19316
Mining and Quarrying	224	580	220	350	640	1172	1343	1751	2102	2502	3085	8711
Manufacturing	19693	17387	25720	54741	66588	86764	102911	136911	139134	140116	146171	165097
Electricity and Water	12916	20198	28717	38069	45485	54724	65463	76366	84660	93010	105850	119555
Construction	7910	7730	10995	25757	31218	42675	50937	68399	75828	83306	11608	234242
Trade, Hotels and Restaurants	1035	4141	2478	2044	2955	3022	4056	5562	5128	4704	4461	4409
Transport and Communication	22338	23017	32289	72709	88708	119518	142341	188101	206795	225295	254260	233335
Finance, Insurance, Real Estate	1153	3092	4456	4376	19207	21308	17885	24919	23022	21077	19988	18343
Public Admin. & Other Services	3670	3162	4484	9088	13921	23165	27059	35443	32744	29978	28430	24083
Gross Fixed Capital Formation	**71059**	**81453**	**112207**	**213984**	**282427**	**369368**	**429546**	**561819**	**591935**	**620597**	**692400**	**827092**
Memo Items:												
Agriculture	2119	2146	2849	6851	13438	17020	17552	24367	22511	20609	19545	19316
Industry	40743	45895	65652	118917	143931	185335	220654	283427	301724	318934	376573	..
Services	28196	33412	43707	88217	124791	163991	187285	248463	262561	276350	311666	..

Note: In calendar years.
Source: Bureau of Statistics, Planning Commission, *National Accounts of Tanzania, 1987–97* (1999).

Table 2.7. Incremental Gross Capital to Output Ratio

Year	Gross Capital 1yrMA (Tshs m)	Gross Capital 3yrMA (Tshs m)	Gross Capital 5yrMA (Tshs m)	GDP at f.c. (TSh m)	Incremental Output 1yrMA (Tshs m)	Incremental Output 3yrMA (Tshs m)	Incremental Output 5yrMA (Tshs m)	1-year ICOR	3-year ICOR	5-year ICOR
1987	328948.0			1071540.0						
1988	254116.0	278736.3		1119017.0	47477.0			6.9		
1989	253145.0	282505.7	311314.4	1147745.0	28728.0	49232.0		8.8	5.7	
1990	340256.0	324502.7	320133.4	1219236.0	71491.0	44705.7	40875.4	3.5	6.3	7.6
1991	380107.0	364468.7	335469.2	1253134.0	33898.0	42724.0	32397.8	10.0	7.6	9.9
1992	373043.0	361315.0	351806.0	1275917.0	22783.0	20590.0	30239.6	16.7	17.7	11.1
1993	330795.0	346222.3	340866.4	1281006.0	5089.0	15269.7	25202.0	73.3	23.7	14.0
1994	334829.0	317060.7	319288.0	1298943.0	17937.0	23109.7	29715.4	18.4	15.0	11.5
1995	285558.0	297534.0	298540.6	1345246.0	46303.0	40235.0	34434.6	7.2	7.9	9.3
1996	272215.0	275693.0	292596.6	1401711.0	56465.0	49715.7	44964.2	5.1	6.0	6.6
1997	269306.0	280865.3		1448090.0	46379.0	53527.0		5.9	5.2	
1998	301075.0			1505827.0	57737.0			4.7		

1yrMA Stands for 1 year moving average… etc.
Note: At 1992 constant prices.
Source: Bureau of Statistics, Planning Commission, *National Accounts of Tanzania, 1987-97* (1999) and *The Economic Survey* (1998).

Table 2.8. Incremental Fixed Capital to Output Ratio

Year	Gross Investment 1yrMA (Tshs m)	Gross Investment 3yrMA (Tshs m)	Gross Investment 5yrMA (Tshs m)	GDP at f.c. (Tshs m)	Incremental Output 1yrMA (Tshs m)	Incremental Output 3yrMA (Tshs m)	Incremental Output 5yrMA (Tshs m)	1-year ICOR	3-year ICOR	5-year ICOR
1987	325546			1071540						
1988	250648	275268.0		1119017	47477			6.9		
1989	249610	278965.7	307780.8	1147745	28728	49232.0		8.7	5.6	
1990	336639	320903.3	316545.2	1219236	71491	44705.7		3.5	6.2	
1991	376461	360822.7	331833.6	1253134	33898	42724.0	40875.4	9.9	7.5	7.5
1992	369368	357639.7	348130.6	1275917	22783	20590.0	32397.8	16.5	17.5	9.8
1993	327090	342517.7	337161.4	1281006	5089	15269.7	30239.6	72.6	23.4	11.0
1994	331095	313326.0	315553.2	1298943	17937	23109.7	25202.0	18.2	14.8	13.8
1995	281793	293769.3	294776.0	1345246	46303	40235.0	29715.4	7.2	7.8	11.3
1996	268420	271898.3	288802.0	1401711	56465	49715.7	34434.6	5.0	5.9	9.2
1997	265482	277040.7		1448090	46379	53527.0	44964.2	5.8	5.1	6.6
1998	297220			1505827	57737			4.6		

1yrMA Stands for 1 year moving average…. etc.

Note: At 1992 constant prices.

Source: Bureau of Statistics, Planning Commission, *National Accounts of Tanzania, 1987-97* (1999) and *The Economic Survey* (1998).

3. Trade and Balance of Payments

Table 3.1. *Balance of Payments*
(millions of US dollars)

Items	1990	1991	1992	1993	1994	1995	1996	1997	1998
CURRENT ACCOUNT	-558.9	-736.1	-704.3	-1022.0	-711.1	-646.4	-461.3	-589.1	-846.6
Goods	-778.5	-865.3	-915.9	-835.6	-790.0	-657.6	-448.9	-446.6	-588.5
Exports (fob)	407.8	362.3	400.7	439.3	519.4	682.9	763.8	717.1	676.0
Imports (fob)	1186.3	1227.6	1316.6	1274.9	1309.3	1340.5	1212.6	1163.7	1264.5
Services	-157.1	-157.5	-169.0	-389.9	-85.1	-216.9	-278.8	-315.8	-469.9
Receipts	130.6	142.1	167.5	310.8	418.2	582.9	537.1	484.3	531.6
Payments	287.8	299.6	336.6	700.7	503.3	799.8	815.9	800.1	1001.5
Income	-185.0	-184.2	-225.4	-147.6	-122.5	-110.3	-72.0	-122.9	-157.2
Receipts	5.9	7.9	8.1	21.4	30.9	31.8	41.5	44.9	45.8
Payments	190.9	192.1	233.5	169.0	153.4	142.1	113.5	167.8	202.9
Current transfers	561.7	470.9	606.1	351.1	286.5	338.4	338.4	296.2	369.0
Inflows	592.7	503.5	641.1	381.1	311.5	370.7	370.7	363.8	416.2
Government	538.4	480.3	506.2	370.9	215.0	236.0	236.0	265.4	278.0
Private	54.3	23.2	134.8	10.2	96.5	134.7	134.7	98.4	138.1
Outflows	31.0	32.6	35.0	30.0	25.0	32.3	32.3	67.7	47.2

(table continues on the next page)

Table 3.1. Balance of Payments (cont'd)

Items	1990	1991	1992	1993	1994	1995	1996	1997	1998
CAPITAL ACCOUNT									
Capital transfers	327.2	353.1	298.2	200.6	262.6	191.0	191.0	270.9	360.2
Inflows	327.2	353.1	298.2	200.6	262.6	191.0	191.0	270.9	360.2
Outflows	327.2	353.1	298.2	200.6	262.6	191.0	191.0	270.9	360.2
	0.0	0.0	0.0	0.0	0.0	0.0	0.0	0.0	0.0
Acquisition/disposals of non-produced									
non-financial assets	0.0	0.0	0.0	0.0	0.0	0.0	0.0	0.0	0.0
FINANCIAL ACCOUNT									
Direct investment	42.3	117.9	107.3	57.0	-106.8	139.5	0.4	-52.8	-203.2
Abroad	0.0	0.0	12.0	20.0	50.0	150.0	148.5	157.8	172.0
In Tanzania	0.0	0.0	0.0	0.0	0.0	0.0	0.0	0.0	0.0
	0.0	0.0	12.0	20.0	50.0	150.0	148.5	157.8	172.0
Portfolio investment	0.0	0.0	0.0	0.0	0.0	0.0	0.0	0.0	0.0
Other investment	42.3	117.9	95.3	37.0	-156.8	-10.5	-148.2	-210.6	-375.2
Inflow of financial resources	236.9	271.0	331.9	615.4	434.5	437.4	318.6	413.9	307.2
Disbursement of Government loans	223.5	260.5	267.5	372.4	274.2	244.1	224.9	266.5	181.0
Trade credit and other financial flows	13.4	10.5	64.4	143.2	122.1	141.9	77.0	111.5	121.8
Disbursement of loans to other sectors	0.0	0.0	0.0	99.8	38.2	51.4	16.7	36.0	4.4
Outflow of financial resources	194.6	153.1	236.6	578.4	591.3	447.9	466.7	624.6	682.4
Repayment of government loans	168.8	145.7	236.6	498.1	491.3	272.5	361.8	400.6	471.6
Trade credit and other financial flows	25.8	7.4	0.0	68.4	75.6	162.6	43.1	183.3	161.6
Repayment of loans by other sectors	0.0	0.0	0.0	11.9	24.4	12.8	61.8	40.6	49.3
Errors and omissions	47.8	33.1	46.2	27.7	60.2	-75.4	15.5	15.7	68.8

Table 3.1. Balance of Payment (cont'd)

Items	1990	1991	1992	1993	1994	1995	1996	1997	1998
OVERALL BALANCE	-141.6	-232.1	-252.6	-736.7	-495.1	-391.4	-254.5	-355.4	-620.8
FINANCING	-141.6	-232.1	-252.6	736.7	495.1	391.4	254.5	355.4	620.8
Net Reserve assets (- increase)	-139.7	-85.3	-253.5	157.3	-77.0	60.1	-165.3	-84.4	-11.1
LCFAR	0.0	0.0	0.0	0.1	18.6	9.3	23.3	24.9	-49.9
Exceptional financing	281.4	317.4	506.1	579.3	553.5	322.0	396.5	414.9	681.8
Arrears	100.2	344.7	206.7	199.0	296.4	269.4	312.2	-148.2	180.0
Rescheduling	155.8	0.0	138.7	136.6	144.5	0.0	0.0	194.8	194.8
Debt forgiveness	11.0	0.0	25.0	23.5	23.8	0.0	0.0	123.7	123.7
Use of Fund credit	14.4	-27.3	135.7	70.4	15.2	-4.0	-13.8	85.3	29.6
Grants/borrowing for BOP purposes	-	-	-	149.8	73.6	56.5	98.1	159.3	153.7
Financing gap	-	-	-	0.0	0.0	0.0	0.0	0.0	0.0
Memorandum items:									
GDP(mp) Mill.TZS				1607762.0	2125325.0	2796640.0	3452560.0	4281600.0	5047869.8
GDP(mp) Mill. USD	3443.8	3768.1	4042.2	3967.1	4170.4	4865.7	5952.9	6994.7	7594.4
CAB/GDP	-16.2	-19.5	-17.4	-25.8	-17.1	-13.3	-7.7	-8.4	-6.5
CAB/GDP (excl. current official transfers)	-31.9	-32.3	-30.0	-35.1	-22.2	-18.1	-11.7	-12.2	-10.1
Gross Official Reserves	192.8	242.1	394.3	228.3	331.3	270.9	441.1	623.1	599.0
Weeks of Imports	6.8	8.2	12.4	6.0	9.5	6.6	11.3	16.5	13.4

Source: Balance of Payments Department of the Bank of Tanzania.

Table 3.2. *Merchandise Exports – Value and Share*

Value (millions of US dollars)

	1980	1981	1982	1983	1984	1985	1986	1987	1988	1989	1990	1991	1992	1993	1994	1995	1996	1997	1998
Coffee	143.4	164.5	132.9	139.7	153.6	118.5	184.7	109.4	96.7	108.0	85.0	77.3	59.5	96.1	115.4	142.6	137.8	117.4	114.9
Cotton	48.4	77.8	56.1	63.9	49.5	26.6	30.4	43.9	75.3	64.9	74.6	63.4	97.6	78.4	105.1	120.2	137.7	116.5	54.1
Sisal	30.5	33.8	24.0	14.1	10.5	5.9	5.2	5.9	4.9	4.3	4.0	2.2	0.9	3.3	5.1	6.3	4.8	8.5	6.8
Tea	22.1	21.6	18.5	23.9	23.5	17.0	13.6	17.7	16.0	16.6	21.5	21.7	24.1	38.0	39.5	23.4	26.3	30.1	32.2
Tobacco	12.5	18.2	19.1	12.2	10.0	13.6	15.0	12.4	15.4	12.0	10.6	16.7	27.2	17.5	20.6	27.1	47.0	12.9	25.5
Cashew nuts	7.3	34.4	9.9	9.9	21.9	11.5	15.0	12.4	16.1	7.4	5.6	16.7	23.5	23.3	51.2	64.0	93.8	75.1	112.1
Cloves	71.6	52.3	44.2	7.3	10.3	42.0	16.4	5.5	8.1	25.3	7.8	3.6	3.6						
Sub-total	335.7	402.5	304.7	270.8	279.3	235.1	280.3	207.2	232.4	238.5	209.1	201.6	236.4	256.6	336.9	383.6	447.4	360.5	345.6
Petroleum Products	24.9	16.1	13.5	12.8	4.6	13.7	4.6	7.1	12.2	15.1	10.0	7.3	8.0	9.1	5.5	11.0	11.1	12.4	7.4
Minerals	63.1	64.7	43.6	40.9	21.6	21.6	13.0	22.0	15.9	11.9	22.6	41.6	42.4	69.0	30.0	44.9	50.4	92.8	103.0
Manufactured goods	90.2	59.7	42.7	42.6	32.8	32.8	39.1	63.0	72.1	85.8	97.2	70.3	60.8	52.0	77.0	109.3	110.8	104.5	72.1
Other	60.6	69.2	49.4	28.0	22.4	22.4	29.3	54.0	47.6	54.1	68.9	41.6	52.4	53.2	70.0	134.3	142.1	148.7	148.1
Sub-total	238.8	209.7	149.2	124.3	81.4	90.5	86.0	146.1	147.8	166.9	198.7	160.8	163.6	183.3	182.5	299.5	314.4	358.4	330.6
TOTAL	574.5	612.2	453.9	395.2	360.7	325.6	366.3	353.2	380.2	405.4	407.8	362.4	400.0	439.9	519.4	683.1	761.8	718.9	676.2

Table 3.2. Merchandise Exports – Value and Share (cont'd)

	1980	1981	1982	1983	1984	1985	1986	1987	1988	1989	1990	1991	1992	1993	1994	1995	1996	1997	1998[1]
								Share of Total Exports (percent).											
Coffee	25.0	26.9	29.3	35.3	42.6	36.4	50.4	31.0	25.4	26.7	20.8	21.3	14.9	21.8	22.2	20.9	18.1	16.3	17.0
Cotton	8.4	12.7	12.4	16.2	13.7	8.2	8.3	12.4	19.8	16.0	18.3	17.5	24.4	17.8	20.2	17.6	18.1	16.2	8.0
Sisal	5.3	5.5	5.3	3.6	2.9	1.8	1.4	1.7	1.3	1.1	1.0	0.6	0.2	0.8	1.0	0.9	0.6	1.2	1.0
Tea	3.8	3.5	4.1	6.0	6.5	5.2	3.7	5.0	4.2	4.1	5.3	6.0	6.0	8.6	7.6	3.4	3.5	4.2	4.8
Tobacco	2.2	3.0	4.2	3.1	2.8	4.2	4.1	3.5	4.0	3.0	2.6	4.6	6.8	4.0	4.0	4.0	6.2	1.8	3.8
Cashew nuts	1.3	5.6	2.2	2.5	6.1	3.5	4.1	3.5	4.2	1.8	1.4	4.6	5.9	5.3	9.9	9.4	12.3	10.4	16.6
Cloves	12.5	8.5	9.7	1.8	2.8	12.9	4.5	1.5	2.1	6.2	1.9	1.0	0.9	58.3	.0.0	0.0	0.0	0.0	0.0
															0.0	0.0	0.0	0.0	0.0
Sub-total	58.4	65.8	67.1	68.5	77.4	72.2	76.5	58.7	61.1	58.8	51.3	55.6	59.1	58.3	64.9	56.2	58.7	50.1	51.1
Petroleum products	4.3	2.6	3.0	3.2	1.3	4.2	1.3	2.0	3.2	3.7	2.5	2.0	2.0	2.1	1.1	1.6	1.5	1.7	1.1
Minerals	11.0	10.6	9.6	10.4	6.0	6.6	3.5	6.2	4.2	2.9	5.5	11.5	10.6	15.7	5.8	6.6	6.6	12.9	15.2
Manufactured goods	15.7	9.7	9.4	10.8	9.1	10.1	10.7	17.8	19.0	21.2	23.8	19.4	15.2	11.8	14.8	16.0	14.5	14.5	10.7
Other	10.5	11.3	10.9	7.1	6.2	6.9	8.0	15.3	12.5	13.3	16.9	11.5	13.1	12.1	13.5	19.7	18.7	20.7	21.9
Sub-total	41.6	34.2	32.9	31.5	22.6	27.8	23.5	41.3	38.9	41.2	48.7	44.4	40.9	41.7	35.1	43.8	41.3	49.9	48.9
TOTAL	100.0	100.0	100.0	100.0	100.0	100.0	100.0	100.0	100.0	100.0	100.0	100.0	100.0	100.0	100.0	100.0	100.0	100.0	100.0

1 Preliminary estimates.
Source: Customs Department and Crop Boards of Tanzania (provided by Balance of Payments Department of the BOP).

Table 3.3. Volume and Unit Price of Selected Merchandise Exports

	1980	1981	1982	1983	1984	1985	1986	1987	1988	1989	1990	1991	1992	1993	1994	1995	1996	1997	1998[1]
Volume (thousand metric tons).																			
Coffee	43.5	67.9	54.8	55.7	55.0	44.0	50.4	42.4	38.7	49.9	62.7	52.5	51.0	58.6	37.0	48.0	64.0	46.6	53.6
Cotton	31.5	44.5	38.9	42.7	28.9	22.1	31.6	44.8	51.7	48.0	46.3	38.7	71.3	61.2	60.0	70.9	89.7	77.3	38.0
Sisal	48.9	57.5	50.7	29.3	21.5	15.5	15.1	17.8	11.2	8.6	7.7	4.5	4.7	5.0	7.2	11.3	7.6	13.7	10.9
Tea	13.3	15.5	11.9	18.4	11.1	11.7	9.5	11.9	11.2	11.0	14.8	17.5	20.4	19.8	21.7	21.6	24.7	20.4	22.7
Tobacco	8.5	10.9	10.1	5.6	4.6	7.7	7.2	8.2	9.8	7.7	5.9	8.6	12.8	10.6	15.4	17.1	24.0	6.3	12.7
Cashew nuts	9.1	25.1	17.2	17.0	33.5	23.6	17.8	11.2	16.3	9.1	7.4	19.0	29.3	23.9	65.0	75.6	121.2	103.3	140.4
Cloves	8.1	6.8	5.7	10.1	1.5	8.7	3.4	2.1	2.6	13.5	3.5	1.2	1.2	..	..	..	..	..	..
Unit Price (US dollar per kilogram).																			
Coffee	3.29	2.42	2.43	2.51	2.79	2.69	3.67	2.58	2.50	2.17	1.36	1.47	1.17	1.64	3.12	2.97	2.15	2.52	2.14
Cotton	1.54	1.75	1.44	1.49	1.71	1.20	0.96	0.98	1.46	1.35	1.61	1.64	1.37	1.28	1.75	1.70	1.54	1.51	1.42
Sisal	0.62	0.59	0.47	0.48	0.49	0.38	0.35	0.33	0.43	0.50	0.52	0.49	0.19	0.67	0.71	0.56	0.63	0.62	0.62
Tea	1.67	1.40	1.55	1.30	2.11	1.46	1.43	1.48	1.43	1.51	1.45	1.24	1.18	1.93	1.82	1.08	1.07	1.47	1.42
Tobacco	1.46	1.67	1.90	2.19	2.16	1.76	2.09	1.51	1.57	1.56	1.81	1.95	2.13	1.65	1.34	1.59	1.96	2.07	2.01
Cashew nuts	0.81	1.37	0.57	0.58	0.65	1.49	0.84	1.11	0.99	0.81	0.76	0.88	0.80	0.98	0.79	0.85	0.77	0.73	0.80
Cloves	8.85	7.67	7.83	0.72	6.93	4.84	4.81	2.60	3.08	1.87	2.23	3.00	3.00	..	..	..	..	..	..

1 Provisional estimates.
Source: Customs Department and Crop Boards of Tanzania (provided by Balance of Payments Department of the BOT).

Table 3.4. *Indices of Value, Volume and Unit Price of Selected Exports*
(1992 = 100)

Value

	1980	1981	1982	1983	1984	1985	1986	1987	1988	1989	1990	1991	1992	1993	1994	1995	1996	1997	1998
Coffee	240.8	276.3	223.3	234.7	258.1	199.1	310.3	183.8	162.5	181.6	142.8	130.0	100.0	161.4	193.9	239.6	231.5	197.3	193.1
Cotton	49.6	79.7	57.5	65.4	50.8	27.3	31.1	45.0	77.1	66.5	76.5	64.9	100.0	80.3	107.7	123.2	141.2	119.4	55.5
Sisal	3392.2	3753.6	2668.0	1562.7	1171.9	655.6	577.8	653.6	540.5	474.5	444.4	244.4	100.0	369.9	565.0	697.9	531.7	941.6	753.3
Tea	91.6	89.6	76.7	99.0	97.4	70.5	56.5	73.3	66.5	68.8	89.2	90.0	100.0	157.8	163.6	96.9	108.9	124.7	133.4
Tobacco	45.8	67.0	70.3	45.0	36.7	50.0	55.2	45.7	56.4	44.2	38.9	61.4	100.0	64.4	75.9	99.9	173.2	47.5	94.0
Cashew nuts	31.1	146.2	41.9	41.9	93.2	48.9	63.8	52.9	68.3	31.5	23.8	71.1	100.0	99.2	218.4	272.9	400.0	320.3	478.1
Cloves	1986.5	1450.4	1227.5	202.1	284.6	1164.8	454.5	151.3	225.4	701.8	216.5	100.0	100.0	:	:	:	:	:	:
Sub-total	142.0	170.3	128.9	114.5	118.1	99.5	118.6	87.6	98.3	100.9	88.4	85.3	100.0	108.6	142.5	162.3	189.2	152.5	146.2
Petroleum products	310.8	201.0	168.5	160.0	57.9	171.2	57.9	88.1	152.6	189.1	124.9	91.2	100.0	113.7	68.3	136.5	137.7	153.9	91.8
Minerals	148.9	152.6	102.8	96.5	51.0	51.0	30.7	51.9	37.6	28.1	53.3	98.1	100.0	162.7	70.8	105.9	118.9	218.9	243.0
Manufactured goods	148.4	98.1	70.3	70.1	54.0	54.0	64.4	103.6	118.5	141.0	159.9	115.6	100.0	85.5	126.7	179.8	182.3	171.9	118.6
Other	115.7	132.2	94.3	53.5	42.8	42.8	56.0	103.1	90.8	103.2	131.5	79.4	100.0	101.5	133.6	256.4	271.3	283.9	282.7
Sub-total	146.0	128.2	91.2	76.0	49.8	55.4	52.6	89.3	90.4	102.0	121.4	98.3	100.0	112.1	111.5	183.0	192.1	219.0	202.0
TOTAL	143.6	153.1	113.5	98.9	90.2	81.4	91.6	88.3	95.1	101.4	101.9	90.6	100.0	110.0	129.9	170.9	190.5	179.8	169.1

Table 3.4. *Indices of Value, Volume and Unit Price of Selected Exports (Cont'd)*

Value

	1980	1981	1982	1983	1984	1985	1986	1987	1988	1989	1990	1991	1992	1993	1994	1995	1996	1997	1998
Coffee	85.4	133.2	107.5	109.4	107.9	86.4	99.0	83.3	75.9	97.9	123.1	103.1	100.0	115.0	72.7	94.3	125.7	91.5	105.3
Cotton	44.1	62.3	54.5	59.9	40.6	31.0	44.3	62.8	72.5	67.4	64.9	54.2	100.0	85.8	84.1	99.3	125.7	108.3	53.2
Sisal	1046.8	1231.6	1085.6	626.6	460.5	331.9	322.4	380.2	239.5	184.4	165.0	96.6	100.0	107.2	153.8	241.4	162.3	292.6	232.8
Tea	65.0	75.8	58.6	90.1	54.5	57.2	46.8	58.4	54.9	53.9	72.6	85.9	100.0	96.9	106.4	106.1	121.3	100.2	111.5
Tobacco	66.8	85.9	79.0	43.8	36.2	60.7	56.4	64.6	76.8	60.4	45.9	67.3	100.0	83.3	121.2	134.6	188.9	49.6	100.0
Cashew nuts	30.9	85.8	58.7	57.8	114.3	80.6	60.8	38.2	55.5	31.0	25.2	64.8	100.0	81.4	221.6	257.7	413.2	352.2	478.6
Cloves	674.6	568.0	471.1	842.4	123.5	723.1	283.5	175.1	220.1	1125.9	291.9	100.0	100.0	:	:	:	:	:	:
Coffee	281.9	207.3	207.7	214.3	239.3	230.5	313.7	220.8	214.1	185.4	116.1	126.0	100	140.3974	267.0	254.1	184.0	215.6	183.1
Cotton	112.3	127.9	105.5	109.2	125.0	87.9	70.3	71.7	106.4	98.7	117.7	119.7	100	93.62007	128.0	124.4	112.6	110.5	103.9
Sisal	323.3	304.1	245.3	248.9	253.9	197.3	178.7	171.5	224.9	257.1	268.6	253.2	100	344.7684	369.0	291.1	327.5	322.3	322.3
Tea	140.8	118.2	130.9	110.0	178.8	123.5	120.7	125.5	121.2	127.7	122.8	104.9	100	162.8607	154.3	91.6	90.7	124.6	120.4
Tobacco	68.6	78.1	89.1	102.8	101.4	82.4	97.8	70.8	73.5	73.2	84.9	91.3	100	77.33711	62.8	74.6	91.9	97.1	94.3
Cashew nuts	100.6	170.5	71.5	72.6	81.6	60.7	105.0	138.5	123.1	101.2	94.3	109.6	100	121.8837	98.6	106.1	96.1	91.1	99.8
Cloves	294.9	255.7	260.9	24.0	230.9	161.3	160.5	86.5	102.5	62.5	74.3	100.0	100	:	:	:	:	:	:

1 Preliminary estimates.
Source: Tables 3.2 and 3.3.

273

Table 3.5. Merchandise Imports – Value and Share

	1981	1982	1983	1984	1985	1986	1987	1988	1989	1990	1991	1992	1993	1994	1995	1996	1997	1998[a]
								Value (millions of US dollars).										
Capital goods	563.1	485.2	326.0	346.5	434.3	494.0	610.9	405.8	480.7	598.8	680.0	700.5	632.9	656.5	554.2	501.0	496.3	614.7
Transport equipment	131.9	82.8	64.3	87.7	108.4	123.7	185.8	81.3	197.5	184.2	306.2	339.4	262.3	242.3	209.7	202.7	187.4	209.6
Building & construction	92.4	96.6	79.7	88.0	95.1	108.7	130.9	185.6	170.1	200.0	102.8	116.3	103.5	107.5	49.2	42.5	31.8	59.3
Machinery	338.9	305.9	182.1	170.8	230.7	261.6	294.2	138.9	113.1	214.6	271.0	244.8	267.1	306.7	295.3	255.8	277.1	345.8
Intermediate goods	382.2	402.4	344.8	370.3	400.6	341.0	346.7	510.5	556.0	547.2	318.0	337.3	296.2	290.4	609.0	531.0	490.4	395.5
Oil	260.9	251.8	229.9	210.6	223.4	145.0	169.5	146.8	152.4	195.0	159.7	185.4	167.2	149.0	193.8	158.4	187.0	106.1
Crude	134.1	133.7	136.6	135.1	117.9	71.7	92.0	84.5	91.3	110.0	76.9	97.6	72.0	79.8	115.2	69.9	93.5	85.2
Products	126.7	118.1	93.3	75.5	105.6	73.3	77.5	62.3	61.1	85.0	82.9	87.8	95.2	69.2	78.6	88.5	93.5	21.0
Fertilizers	6.3	5.9	3.9	9.6	8.8	11.0	6.4	4.0	5.0	8.5	37.2	16.0	11.3	11.7	11.7	23.3	19.4	15.0
Industrial raw materials	115.1	144.8	111.1	150.1	168.4	185.0	170.8	359.8	398.6	343.7	121.1	135.9	117.7	129.7	403.4	349.3	284.0	274.4
Consumer goods	165.1	159.9	119.0	156.6	162.2	210.0	192.0	275.7	190.8	215.7	319.1	392.5	312.2	359.5	377.7	361.8	351.0	443.2
Food	103.7	108.6	74.2	91.1	78.0	95.0	76.0	106.7	54.8	63.1	0.9	48.9	93.7	127.5	44.2	52.7	57.8	97.2
Other	61.4	51.3	44.8	65.5	84.3	115.0	116.0	169.0	136.0	152.6	318.2	343.6	218.5	232.0	333.5	309.1	293.1	345.9
Unclassified imports	0.7	1.9	1.5	0.6	2.1	2.5	0.4	0.4	2.5	1.8	94.0	83.0	224.1	198.6	0.0	0.0	0.0	0.0
TOTAL	1111.1	1049.4	791.4	874.0	999.2	1047.5	1150.0	1192.4	1230.0	1363.5	1411.1	1513.3	1465.4	1505.0	1540.8	1393.8	1337.7	1453.4

(table continues on the next page)

274

Table 3.5. Merchandise Imports – Value and Share (Cont'd)

	1981	1982	1983	1984	1985	1986	1987	1988	1989	1990	1991	1992	1993	1994	1995	1996	1997	1998[1]
							Share of Total Imports (percent).											
Capital goods	50.7	46.2	41.2	39.6	43.5	47.2	53.1	34.0	39.1	43.9	48.2	46.3	43.2	43.6	36.0	35.9	37.1	42.3
Transport equipment	11.9	7.9	8.1	10.0	10.8	11.8	16.2	6.8	16.1	13.5	21.7	22.4	17.9	16.1	13.6	14.5	14.0	14.4
Building & construction	8.3	9.2	10.1	10.1	9.5	10.4	11.4	15.6	13.8	14.7	7.3	7.7	7.1	7.1	3.2	3.0	2.4	4.1
Machinery	30.5	29.1	23.0	19.5	23.1	25.0	25.6	11.6	9.2	15.7	19.2	16.2	18.2	20.4	19.2	18.4	20.7	23.8
Intermediate goods	34.4	38.3	43.6	42.4	40.1	32.6	30.1	42.8	45.2	40.1	22.5	22.3	20.2	19.3	39.5	38.1	36.7	27.2
Oil	23.5	24.0	29.0	24.1	22.4	13.8	14.7	12.3	12.4	14.3	11.3	12.3	11.4	9.9	12.6	11.4	14.0	7.3
Crude	12.1	12.7	17.3	15.5	11.8	6.8	8.0	7.1	7.4	8.1	5.4	6.4	4.9	5.3	7.5	5.0	7.0	5.9
Products	11.4	11.3	11.8	8.6	10.6	7.0	6.7	5.2	5.0	6.2	5.9	5.8	6.5	4.6	5.1	6.3	7.0	1.4
Fertilizers	0.6	0.6	0.5	1.1	0.9	1.1	0.6	0.3	0.4	0.6	2.6	1.1	0.8	0.8	0.8	1.7	1.5	1.0
Industrial raw materials	10.4	13.8	14.0	17.2	16.8	17.7	14.9	30.2	32.4	25.2	8.6	9.0	8.0	8.6	26.2	25.1	21.2	18.9
Consumer goods	14.9	15.2	15.0	17.9	16.2	20.0	16.7	23.1	15.5	15.8	22.6	25.9	21.3	23.9	24.5	26.0	26.2	30.5
Food	9.3	10.3	9.4	10.4	7.8	9.1	6.6	8.9	4.5	4.6	0.1	3.2	6.4	8.5	2.9	3.8	4.3	6.7
Other	5.5	4.9	5.7	7.5	8.4	11.0	10.1	14.2	11.1	11.2	22.6	22.7	14.9	15.4	21.6	22.2	21.9	23.8
Unclassified imports	0.1	0.2	0.2	0.1	0.2	0.2	0.0	0.0	0.2	0.1	6.7	5.5	15.3	13.2	0.0	0.0	0.0	0.0
TOTAL	100.0	100.0	100.0	100.0	100.0	100.0	100.0	100.0	100.0	100.0	100.0	100.0	100.0	100.0	100.0	100.0	100.0	100.0

1 For the period of January-September 1995.
Source: Customs Department and Crop Boards of Tanzania (provided by Balance of Payments Department of the BOT).

Table 3.6. *Indices of Terms of Trade*
(FY93 = 100)

	FY91	FY92	FY93	FY94	FY95	FY96	FY97	FY98
Value								
Exports	92.30	97.40	100.00	101.50	123.80	145.30	165.70	134.70
Imports	92.80	96.90	100.00	108.10	102.70	93.10	94.30	95.20
Unit Value								
Exports	100.40	103.30	100.00	94.50	118.50	111.40	107.00	112.90
Imports	93.60	98.30	100.00	102.70	100.90	101.60	98.70	90.10
Volume								
Exports	91.60	94.60	100.00	107.30	104.40	130.40	154.90	116.90
Imports	98.90	98.50	100.00	108.00	101.70	88.80	89.20	91.70
Terms of Trade	107.90	105.80	100.00	94.50	117.50	109.70	108.40	125.30

Source: IMF, *Recent Economic Development* (1999).

Table 3.7. *Direction of Trade*
Value (millions of US dollars)

	1985	1986	1987	1988	1989	1990	1991	1992	1993	1994	1995	1996	1997	1998*
Export to :														
OAU countries	24.8	20.4	34.3	30.5	51.6	31.4	46.0	80.0	81.0	82.0	104.0	119.0	121.0	103.0
Kenya	1.6	3.0	8.2	8.6	14.6	11.2	7.0	8.0	8.0	9.0	11.0	13.0	13.0	13.0
Uganda	2.1	5.6	2.8	3.3	3.9	3.9	4.0	5.0	6.0	7.0	8.0	10.0	11.0	9.0
Commonwealth countries	102.3	81.8	80.8	72.8	116.2	70.7	-	-	-	-	-	-	-	-
U.K.	49.1	39.9	30.3	30.4	43.8	35.3	34.0	34.0	35.0	31.0	39.0	41.0	49.0	38.0
Singapore	28.7	12.8	10.9	6.8	18.9	4.2	14.0	12.0	8.0	13.0	14.0	14.0	9.0	5.0
Canada	1.2	1.0	0.9	1.4	1.7	2.1	1.0	2.0	2.0	1.0	3.0	1.0	2.0	-
India	11.6	14.7	21.9	12.8	9.1	3.9	31.0	34.0	40.0	53.0	58.0	73.0	52.0	40.0
EEC countries	181.1	186.8	124.6	131.0	165.4	150.1	-	-	-	-	-	-	-	-
Belgium	7.5	7.3	5.9	10.0	10.4	6.6	22.0	34.0	9.0	16.0	9.0	8.0	25.0	30.0
Germany	69.0	78.2	38.0	40.2	51.9	52.4	62.0	47.0	48.0	50.0	66.0	65.0	60.0	47.0
Italy	15.2	15.8	10.5	12.6	17.3	12.1	13.0	14.0	14.0	9.0	11.0	9.0	9.0	6.0
Netherlands	20.2	22.6	23.9	17.1	20.9	19.3	22.0	20.0	21.0	25.0	36.0	38.0	40.0	32.0
Eastern European countries	6.7	1.8	7.4	2.8	3.8	6.7	-	-	-	-	-	-	-	-
Yugoslavia, Fed. Rep.	1.2	0.6	1.8	1.2	1.9	1.8	1.0	1.0	-	-	-	-	-	-
Other countries	23.7	28.4	72.7	102.0	47.8	99.4	-	-	-	-	-	-	-	-
USA	6.2	6.5	6.3	7.0	11.5	72.4	15.0	11.0	12.0	15.0	22.0	18.0	26.0	22.0
Sweden	0.9	0.8	1.0	1.0	0.7	0.7	1.0	2.0	2.0	2.0	2.0	3.0	2.0	-
Japan	11.0	14.2	11.2	13.7	17.1	15.6	21.0	30.0	37.0	45.0	59.0	59.0	54.0	47.0
China	3.1	1.8	1.9	0.5	0.2	0.0	1.0	1.0	1.0	8.0	9.0	17.0	16.0	8.0
Hong Kong	2.5	5.1	7.2	10.0	15.4	10.8	10.0	10.0	4.0	12.0	15.0	18.0	14.0	5.0
TOTAL EXPORTS	338.5	347.6	347.3	372.1	355.0	426.8	426.0	499.0	498.0	558.0	726.0	805.0	715.0	549.0

Table 3.7. Direction of Trade (Cont'd)

Import from:	1985	1986	1987	1988	1989	1990	1991	1992	1993	1994	1995	1996	1997	1998*
OAU countries	51.6	59.5	50.6	42.7	51.6	33.9	-	-	-	-	-	-	-	-
Kenya	22.1	36.7	30.8	26.7	29.8	11.8	38.0	49.0	103.0	122.0	150.0	176.0	261.0	232.0
Uganda	2.8	1.7	0.2	0.1	0.2	0.1	1.0	1.0	1.0	1.0	2.0	2.0	2.0	3.0
Commonwealth countries	205.9	203.3	226.6	234.7	263.9	218.6	-	-	-	-	-	-	-	-
U.K.	108.1	105.5	130.7	143.1	158.6	141.5	142.0	152.0	180.0	139.0	160.0	141.0	14.0	80.0
Singapore	7.2	9.0	7.9	9.7	24.2	8.6	29.0	41.0	37.0	27.0	48.0	31.0	31.0	16.0
Canada	20.6	10.0	11.7	18.7	38.5	17.2	17.0	14.0	7.0	5.0	10.0	14.0	10.0	11.0
India	13.0	13.1	14.9	15.5	27.9	16.1	53.0	82.0	69.0	76.0	78.0	92.0	78.0	66.0
EEC countries	371.0	371.0	465.3	468.2	522.5	361.3	-	-	-	-	-	-	-	-
Belgium	28.6	25.8	16.1	15.9	27.6	33.6	34.0	55.0	44.0	44.0	43.0	34.0	41.0	14.0
Germany	87.4	93.5	117.2	119.3	151.3	65.3	80.0	124.0	85.0	81.0	59.0	50.0	58.0	49.0
Italy	82.4	58.7	87.6	82.1	119.1	45.9	91.0	74.0	60.0	66.0	62.0	71.0	63.0	48.0
Netherlands	37.7	34.6	47.8	43.7	130.8	34.9	63.0	40.0	39.0	33.0	36.0	35.0	99.0	80.0
Eastern European countries	26.5	28.5	9.2	14.8	21.2	26.7	-	-	-	-	-	-	-	-
Yugoslavia, Fed. Rep.	13.4	19.7	5.9	6.5	1.5	2.8	7.0	7.0	-	-	-	-	-	-
Other countries	294.5	357.4	398.4	432.0	370.5	85.9	-	-	-	-	-	-	-	-
USA	40.6	27.8	33.8	11.9	23.6	9.0	38.0	37.0	36.0	54.0	73.0	55.0	71.0	62.0
Sweden	28.9	27.9	27.8	18.9	54.1	29.4	31.0	34.0	43.0	22.0	30.0	21.0	19.0	15.0
Japan	86.9	101.3	106.0	85.1	162.2	31.1	108.0	120.0	123.0	90.0	119.0	85.0	87.0	63.0
China	18.4	13.7	11.6	14.2	18.3	11.4	31.0	32.0	38.0	72.0	82.0	71.0	93.0	64.0
Hong Kong, China	5.0	7.2	6.8	6.7	22.5	5.0	25.0	33.0	35.0	36.0	39.0	28.0	21.0	9.0
TOTAL IMPORTS	999.2	1047.5	1150.0	1192.0	1230.0	1447.0	1533.0	1510.0	1497.0	1505.0	1619.0	1394.0	1337.0	1100.0

* Until the month of September.

Note: The figures of exports and imports may be different from those in BOP.

Source: The Planning Commission, URT, The Economic Survey, various years and the IMF, Direction of Trade, Year Book (1996).

Table 3.7a. *Direction of Trade as Share of Total*
(percent)

Export to :	1985	1986	1987	1988	1989	1990	1991	1992	1993	1994	1995	1996	1997	1998
OAU countries	7.3	5.9	9.9	8.2	14.5	7.4	10.8	16.0	16.3	14.7	14.3	14.8	16.9	18.8
Kenya	0.5	0.9	2.4	2.3	4.1	2.6	1.6	1.6	1.6	1.6	1.5	1.6	1.8	2.4
Uganda	0.6	1.6	0.8	0.9	1.1	0.9	0.9	1.0	1.2	1.3	1.1	1.2	1.5	1.6
Commonwealth countries	30.2	23.5	23.3	19.6	32.7	16.6	-	-	-	-	-	-	-	-
U.K.	14.5	11.5	8.7	8.2	12.3	8.3	8.0	6.8	7.0	5.6	5.4	5.1	6.9	6.9
Singapore	8.5	3.7	3.1	1.8	5.3	1.0	3.3	2.4	1.6	2.3	1.9	1.7	1.3	0.9
Canada	0.4	0.3	0.3	0.4	0.5	0.5	0.2	0.4	0.4	0.2	0.4	0.1	0.3	-
India	3.4	4.2	6.3	3.4	2.6	0.9	7.3	6.8	8.0	9.5	8.0	9.1	7.3	7.3
EEC countries	53.5	53.7	35.9	35.2	46.6	35.2	-	-	-	-	-	-	-	-
Belgium	2.2	2.1	1.7	2.7	2.9	1.5	5.2	6.8	1.8	2.9	1.2	1.0	3.5	5.5
Germany	20.4	22.5	10.9	10.8	14.6	12.3	14.6	9.4	9.6	9.0	9.1	8.1	8.4	8.6
Italy	4.5	4.5	3.0	3.4	4.9	2.8	3.1	2.8	2.8	1.6	1.5	1.1	1.3	1.1
Netherlands	6.0	6.5	6.9	4.6	5.9	4.5	5.2	4.0	4.2	4.5	5.0	4.7	5.6	5.8
Eastern European countries	2.0	0.5	2.1	0.8	1.1	1.6	-	-	-	-	-	-	-	-
Yugoslavia, Fed. Rep.	0.4	0.2	0.5	0.3	0.5	0.4	0.2	0.2	-	-	-	-	-	-
Other countries	7.0	8.2	20.9	27.4	13.5	23.3	-	-	-	-	-	-	-	-
USA	1.8	1.9	1.8	1.9	3.2	17.0	3.5	2.2	2.4	2.7	3.0	2.2	3.6	4.0
Sweden	0.3	0.2	0.3	0.3	0.2	0.2	0.2	0.4	0.4	0.4	0.3	0.4	0.3	-
Japan	3.2	4.1	3.2	3.7	4.8	3.7	4.9	6.0	7.4	8.1	8.1	7.3	7.6	8.6
China	0.9	0.5	0.5	0.1	0.1	0.0	-	0.2	0.2	1.4	1.2	2.1	2.2	1.5
Hong Kong, China	0.7	1.5	2.1	2.7	4.3	2.5	2.3	2.0	0.8	2.2	2.1	2.2	2.0	0.9
TOTAL EXPORTS	100.0	100.0	100.0	100.0	100.0	100.0	100.0	100.0	100.0	100.0	100.0	100.0	100.0	100.0

Table 3.7a. Direction of Trade as Share of Total (Cont'd)

	1985	1986	1987	1988	1989	1990	1991	1992	1993	1994	1995	1996	1997	1998
Import from:														
OAU countries	5.2	5.7	4.4	3.6	4.2	2.3	-	-	-	-	-	-	-	-
Kenya	2.2	3.5	2.7	2.2	2.4	0.8	2.5	3.2	6.9	8.1	9.3	12.6	19.5	21.1
Uganda	0.3	0.2	0.0	0.0	0.0	0.0	0.1	0.1	0.1	0.1	0.1	0.1	0.1	0.3
Commonwealth countries	20.6	19.4	19.7	19.7	21.5	15.1	-	-	-	-	-	-	-	-
U.K.	10.8	10.1	11.4	12.0	12.9	9.8	9.3	10.1	12.0	9.2	9.9	10.1	1.0	7.3
Singapore	0.7	0.9	0.7	0.8	2.0	0.6	1.9	2.7	2.5	1.8	3.0	2.2	2.3	1.5
Canada	2.1	1.0	1.0	1.6	3.1	1.2	1.1	0.9	0.5	0.3	0.6	1.0	0.7	1.0
India	1.3	1.3	1.3	1.3	2.3	1.1	3.5	5.4	4.6	5.0	4.8	6.6	5.8	6.0
EEC countries	37.1	35.4	40.5	39.3	42.5	25.0	-	-	-	-	-	-	-	-
Belgium	2.9	2.5	1.4	1.3	2.2	2.3	2.2	3.6	2.9	2.9	2.7	2.4	3.1	1.3
Germany	8.7	8.9	10.2	10.0	12.3	4.5	5.2	8.2	5.7	5.4	3.6	3.6	4.3	4.5
Italy	8.2	5.6	7.6	6.9	9.7	3.2	5.9	4.9	4.0	4.4	3.8	5.1	4.7	4.4
Netherlands	3.8	3.3	4.2	3.7	10.6	2.4	4.1	2.6	2.6	2.2	2.2	2.5	7.4	7.3
Eastern European countries	2.7	2.7	0.8	1.2	1.7	1.8	-	-	-	-	-	-	-	-
Yugoslavia, Fed. Rep.	1.3	1.9	0.5	0.5	0.1	0.2	0.5	0.5	-	-	-	-	-	-
Other countries	29.5	34.1	34.6	36.2	30.1	5.9	-	-	-	-	-	-	-	-
USA	4.1	2.7	2.9	1.0	1.9	0.6	2.5	2.5	2.4	3.6	4.5	3.9	5.3	5.6
Sweden	2.9	2.7	2.4	1.6	4.4	2.0	2.0	2.3	2.9	1.5	1.9	1.5	1.4	1.4
Japan	8.7	9.7	9.2	7.1	13.2	2.1	7.0	7.9	8.2	6.0	7.4	6.1	6.5	5.7
China	1.8	1.3	1.0	1.2	1.5	0.8	2.0	2.1	2.5	4.8	5.1	5.1	7.0	5.8
Hong Kong, China	0.5	0.7	0.6	0.6	1.8	0.3	1.6	2.2	2.3	2.4	2.4	2.0	1.6	0.8
TOTAL IMPORTS	100.0	100.0	100.0	100.0	100.0	100.0	100.0	100.0	100.0	100.0	100.0	100.0	100.0	100.0

Source: Table 3.7a.

Table 3.8. *External Reserves*
(millions of US dollars)

	FY87	FY88	FY89	FY90	FY91	FY92	FY93	FY94	FY95	FY96	FY97	FY98
Reserve Level	38.2	132.6	51.4	124.3	209.4	384.9	294.6	306.3	255.1	240.1	460.5	502.5
Bank of Tanzania[2]	-33.8	-94.4	81.2	-72.9	-85.1	-175.5	90.3	-11.7	51.2	15.0	-220.4	-60.8
IMF, net	38.8	33.6	-16.2	9.3	-30.5	58.4	40.9	-10.2	-15.9	-22.2	48.5	12.5
Purchase	..	..	..	0.0	0.0	0.0	0.0	0.0	0.0	0.0	0.0	48.4
SAF/ESAF purchase	..	..	..	27.6	0.0	73.8	44.9	0.0	0.0	0.0	72.7	0.0
Repurchase	..	..	..	18.3	30.5	15.4	4.0	10.2	15.9	-22.2	-24.2	-36.0
Reserve level as months of import of goods only	0.4	1.3	0.5	1.1	1.8	3.2	2.4	2.3	2.0	1.5*	2.8*	3*

1 Provisional.
2 The negative sign means increase.
* Includes non-factor services.
Source: Table 3.1 and IMF, *Recent Economic Development* (various issues).

Table 3.9. Scheduled Debt Service Payments
(millions of US dollars)

	FY82	FY83	FY84	FY85	FY86	FY87	FY88	FY89	FY90	FY91	FY92	FY93	FY94	FY95	FY96	FY97	FY98
Debt service /2	112.1	157.1	279.8	351.1	331.9	351.4	373.3	381	395.7	372	352.4	538.3	525.3	477.6	520.2	506.3	415.8
Interest	52.7	55	72.6	93.3	105.1	148.7	180.6	185.2	190.5	190.8	194.5	177.9	153.8	139.4	143.6	140.8	185.4
Amortization	59.4	102.1	207.2	257.8	226.8	202.7	192.7	195.8	205.2	181.2	157.9	360.4	371.5	338.2	143.6	365.5	230.4
Debt service ratio /3	17.4	30.9	57	78.9	78	79.4	83.6	70.8	76.6	70.4	62.2	88.2	61.9	44.8	44.6	36.9	36.4
Debt service as % of GDP	1.7	2.3	4.6	6.4	4.7	10.2	10.8	9.6	10.2	8.9	8.5	14.4	15.5	11.2	..	..	..

1 Preliminary estimates.
2 Including obligations to the IMF.
3 As percent of exports of goods and non-factor services.
Source: Table 3.1 and various IMF documents.

4. External Debt

Table 4.1. *Summary of External Debt, 1980-98 (as of December 31, 1998)*
(millions of US dollars)

	1980	1981	1982	1983	1984	1985	1986	1987	1988	1989	1990	1991	1992	1993	1994	1995	1996	1997	1998
Debt Outstanding & Disbursed (DOD).	2616	2998	3159	3466	3692	4647	4789	5788	6180	5851	6410	6539	6621	6798	7257	6967	6391	6804	6996
Long-term Debt	2111	2551	2623	2913	3022	3351	4316	5056	5361	5279	5750	5782	5800	5819	6142	6779	6191	6594	6829
Public & Publicly Guranteed	2028	2485	2623	2845	2953	3332	4302	5041	5348	5266	5738	5770	5789	5808	6130	6601	5984	6334	6568
Private Non-guaranteed	84	66	0	67	69	19	13	15	13	13	12	12	12	12	12	178	207	260	261
Use of IMF Credit	171	146	126	92	59	578	71	113	141	129	140	143	221	215	212	188	200	210	167
Short-term Debt	333	301	409	461	611	718	402	619	678	443	520	614	600	764	903	-	-	-	-
of which Interest Arrears on LT Debt	30	5	7	14	57	118	142	319	328	343	404	531	515	703	822	-	-	-	-
Disbursements	432	659	316	387	403	211	340	295	416	230	333	309	474	249	261	295	396	967	202.4
Long-term Debt	366	640	316	387	403	211	301	251	372	230	304	280	383	249	261	295	359	933	202.4
Public& Publicly Guaranteed	335	637	297	374	395	207	298	251	372	230	304	280	383	249	261	247	326	867	201
Private Non-guaranteed	31	3	19	13	8	3	3	0	0	0	0	0	0	0	0	48	33	66	1.4
Use of IMF Credit	66	19	0	0	0	0	39	44	43	0	29	29	90	0	0	0	37	34	0
Principal Payments[1]	81	88	68	92	70	118	95	86	83	115	116	142	169	108	115	159	163	98	217
Long-term Debt	48	57	55	64	41	110	62	70	74	106	88	115	164	102	100	132	141	85	169
Public & Publicly Guaranteed	32	37	40	49	36	107	60	70	74	106	88	115	164	102	100	126	141	82	161
Private Non-guaranteed	16	20	15	15	5	3	2	0	0	0	0	0	0	0	0	2.8	4.4	5.4	12.4
IMF Repurchases	33	31	12	28	29	8	32	16	9	9	28	27	6	6	15	27	22	13	48

Table 4.1. *Summary of External Debt, 1980-98 (as of December 31, 1998) (Cont'd)*

	1980	1981	1982	1983	1984	1985	1986	1987	1988	1989	1990	1991	1992	1993	1994	1995	1996	1997	1998
Interest Payments[1]	81	89	85	73	58	63	69	74	74	61	62	62	62	114	69	78	100	57	102
Long-term Debt	48	49	53	48	33	37	45	50	48	49	47	54	56	110	64	77	99	56	102
Public & Publicly Guaranteed	41	43	48	44	32	36	44	50	48	49	47	54	56	110	64	73	95	49	100
Private Non-guaranteed	7	6	5	5	1	1	1	0	0	0	0	0	0	0	0	4	4	7	2
IMF Charges	7	8	8	6	4	1	4	4	4	5	6	3	1	1	1	1.1	0.9	0.6	0.12
Short-term Debt	26	32	24	19	21	25	20	20	22	7	9	5	5	4	5	-	-	-	-
Memo Items:																			
Total Debt Service[1]	161	177	152	165	128	181	164	159	158	176	178	203	231	222	184	234	267	157	325
Long-term Debt	96	107	108	112	74	147	108	120	122	154	135	169	220	211	163	205	244	143	275
Public & Publicly Guaranteed	73	80	88	92	68	143	104	120	122	154	135	169	220	211	163	198	236	131	261
Private Non-guaranteed	23	27	20	20	6	4	3	0	0	0	0	0	0	0	0	7	8	12	14
IMF Repurchase and Charges	39	39	20	34	33	9	36	19	13	15	34	29	7	7	16	29	23	14	50
Short-term Debt	26	32	24	19	21	25	20	20	22	7	9	5	5	4	5	-	-	-	-
DOD as percent of GDP	50.8	48	47.3	55.5	66.1	72.3	105.5	182.4	167.1	127.9	159.7	150.5	141.5	156.1	178.4	128.71	101.01	90.21	88.11

1 Cash basis. See Table 3.9 for scheduled debt service payments.
Note: Debt data in this section are in calendar year basis, and the figures for disbursements and debt service payments may be different from those in the Balance of Payments. Data on IMF were provided by the IMF.
Source: The World Bank, Debtor Reporting System (DRS), (data extracted in November 1995) and BOT, Debt Department, CS-DRMS (Various Reports).

Table 4.2. External Public Debt Outstanding, Commitment and Disbursement by Creditor Type, 1980-98 (as of December, 1998) (millions of US dollars)

	1980	1981	1982	1983	1984	1985	1986	1987	1988	1989	1990	1991	1992	1993	1994	1995	1996	1997	1998
Debt Outstanding & Disbursed (DOD)	2027.7	2484.5	2623.1	2845.4	2953.2	3331.7	4302.4	5041.1	5347.6	5359.6	5822.0	5859.8	5884.2	5896.6	6231.9	6600.6	5983.9	6334.3	6567.8
Multilateral	564.8	699.1	827.1	912.6	951.5	1108.9	1286.1	1481.2	1665.2	1742.2	1995.7	2171.1	2308.0	2417.9	2642.7	2928.9	3098.0	3187.7	3366.4
IDA	242.1	318.9	414.4	475.3	518.0	568.2	670.1	800.8	914.0	1015.6	1250.3	1433.6	1618.3	1759.0	1997.9	2119.3	2238.5	2309.1	2478.9
IBRD	197.7	210.0	211.1	223.2	206.1	265.7	291.2	324.8	279.4	251.5	242.5	207.7	170.8	139.5	114.4	72.5	44.6	31.1	21.2
Bilateral	1205.6	1478.7	1482.3	1615.0	1667.5	1811.3	2573.9	3064.0	3213.7	3133.6	3353.4	3235.8	3202.0	3098.6	3199.4	3402.0	2639.2	2916.2	2973.6
Private Creditors	257.3	306.7	313.7	317.8	334.3	411.5	442.4	496.0	468.7	483.8	473.0	453.0	374.2	380.0	389.8	269.7	246.7	230.4	227.8
Commercial Bank	30.8	41.3	45.7	47.8	45.5	51.3	53.4	62.2	60.6	59.2	67.8	59.9	46.4	47.6	63.1	110.5	101.2	87.9	85.9
Other Private	226.5	265.4	268.0	270.0	288.7	360.2	389.0	433.7	408.1	424.7	405.3	393.1	327.8	332.4	326.7	159.1	145.5	142.5	141.9
Commitments	741.9	430.3	200.3	405.8	256.6	164.4	354.8	487.5	428.6	209.4	702.7	512.7	279.6	515.8	217.6	139.2	505.3	821.2	123.8
Multilateral	158.1	166.1	95.9	143.6	10.0	53.6	220.0	191.4	250.7	132.1	590.5	442.2	205.1	428.5	190.5	56.2	466.1	248.7	99.2
IDA	109.2	91.3	70.5	80.9	0.0	44.9	184.7	23.4	217.4	73.2	537.4	334.1	59.6	345.2	182.7	12.1	179.1	151.8	21.4
IBRD	0.0	0.0	0.0	0.0	0.0	0.0	0.0	0.0	0.0	0.0	0.0	0.0	0.0	0.0	0.0	-	-	-	-
Bilateral	505.1	185.1	99.0	186.0	241.1	13.2	65.4	292.6	78.4	65.7	98.8	54.4	26.0	38.5	14.0	54.9	39.2	563.4	19.9
Private Creditors	78.7	79.1	5.4	76.2	5.5	97.6	69.3	3.4	99.4	11.7	13.4	16.1	48.5	48.8	13.2	28.1	0.0	9.1	4.7
Commercial Bank	8.1	40.6	1.4	7.1	0.0	0.0	0.6	3.0	0.6	0.2	10.4	8.4	1.5	32.2	4.1	8.8	-	-	-
Other Private	70.6	38.5	4.0	69.1	5.5	97.7	68.7	0.4	98.8	11.4	3.0	7.7	46.9	16.6	9.1	19.3	-	9.1	4.7
Disbursements	335.1	637.0	297.2	373.4	394.9	207.1	298.1	250.7	372.4	227.4	304.6	278.9	385.4	227.3	262.6	247.1	326.0	867.7	202.7
Multilateral	121.6	151.0	146.8	115.0	100.7	78.5	137.4	101.5	278.6	132.4	205.2	225.4	254.8	162.3	204.4	202.7	316.7	306.3	175.1
IDA	35.0	78.2	96.9	65.4	49.5	34.5	85.5	89.8	135.3	115.2	186.5	180.7	234.5	146.1	183.2	151.8	170.1	196.5	109.8
IBRD	34.3	19.3	9.9	24.6	24.6	11.3	6.8	5.2	2.5	0.0	0.0	0.0	0.0	0.0	0.0	0.0	0.0	0.0	0
Bilateral	122.8	403.4	114.5	225.0	259.5	82.9	90.1	104.3	58.1	59.6	82.7	49.8	89.6	20.4	37.0	12.0	8.8	556.6	27.6
Private Creditors	90.8	82.7	36.0	33.4	34.8	45.7	70.7	44.9	35.6	35.4	16.6	3.7	41.0	44.6	21.2	32.4	0.5	4.8	0
Commercial Bank	9.1	13.2	8.3	5.8	1.2	0.4	0.3	1.6	1.5	0.9	3.3	1.7	2.3	11.6	12.2	13.1	0.5	1.2	-
Other Private	81.7	69.5	27.7	27.7	33.5	45.3	70.3	43.3	34.1	34.4	13.3	2.1	38.6	33.0	9.0	19.3	-	3.5	-

Note: Public and publicly guaranteed debt only excluding IMF. See Table 4.5 for obligations to the IMF.
Source: The World Bank, Debtor Reporting System (DRS), (data extracted in November 1995) and BOT, Debt Department, CS-DRMS (Various Reports).

Table 4.2a. *External Public Debt Outstanding, Commitment and Disbursement by Creditor Type* (percent)

	1980	1981	1982	1983	1984	1985	1986	1987	1988	1989	1990	1991	1992	1993	1994	1995	1996	1997	1998
Debt Outstanding & Disbursed (DOD).	100.0	100.0	100.0	100.0	100.0	100.0	100.0	100.0	100.0	100.0	100.0	100.0	100.0	100.0	100.0	100.0	100.0	100.0	100.0
Multilateral	27.9	28.1	31.5	32.1	32.2	33.3	29.9	29.4	31.1	32.5	34.3	37.1	39.2	41.0	42.4	44.4	51.8	50.3	51.3
IDA	11.9	12.8	15.8	16.7	17.5	17.1	15.6	15.9	17.1	18.9	21.5	24.5	27.5	29.8	32.1	32.1	37.4	36.5	37.7
IBRD	9.7	8.5	8.0	7.8	7.0	8.0	6.8	6.4	5.2	4.7	4.2	3.5	2.9	2.4	1.8	1.1	0.7	0.5	0.3
Bilateral	59.5	59.5	56.5	56.8	56.5	54.4	59.8	60.8	60.1	58.5	57.6	55.2	54.4	52.5	51.3	51.5	44.1	46.0	45.3
Private Creditors	12.7	12.3	12.0	11.2	11.3	12.4	10.3	9.8	8.8	9.0	8.1	7.7	6.4	6.4	6.3	4.1	4.1	3.6	3.5
Commercial Bank	1.5	1.7	1.7	1.7	1.5	1.5	1.2	1.2	1.1	1.1	1.2	1.0	0.8	0.8	1.0	1.7	1.7	1.4	1.3
Other Private	11.2	10.7	10.2	9.5	9.8	10.8	9.0	8.6	7.6	7.9	7.0	6.7	5.6	5.6	5.2	2.4	2.4	2.2	2.2
Commitments	100.0	100.0	100.0	100.0	100.0	100.0	100.0	100.0	100.0	100.0	100.0	100.0	100.0	100.0	100.0	100.0	100.0	100.0	100.0
Multilateral	21.3	38.6	47.9	35.4	3.9	32.6	62.0	39.3	58.5	63.1	84.0	86.2	73.4	83.1	87.5	40.4	92.2	30.3	80.1
IDA	14.7	21.2	35.2	19.9	0.0	27.3	52.1	4.8	50.7	35.0	76.5	65.2	21.3	66.9	84.0	8.7	35.4	18.5	17.3
IBRD	0.0	0.0	0.0	0.0	0.0	0.0	0.0	0.0	0.0	0.0	0.0	0.0	0.0	0.0	0.0	-	-	-	-
Bilateral	68.1	43.0	49.4	45.8	94.0	8.0	18.4	60.0	18.3	31.4	14.1	10.6	9.3	7.5	6.4	39.4	7.8	68.6	16.1
Private Creditors	10.6	18.4	2.7	18.8	2.1	59.4	19.5	0.7	23.2	5.6	1.9	3.1	17.3	9.5	6.1	20.2	0.0	1.1	3.8
Commercial Bank	1.1	9.4	0.7	1.7	0.0	0.0	0.2	0.6	0.1	0.1	1.5	1.6	0.5	6.2	1.9	6.3	-	-	-
Other Private	9.5	8.9	2.0	17.0	2.1	59.4	19.4	0.1	23.1	5.4	0.4	1.5	16.8	3.2	4.2	13.9	-	1.1	3.8
Disbursements	100.0	100.0	100.0	100.0	100.0	100.0	100.0	100.0	100.0	100.0	100.0	100.0	100.0	100.0	100.0	100.0	100.0	100.0	100.0
Multilateral	36.3	23.7	49.4	30.8	25.5	37.9	46.1	40.5	74.8	58.2	67.4	80.8	66.1	71.4	77.8	82.0	97.1	35.3	86.4
IDA	10.4	12.3	32.6	17.5	12.5	16.7	28.7	35.8	36.3	50.7	61.2	64.8	60.8	64.3	69.8	61.4	52.2	22.6	54.2
IBRD	10.2	3.0	3.3	6.6	6.2	5.5	2.3	2.1	0.7	0.0	0.0	0.0	0.0	0.0	0.0	0.0	0.0	0.0	0.0
Bilateral	36.6	63.3	38.5	60.3	65.7	40.0	30.2	41.6	15.6	26.2	27.2	17.9	23.2	9.0	14.1	4.9	2.7	64.1	13.6
Private Creditors	27.1	13.0	12.1	8.9	8.8	22.1	23.7	17.9	9.6	15.6	5.4	1.3	10.6	19.6	8.1	13.1	0.2	0.6	0.0
Commercial Bank	2.7	2.1	2.8	1.6	0.3	0.2	0.1	0.6	0.4	0.4	1.1	0.6	0.6	5.1	4.6	5.3	0.2	0.1	-
Other Private	24.4	10.9	9.3	7.4	8.5	21.9	23.6	17.3	9.2	15.1	4.4	0.8	10.0	14.5	3.4	7.8	-	0.4	-

Note: Public and publicly guaranteed debt only excluding IMF. See Table 4.5 for obligations to the IMF.
Source: Table 4.2.

Table 4.3. *External Public Debt Service Payments by Creditor Type, 1980-98 (as of December 31, 1998)* (millions of US dollars)

	1980	1981	1982	1983	1984	1985	1986	1987	1988	1989	1990	1991	1992	1993	1994	1995	1996	1997	1998
Principal Payments[1]	32.2	36.9	40.1	48.6	36.0	107.3	60.3	70.1	73.8	104.8	87.7	115.1	159.7	98.0	90.8	125.8	141.5	82.0	161.3
Multilateral	7.5	10.9	12.9	17.1	20.4	30.9	35.3	37.6	35.7	36.5	43.8	63.9	50.6	52.2	64.3	87.5	103.8	63.5	111.8
IDA	0.6	1.3	1.1	1.3	2.1	2.7	2.9	3.2	3.9	5.2	5.9	7.1	8.4	9.2	10.9	12.7	14.4	15.6	17.2
IBRD	4.8	7.0	8.8	12.5	14.8	24.7	26.1	24.6	23.7	23.1	26.1	36.2	30.5	33.1	32.5	34.8	34.0	16.2	10.5
Bilateral	18.4	19.4	17.0	20.4	14.8	75.9	23.1	27.0	29.4	59.2	32.2	37.9	31.7	35.4	17.6	21.6	17.1	7.2	44.4
Private Creditors	6.3	6.6	10.2	11.1	0.8	0.5	1.9	5.5	8.7	9.1	11.6	13.3	77.4	10.4	8.9	16.7	20.6	11.3	5.1
Commercial Bank	0.5	0.7	0.9	1.1	0.4	0.3	0.3	0.3	0.5	0.6	0.6	3.3	8.0	8.8	0.2	11.8	10.7	7.7	4.2
Other Private	5.8	5.8	9.4	10.0	0.4	0.3	1.6	5.2	8.3	8.5	11.0	10.0	69.5	1.6	8.7	4.9	9.8	3.6	0.9
Interest Payments[1]	41.0	43.1	48.0	43.6	32.4	27.3	36.2	44.1	50.0	48.4	47.3	54.3	55.8	111.2	62.5	72.6	94.7	48.8	99.8
Multilateral	18.3	19.0	20.0	18.6	21.0	21.0	27.0	30.9	30.3	26.8	27.1	33.6	33.1	33.1	33.2	53.2	45.5	40.7	27.9
IDA	1.6	1.9	2.6	3.0	3.3	4.6	4.9	6.6	6.8	6.9	8.2	9.8	10.1	13.5	14.2	14.7	22.8	17.1	18.0
IBRD	15.3	15.5	15.8	14.0	16.3	15.2	20.9	22.6	21.8	18.6	17.4	19.6	14.8	12.0	9.6	11.0	8.1	3.2	2.2
Bilateral	15.8	16.6	17.0	19.0	10.9	6.0	8.1	11.2	15.6	17.3	17.0	17.2	17.8	72.6	28.9	16.1	43.9	4.6	69.7
Private Creditors	6.9	7.5	11.0	6.0	0.4	0.4	1.1	2.0	4.2	4.3	3.2	3.5	4.9	5.5	0.4	3.3	5.3	3.5	2.2
Commercial Bank	1.0	1.5	0.9	0.7	0.1	0.2	0.3	0.4	0.5	0.6	0.2	1.3	3.4	3.6	0.3	3.3	5.3	3.5	2.2
Other Private	6.0	6.0	10.1	5.3	0.3	0.2	0.8	1.6	3.7	3.7	3.0	2.2	1.4	2.0	0.1	-	-	-	-

Table 4.3. External Public Debt Service Payments by Creditor Type, 1980-98 (as of December 31, 1998)(Cont'd).

	1980	1981	1982	1983	1984	1985	1986	1987	1988	1989	1990	1991	1992	1993	1994	1995	1996	1997	1998
Memo Item:																			
Average Terms of New Commitments:																			
All Creditors:																			
Interest Rate (%)	4.1	4.2	2.8	4.4	2.6	1.5	2.1	2.3	2.9	3.8	1.2	1.3	1.0	2.0	1.2	1.7	1.2	-	-
Maturity (years)	24.1	26.8	32.0	23.7	6.8	36.3	34.9	27.4	28.5	30.7	34.7	38.9	33.0	35.2	35.7	17.5	35.5	-	-
Grace period (years)	7.5	5.9	8.1	5.7	1.7	7.7	7.7	7.5	7.7	7.4	9.3	10.8	7.1	8.6	9.4	5.7	9.2	-	-
Grant element (%).	43.4	43.3	57.2	40.3	17.1	65.0	62.0	57.1	54.6	51.6	72.0	75.8	64.9	67.1	73.8	48.3	73.0	-	-
Official Creditors:																			
Interest Rate (%)	3.6	3.6	1.9	3.2	2.5	1.7	1.7	2.2	1.4	3.7	1.1	1.0	1.0	1.6	1.0	1.7	1.2	-	-
Maturity (years)	25.6	29.4	35.3	27.0	6.8	41.6	40.9	27.6	34.1	32.1	35.1	39.7	39.1	38.0	37.6	23.0	35.8	-	-
Grace period (years)	8.0	6.6	8.6	6.1	1.7	8.8	9.1	7.5	9.2	7.8	9.3	11.0	8.3	9.1	9.9	7.4	9.3	-	-
Grant element (%)	47.6	49.0	65.7	49.4	17.3	71.8	71.1	57.5	70.7	54.1	72.4	78.1	75.6	72.1	77.6	61.3	73.7	-	-

1 Cash basis.
Note: Public and publicly guaranteed debt only excluding IMF. See Table 4.5 for obligations to the IMF.
Source: The World Bank, Debtor Reporting System (DRS), (data extracted in November 1995) and BOT, Debt Department, CS-DRMS (Various Reports).

Table 4.3a. Share of External Public Debt Service Payments by Creditor Type (as of December 31, 1998) (percent)

	1980	1981	1982	1983	1984	1985	1986	1987	1988	1989	1990	1991	1992	1993	1994	1995	1996	1997	1998
Principal Payments/1	100.0	100.0	100.0	100.0	100.0	100.0	100.0	100.0	100.0	100.0	100.0	100.0	100.0	100.0	100.0	100.0	100.0	100.0	100.0
Multilateral	23.3	29.5	32.2	35.2	56.7	28.8	58.5	53.6	48.4	34.8	49.9	55.5	31.7	53.3	70.8	69.6	73.4	77.4	69.3
IDA	1.9	3.5	2.7	2.7	5.8	2.5	4.8	4.6	5.3	5.0	6.7	6.2	5.3	9.4	12.0	10.1	10.2	19.0	10.7
IBRD	14.9	19.0	21.9	25.7	41.1	23.0	43.3	35.1	32.1	22.0	29.8	31.5	19.1	33.8	35.8	27.7	24.0	19.8	6.5
Bilateral	57.1	52.6	42.4	42.0	41.1	70.7	38.3	38.5	39.8	56.5	36.7	32.9	19.8	36.1	19.4	17.2	12.1	8.8	27.5
Private Creditors	19.6	17.9	25.4	22.8	2.2	0.5	3.2	7.8	11.8	8.7	13.2	11.6	48.5	10.6	9.8	13.3	14.6	13.8	3.2
Commercial Bank	1.6	1.9	2.2	2.3	1.1	0.3	0.5	0.4	0.7	0.6	0.7	2.9	5.0	9.0	0.2	9.4	7.6	9.4	2.6
Other Private	18.0	15.7	23.4	20.6	1.1	0.3	2.7	7.4	11.2	8.1	12.5	8.7	43.5	1.6	9.6	3.9	6.9	4.4	0.6
Interest Payments/1	100.0	100.0	100.0	100.0	100.0	100.0	100.0	100.0	100.0	100.0	100.0	100.0	100.0	100.0	100.0	100.0	100.0	100.0	100.0
Multilateral	44.6	44.1	41.7	42.7	64.8	76.9	74.6	70.1	60.6	55.4	57.3	61.9	59.3	29.8	53.1	73.3	48.0	83.4	28.0
IDA	3.9	4.4	5.4	6.9	10.2	16.8	13.5	15.0	13.6	14.3	17.3	18.0	18.1	12.1	22.7	20.2	24.1	35.0	18.0
IBRD	37.3	36.0	32.9	32.1	50.3	55.7	57.7	51.2	43.6	38.4	36.8	36.1	26.5	10.8	15.4	15.2	8.6	6.6	2.2
Bilateral	38.5	38.5	35.4	43.6	33.6	22.0	22.4	25.4	31.2	35.7	35.9	31.7	31.9	65.3	46.2	22.2	46.4	9.4	69.8
Private Creditors	16.8	17.4	22.9	13.8	1.2	1.5	3.0	4.5	8.4	8.9	6.8	6.4	8.8	4.9	0.6	4.5	5.6	7.2	2.2
Commercial Bank	2.4	3.5	1.9	1.6	0.3	0.7	0.8	0.9	1.0	1.2	0.4	2.4	6.1	3.2	0.5	4.5	5.6	7.2	2.2
Other Private	14.6	13.9	21.0	12.2	0.9	0.7	2.2	3.6	7.4	7.6	6.3	4.1	2.5	1.8	0.2	-	-	-	-

1 Cash basis.
Note: Public and publicly guaranteed debt only excluding IMF. See Table 4.5 for obligations to the IMF.
Source: Table 4.3.

Table 4.4. External Public Debt Including Undisbursed and Arrears (as of June 30, 1999) (millions of US dollars)

	Disbursed	Undisbursed	Total	Principal	Interest
Multilateral loans	3362.8	1167.4	4530.2	7.7	5.3
of which:					
African Dev. Fund	461.6	261.9	723.5	2.8	2.8
IBRD	21.2	0	21.2	-	-
IDA	2478.5	654	3132.5	2.5	0.1
Bilateral loans	2966.2	185.3	3151.5	1239.4	737.9
of which:					
Belgium	167.7	17.8	185.5	12.7	11
China	130.4	93.4	223.9	38.7	0.4
France	162.7	2.4	165.2	46	41.3
Germany, (former FRG only)	77	0	77	-	0
Japan	708.4	8	716.4	311.2	185.2
Netherlands	89.6	0	89.6	0.5	0.3
U.K.	203	0	203	7.7	0.2
Russian Federation	498.4	-	498.4	488.9	193.9
Commercial bank	261.4	84.7	346.1	115.1	192.3
Exports credit	202.2	20.4	222.6	178.2	131.2
Total	6792.6	1457.8	8250.4	1540.4	1066.7

Source: BOT, Debt Department, CS-DRMS (Reports 208 and 651).

Table 4.5. *Obligations to IMF (as of December 31, 1998)*
(millions of US dollars)

	1980	1981	1982	1983	1984	1985	1986	1987	1988	1989	1990	1991	1992	1993	1994	1995	1996	1997	1998
Use of Fund Credit	171.3	146.3	126.2	92.2	59.0	577.8	71.2	113.5	141.4	128.5	140.0	143.3	220.7	214.6	212.4	188.2	199.8	207.8	166.9
Purchases	66.1	19.0	0.0	0.0	0.0	0.0	38.7	43.8	43.1	0.0	29.0	29.3	90.4	0.0	0.0	-	37.2	33.9	-
Debt Service Obligations	39.1	38.7	20.1	33.7	32.5	8.8	36.0	19.2	13.4	14.7	33.9	29.4	6.5	7.1	15.9	28.5	22.6	13.9	49.7
Repurchases	32.5	31.0	12.5	28.1	28.6	7.6	32.1	15.6	9.4	9.4	28.4	26.8	5.5	6.0	15.3	27.4	21.7	13.2	48.5
Charges	6.6	7.7	7.6	5.6	3.9	1.2	3.9	3.5	4.0	5.4	5.5	2.6	1.0	1.1	0.6	1.1	0.9	0.6	1.3
Net Use of Fund Credit		-25.0	-20.1	-34.0	-33.2	518.8	506.6	42.3	27.9	-12.9	11.5	3.3	77.4	-6.1	-2.1	-24.2	11.6	8.0	-40.9

Note: The original debt figures in SDR were converted into US dollar; the figures may be different from those of the DRS.
Source: Treasury Department of the IMF and BOT, Debt Department, CS-DRMS, Report 728.

5. Public Finance

Table 5.1. Summary of Central Government Operations
(millions of Tanzania shillings)

	FY86	FY87	FY88	FY89	FY90	FY91	FY92	FY93	FY94	FY95	FY96	FY97	FY98	FY99
Total Revenue	20831	31098	46431	71790	94655	133238	173566	164110	242444	331240	448373	572030	619084	700393
Tax revenue	19661	29184	42557	63085	81471	118257	153356	146420	220358	299900	383744	505355	566123	627352
Nontax revenue	1170	1914	3874	8705	13184	14981	20210	17690	22086	31340	64629	66675	52961	73041
Total Expenditure and Net Lending	32373	47445	73368	93994	126242	151863	194891	305059	370910	395607	420522	515099	567778	816223
Recurrent expenditure	26912	35146	51896	78119	103866	135375	162286	240349	296221	345915	415140	486203	543751	680960
Development expenditure and Part of net lending	5461	12299	21472	15875	22376	16488	32605	64710	74689	49692	5382	28896	24027	135263
Overall balance (checks issued)	-11542	-16347	-26937	-22204	-31587	-18625	-21325	-140949	-128466	-64367	27851	56931	51306	-115830
Adjustment to cash and other items (net)	3205	-2036	-2982	-3648	-4129	-8750	-1870	6628	-36753	50649	92485	-36512	-93088	-62952
Overall balance (checks-cleared)	-8337	-18383	-29919	-25852	-35716	-27375	-23195	-134321	-165219	-13618	120336	20419	-41782	-178782
Overall balance (after grants)	..	-4946	-11028	-1219	-3923	4251	11471	-82636	-51557	41225	74733	138347	95605	54116
Financing:	8337	18384	29919	25852	35716	27375	23195	134321	165219	125735	64634	-20419	85034	129484
External grants	..	11401	15909	20985	27664	22876	32796	58313	76909	105592	46882	81416	44299	169946
Foreign Financing, net /1	2222	2401	7318	-3245	1489	8858	22676	29436	47754	-37958	-34900	-49065	37066	-26393
Domestic Borrowing	6115	4582	6692	8112	6563	-4359	-32277	46572	40556	58101	52652	-52770	3669	-14069

(table continues on the next page)

Table 5.1. Summary of Central Government Operations (Cont'd)

	FY86	FY87	FY88	FY89	FY90	FY91	FY92	FY93	FY94	FY95	FY96	FY97	FY98	FY99
Total Revenue		10.3	11.1	12.6	12.9	13.9	14.1	10.6	12.0	12.5	13.2	13.5	12.0	10.5
Tax revenue	7.2	9.6	10.2	11.1	11.1	12.3	12.5	9.5	11.0	11.3	11.3	11.9	11.0	9.4
Nontax revenue	0.4	0.6	0.9	1.5	1.8	1.6	1.6	1.1	1.1	1.2	1.9	1.6	1.0	1.1
Total Expenditure and Net Lending	11.8	15.7	17.6	16.5	17.2	15.8	15.9	19.7	18.4	14.9	12.4	12.2	11.0	12.2
Recurrent expenditure	9.8	11.6	12.4	13.7	14.2	14.1	13.2	15.5	14.7	13.0	12.2	11.5	10.6	10.2
Development expenditure and	2.0	4.1	5.1	2.8	3.1	1.7	2.7	4.2	3.7	1.9	0.2	0.7	0.5	2.0
Part of net lending	..													
Overall balance (checks issued)	-4.2	-5.4	-6.4	-3.9	-4.3	-1.9	-1.7	-9.1	-6.4	-2.4	0.8	1.3	1.0	-1.7
Adjustment to cash and other	1.2	-0.7	-0.7	-0.6	-0.6	-0.9	-0.2	0.4	-1.8	1.9	2.7	-0.9	-1.8	-0.9
items (net)	0.0	0.0	0.0	0.0	0.0	0.0	0.0	0.0	0.0	0.0	0.0	0.0	0.0	0.0
Overall balance (checks-cleared)	-3.0	-6.1	-7.2	-4.5	-4.9	-2.9	-1.9	-8.7	-8.2	-0.5	3.5	0.5	-0.8	-2.7
Overall balance (after grants)	..	-1.6	-2.6	-0.2	-0.5	0.4	0.9	-5.3	-2.6	1.5	2.2	3.3	1.9	0.8
Financing:	3.0	6.1	7.2	4.5	4.9	2.9	1.9	8.7	8.2	4.7	1.9	-0.5	1.7	1.9
External grants	..	3.8	3.8	3.7	3.8	2.4	2.7	3.8	3.8	4.0	1.4	1.9	0.9	2.5
Foreign Financing, net[1]	0.8	0.8	1.8	-0.6	0.2	0.9	1.8	1.9	2.4	-1.4	-1.0	-1.2	0.7	-0.4
Domestic Borrowing	2.2	1.5	1.6	1.4	0.9	-0.5	-2.6	3.0	2.0	2.2	1.6	-1.2	0.1	-0.2

1 Includes foreign grants prior to FY87.
Source: The Tanzanian authorities.

Table 5.2. *Central Government Revenue*
(millions of Tanzania shillings)

	FY86	FY87	FY88	FY89	FY90	FY91	FY92	FY93	FY94	FY95	FY96	FY97	FY98	FY99
Total Revenue	20831	31098	46431	71790	94700	133238	173566	164110	242447	331280	448339	572030	619084	700394
Tax revenue	19661	29184	42557	63085	81516	118257	153356	146420	220359	299940	383752	505355	566123	627352
Income taxes	6176	7018	10878	16601	20195	32413	40143	45455	58505	86684	112261	133182	149787	163938
Individual[1]	2211	2327	2902	3456	3947	4600	6832	10736	13223	27094	32383	47476	47821	55202
Company	3830	4286	7457	12266	15418	9829	9412	14332	38400	43044	51290	54690	54680	69933
Other	135	405	519	879	830	17984	23899	20387	6882	16546	28588	31016	47286	38803
Payroll or manpower taxes	200	320	441	577	807	975	1690	2149	2515	4858	6874	8922	10586	11806
Payroll tax	181	291	405	534	737	872	1584	1748	2308	4377	6122	8515	10586	11806
Training levy	19	29	36	43	70	103	106	401	207	481	752	407	0	0
Property taxes	100	107	116	140	188	317	345	494	891	1009	862	553	572	505
Land rent	62	67	74	97	113	194	183	269	294	387	366	0	0	0
Estate duty	2	2	2	6	33	4	12	9	12	13	16	6	14	0
Motor vehicle transfer tax	36	38	40	37	42	119	150	216	585	609	480	547	558	505
Consumption taxes on goods & services (local)	9736	13090	18087	26059	32955	47225	60385	49407	74455	76847	111358	137300	143143	178859
Local sales taxes/VAT	9288	12576	17429	25124	20124	28613	31045	28198	43730	51272	60668	60668	61736	115580
Excise taxes	..	..	..	..	11474	16375	26839	17919	26658	21372	43983	68593	78783	57797
Entertainment tax	32	29	38	50	47	55	42	19	24	1	0	0	0	0
Business licenses	85	19	62	109	185	380	479	736	766	886	1412	1985	0	2812
Other licenses	21	17	51	59	60	168	206	253	115	38	64	65	11	38
Motor vehicle licenses	189	295	168	191	266	567	629	707	810	477	1377	949	1221	1040
Motor vehicle registration	8	9	19	23	22	81	72	211	407	694	1219	1457	1368	1584
Hotel levy	113	145	320	503	777	986	1073	1364	1945	2107	2635	3583	24	8

(table continues on the next page)

Table 5.2. Central Government Revenue (cont'd)

	FY86	FY87	FY88	FY89	FY90	FY91	FY92	FY93	FY94	FY95	FY96	FY97	FY98	FY99
Tax on international transactions	2837	7608	11006	16467	23110	31768	38617	31637	50230	91249	121242	163079	185699	218994
Import duties	1468	4020	5586	8478	11930	17321	21103	16288	28404	..	61271	78374	82047	88052
Sales tax on imports	1345	3519	5327	7841	8447	10386	13817	12929	19525	..	33829	54909	76445	105510
Excise tax on imports	..	..	..	..	2583	3797	3697	2420	2301	..	26142	29796	22466	25390
Export duties	..	..	..	..	..	..	..	..	..	..	..	..	4741	42
Foreign travel levy	24	69	93	148	150	264	0	0	0	0	0	0	0	0
Other taxes	612	1041	2029	3241	4261	5559	12176	17278	33763	39293	31155	62319	76336	53250
of which : Stamp duty	545	948	2198	5799	3027	3973	6195	8201	11348	14175	18176	30578	32926	11332
Nontax revenue	1170	1914	3874	8705	13184	14981	20210	17690	22088	31340	64587	66675	52961	73042
Dividends[2]	441	957	2198	5799	8990	9490	9338	7406	6725	7624	15243	18376	5512	15489
Other[3]	729	957	1676	2906	4194	5491	10872	10284	15363	23716	49344	48299	47449	57553

1 Includes single trade transaction tax.
2 Includes dividends by the Bank of Tanzania
3 Includes collections by Treasury, other ministries and regions, and appropriations-in-aid.
Note: Detailed items for some fiscal years are unavailable. Thus, for example, sales tax on imports, excise tax on imports, import duties, payroll or manpower and property taxes could be included in income tax.
Source: Tanzania Authorities.

Table 5.2a. Share of Central Government Revenues
(percent)

	FY86	FY87	FY88	FY89	FY90	FY91	FY92	FY93	FY94	FY95	FY96	FY97	FY98	FY99
Total Revenue	**100.0**	**100.0**	**100.0**	**100.0**	**100.0**	**100.0**	**100.0**	**100.0**	**100.0**	**100.0**	**100.0**	**100.0**	**100.0**	**100.0**
Tax revenue	94.4	93.8	91.7	87.9	86.1	88.8	88.4	89.2	90.9	90.5	85.6	88.3	91.4	89.6
Income taxes	29.6	22.6	23.4	23.1	21.3	24.3	23.1	27.7	24.1	26.2	25.0	23.3	24.2	23.4
Individual/1	10.6	7.5	6.3	4.8	4.2	3.5	3.9	6.5	5.5	8.2	7.2	8.3	7.7	7.9
Company	18.4	13.8	16.1	17.1	16.3	7.4	5.4	8.7	15.8	13.0	11.4	9.6	8.8	10.0
Other	0.6	1.3	1.1	1.2	0.9	13.5	13.8	12.4	2.8	5.0	6.4	5.4	7.6	5.5
Payroll or manpower taxes	1.0	1.0	0.9	0.8	0.9	0.7	1.0	1.3	1.0	1.5	1.5	1.6	1.7	1.7
Payroll tax	0.9	0.9	0.9	0.7	0.8	0.7	0.9	1.1	1.0	1.3	1.4	1.5	1.7	1.7
Training levy	0.1	0.1	0.1	0.1	0.1	0.1	0.1	0.2	0.1	0.1	0.2	0.1	..	0.0
Property taxes	0.5	0.3	0.2	0.2	0.2	0.2	0.2	0.3	0.4	0.3	0.2	0.1	0.1	0.1
Land rent	0.3	0.2	0.2	0.1	0.1	0.1	0.1	0.2	0.1	0.1	0.1	..	..	0.0
Estate duty	0.0	0.0	0.0	0.0	0.0	0.0	0.0	0.0	0.0	0.0	0.0	0.0	..	0.0
Motor vehicle transfer tax	0.2	0.1	0.1	0.1	0.0	0.1	0.1	0.1	0.2	0.2	0.1	0.1	0.1	0.1
Consumption taxes on goods & services (local)	46.7	42.1	39.0	36.3	34.8	35.4	34.8	30.1	30.7	23.2	24.8	24.0	23.1	25.5
Local sales taxes	44.6	40.4	37.5	35.0	21.3	21.5	17.9	17.2	18.0	15.5	13.5	10.8	18.7	16.5
Excise taxes	..	..	..	..	12.1	12.3	15.5	10.9	11.0	6.5	9.8	13.8	9.3	8.3
Entertainment tax	0.2	0.1	0.1	0.1	0.0	0.0	0.0	0.0	0.0	0.0	0.0	0.0	0.0	0.0
Business licenses	0.4	0.1	0.1	0.2	0.2	0.3	0.3	0.4	0.3	0.3	0.3	0.0	0.5	0.4

(table continues on the next page)

Table 5.2a. *Share of Central Government Revenues (Cont'd)*

	FY86	FY87	FY88	FY89	FY90	FY91	FY92	FY93	FY94	FY95	FY96	FY97	FY98	FY99
Other licenses	0.1	0.1	0.1	0.1	0.1	0.1	0.1	0.2	0.0	0.0	0.0	0.0	0.0	0.0
Motor vehicle licenses	0.9	0.9	0.4	0.3	0.3	0.4	0.4	0.4	0.3	0.1	0.3	0.2	0.2	0.1
Motor vehicle registration	0.0	0.0	0.0	0.0	0.0	0.1	0.0	0.1	0.2	0.2	0.3	0.2	0.3	0.2
Hotel levy	0.5	0.5	0.7	0.7	0.8	0.7	0.6	0.8	0.8	0.6	0.6	0.0	0.0	0.0
Tax on international transactions	13.6	24.5	23.7	22.9	24.4	23.8	22.2	19.3	20.7	27.5	27.0	28.5	30.0	31.3
Import duties	7.0	12.9	12.0	11.8	12.6	13.0	12.2	9.9	11.7	..	13.7	14.3	14.2	12.6
Sales tax on imports	6.5	11.3	11.5	10.9	8.9	7.8	8.0	7.9	8.1	..	7.5	13.4	17.0	15.1
Excise tax on imports	..	..	..	..	2.7	2.8	2.1	1.5	0.9	..	5.8	3.9	4.1	3.6
Export duties	..	..	..	..			..	..	..	..	..	..	..	..
Foreign travel levy	0.1	0.2	0.2	0.2	0.2	0.2	..	..	..	..	..	..	..	..
Other taxes	2.9	3.3	4.4	4.5	4.5	4.2	7.0	10.5	13.9	11.9	6.9	10.9	12.3	7.6
of which: Stamp duty	2.6	3.0	4.7	8.1	3.2	3.0	3.6	5.0	4.7	4.3	4.1	5.3	5.3	1.6
Nontax revenue	5.6	6.2	8.3	12.1	13.9	11.2	11.6	10.8	9.1	9.5	14.4	11.7	8.6	10.4
Dividends/2	2.1	3.1	4.7	8.1	9.5	7.1	5.4	4.5	2.8	2.3	3.4	8.4	7.7	2.2
Other/3	3.5	3.1	3.6	4.0	4.4	4.1	6.3	6.3	6.3	7.2	11.0	8.4	7.7	8.2

1 Includes single trade transaction tax.
2 Includes dividends by the Bank of Tanzania.
3 Includes collections by Treasury, other ministries and regions, and appropriations-in-aid.
Note: Detailed items for some fiscal years are unavailable. Thus, for example, sales tax on imports, import duties, excise tax on imports, payroll or manpower and property taxes could be included in income taxes.
Source: Table 5.2.

Table 5.3. *Central Government Expenditure*
(millions of Tanzania shillings)

	FY86	FY87	FY88	FY89	FY90	FY91	FY92	FY93	FY94	FY95	FY96	FY97	FY98	FY99
Total Expenditure and Net Lending	32373	47445	73368	93994	126242	151863	194893	305059	370910	395607	420522	515098	567779	816222
Recurrent expenditure	26912	35146	51896	78119	103866	135375	162288	240349	296221	345915	415140	486202	543752	680959
Wages and salaries	8015	9004	11920	20128	26834	30439	37535	57946	73779	109680	156087	199228	218807	220478
Interest payments	2815	6480	10449	14649	16628	20101	23700	39414	51524	47520	59606	113647	101182	93999
Domestic	2033	4156	5480	6456	8441	8614	10564	22976	31725	25370	34160	75567	53215	33517
Foreign	782	2324	4969	8193	8187	11486	13136	16438	19799	22150	25446	38080	47967	60482
Other	16082	19662	29527	43342	60404	84835	101053	142989	170918	188715	199447	173327	223763	366482
Other goods and services	12729	15069	20774	30387	33051	61023	70585	142989	170918	188715	199447	173327	223763	366482
Transfers	3353	4593	8753	12955	27353	23812	30466	::	::	::	::	::	::	::
Crop Authorities[1]	715	715	1169	1500	3501	2872	::	::	::	::	::	::	::	::
Parastatals	::	::	1087	2061	4414	4134	::	::	::	::	::	::	::	::
Other domestic	2456	3448	6068	8472	14794	15555	::	::	::	::	::	::	::	::
Foreign	187	430	429	922	1588	1251	::	::	::	::	::	::	::	::
Development expenditure and Part of net lending	5461	12299	21472	15875	22376	16488	32605	64710	74689	49692	5382	28896	24027	135263

1 Includes Strategic Grain Reserve Management.
Source: Tanzanian authorities.

Table 5.3a. *Share of Central Government Expenditure* (percent)

	FY86	FY87	FY88	FY89	FY90	FY91	FY92	FY93	FY94	FY95	FY96	FY97	FY98	FY99
Total Expenditure and Net Lending	100.0	100.0	100.0	100.0	100.0	100.0	100.0	100.0	100.0	100.0	100.0	100.0	100.0	100.0
Recurrent expenditure	83.1	74.1	70.7	83.1	82.3	89.1	83.3	78.8	79.9	87.4	98.7	94.4	95.8	83.4
Wages and salaries	24.8	19.0	16.2	21.4	21.3	20.0	19.3	19.0	19.9	27.7	37.1	38.7	38.5	27.0
Interest payments	8.7	13.7	14.2	15.6	13.2	13.2	12.2	12.9	13.9	12.0	14.2	22.1	17.8	11.5
Domestic	6.3	8.8	7.5	6.9	6.7	5.7	5.4	7.5	8.6	6.4	8.1	14.7	9.4	4.1
Foreign	2.4	4.9	6.8	8.7	6.5	7.6	6.7	5.4	5.3	5.6	6.1	7.4	8.4	7.4
Other	49.7	41.4	40.2	46.1	47.8	55.9	51.9	46.9	46.1	47.7	47.4	33.6	39.4	44.9
Other goods and services	39.3	31.8	28.3	32.3	26.2	40.2	36.2	..	..	..	..	..	..	..
Transfers	10.4	9.7	11.9	13.8	21.7	15.7	15.6	..	..	..	..	..	..	..
Crop Authorities/1	2.2	1.5	1.6	1.6	2.8	1.9	..	..	..	..	..	..	..	..
Parastatals	..	..	1.5	2.2	3.5	2.7	..	..	..	..	..	..	..	..
Other domestic	7.6	7.3	8.3	9.0	11.7	10.2	..	..	..	..	..	..	..	..
Foreign	0.6	0.9	0.6	1.0	1.3	0.8	..	..	..	..	..	..	..	..
Development expenditure and Part of net lending	16.9	25.9	29.3	16.9	17.7	10.9	16.7	21.2	20.1	12.6	1.3	5.6	4.2	16.6

1 Includes Strategic Grain Reserve Management.
Source: Table 5.3

Table 5.4. *Central Government Expenditure by Economic Function* (millions of Tanzania shillings)

	FY86	FY87	FY88	FY89	FY90	FY91	FY92	FY93	FY94	FY95	FY96	FY97	FY98*	FY99**
Recurrent	27081	40863	62107	93365	117992	160001	172645	260242	312712	362799	470016	606309	683181	764537
General public services[1]	9048	12114	18408	26671	39458	42385	49427	89761	110757	106000	141918	183071	173679	199914
Defense	4428	6335	6709	9109	11419	10561	15401	19668	16926	30272	40937	52808	82430	81965
Social services	4101	5890	8677	12328	16575	23651	26831	43075	54707	44263	49690	64099	151821	184084
Education	1883	2491	3364	5403	8001	11453	14062	19888	25464	18608	24122	31117	105189	125714
Health	1427	2115	3115	4256	6274	7860	9601	15737	20054	21762	17572	22667	41346	52285
Other social services[2]	791	1283	2197	2669	2301	4338	3168	7450	9189	3893	7996	10315	5286	6085
Economic services	2452	3894	4969	7806	10351	14591	15346	18505	24397	29122	31407	40513	56926	76000
Agriculture, fishing and Forestry	911	1353	1627	2731	3179	4852	6002	5554	7489	7430	6308	8137	15926	19889
Mining, manufacturing and Construction	285	264	346	421	1415	1378	1110	1238	4722	1537	1302	1679	1396	2215
Water and electricity	220	452	566	1042	1400	1677	2054	2693	3265	2739	410	528	891	2019
Roads and bridges	450	794	920	1499	1685	3097	1676	510	660	12302	..	..	..	..
Transport and communication	329	649	975	1304	1266	2027	2367	3502	4242	1701	17987	23203	30254	45018
Other economic service	258	382	536	808	1407	1561	2138	5008	4019	3413	5400	6966	8459	6859
Others[3]	7052	12631	23345	37453	40190	68813	65640	89233	105925	153142	206064	265818	218325	222574
Public debt	6699	12392	22976	33767	34471	61784	57369	75825	80468	121134	..	..	168046	169930

(table continues on the next page)

300

Table 5.4. Central Government Expenditure by Economic Function (Cont'd)

	FY86	FY87	FY88	FY89	FY90	FY91	FY92	FY93	FY94	FY95	FY96	FY97	FY98*	FY99**
Development	6221	8859	10890	17857	16699	46999	35600	76612	95725	151486	30103	124570	230881	264566
General public services[1]	842	1485	1951	2799	2657	6142	4641	5471	5846	9489	3591	14860	102709	52347
Defense	551	865	928	966	153	2259	2819	3203	3015	2400	0	0	0	0
Social services	712	1120	1364	3175	2778	7351	8158	10331	17575	33238	14468	59869	41060	68953
Education	421	700	626	935	867	2930	2509	5258	5376	20357	9904	40983	10583	14169
Health	65	142	158	1253	359	2353	3725	3308	9207	10412	920	3805	18224	14693
Other social services[2]	227	277	580	987	1553	2069	1924	1765	2992	2469	3644	15081	12253	40091
Economic services	4115	5389	6647	10918	11110	31247	19982	57607	69289	106359	11906	49270	86866	143118
Agriculture, fishing and Forestry	1041	1845	2054	3306	2724	7028	4980	8064	10022	14543	1301	5385	11436	22582
Mining, manufacturing and Construction	1201	1146	1457	1947	1139	4913	2890	4110	3736	4463	6901	28557	1308	8053
Water and electricity	269	548	768	1444	1704	3912	2171	2909	19936	24100	0	0	14642	23780
Roads and bridges	559	679	1229	1211	2447	6265	6175	19950	25958	27294	..	..	..	..
Transport and communication	439	561	402	1159	408	5487	2703	17672	5884	30716	2566	10617	40520	59942
Other economic service	606	610	737	1851	2689	3643	1064	4902	3753	5243	1138	4711	18960	28761
Others[3]	..	..	..	..	..	..	..	..	..	..	138	571	246	148

Table 5.4. *Central Government Expenditure by Economic Function (Cont'd)*

	FY86	FY87	FY88	FY89	FY90	FY91	FY92	FY93	FY94	FY95	FY96	FY97	FY98*	FY99**
Total Expenditure	**33302**	**49722**	**72997**	**111223**	**134691**	**207000**	**208245**	**336854**	**408437**	**514285**	**500119**	**730879**	**914062**	**1029103**
General public services[1]	9890	13598	20359	29469	42115	48527	54068	95232	116603	115489	145509	197931	276388	252261
Defense	4979	7200	7636	10074	11572	12820	18220	22871	19941	32672	40937	52808	82430	81965
Social services	4813	7009	10041	15503	19353	31002	34989	53406	72282	77501	64158	123968	192881	253037
Education	2303	3191	3990	6338	8868	14383	16571	25146	30840	38965	34026	72100	115772	139883
Health	1492	2257	3273	5509	6632	10213	13326	19045	29261	32174	18492	26472	59570	66978
Other social services[2]	1018	1561	2777	3657	3853	6406	5092	9215	12181	6362	11640	25396	17539	46176
Economic services	6568	9283	11616	18724	21461	45838	35328	76112	93686	135481	43313	89783	143792	219118
Agriculture, fishing and Forestry	1951	3198	3680	6037	5903	11880	10981	13618	17511	21973	7609	13522	27362	42471
Mining, manufacturing and Construction	1487	1410	1803	2368	2554	6290	4000	5348	8458	6000	8203	30236	2704	10268
Water and electricity	489	1000	1334	2486	3103	5589	4225	5602	23201	26839	410	528	15533	25799
Roads and bridges	1009	1473	2148	2711	4131	9362	7851	20460	26618	39596	..	..	..	..
Transport and communication	768	1210	1377	2464	1674	7513	5070	21174	10126	32417	20553	33820	70774	104960
Other economic service	864	992	1273	2659	4096	5204	3201	9910	7772	8656	6538	11677	27419	35620
Others[3]	7052	12631	23345	37453	40190	68813	65640	89233	105925	153142	206202	266389	218571	222722
Public debt	6699	12392	22976	33767	34471	61784	57369	75825	80468	121134	..	..	168046	169930

1 Includes general administration, external affairs and public order and safety.
2 Including housing, community amenities, community development and sanitary services.
3 Includes public debt, financial and capital subscriptions, and pension and gratuity
* Adjusted estimates.
** Estimates.
Note: The expenditure figures are different from those in the preceding tables due to the different source.
Source: The Planning Commission, The United Republic of Tanzania, *The Economic Survey* (various issues).

Table 5.4a. Share of Total Central Government Expenditure by Economic Function (percent)

	FY86	FY87	FY88	FY89	FY90	FY91	FY92	FY93	FY94	FY95	FY96	FY97	FY98*	FY99**
Recurrent	**81.3**	**82.2**	**85.1**	**83.9**	**87.6**	**77.3**	**82.9**	**77.3**	**76.6**	**70.5**	**94.0**	**83.0**	**74.7**	**74.3**
General public services[1]	27.2	24.4	25.2	24.0	29.3	20.5	23.7	26.6	27.1	20.6	28.4	25.0	19.0	19.4
Defense	13.3	12.7	9.2	8.2	8.5	5.1	7.4	5.8	4.1	5.9	8.2	7.2	9.0	8.0
Social services	12.3	11.8	11.9	11.1	12.3	11.4	12.9	12.8	13.4	8.6	9.9	8.8	16.6	17.9
Education	5.7	5.0	4.6	4.9	5.9	5.5	6.8	5.9	6.2	3.6	4.8	4.3	11.5	12.2
Health	4.3	4.3	4.3	3.8	4.7	3.8	4.6	4.7	4.9	4.2	3.5	3.1	4.5	5.1
Other social services[2]	2.4	2.6	3.0	2.4	1.7	2.1	1.5	2.2	2.2	0.8	1.6	1.4	0.6	0.6
Economic services	7.4	7.8	6.8	7.0	7.7	7.0	7.4	5.5	6.0	5.7	6.3	5.5	6.2	7.4
Agriculture, fishing and Forestry	2.7	2.7	2.2	2.5	2.4	2.3	2.9	1.6	1.8	1.4	1.3	1.1	1.7	1.9
Mining, manufacturing and Construction	0.9	0.5	0.5	0.4	1.1	0.7	0.5	0.4	1.2	0.3	0.3	0.2	0.2	0.2
Water and electricity	0.7	0.9	0.8	0.9	1.0	0.8	1.0	0.8	0.8	0.5	0.1	0.1	0.1	0.2
Roads and bridges	1.4	1.6	1.3	1.3	1.3	1.5	0.8	0.2	0.2	2.4				
Transport and communication	1.0	1.3	1.3	1.2	0.9	1.0	1.1	1.0	1.0	0.3	3.6	3.2	3.3	4.4
Other economic service	0.8	0.8	0.7	0.7	1.0	0.8	1.0	1.5	1.0	0.7	1.1	1.0	0.9	0.7
Others[3]	21.2	25.4	32.0	33.7	29.8	33.2	31.5	26.5	25.9	29.8	41.2	36.4	23.9	21.6
Public debt	20.1	24.9	31.5	30.4	25.6	29.8	27.5	22.5	19.7	23.6	..	..	18.4	16.5

Table 5.4a. Share of Total Central Government Expenditure by Economic Function (Cont'd)

	FY86	FY87	FY88	FY89	FY90	FY91	FY92	FY93	FY94	FY95	FY96	FY97	FY98*	FY99**
Development	**18.7**	**17.8**	**14.9**	**16.1**	**12.4**	**22.7**	**17.1**	**22.7**	**23.4**	**29.5**	**6.0**	**17.0**	**25.3**	**25.7**
General public services[1]	2.5	3.0	2.7	2.5	2.0	3.0	2.2	1.6	1.4	1.8	0.7	2.0	11.2	5.1
Defense	1.7	1.7	1.3	0.9	0.1	1.1	1.4	1.0	0.7	0.5	0.0	0.0	0.0	0.0
Social services	2.1	2.3	1.9	2.9	2.1	3.6	3.9	3.1	4.3	6.5	2.9	8.2	4.5	6.7
Education	1.3	1.4	0.9	0.8	0.6	1.4	1.2	1.6	1.3	4.0	2.0	5.6	1.2	1.4
Health	0.2	0.3	0.2	1.1	0.3	1.1	1.8	1.0	2.3	2.0	0.2	0.5	2.0	1.4
Other social services[2]	0.7	0.6	0.8	0.9	1.2	1.0	0.9	0.5	0.7	0.5	0.7	2.1	1.3	3.9
Economic services	12.4	10.8	9.1	9.8	8.2	15.1	9.6	17.1	17.0	20.7	2.4	6.7	9.5	13.9
Agriculture, fishing and Forestry	3.1	3.7	2.8	3.0	2.0	3.4	2.4	2.4	2.5	2.8	0.3	0.7	1.3	2.2
Mining, manufacturing and Construction	3.6	2.3	2.0	1.8	0.8	2.4	1.4	1.2	0.9	0.9	1.4	3.9	0.1	0.8
Water and electricity	0.8	1.1	1.1	1.3	1.3	1.9	1.0	0.9	4.9	4.7	0.0	0.0	1.6	2.3
Roads and bridges	1.7	1.4	1.7	1.1	1.8	3.0	3.0	5.9	6.4	5.3				
Transport and communication	1.3	1.1	0.6	1.0	0.3	2.7	1.3	5.2	1.4	6.0	0.5	1.5	4.4	5.8
Other economic service	1.8	1.2	1.0	1.7	2.0	1.8	0.5	1.5	0.9	1.0	0.2	0.6	2.1	2.8
Others[3]	..	..	..	..	..	..	..	..	..	..	0.0	0.1	0.0	0.0

(table continues on the next page)

Table 5.4a. Share of Total Central Government Expenditure by Economic Function (Cont'd)

	FY86	FY87	FY88	FY89	FY90	FY91	FY92	FY93	FY94	FY95	FY96	FY97	FY98*	FY99**
Total Expenditure	100.0	100.0	100.0	100.0	100.0	100.0	100.0	100.0	100.0	100.0	100.0	100.0	100.0	100.0
General public services [1]	29.7	27.3	27.9	26.5	31.3	23.4	26.0	28.3	28.5	22.5	29.1	27.1	30.2	24.5
Defense	15.0	14.5	10.5	9.1	8.6	6.2	8.7	6.8	4.9	6.4	8.2	7.2	9.0	8.0
Social services	14.5	14.1	13.8	13.9	14.4	15.0	16.8	15.9	17.7	15.1	12.8	17.0	21.1	24.6
Education	6.9	6.4	5.5	5.7	6.6	6.9	8.0	7.5	7.6	7.6	6.8	9.9	12.7	13.6
Health	4.5	4.5	4.5	5.0	4.9	4.9	6.4	5.7	7.2	6.3	3.7	3.6	6.5	6.5
Other social services [2]	3.1	3.1	3.8	3.3	2.9	3.1	2.4	2.7	3.0	1.2	2.3	3.5	1.9	4.5
Economic services	19.7	18.7	15.9	16.8	15.9	22.1	17.0	22.6	22.9	26.3	8.7	12.3	15.7	21.3
Agriculture, fishing and Forestry	5.9	6.4	5.0	5.4	4.4	5.7	5.3	4.0	4.3	4.3	1.5	1.9	3.0	4.1
Mining, manufacturing and Construction	4.5	2.8	2.5	2.1	1.9	3.0	1.9	1.6	2.1	1.2	1.6	4.1	0.3	1.0
Water and electricity	1.5	2.0	1.8	2.2	2.3	2.7	2.0	1.7	5.7	5.2	0.1	0.1	1.7	2.5
Roads and bridges	3.0	3.0	2.9	2.4	3.1	4.5	3.8	6.1	6.5	7.7	4.1	4.6	7.7	10.2
Transport and communication	2.3	2.4	1.9	2.2	1.2	3.6	2.4	6.3	2.5	6.3	1.3	1.6	3.0	3.5
Other economic service	2.6	2.0	1.7	2.4	3.0	2.5	1.5	2.9	1.9	1.7				
Others [3]	21.2	25.4	32.0	33.7	29.8	33.2	31.5	26.5	25.9	29.8	41.2	36.4	23.9	21.6
Public debt	20.1	24.9	31.5	30.4	25.6	29.8	27.5	22.5	19.7	23.6	..		18.4	16.5

1 Includes general administration, external affairs and public order and safety.
2 Including housing, community amenities, community development and sanitary services.
3 Includes public debt, financial and capital subscriptions, and pension and gratuity.
* Adjusted estimates.
** Estimates.

Table 5.4b. *Distribution of Central Government Expenditure by Economic Function*
(percent)

Recurrent	FY86	FY87	FY88	FY89	FY90	FY91	FY92	FY93	FY94	FY95	FY96	FY97	FY98*	FY99**
	100.0	100.0	100.0	100.0	100.0	100.0	100.0	100.0	100.0	100.0	100.0	100.0	100.0	100.0
General public services[1]	33.4	29.6	29.6	28.6	33.4	26.5	28.6	34.5	35.4	29.2	30.2	30.2	25.4	26.1
Defense	16.4	15.5	10.8	9.8	9.7	6.6	8.9	7.6	5.4	8.3	8.7	8.7	12.1	10.7
Social services	15.1	14.4	14.0	13.2	14.0	14.8	15.5	16.6	17.5	12.2	10.6	10.6	22.2	24.1
Education	7.0	6.1	5.4	5.8	6.8	7.2	8.1	7.6	8.1	5.1	5.1	5.1	15.4	16.4
Health	5.3	5.2	5.0	4.6	5.3	4.9	5.6	6.0	6.4	6.0	3.7	3.7	6.1	6.8
Other social services[2]	2.9	3.1	3.5	2.9	1.9	2.7	1.8	2.9	2.9	1.1	1.7	1.7	0.8	0.8
Economic services	9.1	9.5	8.0	8.4	8.8	9.1	8.9	7.1	7.8	8.0	6.7	6.7	8.3	9.9
Agriculture, fishing and Forestry	3.4	3.3	2.6	2.9	2.7	3.0	3.5	2.1	2.4	2.0	1.3	1.3	2.3	2.6
Mining, manufacturing and Construction	1.1	0.6	0.6	0.5	1.2	0.9	0.6	0.5	1.5	0.4	0.3	0.3	0.2	0.3
Water and electricity	0.8	1.1	0.9	1.1	1.2	1.0	1.2	1.0	1.0	0.8	0.1	0.1	0.1	0.3
Roads and bridges	1.7	1.9	1.5	1.6	1.4	1.9	1.0	0.2	0.2	3.4	..	..	..	..
Transport and communication	1.2	1.6	1.6	1.4	1.1	1.3	1.4	1.3	1.4	0.5	3.8	3.8	4.4	5.9
Other economic service	1.0	0.9	0.9	0.9	1.2	1.0	1.2	1.9	1.3	0.9	1.1	1.1	1.2	0.9
Others[3]	26.0	30.9	37.6	40.1	34.1	43.0	38.0	34.3	33.9	42.2	43.8	43.8	32.0	29.1
Public debt	24.7	30.3	37.0	36.2	29.2	38.6	33.2	29.1	25.7	33.4	..	..	..	..

(table continues on the next page)

Table 5.4b. Distribution of Central Government Expenditure by Economic Function (Cont'd)

Development	FY86	FY87	FY88	FY89	FY90	FY91	FY92	FY93	FY94	FY95	FY96	FY97	FY98*	FY99**
	100.0	100.0	100.0	100.0	100.0	100.0	100.0	100.0	100.0	100.0	100.0	100.0	100.0	100.0
General public services[1]	13.5	16.8	17.9	15.7	15.9	13.1	13.0	7.1	6.1	6.3	11.9	11.9	44.5	19.8
Defense	8.9	9.8	8.5	5.4	0.9	4.8	7.9	4.2	3.1	1.6	0.0	0.0	0.0	0.0
Social services	11.4	12.6	12.5	17.8	16.6	15.6	22.9	13.5	18.4	21.9	48.1	48.1	17.8	26.1
Education	6.8	7.9	5.7	5.2	5.2	6.2	7.0	6.9	5.6	13.4	32.9	32.9	4.6	5.4
Health	1.0	1.6	1.5	7.0	2.1	5.0	10.5	4.3	9.6	6.9	3.1	3.1	7.9	5.6
Other social services[2]	3.6	3.1	5.3	5.5	9.3	4.4	5.4	2.3	3.1	1.6	12.1	12.1	5.3	15.2
Economic services	66.2	60.8	61.0	61.1	66.5	66.5	56.1	75.2	72.4	70.2	39.6	39.6	37.6	54.1
Agriculture, fishing and Forestry	16.7	20.8	18.9	18.5	16.3	15.0	14.0	10.5	10.5	9.6	4.3	4.3	5.0	8.5
Mining, manufacturing and Construction	19.3	12.9	13.4	10.9	6.8	10.5	8.1	5.4	3.9	2.9	22.9	22.9	0.6	3.0
Water and electricity	4.3	6.2	7.1	8.1	10.2	8.3	6.1	3.8	20.8	15.9	0.0	0.0	6.3	9.0
Roads and bridges	9.0	7.7	11.3	6.8	14.7	13.3	17.3	26.0	27.1	18.0	..	..	..	..
Transport and communication	7.1	6.3	3.7	6.5	2.4	11.7	7.6	23.1	6.1	20.3	8.5	8.5	17.6	22.7
Other economic service	9.7	6.9	6.8	10.4	16.1	7.8	3.0	6.4	3.9	3.5	3.8	3.8	8.2	10.9
	0.0													
Others[3]	..	..	..	..	..	..	..	..	..	..	0.5	0.5	0.1	0.1

1 Includes general administration, external affairs and public order and safety.
2 Including housing, community amenities, community development and sanitary services.
3 Includes public debt, financial and capital subscriptions, and pension and gratuity.
* Adjusted estimates.
** Estimates.
Source: Table 5.4.

Table 5.4c. Central Government Expenditure by Economic Function as Share of GDP (percent)

	FY86	FY87	FY88	FY89	FY90	FY91	FY92	FY93	FY94	FY95	FY96	FY97	FY98*
Recurrent	**9.9**	**13.5**	**14.9**	**16.4**	**16.1**	**16.7**	**14.1**	**16.8**	**15.5**	**13.6**	**13.8**	**14.3**	**13.3**
General public services[1]	3.3	4.0	4.4	4.7	5.4	4.4	4.0	5.8	5.5	4.0	4.2	4.3	3.4
Defense	1.6	2.1	1.6	1.6	1.6	1.1	1.3	1.3	0.8	1.1	1.2	1.2	1.6
Social services	1.5	1.9	2.1	2.2	2.3	2.5	2.2	2.8	2.7	1.7	1.5	1.5	3.0
Education	0.7	0.8	0.8	0.9	1.1	1.2	1.1	1.3	1.3	0.7	0.7	0.7	2.0
Health	0.5	0.7	0.7	0.7	0.9	0.8	0.8	1.0	1.0	0.8	0.5	0.5	0.8
Other social services[2]	0.3	0.4	0.5	0.5	0.3	0.5	0.3	0.5	0.5	0.1	0.2	0.2	0.1
Economic services	0.9	1.3	1.2	1.4	1.4	1.5	1.2	1.2	1.2	1.1	0.9	1.0	1.1
Agriculture, fishing and Forestry	0.3	0.4	0.4	0.5	0.4	0.5	0.5	0.4	0.4	0.3	0.2	0.2	0.3
Mining, manufacturing and Construction	0.1	0.1	0.1	0.1	0.2	0.1	0.1	0.1	0.2	0.1	0.0	0.0	0.0
Water and electricity	0.1	0.1	0.1	0.2	0.2	0.2	0.2	0.2	0.2	0.1	0.0	0.0	0.0
Roads and bridges	0.2	0.3	0.2	0.3	0.2	0.3	0.1	0.0	0.0	0.5	:	:	:
Transport and communication	0.1	0.2	0.2	0.2	0.2	0.2	0.2	0.2	0.2	0.1	0.5	0.5	0.6
Other economic service	0.1	0.1	0.1	0.1	0.2	0.2	0.2	0.3	0.2	0.1	0.2	0.2	0.2
Others[3]	2.6	4.2	5.6	6.6	5.5	7.2	5.3	5.8	5.3	5.8	6.1	6.3	4.2
Public debt	2.4	4.1	5.5	5.9	4.7	6.4	4.7	4.9	4.0	4.6	:	:	:

(table continues on the next page)

Table 5.4c. Central Government Expenditure by Economic Function as Share of GDP (Cont'd)

	FY86	FY87	FY88	FY89	FY90	FY91	FY92	FY93	FY94	FY95	FY96	FY97	FY98*
Development	2.3	2.9	2.6	3.1	2.3	4.9	2.9	5.0	4.8	5.7	0.9	2.9	4.5
General public services[1]	0.0	0.0	0.0	0.0	0.0	0.0	0.0	0.0	0.0	0.0	0.0	0.0	0.0
Defense	0.3	0.5	0.5	0.5	0.4	0.6	0.4	0.4	0.3	0.4	0.1	0.4	2.0
	0.2	0.3	0.2	0.2	0.0	0.2	0.2	0.2	0.1	0.1	0.0	0.0	0.0
Social services	0.3	0.4	0.3	0.6	0.4	0.8	0.7	0.7	0.9	1.2	0.4	1.4	0.8
Education	0.2	0.2	0.1	0.2	0.1	0.3	0.2	0.3	0.3	0.8	0.3	1.0	0.2
Health	0.0	0.0	0.0	0.2	0.0	0.2	0.3	0.2	0.5	0.4	0.0	0.1	0.4
Other social services[2]	0.1	0.1	0.1	0.2	0.2	0.2	0.2	0.1	0.1	0.1	0.1	0.4	0.2
Economic services	1.5	1.8	1.6	1.9	1.5	3.3	1.6	3.7	3.4	4.0	0.4	1.2	1.7
Agriculture, fishing and Forestry	0.4	0.6	0.5	0.6	0.4	0.7	0.4	0.5	0.5	0.5	0.0	0.1	0.2
Mining, manufacturing and Construction	0.4	0.4	0.3	0.3	0.2	0.5	0.2	0.3	0.2	0.2	0.2	0.7	0.0
Water and electricity	0.1	0.2	0.2	0.3	0.2	0.4	0.2	0.2	1.0	0.9	0.0	0.0	0.3
Roads and bridges	0.2	0.2	0.3	0.2	0.3	0.7	0.5	1.3	1.3	1.0	..	..	..
Transport and communication	0.2	0.2	0.1	0.2	0.1	0.6	0.2	1.1	0.3	1.2	0.1	0.3	0.8
Other economic service	0.2	0.2	0.2	0.3	0.4	0.4	0.1	0.3	0.2	0.2	0.0	0.1	0.4

Table 5.4c. Central Government Expenditure by Economic Function as Share of GDP (Cont'd)

	FY86	FY87	FY88	FY89	FY90	FY91	FY92	FY93	FY94	FY95	FY96	FY97	FY98*
Total Expenditure	**12.2**	**16.4**	**17.5**	**19.5**	**18.4**	**21.6**	**17.0**	**21.8**	**20.3**	**19.3**	**14.7**	**17.2**	**17.8**
	0.0	0.0	0.0	0.0	0.0	0.0	0.0	0.0	0.0	0.0	0.0	0.0	0.0
General public services[1]	3.6	4.5	4.9	5.2	5.8	5.1	4.4	6.2	5.8	4.3	4.3	4.7	5.4
Defense	1.8	2.4	1.8	1.8	1.6	1.3	1.5	1.5	1.0	1.2	1.2	1.2	1.6
Social services	1.8	2.3	2.4	2.7	2.6	3.2	2.8	3.5	3.6	2.9	1.9	2.9	3.8
Education	0.8	1.1	1.0	1.1	1.2	1.5	1.3	1.6	1.5	1.5	1.0	1.7	2.3
Health	0.5	0.7	0.8	1.0	0.9	1.1	1.1	1.2	1.5	1.2	0.5	0.6	1.2
Other social services[2]	0.4	0.5	0.7	0.6	0.5	0.7	0.4	0.6	0.6	0.2	0.3	0.6	0.3
Economic services	2.4	3.1	2.8	3.3	2.9	4.8	2.9	4.9	4.7	5.1	1.3	2.1	2.8
Agriculture, fishing and Forestry	0.7	1.1	0.9	1.1	0.8	1.2	0.9	0.9	0.9	0.8	0.2	0.3	0.5
Mining, manufacturing and Construction	0.5	0.5	0.4	0.4	0.3	0.7	0.3	0.3	0.4	0.2	0.2	0.7	0.1
Water and electricity	0.2	0.3	0.3	0.4	0.4	0.6	0.3	0.4	1.2	1.0	0.0	0.0	0.3
Roads and bridges	0.4	0.5	0.5	0.5	0.6	1.0	0.6	1.3	1.3	1.5	..	..	..
Transport and communication	0.3	0.4	0.3	0.4	0.2	0.8	0.4	1.4	0.5	1.2	0.6	0.8	1.4
Other economic service	0.3	0.3	0.3	0.5	0.6	0.5	0.3	0.6	0.4	0.3	0.2	0.3	0.5
Others[3]	2.6	4.2	5.6	6.6	5.5	7.2	5.3	5.8	5.3	5.8	6.1	6.3	4.3
Public debt	2.4	4.1	5.5	5.9	4.7	6.4	4.7	4.9	4.0	4.6	..	..	..

1 Includes general administration, external affairs and public order and safety.
2 Including housing, community amenities, community development and sanitary services.
3 Includes public debt, financial and capital subscriptions, and pension and gratuity.
* Adjusted estimates.
Source: Table 5.4.

310

6. Monetary Survey

Table 6.1. Monetary Survey

	FY86	FY87	FY88	FY89	FY90	FY91	FY92	FY93	FY94	FY95	FY96	FY97	FY98	FY99
Net foreign assets	..	-17459	-15466	-31731	-19581	8091	50082	36482	78599	150179	204147	372876	411235	472342
Assets	..	..	..	-9405	1663	21761	63752	50152	214874	301048	362083	538730	581912	718936
Bank of Tanzania	..	..	..	-13891	-5270	20351	57595	25056	159111	153795	148894	287672	334402	445798
Commercial banks	..	..	..	4486	6933	1409	6157	25096	55763	147253	213189	251058	247510	273138
Liabilities	..	..	..	22327	21244	13670	13670	13670	136275	150869	157936	165854	170677	246594
Bank of Tanzania	..	..	..	12952	11869	4295	4295	4295	132552	143329	153375	162423	168813	246088
Commercial banks	..	..	..	9375	9375	9375	9375	9375	3723	7540	4561	3431	1864	506
Medium-term foreign liabilities	..	4645	22762	39443	53484	47793	49915	49521	43227	39981	44192	43865	43587	43613
Net domestic assets	49895	62568	91857	135636	174590	185683	227383	341470	443664	548987	593202	587541	640587	669773
Domestic credit	49675	63359	96519	129938	157879	181012	181580	272145	414388	474221	435285	417549	454032	593606
Public sector	..	..	..	108336	131379	140294	128370	193811	239497	302611	331368	306386	265340	320562
Government (net)	32271	33928	52029	57451	60284	48756	50220	93309	151141	212149	305905	287547	255353	314109
Non-financial public Enterprises	17404	29432	44490	50885	71095	91537	78150	100502	88356	90462	25463	18839	9987	6453
Private sector	..	..	..	21602	26500	40718	53209	78334	170891	171610	103917	111163	188692	273044
Other items (net)	220	-791	-4662	5698	16712	4671	45803	69325	29276	74766	157917	169992	186555	76167
External arrears counterpart	..	..	..	-52436	-7574	..	..	..	..	..	..	..	..	..
Broad money (M3)	38735	46566	62794	86219	125344	159058	223483	321481	470289	640148	744177	879394	947394	1034895
Money	25573	32233	44785	60137	83346	102811	141273	191261	262176	338176	383564	472621	481642	508994
Quasi-money	13162	14333	18009	26082	41998	56247	82210	130220	208113	301973	360613	407341	465752	525900
Valuation	-3304	-6102	-9165	-13100	-16245	-13077	4067	6950	8748	6890	8579	36890	59834	63570

Note: Ending June 30 unless indicated otherwise; prior to June 1988, domestic credit to private sector was included in non-financial public enterprises; from December 1993 the monetary survey includes all commercial banks.

Source: Bank of Tanzania.

Table 6.1a. *Change in Money Supply and Sources of Change*

	FY88	FY89	FY90	FY91	FY92	FY93	FY94	FY95	FY96	FY97	FY98	FY99
Net foreign assets	..	4.3	-25.9	14.1	22.1	26.4	-6.1	13.1	15.2	8.4	22.7	4.4
Medium-term foreign liabilities	..	-46.8	-35.8	-22.4	6.6	-1.7	0.2	2.8	1.0	-0.9	0.1	0.0
Net domestic assets	32.7	62.9	69.7	45.2	8.8	26.2	51.0	31.8	22.4	6.9	-0.8	6.0
Domestic credit	35.3	71.2	53.2	32.4	18.5	0.4	40.5	44.2	12.7	-6.1	-2.4	4.1
Public sector	..	..	..	26.7	7.1	-7.5	29.3	14.2	13.4	4.5	-3.4	-4.7
Government (net)	4.3	38.9	8.6	3.3	-9.2	0.9	19.3	18.0	13.0	14.6	-2.5	-3.7
Non-financial public Enterprises	31.1	32.3	10.2	23.4	16.3	-8.4	10.0	-3.8	0.4	-10.2	-0.9	-1.0
Private sector	..	..	..	5.7	11.3	7.9	11.2	28.8	0.2	-10.6	1.0	8.8
Other items (net)	-2.6	-8.3	16.5	12.8	-9.6	25.9	10.5	-12.5	9.7	13.0	1.6	1.9
External arrears counterpart	..	..	..	52.0	..	..	..	..	..	..	..	..
Broad money (M3)	20.2	34.8	37.3	45.4	26.9	40.5	43.9	46.3	36.1	16.3	18.2	7.7
Money	17.2	27.0	24.4	26.9	15.5	24.2	22.4	22.1	16.2	7.1	12.0	1.0
Quasi-money	3.0	7.9	12.9	18.5	11.4	16.3	21.5	24.2	20.0	9.2	6.3	6.6
Valuation	-7.2	-6.6	-6.3	-3.6	2.5	10.8	1.3	0.6	-0.4	0.3	3.8	2.6

Note: Ending June 30 unless indicated otherwise; prior to June 1988, domestic credit to private sector was included in non-financial public enterprises; from December 1993 the monetary survey includes all commercial banks.
Source: Table 6.1.

Table 6.2. *Balance Sheet of Bank of Tanzania*
(millions of Tanzania shillings)

	1985	1986	1987	1988	1989	1990	1991	1992	1993	1994	1995	1996	1997	1998	1999
Assets	32674	46829	95778	156389	202851	224939	379680	511828	773606	912619	982722	977544	898828	924765	1036680
Foreign assets	264	2870	2725	9724	10645	24523	98251	129270	111688	154467	178572	155449	287821	325211	441902
Foreign exchange	264	2247	2650	9710	10425	24189	42763	110773	87939	129180	160596	137541	268582	304402	418474
Gold reserves	0	0	0	0	0	0	55387	18452	23653	21491	17929	17596	19187	20622	23182
SDR holdings	0	623	75	14	220	334	101	45	96	3796	47	312	52	187	246
Quota in IMF resources	1875	6360	11101	17865	28209	27433	32274	46107	80953	110700	138267	131441	127732	129942	195601
Claims on government	24565	30953	33697	33020	44470	40340	31901	28218	140298	245962	310747	306512	288702	250107	232759
Loans and advances	4391	0	501	1416	11670	7575	2396	420	41643	600	64838	0	0	0	0
Treasury bills	7	8866	8866	0	0	0	0	0	0	0	0	0	0	0	0
Other securities	20167	22087	24330	31604	32800	32765	29505	27798	98655	245362	245909	306512	288702	250107	232759
Lending to banks	11	1726	19782	43982	49523	51131	5798	2502	2480	0	5455	5455	4613	4611	2590
Revaluation	948	2733	18986	39728	49539	61775	117861	174525	265227	291016	285533	286293	80626	76343	60329
Others	5275	5057	12212	21794	31110	44260	191846	260476	284648	264941	242721	247843	397155	463762	545401
Liabilities	32674	46829	95778	156389	202851	224939	379680	511828	773606	912619	982722	977544	898828	924765	1036678
Currency in circulation	13557	19452	26329	33817	43762	47633	55866	80610	82707	133851	197701	233116	276861	296539	306836
Central Gov't deposits	-81	1611	2229	289	-1124	-373	5332	30063	27257	38751	39106	53247	70917	78684	59093
Banks deposits	473	270	1554	2360	-6034	-15754	-35604	-65693	26172	30688	64060	39901	60140	83587	80630
Foreign liabilities	2935	7614	29724	68257	96087	112342	187068	292277	362403	445188	432454	404809	210024	169093	248398
Use of IMF resources	2211	6615	11796	20022	26590	35355	32956	45340	70981	97146	118605	109275	112859	122440	180886
Allocation of SDRs	550	1865	3255	5238	8271	8027	9486	13518	17288	23641	29528	28071	27279	27751	30852
Other	13029	9402	20891	26406	35299	37709	124576	115713	186798	143354	101268	109125	140748	146671	129983

Note: Year ending June 30.
Source: Bank of Tanzania, Economic and Operations Report for the Year Ended June 1999.

Table 6.3. *Balance Sheet of Commercial Banks*
(millions of Tanzania shillings)

	1985	1986	1987	1988	1989	1990	1991	1992	1993	1994	1995	1996	1997	1998	1999
Assets	35681	42377	77151	126032	262156	333128	345563	330820	369303	632508	1397629	1131951	990617	1316155	1712285
Domestic assets	33853	38536	72816	121929	248574	310952	327672	301625	332705	529516	1197592	862027	679236	1024119	1393359
Cash	838	1142	1778	2116	2667	4366	4388	5014	5999	5652	10461	13450	19946	23873	26964
Deposit with BOT	780	93	1316	3075	2163	2524	2768	6493	10664	31233	56948	40152	60870	93222	76941
Treasury bills	5050	0	0	0	0	0	0	0	5000	7931	14397	58786	86274	71047	64370
Other securities	3349	3723	3642	3589	3589	3589	3512	22651	27520	99977	113031	166728	165353	176005	260603
Loans and bills	17529	27690	54990	88846	119598	156906	168845	171258	243586	270376	270356	134906	134586	201412	282589
Other	6307	5888	11091	24303	120558	143568	148159	96209	39936	114347	732399	448005	212207	458560	681892
Foreign assets	865	2052	1570	103	6964	11995	4863	10631	20281	55763	147253	213189	251058	247510	273138
Liquid	865	2052	1570	103	6964	11995	4863	10631	20281	54323	145252	211751	243285	226680	267296
Other	0	0	0	0	0	0	0	0	0	1440	2001	1438	7773	20830	5842
Fixed assets	964	1789	2765	4000	6618	10181	13210	18563	26172	47230	52786	56736	60323	44528	45789
Other	0	0	0	0	0	0	-182	1	-9855	-1	-2	-1	0	-2	-1
Liabilities	35681	42377	77145	126031	261979	333128	345565	330820	369303	632508	1397629	1131952	990618	1316155	1712285
Domestic liabilities	33412	39267	72343	118416	252082	320385	328729	308373	317618	532467	1336718	1084053	1019327	1281203	1671337
Deposits	27835	32448	43239	58862	75450	107416	125583	164684	223842	351085	486215	541303	647617	694390	780764
Liability to BOT	503	1241	18090	39918	51448	62677	38896	70793	1345	9386	1338	1768	585	1656	500
Liabilities to other banks	68	41	66	53	110	277	55	418	1839	1655	3642	1045	4977	5803	5674
Other	5006	5537	10948	20183	125074	150015	164195	72478	90592	170341	845523	539937	366148	579354	884399
Foreign liabilities	2270	3110	4802	7616	9898	4071	5612	10025	32111	7360	26451	4560	3430	2871	506
Liabilities to foreign banks	254	452	665	261	187	550	276	1078	2086	2959	6939	2857	2630	1743	417
Liabilities to others	25	118	306	470	1489	3521	5336	8947	30025	4401	19512	1703	800	1128	89
Capital and reserves	1990	2541	3830	6885	8222	8672	11224	12422	19575	92681	34460	43339	-32139	32081	40442

Note: Year ending June 30.
Source: Bank of Tanzania, Economic and Operations Report for the Year Ended June 1999.

Table 6.4. Commercial Banks Domestic Lending by Economic Sector

End of Period	1986	1987	1988	1989	1990	1991	1992	1993	1994	1995	1996	1997	1998	1999[2]
					Lending Amount (millions of Tanzania shillings)									
Production	2865	10460	20726	29586	50047	65916	62393	74049	102735	78421	55423	60231	79055	100595
Agricultural production	1362	4039	6020	6612	13224	20074	16685	17883	24433	21086	17236	13920	18826	16668
Mining and manufacturing	1451	6263	14430	22430	35563	43855	40941	50885	72709	55345	37129	43703	57914	81039
Tourism	51	158	276	544	1260	1986	4767	5280	5593	1990	1058	2608	2315	2888
Trade	21945	42188	49026	65228	84037	104807	110233	138733	158076	103310	34391	49766	73758	76525
Marketing of agricultural produce	5150	35221	37324	48361	49220	76531	52925	68645	73004	51294	8820	2675	6419	5503
Export of agricultural produce	221	301	618	744	2085	2834	7009	6266	9126	5131	3505	3117	1954	1876
Trade in capital goods	265	72	133	213	426	662	2319	2376	2649	12	8	438	71	0
Trade in non-capital goods	16309	6595	10952	15911	32307	24781	47981	61446	73298	46873	22058	43536	65314	69146
Other	2880	2342	19094	24784	22821	24644	27656	59504	10428	79109	57483	74845	98267	105469
Building and construction	427	522	634	2542	1565	2593	4946	6601	3532	3385	4317	4316	5748	6682
Transport sector	414	1097	1539	2224	3838	4633	5292	10561	10597	4774	8656	15016	22777	39823
Other/1	2039	723	16920	20018	17418	17418	17418	42343	-3702	70941	44510	55513	69742	58964
Total	27690	54990	88846	119598	156905	195366	200282	272286	271239	260831	147297	184842	251080	282589
					As Share of Total (percent)									
Production	10.3	19.0	23.3	24.7	31.9	33.7	31.2	27.2	37.9	30.1	37.6	32.6	31.5	35.6
Agricultural production	4.9	7.3	6.8	5.5	8.4	10.3	8.3	6.6	9.0	8.1	11.7	7.5	7.5	5.9
Mining and manufacturing	5.2	11.4	16.2	18.8	22.7	22.4	20.4	18.7	26.8	21.2	25.2	23.6	23.1	28.7
Tourism	0.2	0.3	0.3	0.5	0.8	1.0	2.4	1.9	2.1	0.8	0.7	1.4	0.9	1.0
Trade	79.3	76.7	55.2	54.5	53.6	53.6	55.0	51.0	58.3	39.6	23.3	26.9	29.4	27.1
Marketing of agricultural produce	18.6	64.0	42.0	40.4	31.4	39.2	26.4	25.2	26.9	19.7	6.0	1.4	2.6	1.9
Export of agricultural produce	0.8	0.5	0.7	0.6	1.3	1.5	3.5	2.3	3.4	2.0	2.4	1.7	0.8	0.7
Trade in capital goods	1.0	0.1	0.1	0.2	0.3	0.3	1.2	0.9	1.0	0.0	0.0	0.2	0.0	0.0
Trade in non-capital goods	58.9	12.0	12.3	13.3	20.6	12.7	24.0	22.6	27.0	18.0	15.0	23.6	26.0	24.5

Table 6.4. Commercial Banks Domestic Lending by Economic Sector (Cont'd)

End of Period	1986	1987	1988	1989	1990	1991	1992	1993	1994	1995	1996	1997	1998	1999[2]
Other	10.4	4.3	21.5	20.7	14.5	12.6	13.8	21.9	3.8	30.3	39.0	40.5	39.1	37.3
Building and construction	1.5	0.9	0.7	2.1	1.0	1.3	2.5	2.4	1.3	1.3	2.9	2.3	2.3	2.4
Transport sector	1.5	2.0	1.7	1.9	2.4	2.4	2.6	3.9	3.9	1.8	5.9	8.1	9.1	14.1
Other/1	7.4	1.3	19.0	16.7	11.1	8.9	8.7	15.6	-1.4	27.2	30.2	30.0	27.8	20.9
Total	100.0	100.0	100.0	100.0	100.0	100.0	100.0	100.0	100.0	100.0	100.0	100.0	100.0	100.0
Annual Changes from the Previous Year (percent)														
Production	35.4	265.1	98.1	42.7	69.2	31.7	-5.3	18.7	38.7	-23.7	-29.3	8.7	31.3	27.2
Agricultural production	112.0	196.5	49.0	9.8	100.0	51.8	-16.9	7.2	36.6	-13.7	-18.3	-19.2	35.2	-11.5
Mining and manufacturing	0.6	331.5	130.4	55.4	58.6	23.3	-6.6	24.3	42.9	-23.9	-32.9	17.7	32.5	39.9
Tourism	66.0	208.0	74.8	96.8	131.9	57.6	140.0	10.8	5.9	-64.4	-46.8	146.5	-11.2	24.8
Trade	53.6	92.2	16.2	33.0	28.8	24.7	5.2	25.9	13.9	-34.6	-66.7	44.7	48.2	3.8
Marketing of agricultural produce	-47.4	584.0	6.0	29.6	1.8	55.5	-30.8	29.7	6.3	-29.7	-82.8	-69.7	140.0	-14.3
Export of agricultural produce	-50.6	36.2	105.5	20.4	180.3	35.9	147.3	-10.6	45.6	-43.8	-31.7	-11.1	-37.3	-4.0
Trade in capital goods	223.8	-73.0	85.8	60.4	99.5	55.5	250.6	2.5	11.5	-99.5	-33.3	5375.0	-83.8	-100.0
Trade in non-capital goods	310.5	-59.6	66.1	45.3	103.1	-23.3	93.6	28.1	19.3	-36.1	-52.9	97.4	50.0	5.9
Other	156.8	-18.7	715.3	29.8	-7.9	8.0	12.2	115.2	-82.5	658.6	-27.3	30.2	31.3	7.3
Building and construction	36.0	22.4	21.5	300.7	-38.4	65.7	90.8	33.4	-46.5	-4.2	27.5	0.0	33.2	16.2
Transport sector	12.8	164.8	40.3	44.5	72.6	20.7	14.2	99.6	0.3	-55.0	81.3	73.5	51.7	74.8
Other/1	362.8	-64.6	2241.0	18.3	-13.0	0.0	0.0	143.1	-108.7	-2016.3	-37.3	24.7	25.6	-15.5
Total	58.0	98.6	61.6	34.6	31.2	24.5	2.5	36.0	-0.4	-3.8	-43.5	25.5	35.8	12.5

1 Includes public administration and financial institutions.
2 Month of June 1999.
Source: The Bank of Tanzania, *Economic Bulletin* (various issues).

Table 5.5. *Interest Rate Structure*
(percent)

	1985	1986	1987	1988	1989	1990	1991	1992	1993	1994	1995	1996	1997	1998	1999[2]
Bank of Tanzania:															
Discount rate[1]	6.0	6.0	9.0	22.0	22.0	22.0	22.0	22.0	22.0-27.0	27.0-67.5	39.9-50.0	14.9-40.8	10.7-20.5	15.5-20.7	11.8-16.6
Commercial Banks:															
Deposit rates															
Savings	10.0	10.0	21.5	21.5	26.0	26.0	26.0	26.0	24.0	24.0-26.0	15.0-27.0	11.1-22.3	7.3-12.8	2.0-12.0	5.0-12.0
Short-term (31-91 days)	5.00	5.00	14.50	14.50	16.00	16.00	16.00	16.00	16.8-18.0	16.0-19.0	13.0-33.0	2.0-33.0	3.5-13.5	2.5-13.5	2.8-12.3
Fixed (3-6 months)	6.0-14.0	6.0-14.1	15.5-27.0	15.5-27.0	17.0-29.0	17.0-29.0	17.0-29.0	17.0-30.3	22.0-25.0	17.0-30.5	15.0-35.0	8.0-34.0	2.5-29.0	4.0-13.1	
Lending rates															
Short-term	11.0-16.0	11.0-16.0	18.0-29.0	18.0-29.0	20.0-31.0	20.0-31.0	20.0-31.0	18.0-31.0	22.0-31.0	27.7-39.0	27.7-45.0	28.0-46.0	21.0-28.0	15.0-30.0	17.5-30.0
Medium and long-term	11.0-16.0	11.0-16.0	19.0-29.0	19.0-29.0	21.0-31.0	21.0-31.0	21.0-31.0	29.0-31.0	21.0-39.0	24.0-39.0	31.0-40.0	29.0-38.0	21.0-32.0	20.0-32.0	20.0-22.0
Housing mortgage	8.0-16.	8.0-16.0	7.0-29.0	9.0-29.0	9.0-29.0	9.0-29.0	-29.00	9.0-29.0	9.0-29.0	29.0-33.0	29.0-33.0	**	**	**	**

317

Table 6.5. *Interest Rate Structure (Cont'd)*

	1985	1986	1987	1988	1989	1990	1991	1992	1993	1994	1995	1996	1997	1998	1999³
Government securities															
Direct advances	4.0	5.0	5.0	11.3	11.3	14.5	14.5	14.5	14.5	30.0-67.5	39.9-50.0	14.9-40.8	10.7-20.5	15.5-20.7	11.8-16.6
Treasury bills															
Tap	5.3-6.0	5.3-6.0	11.3-12.0	11.3-12.0	14.5-15.5	14.5-15.5	14.5-15.5	12.5-13.5	28.9-75.7	21.3-41.7	..	..	..	..	..
Auction 35 days									28.9-75.7	21.3-46.7	..	..	..	..	..
Auction 91 days									32.2-58.8	30.2-71.6	25.6-71.8	7.3-28.1	5.0-14.9	7.8-15.6	5.5-9.7
Auction 182 days										33.5-64.8	29.9-71.5	9.0-37.3	4.2-15.5	9.2-16.4	6.3-11.8
Treasury notes	10.0	10.0	18.5	18.5	18.5	23.0	23.0	23.0	23.0	23.0					
Stocks	7.5-8.5	12.0-16.0	21.5-27.5	21.5-27.5	24.0-29.0	24.0-29.0	24.0-29.0	24.0-29.0	15.0-24.5	15.0-24.5	15.0-24.5	15.0-24.5	15.0-24.5	15.0-24.5	15.0-24.5
Tax reserve certificate	6.0	9.5	13.0	13.5	16.5	16.5	16.5	16.5	16.5	16.5	16.5	16.5	16.5	16.5	16.5
Memo item:															
Real interest rate²	-17.50	-16.92	-6.53	-7.40	0.14	5.25	3.04	3.22	0.45	-7.5--6.0	-8.8--4.2	-4.3--14.6	-8.1--8.9	-2.5--10.8	-3.2--3.8

1 Discount rate has been determined by the movement of marginal yields of 91-day treasury bills.
2 Derived based on the deposit interest rate on savings offered by the commercial banks.
3 Month of June 1999.
** No Mortgage rates after the collapse of Tanzania Housing Bank (THB).
Source: Bank of Tanzania, *Economic Bulletin* (various issues).

318

Table 6.6. Exchange Rate Movement

	1985	1986	1987	1988	1989	1990	1991	1992	1993	1994	1995	1996	1997	1998	1999[2]
Period average															
TSh/SDR	17.74	38.36	83.09	133.44	183.78	264.65	299.85	419.29	565.89	729.64	871.91	842.01	842.28	901.83	994.08
TSh/US$	17.47	32.70	64.26	99.29	143.38	195.06	219.16	297.71	405.27	509.63	574.76	579.98	612.12	664.67	727.22
US$/TSh 100.00	5.72	3.06	1.56	1.01	0.70	0.51	0.46	0.34	0.25	0.20	0.17	0.17	0.16	0.15	0.14
End of period															
TSh/SDR	18.12	63.26	118.77	168.21	252.71	279.69	334.58	460.63	659.13	764.16	818.10	856.51	842.7	958.87	1107.24
TSh/US$	16.50	51.72	83.72	125.00	192.30	196.60	233.90	335.00	479.87	523.45	550.36	595.64	624.57	681.00	797.90
US$/TSh 100.00	6.06	1.93	1.19	0.80	0.52	0.51	0.43	0.30	0.21	0.19	0.18	0.17	0.16	0.15	0.13
Indices (1994=100)															
Real effective exchange rate	21.56	35.97	61.67	78.03	89.04	97.81	87.68	104.14	101.42	100.00	95.85	80.70	71.55	67.83	..
Annual % change	-15.97	66.88	71.42	26.53	14.10	9.85	-10.36	18.78	-2.61	-1.40	-4.15	-15.81	-11.34	-5.19	..

Memo item:

	FY85	FY86	FY87	FY88	FY89	FY90	FY91	FY92	FY93	FY94	FY95	FY96	FY97	FY98	FY99
Period average[1]															
TSh/US$	17.47	25.09	48.48	81.78	121.34	169.22	207.11	258.44	351.49	457.42	542.17	577.37	596.05	638.40	685.025

Average US$/SDR: 1.30153 1.17916 1.10401 1.069 1.02501 1.01534 1.17317 1.29307 1.34392 1.28176 1.35675 1.36816 1.40838 1.39633 1.4317 1.517 1.4518 1.376 1.35681 1.366961818

1 Fiscal year basis.
2 Up to the third quarter.
Source: IMF, *International Finance Statistics*.

7. Agriculture Sector

Table 7.1. Production of Principal Cash Crops and Food Crops (thousand tons)

	FY81	FY82	FY83	FY84	FY85	FY86	FY87	FY88	FY89	FY90	FY91	FY92	FY93	FY94	FY95	FY/96	FY97	FY98	FY99
Cash Crops																			
Coffee	54.9	54.1	53.8	49.5	49	54.8	41	45.5	48.8	37.1	37.7	52.2	57.4	38.4	44	55	34.1	37	40
Cotton**	174.6	48.9	42.9	47	51.9	105.9	214.6	254.9	189.2	112.9	149.1	26.9	307.4	156.6	126.1	251.2	253.3	208.2	92.7
Tea	17.6	17.4	17.5	11.9	16.8	15.5	14.1	15.9	16	19.2	18.1	18.3	21.1	23	16.6	23	19.8	26.2	21.9
Cashew nuts	54	40	32.5	47	32.4	19.2	18.5	22.5	19.3	16.5	28.7	41.2	39.1	46.6	60	81.7	65.4	93.2	100
Tobacco	14.8	14.2	13.9	11	13.4	12.5	16.5	12.9	11.6	11.1	11.8	16.5	23.3	26.1	22.1	28.4	35.4	51	37.8
Sisal	82.5	70	60	40.2	38	32.8	30.2	33.2	33.3	33.7	36	24.2	24.3	29.6	34.5	32	20.5	20	15
Pyrethrum	2.7	1.8	1.6	1.4	1.4	1.4	1.2	1.4	1.3	1.6	1.7	2.2	1.95	0.5	0.314	1.5	0.4	0.4	4
Food Crops																			
Maize	1839.6	1954.1	2323.8	2546.9	1860	2670.7	2244.5	2423.3	2428.1	2445	2332.2	2226.4	2432	1812	2567	2663	1879	1835	2685
Paddy	349.5	414.9	409.1	511.2	472	417.8	510.8	782.3	767.2	740	624	394	600	614	722	734	528	550	676
Wheat	90.5	95	70.5	71.5	80.5	97.9	71.6	75.2	81.3	106	84	64	78	59	75	84	-380	78	112
Pulses	271.6	296.8	281.9	281.1	304.8	432.1	251.4	379.2	385.3	388	425	312	508	187	378	475	360	374	462

p Provisional.
** Before removing the seeds.
Source: Ministry of Agriculture (published in *Economic and Operations Report* (various issues) and Planning Commission, *The Economic Survey* (1998).

Table 7.1a. *Selected Agricultural Production Indices*
(FY92 = 100)

	FY82	FY83	FY84	FY85	FY86	FY87	FY88	FY89	FY90	FY91	FY92	FY93	FY94	FY95	FY96	FY97	FY98	FY99p
Food Crops																		
Maize	87.8	104.4	114.4	83.5	120.0	100.8	108.8	109.1	109.8	104.8	100.0	109.2	81.4	115.3	119.6	84.4	82.4	120.6
Paddy	105.3	103.8	129.7	119.8	106.0	129.6	198.6	194.7	187.8	158.4	100.0	152.3	155.8	183.2	186.3	134.0	139.6	171.6
Wheat	148.4	110.2	111.7	125.8	153.0	111.9	117.5	127.0	165.6	131.3	100.0	121.9	92.2	117.2	131.3	-593.8	121.9	175.0
Pulses	95.1	90.4	90.1	97.7	138.5	80.6	121.5	123.5	124.4	136.2	100.0	162.8	59.9	121.2	152.2	115.4	119.9	148.1
Cash Crops																		
Coffee	103.6	103.1	94.8	93.9	105.0	78.5	87.2	93.5	71.1	72.2	100.0	110.0	73.6	84.3	105.4	65.3	70.9	76.6
Cotton	181.8	159.5	174.7	192.9	393.7	797.8	947.6	703.3	419.7	554.3	100.0	1142.8	582.2	468.8	933.8	941.6	774.0	344.6
Tea	95.1	95.6	65.0	91.8	84.7	77.0	86.9	87.4	104.9	98.9	100.0	115.3	125.7	90.7	125.7	108.2	143.2	119.7
Cashew nuts	97.1	78.9	114.1	78.6	46.6	44.9	54.6	46.8	40.0	69.7	100.0	94.9	113.1	145.6	198.3	158.7	226.2	242.7
Tobacco	86.1	84.2	66.7	81.2	75.8	100.0	78.2	70.3	67.3	71.5	100.0	141.2	158.2	133.9	172.1	214.5	309.1	229.1
Sisal	289.3	247.9	166.1	157.0	135.5	124.8	137.2	137.6	139.3	148.8	100.0	100.4	122.3	142.6	132.2	84.7	82.6	62.0
Pyrethrum	81.8	72.7	63.6	63.6	63.6	54.5	63.6	59.1	72.7	77.3	100.0	88.6	22.7	14.3	68.2	18.2	18.2	181.8

p Preliminary estimate.
Source: Table 7.1.

Table 7.2. Producer Price of Selected Cash Crops and Food Crops
(TSh per kg)

	1983-84	1984-85	1985-86	1986-87	1987-88	1988-89	1989-90	1990-91	1991-92	1992-93	1993-94	1994-95	1995-96	1996-97	1997-98	1998-99
Cash Crops																
Coffee[1]	21.1	25.9	39.4	43.5	57.9	80.2	127.8	134.8	194.8	261.7	875.3	1842.0	1220.1	1323.0	..	..
Cotton[1]	5.9	8.3	12.5	16.8	19.3	22.0	27.9	40.8	70.0	57.7	80.0	120.0	200.0	168.0	200.0	205.0
Tea	2.8	4.1	4.9	7.6	9.9	13.4	17.0	28.0	40.0	40.0	45.0	50.0	55.0	55.0	55.0	55.0
Cashewnuts[1]	6.9	9.7	10.1	17.8	29.6	39.5	83.6	108.1	130.1	149.1	200.0	330.0	380.0	300.0	330.0	460.0
Tobacco[1]	16.8	23.3	37.4	47.5	59.9	72.6	88.3	107.9	243.7	229.3	330.0	523.7	547.2	654.5	672.0	515.9
Sisal	6.4	7.2	16.1	19.5	38.8	64.6	94.0	89.6	87.8	84.0	163.5	216.0	370.9	..	..	..
Pyrethrum	14.0	19.5	21.1	29.5	35.4	47.8	60.0	120.0	230.0	230.0	230.0	300.0	300.0	300.0	300.0	320.0
Sugar cane	0.2	0.3	0.4	0.5	0.6	0.8	1.7	2.5	3.5	5.3	6.2	8.6	8.9	9.5	10.5	10.5
Food Crops																
Maize	2.2	4.0	5.3	6.3	8.2	9.0	11.0	13.0	15.0	..	..	..	..	..	..	..
Paddy	4.0	6.0	8.0	9.6	14.4	17.3	19.0	26.0	31.4	..	..	..	..	..	..	..
Wheat	3.0	4.5	6.0	7.2	9.0	10.4	13.0	32.0	38.4	..	..	..	..	..	..	..
Pulses	5.0	8.0	12.0	14.4	21.6	24.9	27.3	35.0	..	..	..	..	..	..	..	..

1 Weighted average price except the prices for cotton and cashew nuts since 1994-95.
.. Not available.
Source: The Planning Commission, The United Republic of Tanzania, *The Economic Survey* (various issues).

322

Table 7.2a. *Producer Price Index of Selected Cash Crops and Food Crops*
(FY92 = 100)

	FY84	FY85	FY86	FY87	FY88	FY89	FY90	FY91	FY92	FY93	FY94	FY95	FY96	FY97	FY98	FY99
Cash Crops																
Coffee[1]	10.8	13.3	20.2	22.3	29.7	41.2	65.6	69.2	100.0	134.3	449.4	945.7	626.4	679.2	..	..
Cotton[1]	8.5	11.8	17.9	23.9	27.6	31.5	39.9	58.3	100.0	82.4	114.3	171.4	285.7	240.0	285.7	292.9
Tea	7.0	10.3	12.3	19.0	24.8	33.5	42.5	70.0	100.0	100.0	112.5	125.0	137.5	137.5	137.5	137.5
Cashew nuts[1]	5.3	7.5	7.8	13.7	22.7	30.4	64.3	83.1	100.0	114.6	153.7	253.6	292.0	230.5	253.6	353.5
Tobacco[1]	6.9	9.6	15.3	19.5	24.6	29.8	36.3	44.3	100.0	94.1	135.4	214.9	224.6	268.6	275.8	211.7
Sisal	7.3	8.2	18.3	22.2	44.1	73.6	107.0	102.1	100.0	95.7	186.2	246.0	422.3	..	..	..
Pyrethrum	6.1	8.5	9.2	12.8	15.4	20.8	26.1	52.2	100.0	100.0	100.0	130.4	130.4	130.4	130.4	139.1
Sugar cane	6.8	9.3	10.1	13.3	17.3	21.6	50.3	72.6	100.0	151.5	178.3	247.4	256.0	273.2	302.0	302.0
Food Crops																
Maize	14.7	26.7	35.0	42.0	54.7	60.0	73.3	86.7	100.0	..	..	..	..	..	..	..
Paddy	12.7	19.1	25.5	30.6	45.9	55.1	60.5	82.8	100.0	..	..	..	..	..	..	..
Wheat	7.8	11.7	15.6	18.8	23.4	27.0	33.9	83.3	100.0	..	..	..	..	..	..	..

1 Weighted average price.
Source: Table 7.2.

323

Table 7.3 *Average Yield per Hectare for Tea and Sisal*
(tons per hectare)

		FY83	FY84	FY85	FY86	FY87	FY88	FY89	FY90	FY91	FY92	FY93	FY94	FY95	FY96	FY97	FY98	FY99p
Tea:	Average	4.52101	3.86395	4.09143	3.78639	3.42731	3.37052	3.76499	4.92032	4.40893	4.75826	5.33110	5.32560	6.00894	0.8091	4.35755	5.77696	5.07020
	Estates	7.04671	5.30394	5.74079	5.38931	4.82029	4.71914	5.38137	7.26281	6.49489	8.01402	8.34065	8.09243	9.22337	0.75050	7.26786	9.93763	8.65451
	Smallholder	2.02146	2.34205	2.348261	2.09229	1.95510	1.94518	2.05666	2.44458	2.20431	1.31731	2.16744	2.30847	2.46178	1.47910	0.84213	0.75124	0.74066
Sisal/g		0.45714	0.46134	0.43516	0.37126	0.40843	0.61838	0.41241	0.40848	0.42050	0.28393	0.24786	0.53229	0.46675	0.55561	0.4958	0.45502	0.15295

Note: Provisional refers to only the matured plants.
Source: The Planning Commission, The United Republic of Tanzania, *The Economic Survey* (various issues).

Table 7.4. *Coffee Production*
(tons)

	FY86	FY87	FY88	FY89	FY90	FY91	FY92	FY93	FY94	FY95	FY96	FY97	FY98p
Mild	41042	39060	32804	41230	34945	31304	37065	36901	26361	27137	35142	32933	19789
Arabica	2820	2702	2514	2280	1702	1416	1926	2128	2448	1542	2096	1279	1894
Robusta	11285	16975	10389	11620	16427	11403	8996	12217	7577	7157	9710	9279	9165
Total	55147	58737	45707	55130	53074	44123	47987	51246	36386	35836	46948	43491	30848

Source: The Planning Commission, The United Republic of Tanzania, *The Economic Survey* (various issues).

8. Industrial Sector

Table 8.1. Employment and Labor Cost in Manufacturing Enterprises

ISIC Code	Industry Activities	1984	1985	1986	1987	1988	1989	1990	1991	1992	1993	1994	1995	1996	1997	1998
								Number of People Engaged								
3112, 2	Food processing	20251	17727	27730	28812	32430	35291	36073	36441	36879	36821	36763	36802	36434	37162	38648
313	Beverages	3620	3727	3832	4406	4424	5038	6406	6472	6549	6534	6519	6526	6461	6590	6853
314	Tobacco and cigarette	3375	5019	4970	4918	5060	4952	5008	5058	5119	5124.5	5130	5135	5084	5186	5393
321, 2	Textile manufacture	34112	32789	35787	36596	35060	33817	34025	34383	34797	34595.5	34394	34430	34086	34767	36158
323	Leather products	1846	1816	1628	1728	1465	1275	882	891	902	899.5	897	898	889	907	943
324	Footwear	3890	3728	3690	3321	3321	3036	2767	2796	2829	2818.5	2808	2811	2783	2838	2952
331	Furniture	1858	1795	1873	1800	1787	3014	3204	3280	3323	4108	4893	4898	4849	4946	5144
332	Wood products	3386	3205	3434	3161	3525	4423	5194	5263	5327	3745	2163	2165	2144	2186	2274
341, 2	Paper products, publishing and printing	4413	4386	4715	5165	5607	7256	7501	7582	7673	7605.5	7538	7546	7470	7620	7925
351, 2, 3	Petroleum refining and chemicals	5734	4883	5132	5344	5116	4967	4889	4939	4999	4987	4975	4980	4930	5029	5230
355	Rubber products	842	898	910	905	920	941	869	878	889	883.5	878	879	870	888	923
356	Plastic products	656	576	526	504	504	769	776	784	794	790	786	789	779	795	826
361, 2, 9	Non-Metallic products	3233	3472	5065	4332	4350	5069	4237	4286	4338	4254.5	4171	4175	4134	4216	4385
371, 72, 81	Basic metal industry and metal products	4427	4526	4877	4981	4999	6637	6355	6431	6510	6347.5	6185	6182	6130	6252	6502

(table continues on the next page)

326

Table 8.1. Employment and Labor Cost in Manufacturing Enterprises (Cont'd)

ISIC Code	Industry Activities	1984	1985	1986	1987	1988	1989	1990	1991	1992	1993	1994	1995	1996	1997	1998
385, 390	Miscellaneous manufacturing	883	885	969	966	973	1289	1221	1236	1252	1211	1170	1171	1160	1183	1230
	Total	98983	95289	110004	111580	114163	124161	126042	127427	128968	127444	125920	126044	124794	127287	132377
	Labor Cost (millions of Tanzania shillings)[1]															
3112, 2	Food processing	303	360	314	439	547	1825	2456	3049	3793	3770.5	3748	4496	5396	6475	8094
313	Beverages	74	80	87	120	131	635	700	883	1117	963	809	970	1165	1397	1747
314	Tobacco and cigarette	49	78	79	114	148	283	507	627	778	431.5	85	102	122	147	184
321, 2	Textile manufacture	456	574	701	1003	1025	1833	2149	2664	3307	3235.5	3164	3796	4555	5466	6832
323	Leather products	39	44	49	59	57	94	89	113	143	186	229	275	330	396	495
324	Footwear	107	106	134	131	131	211	195	242	301	163.5	26	31	37	45	56
331	Furniture	21	22	25	31	35	177	528	691	909	682	455	546	655	786	983
332	Wood products	50	55	83	97	108	321	312	387	478	346	214	257	308	370	462

327

Table 8.1. *Employment and Labor Cost in Manufacturing Enterprises (Cont'd)*

ISIC Code	Industry Activities	1984	1985	1986	1987	1988	1989	1990	1991	1992	1993	1994	1995	1996	1997	1998
341, 2	Paper products, publishing and printing	108	127	153	181	240	697	874	1107	1406	1241	1076	1291	1549	1859	2323
351, 2, 3	Petroleum refining and chemicals	180	204	222	298	319	626	885	1133	1438	1079.5	721	865	1038	1245	1557
355	Rubber products	31	34	31	42	87	191	175	223	283	340	397	476	571	686	857
356	Plastic products	11	23	23	28	28	96	120	153	192	167	142	170	204	245	307
361, 2, 9	Non-Metallic products	110	136	219	228	252	483	410	516	652	610	568	681	818	981	1226
371, 72, 81	Basic metal industry and metal products	147	180	208	273	294	571	692	869	1095	1115.5	1136	1363	1635	1962	2453
382, 3	Manufacture and repair of machinery	71	88	99	113	121	315	388	487	615	529.5	444	533	369	767	959
384	Assembly and repairs of transport equipment	53	69	103	127	144	340	383	480	602	539	476	571	385	822	1028
285, 390	Miscellaneous manufacturing	16	17	23	24	24	96	128	177	224	188	152	182	219	263	328
	Total	1826	2197	2553	3308	3691	8794	10991	13801	17333	15587.5	13842	16605	19356	23912	29891

1 This labor cost should be interpreted with caution because of the augmented coverage of the industry for the survey and decontrol of wage rates since 1989.
Source: The Planning Commission, The United Republic of Tanzania, *Statistical Abstract* (1995) and *The Economic Survey* (1998).

Table 8.2. Production f Selected Manufactured Commodities

Commodity	Unit	1984	1985	1986	1987	1988	1989	1990	1991	1992	1993	1994	1995	1996	1997	1998*
Canned beef	tons	169	129	109	132	171	34	26	12	..	..	..	..	..	..	..
Biscuits and macaroni	tons	..	989	1534	1411	1206	1315	1141	739	497	378	241	246	71	288	805
Sugar	000 tons	112.4	99.7	96.8	106.6	98.2	96.2	107	125.3	111.9	123.4	97.5	105	104.1	..	..
Wheat flour	million tons	35	39	39.786	22.382	29.9	11.147	12.14	2.94	15.999	7.544	11.565	11.512	33.9979	77.598	87.7
Konyagi (spirit)	000 litres	872	682	713	809	1069	1164	1203	1505	1879	1882	1988	2011	1832	1849	1994
Beer	million litres	69.5	76.2	65.2	58.8	53	53.7	45	50	49.4	57.1	56.8	89.3	125.7	148.3	170.7
Chibuku	million litres	15.3	10.9	29.5	12.3	15.2	16.3	14	15.2	13.2	14.8	10.7	11.3	14.031	13.68	11.99
Cigarettes	million pcs	2666	2666	2748	2635	2967	2846	3742	3816	3789	3892	3383	3699	3733.3	4710	3933
Textiles	million Sq. m.	68.002	58.072	61.9	60.8	64.3	70.9	63.3	62.8	73.2	60.3	51.4	31.201	33.4356	41.7	45.5
Sisal ropes	000 tons	22	15	19.187	16.37	18.498	18.393	20.208	18.367	21.807	24.8	21.306	17.323	11.1784	4.919	4.3
Fish nets	tons	67	96	124	916	156	138	152	146	96	93	123	108	125.5	70	35
Plywood	000 cu. m.	1892	1589	1938	2094	2250	1687	1525	1642	1162	673	487	284	315	115	..
Pyrethrum	000 tons	54	39	40	41	44	40	40	54	49	35	24	21	10.5	3	9
Fertilizers	000 tons	52	41	47.032	19.276	5.989	27.03	17.426	20.62	..	..	..	..	..	..	..
Paints	000 litres	551	1127	1659	2374	1991	2037	2199	3321	2375	2129	2016	3228	5205.4	4986	4943
Petroleum products	000 tons	637	572	370	372	438	441	337	337	357	348	340	398	336.6	313	312
Cement	000 tons	364	373	435	498	592	595	664	1023	977	749	986	739	725.8	621	778
Rolled steel	000 tons	10	11	11.289	9.61	10.45	15.327	9.129	7.568	6.097	7.104	7.002	2.518	7.733	12.5	9.5
Iron sheets	000 tons	23.012	22.151	8.9	16.56	14.713	20.1	21.7	23.4	24.1	25.9	22.9	18.142	6.422	15.218	14.9
Aluminum	tons	1515	2283	1486	2659	2598	1489	2537	2568	2845	3245	2659	1158	359.9	117	180
Radios	000 unit	40	69	48	72	102	56	71	102	108	95	55	76	56	56	15
Radiators	pieces	5810	8215	6681	5665	4920	3627	3349	2835	2962	2209	2017	..	..	..	..
Battery (dry cell)	million unit	41.39	44.077	44.289	26.32	23.941	35.476	28.811	33.012	47.504	48.603	57.263	59	65.6	43	46
Battery (M/vehicles)	000 pieces	13.628	13.963	22.133	27.088	22.583	31.582	20.136	17.253	11.305	8.709	7.06	7.08	1.85	..	..
Battery	million unit	..	27	27	26	24	35	21	44	47	43	57	59	66	43	46

* Provisional estimates.
Figures not available.
Source: The Planning Commission, The United Republic of Tanzania, The Economic Survey and Statistical Abstract (various issues).

Table 8.3. Mineral Production

Mineral	Unit	1984	1985	1986	1987	1988	1989	1990	1991	1992	1993	1994	1995	1996	1997	1998
Diamond	000 carat	277	255.5	190	126	88	77.5	69.5	72	67.5	40.8	25.5	49.5	12.7	12.3	97.8
Salt	000 tons	29.9	21.1	15.3	41.1	30.1	21.3	28	30.8	18.6	83.4	84.3	105	86.7	72.5	75
Phosphate	000 tons	14.5	26.5	21	18.4	13	8.451	25.066	2.4	4.9	2.2	..	6.7	0.72	2.12	..
Gemstone	Kgs	388.8	645.7	300	9053	9053	24621	32292	59625.7	26678	32979	48507	111403.8	142160	509489	48518
Tin	000 tons	0.3	1.8	2.1	5.4	14.2	14.7	13.5	6.4	7.5	12	9	3	:	:	
Gold	Kgs	39.5	55.2	46.9	201.1	164.4	116	1650	5435.9	8555.2	3370	2861	320	318	323	427
Gypsum	000 tons	7.6	14.4	12.9	29.6	19.6	5.9	36.2	5.3	15	52.2	53	42	55.4	46.3	59.1
Kaolin	000 tons	1.7	1.6	2.3	2.5	1.6	1.6	2	1.7	1.4	474	541	596	1332	898	..
Galactic	000 tons	2.2	3.5	3.5	2.9	1.7	2.5	1.5	0.8	..	..	..	..	:	:	..
Coal	000 tons	8.2	6.6	3.6	2.9	3.3	15.14	16.929	33.213	31.14	40.248	45	43.189	52	28.4	..
Glass sand	000 tons	10	9.3	7.6	6.1	12	13.101	6.365	4.262	..	0.916	0.607	0.596	0.715	0.797	..
Limestone	000 tons	138.8	247	457.4	680.7	792.5	986.5	861.3	553.4	990.5	1618	1740	1062.1	1200	1282.5	1182
Production Index (1991=100)																
Diamond		384.7	354.9	263.9	175.0	122.2	107.6	96.5	100.0	93.8	56.7	35.4	68.8	17.6	17.1	135.8
Salt		97.1	68.5	49.7	133.4	97.7	69.2	90.9	100.0	60.4	270.8	273.7	340.9	281.5	235.4	243.5
Phosphate		604.2	1104.2	875.0	766.7	541.7	352.1	1044.4	100.0	204.2	91.7	..	279.2	30.0	88.3	..
Gemstone		0.7	1.1	0.5	15.2	15.2	41.3	54.2	100.0	44.7	55.3	81.4	186.8	238.4	854.5	81.4
Tin		4.7	28.1	32.8	84.4	221.9	229.7	210.9	100.0	117.2	187.5	140.6	46.9	:	:	..
Gold		0.7	1.0	0.9	3.7	3.0	2.1	30.4	100.0	157.4	62.0	52.6	5.9	5.8	5.9	7.9
Gypsum		143.4	271.7	243.4	558.5	369.8	111.3	683.0	100.0	283.0	984.9	1000.0	792.5	1045.3	873.6	1115.1
Kaolin		94.1	94.1	135.3	147.1	94.1	94.1	117.6	100.0	82.4	27882.4	31823.5	35058.8	78352.9	52823.5	..
Galactic		275.0	437.5	437.5	362.5	212.5	312.5	187.5	100.0				:	:		..
Coal		24.7	19.9	10.8	8.7	9.9	45.6	51.0	100.0	93.8	121.2	135.5	130.0	156.6	85.5	..
Glass sand		234.6	218.2	178.3	143.1	281.6	307.4	149.3	100.0	..	21.5	14.2	14.0	16.8	18.7	..
Limestone		25.1	44.6	82.7	123.0	143.2	178.3	155.6	100.0	179.0	292.4	314.4	191.9	216.8	231.7	213.6

Source: The Planning Commission, The United Republic of Tanzania, *The Economic Survey*, various issues and Bank of Tanzania, *Economic and Operations Report for the Year Ended 30th June 1998.*

Table 8.4. *Nominal Retail Price of Petroleum Products*

	1985	1986	1987	1988	1989	1990	1991	1992	1993	1994	1995	1996**	1997*	1998*
Motor spirit super	19.8	30.5	43.7	67	96	157	157	201	271	325	335	360	420	420
Motor spirit regular	16.7	25.25	37.9	61	92	152	149	191	259	315	325	350	410	410
Illuminating kerosene	10	11.25	16.9	20	37	83	83	92	148	160	160	170	257	257
Gas oil	8.65	14	19.5	22.5	39	92	92	129	211	256	266	285	330	330
Industrial diesel oil	9.452	11.82	19.51	21.35	33.25	85	85	110.92	202	252	252	265	380	380
Retail Price Index (1992=100)														
Motor spirit super	9.9	15.2	21.7	33.3	47.8	78.1	78.1	100.0	134.8	161.7	166.7	179.1	209.0	209.0
Motor spirit regular	8.7	13.2	19.8	31.9	48.2	79.6	78.0	100.0	135.6	164.9	170.2	183.2	214.7	214.7
Illuminating kerosene	10.9	12.2	18.4	21.7	40.2	90.2	90.2	100.0	160.9	173.9	173.9	184.8	279.3	279.3
Gas oil	6.7	10.9	15.1	17.4	30.2	71.3	71.3	100.0	163.6	198.4	206.2	220.9	255.8	255.8
Industrial diesel oil	8.5	10.7	17.6	19.2	30.0	76.6	76.6	100.0	182.1	227.2	227.2	238.9	342.6	342.6

** and * refers to prices in September and July respectively.
Source: Tanzania Petroleum Development Corporation.

331

9. Prices

Table 9.1. National Consumer Price Index

	Weights	1990	1991	1992	1993	1994	1995	1996	1997	1998	1999
				Retail Price Index (1994=100)							
General index	100.0	34.5	44.4	54.1	67.8	90.2	115.8	140.1	162.6	183.5	200.4
Food	64.2	33.2	43.8	53.1	63.8	88.8	115.1	138.6	162.8	185.3	185.7
Drinks and tobacco	2.5	39.4	43.7	56.7	70.9	91.5	114.6	143.1	151.2	165.5	169.1
Rent	4.9	25.1	30.5	35.7	40.1	94.3	106.7	137.4	158.4	176.0	180.3
Fuel light and water	7.6	34.0	41.4	51.0	70.4	92.0	126.5	166.1	198.2	232.0	248.7
Clothing and footwear	9.9	42.4	51.1	62.7	81.5	95.2	114.2	136.3	154.1	165.9	176.9
Furniture and utensils	1.4	41.7	52.2	63.4	73.6	93.4	114.4	144.1	161.4	184.8	188.0
Household operations	3.4	41.8	48.8	67.7	74.8	95.7	120.1	138.7	148.6	156.2	158.8
Personal care and health	1.3	52.1	67.0	76.2	112.2	93.5	102.4	118.2	135.7	143.1	144.1
Recreation and entertainment	0.7	19.2	26.6	38.9	62.8	93.9	113.6	129.5	142.3	156.7	161.3
Transportation	4.1	35.2	47.3	52.2	74.5	95.2	126.7	162.4	198.7	222.5	226.3

(table continues on the next page)

332

Table 9.1. National Consumer Price Index (Cont'd)

	1990	1991	1992	1993	1994	1995	1996	1997	1998	1999[1]
Annual Retail Price Changes (percent)										
General index		28.7	21.8	25.3	33.0	28.4	21.0	16.1	12.9	8.2
Food		31.9	21.2	20.2	39.2	29.6	20.4	17.5	13.8	8.5
Drinks and tobacco		10.9	29.7	25.0	29.1	25.2	24.9	5.7	9.5	7.3
Rent		21.5	17.0	12.3	135.2	13.1	28.8	15.3	11.1	5.8
Fuel light and water		21.8	23.2	38.0	30.7	37.5	31.3	19.3	17.1	11.6
Clothing and footwear		20.5	22.7	30.0	16.8	20.0	19.4	13.1	7.7	13.9
Furniture and utensils		25.2	21.5	16.1	26.9	22.5	26.0	12.0	14.5	6.5
Household operations		16.7	38.7	10.5	27.9	25.5	15.5	7.1	5.1	5.4
Persnoal care and health		28.6	13.7	47.2	-16.7	9.5	15.4	14.8	5.5	3.2
Recreation and entertainment		38.5	46.2	61.4	49.5	21.0	14.0	9.9	10.1	8.2
Transportation		34.4	10.4	42.7	27.8	33.1	28.2	22.4	12.0	5.4

1 Second quarter.

Note: Based on wage earners with incomes between TSh 17,500 and Tshs 40,000 per month. Only December 1994=100, otherwise the annual average is used which was not equal to 100 in 1994.

Source: Bureau of Statistics of The Planning Commission, presented in *Economic Bulletin* of Bank of Tanzania.

Table **9.2.** *Dar Es Salaam Cost of Living Index - Middle Income Group*

	Weight	1987	1988	1989	1990	1991	1992	1993	1994	1995	1996	1997	1998
Living Cost Index (1994=100)													
General	100	15.6	20.8	27.1	34.0	48.1	61.1	74.6	100.0	125.9	132.8	141.2	148.0
Food	76.9	15.9	20.8	26.5	32.8	46.2	56.2	72.4	100.0	127.0	128.0	134.2	140.7
Non food	23.1	14.7	21.0	29.5	39.0	55.3	64.0	83.4	100.0	143.4	146.3	161.1	170.8
Annual Living Cost Change (percent)													
General			33.3	30.3	25.5	41.5	27.0	22.1	34.0	25.9	5.5	6.3	4.8
Food			30.8	27.4	23.8	40.9	21.6	28.8	38.1	27.0	0.8	4.8	4.8
Non food			42.9	40.5	32.2	41.8	15.7	30.3	19.9	43.4	2.0	10.1	6.0

Note: Middle income group consists of wage earners with incomes over TShs 17,500, and up to TShs 40,000 per month.
Source: Bureau of Statistics of The Planning Commission, presented in *Economic Bulletin* of Bank of Tanzania.

Table 9.3. Dar es Salaam Retail Price Index

	1984	1985	1986	1987	1988	1989	1990	1991	1992	1993	1994	1995	1996	1997	1998
Retail Price Index (1994=100)															
Total	6.8	9.0	12.3	15.5	20.2	26.4	34.0	46.4	57.3	73.0	100.0	101.7	128.7	137.4	146.8
Food	1.6	6.5	8.6	12.3	15.2	20.2	25.6	32.3	54.4	69.3	100.0	101.8	123.3	129.3	137.6
Drinks and tobacco	1.5	7.2	7.7	10.7	17.4	19.1	29.1	43.7	59.2	94.3	100.0	98.0	163.0	175.8	181.6
Fuel and soap	6.0	6.4	8.9	14.4	15.8	24.1	36.2	49.0	57.2	79.2	100.0	109.2	128.8	159.0	188.4
Clothing	9.4	14.3	16.0	18.7	23.6	33.7	44.2	65.3	77.8	91.6	100.0	99.1	140.1	154.7	156.3
Households	12.5	11.3	16.8	18.5	27.8	42.7	55.1	67.0	81.8	99.5	100.0	102.9	127.8	126.3	133.5
Annual Retail Price Changes (percent)															
Total		32.4	36.7	26.0	30.3	30.7	28.8	36.5	23.5	27.4	37.0	1.7	26.5	6.8	6.8
Food		306.3	32.3	43.0	23.6	32.9	26.7	26.2	68.4	27.4	44.3	1.8	21.1	4.9	6.4
Drinks and tobacco		380.0	6.9	39.0	62.6	9.8	52.4	50.2	35.5	59.3	6.0	-2.0	66.3	7.9	3.3
Fuel and soap		6.7	39.1	61.8	9.7	52.5	50.2	35.4	16.7	38.5	26.3	9.2	17.9	23.4	18.5
Clothing		52.1	11.9	16.9	26.2	42.8	31.2	47.7	19.1	17.7	9.2	-0.9	41.4	10.4	1.0
Households		-9.6	48.7	10.1	50.3	53.6	29.0	21.6	22.1	21.6	0.5	2.9	24.2	-1.2	5.7

Note: Based on wage earners with income up to TSh17,500 per month.
Source: Bureau of Statistics of The Planning Commission, presented in *Economic Bulletin* of Bank of Tanzania.

REFERENCES

The word "processed" describes informally reproduced works that may not be commonly available through libraries.

Adam, Christopher S., and Stephen A. O'Connell. 1998. "Aid, Taxation, and Development: Analytical Perspectives on Aid Effectiveness in Sub-Saharan Africa." Policy Research Working Paper no. 1885. World Bank, Washington, D.C.

Alter, R. 1991. "Lessons from the Export Processing Zone in Mauritius." *Finance and Development* (December): 7–9.

Appleton, S., and A. Balihuta. 1996. "Education and Agricultural Productivity in Uganda." Center for the Study of African Economies Working Paper Series no. WPS/96 5.

Appleton, S., and J. Mackinon. 1996. "Enhancing Human Capacities in Africa." In B. Ndulu and N. Van de Walle (eds.), *Agenda for Africa's Economic Renewal.* New Brunswick, New Jersey and Oxford, U.K.: Transaction.

Ballali, D. T. S. 1999. Keynote Address to the 11th Conference of Financial Institutions, AICC, February 15, Arusha, Tanzania.

Banda, T. 1997. "Some of the Critical Preconditions for Agricultural Take-Off in Tanzania." In J. Shitundu and N. Luvanga, eds., *Economic Management in Tanzania.* Dar es Salaam: TEMA Publishers.

Bank of Tanzania. 1996. *Economic Bulletin for the Quarter Ended 31ˢᵗ March, 1996,* vol. XXV, no. 1. Dar es Salaam.

_____. 1997 and various years. *Economic and Operations Report.* Dar es Salaam.

Barro, Robert J., and Jong-Wha Lee. 1993. "International Comparisons of Educational Attainment. 1993." *Journal of Monetary Economics* 32(3):363–94.

_____. 1996. "International Measures of Schooling Years and Schooling Quality." *American Economic Review, Papers and Proceedings* 86(2): 218–23.

Bedi, Arjun S. 1999. *The Role of Information and Communication Technologies in Economic Development.* Discussion Papers on Development Policy no. 7. Bonn: Center for Development Research.

Bevan, D., Paul Collier, and Jan Willem Gunning. 1989. *Peasants and Governments.* Oxford, U.K.: Clarendon Press.

Bevan, D., Paul Collier, David Bevan, Jan Willem Gunning with Arne Bigsten and Paul Horsnell. 1990. *Controlled Open Economies: A Neoclassical Approach to Structuralism.* Oxford, U.K.: Clarendon Press.

Bienefeld, M. 1995. "Structural Adjustment and Tanzania's Peasantry: Assessing the Likely Long-Term Impact." In V. Jamal, ed., *Structural Adjustment and Rural Labour Markets in Africa.* New York: St. Martin's Press, Inc.

Bloom, D. E., and J. D. Sachs. 1998. *Geography, Demography, and Economic Growth in Africa.* Brookings Papers on Economic Activity. Washington, D.C.: The Brookings Institution.

Bonnel, Rene. 2000. *HIV/AIDS: Does it Increase or Decrease Growth? What Makes an Economy HIV-Resistant?* Washington, D.C.: World Bank, AIDS Campaign Team. Africa. Processed.

Bratton, Michael, and Nicolas van de Walle. 1997. *Democratic Experiments in Africa: Regime Transitions in Comparative Perspective.* Cambridge, U.K. and New York: Cambridge University Press.

Collins, Susan M., and Barry P. Bosworth. 1996. "Economic Growth in East Asia: Accumulation Versus Assimilation." Brookings Papers on Economic Activity (2):135–203.

Cross-Border Initiative. 2000. *Road Map For Investment Facilitation.* Report for the Fourth Ministerial Meeting in Mauritius, October 1999. Prepared by the cosponsors in consultation with the technical working groups of the Cross-Border Initiative participating countries. Washington, D.C.

Cuddington, J. T. 1993. "Modeling the Macroeconomic Effects of AIDS with an Application to Tanzania." *The World Bank Economic Review* 7(2):173–188.

Dayal-Gulati, Anuradha, and Christian Thirmann. 1997. "Saving in Southeast Asia and Latin America Compared: Searching for Policy Lessons." IMF Working Paper. WP/97/110. International Monetary Fund, Washington, D.C.

Demery, L., and L. Squire. 1996. "Macroeconomic Adjustment and Poverty in Africa: An Emerging Picture." *The World Bank Research Observer* 11(1):39–59.

Devarajan, Shantayanan, William Easterly, and Howard Pack. 1999. "Is Investment in Africa too Low or too High?" World Bank, Washington, D.C. Processed.

Due, J. F., and C. Meyer. 1989. "Major Determinants of Tax Structures of Market Economy Countries." *Tanzania Journal of Economics* 1(1): 47–66.

Easterly, William. 1999. "The Lost Decades: Explaining Developing Countries' Stagnation 1980–1998." World Bank, Washington, D.C. Processed.

Easterly, William, and Ross Levine. 1997. "Africa's Growth Strategy: Policies and Ethnic Divisions." *Quarterly Journal of Economics* 112: 1203–50.

_____. 2000. "It's Not Factor Accumulation: Stylized Facts and Growth Models." International Monetary Fund Seminar Series (International) no. 2000–12. International Monetary Fund, Washington, D.C.

_____. 1998. "Troubles with the Neighbours: Africa's Problem, Africa's Opportunity." *Journal of African Economies* 7(1):120–142

Eele, G., J. Semboja, S. B. Likwelile, L. Rutasitara, and S. Akroyd. 1999. *Meeting the International Development Targets in Tanzania.* Draft report. Dar es Salaam: REPOA and Oxford Policy Management.

Elbadawi, I., B. Ndulu, and N. Ndung'u. 1997. "Risks, Uncertainties, and Debt Overhang as Determinants of Private Investment in Sub-Saharan Africa." Paper presented at the 10th Anniversary Conference of the CSAE, April 17–18, University of Oxford, Oxford, U.K.

ERB (Economic Research Bureau). 1993. "Macroeconomic Perspectives: The Zanzibar Economy." *Tanzania Economic Trends: A Quarterly Review of the Economy* 2(2): 6–13.

Euromoney. 1999. "Has the World Bank Lost its Way?" (December).

Fallon, Peter. 1998. "Dispersion of Subnational Regional Income per Capita." KMS note. World Bank, Washington, D.C.

Filmer, Deon. 1999. *Educational Attainment and Enrollment Profiles: A Resource "Book" Based on an Analysis of Demographic and Health Survey Data.* Washington, D.C.: World Bank.

Financial Times. 1999. "Don't Press-Gang the Private Sector." October 13.

Financial Times Survey. 1999. Survey on Tanzania. March 31.

Foster, J., J. Greer, and E. Thorbecke. 1984. "Notes and Comments: A Class of Decomposable Poverty Measures." *Econometrica* 52(3):761–6.

Glen, J. D., and M. A. Sumlinski. 1995. *Trends in Private Investment in Developing Countries 1995: Statistics for 1980–93.* Discussion Paper no. 25. Washington, D.C.: International Finance Corporation.

Government of Zanzibar. 1992. *Annual Price Review, Cloves and Chilies, FY93.* Ministry of Agriculture, Livestock Development, and Natural Resources.

_____. 1999a. "Rolling Plan and Forward Budget." President's Office: Planning and Privatization.

_____. 1999b. *Zanzibar Statistical Abstract, 1997.* President's Office: Planning and Privatization.

_____. 1999c. "Agricultural Sector Survey." Project no. TCPI/URT/67/6. Ministry of Agriculture, Livestock, and Natural Resources, with the Food and Agriculture Organization of the United Nations, final draft.

_____. 1999d. "Agricultural Sector Policy." Ministry of Agriculture, Livestock, and Natural Resources.

_____. Various years. *Zanzibar Statistical Abstract.* President's Office: Planning and Privatization.

Husain, Ishrat, and John Underwood, eds. 1991. *African External Finance in the 1990s.* Washington, D.C.: The World Bank.

IDA and IMF (International Development Association and International Monetary Fund) 2000. *Tanzania: Decision Point Under the Enhanced Heavily Indebted Poor Countries (HIPC) Initiative.* Washington, D.C.

IDC (Investment Development Consultancy). 1996. *Evaluation of the EU Structural Adjustment Support Programme in Tanzania (1992–1995).* Brussels.

IFC (International Finance Corporation). 1994. *Building the Private Sector in Africa.* Washington, D.C.

ILO and JASPA (International Labour Organisation and Jobs and Skills Programme for Africa). 1982. *Basic Needs in Danger—A Basic Needs Oriented Development Strategy for Tanzania.* Addis Ababa.

IMF (International Monetary Fund). 1999a. "Tanzania: Recent Economic Developments." Report to the Members of the IMF Executive Board, SM/99/20. Washington, D.C.

_____. 1999b. *Annual Report on Exchange Rate Arrangements and Exchange Restrictions 1999*. Washington, D.C.

_____. Various. *World Economic Outlook*. Washington, D.C.

_____. Various issues. 1996. *Tanzania: Selected Issues and Statistical Appendix*. Washington, D.C.

Jaspersen, F. Z., Anthony H. Aylward, and Mariusz Sumlinksi. 1995. *Trends in Private Investment in Developing Countries: Statistics from 1970–94*. Discussion Paper no. 28. Washington, D.C.: International Finance Corporation.

Kahama, George. 1995. *Tanzania in the 21st Century*. Dar es Salaam: Tanzania Publishing House.

Kapunda, Steven M. 1988. "Consumption Patterns and Tanzanian Economic Development." PhD thesis, University of Dar es Salaam.

Kaufmann, D., and S. A. O'Connell. 1999. "The Macroeconomics of Delayed Exchange Rate Unification: Theory and Evidence from Tanzania." Policy Research Working Paper no. 2060. World Bank, Washington, D.C.

Kenny, C., and M. Syrquin. 1999. "Growth and Transformation in East Africa." In S. Yusuf, ed., *Tanzania Peri-urban Development in the African Mirror*, vol. 2. Report no. 1952TA. Washington, D.C.: World Bank.

Kilindo, A. 1992. "Inflationary Finance and the Dynamics of Inflation in Tanzania." Ph.D diss., University of Dar es Salaam, Dar es Salaam.

Lipton, R., and M. Ravallion. 1995. "Poverty and Policy." In J. Behrman and T. N. Srinivasan, eds., *Handbook of Development Economics*, vol. III. North-Holland, New York, NY.Luvanga, N., and D. Bol. 1999. *The Impact of Tanzania's Trade and Exchange Regime on Exports*.

Maasdorp, G. G., and R. Hess. 1999. *The Establishment of an East African Trade Regime*. For the Secretariat of the Commission for East African Cooperation. Arusha, Tanzania

Mabele R. B., and H. Mwinyimvua. 1998. "An Analysis of the Impact of Introducing Value Added Tax (VAT) in Zanzibar." Report prepared for the Tanzania Revenue Authority. University of Dar es Salaam, Economic Research Bureau, Dar es Salaam.

Madani, D. A. 1998. *Review of the Role and Impact of Export Processing Zones*. Washington, D.C.: World Bank.

Mbilinyi, M. 1993. *Review of Women's Conditions and Positions in Tanzania: Issues and Methodology*. Background paper prepared for the Tanzania Gender Networking Program. Dar es Salaam, Tanzania

McKinnon, R. 1973. *Money and Capital in Economic Development*. Washington, D. C.: The Brookings Institution.

Megyery, Kathy, and Frank Sader. *Facilitating Foreign Participation in Privatization*. Occasional Paper 8. Washington, D.C.: Foreign Investment Advisory Service.

Mkai, C. and Mwisomba. 1998. "Tanzania: Poverty Line." Commissioned Report to Research on Poverty Alleviation, Dar es Saalam..

Mtatifikolo, F. P., and A. L. Kilindo. 1993. "The Public Revenue and Expenditure Systems of Zanzibar." *Tanzania Economic Trends, A Quarterly Review of the Economy*, vol. 6, nos. 1 and 2. Dar es Salaam: University of Dar es Salaam, Economic Research Bureau.

Mtatifikolo F. P., R. B. Mabele, and A. L. Kilindo. 1993. "The Economy of Zanzibar." Processed.

Ndulu, B. J. 1994. "Tanzania's Economic Development: Lessons from the Experience and Challenges for the Future." In L. A. Msambichaka, H. P. B. Moshi, and F. P. Mtatifikolo, eds., *Development Challenges and Strategies for Tanzania: An Agenda for 21st Century*, Dar es Salaam: University of Dar es Salaam.

_____. 1986. "Investment, Output Growth, and Capacity Utilization in an African Economy: The Case of the Manufacturing Sector in Tanzania." *East African Economic Review* 2.

Ndulu, B., and M. Hyuha. 1989. "Inflation and Economic Recovery in Tanzania: Some Empirical Evidence." *UCHUMI* 2(1).

Ndulu, B., and S. O'Connell. 1999. "Governance and Growth in Sub-Saharan Africa." *Journal of Economic Perspectives* 13(3): 41–66.

Ndulu, B. J., and S. M. Wangwe. 1997. "Managing the Tanzania Economy in Transition to Sustained Development." In D. Bol, N. Luvanga, and J. Shitundu, eds., *Economic Management in Tanzania*. Dar es Salaam: TEMA Publishers.

Parente, Stephen L., and Edward C. Prescott. 1999. "Monopoly Rights: A Barrier to Riches." *American Economic Review* 89(5):1216–33.

Pfeffermann, Guy P., Gregory V. Kisunko, and Mariusz A. Sumlinski. 1999. *Trends in Private Investment in Developing Countries—Statistics for 1970–97*. Discussion Paper no. 37. Washington, D.C.: International Finance Corporation.

Pinto, B. 1989. "Black Market Premia, Exchange Rate Unification, and Inflation in Sub-Saharan Africa." *The World Bank Economic Review* 3(3).

_____. 1991. "Black Markets for Foreign Exchange Rate, Real Exchange Rates, and Inflation." *Journal of International Economics* 30.

Price Waterhouse Coopers and Lybrand. 1997. *Tanzania Investment Roadmap*. Dar es Salaam: USAID/Tanzania.

_____. 1999. *Tanzania Investment Roadmap*, vols. I-V; Private Sector Consultancy Services USAID/Tanzania. Dar es Salaam.

Pritchett, Lant. 1999. "The Tyranny of Concepts: CUDIE (Cumulated, Depreciated, Investment Effort) Is not Capital." Policy Research Working Paper no. 2341. World Bank, Washington, D.C.

Rajaram, A., A. Yeats, N. Ng'eno, F. Musonda, and G. Mwau. 1999. "Putting the Horse before the Cart: on the Appropriate Transition to an East African Customs Union." Final Report for the East African Cooperation Secretariat.

Ravallion, M., and B. Bidani. 1994. "How Robust Is a Poverty Profile?" *World Bank Economic Review* 8(1): 75–102.

REPOA (Research on Poverty Alleviation) 1998. *Economic Policy Changes and Rural Poverty—Survey Data*. Dar es Salaam.

Rhee, Y. W., and others. 1990. *Free Trade Zones in Export Strategies.* Industrial Series Paper no. 36. Washington, D.C.: World Bank.

Rodrik, D. 1997. "Trade Policy and Economic Performance in Sub-Saharan Africa." Prepared for the Ministry of Foreign Affairs, Sweden. Draft.

Roemer, M., and M. K. Gugerty. 1997. *Does Economic Growth Reduce Poverty?* CAER II Discussion Paper no.5. Cambridge, Massachusetts: Harvard Institute for International Development.

Romer, P. 1993. "Idea Gaps and Object Gaps in Economic Development." *Journal of Monetary Economics* 32: 543.

Rutasitara, L. 1997. "Recipient Views on Poverty Reduction Projects and Programmes of European Donors in Tanzania: Cases of Zanzibar Forestry (Finland), Stabex for Coffee, Kilimanjaro Region (EU), and PRIDE Tanzania (Norway)." Research report to Research on Poverty Alleviation. Dar es Salaam.

Rweyemamu, J. 1973. *Underdevelopment and Industrialization in Tanzania: A Study of Perverse Capitalist Industrial Development.* Oxford, U.K.: Oxford University Press.

Sadig, Rasheed. 1996. *A New Africa in the 21st Century: What Policy Agenda, What Conditions.* Policy Management Report No. 4. European Center for Development Policy Management.

Sahn, D., and S. Younger. 1997. *Structural Adjustment Reconsidered.* Cambridge, U.K.

Sahn, D., D. Stifel, and S. Younger. 1999. *Intertemporal Changes in Welfare: Preliminary Results from Nine African Countries.* Ithaca, New York: Cornell University.

Schmidt-Hebbel, Klaus, and Luis Serven. 1997. *Saving Across the World: Puzzles and Policies.* Discussion Paper no. 354. Washington, D.C.: World Bank.

Semboja, Joseph, Amon Chaligha, Godwin Mjema, Joseph Shitundu, and Servacius Likwelile. 1999. *Restarting and Sustaining Growth and Development in Tanzania.* Dar es Salaam.

Semboja, J., and S. Likwelile. 1999. "The Changing Character of Gender Inequality in Tanzania: Lessons from the 1998 National Form Four Certificate Examination Results." *REPOA* (Research on Poverty Alleviation) *Newsletter* (10).

Shaw, E. 1973. *Financial Deepening in Economic Development.* New York: Oxford University Press.

Steward, F., and W. van der Geest. 1994. *Adjustment and Social Funds: Political Panacea or Effective Poverty Reduction?* Employment Papers 2. Geneva: International Labour Organisation.

The Economist. 2000. Various issues.

Tinios P., A. Sarris, H. K. R. Amani, W. Maro, and S. Zografakis. 1993. *Households, Consumption and Poverty in Tanzania: Results from the 1991 National Cornell-ERB Survey.* Ithaca, New York: Cornell Food and Nutrition Program.

Towo, Esther. 1989. "Consumption Patterns: The Case of Zanzibar." MA dissertation, University of Dar es Salaam.

UNDP (United Nations Development Programme). 1997. *Human Development Report.* New York.

UNECA (United Nations Economic Commission for Africa). 1998, 1999. *Economic Report on Africa* UNECA–Addis Ababa. University Press.

URT (United Republic of Tanzania). 1986. *Economic Recovery Programme (ERP)*. Dar es Salaam.

_____. 1992. *Agricultural Statistical Bulletin*, Issue No. 3, Ministry of Agriculture.

_____. 1993. *The Labor Force Survey FY91*. Dar es Salaam: Bureau of Statistics.

_____. 1995. *National Accounts of Tanzania 1966-1994*. Dar es Salaam: Bureau of Statistics.

_____. 1996. *The Composite Development Goal–for the Long Term Development Perspective* Dar es Salaam: Planning Commission.

_____. 1997a. *Demographic and Health Survey 1996*. Bureau of Statistics, Commission and Demographic and Health Surveys. Macro International.

_____. 1997b. *Revised National Accounts of Tanzania 1987–1996*. Dar es Salaam.

_____. 1997c. *Adult Morbidity and Mortality Project (AAMP) Report*. Dar es Salaam: Ministry of Health

_____. 1997d. "Wariba Report on Corruption in Tanzania." Dar es Salaam.

_____. 1998a. *The National Poverty Eradication Strategy*. Dar es Salaam: Government printer.

_____. 1998b. *The Tanzania Development Vision 2025*. Dar es Salaam: Planning Commission

_____. 1998c. *National AIDS Control Programme: Strategic Framework for the Third Medium Term Plan for Prevention and Control of HIV/AIDS/STDs 1998-2002* Dar es Salaam: Ministry of Health

_____. 1999a. "Consultation on Trade-related Assistance." Report prepared by the Ministry of Industry and Commerce in consultation with other concerned ministries and private sector organizations. Draft.

_____. 1999b. *The Economic Survey 1998*. Dar es Salaam: Planning Commission.

_____. 1999c. *Revised National Accounts for Tanzania (1987–1997)*.Dar es Salaam: Bureau of Statistics

_____. 1999d. *Public Expenditure Review*, 2 vols. Report no. 19898. Washington, D.C.: Government of Tanzania and World Bank.

_____.2000. "Poverty Analysis: Summary Results." A Presentation at the Poverty Reduction Strategy Workshop, April 4, Dar es Salaam. National Bureau of Statistics.

_____. 2001. "Public Expenditure Review," 2 vols. Government of Tanzania and World Bank, Washington, D.C. Draft.

_____. Various. *National Accounts of Tanzania*. Dar es Salaam: Bureau of Statistics

_____. Various years. *The Economic Survey*. Dar es Salaam: Planning Commission.

URT, World Bank, and IMF. Tanzania: Policy Framework Papers, various issues for various years. Dar es Salaam.

USAID (United States Agency for International Development). 1999. *Investor Roadmap Reports*, vol. I–V. Private Sector Consultancy Services.

Wagao, J. 1992. "Adjustment Policies in Tanzania, 1981–90: The Impact on Growth, Structure and Human Welfare" In G. A. Cornia, R. van der Hoeven, and P. T. Mkandawire, eds.,

Africa's Recovery in the 1990s: From Stagnation and Adjustment to Human Development. London: St. Martin's Press.Wangwe, S. M. 1998. "Review of the Economic Recovery Programme: Case of Industry." Paper presented at the Fififth Economic Policy Workshop, May 23–25, Dar es Salaam.

WEC and CID (World Economic Forum and Center for International Development). 2000. *The Africa Competitiveness Report 2000/2001.* Cambridge, Massachusetts.

WEC and HIID (World Economic Forum and Harvard Institute for International Development). 1998. *The Africa Competitiveness Report FY98.* Cambridge, Massachusetts.

World Bank. 1991a. *Developing the Private Sector—The World Bank's Experience and Approach.* Washington, D.C.

_____. 1991b. *Tanzania Economic Report: Towards Sustainable Development in the 1990s.* Washington, D.C.

_____. 1993. *Tanzania: A Poverty Profile.* Washington, D.C.

_____. 1995. *Challenges of Reform, Growth, Incomes and Welfare.*

_____. 1996a. "Neglected Tradeoffs in Poverty Measurement," *IDS Bulletin* 27(1).

_____. 1996b. *Tanzania: The Challenge of Reforms: Growth, Income and Welfare.* Washington, D.C.

_____. 1997a. "Technical and Higher Education and Training in Tanzania: Investment, Returns, and Future Opportunities." Africa Region, Human Development Group 1, Washington, D.C. Processed.

_____. 1997b. *World Development Report 1997.* New York: Oxford University Press.

_____. 1998a. *Africa can Compete! A Framework for World Bank Group Support for Private Sector Development in Sub-Saharan Africa.* Washington, D.C.

_____. 1998b. *World Development Report 1998: Knowledge for Development.* New York: Oxford University Press.

_____. 1998c. *Assessing Aid: What Works, What Doesn't Work, and Why.* New York: Oxford University Press.

_____. 1998d. The Economic Survey. Dar es Salaam: Planning Commission

_____. 1999a. *African Development Indicators FY99.* Washington, D.C.

_____. 1999b. *Africa Regional Database 1999 (SIMA).* Washington, D.C.

_____. 1999c. *Global Development Finance.* Washington, D.C.

_____. 1999d. "Interim Poverty Reduction Strategy Paper (PRSP)". Draft proposal.

_____. 1999e. *Mpango wa Maendeleo na Bajeti Tangulizi (Rolling Plan and Forward Budget),* vol. 2., *Programmes and Budget, Ministry of State Planning and Investment.* Zanzibar: Government of Zanzibar.

_____. 1999f. Speech of the Minister of State for Planning to Parliament, Planning Commission, DSM. June.

_____. 1999g. "SADC Regional Integration—The Bank Group Role in Spatial Development Initiatives, Transport/Development Corridors, and Growth Triangles." Discussion notes. Washington, D.C.

_____. 1999h. *Preparatory Workshop for Developing Tools for Home Based Care Services in Tanzania*. Ministry of Health. Dar es Salaam.

_____. 1999i. *World Development Report 1999*. New York: Oxford University Press.

_____. 1999j. "Tanzania: Peri Urban Development in the African Mirror," 2 vols. Report no. 19526 TA. Washington, D.C.

_____. 2000 "Agriculture in Tanzania Since 1986: Follower or Leader of Growth?" Washington, D.C.

_____. 2000a. "Export Diversification, Trade Policy and Regional Integration," In *Africa in the 21st Century*. draft.

_____. 2000b. *Greening Industry, New Roles for Communities, Markets and Governments*. Washington, D.C.

_____. 2000c. *Tanzania Country Assistance Strategy*. Washington, D.C.

_____. 2000d. "Botswana: An Example of Prudent Economic Policy and Growth." *Infobrief* no. 161. Washington, D.C.: Africa Region.

_____. 2000e. "Africa in the 21st Century." Draft. Washington, D.C.

_____. 2000f. *African Development Indicators*. Washington D.C.

_____. 2001. "Tanzania a the Turn of the Century from Reforms to Sustained Growth and Poverty Reduction". Washington, D.C.

_____. Various. *African Development Indicators*. Washington, D.C.

_____. Various. *World Development Indicators*. Various issues, 1998–2000. Washington, D.C.

MAP SECTION